THE FIRST URBAN CHURCHES 5
COLOSSAE, HIERAPOLIS, AND LAODICEA

WRITINGS FROM THE GRECO-ROMAN WORLD
SUPPLEMENT SERIES

Clare K. Rothschild, General Editor

Number 16

THE FIRST URBAN CHURCHES 5
COLOSSAE, HIERAPOLIS, AND LAODICEA

Edited by
James R. Harrison and L. L. Welborn

Atlanta

Copyright © 2019 by Society of Biblical Literature

All rights reserved. No part of this work may be reproduced or transmitted in any form or by any means, electronic or mechanical, including photocopying and recording, or by means of any information storage or retrieval system, except as may be expressly permitted by the 1976 Copyright Act or in writing from the publisher. Requests for permission should be addressed in writing to the Rights and Permissions Office, SBL Press, 825 Houston Mill Road, Atlanta, GA 30329 USA.

Library of Congress Cataloging-in-Publication Data

First urban churches / edited by James R. Harrison and L. L. Welborn.
    volumes cm. — (Society of Biblical Literature. Writings from the Greco-Roman world Supplement series ; Number 7)
    Includes bibliographical references.

    ISBN 978-1-62837-102-4 (v. 1 : pbk. : alk. paper) — ISBN 978-1-62837-104-8 (v. 1 : ebook) — ISBN 978-1-62837-103-1 (v. 1 : hardcover : alk. paper)
    ISBN 978-0-88414-111-2 (v. 2 : pbk. : alk. paper) — ISBN 978-0-88414-112-9 (v. 2 : ebook) — ISBN 978-0-88414-113-6 (v. 2 : hardcover : alk. paper)
    ISBN 978-0-88414-234-8 (v. 3 : pbk. : alk. paper) — ISBN 978-0-88414-235-5 (v. 3 : ebook) — ISBN 978-0-88414-236-2 (v. 3 : hardcover : alk. paper)
    ISBN 978-1-62837-226-7 (v. 4 : pbk. : alk. paper) — ISBN 978-0-88414-337-6 (v. 4 : ebook) — ISBN 978-0-88414-336-9 (v. 4 : hardcover : alk. paper)
    ISBN 978-1-62837-261-8 (v. 5 : pbk. : alk. paper) — ISBN 978-0-88414-418-2 (v. 5 : ebook) — ISBN 978-0-88414-419-9 (v. 5 : hardcover : alk. paper)
    1. City churches. 2. Church history—Primitive and early church, ca. 30–600. 3. Cities and towns—Religious aspects—Christianity. I. Harrison, James R., 1952– editor.
    BV637.F57 2015
    270.109173'2—dc23   2015021858

Contents

Abbreviations vii

Part 1. Introduction to the Lycus Valley

Perspectives on the Lycus Valley: An Inscriptional, Archaeological, Numismatic, and Iconographic Approach
    Alan H. Cadwallader and James R. Harrison 3

Part 2. Responses to Ulrich Huttner's Perspectives on the Lycus Valley

Colossians, Hierapolitan Coins—and the Young Bearers of Hope
    Ulrich Huttner 73

Unraveling the Threads of Identity: Cloth and Clothing in the Lycus Valley
    Rosemary Canavan 81

On the Question of Comparative Method in Historical Research: Colossae and Chonai in Larger Frame
    Alan H. Cadwallader 105

Salience, Multiple Affiliation, and Christ Belief in the Lycus Valley: A Conversation with Ulrich Huttner's *Early Christianity in the Lycus Valley*
    Harry O. Maier 153

Part 3. Thematic Essays on the Lycus Valley

Initiation, Vision, and Spiritual Power: The Hellenistic Dimensions of the Problem at Colossae
    Clinton E. Arnold 173

Everyday Life in a Roman Town Like Colossae:
The Papyrological Evidence
    Peter Arzt-Grabner 187

A City with a Message: Colossae and Colossians
    Angela Standhartinger..239

Employing Numismatic Evidence in Discussions of Early
Christianity in the Lycus Valley: A Case Study from Laodicea
    Michael P. Theophilos..257

Rome's Market Economy in the Lycus Valley: Soundings
from Laodicea and Colossae
    Michael Trainor 293

Has the Vita Abercii Misled Epigraphists in the
Reconstruction of the Inscription?
    Allen Brent 325

The Inscriptions and Oracular Prophecy in the Eastern
Mediterranean Basin: Assessing the Book of Revelation in
Its Graeco-Roman Revelatory Context
    James R. Harrison 363

Contributors...417
Primary Sources Index 421
Modern Authors Index..447

Abbreviations

Primary Sources

2 Clem.	2 Clement
Acts Phil.	Acts of Philip
Adv. pag.	Orosius, *Adversus paganos*
Aen.	Vergil, *Aeneid*
A.J.	Josephus, *Antiquitates judaicae*
Alex.	Lucian, *Alexander*
Amic.	Cicero, *De amicitia*
Anab.	Arrian, *Anabasis*; Xenophon, *Anabasis*
Ann.	Tacitus, *Annales*
Anth. Pal.	Palatine Anthology
Apol.	Seneca, Apolocyntosis; Apuleius, *Apologia*
Arch.	Vitruvius, *De architectura*
Att.	Cicero, *Epistulae ad Atticum*
Avod. Zar.	Avodah Zarah
Bapt.	Tertullian, *De baptismo*
Bell. Mith.	Appian, *Bellum Mithridaticum*
Bib. hist.	Diodorus Siculus, *Bibliotheca historica*
C	Codex Coislinianus
Carm.	Horace, *Carmina*
Chron.	Eusebius, *Chronicon*; John Malalas, *Chronicle*; Michael Choniates, *Chronicon*, Theophanes, *Chronicle*
Civ.	Augustine, *De civitate Dei*
Clem.	Seneca, *De clementia*
Comm.	Commodus
Cor.	Clemens Romanus, *Epistula ad Corinthios*
Descr.	Pausanias, *Graeciae descriptio*
Dial.	Justin Martyr, *Dialogus*

Dig.	Digest
Disc.	Epictetus, *Discourses*
Dom.	Suetonius, *Domitianus*
Ecl.	Calpunius Siculus, *Eclogue*; Titus Calpurnius, *Eclogues*; Vergil, *Eclogae*
Eleg.	Propertius, *Eligiae*
Ep.	*Epistle*
Eph.	Ignatius, *To the Ephesians*
Epigr.	Martial, *Epigrams*
Epist.	Justin, *Epitome historiarum Trogi Pompeii*
Ethn.	Stephanus, *Ethnica*
Fam.	Cicero, *Epistulae ad familares*
Flac.	Cicero, *Pro Flacco*
Flacc.	Philo, *In Flaccum*
Frag. ep.	Julian, *Fragmentum epistolae*
Gal.	Julian, *Contra Galilaeos*
Geogr.	Strabo, *Geographica*
H	Codex Hierosolymitanus Sabaiticus
Hipp.	Apollonius Citensis, *In Hippocratis de articulis commentarius*
Hist.	Herodian, *History of the Empire*; Herodotus, *Historiae*; Polybius, *Histories*; Tacitus, *Histories*; Zonaras, *Epitome historiarum*
Hist. Aug.	Historia Augusta
Hist. eccl.	Eusebius, *Historia ecclesiastica*; Socrates; *Historia ecclesiastica*; Sozmen, *Historia ecclesiastica*; Theodoret, *Historia ecclesiastica*
Hist. rom.	Dio Cassius, *Historiae romanae*
Hom.	Asterius of Amasea, *Homilies*
Hom. Col.	John Chrysostomus, *Homilies on Colossians*
Leg.	Philo, *Legum allegoriae*
Legat.	Philo, *Legatio ad Gaium*
LXX	Septuagint
m.	Mishnah
M	Codex Mosquensis
Magn.	Ignatius, *To the Magnesians*
Mart. Phil.	Martyrdom of Philip
Metam.	Apuleius, *Metamorphoses*
Myst.	Iamblicus, *De mysteriis*

Nat.	Pliny, *Naturalist historia*
Od.	Homer, *Odyssey*
Or.	Aelius Aristides, *Orationes*; Dio Chrysostom, *Orations*; Julian, *Orations*; Gregory of Nazianzus, *Orations*
P	Codex Parisianus graecus
Pasch.	Melito of Sardis, *Peri pascha*
Phld.	Ignatius, *To the Philadelphians*
Phil.	Polycarp, *To the Philippians*
Pol.	Ignatius, *To Polycarp*
Protr.	Clement, *Protrepticus*
Quaest. conv.	Plutarch, *Quaestionum convivialum libri IX*
Ref.	Hippolytus, *Refutatio omnia haeresium*
Res. gest. divi Aug.	Res gestae divi Augusti
Sib. Or.	Sibylline Oracle
Sim.	Shepherd of Hermas, *Similitudes*
Smyrn.	Ignatius, *To the Smyrnaeans*
Strateg.	Polyaenus, *Strategemata*
Them.	Constantine Porphyrogenitus, *De thematibus*
Tib.	Suetonius, *Tiberius*
Trall.	Ignatius, *To the Trallians*
Trist.	Ovid, *Tristia*
Vit. Aberc.	Vita Abercii
Vit. soph.	Philostratus, *Vita sophistarum*

Secondary Sources

AA	*Archäologischer Anzeiger*
AAT	*Atti della Accademia delle Scienze di Torino*
AB	Anchor Bible
ABR	*Australian Biblical Review*
AÉ	Cagnat, Ren., et al., ed. *L'Année Épigraphique.* Paris: Presses universitaires de France, 1888–.
Aeg	*Aegyptus*
Aev	*Aevum: Rassegna de scienze, storiche, linguistiche, e filologiche*
AJA	*American Journal of Archaeology*
AJEC	Ancient Judaism and Early Christianity
AJP	*American Journal of Philology*

AKG	Arbeiten zur Kirchengeschichte
AncSoc	*Ancient Society*
Annales	*Annales: Histoire, Sciences Sociale*
ANRW	Temporini, Hildegard, and Wolfgang Haase, eds. *Aufstieg und Niedergang der römischen Welt: Geschichte und Kultur Rom sim Spiegel der neueren Forschung*. Part 2: *Principat*. Berlin: de Gruyter, 1972–.
APB	*Acta Patristica et Byzantina*
APF	*Archiv für Papyrusforschung*
AS	*Anatolian Studies*
BAR	*Biblical Archaeology Review*
BARIS	British Archaeological Reports International Series
BASP	Bulletin of the American Society of Papyrologists
BCH	*Bulletin de correspondance hellénique*
BE	*Bulletin épigraphique*
BECNT	Baker Exegetical Commentary on the New Testament
BETL	Bibliotheca Ephemeridum Theologicarum Lovaniensium
BGU	Schubart, W., et. al., eds. *Aegyptische Urkunden aus den Königlichen* (later *Staatlichen*) *Museen zu Berlin, Griechische Urkunden*. Berlin, 1895–2005.
Bib	*Biblica*
BL	Preisigke, Friedrich, et al., eds. *Berichtigungsliste der griechischen Papyrusurkunden aus Ägypten*. 12 vols. Leiden: Brill, 1922–2009.
BL Add MS	British Library Additional Manuscript
BMC Phrygia	Head, Barclay V. *A Catalogue of the Greek Coins in the British Museum: Phrygia*. London: British Museum, 1906.
BMC Sicily	Poole, R. S., ed. *A Catalog of the Greek Coins in the British Museum: Sicily*. London: British Museum, 1876.
BN	*Biblische Notizen*
BNP	*Brill's Neue Pauly*
BNTC	Black's New Testament Commentaries
BR	*Biblical Research*
BSac	*Bibliotheca Sacra*

BTB	*Biblical Theology Bulletin*
BZNW	Beihefte zur Zeitschrift für die neutestamentlich Wissenschaft
C.Epist.Lat.	Cugusi, P., ed. *Corpus Epistolarum Latinarum, papyris tabulis ostracis servatarum.* 3 vols. Florence: Gonnelli, 1992–2002.
C.Ptol.Sklav.	Scholl, R., ed. *Corpus der ptolemäischen Sklaventexte.* Stuttgart: Steiner, 1990.
CBQ	*Catholic Biblical Quarterly*
CdE	*Chronique d'Égypte*
Ch.L.A.	Bruckner, A., et al., eds. *Chartae Latinae Antiquiores.* 49 vols. Basel: Dietikon-Zurich, 1954–1998.
CIG	Boeckh, August, ed. *Corpus Inscriptionum Graecarum.* 4 vols. Berlin: Reimer, 1828–1877.
CIJ	*Corpus inscriptionum judacarum.* Vatican City: Pontificio Instituto di Archeologia Christiana, 1936–1952.
CIL	*Corpus inscriptionum Latinarium.* Berlin, 1862–.
ClQ	*Classical Quarterly*
CP	*Classical Philology*
CPR	Corpus Papyrorum Raineri
CurBR	*Currents in Biblical Research*
DEG	Chantraine, Pierre. *Dictionnaire étymologique de langue grecque: Histoire des mots.* 5 vols. Librairie Klincksieck: Serie Linguistique. Paris: Klincksieck, 1968–1980.
DNP	Cancik, Hubert, and Helmuth Schneider, eds. *Der neue Pauly: Enzyklopädie der Antike.* Stuttgart: Metzler, 1996–.
EA	*Epigraphica Anatolica*
EBGR	*Epigraphic Bulletin for Greek Religion*
ECAM	Early Christianity in Asia Minor
ECL	Early Christianity and Its Literature
EJJS	*European Journal of Jewish Studies*
GCS	Die griechischen christlichen Schriftsteller der ersten drei Jahrhunderte
GRBS	*Greek, Roman, and Byzantine Studies*
HNT	Handbuch zum Neuen Testament

HThKNT	Herders Theogischer Kommentar zum Neuen Testament
HTR	*Harvard Theological Review*
HTS	Harvard Theological Studies
ICC	International Critical Commentary
ICUR	Inscriptiones christianae Urbis Romae
IBoubon	Kokkinia, Christina, ed. *Boubon: The Inscriptions and Archaeological Remains, a Survey 2004–2006*. Meletemata 60. Athens: de Boccard, 2008.
IDidyma	Rehm, R., ed. *Die Inschriften*. Vol. 2 of *Didyma*. Berlin: Mann, 1958.
IDenizli	Ritti, Tullia, ed. *Museo archeologico di Denizli-Hierapolis: Catálogo delle iscrizioni greche e latine; Distretto di Denizli*. Napoli: Liguori Editore, 2008.
IEph	Wankel, Hermann, et al., eds. *Die Inschriften von Ephesos*. 8 vols. Bonn: Habelt, 1979–1984.
IG	*Inscriptiones Graecae*. Editio Minor. Berlin: de Gruyter, 1924–
IGBulg	Mihailov, Georgi. *Inscriptiones Graecae in Bulgaria pertae*. Sofia: Academiae Litterarum Bulgaricae, 1956–1970.
IGRR	Cagnat, René, J. Touvain, Pierre Jouguet, and Georges Lafaye, eds. *Inscriptiones graecae ad res romanas pertinentes*. 4 vols. Paris: Leroux; Rome: Bretschneider, 1906–1964.
IGSK	Inschriften griechischer Städte aus Kleinasien
IJO	Noy, David, et al., eds. *Inscriptiones Judaicae Orientis*. 3 vols. TSAJ 99, 101, 102. Tübingen: Mohr Siebeck, 2004.
IK	Inschriften griechischer Städte aus Kleinasien
IstForsch	Istanbuler Forschungen
IstMitt	Istanbuler Mitteilungen
ILaodikeia	Corsten, Thomas. *Die Inschriften von Laodikeia am Lykos*. Inschriften griechischer Städte aus Kleinasien 49. Bonn: Habelt, 1997. For the texts, see https://inscriptions.packhum.org/book/607?location=14.
IMagnesia	Kern, Otto. *Die Inschriften von Magnesia am Maeander*. Berlin: Spemann, 1900.

IMilet	Rehm, Albert. *Milet.* 9 vols. Berlin: de Gruyter, 1908–1928.
IMylasa	Blümel, Wolfgang. *Die Inschriften von Mylasa.* 2 vols. Bonn: Habelt, 1987–1988.
Int	*Interpretation*
IPergamon	Fränkel, N. and C. Habicht. *Altertümer von Pergamon.* 3 vols. Berlin: de Gruyter, 1890–1969.
ISardBR	Buckler, W. H., and D. M. Robinson. *Greek and Latin Inscriptions.* Vol. 7 of *Sardis.* Leiden: Brill, 1932.
ISmyrna	Petzl, G., ed. *Die Inschriften von Smyrna.* Bonn: Habelt, 1982–1990.
IStratonikeia	Şahin, Mehmet Çetin. *The Inscriptions of Stratonikeia.* IGSK 68. Bonn: Habelt, 2010.
JAAR	*Journal of the American Academy of Religion*
JAC	*Jahrbuch für Antike und Christentum*
JBL	*Journal of Biblical Literature*
JECH	*Journal of Early Christian History*
JHS	*Journal of Hellenic Studies*
JGRChJ	*Journal of Greco-Roman Judaism and Christianity*
JIWE	Noy, David. *Jewish Inscriptions of Western Europe.* 2 vols. Cambridge: Cambridge University Press, 1993–1995.
JNG	*Jahrbuch für Numismatik und Geldgeschichte*
JJP	*Journal of Juristic Papyrology*
JÖAI	*Jahreshefte des Österreichischen Archäologischen Instituts in Wien*
JQR	*Jewish Quarterly Review*
JRA	*Journal of Roman Archaeology*
JRASup	Journal of Roman Archaeology Supplement Series
JRS	*Journal of Roman Studies*
JSJSup	Journal for the Study of Judaism in the Persian, Hellenistic, and Roman Periods Supplement Series
JSNT	*Journal for the Study of the New Testament*
JSNTSup	Journal for the Study of the New Testament Supplement Series
JTS	*Journal of Theological Studies*
Jur.Pap.	Meyer, Paul Martin, ed. *Juristische Papyri.* Berlin: Weidmann, 1920.

KEK	Kritish-exegetische Kommentar über das Neue Testament
LBW	Le Bas, Philippe, and William Henry Waddington, eds. *Inscriptions grecques et latines*. Paris: Didot, 1870.
LGPN	Balzat, Jean-Sébastien, Richard W. V. Catling, Édouard Chiricat, and Thomas Corsten. *Lexicon of Greek Personal Names*. Oxford: Clarendon, 2018.
Lives	Diogenes Laertius, *Lives and Opinions of Eminent Philosophers*
LNTS	Library of New Testament Studies
LSAM	Sokolowski, Franciszek, ed. *Lois sacrées d l'Asie Mineure*. Paris: de Boccard, 1955.
LSJ	Liddell, Henry George, Robert Scott, Henry Stuart Jones, and Roderick McKenzie. *A Greek-English Lexicon*. 9th ed. Oxford: Oxford University Press, 1996.
MAMA	Calder, W. M., Alan Cameron, J. Cullen, and Barbara Levick, eds. *Monumenta Asiae Minoris antiqua*. London: Manchester University Press; Longmans, Green, 1928–.
MBAH	*Marburger Beiträge zur Antiken Handels-, Wirtschafts- und Sozialgeschichte*
MBPF	Münchener Beiträge zur Papyrusforschung und antiken Rechtsgeschichte
MDAIA	*Mitteilungen des Deutschen Archaeologischen Instituts, Atheniasche Abteilung*
Med Arch	*Mediterranean Archaeology*
MOTP	Bauckham, Richard, James R. Davila, and Alexander Panayotov, eds. *Old Testament Pseudepigrapha: More Noncanonical Scriptures*. 2 vols. Grand Rapids: Eerdmans, 2013–.
NCB	New Century Bible
NCBC	New Cambridge Bible Commentary
NEASB	*Near East Archaeological Society Bulletin*
NewDocs	Horsley, G. H. R., et al., eds. *New Documents Illustrating Early Christianity*. Edited by North Ryde, NSW: The Ancient History Documentary Research Centre, Macquarie University, 1981–.

NICNT	New International Commentary on the New Testament
NIGTC	New International Greek Testament Commentary
NTOA	Novum Testamentum et Orbis Antiquus
NTS	*New Testament Studies*
NovTSup	Novum Testamentum Supplement
NTTSD	New Testament Tools, Studies and Documents
NumC	*Numismatic Chronicle*
O.BuNjem	Marichal, R., ed. *Les Ostraca de Bu Njem*. Tripoli: Grande Jamahira arabe, libyenne, populaire et socialiste, Dépt. des antiquities, 1992.
O.Cret.Chers.	Litinas, N., ed. *Greek Ostraka from Chersonesos: Ostraca Cretica Chersonesi*. Vienna: Holzhausen, 2009.
O.Brux.	Bingen, J., ed. *Au Temps ou on lisait le grec en Égypte*. Brussels: Fondation égyptologique Reine Élisabeth, 1977.
O.Did.	Ostracon Didymoi
OGIS	Dittenberger, Wilhelm, ed. *Orientis Graeci Inscriptiones Selectae*. 2 vols. Leipzig: Hirzel, 1903–1905.
OLA	Orientalia Lovaniensia Analecta
ÖTK	Ökumensicher Taschenbuch-Kommentar
P.Abinn.	Bell, H. I., V. Martin, E. G. Turner, D. van Berchem, eds. *The Abinnaeus Archive: Papers of a Roman Officer in the Reign of Constantius II*. Oxford: Clarendon, 1962.
P.Amh.	Grenfell, B. P., and A. S. Hunt, ed. *The Amherst Papyri, Being an Account of the Greek Papyri in the Collection of the Right Hon. Lord Amherst of Hackney, F.S.A. at Didlington Hall, Norfolk*. 2 vols. London: Frowde, 1900–1901.
P.Ant.	Roberts, C. H., J. W. B. Barns, and H. Zilliacus, eds. *The Antinoopolis Papyri*. London: Egypt Exploration Society, 1950–1967.
P.Berl.Cohen	Cohen, Nahum, ed. *Greek Documentary Papyri from Egypt in the Berlin Aegyptisches Museum*. Oakville, CT: American Studies in Papyrology, 2007.
P.Bingen	Melaerts, H, ed. *Papyri in Honorem Johannis Bingen Octogenarii*. Leuven: Peeters, 2000.

P.Cair.Masp.	Maspero, Jean, ed. *Papyrus grecs d'époque byzantine, Catalogue général des antiquités égyptiennes du Musée du Caire*. 3 vols. Cairo: Impr. de l'Institut français d'archéologie orientale, 1911–1916.
P.Cair.Preis.	Preisigke, F., ed. *Griechische Urkunden des Aegyptischen Museums zu Kairo*. Strassburg: Trübner, 1911.
P.Cair.Zen.	Edgar, C.C., ed. *Zenon Papyri, Catalogue général des antiquités égyptiennes du Musée du Caire*. 5 vols. Cairo: Institut français d'archéologie orientale, 1925–1940.
P.Choix	Malinine, Michel, ed. *Choix de textes juridiques en hiératique "anormal" et en démotique*. 2 vols. Paris: Champion; Cairo: Institut français d'archéologie orientale du Caire, 1953–1983.
P.Col.	Westermann, W. L., et al., eds. *Columbia Papyri*. 11 vols. New York: Columbia University Press, 1929–1998.
P.Corn.	Westermann, William Linn, and Casper John Kraemer Jr., eds. *Greek Papyri in the Library of Cornell University*. New York: Columbia University Press, 1926.
P.Diog.	Schubert, P., ed. *Les archives de Marcus Lucretius Diogenes et textes apparentés*. Bonn: Habelt, 1990.
P.Dime	Lippert, S. L., and M. Schentuleit. *Demotische Dokumente aus Dime I: Ostraka,* Wiesbaden: Harrassowitz, 2006.
P.Dura	Welles, C. B., R. O. Fink, and J. F. Gilliam, eds. *The Parchments and Papyri*. Vol. 5.1 of *The Excavations at Dura-Europos conducted by Yale University and the French Academy of Inscriptions and Letters: Final Report*. New Haven: Yale University Press, 1959.
P.Euphrates	Feissel, D., and J. Gascou. "Documents d'archives romains inédits du Moyen Euphrates." *Journal des Savants* (1995): 65–119; (1997): 3–47; (2000): 157–208.
P.Fam.Tebt.	van Groningen, B. A., ed. *A Family Archive from Tebtunis*. Leiden: Brill, 1950.

P.Fay.	Grenfell, B. P., A. S. Hunt, and D. G. Hogarth, eds. *Fayum Towns and their Papyri*. London: Egypt Exploration Society, 1900.
P.FuadUniv.	Crawford, D. S., eds. *Fuad I University Papyri*. Alexandria: Société de Publications égyptiennes, 1949.
P.Gen.	Nicole, J., et al., eds. *Les Papyrus de Genève*. 6 vols. Geneva: Bibliothèque Publique et Universitaire, 1896–2010.
P.Hamb.	Meyer, P. M., et al., eds. *Griechische Papyrusurkunden der Hamburger Staats- und Universitätsbibliothek*. 4 vols. Leipzig: Teubner; Hamburg: Augustin, 1911–1998.
P.Hever	Cotton, H. M., and A. Yardeni, eds. *Aramaic, Hebrew and Greek Documentary Texts from Nahal Hever and Other Sites, with an Appendix containing Alleged Qumran Texts (The Seiyâl Collection II)*. Oxford: Clarendon, 1997.
P.Jud.Des.Misc.	Charles, James H., et al., eds. *Miscellaneous Texts from the Judaean Desert*. Oxford: Clarendon, 2000.
P.Köln	Kramer, B., et al., eds. *Kölner Papyri*. Opladen: Westdeutscher Verlag; Paderborn: Schöningh, 1976–2007.
P.Laur.	Pintaudi, R., and G. M. Browne, eds. *Dai Papiri della Biblioteca Medicea Laurenziana*. 5 vols. Florence: Gonnelli, 1976–1984.
P.Lond.	Kenyon, F. G., et al., eds. *Greek Papyri in the British Museum*. 7 vols. London: British Museum, 1893–1974.
P.Masada	Cotton, H. M., and J. Geiger, eds. *Masada II: The Yigael Yadin Excavations 1963—1965; Final Reports: The Latin and Greek Documents*. Jerusalem: Israel Exploration Society, 1989.
P.Mich.	Edgar, C. C., et. al., eds. *Michigan Papyri*. 29 vols. Ann Arbor: University of Michigan Press; Cleveland: American Philological Association; Toronto: Oxbow; Zutphen: Terra; Atlanta: Scholars Press; Amsterdam; Stuttgart: Tuebner, 1931–1999.
P.Michael.	Crawford, David Steward, eds. *Papyri Michaelidae, being a Catalogue of Greek and Latin Papyri, Tablets*

	and Ostraca in the Library of Mr G.A. Michailidis of Cairo. Aberdeen: Egypt Exploration Society, 1955.
P.Münch.	Heisenberg, A., et al., eds. *Die Papyri der Bayerischen Staatsbibliothek München.* 3 vols. Stuttgart: Teubner, 1986.
P.Murabba'ât	Benoit, P., J. T. Milik, and R. de Vaux. *Les grottes de Murabba'ât.* Oxford: Clarendon, 1961.
P.Oxy.	Grenfell, Bernard P., et al., eds. *The Oxyrhynchus Papyri.* London: Egypt Exploration Fund, 1898–.
P.Oxy.Hels.	Zilliacus, H., J. Frösén, P. Hohti, J. Kaimio, and M. Kaimio, eds. *Fifty Oxyrhynchus Papyri.* Helsinki: Societas Scientiarum Fennica, 1979.
P.Petra	Frösen, J., et al., eds. *The Petra Papyri.* Amman: American Center of Oriental Research, 2002, 2007.
P.Petaus	Hagedorn, Ursula, Dietr Hagedorn, Louise C. Youtie, and Herbert C. Youtie. *Das Archiv des Petaus.* Opladen: Westdeutscher Verlag, 1969.
P.Rain.Cent.	Loebenstein, Helene. *Festschrift zum 100-jährigen Bestehen der Papyrussammlung der Österreichischen Nationalbibliothek, Papyrus Erzherzog Rainer.* Wein: Brüder Hollinek, 1983.
P.Ryl.	Hunt, A., et al., eds. *Catalogue of the Greek and Latin Papyri in the John Rylands Library, Manchester.* Manchester: Manchester University Press, 1911–1952.
P.Scholl.	Popko, Lutz, Nadine Quenouille, and Michaela Rücker, eds. *Von Sklaven, Pächtern und Politikern: Beiträge zum Alltag in Ägypten, Griechenland und Rom.* Archiv für Papyrusforschung und verwandte Gebiete 33. Berlin: De Gruyter, 2012.
P.Sijp.	Sirks, Adriaan Johan Boudewijn, and K. A. Worp, eds. *Papyri in Memory of P. J. Sijpesteijn,* Oakville, CT: American Society of Papyrologists, 2007.
P.Stras.	Preisigke, F., ed. *Griechische Papyrus der Kaiserlichen Universitäts- und Landes-bibliothek zu Strassburg.* 9 vols. Leipzig: Hinrichs, 1912–1989.
P.Tebt.	Grenfell, B. P., et al., eds. *The Tebtunis Papyri.* 5 vols. London, 1902–2005.

P.Turner	Parsons, Patricia J., and Helen Cockle, eds. *Papyri Greek and Egyptian Edited by Various Hands in Honour of Eric Gardner Turner on the Occasion of His Seventieth Birthday*. London: Egypt Exploration Society, 1981.
P.Ups.Frid.	Frid, Bo, ed. *Ten Uppsala Papyri*. Bonn: Habelt, 1981.
P.Vind.Bosw.	Boswinkel, E., ed. *Einige Wiener Papyri*. Leiden: Brill, 1942.
P.Warr.	David, M., B. A. van Groningen, and J. C. van Oven, eds. *The Warren Papyri*. Leiden: Lugduni Batavorum, 1941.
P.Wisc.	Sijpesteijn, P. J., ed. *The Wisconsin Papyri*. 2 vols. Leiden: Brill, 1967; Zutphen: Terra, 1977.
P.Yadin	Levine, Baruch A., et. al., eds. *The Documents from the Bar Kochba Period in the Cave of Letters*. 2 vols. Jerusalem: Israel Exploration Society, 1963–2002.
PapyLup	*Papyrologica Lupiensia*
PfMb	Pfuhl, Ernst, and Hans Möbius, eds. *Die ostgriechischen Grabreliefs*. 2 vols. Mainz am Rhein: von Zabern, 1977–1979.
PG	Patrologia Graeca
PGM	Preisendanz, Karl, ed. and trans. *Papyri Graecae Magicae: Die griechischen Zauberpapyri*. 3 vols. Leipzig: Teubner, 1928–1941.
PIR	*Prosopographia Imperii Romani*
PKNT	Papyrologische Kommentare zum Neuen Testament
PSI	Vitelli, G., et al., eds. *Papiri greci e latini*. 15 vols. Florence: Pubblicazioni della Società Italiana per la ricerca dei papiri greci e latini in Egitto, 1912–1957.
PzB	*Protokolle zur Bibel*
RBPH	*Revue belge de Philologie et d'Histoire*
RECAM	Regional Epigraphic Catalogues of Asia Minor
RevExp	*Review and Expositor*
RGRW	Religions in the Graeco-Roman World
RIC 1	Sutherland, C. H. V. *31 BC to AD 69, Augustus to Vitellius*. Vol. 1 of *Roman Imperial Coinage*. London: Spink, 1984.

RIC 2	Mattingly, Harold, et al. *Vespasian to Hadrian*. Vol. 2 of *The Roman Imperial Coinage*. London: Spink, 1972.
RPC	Amandry, M., and A. Burnett. *Roman Provincial Coinage*. London: British Museum; Paris: Bibliothéque nationale de France, 1992–.
RPC CS	Ripollès, P., A. Burnett, M. Amandry, I. Carradice, and M. Spoerri. *Roman Provincial Coinage, Consolidated Supplement I–III*. Oxford: Ashmolean Museum, 1992–2015.
RPC Supp. 1	Burnett, A., M. Amandry, and P. P. Ripolles. *Roman Provincial Coinage, Supplement I*. Paris, Bibliothèque Nationale de France, 1999.
RPC Supp. 2	Burnett, A., M. Amandry, P. P. Ripollès, and I. Carradice. *Roman Provincial Coinage, Supplement II*. London: British Museum Press, 2006.
RPC Supp. 3	Burnett, A., M. Amandry, I. Carradice, P. P. Ripollès, and M. Spoerri. *Roman Provincial Coinage, Supplement III*. New York: The American Numismatic Society, 2014.
RPC Supp. 4	Amandry, M., A. Burnett, A. Hostein, J. Mairat, P. P. Ripollès, and M. S. Butcher. *Roman Provincial Coinage, Supplement 4*. London: British Museum Press, 2017.
RPC Supp. 5	Amandry, M., A. Burnett, A. Hostein, J. Mairat, P. P. Ripollès, and M. S. Butcher. *Roman Provincial Coinage, Supplement 5*. London: British Museum Press, 2019.
RRA	Rhetoric of Religious Antiquity
SB	Sammelbuch griechischer Urkunden aus Aegypten
SBLSBS	Society of Biblical Literature Sources for Biblical Study
SBLSP	Society of Biblical Literature Seminar Papers
SEG	*Supplementum Epigraphicum Graecum*
SIG	Dittenberger, Wilhelm. *Sylloge inscriptonum graecarum*. 4 vols. 3rd ed. Leipzig: Hirzel, 1915–1924.
SNG	Sylloge Nummorum Graecorum
SNTSMS	Society for New Testament Studies Monograph Series

SNTSU	Studien zum Neuen Testament und seiner Umwelt
SP	Sacra pagina
SPP	Wessely, C. *Studien zur Palaeographie und Papyruskunde.* Leipzig: Avenarius, 1901—1924.
STOA	Studien zur Umwelt des Neuen Testaments
StPatr	*Studia Patristica*
SUNT	Studien zur Umwelt des Neuen Testaments
T.Dacia	Russu, I. I., ed. *Tablitele Cerate Dacice.* Bucharest: Editura Academiei Republicii Socialiste România, 1975.
T.Hercul.	Camodeca, Giuseppe. "Tabulae Herculanenses: Riedizione delle emptiones di schiavi (TH 59–62)." Pages 53–76 in *Quaestiones Iuris: Festschrift für Joseph Georg Wolf zum 70. Geburtstag.* Edited by Ulrich Manthe and Christoph Krampe. Freiburger rechtsgeschichtliche Abhandlungen 2/36. Berlin: Duncker & Humblot, 2000.
T.Jucundus	Zangemeister, K., ed. *Tabulae ceratae Pompeis repertae annis MCCCLXXV et MCCCLXXXVII.* CILSup 4.1. Berlin: de Gruyter, 1898.
T.Sulpicii	Camodeca, G., ed. *Tabulae Pompeianae Sulpiciorum: Edizione critica dell'archivio puteolano dei Sulpicii.* 2 vols. Rome: Quasar, 1999.
T.Vind.	Speidel, Michael Alexander, ed. *Die römischen Schreibtafeln von Vindonissa.* Brugg: Gesellschaft Pro Vindonissa, 1996.
T.Vindol.	Bowman, A. K., an J. D. Thomas, ed. *Vindolanda: The Latin Writing Tablets.* 3 vols. London: Society for the Promotion of Roman Studies, 1983–2003.
TAM	Kalinka, E., et al., eds. *Tituli Asiae Minoris.* 5 vols. Vindobonae: Hoelder-Pichler-Tempsky; 1920–1989.
THKNT	Theologischer Handkommentar zum Neuen Testament
TPINTC	TPI New Testament Commentaries
TSAJ	Texte und Studien zum antiken Judentum
TU	Texte und Untersuchungen
TynBul	*Tyndale Bulletin*
VCSup	Supplements to Vigiliae Christianae

VeEc	*Verbum et Ecclesia*
W.Chr.	Mitteis, L., and U. Wilcken, eds. *Grundzüge und Chrestomathie der Papyruskunde*. 2 vols. Leipzig: Teubner, 1912.
WBC	Word Biblical Commentary
WD	*Wort und Dienst*
WUNT	Wisssenschaftliche Untersuchungenzum Neuen Testament
ZKT	*Zeitschrift für katholische Theologie*
ZNW	*Zeitschrift für die neutestamentliche Wissenschaft und die Kunde der älteren Kirche*
ZPE	*Zeitschrift für Papyrologie und Epigraphik*
ZSS	*Zeitschrift der Savigny-Stiftung für Rechtsgeschichte*

Part 1
Introduction to the Lycus Valley

Perspectives on the Lycus Valley: An Inscriptional, Archaeological, Numismatic, and Iconographic Approach

Alan H. Cadwallader and James R. Harrison

This chapter discusses the archaeology, epigraphy, numismatics, and iconography of the Lycus Valley and its famous three New Testament cities (Colossae, Laodicea, Hierapolis). Part 1 of the chapter, written by Alan H. Cadwallader, is an epigraphic portrait of Colossae. Crucially, among other important contributions, Cadwallader provides an up-to-date list of the thirty-one Colossian inscriptions available for New Testament researchers on ancient Colossae. What is known archaeologically about the (as yet) unexcavated city may be found in his book on the few archaeological fragments that we do have, as well as the collection of essays on the city, edited with Michael Trainor.[1]

Parts 2 and 3 have been written by James R. Harrison. Part 2 explores the history of Laodicea and its archaeological excavation, proceeding then to an archaeological, epigraphic, numismatic, and iconographic investigation of the site. The reason for such a comprehensive approach is that the publications on the archaeological excavation of the city are either in French, Italian, or Turkish. Gratifyingly a small but helpful collection of English essays on Laodicea and Hierapolis has recently appeared.[2] In

---

1. Alan H. Cadwallader, *Fragments of Colossae: Sifting through the Traces* (Hindmarsh: ATF Press, 2015); Cadwallader and Michael Trainor, eds., *Colossae in Space and Time: Linking to an Ancient City* (Göttingen: Vandenhoeck & Ruprecht, 2011). Note most recently his authoritative essay: Alan H. Cadwallader, "The Historical Sweep of the Life of Kolossai," in *Epigraphical Evidence Illustrating Paul's Letter to the Colossians*, ed. Joseph Verheyden, Marcus Öhler, and Thomas Corsten, WUNT 411 (Tübingen: Mohr Siebeck, 2018), 25–67.

2. Celal Şimşek and Francesco D'Andria, eds., *Landscape and History in the Lykos*

Harrison's treatment, he draws attention to the intersection of the material evidence of Laodicea and Hierapolis with the New Testament at various places.

Part 3 adopts a more constricted approach to the evidence of Hierapolis, examining the Severan theater reliefs at Hierapolis and their significance for the city's identity in the Second Sophistic period, as well as several epigraphic vignettes of its urban life. Although the results of the archaeological and epigraphic investigation of Hierapolis continue to be published in the ever-expanding Italian series *Hierapolis Di Frigia*, eleven volumes having appeared so far, there are for the English reader two invaluable publications on the archaeology of Hierapolis and its epigraphy.[3] The history of the city and of the archaeological teams who unearthed its remains can also be consulted there.[4] The coinage of the city has also received detailed attention in English scholarship over the years.[5] This allows us to pursue the more focused approach adopted in this section. However, for specialists, the technical study of the city's epigraphy is exceptionally well served by several publications of the highest quality.[6]

In 2013 the pioneering publication of Ulrich Huttner on the history of early Christianity in the Lycus Valley appeared to subsequent critical acclaim. The current volume pays homage to his scholarly contribution

---

Valley: Laodikeia and Hierapolis in Phrygia (Newcastle upon Tyne: Cambridge Scholars, 2017). Additionally, Francesco D'Andria, "Hierapolis of Phrygia: Its Evolution in Hellenistic and Roman Times," in *Urbanism in Western Asia Minor: New Studies on Aphrodisias, Ephesos, Hierapolis, Pergamon, Perge and Xanthos*, ed. David Parrish, JRASup 45 (Portsmouth: Journal of Roman Archaeology, 2001), 96–115.

3. Tullia Ritti, *An Epigraphic Guide to Hierapolis (Pamukkale)* (Istanbul: Ege Yayinlari, 2006); Francesco D'Andria, *Hierapolis of Phrygia (Pamukkale): An Archaeological Guide*, trans. P. Arthur (Istanbul: Ege Yayinlari, 2010). Additionally, D'Andria, "Hierapolis of Phrygia," 96–115.

4. D'Andria, *Hierapolis of Phrygia*, 9–13, 17–19.

5. See Leo Weber, "The Coins of Hierapolis in Phrygia," *NumC* 13 (1913): 1–30, 161; Weber, "The Coins of Hierapolis in Phrygia (Continued)," *NumC* 13 (1913): 133–61; Ann Johnston, "Hierapolis Revisited," *NumC* 144 (1984): 52–80.

6. Carl Humann, et al., ed. *Altertümer von Hierapolis* (Berlin: Reimer, 1898); Tullia Ritti, *Hierapolis I: Fonti Letterarie ed Epigrafiche*, Archeologica 30 (Rome: Giorgio Bretschneider, 1985); Ritti, *Epigraphic Guide to Hierapolis*; Ritti et al., *Museo Archaeologicodi Denizli-Hierapolis: Catalogo delle iscrizioni greche e latine* (Naples: Liguori, 2008); Ritti, *Hierapolis di Frigia IX: Storia e istituzioni di Hierapolis* (Istanbul: Ege YayinLari, 2017). For the documentary evidence regarding Asian Jews, including those at Laodicea and Hierapolis, see *IJO* 2.

with three incisive responses to his work from seasoned Lycus Valley scholars.[7] As a further contribution in this volume, Huttner brings the coins of Hierapolis into dialogue with the Epistle to the Colossians. Rosemary Canavan, Alan H. Cadwallader, and Harry O. Maier respond to Huttner's magnum opus from various viewpoints and methodologies, appreciatively highlighting his enormous contribution to the discipline, while posing new questions about his arguments, use of evidence, and conclusions. The remaining essays in the volume—authored by Clinton E. Arnold, Peter Arzt-Grabner, Angela Standhartinger, Michael P. Theophilos, Michael Trainor, Allen Brent, and James R. Harrison—present thematic and exegetical essays on aspects of the historical, social, and religious life in the Lycus Valley from a variety of methodological viewpoints involving the material and documentary evidence.

Part 1. An Epigraphic Portrait of Colossae

Colossae is frequently represented as the poor relative of the major triad of cities in the Lycus Valley: that is, of Hierapolis, Laodikeia, and Colossae. Hierapolis and Laodikeia have received extensive excavations and analysis (see above). Their inventories of inscriptions are significant and expanding (see above), but, perhaps significantly, have yet to reveal any epigraphical mention of their neighbor to the east, at the entrance to the valley. Rather, they carry mutual references (both affirming and contesting),[8] in addition to their many connections with other cities, villages, and sanctuaries in ever-widening circles across Asia Minor (and occasionally beyond). This mutuality of notice seems to be mirrored in the Roman institutional perspective that at times grouped Laodikeia and Hierapolis as a pair[9] but neglected any grouping of these cities with Colossae. No Colossian-minted bronzes have been found thus far in the coins discovered in finds from

---

7. Ulrich Huttner, *Early Christianity in the Lycus Valley*, trans. David Green, AJEC 85; Early Christianity in Asia Minor 1 (Leiden: Brill, 2013).

8. For conflict (over fishing taxes/rights) between the two cities (with Tripolis joining Hierapolis in the dispute), see Ritti, *Hierapolis di Frigia IX*, 388–95; for (a form of) cooperation, see the Laodikeian northern theater seat-allocation to the famed association of purple-dyers: Celal Şimşek and M. A. Sezgin, "Laodikeia Kuzey Tiyatrosu (The North Theatre at Laodikeia)," *Olba* 19 (2011): 186.

9. See Michel Christol and Thomas Drew-Bear, "Un sénateur de Xanthos," *Journal des Savants* 3 (1991): 195–226, especially at 213; see also *TAM* 2:194.

Laodikeia or Hierapolis, even though the latter boasts at least twenty-eight other cities among those civic coins found in excavations at the ancient site.[10] References to either city in a Colossian connection must await a fourth century date.[11] This is not to suggest that Colossae was either isolationist or reduced to the decaying rump that earlier scholarship predicated of the city.[12] Even with the minimal amount of evidence that we possess, Colossae can be demonstrated to have enjoyed contact with other cities such as Apameia, Aphrodisias, Attouda, Boubon, Ephesus, Eumeneia, Keretapa, Sardis, Smyrna, and Tripolis. Other cities might reasonably be affirmed to be connected with Colossae by reason of road networks. Certainly, the Roman army, when passing the city, seems to have relied on supplies from her civic warehouses (*IGRR* 4.870.9).

Colossae's list of inscriptions has witnessed only small increments since the initial discoveries of Francis Arundell in 1826, and the fixing of the site itself by William Hamilton in 1836.[13] It is clear that earlier epigraphic evidence was seen,[14] but transcriptions were not executed. To

---

10. A. Travaglini and V. G. Camilleri, *Hierapolis di Frigia, Le Monete: Campagne di Scavo 1957–2004* (Istanbul: Ege, 2010), 9–12, 23.

11. A positive reference to Hierapolis occurs in the early Byzantine story, The Miracle of St Michael of Chonai, which probably originates in the late fourth century as a popular reaction to the implicit Laodikeian impugning of Colossian religious practices in the Synod of Laodikeia canon 35; see Alan H. Cadwallader, "Inter-City Conflict in the Story of St Michael of Chonai," in *Religious Conflict from Early Christianity to the Rise of Islam*, ed. Wendy Mayer and Bronwyn Neil (Tübingen: de Gruyter, 2013), 109–28.

12. See Cadwallader, *Fragments of Colossae*, 5–24.

13. Published in F. V. J. Arundell, *A Visit to the Seven Churches of Asia Minor with an Excursion into Pisidia* (London: John Rodwell, 1828), 98, 156; Arundell, *Discoveries in Asia Minor*, 2 vols. (London: R. Bentley, 1834), 170; W. J. Hamilton, *Researches in Asia Minor, Pontus and Armenia*, 2 vols. (London: J. Murray, 1842).

14. In 1750, Robert Wood mentions an inscription when he was journeying from Laodikeia that caused him to surmise that Colossae was nearby; this suggests a milestone: journal 6, fol.67 (Joint Library of the Hellenic and Roman Societies, University of London). The Italian explorer, Antonino Picenini, in 1705, commented on many columns, inscriptions, and other remains strewn along the space of a mile, but he provided no more than this general observation: travel diary, Asia Minor, fols. 68–69 (BL Add MS 6269). In 1828, Francis Arundell relayed a report from a Greek correspondent that an inscription was to be seen high on a cliff face above two artificial caves that were probably used by religious ascetics overlooking the Saint Michael shrine at what is now the Göz picnic ground between Honaz and Emirazizli. Investigations by

date, thirty-one inscriptions are known if two inscriptions from elsewhere (Smyrna, Boubon) that mention Colossae are added.[15] Also included in this number is an inscription on a recently rediscovered double-sided intaglio gem held in a swivel ring—"Tyche Protogeneia of the Colossians." The extensively carved cornelian was first published in 1780 but was thought to be lost.[16] Some efforts to expand the list have been encouraged by the misleading descriptions in the collection of epitaphs published by Ernst Pfuhl and Hans Möbius, who referred to a number of discoveries as somehow related to Colossae.[17] The stylistic similarities in funerary stelae from Colossae and Attouda are manifest, but stylistic similarities can also be found in the funerary *bomoi* (altar-like tombstones) from Colossae and Eumeneia without suggesting that the Eumeneian *bomoi* should be included as those of Colossae. When the original publications of the stelae and their inscriptions are traced, it is clear that they are to be assigned to Attouda and its surrounding region, not to Colossae.[18]

This small (but for that reason treasured) aggregate provides scholarly analysis of Colossae with an even more penurious supply than that

---

the author of this section revealed the carved cavities but no inscription. It may well have been painted. See Arundell, *Visit to the Seven Churches of Asia Minor*, 318–20.

15. IK 23.440 (Smyrna); Milner, *Epigraphical Survey*, 3.4.11 (Balboura). See the list following in the main text.

16. A. Belley, "Observations sur une Cornaline Antique du Cabinet de Mgr le Duc D'Orléans," in *Histoire des Ouvrages de l'Academie Royale des Inscriptions et Belles-Lettres* (Paris: Panckoucke, 1780), 17–27; P. G. P. Meyboom, *The Nile Mosaic of Palestrina* (Leiden: Brill, 1995), 210 n. 37. Cadwallader announced the "rediscovery" at the Annual Meeting of the Society of Biblical Literature in Atlanta in 2016: "A forgotten intaglio gem of Colossae: exploring religious aggregation in a first-century polis of Asia Minor." However, the gem had remained secure at The Hermitage Museum in Saint Petersburg for more than two hundred years. It was included as part of a special exhibition of the Duc d'Orléans collection in 2001 and published in a Russian-French catalogue to the exhibition; see Y. O. Kagan and O. Y. Neverov, *Le Destin d'une Collection: 500 pierres gravées du Duc d'Orléans* (Saintt Petersburg: Musée de l'Hermitage, 2001), §274/92.

17. So "aus der Gegend von Attouda bis Kolossai"; see Ernst Pfuhl and Hans Möbius, *Die Ostgriechischen Grabreliefs*, 4 vols (Mainz: von Zabern, 1977–1979), nos. 236, 1607, 1634, 1665b, 1920, 1973, 2005.

18. This requires that one funerary stela for Zeuxis, son of Zeuxis (Pfuhl and Möbius, *Die Ostgriechischen Grabreliefs*, no. 1920), now found at the Basmahane museum at Izmir and listed there as from Colossae (sometimes so found on the web), should be corrected.

of Lystra,[19] a similarly unexcavated site of particular interest to New Testament commentators. There has been no collation of the discoveries to date. The published transcriptions of Arundell and Edward T. Daniell were incorporated into the early massive compilation, the four-volume *Corpus Inscriptionum Graecarum*.[20] Subsequently, several more inscriptions were published in various journals.

The largest number of inscriptions was provided by William Buckler and William Calder in 1939, the result of half a day's on-site coverage in 1933, with a handful of further days spent scouring Denizli and Honaz.[21] The resultant publication contained twelve new inscriptions (*MAMA* 6.38–49), along with two broken funerary stones (a stela and a sarcophagus side), both of which could be expected to have contained an inscription on lost fragments of the respective installations (*MAMA* 6.50, 51). One item found on site was adjudged to be too fragmentary for inclusion.[22] Calder and Buckler also provided a list of all inscriptions of Colossae up to the time of their publication, a further eight inscriptions.[23] These are indicated by an asterisk in the list below. The inscribed swivel-ring carnelian gem was not included in their list.

Since 1939, a small number of inscriptions have been published and previously published inscriptions have been revised in their readings, translations, and analyses. Noteworthy has been Tullia Ritti's inclusion of a number of inscriptions from Colossae that are now held in the Denizli Museum at Hierapolis.[24] For the sake of providing the most up-to-date (compressed) concordance of inscriptions for ongoing research, the following list has been compiled.[25] The abbreviated publication references

---

19. For the number of inscriptions assigned to Lystra, much depends on the designation of the catchment area. *MAMA* 8 lists fifty-one inscriptions for Lystra itself, with another forty-seven if the region includes the territory bordered by the Çarşamba River.

20. *CIG* 3955, 3956, 4380k^3. A selection of Daniell's Inscriptions were also published in T. A. B. Spratt and E. Forbes, *Travels in Lycia, Milyas and the Cibyratis in company with the late Rev. E. T. Daniell*, 2 vols. (London: John van Hoorst, 1847).

21. See Alan H. Cadwallader, "Revisiting Calder on Colossae," *AS* 56 (2006): 103–11.

22. Cadwallader, "Revisiting Calder on Colossae," 108.

23. *MAMA* 6:142.

24. Ritti et al., *Museo Archaeologicodi Denizli-Hierapolis*, nos. 59, 73, 80 (= *MAMA* 6.50, anepigraphic), 113.

25. There are possible additions to this list. High up the monolith above the

may be checked against the list of abbreviations and the bibliography to obtain full details.[26]

1. Belley, "Observations," 17–27 = Belley 1784, 11–14 = Kagan Neverov, *Destin d'une Collection*, 274/92. Tyche Protogeneia of the Kolossians (intaglio gem).
2. *MAMA* 6.45. Epitaph for Trophimos and his wife.
3. *MAMA* 6.44 = Cadwallader, "New Inscription," 40.112 §2 = *SEG* 57.1385. Epitaph for Dion the leatherworker.
4. *CIG* 3956 = Arundell, *Discoveries in Asia Minor*, 170 = Arundell, *Visit to the Seven Churches of Asia Minor*, 98 = *MAMA* 6.51 = Cadwallader, "New Inscription," 40.114 = *SEG* 57.1383. Tomb of Datys (?) son of Zenon.
5. *MAMA* 6.46. Epitaph for Damokrates by Testamentary Disposition.
6. *MAMA* 6.41. Honour for Herakleon.
7. *CIG* 3955 = Arundell, *Visit to the Seven Churches of Asia Minor*, 156 = *MAMA* 6.53*. Epitaph (?).

---

spring that was likely the site of the Saint Michael hagiasma, there appears to be the letters T H P carved vertically. Confidence is impossible, but it may suggest ὁ σωτήρ, which would fit with the story of Saint Michael of Chonai and its possible forebears in a Zeus cult. See Alan H. Cadwallader, "'As If in a Vision of the Night…': Authorising the Healing Spring of Chonai," in *Dreams, Memory and Imagination in Byzantium*, ed. Bronwyn Neil and Eva Anagnostou-Laoutides (Leiden: Brill, 2018), 265–92. The Ak khan caravanserai outside Denizli (built in 1253–1254) made extensive use of materials quarried from ancient sites. There are reasons to suspect that Colossae rather than Laodikeia was a preferred source. The wall contains two re-used fragmentary inscriptions. See Alan H. Cadwallader, "One Man, Two Women, One Grave: Complicating Family Life at Colossae," in *Stones, Bones and the Sacred: Essays on Material Culture and Ancient Religion in Honor of Dennis E. Smith*, ed. Alan H. Cadwallader (Atlanta: SBL Press, 2016), 165 n. 36. Two other references to inscriptional evidence have been made, a stone reused in the old Moslem cemetery adjacent to the fortress above the town of Honaz seen by George Lampakis in 1909; the other noted by Harold Mare in 1976. Both inscriptions were said to be too abraded for recording. See G. Lampakis, Οἱ ἑπτά ἀστέρες τῆς Ἀποκαλύψεως [The seven stars of Revelation] (Athens: Tzabella, 1909), 452–54; W. Harold Mare, "Archaeological Prospects at Colossae," *NEASB* 7 (1976): 39–59. One *bomos* with relief, situated in a Honaz café, is heavily weathered but could be expected to have contained a funerary inscription when pristine; see Cadwallader, "One Man, Two Women, One Grave," 167.

26. References to the journals *JHS*, *BE*, *GRBS*, *MDAIA*, and *BCH* include only the volume and pages.

8. Clerc, "Inscriptions de la vallée du Méandre," 11.353 §11 = *MAMA* 6.40 = Magie, *Roman Rule*, 1523 n. 57. Games honors for Zenon.
9. *MAMA* 6.48 = PfMb 2.1974 = *BE* 1979:15 = *SEG* 29.1391 = Ritti et al., *Museo Archaeologicodi Denizli-Hierapolis*, §73 = Huttner, *Early Christianity in the Lycus Valley*, 31. Epitaph for Tatianos.
10. *IGRR* 4.869 = *JHS* 18:90 §25 = *MAMA* 6.47* = Magie, *Roman Rule*, 1479 n. 28 = Pflaum, *Les Carrières*, 1.262 §109. Dedication to the Emperor Hadrian.
11. *JHS* 18:90 §26 = *MAMA* 6.50* = Merkelbach and Stauber, *Steinepigramme*, 1.02.15.01. Kastor the pugilist.
12. *MAMA* 6.49 = *GRBS* 48:334. Offering at Saint Theodore's Church (?).
13. *MDAIA* 16:199 = *IGRR* 4.871 = *MAMA* 6.52*. Epitaph of Karpon.
14. *MAMA* 6.42 = Robert, "Les inscriptions," 328. Epitaph of Aurelios Herakleon.
15. *MAMA* 6.38 = Foss, *History*, 2.483. Dedication to Constantius I, Diocletian, and Maximian.
16. *LBW* 1693b = *IGRR* 4.870 = Ramsay, *Cities and Bishopric*, 212 = *MAMA* 6.48* = Robert, "Les inscriptions," 269 = *BE* 1970:584 = Magie, *Roman Rule*, 986 n. 22. Honor for a Boularch.
17. Cadwallader, "Revisiting Calder," 56.108. A cautionary (funerary) fine to the fiskos.
18. *MDAIA* 18:206 §3 = Bell, "Archives," F210 = Wilson, *Handbooks*, 104. Funerary *bomos* for Dionysios and family.
19. Clerc, "Inscriptions de la vallée du Méandre," 11.354 §12 = *IGRR* 4.868 = *MAMA* 6.46* = Robert, "Les inscriptions," 278. Votive (road marker?) to Trajan.
20. Clerc, "Inscriptions de la vallée du Méandre," 11.353 §10 = *MAMA* 6.49*. Priest of Dionysos.
21. *MDAIA* 18:207 §4 = *MAMA* 6.43 = IK 49.104 = Emrys-Evans, "Notes on the Consonants," 12.162. Epitaph for Markos.
22. Cadwallader, "New Inscription," 40.114 §3 [109 §1] = *EBGR* 2007:25 = *SEG* 57.1382. Honor for Markos, chief translator of Colossae.
23. *MAMA* 6.47 = *BE* 1939:392 = PfMb 1.594 = Ritti et al., *Museo Archaeologicodi Denizli-Hierapolis*, §113. Epitaph for Glykon.
24. Cadwallader, "New Inscription," 40.109 §1 = *SEG* 57.1384. Epitaph for Karpos and his family.

25. *MAMA* 6.39 = Ritti et al., *Museo Archaeologicodi Denizli-Hierapolis*, §59. Funerary honor for Crispinus.
26. Spratt and Forbes, *Travels in Lycia*, 2.289 = *LBW* 1220 = *CIG* 3.4380k^3 = *BCH* 107:552 n. 9 = Milner, *Epigraphical Survey*, 3.4.11 = *IBoubon* 102. Epitaph for (Arphias/Apphias/)Aphias.
27. IK 23.440 = Michon, "Erwerbungen," 1900.156 §24 = Dain *Inscr* §53 = Robert, *Opera Minores*, 3.1587 §53. Epitaph for Diodotos the Colossian.
28. Konakçi-Duman *Denizli Sempozyumu* 1.61 §8 (pl. 12b). A votive altar for Bacchus?
29. Cadwallader, "Honouring the Repairer of the Baths," 2012 = *NewDocs* 10.17 = *AÉ* 2011.1347 = *BE* 2013:407 = *SEG* 61.1160 = *SEG* 62.1235 = Reasoner, *Roman Imperial Texts*, 138–39. Honour for Korymbos for the repair of the baths.
30. Cadwallader, "One Man, Two Women," 168. Epitaph for Epictetus and Ariste.
31. Cadwallader, "One Man, Two Women," 171. Epitaph for Meniandros, Zenonis and Hieikis (?).

The inscriptions span a period from perhaps the first century before the common era (no. 5) to the fifth or early sixth century (no. 12). So the inscriptions, though few, witness to six hundred years of epigraphical activity, even without any archaeological excavations. The majority (eighteen) are epitaphs or funerary memorializations. Only one inscription is in Latin (no. 15, an imperial reuse of a Greek memorialization, no. 14, executed barely sixty years previously). The inscriptions in their style and geographical context have also enabled some insights into the religious, political, and social structures and influences within Colossian society.

Most significant for the interpretation of the history of Colossae in the first century has been the discovery of a large honorific pedestal that acknowledges the beneficence of a certain Korymbos in repairing the baths and extending the water infrastructure of the city (no. 29). The inscription is dated to the late first century to early second century CE on the basis of letter style and the Hellenistic naming formulae of the thirty honorands.[27] This has laid to rest the axiom that Colossae was either destroyed or set

---

27. Alan H. Cadwallader, "Honouring the Repairer of the Baths: A New Inscription from Kolossai," *Antichthon* 46 (2012): 150–83.

into a terminal spiral by the earthquake of 60 CE that hit the Lycus Valley.[28] It has revived attention directed toward other inscriptions that belong to the second and third centuries. Most important in this regard has been the short honorific inscription (*IGRR* 4.869) for the emperor Hadrian set up at Colossae by one of the commanders of Hadrian's military escort Loukius (Statius) Makedo.[29] Hadrian's pan-Hellenic tour of 129 CE brought special contact with those ancient cities that had a proud heritage of the worship of Zeus. Colossae seems to have been one of the stations for this propaganda extravaganza. How important was the honor of an imperial adventus for the city can be witnessed in its coins. Two separate benefactors sponsored the minting of bronzes that accorded Hadrian the key title marking his tour—Olympios. One coin, struck by the named benefactor, Hieronymos, has already been published. It has a bare-headed Hadrian, wearing a paludamentum and featuring the legend "Olympian Hadrian."[30] Hieronymos was responsible for eight different coins struck from the Colossian mint, so one might expect him to have joined the honor roll exalting Hadrian. But he was joined by another benefactor, Octavios Apollonios, son of Valerianos or Valerios. (He seems concerned to give his full identification on his coins.) Four of his civic coins, running through to the end of Hadrian's reign have been published.[31] Recently, a fifth has come to light that probably indicates the enthusiasm of Colossae's ruling elite to join the celebrations honoring Hadrian on tour. Apollonios also

---

28. Alan H. Cadwallader, "Refuting an Axiom of Scholarship on Colossae: Fresh Insights from New and Old Inscriptions," in Cadwallader and Trainor, *Colossae in Space and Time*, 151–79; Lukas Bormann, *Der Brief des Paulus an die Kolosser*, ThHK 10.1 (Leipzig: Evangelische Verlagsanstalt, 2012), 12–28; Paul Foster, *Colossians*, BNTC (London: T&T Clark, 2016), 1–24; Janice C. Anderson, *Colossians: An Introduction and Study Guide: Authorship, Rhetoric, and Code* (London: T&T Clark, 2018), 20–21, 55–58.

29. See H-G. Pflaum, *Les Carrières Procuratoriennes Équestres sous le Haut-Empire romain*, (Paris: P. Geuthner, 1960), 1.109 (262–64); H. Halfmann *Itinera principum: Geschichte und Typologie der Kaiserreisen im Römischen Reich* (Stuttgart: Steiner, 1986), 206; Anthony R. Birley, *Hadrian: The Restless Emperor* (London: Routledge, 1997), 216–20.

30. Hans von Aulock, *Münzen und Städte Phrygiens*, 2 vols., IstMitt 25, 27. (Tübingen: Wasmuth, 1980, 1987), 2.547; *RPC* 3.2309.

31. See von Aulock, *Münzen und Städte Phrygiens* 2.447, 550, 551. On the coins from Colossae for the reign of Hadrian, see Alan H. Cadwallader, "Wealthy, Widowed, Astute and Beneficent: Claudia Eugenetoriane and the Second Century Revival of the Colossian Mint," *New Docs* 12 (forthcoming).

minted a coin bearing the Colossian banner, his own name, and honoring "Olympian Hadrian." The iconography is virtually identical to that minted by Hieronymos.[32] This evidence shows clearly that Colossae remained a vibrant city into the second century (and beyond). In fact, the evidence of coins, including a homonoia coin indicating an alliance with Aphrodisias struck early in the reign of the emperor Commodus, plus that of inscriptions, suggests that Colossae, along with a number of cities in Asia Minor, experienced a substantial increase in its prosperity in this period.[33]

The yield of names (of subscribers, with their genealogies) from this inscription amounts to sixty-six that survive in whole or in part on the damaged shaft of the *bomos*. It probably originally contained about one hundred names. This list has substantially bolstered the onomastic stock of Colossae, so as to make a significant contribution to the *Lexicon of Greek Personal Names*.[34] The Hellenistic-style genealogies sometimes run to five generations and so provide the names of Colossian citizens, some dating back to the turn of the common era. Scholarly interaction since the publication of the *editio princeps* has made a few valuable suggestions as to alternate onomastic forms and their origins.[35] But this list enables tentative assessments of the shifting identities and ethnic origins of the Colossian population. Particularly interesting is that the dedicants all have Greek names, even one, named Theodore, who could claim a Roman name (Likinnios) belonging to a (servile?) forebear. At the same time, the names in the genealogies for these dedicants occasionally reveal indigenous Phrygian, Thracian, and perhaps Scythian, Lycian, Carian, and Lydian names. This suggests that ethnicity was somewhat fluid in this period, with a clear preference for Greek identification. Colossians were self-curating as Greek, none more so than the family that gave a son the rare name of a Homeric character, Tudeides. None of these Colossian citizens either has or wants to display a Roman citizenry name, and all proudly display stability in their family lines (at Colossae) with a clear adherence to "Greekness."[36] This

---

32. RPC 3.2310A online.

33. See generally, Cadwallader, "Historical Sweep of the Life of Kolossai."

34. See *LGPN* 5C., e.g., s.v. "Κόρυμβος."

35. See especially the comments of Patrice Hamon in *BE* 2013.407, who suggests Τρυφωνίων for Τρυφωνίωνος in l. 27.

36. See Harry O. Maier, *Picturing Paul in Empire: Imperials Image, Text and Persuasion in Colossians, Ephesians and the Pastoral Epistles* (London: T&T Clark, 2013), 92–93.

valorization of Greek identity may explain the unique occurrence in the New Testament of Greek being placed before Jew in Col 3:11, a recognition of the dominant cultural commitment permeating Colossian society.[37] This seems to be corroborated by one Colossian youth who ventured to Smyrna for further education in philosophy (no. 27), perhaps at the feet of the renowned cosmological theorist, Theon, and the reliance on Greek epiphany stories and foundation narratives for a pagan and Greek shrine that is reflected in the early Byzantine text related to the site, called The Miracle of Saint Michael (the Archangel) of Chonai.[38]

One inscription (no. 22) has received considerable attention since it was first published in 2007.[39] The slightly incomplete text reads (as first published) Μάρκωι Μάρκου | Κολοσσηνῶν | ἀρχερμηνεῖ | καὶ ἐξηγητῆ[ι] …; "[… dedicated this] to Markos son of Markos, chief interpreter and translator for the Colossians." The limestone pedestal was found wedged in mud low in the northern bank of the Ak Su (Lycus River) near the site traditionally designated the Church of Saint Michael, to the east of the höyük (artificial mound) and across the river from the western edge of the building remains identified by locals as the Roman baths.[40] The initial analysis of the inscription took the pedestal as an agora installation honoring an official largely responsible for commercial, administrative matters, though recognizing that a wide range of tasks (including military, imperial, or religious responsibilities) might be envisaged. The ἀρχ- compound was taken as suggesting a leadership position, perhaps the head of a bureau with "a focus on the activities of the commercial and civic agoras," especially in

---

37. See Alan H. Cadwallader, "Greeks in Colossae: Shifting Allegiances in the Letter to the Colossians and Its Context," in *Attitudes to Gentiles in Ancient Judaism and Early Christianity*, ed. David C. Sim and James S. McLaren (London: Bloomsbury, 2013), 224–41. Compare Mark Reasoner, *Roman Imperial Texts: A Sourcebook* (Minneapolis, MN: Fortress, 2013), 139.

38. See Leonard L. Thompson, "ISmyrna753: Gods and the One God," in *Reading Religions in the Ancient World: Essays Presented to Robert McQueen Grant*, ed. David E. Aune and Robin Darling Young (Leiden: Brill, 2007), 101–24.

39. Alan H. Cadwallader, "A New Inscription, A Correction and a Confirmed Sighting," *EA* 40 (2007): 112–18 (no. 3).

40. Unfortunately, the spring rains and melting snows subsequent to the summer low water level apparently washed the pedestal away. The discovery had been made following information from a local farmer that he had pushed a cylindrical, carved stone from his field into the river.

a region where multiple languages operated.[41] The inscription was seen as making a contribution to and informed by the monograph on ancient translation by Claudia Wiotte-Franz.[42]

While a number of commentators have adopted this line of interpretation,[43] there have been two alternate readings provided. Angelos Chaniotis argued that the inscription honors a temple official and that the work envisaged in the phrase ἀρχερμηνεύς καὶ ἐξηγητής was religious in nature, the interpretation of oracles, a position specifically rejected in the *editio princeps* interpretation.[44] However, one should be mindful that the rigid demarcation of categories, such as religious and commercial, is artificial. Chaniotis's reason was that "it is not very likely that the translation needs of Kolossai were so substantial as to require a board of translators."[45] Here Chaniotis has clearly been influenced by the received convention that Colossae was a shadow of its former pre-Laodikeia days. Laodikeia was manifestly the largest city in the Lycus Valley, but Colossae had maintained its civic pride and, as noted above, had enjoyed considerable prosperity, ascendant in the second century but, from the number of paraded long genealogies, built at least during the previous decades. More important, Colossae was the gateway to and from the Phrygian highlands to the east and had an institutional memory of the past far longer than the other main cities of the Lycus. Nevertheless, Chaniotis's interpretation has been endorsed by his coeditor in the *Supplementum epigraphicum graecum* series, H. W. Pleket.[46]

A recent examination by Lukas Bormann has challenged this religious reading.[47] Bormann suggests that the compound ἀρχερμηνεύς is an honorific title indicative of status rather than a hierarchical position, much

---

41. Cadwallader, "New Inscription," 116.

42. C. Wiotte-Franz, *Hermeneus und Interpres: Zum Dolmetscherwesen in der Antike* (Saarbrücken: Saarbrücker Druckerei und Verlag, 2001).

43. See Rick Strelan, "The Languages of the Lycus Valley," in Cadwallader and Trainor, *Colossae in Space and Time*, 91; Foster, *Colossians*, 7; Rosemary Canavan, *Clothing the Body of Christ at Colossae: A Visual Construction of Identity*, WUNT 2/334 (Tübingen: Mohr Siebeck, 2012), 13–14.

44. Cadwallader, "New Inscription," 116 n. 21.

45. Angelos Chaniotis, "Epigraphic Bulletin for Greek Religion," *Kernos* 23 (2010): 285–86, no. 25. This is repeated at *SEG* 57.1382.

46. See Pleket's comment at the conclusion of the entry for *SEG* 61.1160.

47. Lukas Bormann, "Barbaren und Skythen im Lykostal? Epigraphischer Kommentar zu Kol 3:11," in Verheyden, Öhler, and Corsten, *Epigraphical Evidence*, 193–96.

like ἀρχισυνάγωγος. However, he does not use this parallel to authenticate a religious connection, even though he does not examine how the element ἀρχ- operates in other contexts, apart from an undeveloped aside to ἀρχιγεωργός in P.Oxy. 477. He also seems to place undue weight on the languages of the few inscriptions that we currently have from Colossae, namely, Greek and Latin, to argue that translational demands were far more limited than Rick Strelan assumed. But Strelan had been careful to underscore that inscriptional language cannot be taken as indicating the range of languages that might be heard in the Colossian marketplace and environs.[48] Indeed, a Greek name is no guarantee that the bearer can actually speak Greek, as P.Oxy. 237 demonstrates.[49]

Bormann's alternative to both previous interpretations is to take the Greek and Latin of the published inscriptions as an indication of the much-needed assistance for the interpretation and translation of imperial administrative and legal requirements. He claims that only the name Apphia (no. 19; cf. Phlm 2) might claim a Phrygian background but consigns this to rural areas. However, he neglects those theonyms built on the Phrygian god Mên in the Korymbos inscription (Menas and especially Menogas) as well as the likelihood of a Phrygian origin in the name Minnion.[50] The multitude of inscriptions from neighboring Laodikeia even more indicates the presence of Phrygian names, especially held by those who often maintained family histories and allegiances, namely, women.[51] Moreover, he makes no reference to the Phrygian influence to be found in grave stylistics. Of course, this does not necessarily collate to the survival of the Phrygian language, but it does provide a fertile support.

Certainly, the demand for services to cope with the legal pluralism of the empire was considerable in the eastern empire, where cities such as Colossae had a long history of development of their own constitutional and jurisprudential frameworks.[52] Though Bormann does not mention it,

---

48. Strelan, "Languages of the Lycus Valley," 79–82.

49. In a dispute over a will, a certain Dionysia, daughter of Chaeremon, was apparently so non- or ill-versed in Greek, that an interpreter had to be appointed for the hearing of her case.

50. So Ladislav Zgusta, *Kleinasiatische Personennamen* (Prague: Czechoslovakian Academy, 1964), 318, 522.

51. See P. O. Aytaçlar and E. Akıncı, "A List of Female Names from Laodicea on the Lycus," *EA* 39 (2006): 113–16.

52. See Alan H. Cadwallader, "Complicating Class in the Letter to Philemon: A Prolegomenon," in *The Struggle over Class: Socioeconomic Analysis of Ancient Jewish*

the names surviving on the inscription, Markos and Markos, are suggestive of a Roman connection (perhaps servile in origin, given the use of a common praenomen without elaboration).[53] His interpretation is suggestive and has the value of comparative support. However, his reliance on the languages of the small number of extant Colossian inscriptions and a failure to consider the valuable work of Wiotte-Franz means that the sociopolitical setting in the interpretation of this inscription must be considered as still debatable.

Of course, the limited number of inscriptions demands circumspection about too-encompassing assertions about the overarching characteristics of Colossian society. The small cache has fostered scrutinization of any other material that may assist in filling in the sketchy outline we can form. This has meant a sifting of the coins, a careful appraisal of the layout of the site itself, and analysis of anepigraphic finds that have surfaced—primarily ceramics.[54] Numismatics has historically been separated from epigraphy but, like gems, can offer pertinent insights through their legends and iconography. Colossae is well-served in this regard by the catalogue assiduously compiled by Hans von Aulock.[55] Since the publication of his work, several new coin types have surfaced, mainly through auction rooms. One type (the two "Olympian Hadrian" coins) has already been mentioned. These discoveries have expanded the range of key benefactors and magistrates exerting their influence in Colossian society in the second and third centuries, including one named Epaphras (unrecognized by von Aulock) and a woman named Eugenetoriane (who designated herself "widow" on one legend of the three coin types she sponsored). The coins have begun to be analyzed for more than the simple equation of their iconography with the range of deities worshiped at Colossae, though the recent discovery of two coins displaying a Silenus typology,[56] combined with a (probably) votive altar to Bacchus (no. 28, an

---

and Christian Texts, ed. G. Anthony Keddie, M. Flexsenhar, and Steven J. Friesen (Atlanta: SBL Press, forthcoming).

53. The name is common in the region of Phrygia though often as part of a citizenry formula. See *LGPN* V.C, s.v. "Μᾶρκος."

54. See B. Duman and E. Konakçi, "The Silent Witness of the Mound of Colossae: Pottery Remains," in Cadwallader and Trainor, *Colossae in Space and Time*, 247–81, and, generally, Cadwallader, *Fragments of Colossae*.

55. Von Aulock, *Münzen und Städte Phrygiens*, 2.83–94.

56. The small denomination coin (probably worth a quarter of an assarion, that is, about a quadrans) was minted under the auspices of (Tiberius Claudius) Sacerdos, who,

inscription yet to be critically published), has increased the likelihood of a significant Dionysian cult in the city. The role of benefaction in undergirding civic mints and the subtle political posturing of Hellenistic cities in relation to their imperial masters have begun to be explored. There is greater awareness of the delicate imperative on Colossian leadership to balance civic and imperial institutions (such as the local demos and the imperial senate, as well as the emperor and his family) and to cultivate productive and cohesive inter-city relations. The detailed research of Andrea Armstrong, Katharina Martin, and Robert Bennett is critical and exemplary for extracting an invaluable yield from numismatics.[57]

A second broad vein of materials has been mined in the effort to supplement and color our picture of Colossae. This is the harvesting of potentially relevant evidence from sources outside of the ancient city. This utilization of *comparanda* (in papyri, inscriptions, and coins in the main, with occasional reference to literary sources outside of testimonia) is particularly to be found in the ground-breaking work of Arnold, though its progenitor in the work of the classicist David Magie is still worth sifting.[58] The methodology has gained increasing refinement and diversification in the two decades since 1996, notably in the publications of Standhartinger, Maier, Canavan, Huttner, and, most recently, a collection that focuses on epigraphical contributions to the understanding of the letter to the Colossians.[59] We eagerly await the eventual publication of the contribution on

---

on other coins, is self-identified as *archon* of the Colossians. One coin (2.62 g, 14 mm) was sold as Lot 227 at the Kölner Auction in October 2017 (misidentifying the magistrate as Aristides); a second (1.95 g, 15 mm) was sold as Lot 259 at the Savoca Silver Auction, 29 December 2018. The obverse features the head of Silenus, facing right, with the legend ΚΟΛΟCCHNΩN; the reverse has a running boar, facing right, with the legend CAKEPΔΩC, the sponsoring magistrates—on other coins designated an *archon*.

57. Andrea J. Armstrong, "Roman Phrygia: Cities and Their Coinage" (PhD thesis, University College, London 1998); Katharina Martin, *Demos—Boule—Gerousia: Personifikationen städtischer Institutionen auf kaiserzeitlichen Münzen aus Kleinasien*, 2 vols (Bonn: Habelt, 2013); Robert Bennett, *Local Elites and Local Coinage: Elite Self-Representation on the Provincial Coinage of Asia, 31 BC to AD 275* (London: Royal Numismatic Society, 2014).

58. Clinton E. Arnold, *The Colossian Syncretism: The Interface between Christianity and Folk Belief at Colossae* (Grand Rapids: Baker, 1996); David Magie, *Roman Rule in Asia Minor to the End of the Third Century after Christ*, 2 vols. (Princeton: Princeton University Press, 1950).

59. Angela Standhartinger, *Studien zur Entstehungsgeschichte und Intention des Kolosserbriefs* (Leiden: Brill, 1998); "Kolosserbrief," *Das wissenschaftliche Bibelpor-*

Colossians in the Papyrologische Kommentare zum Neuen Testament series.. Of course, there is a fine balance to be struck between the survey of *comparanda* and the explicit evidence deriving from the city itself.[60] Equally the importance of material culture generally as a corrective to a narrow concentration on a New Testament letter cannot be underestimated and one can only repeat a century-long hope that Colossae will be permitted to be fully surveyed in preparation for excavation.

Part 2. An Archaeological, Numismatic and Epigraphic Portrait of Laodicea

1. The History of Laodicea

The prehistory of the Lycus Valley stretches back to the Neolithic and early Chalcolithic periods.[61] Laodicea itself was founded by King Antiochus II on behalf of his wife Laodike.[62] This means that the city was so named before 253 BCE, when Laodike was divorced. An alternative tradition claims that the city was named after the sister of Antiochus I, called Laodike. But, as Magie notes, "there is no record of any sister of Antiochus

---

tal der Deutschen Bibelgesellschaft (2010): https://www.bibelwissenschaft.de/stichwort/51912/; Maier, *Picturing Paul in Empire*; Canavan, *Clothing the Body of Christ*; Huttner, *Early Christianity in the Lycus Valley*; Verheyden, Öhler, and Corsten, *Epigraphical Evidence, loc. cit.* See also Paul McKechnie, *Elect Cities: Christianity in Phrygia from the First Century to the Great Persecution* (Cambridge: Cambridge University Press, 2019);

60. See Alan H. Cadwallader, "On the Question of Comparative Method in Historical Research: Colossae and Chonae in Larger Frame," in this volume.

61. See Ali Ozan et al., "Prehistory of the Lykos Valley," and Erim Konakci, "The Lykos Valley during the Second Millenium BC," in *Landscape and History in the Lykos Valley: Laodikeia and Hierapolis in Phrygia*, ed. Celal Şimşek and Francesco D'Andria (Newcastle upon Tyne: Cambridge Scholars, 2017), 53–77 and 79–107.

62. For discussions of the history of Laodicea, see Jean des Gagniers, "Première partie: Introduction historique," in *Laodicée du Lycos: Le Nymphée Campagnes 1961–1963*, ed. Jean des Gagniers et al. (Paris: Éditions E. De Boccard, 1969), 1–11; Giogio Bejor, "Per Una Ricerca Di Laiodicea Ellenistica," in *Laodicea Di Frigia I*, ed. Gustavo Traversari, RDASup 24 (Rome: Bretschneider, 2000), 15–23; Celal Şimşek, "Urban Planning of Laodikeia on the Lykos in the Light of New Evidence," in *Landscape and History in the Lykos Valley: Laodikeia and Hierapolis in Phrygia*, ed. Celal Şimşek and Francesco D'Andria (Newcastle upon Tyne: Cambridge Scholars, 2017), 2–7.

with this name, and her existence is very doubtful."[63] Pliny the Elder tells us that the city was first called Diospolis ("city of Zeus") and later renamed Rhoas, before its eventual Hellenistic foundation by Antiochus (Pliny the Elder, *Nat.* 5.105). The name "Diospolis" explains the strong attachment of Laodicea to Zeus in its coinage.[64] The strategic geographic position of the city, situated in a fertile plain,[65] cannot be understated: "Roads ran west along the Lycus and Maeander valleys to Ephesus, south east to Apamaea and Cibyra, beyond to Syria, and southeast to Pamphylia."[66] Later, the first Roman governor of Asia, M. Aquillius, erected milestones along the roads between 129–126 BCE, several of which have been found.[67]

Our earliest inscription from the Hellenistic age of Laodicea (January 267 BCE, the reign of Antiochus I) is an honorific decree eulogizing two officials from the villages of Neoteichos and Kiddoukome in Asia Minor (ILaodikeia 1.6, 31), both near the foundation site of Laodicea (ILaodikeia 1).[68] The officials are praised for administering the property of Achaeus, who was probably the younger brother of Antiochus I.[69] Several other

---

63. Magie, *Roman Rule*, 2:986 n. 23.
64. Armstrong, *Roman Phrygia*.
65. Gagniers, "Première partie," 2.
66. Stephen Mitchell, "Italian and Turkish Archaeological Work in the Lycus Valley around Laodicea and Hierapolis," *JRA* 14 (2001): 632. Armstrong writes: "The position of Laodicea near these major routes would ensure that both goods and personnel would pass by in the vicinity of the city and in turn this would ensure the city's growth and development" (*Roman Phrygia*, 35–36).
67. David French, *Roman Roads and Milestones of Asia Minor: An Interim Catalogue of Milestones*, vol. 2.1, BARIS 392 (Oxford: British Institute of Archaeology at Ankara, 1988), 101 no. 266; 106 no. 279; 111 nos. 294–295.
68. Translated by Michel M. Austin, *The Hellenistic World from Alexander to the Roman Conquest: A Selection of Sources in Translation*, 2nd ed. (Cambridge: Cambridge University Press, 2007), §168. For usages of κώμη ("village") in this Hellenistic inscription that refer to other small local settlements outside of the city of Laodicea, see ILaodikeia 1, 19 (Βάβα κώμη), 21/29 (Κιδδίου κώμη). There are no further references to villages in Corsten's collection of the Laodicean inscriptions. For a discussion of the villages and communities in the territory of Hierapolis, including their religious affiliations, see Ritti, *Hierapolis di Frigia IX*, 35–36. Note especially the revealing clash between shepherds and vineyard owners over vines damaged by grazing cattle and sheep in the Hieropolitan village of Kagyetteia (MAMA 4.297: 250 CE). For a translation, see Peter Thonemann, *The Maeander Valley: A Historical Geography from Antiquity to Byzantium* (Cambridge: Cambridge University Press, 2011), 194.
69. See Michael Wörrle, "Antiochus I., Achaios der Ältere und die Galater: Eine neue Inschrift in Denizli," *Chiron* 5 (1975): 59–97.

inscriptions illustrate the daily life of Laodicea in the Hellenistic Age: a decree in honor of three Laodicean citizens for erecting public buildings (ILaodikeia 2); a decree of Laodicea recognizing the asylum of Artemis Leukophryne in Magnesia on Meander (ILaodikeia 4); last, a decree in honor of three judges from Priene for their legal work in Laodicea (ILaodikeia 5), among several other very fragmentary decrees.

However, political stability was not necessarily assured at this time and ultimately Laodicea would transition, along with rest of Asia Minor, to be under Roman rule. Polybius writes regarding Achaeus who chose Laodicea as the site in 200 BCE to rebel against his nephew Antiochus III (*Hist.* 5.57.5). This would-be king was executed and Anatolia was returned to the Seleucid rule of Antiochis III. Two years later Garsyeris, the general of Achaeus, led the Seleucid forces southwest from Laodicea to fight a war against Pisidian Selge (Polybius, *Hist.* 5.772). Laodicea remained under Seleucid rule until 190 BCE when, after the battle of Magnesia, the victorious Romans prized Laodicea from Seleucid rule and placed its newly acquired territory under the control of the Pergameme dynasty, client-kings and allies of Rome, as agreed under the terms of the Treaty of Apameia (180 BCE).

Eventually, however, Pergamum—and therefore Laodicea—was annexed to Rome in line with the specifications of the will of Attalos III in 133 BCE, with the result that the Roman province of Asia was established in 129 BCE (Strabo, *Geogr.* 13.4.2). But Laodicea was not yet immune from external threat. The Pontic armies under Mithridates VI besieged the city during the First Mithridatic War (87–85 BCE) until a peace treaty was formalized between Rome and Mithridates in 85 (Appian, *Bell. Mith.* 20).[70] The Roman consul Sulla demanded that five years of unpaid taxes be paid, along with war reparations, by the Asian cities. Consequently, cities were impoverished, borrowed money at high interest, and mortgaged their public buildings (Appian, *Bell. Mith.* 62–63). Notwithstanding, the Laodiceans astutely offered a bilingual inscription to the city of Rome as an appeasement to the Roman people, "which have become its saviour and benefactor because of their virtue and good will towards it."[71]

---

70. Appian's historical account is truncated when viewed against the inscriptional evidence of Aphrodisias. See Armstrong, *Roman Phrygia*, 26.

71. For translation, see E. H. Warmington, *Remains of Old Latin IV: Archaic Inscriptions*, LCL (London: Heinmann, 1940), "1. Inscriptions Proper: Honorary Inscriptions" §23.

Economic problems still continued for Laodicea, Hierapolis, and Colossae during Cicero's governorship of Cilicia, though caution is required with his evidence because Cicero is highlighting his success as a governor (*Att.* 5.16).[72] Further difficulties resulted from the occurrence of an earthquake in the 20s BCE (Suetonius, *Tib.* 8). But, despite the troubles, wealth increasingly accrued to Laodicea in the imperial age (Strabo, *Geogr.* 12.8.13; 12.18.16) and the city became famous for its wool and the production of woolen fabrics (Pliny the Elder, *Nat.* 21.9.27; 25.9.67; Vitruvius, *Arch.* 8.13.14; Cicero, *Fam* 2.17.2; 3.5.4; Strabo, *Geogr.* 12.8.13). It is perhaps this economic self-sufficiency and its seductive dangers spiritually in the first century CE that John of Patmos pinpoints in his critique of the Laodicean church (Rev 3:17–18). Indeed, Laodicea recovered from further severe earthquakes in the Lycus Valley in 60 CE and did not require imperial munificence like Hierapolis to recover (Tacitus, *Ann.* 14.27).[73]

Laodicea grew in political and civic status as well in the imperial age. The city, Pliny writes (*Nat.* 5.105), became famous in the Cibyratic *conventus*, one of the Asian juridical districts. Hadrian also visited the city, one of his letters reveals (*IGRR* 4.1033: 129 CE), during his eastern tour of Asia, Lycia, and Syria. In the frenetic competition for imperial patronage among the Asian cities, Laodicea became a *neokoros* city during the reigns of (possibly) Hadrian, (possibly) Commodus, Caracalla, and Severus Alexander.[74]

---

72. Armstrong, *Roman Phrygia*, 28.

73. Note Sib. Or. 4.106: "Wretched Laodicea, at some time an earthquake will throw you headlong and spread you flat, but you will be founded again as a city, and stand." For discussion of earthquakes in the region, see Armstrong, *Roman Phrygia*, 31–33; Halil Kumsar, "Historical Earthquakes that Damaged Hierapolis and Laodikeia Antique Cities and Their Implications for Earthquake Potential of Denizli Basin in Western Turkey," *Bulletin of Engineering Geology and the Environment* 75 (2016): 519–36.

74. The attribution of neokorate status to Laodicea under Hadrian and Commodus finds *no explicit published* epigraphic or numismatic confirmation, despite the claim of Şimşek ("Urban Planning of Laodikeia," 4) to the contrary. Does Şimşek know of unpublished inscriptions in each case? But, as Cadwallader notes in private correspondence, "Certainly there is no 'twice/thrice neokoros' statement in the evidence which one would expect if there were separate awards." Possibly the Hadrianic neokorate status is inferred on the basis of ILaodikeia 53 below, though, I would note, precise dating of the inscription is debateable. I am grateful to Cadwallader for his methodological cautions regarding Şimşek's arguments. The Laodicean coins minted under the reigns of Caracalla, and Severus Alexander emphasize the neokorate status either on the obverse or reverse (ΛΑΟΔΙΚΕΩΝ ΝΕΩΚΟΡΩΝ). For the coins, see

Moreover, the Laodiceans enthusiastically adopted Roman habits such as bathing, demonstrated by the proliferation of bathhouses in the city.[75] Furthermore, games in honor of the imperial rulers were held at Laodicea,[76] and the adoption of Roman gladiatorial spectacles in the Greek East and the Lycus Valley in particular, discussed below, also became highly popular. But one last earthquake levelled the city in 494 CE.

Finally, the place of Jews in Laodicean society, as revealed in the epigraphy, will be discussed in our last section.[77] We now turn to the history of excavation of the city.

2. History of the Excavations of Laodicea

Prior to the major excavations conducted at Laodicea from the mid-twentieth century onward, there were many individuals, too many for us to list here,[78] who had visited the site from 1671–1939, often as part of a wider itinerary of visits to ancient sites in Asia generally. They wrote journals and

---

Armstrong, *Roman Phrygia*, 268–70 §§95–110 (Julia Domna in the reign of Caracalla), 271–76 §§120–158 (Caracalla), 279 §§173–174 (Severus Alexander). Note, too, ILaodikeia 135 (third century CE): "the Augustus-loving temple-warden (νεωχόρ[ος]) metropolis of Asia, the city of Laodicea"; cf. ILaodikeia 50 (third century CE), ILaodikeia 136 (third century CE). Additionally, the honorific inscription of Antonia from the Zenon family underscores neokorate status: "Antonia, daughter of L(ucius) Antonius Zeno, the greatest high priest of Asia, priest of the city … gymnasiarch … best wife, temple-warden (νε[ωχόρον]) and high-priestess of Asia and priestess of … gymnasiarch" (ILaodikeia 53 [first–second century CE]).

75. Armstrong, *Roman Phrygia*, 150.

76. An inscription (second–third century CE) mentions the games in honor of the emperor Commodus held at Laodicea (ILaodikeia 59: "high priest and agonothete of the five-year festival of the great games Dia Kommodeia"). On the role of the agonothete, see James R. Harrison, "Paul and the *agōnothetai* at Corinth: Engaging the Civic Values of Antiquity," in *The First Urban Churches 2: Roman Corinth*, ed. James R. Harrison and L. L. Welborn (Atlanta: SBL Press, 2016), 271–326.

77. For an excellent discussion of the Jewish community in the Lycus Valley, see F. F. Bruce, "The Jews and Christians in the Lycus Valley," *BSac* 141 (1985): 3–15. On Jews in Phrygia more generally, see William M. Ramsay, *The Lycos Valley and South-Western Phrygia*, vol. 1.2 of *The Cities and Bishoprics of Phrygia* (Oxford: Clarendon, 1895), 667–76.

78. For a detailed history of the visitation and excavation of the site from 1671–2008 onwards, see Celal Şimşek, *Laodikeia (Laodicea ad Lycum)* [Turkish], Laodikeia Calismalari 2 (Istanbul: Ege Yayinlari, 2013), 23–26.

books on what they saw, conducted preliminary investigations of features of the site (e.g., W. J. Hamilton), or catalogued the extant epigraphy on public monuments and tombstones.[79]

The first major excavation of an important Laodicean complex commenced with the 1961–1963 campaigns carried out by L'Université Laval, Québec, Canada. The team, under the direction of Professor Jean des Gagniers, excavated the Caracalla Nymphaeum, with the archaeological results being published in 1969. In a wide-ranging coverage, Gagniers and his collaborators, including the formidable epigraphist Louis Robert, discussed the history and geography of Laodicea, as well as the sculptures, ceramics, lamps, and inscriptions of the Nymphaeum.[80] Robert's superb coverage of the epigraphy remains as authoritative, insightful, and penetrating as the day it was written.[81] Robert's masterful coverage was eventually crowned in 1997 by Thomas Corsten's pioneering publication of the entire corpus of Laodicean inscriptions, accompanied by German translations and commentaries on each of the 126 documents. Standing now on the shoulders of Buckler and Calder, Robert, and Corsten, classical and New Testament scholars are well placed to establish a clear epigraphic portrait of the city from Hellenistic times to the late imperial period, notwithstanding the relative poverty of our Laodicean epigraphic resources in comparison to the eight volumes of inscriptions from Ephesus.[82]

---

79. E.g., F. V. J. Arundell, R. Chandler, W. Cochran, C. Fellows, W. M. Leake, R. Pococke, W. M. Ramsay, G. Weber, among others. For a list of their publications, see Şimşek, *Laodikeia*, 521–22. Sherman E. Johnson writes appreciatively: "Early travellers, such Pockocke, Hamilton, and Fellows, laid the basis for later archaeological and topographical study of Asia Minor." Sherman E. Johnson, "Early Christianity in Asia Minor," *JBL* 77 (1958): 1. Note especially the pivotal English publication of Ramsay, *Lycos Valley and South-Western Phrygia*; Ramsay, *St Paul the Traveller and the Roman Citizen* (London: Hodder & Stoughton, 1897). Şimşek notes that W. J. Hamilton visited Laodicea during his tour through Anatolia, investigating "the post-earthquake situation of the city and the remaining structures like the stadium, gymnasium, theatre and aqueduct" (*Laodikeia*, 23; see Hamilton, *Researches in Asia Minor, Pontus, and Armenia*). For the Laodicean inscriptions available before World War II, see *MAMA* 6.1–37.

80. Gagniers et al., *Laodicée du Lycos*.

81. Louis Robert, ed. "Les inscriptions," in Gagniers et al., *Laodicée du Lycos*, 247–389.

82. Thomas Corsten, *Die Inschriften von Laodikeia am Lykos* (Bonn: Habelt, 1997); James R. Harrison, "An Epigraphic Portrait of Ephesus and Its Villages," in *The First Urban Churches 3: Ephesus*, ed. James R. Harrison and L. L. Welborn (Atlanta: SBL Press, 2018), 1–67.

The next major excavation of Laodicea occurred under the auspices of Ca'Foscari University of Venice, under the direction of Professor G. Traversari. Surveys of the city were carried out by the archaeological team from 1995 to 2002. New topographical maps of the city were undertaken, its structures then imposed upon the new plan and then related back to the initial survey. The results were published in Italian in 2000, though to some critical reviews.[83] The aerial photographs of the site are nonetheless spectacular, and the coverage of the southern complex of monuments in the city (i.e., bouleterion, bath-gymnasium, stadium) is very helpful because it also draws on previous archaeological reports as much as the evidence of the new Italian reports.[84]

An entirely new Turkish archaeological campaign, including major restorations of existing monuments at the site as well as new excavations, has been carried out since 2003 by Professor Celal Şimşek of Pamukkale University, in cooperation with the Ministry of Culture and Tourism. On any day onsite, Şimşek has a team of fifteen archaeologists, eight restoration specialists, and master craftsmen specializing in stonework and masonry.[85] There would also be a continuous stream of doctoral candidates from Pamukkale University present as well. From 2008 there has been established a protocol between the Denizli Metropolitan Municipality and Ministry of Culture and Tourism, where the municipality acts as a benefactor of the campaign in twelve month turnovers, ensuring a continuous advancement of new excavations and restorations through the provision of secure funding. The impressive list of what had been accomplished since 2003 can be found on the UNESCO World Heritage List website.[86] Most recently, in 2018 the Denizli Metropolitan Municipality has announced that, under the guidance of Şimşek, the 2,200-year-old

---

83. See Luigi Sperti, "Ricognizione Archaeologica a Laodicea di Frigia 1993–1998," in Traversari, *Laodicea Di Frigia I*, 29–102. For critical reviews, see, e.g., Mitchell, who bluntly states: "The first publication results from the Italian survey at Laodicea on the Lycus is extremely disappointing" ("Italian and Turkish Archaeological Work," 632).

84. Traversari, *Laodicea Di Frigia I*, pls. I–XVI; Sperti, "Ricognizione Archaeologica a Laodicea di Frigia 1993–1998," 29–102.

85. Mark R. Fairchild, "Laodicea's 'Lukewarm' Legacy: Conflicts of Prosperity in an Ancient Christian City," *BAR* (March/April 2017): 36.

86. See the section on "Statements of Authenticity and/or Integrity" on "Archaeological Site of Laodikeia," UNESCO World Heritage Centre," https://tinyurl.com/SBL4218a.

western theater, with a capacity for 15,000 people and operative in Hellenistic and Roman times, will be restored in a three-year project, with a view to hosting in the theater various cultural and arts events.[87]

As a result, there has been an explosion in scholarship on the archaeology of Laodicea since 2003. First, there has appeared a massive two-volume study, published in Turkish, of the necropolis surrounding the city in all directions, comprising some 283 tombs.[88] Second, the results of the archaeological campaigns in Laodicea from 2003–2013 were published in 2014.[89] Third, this has been followed by Şimşek's definitive archaeological guide to the city, incorporating the excavation and new finds until 2013, written in Turkish, but needing translation into English so that its scholarly riches can be more widely accessed.[90] Fourth, this guide has been most recently followed up by a helpful English collection of essays on Laodicea and Hierapolis, edited by Şimşek and Francesco D'Andria.[91] Fifth, a volume on the amphorae of Laodicea also appeared in the same year.[92] Sixth, another volume explores how Laodicea became a venue of religious pilgrimage from the fourth century CE onwards. Christian churches spread as architectural monuments across the city and family chapels were established in private houses. The main focus of the study, however, is upon the 2010 excavation of the Church of Laodicea, with its various architectural elements, and the development of a Christian quarter around it.[93] In sum, the appearance of the four volumes of the Laodikeia Çalismalari series, as well as Şimşek's various archaeological guides to the city in its Graeco-Roman and Christian expressions, testifies to the momentum and continuing vitality of the archaeological campaigns at Laodicea and their scholarly

---

87. "Laodikeia's Western Theatre to Be Restored," *Hurriyet Daily News*, 23 March 2018, https://tinyurl.com/SBL4218b.

88. Celal Şimşek, M. Okunak and M. Bilgin, *Laodikeia Nekropulü (2004–2010 Yillari)*, Laodikeia Çalismalari 1.1–2 (Istanbul: Ege Yayinlari, 2011).

89. Celal Şimşek, *10. Yilinda Laodikeia (2003–2013 Yillari)*, Laodikeia Çalismalari 3 (Istanbul: Ege Yayinlari, 2014).

90. Şimşek, *Laodikeia*. The dated chapter of Edwin Yamauchi on Laodicea (*The Archaeology of New Testament Cities in Western Asia Minor* [Grand Rapids: Baker, 1980], 135–46) still retains some value.

91. Şimşek and D'Andria, *Landscape and History in the Lykos Valley*.

92. C. Şimşek, A. Alkac, and B. Duman, *Laodikeia amphora mühürleri*, Laodikeia Çalismalari 4 (Istanbul: Ege Yayinlari, 2017).

93. Celal Şimşek, *Church of Laodikeia: Christianity in the Lykos Valley* (Istanbul: Ege Yayinlari, 2015).

significance for our understanding of Phrygian society, culture, and history. It is therefore not surprising that the site of ancient Laodicea, with several other archaeological sites, was added to UNESCO's World Tentative Heritage List in June 2013.

3. The Main Structures of Laodicea: The Archaeological, Epigraphic and Iconographic Evidence

What are the main structures of the city?[94] The structures discussed below were highlighted as significant features in Laodicea's UNESCO's World Heritage Temporary List application.[95] However, we will only discuss those sites where there are intersections between the inscriptional, iconographic, and archaeological evidence (though, *pace*, the Church of Laodikeia, omitted below, where such intersections exist).[96] This means that the following structures will not be discussed: (1) the conjectural identification of the council house (*bouleuterion*) or, possibly, *odeon*; (2) houses with a peristyle design (house A complexes, peristyle house with church [Oratory]); (3) temples (Temple A); and (4) churches (East, North, West, Central, Southwest Churches, and Laodikeia Church).[97] S. Mitchell assesses the importance of Laodicea in comparison to its nearby neighbor in these words: "The remains of Laodicea, compared to those of Hierapolis, are unspectacular and attract few tourists, but the city was

---

94. See now the excellent English coverage of Şimşek, "Urban Planning of Laodikeia."

95. See "Archaeological Site of Laodikeia."

96. There are several inscriptions in the Laodikeia Church, now conveniently translated into English with Greek texts supplied (Şimşek, *Church of Laodikeia*, 37, 45). Three inscriptions are found on the altar table pieces, a marble vessel, and the ambo of the church's nave: specifically, an honorific memorial of family members, a vow, and the names of the presbyters at the time of the pulpit restoration. There are also two honorific mosaic inscriptions accompanied by a cross on the south aisle of the church, citing in each case the name of the benefactor deacon, including the status conscious "first deacon Polykarpos" (Şimşek, *Church of Laodikeia*, 75 figs. 108–109).

97. For identification as *bouleuterion* or *odeon*, see Traversari, *Laodicea Di Frigia I*, 42–54; Şimşek, *Laodikeia*, 240–43. For house A complexes, see Şimşek, *Laodikeia*, 307–19; Şimşek, "Urban Planning of Laodikeia," 13–14, 18–19. For the peristyle house with church (Oratory), see Şimşek, "Urban Planning of Laodikeia," 45–46, figs. 34–35. For Temple A with chapel in courtyard, see Şimşek, "Urban Planning of Laodikeia," 46, fig. 36. For plan of Laodikeia Church, see Şimşek, "Urban Planning of Laodikeia," 47 fig. 37. For basilicas north and south, see Traversari, *Laodicea Di Frigia I*, 95–97.

not simply a centre of regional significance but one of the key cities of Asia Minor."[98]

At the outset, it should be noted that the city was surrounded by rivers (Maeander, Lycos) and minor creeks (Kadmos, Asopos) on three sides.[99] However, the absence of any springs within the urban territory of Laodicea meant that complex water supply systems had to be devised to secure the city's water needs. These consisted of two water distribution terminals, as well as an elaborate piping system, comprising thick-walled terracotta pipes in the Hellenistic Age and travertine pipes (less susceptible to pressure) in Roman times.[100] Aqueducts and open channels also contributed to the overall water distribution system.

In terms of urban planning, the city had three main streets (Syria, Stadium, Ephesus), each flanked with porticoes that had shops behind them.[101] There were two monumental gates (Ephesus and Syria),[102] as well as six other city gates. What, then, do we learn from the city's major sites?

3.1. The Stadium

The doubled-ended Laodicean stadium, a structure 285 m long and 70 m high, was the largest in Anatolia.[103] Its enclosed structure hosted gladiatorial combats, as we learn from Cicero who had privately criticized the young Hortensius for behaving badly with gladiators while he was

---

98. Mitchell, "Italian and Turkish Archaeological Work," 632.

99. On the reverse of a Laodicean coin (Henry Clay Lindgren and Frank L. Kovacs, *Ancient Bronze Coins of Asia Minor and the Levant from the Lindgren Collection* [San Mateo: Chrysopylon, 1985], §599), we see a reclining river god holding a flower (or branch) in his hand and reed in his left, while water flows from an inverted vase poised on his right arm.

100. See Şimşek, "Urban Planning of Laodikeia," 10; for travertine pipes, see 36 fig. 19.

101. On each street, see Şimşek, "Urban Planning of Laodikeia," 10–13.

102. The Syria gate is dated by an inscription (ILaodikeia 24) to 84/85 CE, discussed below. On the Ephesian monumental propyla (gate) in the Western Agora, see Giorgio Bejor and Jacopo Bonetto, "Recognizione del 1999: Dalla Porta Efesia All'Agora Occidentale" in Traversari, *Laodicea Di Frigia I*, 105–24. For the monumental propylon of the Northern Agora, see Şimşek, *Laodikeia*, 276–77, figs. 371, 373. Pholostratus (*Vit. soph.* 1.25) refers to the Syrian gates of Laodicea, the eastern entrance to the city.

103. On the stadium, see Traversari, *Laodicea Di Frigia I*, 63–74 (figs. 30–32); Şimşek, *Laodikeia*, 208–18 (plates 275–79).

at Laodicea (Cicero, *Att.* 6.3.9). There are nine extant gladiator inscriptions at Laodicea, with rich accompanying iconographic evidence in some cases.[104] Four examples will suffice.

On a first–second-century CE inscription, the stela depicts a loinclothed and belted gladiator whose left hand is placed on his shield, whereas his right hand holds a palm branch. To his right a small dog stands away from the gladiator, but the animal looks back towards him. The gladiatorial contests of the gladiator are honored thus: "[N.N. erected this stela] for Kallimorphos, her own husband, from Thyateira, out of her own means in memory (of him). Kallimorphos the Beautiful greets the passers-by."[105] Elsewhere, in a first-century CE (?) inscription, gladiators are honored for the contests, sponsored by the high status imperial priest of the city, in which they have participated: "(This monument) of the gladiators (is) given by the *archierus* and *stephanephoros*, Diokles, the son of Metrophilos."[106] Finally, we see panelled reliefs of *venatio* contests where the wild animals to be fought included a wild bull, depicted as falling forwards, and a bear.[107] The relevance of this background for New Testament studies has not escaped the attention of scholars. In this regard, Paul's strategic use of gladiatorial imagery in his epistles has been exhaustively demonstrated by James R. Unwin, along with forays from other scholars.[108]

Finally, there are three inscriptions of a wealthy and elite Laodicean family whose members had acted as benefactors in various civic liturgies

---

104. ILaodikeia 73–78, 81A; Louis Robert, "Monuments des gladiateurs dans l'Orient grec," *Hellenica* 7 (1949): 140 (plate 16, 1); Robert, *Les gladiateurs dans l'orient grec* (Paris: Champion, 1940), 151, no. 116. For Laodicean gladiator inscriptions and their iconography, see Michael J. D. Carter, *The Presentation of Gladiatorial Spectacles in the Greek East: Roman Culture and Greek Identity* (PhD thesis, McMaster University, 1999), "Catalogue of Inscriptions," §§351, 352, 353, 354, 355, 355a.

105. ILaodikeia 75. Throughout I am indebted to the German translations of Corsten, *Die Inschriften von Laodikeia am Lykos.*

106. ILaodikeia 73.

107. ILaodikeia 78; Robert, "Monuments des gladiateurs dans l'Orient grec," 140 (plate 16, 1).

108. James R. Unwin, *Subversive Spectacles: The Struggles and Deaths of Paul and Seneca* (PhD thesis, Macquarie University, 2017). Note also C. W. Concannon, "'Not for an Olive Wreath, but Our Lives': Gladiators, Athletes, and Early Christian Bodies," *JBL* 133 (2014): 193–214; Alan H. Cadwallader, "Paul and the Games," in *Paul in the Greco-Roman World: A Handbook*, ed. J. Paul Sampley, vol. 1 (London: T&T Clark Bloomsbury, 2016), 363–90.

from Vespasian's reign to the first half of the second century CE.[109] An inscription honors Nikostratos, the son of Lykios, for his role in the completion of the incomplete parts of the stadium at the time of the inscription in 79 CE:

> To Imperator Titus Caesar Augustus Vespasianus, consul for the seventh time, son of the divine Caesar Vespasianus, and the (Laodicean) people: Nikostratos, the son of Lykios, the son of Nikostratos, has consecrated the amphitheatre stadium in white marble from his own funds, (with) Nicostratos' inheritance being, (in the estimate of posterity), that he completed the parts of the structure not yet completed, and the proconsul Marcus Ulpius Traianus made the consecration.[110]

Subsequent family members up to first half of the second century CE—the time of the premature death of Tatia in our honorific inscription below—had continued to exercise civic beneficence in the city and serve in various magistracies as required. The granduncle of deceased Tatia below, for example, had assumed the prestigious position of priest of the city and had performed the same role as his forebears in conserving the stadium for future generations by maintaining its white marble facades:[111]

> The Council and the people have honoured Tatia, daughter of Nicostratos, son of Pericles, who died young, for the sake of the magistracies, services, and supervision of public works filled by her father and for the cause of his granduncle Nicostratos, who, in other services, had been priest of the city and has consecrated the amphitheatre stadium in white marble.[112]

---

109. For the family tree, see Corsten, *Die Inschriften von Laodikeia am Lykos*, referring to the following inscriptions: ILaodikeia 9, 13, 83. We will not discuss the statue inscription in honor of Vespasian erected by the "Caesar-loving" Nicostratos, son of Nicostratos Theagenes (ILaodikeia 9).

110. ILaodikeia 15. The editors of *RPC* 2.194, suggest that the appearance of an athletic designs on the reverses of the coins of Titus (*RPC* 2.1272–1280) "can be plausibly connected to the building of a new stadium at Laodicea in 78/80."

111. On the importance of the marble trade in Asia Minor, see Lea Emilia Long, *Urbanism, Art, and Economy: The Marble Quarrying Industries of Aphrodisias and Roman Asia Minor* (PhD diss., University of Michigan, 2012). Şimşek ("Urban Planning of Laodikeia," 9) notes that Laodicea had its marble and travertine quarries at the foot of Mount Cökelez in the north, Mount Salbakos in the south, and Mount Kadmos in the southeast.

112. ILaodikeia 83 (first half of the second century CE). Translated by Yamauchi, *Archaeology of New Testament Cities*, 142.

Here we see how certain Laodicean elites maintained their prestige over several generations not only by exercising beneficence and assuming magistracies, but also by continuing to care for particular sites in the city, such as the stadium, reputed over time to be their peculiar preserve as benefactors.

3.2. Two Theaters (Western, Northern)

The western theater was constructed in the Hellenistic Age whereas the northern theater was built in the second century CE.[113] Two Laodicean inscriptions underscore the importance of the theater in civic honorific rituals. Building commissioners and two judges from other cities visiting Laodicea were rewarded with (respectively) the privilege of the front seats in the Hellenistic theater and were crowned with gold crowns before the people at the same site.[114] Şimşek incisively observes that "the existence of two theatres and one of the largest stadia in Anatolia sheds light on the population, and reveals the importance of sports, art and culture."[115]

Like most theaters in antiquity there was reserved seating in the theaters of Laodicea.[116] There are reserved seats for guilds, high-status magistrates ("[Place] of Paulinus, man of consular rank"), and other individuals of whom we only possess the names.[117] By contrast, the teaching of Jesus eschews the ancient quest for public conspicuousness (Matt 6:1–4) and social precedence (Luke 14:7–11; cf. Prov 25:6–7) that was associated with honorific rituals and feasting culture in antiquity. Instead Jesus maintains the priority of personal humility before God and others (Matt 19:30; 20:16; Mark 10:31; Luke 13:30; 18:9–14) and inculcates a culture of honoring of the weak and marginalized (Luke 14:12–14), as opposed to

---

113. For full discussion, see C. Şimşek and M. A. Sezgin, "The West and North Theatres in Laodicea," in *Restoration and Management of Ancient Theatres in Turkey: Methods, Research, Results*, ed. Filippo Masino, Paolo Mighetto, and Giorgio Sobra, Archaeologia e Storia 11 (Lecce: Congedo Editore, 2012), 103–28. Additionally, see Traversari, *Laodicea Di Frigia I*, 81–91; Şimşek, *Laodikeia*, 219–27 (West Theater), 228–40 (North Theater).

114. ILaodikeia 2, 5.

115. Şimşek, "Urban Planning of Laodikeia," 17.

116. On seating in theaters in antiquity, see Tamara Jones, "Seating and Spectacle in the Graeco-Roman World" (PhD diss., McMaster University, 2008).

117. ILaodikeia 32–33 (guilds); ILaodikeia 31 (magistrates); ILaodikeia 29 (Zenon), ILaodikeia 30 (Sacerdotos Pomponianos), ILaodikeia 34 (Titus Varus).

courting the favor of the powerful (Luke 22:25–27). The Pauline epistles similarly invert honorific rituals within the body of Christ (Rom 12:8b, 16b; 1 Cor 12:24b).

3.3. Five Agorae (East, Central, West, South, North)

Despite the wide distribution of agorae throughout the city, there are only two inscriptional references to the ἀγορά (marketplace): both are from the Hellenistic Age and refer to the erection of honorific stone stelae in the most prominent place in the marketplace.[118] Once again, the city's cultivation of honorific culture had to be publicly conspicuous for the honorand to be properly reciprocated for his civic favors to the people.[119]

3.4. Five Fountains (*Nymphaea*), Latrines, Bath Complexes (East, Central, West), and Two Large Water Distribution Terminals

Under this diverse group of structures in the city we are concentrating upon the importance of water distribution throughout the city. There are five Laodicean fountains (*nymphaea*), each situated on one of the main streets: (1) the Caracalla Nymphaeum and Septimus Severus Nymphaeum (Nymphaeum A) on Syria Street; (2) the Trajan Nymphaeum and Nymphaeum B on Stadium Street; and (3) the West Nymphaeum on Ephesus Street.[120] The *nymphaea* at Laodicea were one or two-story structures situated on the corners of main streets or in plazas.[121] Three inscriptions survive from the *nymphaea*, two of them too fragmentary to be comprehensible,[122] but the third is sufficiently legible for the honorific epigram eulogizing governor Skylakios (340–359 CE) to be understood: "There are many miracles of older (times); but now, as the greatest of our generation in his tenure as

---

118. ILaodikeia 2.22; 4b.12–13.

119. Note in this regard the boastful epigraphic dedication of the governor (or high official) of Syria called Dyscolius (317–24 CE) on a statue base found in the southwest stoa of the so-called Temple A: "Dyscolius, by far the best of governors, dedicated the wonderful statue of me, Artemis." See Celal Şimşek and F. Guizzi, "A Dedication of the Praeses Dyscolius from Laodikeia on the Lykos," *Mediterraneo Antico* 14.1–2 (2012): 511–18.

120. On the nymphaea, see Gagniers, *Laodicée du Lycos, passim*. Additionally, see Traversari, *Laodicea Di Frigia I*, 63–74; Şimşek, *Laodikeia*, 143–76.

121. Şimşek, "Urban Planning of Laodikeia," 16.

122. ILaodikeia 16–17.

eparchos, with wisdom built this edifice in just twelve months, he who has done no harm to anyone, Aiakide Skylakios."[123] Of fundamental importance among the many fragments of sculpture found among the *nymphaea* is a superbly rendered and undamaged statue of the Egyptian goddess Isis.[124]

With such an abundance of water at these sites, it should not surprise us that there were also latrines at Nymphaeum B on Stadium Street.[125] In a latrine vestibule at Laodicea the remains of a fragmentary but beautifully colored geometric mosaic, with a wonderfully rendered goat, shows how pleasant such facilities could be visually.[126]

Regarding the bath complexes, of which there were three, Şimşek encapsulates their significance well in a 2014 interview at the archaeological site:

> Baths were prepared at noon for people to wash and later served as a school in the afternoon. They were places for young people at the same time. The baths also hosted between 20–30 people for private meetings. The baths were very important in that era because they were the places for meeting and education, as well as trade centres.[127]

Finally, we turn to the two large water distribution terminals and the important question of how adequately the city maintained its water supply.[128] An inscribed fragment of a marble architrave block found in the north-western moor of the water tower retains this crucial phrase: "he made the reservoir from his own funds."[129] Furthermore, several scholars have argued that an inscribed block, found on a block at the foot of a water tower, represents the dedication of the freedman Hedychrus to his patron: "He, Hedychrus, built me and he called me 'Hedychrus' by establishing

---

123. ILaodikeia 18.

124. See Lilly Kahil, "La Sculpture," in *Laodicée du Lycos: Le Nymphée Campagnes 1961–1963*, ed. Jean des Gagniers et al. (Paris: de Boccard, 1969), 189–92, with plate opposite 190.

125. On the latrines, see Şimşek, *Laodikeia*, 177–79.

126. Şimşek, *Laodikeia*, 178 plate 232.

127. "Ancient Baths Double as Schools in Laodicea," *Hurriyet Daily News*, 11 June 2014, https://tinyurl.com/SBL4218c.

128. For the large water distribution terminals, see Traversari, *Laodicea Di Frigia I*, 63, figs. 19 and 20; Şimşek, "Urban Planning of Laodikeia," fig. 20. For the travertine pipes, see fig. 19.

129. ILaodikeia 12 (first century CE).

me for his masters as the fruit of their labours."[130] Craig Koester helpfully writes that the name Hedychrus, "which means 'sweet complexioned', apparently suited the pleasing quality of the water provided by the city's first-century water system."[131] This is confirmed by a Laodicean epigram (fourth–fifth century CE), probably belonging to a fountain house, which speaks of its high quality water in this manner: "To good fortune. We, the nymphs of the spring, have the sweet, clear water of the Aldiskos."[132]

But perhaps the most revealing find is a new inscription, excavated by Şimşek and announced in a popular 2015 Turkish publication,[133] though, disappointingly, without the provision of the Greek text or a translation. Şimşek elaborates upon the pivotal significance of the inscription thus: "This inscription, which is of utmost importance, addresses issues such as maintenance of waterways to Laodikeia, their destruction, keeping the water uncontaminated and unlittered, and its use for orchard irrigation, as well as indicating severe fines for illegal use."[134] The prominent inscription was inscribed on the eastern wing of the façade of Trajan's nymphaeum, overlooking the public square.

In a 2018 publication,[135] Şimşek helpfully summarizes the content of the water law. Initially, the law deals with the illegal retention of public water from the city for private interests by means of its re-routing (ll. 7–9). People who illegally use the city water for personal use will be fined 5000 denarii (ll. 9–11), as will corrupt public officials who siphon off water to private individuals (ll. 11–12). However, those who legally

---

130. ILaodikeia 13. For discussion, see pp. 362–63.

131. Craig R. Koester, "The Message to Laodicea and the Problem of Its Local Context: A Study of the Imagery in Rev 3:14–22," NTS 49 (2003): 410. See also the methodological discussion of the proper use of archaeological evidence in Lynn R. Huber, "Making Men in Rev 2–3: Reading the Seven Messages in the Bath-Gymnasiums of Asia Minor," in *Stones, Bones, and the Sacred: Essays on Material Culture and Ancient Religion in Honor of Dennis E. Smith*, ed. Alan H. Cadwallader, ECL 21 (Atlanta: SBL Press, 2016), 101–28.

132. ILaodikeia 11.1–3. Trans. Koester, "Message to Laodicea," n. 6.

133. Celal Şimşek, "1900 Yillik Su Yasasi Balundu," *Tübitak Bilim ve Teknik* 49.576 (2015): 66–67, here 67.

134. Şimşek, "Urban Planning of Laodikeia," 8.

135. Celal Şimşek, "Laodikeia Water Law," in *Future Cities: Second International Urban Environment Health Congress. 16–29 April, 2018 Cappadocia*, 199. The article is found on Şimşek's academia.edu website. The publication is in Turkish, with a brief English abstract.

buy water for their homes, gardens, and farms do not violate the imperial edict (ll. 12–14). In terms of the care of the water supply, the diameter of pipes for the water reservoir has very clear specifications (ll. 14–15); but, conversely, the illegal use of piped water for gold digging is fined (ll. 15–16). Moreover, 30,000 denarii are allocated for closing the top of the city water reservoir in order to protect this valuable resource (ll. 16–19). At an administrative level, any magistrate or city official who removes any work on the pipes will be fined 12,500 denarii (ll. 19–20). Two honorable citizens from the city attend to the safety of the urban water supply (ll. 20–22), whereas the governor of the aqueduct and waterways ensures the security of provincial people's water as much as the water destined for the city center (ll. 23–25). In sum, the "magnificent cities" water formula creates equity for all (ll. 25–27).

This new evidence is pertinent for an important debate opened up by Koester.[136] The great care that Laodicea took in maintaining the high quality of its water supply has been clearly demonstrated by the archaeological and epigraphic evidence. Consequently, Koester has justifiably called into question the suggestion that the so-called lukewarm water of Laodicea in Rev 3:16 was undrinkable. Certainly Strabo did not think so: his telling concession, "although their water was drinkable," proves otherwise (*Geogr.* 13.4.14). Nevertheless, Revelation commentators have often proposed that the Laodicean water changed its temperature from being cool to being lukewarm because it was channeled to the city from its springs source by means of an aqueduct: this, they claim, was the local origin of John's imagery. Alternatively, other scholars, as Lynn R. Huber notes, find the origin of the image to be drawn from Hierapolis: Laodicea piped in her water from her neighbor, with the result that the water was "medicinal tasting and nauseous."[137]

But, if these suggestions founder on the local evidence available, noted above, is there another ancient context that might be invoked to explain John's imagery? Koester suggests that the lukewarm imagery should be understood against the backdrop of the hospitality rituals of antiquity where wine was served either chilled or warmed.[138] The idea of a host offering lukewarm wine to his guests would have been highly insulting, and, therefore, the wine would be justifiably spat out of the mouth of its

---

136. Koester, "Message to Laodicea," 409–11.
137. Huber, "Making Men in Rev 2–3," 104.
138. Koester, "Message to Laodicea," 411–16.

recipients. Thus the context of the metaphor is one of ancient feasting rituals as opposed to Laodicea's water distribution system. This is reinforced by John's later invitation to the auditors of his apocalypse to accept the invitation to the Lamb's wedding feast (Rev 19:7–10).

3.5. A Gymnasium

The South Bath-Gymnasium complex, adjacent to the stadium, finds equivocal confirmation in the epigraphic evidence.[139] In a 135 CE inscription the Greek word for "gymnasium" (γυμνάσιον) has been entirely restored by the editor: "To imperator Traianus Hadrianus Caesar Augustus and to Sabina Augusta: the council and people of Laaodicea dedicated the [gymnasium?] … when Gargilius Antiquus was proconsul."[140] However, given the amount of spaces available on the stone, the editor Corsten also suggests that the original word could also be restored as βαλανεῖον ("bath").[141] However, an inscription of the Zenon family, in a dedication to Antonia (first half of first century CE), there is reference to the "priest and gymnasiarch of the city."[142] We have here, at the very least, epigraphic confirmation of the officials belonging to the gymnasium.[143]

The hermeneutical potential of bringing a bath-gymnasium perspective to Rev 2–3—enculturated as John's auditors were to the values of the gymnasium which was devoted to the construction of elite male identity—has been demonstrated by Huber. Although the values of the ancient gymnasium and early Christian communities are different, there are nonetheless interesting resonances in the rhetorical topoi employed in Revelation: that is, the construction of community identity, endurance in the face of hardship, valorized virtue, and the coronal awards of honorific culture, though postponed to the eschaton, to name a few.[144] Did John decide to pitch his summons to faithfulness to the risen Christ on

---

139. On the South Bath-Gymnasium complex, see Şimşek, *Laodikeia*, 196–201.
140. ILaodikeia 14.2.
141. Corsten, *Die Inschriften von Laodikeia am Lykos*, 50.
142. ILaodikeia 53.3; see also ILaodikeia 28.1; 47.4.
143. See James R. Harrison, "Paul and the Gymnasiarchs: Two Approaches to Pastoral Formation in Antiquity," in *Paul: Jew, Greek, and Roman; Pauline Studies*, ed. Stanley E. Porter, vol. 5 (Leiden: Brill, 2008), 141–78.
144. Huber, "Making Men in Rev 2–3," 108–25. On honorific crowning, see James R. Harrison, "'The Fading Crown': Divine Honour and the Early Christians," *JTS* 54 (2003): 493–529.

the part of the Asian churches (Rev 2:1, 8, 12, 18; 3:1, 7, 14) in terms that, while resonating in familiar rhetorical ways, were designed to challenge the dominant values of the Asian elites and their *paideia* as much as the hegemony of the imperial beast?

3.6. The Cemeteries (*Necropoleis*) Surrounding the City on Its Four Sides

The grave contents of the Laodicean *necropoleis* are typical of burial sites: bowls, ceramic lamps, coins, beads, jewellery, et cetera. Sometimes we find figurines of deities accompanying the deceased (e.g., Dionysius, Aphrodite).[145] But what religious beliefs undergirded such practices are difficult to identify. The quality of the other figurines found among the grave goods, including models of theater masks, is generally high.[146] However, it is especially surprising that out the 1603 *necropoleis* finds catalogued by Şimşek only five inscriptions appear. Some of these merely comprise a list of three names with patronymics, accompanied by the traditional farewell of the deceased (XAIPETE).[147]

Another inscription imposes a fine upon anyone who violates the burial site by burying corpses other than the immediate family of the deceased.[148] The heaviness of the fine and the preservation of the funerary epigraphic record in the public archives, while entirely conventional, demonstrates the seriousness with which such grave violations were viewed in antiquity:

> Neratia Eutyche is buried in the coffin.
> No one else can be buried in it
> except Aurelius Zosimianus and Neratius.
> If anyone violates this (prohibition),
> the (fine) will be 2500 denarii

---

145. Şimşek, Okunak, and Bilgen, *Laodikeia Nekropulü*, §912 (Dionsius), §1531 (Aphrodite).

146. Şimşek, Okunak, and Bilgen, *Laodikeia Nekropulü*, §§605, 795, 913, 1506–1508.

147. Şimşek, Okunak, and Bilgen, *Laodikeia Nekropulü*, §1149. Similarly, the inscription of the deceased Apollonides (p. 416). Sometimes the claim to possession of the burial site is made with great brevity (p. 414): "The sarcophagus belongs to Maustaria Aurelius Dionysius, who lived in Laodicea."

148. On the violation of tombs generally, see Dig. 47.12. I am indebted to Cadwallader for this reference.

to the sacred treasury.
A copy of this (inscription) is placed
in the (public) archives.[149]

Finally, there is in the necropolis of Laodicea an intriguing variation to conventional funeral practices, registered in our final inscription below.[150] As we have seen from the inscription above, only family members were to be interred in allocated grave sites, with the possibility of penalties being invoked if this procedure was violated. But, in this case, a nonfamily member, as far as we can discern, is allowed to be buried in the grave of the very much alive grave-owner called Marcus. Marcus accedes to the corpse of Tatas being placed in his own grave site and donates the stela in memory of the deceased Tatas because of the public virtue (ἀρετή) of Tatas's two sons, Zosimos and Nikanor.

The inscription is silent as to whether there was a prior connection between the family of Tatas and the family of Marcus. Were they distant relations or perhaps close family friends? Was Marcus reciprocating a prior favor of Tatas and his sons? Was he ingratiating himself with the two sons for reasons unknown to us? Was he simply struck by the virtue of the family and helped these worthy fellow citizens of Laodicea in a time of crisis? Nevertheless, ancient readers may have been surprised by this departure from traditional burial rites on Marcus's part and would have responded to the grave-owner's own display of ἀρετή as much as the virtue of Tatas's two sons eulogized on the stone.

4. The Numismatic Identity of Laodicea

In this section, for the sake of brevity, we will only focus on the Laodicean numismatic evidence from the death of Caesar to Domitian (44 BCE–CE 96), roughly corresponding to the period of the first two generations of the early Christians at Laodicea.[151]

In terms of the Julio-Claudian coins, we have already highlighted the strong association of Laodicea with Zeus through its original village, Dio-

---

149. Şimşek, Okunak, and Bilgen, *Laodikeia Nekropulü*, p. 506.
150. Şimşek, Okunak, and Bilgen, *Laodikeia Nekropulü*, §229.
151. For a much wider-ranging discussion of all the Laodicean coins, see Armstrong, *Roman Phrygia*, 156–249. For a convenient list of all the available coins, see the "Catologue" therein, 254–358.

spolis. This is heavily reinforced on the reverse of the Julio-Claudian and Flavian coins which depict Zeus Laodiceus standing to the left, accompanied by an eagle and staff.[152] The Phrygian culture of Laodicea is also foregrounded with the reverse side showing its main deity, Men, wearing a Phrygian cap.[153] On the Julio-Claudian and Flavian coins Apollo (obverse) is accompanied by Isis (reverse), underscoring the importance of the Apolline oracular sites and the revelation dispensed there for Laodicea and Hierapolis.[154] Other deities such as Aphrodite appear during the Julio-Claudian period, whereas Nike first appears on the Domitianic issues.[155] The civic institutions of Laodicea receive attention too. Notably, the importance of the Laodicean *demos*, appearing on a republican coin issue and reappearing on an issue from the reign of Nero, predates the much later personification of the Roman senate, which is found on the coins of Caracalla.[156]

So far, the Julio-Claudian coin issues on their reverses have maintained local Phrygian and Laodicean referents notwithstanding the recognition of the Julio-Claudian and Flavian rulers on the obverse. Nonetheless, the Julio-Claudian obverses acknowledge the Augustan imperial age of blessing (ΣΕΒΑΣΤΟΣ), symbolized on one issue by the cornucopia of plenty and the astrological auspiciousness of Capricorn, Augustus's birth sign.[157] Other Julio-Claudian and Flavian relatives such as Agrippina II and Domi-

---

152. Augustus: *RPC* 1.2893–2896, 2898; Tiberius: *RPC* 1.2901, 2905, 2908, 2911; Claudius: *RPC* 1.2912–2914; Nero: *RPC* 1.2917–2923, 2926; Vespasian: *RPC* 2.1268–1270; Domitian: *RPC* 2.1282 [Hera facing Zeus Laodicus], 1288, 1292.

153. *RPC* 1.2907, 2927. Issues showing the Phrygian deity Men drop out in the Flavian period.

154. *RPC* 1.1294, 2903, 2905, 2909. See James R. Harrison, "The Inscriptions and Oracular Prophecy in the Eastern Mediterranean Basin: Assessing the Book of Revelation in Its Graeco-Roman Revelatory Context" in this volume.

155. Aphrodite: *RPC* 1.2910, 2924–2925. Nike: *RPC* 2.1286, 1293.

156. For coins of Nero, see Armstrong, *Roman Phrygia*, 199; *RPC* 1.2892 (first century BCE?): the laureate head of Demos with drapery on shoulder; *RPC* 1.2928: the Demoi of Laodicea and Smyrna face each other, clasping hands and holding scepters. For the Flavian period, see *RPC* 2.1271, 1276–1278. For coins of Caracalla, see Armstrong, *Roman Phrygia*, 179–219, "Catalogue," §§B65–66. For discussion of personifications, indigenous (e.g., Hierapolis and Tyche; Demos; Gerousia; Boule) and Roman (e.g., Roman senate; goddess Roma), in the inscriptions, numismatics and iconography of Hierapolis, see Ritti, *Hierapolis di Frigia IX*, 129–32.

157. *RPC* 1.2897. See Tamsyn Barton, "Augustus and Capricorn: Astrological Polyvalency and Imperial Rhetoric," *JRS* 85 (1995): 33–51.

tia are also honored, and the potential future heirs to imperial power in the Claudian era, Brittanicus and Nero, are similarly acknowledged.[158] The goddess Roma makes her appearance from the Flavian period onwards.[159] The three deities Zeus, Hera, and Athena make their first appearance on a coin of Domitian and correspond to the Capitoline deities (Jupiter, Juno, Minerva) at Rome.[160] On a Domitianic era coin with Roma on the obverse, the wolf and twins of Roman mythological origins are found on the reverse.[161] Here we see a seamless interplay between the Julio-Claudian realities of political power in Asia Minor and the Laodicean commitment to their indigenous religious identities of the city.

Last, an intriguing coin issue emanates from the Neronian period, already noted. Purportedly, it shows on the reverse the Demoi of Laodicea facing each other, who mutually clasp hands, while holding scepters.[162] What has grabbed scholarly attention and has divided interpreters is the legend on the reverse: ΑΝΤΩ ΖΗΝΩΝΟΣ ΖΗΝΩΝ ΥΙΟΣ ΛΑΟΔΙΚΕΩΝ ΖΜΥΡΝΑΙΩΝ ΟΜΗΡΟΣ. The odd order of the words, the difficulties posed by their interrelation, and where the punctuation should be placed has led to competing translations of the legend. This also affects how we understand the identity of the two figures on the coin's reverse and how we understand the intention of the coin. We cannot enter here into the reasons for the differing translations, but the reader is referred to the comments in the *Roman Provincial Coinage* (vol. 1) and in the doctoral thesis of Armstrong.[163] Three alternate translations have been proposed:

1. Antonius Zenon, Son of Zenon. Peace pledge [ΟΜΗΡΟΣ] of the Laodicians and of the Smyrnans.[164]
2. Zenon, son of Antonius Zenon. Peace pledge [ΟΜΗΡΟΣ] of the Laodicians and of the Smyrnans.
3. Antonius Zenon. Zenon, son of the Laodicians. Homer [ΟΜΗΡΟΣ], (son) of the Smyrnans.

---

158. Agrippina II: *RPC* 1.2918; Domitia: *RPC* 2.1281–1285, 1290–1292; Brittanicus: *RPC* 1.2915; Nero: *RPC* 1.2915.
159. *RPC* 2.1279–1280, 1293–1295. See Armstrong, *Roman Phrygia*, 220–49.
160. *RPC* 2.1282–1283. See Armstrong, *Roman Phrygia*, 165–78.
161. *RPC* 2.1295.
162. *RPC* 1.2928.
163. *RPC* 1.2928 (notes); Armstrong, *Roman Phrygia*, 156–63.
164. For discussion of Antonius, see Thonemann, *Maeander Valley*, 210–12.

At the outset, it must be acknowledged that certainty of interpretation in the case of this coin is impossible. In translations (1) and (2), the first named figure—however we translate his name—is the magistrate responsible for the coin's minting (i.e., the moneyer). The word ΟΜΗΡΟΣ, translated here as "peace pledge," is arguably the precursor of the later abstraction ΟΜΟΝΟΙΑ ("sameness of mind," "unity"), a word which is found on coins establishing concord between the cities of Asia Minor (e.g., Hierapolis and Ephesus; Laodicea and Smyrna).[165] Hence the figures on the reverse represent the Demoi of Laodicea and Smyrna, who demonstrate their unity by facing each other and clasping hands, while retaining the symbols of their independence by holding scepters. Thus the potential conflicts aroused by interstate rivalries in Asia Minor are overcome by this act of *homonoia*. Notably, as John Lotz has argued, the peace and unity articulated in Eph 1:21 represents an alternative construct to the political model espoused in Asia Minor.[166]

In translation (3), the first named individual is the moneyer. The next two individuals are Zenon, a member of a wealthy family from Laodicea,[167] and Homer, the famous Greek epic poet whose home town was, according to tradition, Smyrna. Thus, as Strong argues, the coin reveals Laodicea's concern with its own status and identity. This Laodicean coin "is a definitive statement about its own Hellenism and cultural importance."[168] Simultaneously, however, the legend on the reverse on this Neronian coin, represents an astute nod to Nero's phihellenism on the part of Laodicea.

5. Epigraphic Vignettes of Laodicea: Gods, Benefactors, the Heroic Past, and the Jewish Community

So far we have touched upon many Laodicean inscriptional motifs: the relation of archaeological sites to their inscriptions, spectacles and gladiators, theater seating, funeral culture, and water distribution, among others.

---

165. See John Paul Lotz, "The *HOMONOIA* Coins of Asia Minor and Ephesians 1:21," *TynBul* 50.2 (1999): 173–88; Armstrong, *Roman Phrygia*, 294–300 (Laodicea), 338–48 (Hierapolis), 349 (Colossae).

166. Lotz, "*HOMONOIA* Coins." See the fragmentary letter of an unidentified Caesar or governor on rivalries between states: ILaodikeia 10.

167. For the evidence, see Armstrong, *Roman Phrygia*, 163.

168. Armstrong, *Roman Phrygia*, 164.

In our final section we will explore four inscriptional vignettes that throw further light on Laodicean society.

5.1. The Gods

The divine world is always at the center of Laodicean society, an emphasis which the inscriptions consistently reveal. First, the involvement of Laodikeia in the Apolline cult at Claros surfaces in several inscriptions. There is mention of a prophet, Lucius Antonius Aurelianus, in an honorific dedication.[169] Among the twenty-five inscriptions discussed by Robert, each of which records the arrival of a Laodicean delegation to the oracular sanctuary of Apollo of Claros, there is mention of various prophets of Laodicea among the delegates.[170] Last, a fragmentary oracle of Claros and a lot oracle have also been discovered at Laodicea.[171]

Second, an inscriptional dedication links the Roman ruler to the tutelary deity of Laodicea in an address to Domitian, whose name has been erased from the inscription in *damnatio memoriae*: "for Zeus Megistos Soter and Imperator [[Domitian]] Caesar Augustus Germanicus."[172] Elsewhere there is another dedication to Zeus Soter and the divine Augusti.[173] Significantly, in both dedications above, the address to Zeus precedes the address to the Roman ruler: the founding god of the city, therefore, had preeminence. There are also dedications to Zeus Patrios by himself or in conjunction with other closely associated deities, as seen in a splendid relief of Zeus and Hermes on the stela of an inscription (cf. Acts 14:11–12).[174]

Third, in a fragmentary inscription, an unnamed Laodicean dedicates gilded statues to the Erotes for his "night generalship,"[175] which, in his case, was carried out according to decree in his role as a night police offi-

---

169. ILaodikeia 67. See the exhaustive discussion on pp. 289–312.

170. ILaodikeia 1, 3, 4, 5, 8, 11, 12, 13, 14, 15, 18, 19, 21 [restored], 22, 23, 24; see also the discussion on pp. 299–303.

171. ILaodikeia 68–69.

172. ILaodikeia 24. For discussion, see Rosalinde A. Kearsley, "Epigraphic Evidence for the Social Impact of Roman Government in Laodicea and Hierapolis," in Cadwallader and Trainor, *Colossae in Space and Time*, 132–38. On erasure in antiquity, see James R. Harrison, "The Erasure of Honour: Paul and the Politics of Dishonour," *TynBul* 66.2 (2016): 161–84.

173. ILaodikeia 62A.

174. Zeus: ILaodikeia 26; see also 62. Zeus and Hermes: ILaodikeia 125, with plate.

175. ILaodikeia 70.

cer. Importantly, the fear of night crime in antiquity is also reflected in Jesus's brief parable on the thief in the night (Matt 24:43)

Fourth, an honorific inscription employs the language of mercy to describe the goddess, Hestia, whose role of protecting home, family and state is enlisted for the fatherland. What is slightly unusual is that mercy or pity is not readily granted by the gods in antiquity:

> [–] Terentius Longinus (consecrated) the gracious [ἴλεων] goddess Hestia to the fatherland with the base and altar for the office over and above the revenues; he has also twice gone on an embassy at his own expense, both to Lucius Caesar and to the great Imperator Titus Aelius Hadrianus Antoninus Augustus Pius to Rome for the time of (his) office.[176]

5.2. Benefactors

Our epigraphic evidence provides us insight into the benefaction culture of the elite citizens of Laodicea. Building programs and monetary foundations were the substance of their munificent activity. We have already referred to the role that the family of Nikostratos played across the generations in the building and maintenance of the stadium amphitheater at Laodicea. Other examples surface in our inscriptions. Q. Pomponius Flaccus is honored by the city because he "has laid out a marble pavement for Zeus at his own expense."[177] Ti Claudius Tryphon, freedman of Tiberius Claudius Augustus, "built the walls and towers and the triple gate."[178] Pythadoros gives 3000 drachmae for "a crown for the Apollonis tribe of the council."[179]

However, other types of activities such as embassies and night-policing on behalf of the city were also conducted at the expense of the benefactor, as the previously mentioned honorific inscription to Terentius Longinus, ambassador of the city, demonstrates. The honorific decree of Q. Pomponius Flaccus, also mentioned above, sums up his night-policing role and ambassadorship on behalf of Laodicea thus: "who, according to the laws,

---

176. ILaodikeia 65. David Konstan (*Pity Transformed* [London: Duckworth, 2001], 110) writes: "Divine pity, however, is not a quality on which human beings can rely safely. In general, characters in Homer do not ask the gods for pity, and when they do, it is always with the recognition that the result of such petition is at best doubtful."
177. ILaodikeia 82.11–12.
178. ILaodikeia 24b.3.
179. ILaodikeia 84.7–8.

was a night general and undertook at his own expense an embassy for his hometown to Rome."[180] We have also already seen that a dedication of gilded statues to the Erotes was made for the worshiper's (presumably dangerous) role as a night policeman. Benefactors, it seems, were as concerned for the city's civic safety as much for its buildings and grain provision.

5.3. The Heroic Past Reborn

An epigram from a tomb at Laodikeia praises the σωφροσύνη and the appearance of its honorand, Epigonos, claiming that he is superior in virtue and descent to the mythological heroes of the Trojan war: namely, the Greek Achilleus and the Trojan Hector.[181] The inflated claim is bold when one remembers that Rome derived her mythological origins solely from the Trojan heroes, Aeneas and his family, who had fled the war upon the sack of the city by the Greeks:

> Tomb none other you see, passers by, than that of Epigonos, whose virtue [τὰν ἀρετάν] Time will not quench, leaving behind first place in the presence of the living on account of his prudence [σωφροσύνας] and his most godlike shape [θειοτάτος μορφᾶς]; even Achilleus, Hector, son of Priam, and Hippolytus, who fled his father's marriage bed, were not as Epigonos, the son of Andreas, the well-born [εὐγενέτα], a king of same father. But Epigonos remains with the survivors on a monument; also Achilleus the son of Thetis, did not escape Fate [μοιρ(ᾶ)ν].[182]

Whereas Fate had triumphed over the Greek hero Achilleus, the virtue of Epigonos not only trumps Time itself but also outshines the illustrious reputation of all Homeric heroes, Greek and Trojan. But that is not the end of the mythological allusions in the epigram. Hippolytus, the illegitimate

---

180. ILaodikeia 82.10–12.
181. ILaodikeia 81.
182. For another Homeric epigraphic example, see *IG* 10051 in Stephen Mitchell, "The Ionians of Paphlagonia," in *Local Knowledge and Microidentities in the Imperial Greek World*, ed. Tim Whitmarsh (Cambridge: Cambridge University Press, 2010), 95. See also G. H. R. Horsley, "Homer in Pisidia: Aspects of the History of Greek Education in a Remote Roman Province," *Antichthon* 34 (2000): 46–81. For a hero cult inscription at Philippi, see James R. Harrison, "Excavating the Urban and Country Life of Roman Philippi and Its Territory," in *The First Urban Churches 4: Roman Philippi*, ed. James R. Harrison and L. L. Welborn (Atlanta: SBL Press, 2018), 29.

son of the Athenian king Theseus, was killed after rejecting the sexual advances of his stepmother Phaedra ("who fled his father's marriage bed"). Once again, Epigonos is not only vastly superior in virtue to the adulterous royal house of Athens but also, in contrast to its tragic illegitimate prince Hippolytus, is "well-born." In reality, this pretentious funerary epigram was a curious expression of a wider phenomenon of the Second Sophistic, best exemplified by Philostratus's *On Heroes*. In that literary work, readers were exposed to what was claimed to be a truer and more accurate version of the Trojan War than Homer's version, reflecting through the epic tradition the continuing historical importance of hero cults in the third century CE.[183]

5.4. The Jewish Community of Laodicea

The Jewish inscriptions at Laodicea are especially sparse. Only two inscriptions are extant: *IJO* 2.212–213, but, importantly, the sarcophagus of L. Nonius Glycon (*IJO* 2.213) refers to the stipulations of Deuteronomy in issuing a warning against the unauthorized use of the grave: "to him (will come) the curses that are written in Deuteronomy." This feature was also found at Jewish graves in Acmonia in Phrygia (*CIJ* 760; cf. *MAMA* 6.335).[184] Not only is the explicit reference to the Old Testament Scriptures significant, but also the fact that is assumed that the Jewish reader knows to which section of Deuteronomy is being referred: Peter W. van der Horst postulates Deut 28:22, 28–29.[185] We are dealing with a diaspora community that draws its identity and ethics from the Old Testament scriptures in its urban context and which demonstrates its piety by warning (presumably) other Jews about the divine wrath facing those who violate the Deuteronomic commandments.[186] Graeco-Roman readers would have been puzzled by

---

183. Flavius Philostratus, *On Heroes*, trans. Ellen Bradshaw Aitken and Jennifer K. Berenson McLean (Atlanta: Society of Biblical Literature, 2001).

184. See Peter W. van der Horst, *Ancient Jewish Epitaphs: An Introductory Survey of a Millennium of Jewish Funerary Epigraphy (300 BCE–700 CE)* (Kampen: Kok Pharos, 1991), 56–57.

185. Van der Horst, *Ancient Jewish Epitaphs*, 56; see also Paul Trebilco, *Jewish Communities in Asia Minor*, SNTSMS 69 (Cambridge: Cambridge University Press, 1991), 62–69.

186. Trebilco (*Jewish Communities in Asia Minor*, 65–66) rejects the suggestion that this is a magical use of the Deuteronomic text, arguing that the Jewish community "was acting in accord with the intent of the passage" (66).

the Deuteronomic reference but, in line with their culture, they would have understood the prohibition perfectly well at a general level. But the very specificity of the Deuteronomic reference poses the question whether the prohibition is only intended for intra-mural consumption.

Furthermore, historical caution is required regarding the distinctiveness of such sentiments among Jews living in the Lycus Valley. As we have seen from an inscription from the Laodicean necropolis, noted above, warnings regarding the violation of tombs were widespread in antiquity. It seems probable, then, that the Jewish community at Laodicea adapted culturally to well-known Graeco-Roman funeral customs in Asia Minor, but in their case articulated these practices from an Old Testament perspective.[187]

However, it is *not* the case at nearby Hierapolis that warnings regarding violations of Jewish tombs carried a reference to the Deuteronomic commandments.[188] This textual reference is a predilection of Acmonia and Laodicea *alone* in Phrygia, both of whom, seemingly, felt that they had to redefine existing funeral conventions by reference to Scripture. Why, then, did Jews in Laodicea resort to this scriptural strategy whereas other Jews living in the same valley at Hierapolis did not? We do not know the answer other than the variegation with diaspora Judaism in Asia Minor.

Part 3. Hierapolis: An Iconographic and Epigraphic Portrait

1. Iconography, Mythology, and the Civic Identity of Hierapolis

The cities of the Greek East, in the period of the Second Sophistic, turned to the mythic past and their traditional gods in negotiating place for their own civic identity in the Roman Empire. Various manifestations of cultural archaism in the Greek world occurred during the period of the Second Sophistic (late first century CE–early third century CE) and were also facilitated by the philhellenism of Hadrian. This movement was not

---

187. Walter Ameling ("The Epigraphic Habit and the Jewish Diasporas of Asia Minor and Syria," in *From Hellenism to Islam: Cultural and Linguistic Change in the Roman Near East*, ed. Hannah M. Cotton et al. [Cambridge: Cambridge University Press, 2009], 207–8) argues that the Jews of Laodicea adapted to the Phrygian cultural custom of "cursing" in funerary epitaphs.

188. Richard S. Ascough, Philip A. Harland, and John S. Kloppenborg, *Associations in the Greco-Roman World* (Waco, TX: Baylor University Press; Berlin: de Gruyter, 2012), §§150–151.

only confined to linguistic Atticism and *paideia* but also demonstrated increased concern for the mythical past and local religious traditions, including the continuing vitality of the Greek oracular sanctuaries. Elite benefactors in the Greek East vied with each other to build large urban monuments and sponsor elaborate civic processions that honored their city's protecting deities and celebrated the founder traditions associated with local myths.[189] However, Roman rule and its cult were not supplanted by the elite endorsement of Greek religious traditions relating to the civic identity of each Asian city. Rather the elites worked cooperatively with their Roman overlords, acquiring additional status through imperial priesthoods and by integrating local religious traditions with the realities of Roman power and patronage.

The theater reliefs at Hierapolis, finished during the Severan period (206 CE), are found on the large richly decorated *scaenae frons*, which provides a spectacular backdrop to the stage (*logeion*).[190] The originals, housed in the Pamukkale Museum, "present a narrative through images of the myths tied to the two most important deities at Hierapolis and, indeed, in the whole of Asia Minor."[191] At the central exedra, the Apollo cycle of reliefs radiates to the right whereas the Artemis cycle radiates to the left. The details of the reliefs are set out below.

(1) The Apollo cycle of reliefs commences with the sacred wedding of Zeus and Leto and moves to the birth of the child Apollo and his training from infancy to adulthood, highlighting Apollo's maturation in his punish-

---

189. For discussion of processions at Hierapolis, see Ritti, *Hierapolis di Frigia IX*, 139–42.

190. See D'Andria, *Hierapolis of Phrygia*, 157, figs. 135, 137. For discussion, see Ritti, *Hierapolis I*, 55–77, 105–25; Francesco D'Andria and Tullia Ritti, *Hierapolis II: Le sculture del teatro; I rilievi con I cicli di Apollo e Artemide*, Archaeologica 54 (Rome: Bretschneider, 1985); Simon Price, "Local Mythologies in the Greek East," in *Coinage and Identity in the Roman Provinces*, ed. Christopher Howgego, Volker Heuchert, and Andrew Burnett (Oxford: Oxford University Press, 2005), 118–19; Diana Yi-man Ng, *Manipulation of Memory: Public Buildings and Decorative Programs in Roman Cities of Asia Minor* (PhD Thesis, University of Michigan, 2007), esp. 97–143; D'Andria, *Hierapolis of Phrygia*, 147–81; Bailey Benson, *The Creation of Shared Memory: The Theater Reliefs from Hierapolis* (MA thesis, Chapel Hill, 2014). On the theater and stage at Hierapolis, note the fragmentary inscription: "and [author of] contributions of theater and stage […]" (Tullia Ritti, *Fonti Letterarie ed Epigraphi: Hierapolis Scavi e Ricerche* [Rome: Bretschneider, 1985], 91–92, pl. 9a).

191. D'Andria, *Hierapolis of Phrygia*, 161.

ment of the hubristic Adonis and his triumph over a serpent-like giant on a griffin-led chariot.[192] From here the relief concentrates on the local Asian Marsyas myth, with another scene of the punishment of *hybris*, leading to the eventual apotheosis of Apollo and his crowning by the nymphs.[193] In the final section of the relief, Apollo is identified as the god of purification and as the god Musagetes, the conductor of the choir of the Muses.[194] The relief culminates in the personification of Tyche (Fortune) of Hierapolis.[195]

(2) The Artemis cycle of reliefs parallels the progression of the Apollo cycle.[196] The birth of Artemis progresses from her infancy to her maturation as the huntress goddess, symbolized by another chariot scene with Artemis as the driver.[197] Another example of the punishment of *hybris* is displayed in the images of Artemis killing the fleeing daughters of Niobe.[198] The local Anatolian myths about Artemis are preferred to classical traditions about the goddess, with imagery derived from the annual procession from Ephesus, along the Sacred Way, to Artemis's sanctuary, as well as scenes of cultic sacrifice and the divinities (Dike, Nemesis) from the Asian athletic contests.[199]

(3) Further reliefs, found on the upper orders of the theater, show the god Dionysos. His presence on these reliefs is appropriate because he is the god "who presides over all dramatic performance, (and) reinforces the significance of the Muses."[200] The allusion back to the deities Musagetes and the Muses in the Apollo cycle is clear enough.

(4) On the central block of the Porta Regia above the doorway, various reliefs of the imperial family of Septimius Severus are depicted.[201] Rather than the Roman ruler in Rome being personally disconnected from the

---

192. D'Andria, *Hierapolis of Phrygia*, 162–165, figs. 142a and 142b.
193. D'Andria, *Hierapolis of Phrygia*, 162, figs. 142a 6, 7 and 163, figs. 142a 8, 9, 10. For details of the myth, see Price, "Local Mythologies in the Greek East," 118.
194. D'Andria, *Hierapolis of Phrygia*, 164–5, fig. 142b.
195. D'Andria, *Hierapolis of Phrygia*, 165, fig. 142b 16.
196. D'Andria, *Hierapolis of Phrygia*, 171–75, esp. figs. 150a and 150b.
197. D'Andria, *Hierapolis of Phrygia*, 172, fig. 150a 1, 2 and 173, fig. 150a 3.
198. D'Andria, *Hierapolis of Phrygia*, 172, fig. 150a 4. For details of the myth, see Price, "Local Mythologies in the Greek East," 118–19.
199. D'Andria, *Hierapolis of Phrygia*, 175, fig. 150b 5, 6, 7, 8; 176.
200. D'Andria, *Hierapolis of Phrygia*, 139.
201. On the central section, Ng, *Manipulation of Memory*, 127–35; Benson, *Creation of Shared Memory*, 34–38. On the left and right sections of the Port Regia reliefs, omitted here, 30–34.

eastern provinces, this relief probably alludes to Severus's visits to the province of Asia in 194 and 202 CE.[202] Hierapolis was intimately connected to the imperial family by virtue of the fact that one of their prominent citizens, the sophist Aelieus Antipater, was tutor to Severus's sons Geta and Caracalla (Philostratus, *Vit. soph.* 2.24). Finally, other nearby figures show (probably) Agon crowning himself and a figure epigraphically identified as Agonothesia (Αγωνο[θε]σία), alluding to the local Pythian games.[203] Another figure personifies the city Hierapolis, placed alongside the local god of the Chrysorhoas river.[204]

What do we make of this rich interplay of Apolline, Artemesian, and imperial motifs at the theater of Hierapolis? The Apolline connection underscores the presence of the oracular at Hierapolis and Apollo's healing and purifying powers over a local plague.[205] This connection was also present in an oracle articulating the triumph of Artemis over (the perceived) sorcerer's infliction of a plague at Sardis.[206] Specific motifs from local myth are emphasized in the cycles of Apollo and Artemis as opposed to the generic myths ubiquitously found abroad. The punishment of *hybris* in each cycle warns Hierapolis to be faithful and submissive to her local gods and goddesses. The local Artemis traditions of Hierapolis are brought into dialogue with the Artemis traditions of Ephesus, conveying the impression of a shared past.[207] The crowning of Artemis by the nymphs would link the myth directly with the Nymphaeum of the Tritons, which was soon afterwards dedicated at Hierapolis (ca. 218–236 CE).[208]

---

202. Benson, *Creation of Shared Memory*, 39–42.
203. Ritti, *Hierapolis I*, 61, pl. 2a.
204. Note the two inscriptional acclamations of Hierapolis: "Prosper, o Hierapolis!"; "Great fortune of the city!" (Ritti, *Epigraphic Guide to Hierapolis*, §22). See also Ritti, *Hierapolis I*, 62, pl. 2a.
205. Ritti, *Epigraphic Guide to Hierapolis*, §§16, 38.
206. James R. Harrison, "Artemis Triumphs over a Sorcerer's Evil Art," *NewDocs* 10 (2012): 37–47.
207. Benson, *Creation of Shared Memory*, 27.
208. See Francesco D'Andria, "Gods and Amazons in the Nymphaeums of Hierapolis," in *Roman Sculpture in Asia Minor: Proceedings of the International Conference, May 24–26, 2007, Cavallino (Lecce)*, ed. Francesco D'Andria and Ilaria Romeo, JRASup81 (Portsmouth: Journal of Roman Archaeology, 2011), 150–72. For the Nymphaeum's dedications, see Ritti, *Epigraphic Guide to Hierapolis*, §12. Note the third century epigram honoring Hierapolis for its nymphs (§21): "Sacred town, town of

Last, these mythic traditions are entwined with imperial cult, given resonance by the Roman ruler's visits to Asia and the strong connection of Hierapolis with the imperial family. D. Yi-man Ng proposes that the emperor "is shown as but one of the devotees, albeit the most exalted one, of Hierapolis' local cults."[209] While this interpretation is possible in terms of the iconography, the dedicatory inscription in the theater points to the status equivalence of Septimius Severus, Marcus Aurelius, Septimius Geta, and Julia Domna with Apollo Archegetes and the ancestral gods.[210] The central position of Septimius Severus and his family in the upper level of the theater's decoration, with the personified Hierapolis to the imperial family's left, reinforces the message of equivalence. Elsewhere in the theater, reliefs of the old Pergameme kings, Attalus and Eumenes, also appear, affirming the fact that the Romans and their gods are the legitimate successors to the ruler cult of the Pergameme royalty.[211]

2. Epigraphic Vignettes of Hierapolis

2.1. The Indigenous Gods of Hierapolis

At the outset we might ask how worship of the indigenous gods adapted to the arrival of the imperial cult at Hierapolis.[212] While there are dedications to the Roman rulers for their beneficence at Hierapolis and honorific monuments erected by their clients at Laodicea,[213] the inscriptions of Hierapolis are fascinating for the way that the Roman rulers and their family are often linked with the indigenous deities in the initial address to the ruler: for example, Gaius Caesar, son of Augustus, and Zeus; Apollo

---

gold, may you own the most advantageous territory of all of vast Asia, lady of the Nymphs, adorned by the splendour of (your) waters."

209. Ng, *Manipulation of Memory*, 142–43.

210. Ng, *Manipulation of Memory*, 236–37; Ritti, *Epigraphic Guide to Hierapolis*, §24 (206–208 CE).

211. Ritti, *Hierapolis I*, 119–20; Price, "Local Mythologies in the Greek East," 124.

212. For discussion of the imperial cult at Hierapolis, see Ritti, *Hierapolis di Frigia IX*, 132–37.

213. E.g., Titus: ILaodikeia 9 [l. 9: φιλόκαισαρ ἐκ τῶν ἰδίων]; Domitian: ILaodikeia 24. Ritti, *Epigraphic Guide to Hierapolis*, §10. Note also the dedication to apotheosized Livia (Λιβίαν θεάν) in Tullia Ritti and H. Hüseyin Baysal, eds., *Museo Archeologico di Denizli-Hierapolis: Catalogo delle iscrizioni greche e latine* (Naples: Liguori Editore, 2008), §48: For Hadrian, see §19: "to [Hadrian] Olympios and Panhellenios."

Archegetes, the protecting deity of the city, and Severus Alexander; Zeus Olympios, the ancestral gods, and Hadrian.[214] From the beginning of the Julio-Claudian era, some of the local Asian mints either identify the Roman ruler and his family with various deities or the local deity with the goddess Roma on their coins.[215]

The Roman rulers were also occasionally involved in official decisions regarding the rights of the indigenous cults. In a letter of Hadrian to Hierapolis, which was returned with the city's ambassadors upon their congratulating him at Rome with a gold crown at his accession to power, the Roman ruler reaffirmed the rights of shelter (*asylium*: "place of refuge") at their sanctuaries.[216] This was a prestigious honor and a rare privilege, given that Tiberius had formerly abolished such rights in Asia (Tacitus, *Ann.* 3.60–63; Suetonius, *Tib.* 37). Furthermore, Hadrian sent back the crown with the ambassadors, not because he was snubbing Hierapolis (indeed, contra: "feeling satisfied by the honor"), but rather, on account of the enormous expense of the crown, he was returning it as an unexpected benefaction.

In addition to dispensing asylum, the indigenous gods could dispense punishment.[217] Insight into the invocation of the retribution of the indig-

---

214. Gaius Caesar: Ritti, *Epigraphic Guide to Hierapolis*, §34. Apollo Archegetes: Note the prayer: "May the Archegetes be propitious to you" (Ritti, *Epigraphic Guide to Hierapolis*, §22). Severus Alexander: Ritti, *Epigraphic Guide to Hierapolis*, §12; see also §14 [unnamed emperor]). See also Ritti and Baysal, *Museo Archeologico di Denizli-Hierapolis*, §29: "to Zeus Sotēr and to the divine Augusti." Zeus Olympios: Ritti, *Epigraphic Guide to Hierapolis*, §20.

215. For example, on the reverse of a leaded bronze coin from Smyrna, Livia is shown as Aphrodite (*RPC* 1.1.2467 [Augusta]), Drusilla as Persephone (*RPC* 1.1.2473 [Caligulan]), and Poppaea as Nike (*RPC* 1.1.2486 [Neronian]). In the case of Ephesus, on the reverse of a copper coin Roma stands, holding the scepter and cult statue of Artemis (*RPC* 1.1.2632). Sometimes an entirely Roman emphasis is articulated. On a brass coin of Tiberius from Smyrna (*RPC* 1.1.2469), the obverse displays the Senate and Livia, whereas the reverse renders a temple with four columns enclosing a statue of the emperor as Pontifex. No identification with any indigenous deity is made in this instance. The Flavian coins from Asia universally identify the Roman ruler or family member with indigenous deities by coupling his/her image on the obverse with a deity on the reverse.

216. Ritti, *Epigraphic Guide to Hierapolis*, §36: Hadrian says, "As far as the rights of asylum that were given to your ancestral gods by the kings and emperors and senate, that have been ratified even by the divine Trajan, I [confirm] them as well."

217. For the inscriptions of the indigenous deities at Hierapolis, see Ritti and

enous gods is afforded by the imprecation of P. Ail. Apollinarios Makedon against potential desecrators of his and his wife's tomb at Hierapolis. After outlining the fines against those who might interfere with the burial site, the inscription (second half of second century CE) on the blocks beneath the entablature above the tomb's entrance then says:

> The man who does anything against the prescriptions will be liable to fines, and may he not know the pleasure of children and of life, may the earth be not accessible and the sea not navigable, but may he die with all sufferings, childless [ἄκτενος] and destitute [ἄβιος] and deformed [πήρος], and may he find after his death the gods of the underworld punishing and enraged, both the man who has ordered it to be built or made, and the workman.[218]

The unusual savagery of the retributive justice invoked in this particular inscription can be deduced from the fact that among J. Strubbe's collection of 404 imprecations,[219] ἄβιος and πήρος (literally, "disabled in a limb," "maimed") are only found in this inscription. Otherwise the imprecation is entirely conventional.

Last, usually little is revealed in the honorific inscriptions regarding the rituals of the indigenous cults, other than the glimpses we receive, for example, in the honoring of an Ephesian priestess of Artemis, whom I have discussed elsewhere (IEph 3.987).[220] But an inscription from Hierapolis reveals on what days the priest Tiberius Julius Myndios was to make libations and sacrifices to Zeus, presentations of new roses, bathing for Zeus, and sacrifices for the Deia after the Augustus day.[221] Such cultic knowl-

---

Baysal, *Museo Archeologico di Denizli-Hierapolis*, §§27–47. See also their accompanying iconography in plates §§31A, 31B, 32–34, 42. For discussion, see Ritti, *Hierapolis di Frigia IX*, 99–129.

218. Johann Strubbe, ed., APAI EPITYMBIOI: *Imprecation against Desecrators of the Grave in the Greek Epitaphs of Asia Minor; A Catalogue* (Bonn: Rudolf Habelt, 1997), §285.9–12 (= Walther Judeich, "Inschriften," in *Altertümer von Hierapolis*, ed. Carl Humann [Berlin: Reimer, 1898], §339). For a picture of the tomb and the entablature on which the inscription is, see Ritti, *Epigraphic Guide to Hierapolis*, 57.

219. Strubbe, APAI EPITYMBIOI, *passim*. Note the Ephesian curse against impiety and sacrilege in a synhedrion decree regulating the annual sacrifices to the emperor Commodus for his eternal continuance (IEph Ia 26.10, 22–23).

220. James R. Harrison, "Family Honour of a Priestess of Artemis," *NewDocs* 10 (2012): 34–35.

221. Ritti, *Epigraphic Guide to Hierapolis*, §37 (117–137 CE).

edge, taken for granted by its adherents and casual observers, is seldom revealed epigraphically. Finally, it is important to realize that benefactors of the indigenous private associations could also be sponsors of the imperial cult in various capacities in the public sphere: the elites sought honor on multiple fronts.

2.2. Benefactors of Hierapolis

In the case of Hierapolis, an *archgallos*, the head of the college of worshipers of Cybele and Attis, "has taken decorous care and has served the gods in a way worthy of the praise."[222] Again at Hierapolis, the Latin-named Pompeianus dedicates a statue of Tyche to Apollo Archegetes for his position of *stephanephoros* (holder of Apollo's sacred crown) and *agoranomos* (inspector of the market).[223] Without the eastern Mediterranean elites heavily funding the official civic cults and festivals, local association activities, the gods of the gymnasia and the games, including filling their various priesthoods, we would not be witnessing the strong revitalization of traditional indigenous religion during the first three centuries CE. Examples of other traditional civic benefactions can also be cited, such as the honorific list of the financiers of a building or the temple and stoas funded by Glykon, son of the priest Teimoxenos.[224] Again, without the wealthy elites and the honorific culture driving them, the city would not have been able to afford the beautifying of its public spaces.[225]

---

222. Ritti, *Epigraphic Guide to Hierapolis*, §27. On the archaeology of the Plutonium ("place of Pluto") and the castrated priests of Cybele who descended into the small cave at Hierapolis, see Francesco D'Andria, *Cehennem'Den Cennet'e Hierapolis (Pamukkale): Ploutonion Aziz Philippus'un Mezari ve Kutsal Alani* (Istanbul: Ege Yayinlari, 2014), written in Turkish; D'Andria, "Nature and Cult in the *Ploutonion* of Hierapolis before and after the Colony," in *Landscape and History in the Lykos Valley: Laodikeia and Hierapolis in Phrygia*, eds. Celal Şimşek and Francesco D'Andria (Newcastle upon Tyne: Cambridge Scholars Publishing, 2017), 207–40. Larry J. Kreitzer ("The Plutonium of Hierapolis and the Descent of Christ into the 'Lowermost Parts of the Earth' (Ephesians 4:9)," *Bib* 79 [1998]: 381–93) has argued that the Plutonium is the geographical location that Paul wants his Ephesian auditors to imagine when he speaks of Christ entering the lowermost parts of the earth (Eph 4:9). For a picture of the entrance to the Plutonium, see D'Andria, *Hierapolis of Phrygia*, 142, fig. 125.

223. Ritti, *Epigraphic Guide to Hierapolis*, §43.
224. Ritti et al., *Museo Archaeologicodi Denizli-Hierapolis*, §§22–23.
225. It would be unwise to restrict the contribution of building at Hierapolis to

2.3. Spectacles at Hierapolis

We have already discussed the gladiatorial spectacles that were held at Laodicea's stadium, along with the gladiator inscriptions and the iconography of their funeral stelae in the city. We have a similar wealth of information for spectacles at Hierapolis.[226] Several examples will suffice.

A singular epigram from a gladiator stela at Hierapolis reveals how its honorand, Stephanos, died. The epigram arouses pathos through its explanation of the circumstances leading up to his death. Despite his display of courage and being crowned for victories in ten contests, Stephanos is nevertheless disconsolate. The reason, it seems, is that before he died he had to kill, probably in gladiatorial combat, a companion who had saved his life on another occasion. The gladiatorial cycle of bouts, if the competitor was to survive and be successful, sometimes involved heart-wrenching decisions for the combatant:

> First celebrated in stadiums, I met death
> after killing an opponent filled with unreasoning hate.
> My name is Stephanos; crowned ten times in contest,
> I die and in the long ages I will remain encircled
> in the womb of the earth; but my courage never left me,
> before with my hands I had to come to kill the defender of my life.
> Polychronis made the inscription in memory.[227]

---

the elite benefactors alone. Note the inscription dedicated to the citizen of Herapolis, M. Aur. Ammianos, who devised a water-powered twin saw for cutting stones for civic building projects. For the third century CE inscription and the iconography of the device on the sarcophagus relief, see Tullia Ritti, Klaus Grewe and Paul Kessner, "A Relief of a Water-Powered Stone Saw Mill on a Sarcophagus at Hierapolis and Its Implications," *JRA* 20 (2007): 139–63.

226. For the inscriptions, see Ritti, *Fonti Letterarie ed Epigraphi*, 97–101; Robert, *Les gladiateurs dans l'orient grec*, §§121–126. See also Ritti et al., *Museo Archaeologicodi Denizli-Hierapolis*, §§62–63, plates 62–63. For description of the iconography, see Carter, *Presentation of Gladiatorial Spectacles*, "Catalogue of Inscriptions," §§341–348. On gladiators at Hierapolis, see Tullia Ritti and Salim Yilmaz, *Gladiatori e venationes a Hierapolis di Frigia* (Rome: Accademia Naz. dei Lincei, 1998); Ritti, *Hierapolis di Frigia IX*, 181–86. For victors at the athletic and artistic games held at Hierapolis, see Ritti et al., *Museo Archaeologicodi Denizli-Hierapolis*, §§60–61. For discussion of the games, see Ritti, *Hierapolis di Frigia IX*, 168–81.

227. Ritti, *Fonti Letterarie ed Epigraphi*, 97–98 (= Robert, *Les gladiateurs dans l'orient grec*, §124). The translation is indebted to Ritti.

Last, what light does the iconography of the Hierapolis stelae throw upon the New Testament? We will focus on two important reliefs which depict prisoners condemned to death by the beasts (*damnatio ad bestias*) in the arena.[228] First, a graphic relief shows three loin-clothed men, criminals to be executed in the arena, walking towards the right in a procession with eyes cast down towards the ground. Each man carries a placard over his right shoulder and has a rope draped around his neck.[229] There are, however, no indications of any beasts in the relief, but dismemberment by wild animals would have been a typical punishment. Nevertheless, Paul was well aware of the potency of visual imagery like this throughout the Roman Empire. In 1 Cor 4:9b the dishonored apostles are depicted as shuffling last of all into the Corinthian theater, appointed to die or perform there for the entertainment of the highly honored, including the celestial audience (1 Cor 4:9b). Significantly, the visual dimensions of shame in the Hierapolis relief (placards, downcast eyes, neck rope) are also reflected in the terminology of shame (μωροί, ἀσθενεῖς, ἄτιμοι) that Paul applies to the apostles (1 Cor 4:10) so that, in a paradoxical reversal of status, the Corinthians might become wise (φρόνιμοι), strong (ἰσχυροί), and honorable (ἔνδοξοι) in Christ.[230]

Second, a partially mutilated relief displays the execution of a condemned man. The man, covered by an undergarment, is tied to a pole across his chest, with his legs and arms free. To his left a large bear, clambering up the pole, begins to tear him apart. The horror and cruelty of the scene is not avoided, with greater precision of rendering being given to the bear.[231] Again, in 1 Cor 15:32, the apostle graphically says he fought with wild beasts at Ephesus, so much so that, rather than this merely being a metaphorical reference, some commentators from the past have wondered whether the apostle actually did fight wild animals in the city's amphitheater.[232]

---

228. For a highly weathered relief showing diverse scenes of gladiators and a bound wild animal, see Robert, *Les gladiateurs dans l'orient grec*, §123; Ritti, *Fonti Letterarie ed Epigraphi*, 100 plate 11b; Carter, *Presentation of Gladiatorial Spectacles*, "Catalogue of Inscriptions," §344.

229. Ritti, *Fonti Letterarie ed Epigraphi*, 102 plate 13.

230. See James R. Harrison, "Paul and Ancient Civic Ethics: Redefining the Canon of Honour in the Graeco-Roman World," in *Paul's Graeco-Roman Context*, ed. Cilliers Breytenbach, BETL 277 (Leuven: Peeters, 2015), 75–118.

231. Ritti, *Fonti Letterarie ed Epigraphi*, 102–3, plate 12d.

232. Robert E. Osborne, "Paul and the Wild Beasts," *JBL* 85 (1966): 225–30. More recently, the majority of scholars, however, have regarded the reference in 1 Cor

2.4. The Jews of Hierapolis: The Family Tomb of P. Aelius Glykon and Aurelia Amia in the Northern Necropolis

Philip A. Harland has extensively treated the Jewish inscriptional evidence of Hierapolis.[233] All the Jewish inscriptions are found on either tombs or sarcophagi, either in the northern (*IJO* 2.189, 192–194, 198, 201–203, 205–209) or eastern (*IJO* 2.188, 196) *necropoleis*, or elsewhere in tumuli tombs closer to the city (*IJO* 2.200, 204). These are sometimes accompanied by Jewish symbols such as the menorah (seven-branched candlestick), the lulav (palm branch), the ritual trumpet made from the horn of a ram, and a (messianic?) lion.[234] The inscriptions are entirely conventional. There are the names of the interred, sometimes the explicit identification of the interred as Ἰουδαίου or Ἰουδέων, warnings against the violation of the tomb, the fines to be paid "to the people of the Judaeans" if there were a violation (*IJO* 2.206)[235] and, last, a copy of the inscription in the civic archives (*pace*, a Judean archive: *IJO* 2.205).

The intriguing exception to the rule is the tomb of P. Aelius Glykon[236] and his wife Aurelia Amia, the inscription of which is cited in part below (*IJO* 2.196.5–11: late second–third century CE):

15:30–32 as metaphorical: Abraham J. Malherbe, "The Beasts at Ephesus," in *Paul and the Popular Philosophers* (Minneapolis: Fortress, 1989), 79–89; L. L. Welborn, "Paul's Spectacle Metaphor in 1 Corinthians 15:30–32," *The Bible and Critical Theory* 8 (2012): 39–51.

233. Philip A. Harland, "Acculturation and Identity in the Diaspora: A Jewish Family and 'Pagan' Guilds at Hierapolis," in *The Religious History of the Roman Empire: Pagans, Jews, and Christians*, ed. John A. North and Simon R. F. Price (Oxford: Oxford University Press, 2011), 385–418; Harland, *North Coast of the Black Sea, Asia Minor*, vol. 2 of *Greco-Roman Associations: Texts, Translations and Commentary*, BZNW 204 (Berlin: de Gruyter, 2014), §116. See also A. Thomas Kraabel, *Judaism in Western Asia Minor under the Roman Empire: With a Preliminary Study of the Jewish Community at Sardis, Lydia* (Cambridge: Harvard University Library, 1969), 125–29. Also, see Elena Miranda, "La communità giudaica di Hierapolis di Frigia," *EA* 31 (1999): 109–55.

234. For the tomb of the Jew Mar(cus) Aur(elius) Philoumenos Streneion, with menora, lalav and trumpet symbols flanking the entry, see Ritti, *Epigraphic Guide to Hierapolis*, §54 fig. 18 (= *IJO* 2.203). For messianic lion and menorah on the family "(Grave) of the Judaeans," see Harland, "Acculturation and Identity in the Diaspora," 389, fig. 11.1 (= *IJO* 2.187).

235. Fines were also paid to civic institutions (*IJO* 2.192, 193, 198, 199, 200, 202, 204) and the *gerousia* (*IJO* 2.189).

236. The name could be either "P. Aelius Glykon, son of Zeuxis Aelianus" (Har-

He (Aelius) left behind 200 denarii for the grave-crowning ceremony to the most holy presidency of the purple-dyers, so that it would produce from the interest enough for each to take a share in the seventh month[237] during the festival of the Unleavened Bread. Likewise he also left behind 150 denarii for the grave-crowning ceremony to the association of carpet-weavers, so that the revenues from the interest should be distributed, half to the festival of Kalends on the eighth day of the fourth month[238] and half during the festival of Pentecost.

Here we see depicted a citizen's experience of the religious pluralism and multiple identities of Hierapolis. The competing religious affiliations of the city collide in the social lives of the city's inhabitants and demand allegiance at various levels, depending upon one's professional, cultic, ethnic and client-patron obligations. Note (1) the presence of local trades associations (purple-dyers, carpet-weavers), among which were people of diverse social and ethnic status;[239] (2) the calendrical observance of the traditional festivals by the Jews (Unleavened Bread, Pentecost); (3) the Romanization of Hierapolis evidenced by its observance of the Roman calendar (the celebration of the Roman New Year festival of the Kalends); and (4) the practice of indigenous funerary rituals of Hierapolis (the grave-crowning ceremony).

An important question emerges at this stage, but one without a definitive answer. Is Aelius—most likely a Roman citizen[240]—a native-born Jew, a god-fearer, or a gentile attracted by Jewish customs?[241] Certainty is unachievable. Most probably the family's choice of the festival days of Unleavened Bread and Pentecost for the performance of the grave ceremonies on behalf

---

land, "Acculturation and Identity in the Diaspora," 395 n. 19) or "P. Aelius Glykonianos Zeuxainos Aelianus" (*IJO* 2.196).

237. March–April.

238. 1 January.

239. On whether the ethnic membership of these two associations in our inscription were Jewish, gentile, or a mixture of both, see Harland, "Acculturation and Identity in the Diaspora," 405–9. Harland and Kraabel (*Judaism in Western Asia Minor*, 134–35) opt for a mixed constituency, whereas Miranda ("La communità giudaica di Hierapolis di Frigia," 140–45) opts for a Jewish constituency. For the inscriptions relating to the associations of Hierapolis, see Ascough, *Associations in the Greco-Roman World*, §§148–158.

240. Harland, "Acculturation and Identity in the Diaspora," 397–98.

241. Harland, "Acculturation and Identity in the Diaspora," 396–97.

of the family points to Jewish extraction.²⁴² If this inference is correct, more puzzling is the inclusion of the grave ceremonies on the feast of Kalends, given that various Jewish prohibitions were placed on commerce before and, though disputed by some rabbis, after the Roman festivals, including Kalends (m. Avod. Zar. 1:1–3). However, this sensitivity expressed by the Tannaim in the Mishnah regarding any Jewish association with the gentiles during the Roman festivals was not reflected in the more acculturated and Romanized urban life of Hierapolis. Are we witnessing here a collision between the ideals of Jewish piety and the practical realities of routine urban life in the Jewish diaspora?

Finally, Aelius's arrangements reveal what was the common custom for grave-ceremonies at Hierapolis.²⁴³ One paid the local associations to act as burial societies, arranging the family interment for the grieving relatives and the maintenance of ongoing grave ceremonies for posterity.²⁴⁴ However, the fact that Aelius does not mention that he is a purple-dyer or carpet-weaver in the inscription makes it unlikely that he belonged to either association.²⁴⁵ Aelius's transaction regarding his family burial, therefore, was an entirely financial and organizational matter, reflecting no personal commitment to the local associations of Hierapolis and their associated cults. Consequently, the document is striking testimony to how well the Jews had assimilated to the culture of Asia cities, without compromising their core covenantal identity. Surprisingly, funerary segregation between gentiles and Jews was not the rule in the diaspora, if the Jewish adoption of the burial customs of Hierapolis for their families is representative.²⁴⁶

Conclusion

Although Colossae is characterized as the poor relative among the family of our three Lycus Valley cities, to borrow Cadwallader's words, the epigraphic remains of the city and its coinage reveal a complex and self-assured community, notwithstanding the fact that our knowledge is

---

242. Harland, *North Coast of the Black Sea*, 173.
243. Harland, *North Coast of the Black Sea*, 173.
244. Harland, *North Coast of the Black Sea*, 170–72.
245. Harland, "Acculturation and Identity," 406 n. 49.
246. Éric Rebillard, *The Care of the Dead in Late Antiquity* (Ithaca: Cornell University Press, 2009), 22.

severely hampered by the fact that it awaits excavation in the modern era. The wealth of material and epigraphic evidence available for Hierapolis and Laodicea gives us keen insight into the Romanized Phrygian culture of the valley, including its Jewish communities living within its territory, as well as affording us strong insight into the civic and mythological identity of each *polis*. We have noted several strong intersections with the New Testament documents that help to enrich exegesis of the texts. Until Colossae itself is finally excavated, perhaps the archaeological, epigraphic, numismatic, and iconographic evidence of Hierapolis and Laodicea can continue to provide some indirect light from the Lycus Valley on the epistle to the Colossians.

Bibliography

Anderson, Janice C. *Colossians: An Introduction and Study Guide; Authorship, Rhetoric, and Code*. London: T&T Clark, 2018.

Ameling, Walter. "The Epigraphic Habit and the Jewish Diasporas of Asia Minor and Syria." Pages 203–34 in *From Hellenism to Islam: Cultural and Linguistic Change in the Roman Near East*. Edited by Hannah M. Cotton, Robert G. Hoyland, Jonathan J. Price, and David J. Wasserstein. Cambridge: Cambridge University Press, 2009.

"Ancient Baths Double as Schools in Laodicea." *Hurriyet Daily News*. 11 June 2014. https://tinyurl.com/SBL4218c.

Armstrong, Andrea J. "Roman Phrygia: Cities and Their Coinage." PhD diss., University College, London 1998.

"Archaeological Site of Laodikeia." UNESCO World Heritage Centre," https://tinyurl.com/SBL4218a.

Arnold, Clinton E. *The Colossian Syncretism: The Interface between Christianity and Folk Belief at Colossae*. Grand Rapids: Baker, 1996.

Arundell, F. V. J. *Discoveries in Asia Minor*. 2 vols. London: R. Bentley, 1834.

———. *A Visit to the Seven Churches of Asia Minor with an Excursion into Pisidia*. London: John Rodwell, 1828.

Ascough, Richard S., Philip A. Harland, and John S. Kloppenborg. *Associations in the Greco-Roman World*. Waco, TX: Baylor University Press; Berlin: de Gruyter, 2012.

Aulock, Hans von. *Münzen und Städte Phrygiens*. 2 vols. IstMitt 25, 27. Tübingen: Wasmuth, 1980, 1987.

Austin, Michel M. *The Hellenistic World from Alexander to the Roman Conquest: A Selection of Sources in Translation.* 2nd ed. Cambridge: Cambridge University Press, 2007.

Aytaçlar, P. O., and E. Akıncı. "A List of Female Names from Laodicea on the Lycus." *EA* 39 (2006): 113–16.

Barton, Tamsyn. "Augustus and Capricorn: Astrological Polyvalency and Imperial Rhetoric." *JRS* 85 (1995): 33–51.

Bejor, Giogio. "Per Una Ricerca Di Laiodicea Ellenistica." Pages 15–23 in *Laodicea Di Frigia I*. Edited by Gustavo Traversari. RDASup 24. Rome: Bretschneider , 2000.

Bejor, Giorgio, and Jacopo Bonetto. "Recognizione del 1999: Dalla Porta Efesia All'Agora Occidentale." Pages 105–24 in *Laodicea Di Frigia I*. Edited by Gustavo Traversari. RDASup 24. Rome: Bretschneider, 2000.

Bell, G. "Gertrude Bell Archives." University of Newcastle-on-Tyne.

Belley, A. "Observations sur une Cornaline Antique du Cabinet de Mgr le Duc D'Orléans." Pages 17–27 in *Histoire des Ouvrages de l'Academie Royale des Inscriptions et Belles-Lettres*. Paris: Panckoucke, 1780. Republished in *Mémoires de Littérature, tires des registres de l'Académie royale des inscriptions et Belles-Lettres* 36 (1784): 11–17.

Bennett, Robert. *Local Elites and Local Coinage: Elite Self-Representation on the Provincial Coinage of Asia, 31 BC to AD 275*. London: Royal Numismatic Society, 2014.

Benson, Bailey. *The Creation of Shared Memory: The Theater Reliefs from Hierapolis*. MA thesis, Chapel Hill, 2014.

Birley, Anthony R. *Hadrian: The Restless Emperor*. London: Routledge, 1997.

Bormann, Lukas. "Barbaren und Skythen im Lykostal? Epigraphischer Kommentar zu Kol 3:11." Pages 161–98 in *Epigraphical Evidence Illustrating Paul's Letter to the Colossians*. Edited by Joseph Verheyden, Marcus Öhler, and Thomas Corsten. WUNT 411. Tübingen: Mohr Siebeck, 2018.

———. *Der Brief des Paulus an die Kolosser*. THKNK 10.1. Leipzig: Evangelische Verlagsanstalt, 2012.

Bruce, F. F. "The Jews and Christians in the Lycus Valley." *BSac* 141 (1985): 3–15.

Cadwallader, Alan H. "'As If in a Vision of the Night…': Authorising the Healing Spring of Chonai." Pages 265–92 in *Dreams, Memory and Imagination in Byzantium*. Edited by Bronwen Neil and Eva Anagnostou-Laoutides. Leiden: Brill, 2018.

———. "Complicating Class in the Letter to Philemon: A Prolegomenon." Forthcoming in *The Struggle over Class: Socioeconomic Analysis of Ancient Jewish and Christian Texts*. Edited by G. Anthony Keddie, Michael Flexsenhar, and Steven J. Friesen. Atlanta: SBL Press.

———. *Fragments of Colossae: Sifting through the Traces*. Hindmarsh: ATF Press, 2015.

———. "Greeks in Colossae: Shifting Allegiances in the Letter to the Colossians and Its Context." Pages 224–41 in *Attitudes to Gentiles in Ancient Judaism and Early Christianity*. Edited by David C. Sim and James S. McLaren. London: Bloomsbury, 2013.

———. "The Historical Sweep of the Life of Kolossai." Pages 25–67 in *Epigraphical Evidence Illustrating Paul's Letter to the Colossians*. Edited by Joseph Verheyden, Marcus Öhler, and Thomas Corsten. WUNT 411. Tübingen: Mohr Siebeck, 2018.

———. "Honouring the Repairer of the Baths: A New Inscription from Kolossai." *Antichthon* 46 (2012): 150–83.

———. "Inter-City Conflict in the Story of St Michael of Chonai." Pages 109–28 in *Religious Conflict from Early Christianity to the Rise of Islam*. Edited by Wendy Mayer and Bronwyn Neil. Berlin: de Gruyter, 2013.

———. "A New Inscription, A Correction and a Confirmed Sighting." *EA* 40 (2007): 109–18.

———. "One Man, Two Women, One Grave: Complicating Family Life at Colossae." Pages 157–94 in *Stones, Bones and the Sacred: Essays on Material Culture and Ancient Religion in Honor of Dennis E. Smith*. Edited by Alan H. Cadwallader. ECL 21. Atlanta: SBL Press, 2016.

———. "Paul and the Games." Pages 363–90 in *Paul in the Greco-Roman World: A Handbook*. Edited by J. Paul Sampley. Vol. 1. London: T&T Clark Bloomsbury, 2016.

———. "Refuting an Axiom of Scholarship on Colossae: Fresh Insights from New and Old Inscriptions." Pages 151–79 in *Colossae in Space and Time: Linking to an Ancient City*. Edited by Alan H. Cadwallader and Michael Trainor. NTOA–SUNT 94. Göttingen: Vandenhoeck & Ruprecht, 2011.

———. "Revisiting Calder on Colossae." *AS* 56 (2006): 103–11.

———. "Wealthy, Widowed, Astute and Beneficent: Claudia Eugenetoriane and the Second Century Revival of the Colossian Mint." *NewDocs* 12 (forthcoming).

Cadwallader, Alan H., and Michael Trainor, eds. *Colossae in Space and Time: Linking to an Ancient City*. NTOA–SUNT 94. Göttingen: Vandenhoeck & Ruprecht, 2011.

Canavan, Rosemary. *Clothing the Body of Christ at Colossae: A Visual Construction of Identity*. WUNT 2/334. Tübingen: Mohr Siebeck, 2012.

Carter, Michael J. D. *The Presentation of Gladiatorial Spectacles in the Greek East: Roman Culture and Greek Identity*. PhD thesis, McMaster University, 1999.

Chaniotis, Angelos. "Epigraphic Bulletin for Greek Religion." *Kernos* 23 (2010): 271–327.

Christol, Michel, and Thomas Drew-Bear. "Un sénateur de Xanthos." *Journal des savants* 3 (1991): 195–226.

Clerc, Michel Armand. "Inscriptions de la vallée du Méandre: Tralles, Nysa, Attuda, Laodicée et Colosses." *BCH* 11 (1887): 346–54.

Concannon, C. W. "'Not for an Olive Wreath, but Our Lives': Gladiators, Athletes, and Early Christian Bodies." *JBL* 133 (2014): 193–214.

Corsten, Thomas. *Die Inschriften von Laodikeia am Lykos*. Bonn: Dr Rudolf Habelt GMBH, 1997.

Dain, Alphonse. *Inscriptions grecques du Musée du Louvre: Les textes inédits*. Paris: Belles Lettres, 1933.

D'Andria, Francesco. *Cehennem'Den Cennet'e Hierapolis (Pamukkale): Ploutonion Aziz Philippus'un Mezari ve Kutsal Alani*. Istanbul: Ege Yayinlari, 2014.

———. "Gods and Amazons in the Nymphaeums of Hierapolis." Pages 150–72 in *Roman Sculpture in Asia Minor: Proceedings of the International Conference, May 24–26, 2007, Cavallino (Lecce)*. Edited by Francesco D'Andria and Ilaria Romeo. JRASup 81. Portsmouth: Journal of Roman Archaeology, 2011.

———. "Hierapolis of Phrygia: Its Evolution in Hellenistic and Roman Times." Pages 96–115 in *Urbanism in Western Asia Minor: New Studies on Aphrodisias, Ephesos, Hierapolis, Pergamon, Perge and Xanthos*. Edited by David Parrish. JRASup. 45. Portsmouth, Journal of Roman Archaeology, 2001.

———. *Hierapolis of Phrygia (Pamukkale): An Archaeological Guide*. Translated by P. Arthur. Istanbul: Ege Yayinlari, 2010.

———. "Nature and Cult in the *Ploutonion* of Hierapolis before and after the Colony." Pages 207–40 in *Landscape and History in the Lykos Valley: Laodikeia and Hierapolis in Phrygia*. Edited by Celal Şimşek and Francesco D'Andria. Newcastle upon Tyne: Cambridge Scholars, 2017.

D'Andria, Francesco, and Tullia Ritti. *Hierapolis II: Le sculture del teatro; I rilievi con I cicli di Apollo e Artemide.* Archaeologica 54. Rome: Bretschneider, 1985.

Duman, B., and E. Konakçi. "The Silent Witness of the Mound of Colossae: Pottery Remains." Pages 247–81 in *Colossae in Space and Time: Linking to an Ancient City.* Edited by Alan H. Cadwallader and Michael Trainor. Göttingen: Vandenhoeck & Ruprecht, 2011.

Emrys-Evans, D. "Notes on the Consonants in the Greek of Asia Minor." *ClQ* 12 (1918): 162–70.

Fairchild, Mark R. "Laodicea's 'Lukewarm' Legacy: Conflicts of Prosperity in an Ancient Christian City." *BAR* (March/April 2017): 31–39, 67–68.

Flavius Philostratus. *On Heroes.* Translated by Ellen Bradshaw Aitken and Jennifer K. Berenson McLean. Atlanta: Society of Biblical Literature, 2001.

Foss, C. *History and Archaeology of Byzantine Asia Minor.* Aldershot, Hampshire: Variorum, 1990.

Foster, Paul. *Colossians.* BNTC. London: T&T Clark, 2016.

French, David. *Roman Roads and Milestones of Asia Minor: An Interim Catalogue of Milestones.* Vol. 2.1. BARIS 392. Oxford: British Institute of Archaeology at Ankara, 1988.

Gagniers, Jean des. "Première partie: Introduction historique." Pages 1–11 in *Laodicée du Lycos: Le Nymphée Campagnes 1961–1963.* Edited by Jean des Gagniers et al. Paris: Éditions E. De Boccard, 1969.

Gagniers Jean des, et al. *Laodicée du Lycos: Le Nymphée Campagnes 1961–1963.* Edited by Paris: Éditions E. De Boccard, 1969.

Halfmann, H. *Itinera principum: Geschichte und Typologie der Kaiserreisen im Römischen Reich.* Stuttgart: Steiner, 1986.

Hamilton, W. J. *Researches in Asia Minor, Pontus and Armenia.* 2 vols. London: J. Murray, 1842.

Harland, Philip A. "Acculturation and Identity in the Diaspora: A Jewish Family and 'Pagan' Guilds at Hierapolis." Pages 385–418 in *The Religious History of the Roman Empire: Pagans, Jews, and Christians.* Edited by John A. North and Simon R. F. Price. Oxford: Oxford University Press, 2011.

———. *North Coast of the Black Sea, Asia Minor.* Vol. 2 of *Greco-Roman Associations: Texts, Translations and Commentary.* BZNW 204. Berlin: de Gruyter, 2014.

Harrison, James R. "Artemis Triumphs over a Sorcerer's Evil Art." *NewDocs* 10 (2012): 37–47.

———. "An Epigraphic Portrait of Ephesus and Its Villages." Pages 1–67 in *The First Urban Churches 3: Ephesus*. Edited by James R. Harrison and L. L. Welborn. Atlanta: SBL Press, 2018.

———. "The Erasure of Honour: Paul and the Politics of Dishonour." *TynBul* 66.2 (2016): 161–84.

———. "Excavating the Urban and Country Life of Roman Philippi and Its Territory." Pages 1–61 in *The First Urban Churches 4: Roman Philippi*. Edited by James R. Harrison and L. L. Welborn. Atlanta: SBL Press, 2018.

———. "'The Fading Crown': Divine Honour and the Early Christians." *JTS* 54 (2003): 493–529.

———. "Family Honour of a Priestess of Artemis." *NewDocs* 10 (2012): 30–36.

———. "Paul and the *Agōnothetai* at Corinth: Engaging the Civic Values of Antiquity." Pages 271–326 in *The First Urban Churches 2: Roman Corinth*. Edited by James R. Harrison and L. L. Welborn. Atlanta: SBL Press, 2016.

———. "Paul and Ancient Civic Ethics: Redefining the Canon of Honour in the Graeco-Roman World." Pages 75–118 in *Paul's Graeco-Roman Context*. Edited by Cilliers Breytenbach. BETL 277. Leuven: Peeters, 2015.

———. "Paul and the Gymnasiarchs: Two Approaches to Pastoral Formation in Antiquity." Pages 141–78 in *Paul: Jew, Greek, and Roman; Pauline Studies*. Edited by Stanley E. Porter. Vol. 5. Leiden: Brill, 2008.

Horsley, G. H. R. "Homer in Pisidia: Aspects of the History of Greek Education in a Remote Roman Province." *Antichthon* 34 (2000): 46–81.

Horst, Peter W. van der. *Ancient Jewish Epitaphs: An Introductory Survey of a Millennium of Jewish Funerary Epigraphy (300 BCE–700 CE)*. Kampen: Kok Pharos, 1991.

Huber, Lynn R. "Making Men in Rev 2–3: Reading the Seven Messages in the Bath-Gymnasiums of Asia Minor." Pages 101–28 in *Stones, Bones, and the Sacred: Essays on Material Culture and Ancient Religion in Honor of Dennis E. Smith*. Edited by Alan H. Cadwallader. ECL 21. Atlanta: SBL Press, 2016.

Humann, Carl, et al., eds. *Altertümer von Hierapolis*. Berlin: Reimer, 1898.

Huttner, Ulrich. *Early Christianity in the Lycus Valley*. Translated by David Green. AJEC 85; Early Christianity in Asia Minor 1. Leiden: Brill, 2013.

Johnson, Sherman E. "Early Christianity in Asia Minor." *JBL* 77 (1958): 1–17.
Johnston, Ann. "Hierapolis Revisited." *NumC* 144 (1984): 52–80.
Jones, Tamara. "Seating and Spectacle in the Graeco-Roman World." PhD diss., McMaster University, 2008.
Judeich, Walther. "Inschriften." Pages 67–179 in *Altertümer von Hierapolis*. Edited by Carl Humann. Berlin: Reimer, 1898.
Kagan, Y. O., and O. Y. Neverov. *Le Destin d'une Collection: 500 pierres gravées du Duc d'Orléans*. Saint Petersburg: Musée de l'Hermitage, 2001.
Kahil, Lilly. "La Sculpture." Pages 187–226 in *Laodicée du Lycos: Le Nymphée Campagnes 1961–1963*. Edited by Jean des Gagniers et al. Paris: de Boccard, 1969.
Kearsley, Rosalinde A. "Epigraphic Evidence for the Social Impact of Roman Government in Laodicea and Hierapolis." Pages 130–50 in *Colossae in Space and Time: Linking to an Ancient City*. Edited by Alan H. Cadwallader and Michael Trainor. NTOA 94. Göttingen: Vandenhoeck & Ruprecht, 2011.
Koester, Craig R. "The Message to Laodicea and the Problem of Its Local Context: A Study of the Imagery in Rev 3:14–22." *NTS* 49 (2003): 407–24.
Kokkinia, Christina. "The Inscriptions of Boubon: A Catalogue." Pages 27–126 in *Boubon: The Inscriptions and Archaeological Remains; A Survey 2004–2006*. Edited by C. Kokkinia. ΜΕΛΕΤΗΜΑΤΑ 60. Athens: de Boccard, 2008.
Konakçi, Erim. "The Lykos Valley during the Second Millenium BC." Pages 79–107 in *Landscape and History in the Lykos Valley: Laodikeia and Hierapolis in Phrygia*. Edited by Celal Şimşek and Francesco D'Andria. Newcastle upon Tyne: Cambridge Scholars, 2017.
Konakçi, Erim, and Bahadır Duman, "Arkeolojik ve Yazılı Kanıtlar Işığında Kolossai" [Colossae in the light of archaeological and historical evidence]. Pages 57–67 in vol. 2 of *Uluslararası Denizli ve Çevresi: Tarih ve Kültür Sempozyumu* [International symposium on the history and culture of Denizli and its surroundings]. 2 vols. Denizli: Pamukkale University, 2007.
Konstan, David. *Pity Transformed*. London: Duckworth, 2001.
Kraabel, A. Thomas. *Judaism in Western Asia Minor under the Roman Empire: With a Preliminary Study of the Jewish Community at Sardis, Lydia*. Cambridge: Harvard University Library, 1969.

Kreitzer Larry J. "The Plutonium of Hierapolis and the Descent of Christ into the 'Lowermost Parts of the Earth' (Ephesians 4:9)." *Bib* 79 (1998): 381–93.

Kumsar, Halil. "Historical Earthquakes that Damaged Hierapolis and Laodikeia Antique Cities and Their Implications for Earthquake Potential of Denizli Basin in Western Turkey." *Bulletin of Engineering Geology and the Environment* 75 (2016): 519–36.

Lampakis, G. *Οἱ ἑπτά ἀστέρες τῆς Ἀποκαλύψεως* [The seven stars of Revelation]. Athens: Tzabella, 1909.

"Laodikeia's Western Theatre to Be Restored." *Hurriyet Daily News*. 23 March 2018. https://tinyurl.com/SBL4218b.

Lindgren, Henry Clay, and Frank L. Kovacs. *Ancient Bronze Coins of Asia Minor and the Levant from the Lindgren Collection*. San Mateo: Chrysopylon, 1985.

Long, Lea Emilia. *Urbanism, Art, and Economy: The Marble Quarrying Industries of Aphrodisias and Roman Asia Minor*. PhD diss., University of Michigan, 2012.

Lotz, John Paul. "The *HOMONOIA* Coins of Asia Minor and Ephesians 1:21." *TynBul* 50.2 (1999): 173–88.

Magie, David. *Roman Rule in Asia Minor to the End of the Third Century after Christ*. 2 vols. Princeton: Princeton University Press, 1950.

Maier, Harry O. *Picturing Paul in Empire: Imperial Image, Text and Persuasion in Colossians, Ephesians and the Pastoral Epistles*. London: T&T Clark, 2013.

Malherbe, Abraham J. "The Beasts at Ephesus." Pages 79–89 in *Paul and the Popular Philosophers*. Minneapolis: Fortress, 1989.

Mare, W. Harold. "Archaeological Prospects at Colossae." *NEASB* 7 (1976): 39–59.

Martin, Katharina. *Demos—Boule—Gerousia: Personifikationen städtischer Institutionen auf kaiserzeitlichen Münzen aus Kleinasien*. 2 vols. Bonn: Habelt, 2013.

McKechnie, Paul. *Elect Cities: Christianity in Phrygia from the First Century to the Great Persecution*. Cambridge: Cambridge University Press, 2019.

Merkelbach, Reinhold, and Josef Stauber. *Steinepigramme aus dem griechischen Osten*. 5 vols. Stuttgart: de Gruyter, 1998–2004.

Meyboom, P. G. P. *The Nile Mosaic of Palestrina*. Leiden: Brill, 1995.

Michon, E. "Erwerbungen des Louvre im Jahre 1899." *AA* 15 (1900): 155–59.

Milner, N. P. *An Epigraphical Survey in The Kibyra-Olbasa Region*. RECAM 3. London: BIAA, 1998.

Miranda, Elena. "La communità giudaica di Hierapolis di Frigia." *EA* 31 (1999): 109–55.

Mitchell, Stephen. "The Ionians of Paphlagonia." Pages 86–110 in *Local Knowledge and Microidentities in the Imperial Greek World*. Edited by Tim Whitmarsh. Cambridge: Cambridge University Press, 2010.

———. "Italian and Turkish Archaeological Work in the Lycus Valley around Laodicea and Hierapolis." *JRA* 14 (2001): 632–34.

Ng, Diana Yi-man. *Manipulation of Memory: Public Buildings and Decorative Programs in Roman Cities of Asia Minor*. PhD Thesis, University of Michigan, 2007.

Osborne, Robert E. "Paul and the Wild Beasts." *JBL* 85 (1966): 225–30.

Ozan, Ali, et al. "Prehistory of the Lykos Valley." Pages 53–77 in *Landscape and History in the Lykos Valley: Laodikeia and Hierapolis in Phrygia*. Edited by Celal Şimşek and Francesco D'Andria. Newcastle upon Tyne: Cambridge Scholars, 2017.

Pflaum, H-G. *Les Carrières Procuratoriennes Équestres sous le Haut-Empire romain*. Vol. 1. Paris: P. Geuthner, 1960.

Pfuhl, Ernst, and Hans Möbius. *Die Ostgriechischen Grabreliefs*. 4 vols. Mainz: von Zabern, 1977–1979.

Price, Simon. "Local Mythologies in the Greek East." Pages 115–24 in *Coinage and Identity in the Roman Provinces*. Edited by Christopher Howgego, Volker Heuchert, and Andrew Burnett. Oxford: Oxford University Press, 2005.

Ramsay, William M. *The Cities and Bishoprics of Phrygia*. 2 vols. Oxford: Clarendon, 1895, 1897.

———. *The Lycos Valley and South-Western Phrygia*. Vol. 1.2 of *The Cities and Bishoprics of Phrygia*. Oxford: Clarendon, 1895.

———. *St Paul the Traveller and the Roman Citizen*. London: Hodder & Stoughton, 1897.

Reasoner, Mark. *Roman Imperial Texts: A Sourcebook*. Minneapolis: Fortress, 2013.

Rebillard, Éric. *The Care of the Dead in Late Antiquity*. Ithaca: Cornell University Press, 2009.

Ritti, Tullia. *An Epigraphic Guide to Hierapolis (Pamukkale)*. Istanbul: Ege Yayinlari, 2006.

———. *Fonti Letterarie ed Epigraphi: Hierapolis Scavi e Ricerche*. Rome: Bretschneider, 1985.

———. *Hierapolis I: Fonti Letterarie ed Epigrafiche*. Archeologica 30. Rome: Giorgio Bretschneider, 1985.

———. *Hierapolis di Frigia IX: Storia e istituzioni di Hierapolis*. Istanbul: Ege Yayinlari, 2017.

Ritti, Tullia, H. Hüseyin Baysal, Elena Miranda, and Francesco Guizzi, eds. *Museo Archeologico di Denizli-Hierapolis: Catalogo delle iscrizioni greche e latine*. Naples: Liguori Editore, 2008.

Ritti, Tullia, Klaus Grewe and Paul Kessner. "A Relief of a Water-Powered Stone Saw Mill on a Sarcophagus at Hierapolis and Its Implications." *JRA* 20 (2007): 139–63.

Ritti, Tullia, and Salim Yilmaz. *Gladiatori e venationes a Hierapolis di Frigia*. Rome: Accademia Naz. dei Lincei, 1998.

Robert, Louis. "Documents d'Asie Mineure." *BCH* 107 (1983): 497–599.

———. *Les gladiateurs dans l'orient grec*. Paris: Champion, 1940.

———, ed. "Les inscriptions." Pages 247–389 in *Laodicée du Lykos: Le nymphée*. Edited by J. des Gagniers et al. Quebec: L'Université Laval, 1969.

———. "Monuments des gladiateurs dans l'Orient grec." *Hellenica* 7 (1949): 126–51.

———. *Opera Minora Selecta: Épigraphie et antiquités grecques*. 7 vols. Amsterdam: Hakkert, 1969–1990.

Standhartinger, Angela. "Kolosserbrief." *Das wissenschaftliche Bibelportal der Deutschen Bibelgesellschaft* (2010): https://www.bibelwissenschaft.de/stichwort/51912/

———. *Studien zur Entstehungsgeschichte und Intention des Kolosserbriefs*. Leiden: Brill, 1998.

Şimşek, Celal. *10. Yilinda Laodikeia (2003–2013 Yillari)*. Laodikeia Çalismalari 3. Istanbul: Ege Yayinlari, 2014.

———. "1900 Yillik Su Yasasi Balundu." *Tübitak Bilim ve Teknik*. 49.576 (2015): 66–67.

———. *Church of Laodikeia: Christianity in the Lykos Valley*. Istanbul: Ege Yayinlari, 2015.

———. *Laodikeia (Laodicea ad Lycum)* [Turkish]. Laodikeia Çalismalari 2. Istanbul: Ege Yayinlari, 2013.

———. "Laodikeia Water Law." Pages 190–99 in *Future Cities: Second International Urban Environment Health Congress. 16–29 April, 2018 Cappadocia*. N.p.

———. "Urban Planning of Laodikeia on the Lykos in the Light of New Evidence." Pages 1–51 in *Landscape and History in the Lykos Valley:*

Laodikeia and Hierapolis in Phrygia. Edited by Celal Şimşek and Francesco D'Andria. Newcastle upon Tyne: Cambridge Scholars, 2017.

Şimşek, Celal, A. Alkac, and B. Duman. *Laodikeia amphora mühürleri*. Laodikeia Çalismalari 4. Istanbul: Ege Yayinlari, 2017.

Şimşek, Celal, and Francesco D'Andria, eds. *Landscape and History in the Lykos Valley: Laodikeia and Hierapolis in Phrygia*. Newcastle upon Tyne: Cambridge Scholars, 2017.

Şimşek, Celal, and F. Guizzi. "A Dedication of the Praeses Dyscolius from Laodikeia on the Lykos." *Mediterraneo Antico* 14.1–2 (2012): 511–18.

Şimşek, Celal, M. Okunak, and M. Bilgin. *Laodikeia Nekropulü (2004–2010 Yillari)*. 2 vols. Laodikeia Çalismalari 1.1–2. Istanbul: Ege Yayinlari, 2011.

Şimşek, Celal, and M. A. Sezgin. "Laodikeia Kuzey Tiyatrosu (The North Theatre at Laodikeia)." *Olba* 19 (2011): 173–201.

———. "The West and North Theatres in Laodicea." Pages 103–28 in *Restoration and Management of Ancient Theatres in Turkey: Methods, Research, Results*. Edited by Filippo Masino, Paolo Mighetto, and Giorgio Sobra. Archaeologia e Storia 11. Lecce: Congedo Editore, 2012.

Sperti, Luigi. "Ricognizione Archaeologica a Laodicea di Frigia 1993–1998." Pages 29–102 *Laodicea Di Frigia I*. Edited by Gustavo Traversari. RDASup 24. Rome: Bretschneider, 2000.

Spratt, T. A. B., and E. Forbes. *Travels in Lycia, Milyas and the Cibyratis in Company with the Late Rev. E. T. Daniell*. 2 vols. London: John van Hoorst, 1847.

Strelan, Rick. "The Languages of the Lycus Valley." Pages 77–103 in *Colossae in Space and Time: Linking to an Ancient City*. Edited by Alan H. Cadwallader and Michael Trainor. Göttingen: Vandenhoeck & Ruprecht, 2011.

Strubbe, Johann, ed. **APAI EPITYMBIOI**: *Imprecation against Desecrators of the Grave in the Greek Epitaphs of Asia Minor; A Catalogue*. Bonn: Rudolf Habelt, 1997.

Thompson, Leonard L. "ISmyrna753: Gods and the One God." Pages 101–24 in *Reading Religions in the Ancient World: Essays Presented to Robert McQueen Grant*. Edited by David E. Aune and Robin Darling Young. Leiden: Brill, 2007.

Thonemann, Peter. *The Maeander Valley: A Historical Geography from Antiquity to Byzantium*. Cambridge: Cambridge University, 2011.

Travaglini, A., and V. G. Camilleri. *Hierapolis di Frigia, Le Monete: Campagne di Scavo 1957–2004*. Istanbul: Ege Yayinlari, 2010.

Traversari, Gustavo. *Laodicea Di Frigia I*. RDASup 24. Rome: Bretschneider, 2000.

Trebilco, Paul. *Jewish Communities in Asia Minor*. SNTSMS 69 Cambridge: Cambridge University Press, 1991.

Unwin, James R. *Subversive Spectacles: The Struggles and Deaths of Paul and Seneca*. PhD thesis, Macquarie University, 2017.

Verheyden, Joseph, Markus Öhler, and Thomas Corsten, eds. *Epigraphical Evidence Illustrating Paul's Letter to the Colossians*. WUNT 411. Tübingen: Mohr Siebeck, 2018.

Weber, Leo. "The Coins of Hierapolis in Phrygia." *NumC* 13 (1913): 1–30, 161.

———. "The Coins of Hierapolis in Phrygia (Continued)." *NumC* 13 (1913): 133–61.

Warmington, E. H. *Remains of Old Latin IV: Archaic Inscriptions*. LCL. London: Heinmann, 1940.

Weber, Georg. "Inschriften aus Sued-Phrygien." *MDAIA* 18 (1893): 206–7.

———. "Der unterirdische Lauf des Lykos bei Kolossai." *MDAIA* 16 (1891): 194–99.

Welborn, L. L. "Paul's Spectacle Metaphor in 1 Corinthians 15:30–32." *The Bible and Critical Theory* 8 (2012): 39–51.

Wilson, Maj-Gen. Sir C., ed. *Handbooks for Travellers: Asia Minor*. London: John Murray, 1895.

Wiotte-Franz, Claudia. *Hermeneus und Interpres: Zum Dolmetscherwesen in der Antike*. Saarbrücken: Saarbrücker Druckerei und Verlag, 2001.

Wörrle, Michael. "Antiochus I., Achaios der Ältere und die Galater: Eine neue Inschrift in Denizli." *Chiron* 5 (1975): 59–97.

Yamauchi, Edwin, *The Archaeology of New Testament Cities in Western Asia Minor*. Grand Rapids: Baker, 1980.

Zgusta, Ladislav. *Kleinasiatische Personennamen*. Prague: Czechoslovakian Academy, 1964.

Part 2
Responses to Ulrich Huttner's Perspectives on the Lycus Valley

Colossians, Hierapolitan Coins—and the Young Bearers of Hope

Ulrich Huttner

At about the same time when Paul was in contact with the Christian community at Colossae, perhaps some years before, M. Syillios (Suillius) Antiochos, who held the post of a grammateus in Hierapolis, had the responsibility of issuing a series of coins (*RPC* 1.2969-2973) to celebrate the reigning emperor Claudius together with his sons, Britannicus, his own son, and Nero, who had been adopted in 50 CE.[1] Antiochos had kept good relations with senatorial circles, since at the beginning of the fifties P. Suillius Rufus, the then governor of Asia, had rewarded the excellent notable from Hierapolis with Roman citizenship.[2]

Five pieces belong to the series of coins.[3] On the obverse of two of them can be seen the laureate portrait of Claudius, while the reverse shows the god of Hierapolis: Apollo, one classical version with the lyra and another indigenous version with the double axe.[4] On the next two coins can be found the portraits of the princes: Britannicus, about ten

---

Thanks to Julien Ogereau for improving my English.

1. For dating the Letter to Philemon, see Ulrich Huttner, *Early Christianity in the Lycus Valley*, trans. David Green, AJEC 85; Early Christianity in Asia Minor 1 (Leiden: Brill, 2013), 98-102: during the 50s or early 60s of the first century.

2. On P. Suillius Rufus, see Werner Eck, "Suillius 3," *DNP* 11:1092-93; Steven H. Rutledge, *Imperial Inquisitions: Prosecutors and Informants from Tiberius to Domitian* (London: Routledge, 2001), 270-1; *PIR* 7.2² (2006): 357-58. For the grant of Roman citizenship by the governor, see Bernard Holtheide, *Römische Bürgerrechtspolitik und römische Neubürger in der Provinz Asia* (Freiburg: Hochschulverlag, 1983), 20. In the case of M. Suillius Antiochos, Holtheide (*Römische Bürgerrechtspolitik*, 66) thinks of the influence of M. Suillius Nerullinus (cos. 50), the son of P. Suillius Rufus.

3. See the appendix to this chapter.

4. On different forms of Apollo in Hierapolis, see Saskia Kerschbaum, "Die Apol-

years old, and Nero—some years older. They have the faces of boys, while the reverses display cultic motifs: two crowns on a table—the prizes of festival games—and a double axe. The most interesting is the fifth coin, by which the members of the imperial family are both paired with the patron deity and divinized. On the obverse is a head of the god Apollo framed by the name of Suillius, while the reverse represents the front of a temple with six columns and some unidentified figure in the gable. The legend hints at the dedication of the sanctuary: Γένει Σεβαστῶν—"to the family of the Augusti" (*RPC* 1.2973).[5] This is a little bit difficult to interpret, as Claudius is not given the title "Augustus" on the above-mentioned coins, and neither Britannicus nor Nero bore the title in these years at all.[6] In spite of these inconsistencies there cannot be any doubt that the members of the Claudian dynasty were caught up in the aura of sacred reverence dedicated to the first emperors and descending from Augustus. The significance of such temple-buildings in the urban landscape is not to be underestimated: they were monumental examples of the imperial orientation of the cities looking for a place in the political and cultural system of the Roman Empire over which a person with the title of Augustus reigned single-handedly.[7]

Looking at these coins, one can find more than one reference to the text of Colossians composed some years later, soon after the death of Paul during the 60s.[8] During the second, and, above all, during the third century, agonistic motifs on coins were quite normal, but not in the first century.[9] We may conclude that the emblem on the Hierapolis coin was a peculiar representation of a rather special agonistic self-confidence in the Lycus Valley. In several passages of Colossians we read metaphors about Greek games (Col 1:29–2:1; 4:12). This is expressed in particular by the word καταβραβεύειν

---

lines von Hierapolis in Phrygien," *Jahrbuch für Numismatik und Geldgeschichte* 64 (2014): 29–30.

5. Additionally, BMC Phrygia p. 229 n. 11; Simon R. F. Price, *Rituals and Power: The Roman Imperial Cult in Asia Minor* (Cambridge: Cambridge University Press, 1984), 264 n. 85; Kerschbaum, "Die Apollines von Hierapolis in Phrygien," 40 n. 5.

6. Dietmar Kienast, *Römische Kaisertabelle. Grundzüge einer römischen Kaiserchronologie*, 2nd ed. (Darmstadt: Wissenschaftliche Buchgesellschaft, 1996), 93 and 96.

7. Harry O. Maier, *Picturing Paul in Empire: Imperial Image, Text and Persuasion in Colossians, Ephesians and the Pastoral Epistles* (London: Bloomsbury, 2013), 2. See also Price, *Rituals and Power*, 156–62.

8. Huttner, *Early Christianity in the Lycus-Valley*, 113–14.

9. See Wolfgang Leschhorn, "Die Verbreitung von Agonen in den östlichen Provinzen des Römischen Reiches," *Stadion* 24 (1998): 31–58.

used to warn against the authority of the followers of the angels (Col 2:18).[10] The table with the prize crowns would have been part of the symbolic imagery associated with the metaphoric language in Colossians.

Taking the series of five coins issued by Antiochos together, the Hierapolitans perceived a message of trust that can be set in contrast to the message of Colossians: young imperial hope bearers, Nero and Britannicus, took their positions at the side of their father Claudius and also at the side of the familiar Apollo. As divinized members of the imperial family they became prominent figures in the religious and cultic life of Hierapolis. They were young and mighty gods, just like Jesus Christ.

During the years before his accession Nero gained the favor of Greek communities by representing their interests.[11] Apamea, east of Hierapolis, had been destroyed by an earthquake, and it was the prince's public pronouncement in Greek language that exempted the town from taxes (Tacitus, *Ann.* 12.58, with Suetonius, *Nero* 7.2.). At the same time in Apollonia Salbake, to the south of the Lycus Valley, young Nero had already his own priest.[12] How intensely had hope been placed on Nero is indicated by Seneca some years later, who celebrated him as the new star a short time after Claudius had died in autumn 54. In the *Apocolocyntosis*, Seneca's sarcastic pamphlet on the dead emperor, the god Apollo sings verses of hope for the young successor who would provide for a golden future:

> let the duration of human life be surpassed by him who is my like in looks and grace, and my equal in voice and song. He will guarantee an era of prosperity to the weary and break the silence of the laws. Like the Morning Star, as he rises scattering the stars in flight, or like the Evening Star, as he rises when the stars return, like the gleaming Sun, as soon as rosy Dawn has dispelled the shadows and led in the day, as he gazes on the world and begins to whip up his chariot from the starting barrier: such a Caesar is at hand, such a Nero shall Rome now gaze upon. His

---

10. See Lukas Bormann, *Der Brief des Paulus an die Kolosser*, THKNT 10.1 (Leipzig: Evangelische Verlagsanstalt, 2012), 143. On βραβευτής in agonistic contexts, see Christof Schuler, *Ländliche Siedlungen und Gemeinden im hellenistischen und römischen Kleinasien*, Vestigia 50 (Munich: Beck, 1998), 238–39.

11. Christopher Jones, "Nero Speaking," *Harvard Studies of Classical Philology* 100 (2000): 453–54.

12. *MAMA* 6.156. See Jakob Munk Højte, *Roman Imperial Statue Bases from Augustus to Commodus* (Aarhus: Aarhus University Press, 2005), 325–26.

radiant face blazes with gentle brilliance and his shapely neck with flowing hair. (Seneca, *Apol.* 4.21–32 [Eden])

The sixteen-year-old youth was able to play the part of the youthful god of light: Nero was Apollo.

Seneca's verses on Nero belong to a tradition of celebrating messiah-like boys that dates to the beginnings of the Principate—a tradition that has been retraced in a masterly manner by Eduard Norden in his famous book *Die Geburt des Kindes: Geschichte einer religiösen Idee*.[13] One of the paradigmatic poems expressing the hope of a newborn divine prince was written by Virgil in 40 BCE with his fourth eclogue announcing a new era full of peace and happiness. Here also we find Apollo taking the world under his wings (*Ecl.* 4.10). Nobody knows whom Virgil meant with the figure of the divine boy (*puer*), however, as specialists have not succeeded in identifying that bearer of hope.[14] But it is clear that in the first decades of the Principate, similar hopes were placed on young members of the emperor's family again and again.[15] The trail of Virgil's fourth eclogue is followed up by Calpurnius Siculus, who glorifies a youthful peacemaker as well, and there are good reasons to identify this peacemaker with Nero receiving imperial government in 54 (*Ecl.* 1.42–88; 4.84–159).[16]

In Colossians, God's son "is the image of the invisible God" (εἰκὼν τοῦ θεοῦ τοῦ ἀοράτου, 1:15). On the coins the contemporaries became aware of a visible god, that is, the emperor Claudius, and of two divine princes, visible as well, and one can ask with good reason, whether people did not recognize the image of Christ in the portraits of Britannicus and Nero, two rather normal, well-behaved boys, but without doubt great bearers

---

13. Eduard Norden, *Die Geburt des Kindes: Geschichte einer religiösen Idee* (Leipzig: Teubner, 1924).

14. Most reasonable seems the solution of Karl Galinsky, *Augustan Culture: An Interpretive Introduction* (Princeton: Princeton University Press, 1996), 92: "The miraculous child ultimately is no more than a symbol or personification of the new age."

15. See Andreas Alföldi, "Der neue Weltherrscher der Vierten Ekloge Vergils," in *Saeculum Augustum II: Religion und Literatur*, ed. Gerhard Binder (Darmstadt: Wissenschaftliche Buchgesellschaft, 1988), 210–12.

16. For dating the first Eclogue, see Joachim Fugmann, "Nero oder Severus Alexander? Zur Datierung der Eklogen des Calpurnius Siculus," *Philologus* 136 (1992): 202–4; on both John Garthwaite and Beatrice Martin, "Visions of Gold: Hopes for the New Age in Calpurnius Siculus' 'Eclogues,'" in *Writing Politics in Imperial Rome*, ed. William J. Dominik, John Garthwaite, and Paul A. Roche (Leiden: Brill, 2009), 307–8.

of hope in the eyes of the observer. So one can discover points of reference in the visual culture to create a new idea of the relation between God and God's son. Harry Maier reminds us that "Paul represents his teachings with the help of imperial image and vocabulary, often only to reconfigure it."[17] It is clear that the listeners and readers interpreted Pauline texts also "with the help of imperial image and vocabulary," so that we can ask the question whether now and then people's minds would not have provided Jesus Christ with the features of an imperial prince. Paul's addressees were beyond his control, and he did not constantly take into account the divergence between christological monotheism and imperial divinization.[18]

One last remark on M. Sullius Antiochus's coin series in Hierapolis. It may be surprising that this is a purely male series. Agrippina, the empress and symbol of concord of the imperial family,[19] is missing. Presumably it would be too far-fetched to make a connection with the missing reference to male and female in Colossians' enumeration of the opposite identities that will be dissolved by Jesus Christ: gentile versus Jew, circumcised versus uncircumcised, barbarian versus Scythian, slave versus free (Col 3:11), but not male versus female as in Galatians (Gal 3:28). We should not exclude the possibility that Agrippina's portrait was part of the series as well and that no specimen has been discovered until now, since evidence for the Britannicus-type is constituted only by a single coin in the collections of Oxford (*RPC* 1.2971).

Appendix: *RPC* 1.2969-2973:
Series of coins in Hierapolis (ca. 50–54, M. Suillios Antiochos):

2969
Obv.: ΚΛΑΥΔΙΟΣ ΚΑΙΣΑΡ; laureate head, r.
Rev.: Μ ΣΥΙΛΛΙΟΣ ΑΝΤΙΟΧΟΣ ΓΡΑ ΙΕΡΑΠΟΛΙΤΩΝ; Apollo, standing r., playing lyre

---

17. Maier, *Picturing Paul in Empire*, 40. For similar considerations on Luke in the context of the imperial symbolic language of the golden age, see Stefan Schreiber, "Goldene Zeiten? Politische Perspektiven der lukanischen Geburtsgeschichte," in *Neues Testament und politische Theorie: Interdisziplinäre Beiträge zur Zukunft des Politischen*, ed. Eckart Reinmuth (Stuttgart: Kohlhammer, 2011), 83–97.

18. Maier, *Picturing Paul in Empire*, 82.

19. See Anthony A. Barrett, *Agrippina: Sex, Power, and Politics in the Early Empire* (New Haven, CT: Yale University Press, 1996), 108–10; Maier, *Picturing Paul in Empire*, 95–96.

2970
Obv.: ΚΛΑΥΔΙΟΣ ΚΑΙΣΑΡ; laureate head, r.
Rev.: Μ ΣΥΙΛΛΙΟΣ ΑΝΤΙΟΧΟΣ ΓΡΑ ΙΕΡΑΠΟΛΙΤΩΝ; Apollo, on horseback, r., with double axe

2971
Obv.: ΒΡΙΤΑΝΝΙΚΟΣ ΚΑΙΣΑΡ; draped bust of Britannicus, r.
Rev.: ΣΥΙΛΛΙΟΣ ΑΝΤΙΟΧΟΣ ΙΕΡΑΠΟΛΙΤΩΝ; table with two crowns; to r., palm branch

2972
Obv.: ΝΕΡΩΝ ΚΑΙΣΑΡ; draped bust of Nero, r.
Rev.: ΣΥΙΛΛΙΟΣ ΑΝΤΙΟΧΟΣ ΙΕΡΑΠΟΛΙΤΩΝ; double axe on basis, with snake coiled around and surmounted by radiate head (?)

2973
Obv.: Μ ΣΥΙΛΛΙΟΣ ΑΝΤΙΟΧΟΣ ΓΡΑ ΙΕΡΑΠΟΛΙΤΩΝ; draped bust (of Apollo?), r.
Rev.: ΓΕΝΕΙ ΣΕΒΑΣΤΩΝ; temple with six columns

Bibliography

Alföldi, Andreas. "Der neue Weltherrscher der Vierten Ekloge Vergils." Pages 197–215 in *Saeculum Augustum II: Religion und Literatur*. Edited by Gerhard Binder. Darmstadt: Wissenschaftliche Buchgesellschaft, 1988.

Barrett, Anthony A. *Agrippina: Sex, Power, and Politics in the Early Empire*. New Haven, CT: Yale University Press, 1996.

Bormann, Lukas. *Der Brief des Paulus an die Kolosser*. THKNT 10.1. Leipzig: Evangelische Verlagsanstalt, 2012.

Eck, Werner. "Suillius 3." *DNP* 11:1092–93.

Eden, P. T. *Seneca, Apocolocyntosis*. Cambridge: Cambridge University Press, 1984.

Fugmann, Joachim. "Nero oder Severus Alexander? Zur Datierung der Eklogen des Calpurnius Siculus." *Philologus* 136 (1992): 202–7.

Galinsky, Karl. *Augustan Culture: An Interpretive Introduction*. Princeton: Princeton University Press, 1996.

Garthwaite, John, and Beatrice Martin. "Visions of Gold: Hopes for the New Age in Calpurnius Siculus' 'Eclogues.'" Pages 307–22 in *Writing*

Politics in Imperial Rome. Edited by William J. Dominik, John Garthwaite, and Paul A. Roche. Leiden: Brill, 2009.

Holtheide, Bernard. *Römische Bürgerrechtspolitik und römische Neubürger in der Provinz Asia*. Freiburg: Hochschulverlag, 1983.

Højte, Jakob Munk. *Roman Imperial Statue Bases from Augustus to Commodus*. Aarhus: Aarhus University Press, 2005.

Huttner, Ulrich. *Early Christianity in the Lycus Valley*. Translated by David Green. AJEC 85; Early Christianity in Asia Minor 1. Leiden: Brill, 2013.

Jones, Christopher. "Nero Speaking." *Harvard Studies of Classical Philology* 100 (2000): 453–62.

Kerschbaum, Saskia. "Die Apollines von Hierapolis in Phrygien." *Jahrbuch für Numismatik und Geldgeschichte* 64 (2014): 15–42.

Kienast, Dietmar. *Römische Kaisertabelle: Grundzüge einer römischen Kaiserchronologie*. 2nd ed. Darmstadt: Wissenschaftliche Buchgesellschaft, 1996.

Leschhorn, Wolfgang. "Die Verbreitung von Agonen in den östlichen Provinzen des Römischen Reiches." *Stadion* 24 (1998): 31–58.

Maier, Harry O. *Picturing Paul in Empire: Imperial Image, Text and Persuasion in Colossians, Ephesians and the Pastoral Epistles*. London: Bloomsbury, 2013.

Norden, Eduard. *Die Geburt des Kindes. Geschichte einer religiösen Idee*. Leipzig: Teubner, 1924.

Price, Simon R. F. *Rituals and Power: The Roman Imperial Cult in Asia Minor*. Cambridge: Cambridge University Press, 1984.

Rutledge, Steven H. *Imperial Inquisitions: Prosecutors and Informants from Tiberius to Domitian*. London: Routledge, 2001.

Schreiber, Stefan. "Goldene Zeiten? Politische Perspektiven der lukanischen Geburtsgeschichte." Pages 83–97 in *Neues Testament und politische Theorie: Interdisziplinäre Beiträge zur Zukunft des Politischen*. Edited by Eckart Reinmuth. Stuttgart: Kohlhammer, 2011.

Schuler, Christof. *Ländliche Siedlungen und Gemeinden im hellenistischen und römischen Kleinasien*. Vestigia 50. Munich: Beck, 1998.

Unraveling the Threads of Identity: Cloth and Clothing in the Lycus Valley

Rosemary Canavan

When peering into the ancient past, we are sometimes like scavengers, scouring the surviving artifacts and records for scraps and threads in order to piece together the life and times of the ancient peoples. Yet we do not have all the pieces, threads, or fragments. There are many lacunae. This paper engages the scraps and threads of evidence for the textile trade and especially the cloth and clothing industry of the Lycus Valley as well as considers some of the lacunae. I do this in conversation with Ulrich Huttner's volume, *Early Christianity in the Lycus Valley*, to further elucidate the propensity of this industry to act as vivid imagery in identity formation in the Letter to the Colossians.

Huttner's volume is a magnificent compilation of information. While taking a historian's approach, he admits that it is too ambitious to think that he would be embarking on illuminating the "mission and expansion of Christianity" by his focus on the Lycus Valley.[1] Recognizing the fragmentary nature of the sources available, Huttner ponders the questions that might be answered.[2] Determining the Christ followers as a community within a community, Huttner notes that "the collective identity of Christians" becomes the difference between "they" and "us."[3] Of course, it is not that simple, for identity and belonging is multilayered. Huttner

---

This chapter was originally presented by invitation by Dr. Rosemary Canavan, Catholic Theological College, University of Divinity at the Annual Meeting of the Society of Biblical Literature in Atlanta, 22 November 2015.

1. Ulrich Huttner, *Early Christianity in the Lycus Valley*, trans. David Green, AJEC 85; Early Christianity in Asia Minor 1 (Leiden: Brill, 2013), 1.
2. Huttner, *Early Christianity in the Lycus Valley*, 5–7.
3. Huttner, *Early Christianity in the Lycus Valley*, 6–7.

sets out to show how the Christ followers in the Lycus Valley successfully created a "locus," "a space for themselves where they could put their ideas about realizing Jesus' message into practice."

In response I wish to explore some threads of context and material culture that have the propensity for vivid imagery for the hearers of the Letter to the Colossians in the Lycus Valley. Specifically, I will look at the overlay and interconnection of clothing as identity in the production and trade of the clothing and textile industry, religious life and practice, and the associations and guilds of the larger community.

Textile production and trade is not only a major area of life and industry in the Lycus Valley, but it is vital to their identity and survival. It is not surprising to me that clothing becomes the defining metaphor of how the Christ followers are identified in Christ: clothing themselves with the new self, virtues, and love (Col 3:10, 12, 14). Within this the "us" and "them" of other identities is overlaid with their identity in Christ. Before we go much further a word about identity.

Identity Construction

Identity is a twentieth-century concept that can be gainfully employed in describing the belonging of peoples to communities in ancient times. While using identity as a tool, it is vital to retain a sense of how people belonged in the first century. Significantly, families presided over by the patriarch spring to mind. Families were also the determiners of labor skills, mentoring young generations into the skills of their forefathers. Ethnic connection is first and foremost as is kinship, with layers of tribe, intermarriage, and changes of provincial boundaries to be factored in. Then, what about wars and new ruling elites, subjugation to new rulers and exile to foreign lands, and invasion by barbarians and marauding hoards? Captivity and slavery were the fate of many oppressed and conquered peoples. The list of identities in Colossians (3:11) seems to cover some of these happenstances of how people came to be recognized. The nomenclature indicates differentiation between one and another: Greek and Jew, Scythian and barbarian, circumcision and uncircumcision, and slave and free. These divisions indicate difference between ethnic group identity and within categories of barbarians or aliens, within religious groups and along economic and political lines. These differences could be recognized in a number of ways, such as the way they spoke, the way they lived and worked, and the way they practiced religion. It is clothing as an overt and visual means of identification and differentiation of one group from the other that I wish to follow through in the tapestry of the Lycus Valley community identities and the distinction of Christ followers in the larger community.

Context of Clothing and Textile Production

Huttner describes the Lycus River as "a lifeline" bringing water for domestic consumption as well as providing the necessary conditions for productive farming of the area.[4] This river is fed by the Asopas, Capros, and Cadmus, the latter being likely a tributary of the Capros in the first century. Today the Turkish name for this river is Çürüksu, meaning "rotten water," which does not speak well of its quality. In addition to these fresh water streams, there were hot mineral springs whose alkalinity made them undrinkable. This mineral laden water was advantageous to textile trades, being ideal for such processes as bleaching, setting dyes, and bating leather.[5] A recent discovery at the Laodikeia site of a water law dating to 114 CE adds a further perspective. The rule lists fines for interference with the water channels that fed the river water through the arable plain.[6] The water law inscription includes a fine for using this water for agricultural purposes. This fine indicates a priority for this water for consumption as drinking water and imposes penalties to deter landholders, farmers, or other interested parties from hijacking the water to the benefit of their crops, herds, or industry. The institution of such a law implies that such practices were occurring and needed to be controlled.

Trade routes were also determined by the Lycus River providing a natural way through the plains and mountains of the Lycus Valley with Laodikeia as the hub. Routes ran to and from the east, Ephesus, or Miletus via the Lycus Valley to Apamea-Celanae and beyond to Syria or down from Laodikeia to the coast to Attalia (Antalya) and Side.[7] These routes were established as early as the time of Persian rule. Milestones from the

---

4. Huttner, *Early Christianity in the Lycus Valley*, 18.

5. Huttner does not mention the setting of dyes—my addition. See Huttner, *Early Christianity in the Lycus Valley*, 19.

6. "Ancient 'Water Law' Unearthed in Laodicea," *Hurriyet Daily News*, 21 August 2015.

7. Huttner, *Early Christianity in the Lycus Valley*, 19; William M. Ramsay, *The Cities and Bishoprics of Phrygia*, 2 vols. (Oxford: Clarendon, 1895), 1:217; H. A.

Roman Imperial period attest to the continuance of the routes linking Tripolis, Hierapolis, and Laodikeia as well as Tripolis to Philadelphia.[8] These trade routes provided the means for the cloth, clothing, and textile industry to offer viable commodities for interregional and world markets rather than just for local consumption.

Cattle, pigs, sheep, and goats all appear on funerary stelae throughout the area, reflecting the importance of animal husbandry to the livelihood of the community. The breadth of industry ranging from the cloth, clothing, and textiles, to leather, lanolin, rope, and string is too much for this response. I note it here to assist in building the perspective of the people in the cities of the Lycus Valley as being immersed in this industry and in a life that connected their work, religious practice, and familial and social connections.

Religious Life and Practice

Let me move then to the religious life and practice. Huttner recognizes that "the Christian communities emerged within and alongside a cosmos of religious affiliation from which they isolated themselves but which they also sought to penetrate."[9] Isolating from religious practices that were woven into their way of life in the larger Lycus Valley and local Colossian community is likely more difficult than the first fervor of conversion might have seemed. Family, kinship, friendship, and association connections were at stake. Social cohesion would be brought into tension. Philip A. Harland ably embraces this complexity by paying attention to the "principal social network connections" of associations, namely, the familial or household, shared ethnic or geographical origin, neighborhood or locality, and deity worship or ritual links.[10] One association of friends (ἑταῖροι) honored on a stela from Colossae is a prime focus for the visual identity through clothing.[11]

Ormerod, "A Note on the Eastern Trade-Route in Asia Minor," *The Classical Review* 26.3 (1912): 76–77.

8. Huttner, *Early Christianity in the Lycus Valley*, 19.

9. Huttner, *Early Christianity in the Lycus Valley*, 42.

10. Philip A. Harland, *Associations, Synagogues, and Congregations: Claiming a Place in Ancient Mediterranean Society*, 2nd rev. ed. with links to inscriptions (Kitchener, ON: Philip A. Harland, 2013), 19.

11. *MAMA* 6.47, plate 10.

The marble stela was raised in honor of Glyko by the association of friends (ἑταῖροι) and is now housed at the Denizli Archaeological Museum. It is dated to late first to early second century CE.[12] The couple on the stela are dressed with their outer garment, himation, in the arm-sling style portraying a public posture of reserve and discipline.[13] This pose is known from Demosthenes (384–322 BCE) as a model of self-restraint (σοφροσύνης παράδειγμα) (*De Falsa Legatione* 251). Both wear an outer garment, a cloak, made from a specially woven cloth, *trimitos*, a twill woven with three special threads, *mitos*.[14] The weave is more pronounced on the tunic revealed below the cloak on the woman to the left. This garment may be a locally styled tunic of the *trimitos* cloth that is identified as Laodikeian *trimita* by the time of the Price Edict of Diocletian.[15] The mottled appearance is achieved through weaving two finer threads with a thicker one to produce its mottled appearance. This has also been suggested as a web-like pattern implying a link with Cybele and the net of prophecy that is visible in some of her depictions.[16] It may well be possible for a specific style of weave to be used for ritual or religious garments, yet the style appears to have had a broader market than this.

A recent find from Laodikeia of Athena's head reasserts her association with weaving and the textile and clothing industry of the Lycus Valley.[17] In a frieze in the Transitorium in the Forum in Rome, Minerva (Rome's equivalent of Athena) is depicted in a weaving contest with Arachne. Dated to the

---

12. Buckler and Calder, *MAMA* 6.47, plate 10.

13. The arm-sling is one of two styles used in statuary and identified as such in R. R. R. Smith, "Cultural Choice and Political Identity in Honorific Portrait Statues in the Greek East in the Second Century AD," *The Journal of Roman Studies* 88 (1998): 62; Rosemary Canavan, *Clothing the Body of Christ at Colossae: A Visual Construction of Identity*, WUNT 2/334 (Tübingen: Mohr Siebeck, 2012), 97.

14. For twill woven with three heddles, see Liza Cleland, Glenys Davies, and Lloyd Llewellyn-Jones, eds., *Greek and Roman Dress from A to Z* (London: Routledge, 2012), 89, 199.

15. Ramsay likens this material to Greek or Smyrna muslin and links it to the Laodikeian *trimita* tunic. Ramsay, *Cities and Bishoprics of Phrygia*, 1, 41. See also Cleland, Davies, and Llewellyn-Jones, *Greek and Roman Dress*, 89, 126, 99; E. J. W. Barber, *Prehistoric Textiles: The Development of Cloth in the Neolithic and Bronze Age with Special Reference to the Aegean* (Princeton: Princeton University Press, 1991), 107–11.

16. Alan H. Cadwallader, *Fragments of Colossae: Sifting through the Traces* (Hindmarsh: ATF Press, 2015), 51.

17. "Athena's Head Unearthed in Laodicea," *Hurriyet Daily News*, 15 August 2015.

first century CE in the time of Domitian, this frieze affirms a restoration of Roman virtues espousing women in the domestic arena with wool working skills as symbolic of stability and traditional values.[18] This discovery of Athena adds to the current knowledge of the localized manifestation of Zeus, Zeus Ktesis (Ktesios) Patrios, as the god of sheep and shepherds who is depicted in woolen garb and holds an eagle-topped crook on a funerary stela found at Heracleia Salbake (near modern Vakif), not far from Colossae.[19] There is another eagle perched on his other hand. The undergarment or tunic appears to be roughly woven, indicating a course wool weave and the wrap of the cloak shows close folds as of a heavy wool cloth, even perhaps felt, that may indicate a dual function as blanket. To the right of the figure of Zeus is a small representation of a youthful Hermes, protector and patron of herdsmen and trade.

Fig. 3.1. Zeus Ktesis Patrios, Roman Period. Denizli Archaeological Museum. Author's photo.

There are two other images extant in this area: one is a bust, head and shoulders, on the front of an altar with a running dog on one side panel

---

18. Lena Larsson Lovén, "Wool Work as A Gender Symbol in Ancient Rome: Roman Textiles and Ancient Sources," in *Ancient Textiles: Production, Craft and Society*, ed. Carole Gilles and Marie-Louise B. Nosch (Oxford: Oxbow Books, 2007), 234.

19. This funerary stela and the two further depictions of Zeus Ktesis Patrios mentioned are now housed in the Denizli Archaeological Museum. See Rosemary Canavan, "Weaving Threads: Clothing in Colossae," in Cadwallader, *Fragments of Colossae*, 118; Hatice Erdemir, "Woollen Textiles: An International Trade Good in the Lycus Valley in Antiquity," in *Colossae in Space and Time: Linking to an Ancient City*, ed. Alan H. Cadwallader and Michael Trainor (Göttingen: Vandenhoeck & Ruprecht, 2011), 110.

Fig. 3.2. Altar for Zeus Ktesis Patrios. His distinctive woolen clothing visible on the bust. Dog on the side of the altar. Denizli Archaeological Museum. Author's photo.

Fig. 3.3. Bust of Mên in the Anatolian Archaeological Museum, Ankara. Author's photo.

and a thunderbolt on another (see fig. 2[20]); the other is a stone relief showing the god grazing his sheep.

In addition, the god Mên was depicted in lunar iconography with moon-shaped horns on his shoulders. He normally wore a Phrygian cap and a belted tunic. Both the Phrygian cap and the moon-shaped horns identify him on coins minted at Laodikeia and Attouda. The head of Mên graced the obverse of coins minted in Laodikeia, such as one from 14–37 CE with an eagle on the reverse with the name of *Dioskouridēs* magistrate.[21]

---

20. See also *MAMA* 6.87, plate 16.

21. *RPC* 1.2907; BMC Phrygia 64; SNG Copenhagen 513. See an image of the Laodikeian coin at Muenzen and Medaillen Deutschland. Accessed 11 October 2015, see http://www.muenzenundmedaillendeutschland.de. Issued under Roman rule in the time of Nero, Kornelios Aineas, ca. 66–68 CE. AE18 (4.04g). On obverse: ΛΑΟΔΙ-ΚΕΩΝ, draped bust of Mên right, wearing laureate Phrygian hat, and with a crescent

At a sanctuary north of Hierapolis, Mên Karou was also portrayed in this manner. He was associated with healing in this area.²²

These few examples show the distinctiveness of clothing to identity in the valley and its religious connections. Worship of these gods and many more attested in the area in conjunction with festivals to honor them are part of the fabric of the greater community life. In the Letter to the Colossians the community is exhorted to not be condemned for matters of observing festivals, new moons and Sabbaths (2:16), worship of angels, or dwelling on visions (2:18).

Guilds, Associations, and the Social Strata

Huttner identifies some of the extraordinary men and women in the Lycus Valley. These we know from inscriptions, stelae, monuments, and sarcophagi. He elucidates three women of the famous Laodikeian Zenonis family. Julia, Claudia, and Antonia were descendants of Polemon I, son of Zenon, who ruled as king of Pontus under Augustus.²³ Both Julia and Claudia issued city coins, one under Nero honoring Poppea (ca. 62 CE) and the other under Titus (79–81 CE). Antonia stands out particularly as being one of a select few to attain the provincial high priesthood and the only one attested to hold the office of imperial *neokoros* in Asia Minor.²⁴ She held the office of priestess for the province's emperor cult (Ἀρχιέρεια τῆς Ἀσιάς) as well as a priestly office in the city.²⁵

In previous studies I also focused on inscriptions honoring women especially from Asia Minor.²⁶ The names of these women engraved in stone for their benefaction, office-holding, and virtue offered a place of

---

around his shoulders. On the reverse: ΑΙ-ΝΗ-ΑΣ, eagle with open wings standing facing and head left; ΚΟΡ monogram to left.

22. Huttner, *Early Christianity in the Lycus Valley*, 53.

23. For the source of this paragraph, see Huttner, *Early Christianity in the Lycus Valley*, 96–97.

24. Rosalinde A. Kearsley, "Epigraphic Evidence for the Social Impact of Roman Government in Laodicea and Hierapolis," in *Colossae in Time and Space: Linking to an Ancient City*, ed. Alan H. Cadwallader and Michael Trainor (Göttingen: Vandenhoeck & Ruprecht, 2011), 146.

25. Rosalinde A. Kearsley indicates that there is no evidence to affirm that Antonia held both titles concurrently. See Kearsley, "Epigraphic Evidence for the Social Impact of Roman Government," 146.

26. Rosemary Canavan, "Texts, Houses and Public Offices: Investigation of

comparison for the opportunity for women to take leadership positions in the Christ communities of the Lycus Valley and beyond in Asia Minor.

Huttner also shines the spotlight on Aelia Larcia D., honored as "benefactress of her native city" for whom Sosthenes son of Skymos, clothier, raised a statue at his own expense, including the base and pedestal.[27] This honor brings the clothier also into the historical record. Another clothier, a linen-worker supervisor, in nearby Aphrodisias is memorialized on a stela.[28] The inscription is damaged and the remaining words reveal: "[... the] market supervisor, greets the association of linen-workers and the passersby."[29] Robert Smith suggests that this stela was raised by the guild of the local linen-workers for their supervisor (ἐνποριάρχης).[30] The recognition of these men as clothiers indicates the importance of this industry to the region. Their inclusion in the honors also points to the large workforce, formal and informal, male and female, who are engaged in this industry, an industry in which some might rise to honorable levels. Huttner notes that the association of wool-washers or fullers (ἐριοπλύται) and that of purple-dyers (πορφυροβάφεις) honor Tiberius Claudius Zotikos in two separate inscriptions.[31] Zotikos was a member of the highest executive body of the city of Hierapolis in the period from 212 CE: the college of the strategoi.[32] Raising monuments and honoring significant leaders in the community has a dual function in the honor system as those who

---

Women in Leadership in Pauline Communities in Asia Minor in the First Century" (BThHons thesis, Flinders University, 2006).

27. Huttner, *Early Christianity in the Lycus Valley*, 167. Huttner refers to the inscription in Thomas Corsten, *Die Inschriften von Laodikeia am Lykos* (Bonn: Habelt, 1997), 104–7, no. 51.

28. Dated to the late second century CE. Dimensions: Height: 51.5 cm, Width: 33.5 cm, Depth: 17 cm. R. R. R. Smith and Kenan T. Erim, *Aphrodisias Papers 2: The Theatre, a Sculptor's Workshop, Philosophers, and Coin-Types, Including the Papers given at the Third International Aphrodisias Colloquium Held at New York University on 7 and 8 April, 1989*, Journal of Roman Archaeology, Supplementary series (University of Michigan, 1991), 300, R2, plate 154.

29. Smith and Erim, *Aphrodisias Papers 2*, 301.

30. Smith and Erim, *Aphrodisias Papers 2*, 301.

31. Huttner, *Early Christianity in the Lycus Valley*, 166; Richard S. Ascough, Philip A. Harland, and John S. Kloppenborg, *Associations in the Greco-Roman World: A Sourcebook* (Waco, TX: Baylor University Press; Berlin: de Gruyter, 2012), 98–99.

32. Huttner, *Early Christianity in the Lycus Valley*, 166. Huttner refers to the inscriptions in Tullia Ritti, *An Epigraphic Guide to Hierapolis (Pamukkale)* (Istanbul: Ege Yayinlari, 2006), 144–46, 82, no. 32, 44.

supply the inscription and monument are also named and take their place of honor. The profile of wool washers/fullers, purple-dyers, and clothiers is enhanced by their association with important people. Their association or the individual's name and occupation are etched into the public record and raise the status of these associations and individuals. Similarly, the inscription for Publius Aelius Herogenes and Marcus Aurelius Diodorus mentions dyers (βάφεις) and purple dyers (πορφυροβάφεις) respectively.[33] A further large heroon at Hierapolis is inscribed "the association of dyers crowns this heroon."

ΤΟΥΤΟΤΟΗΡΩΟΝ
ΣΤΕΦΑΝΟΙ
ΗΕΡΓΑΣΙΑΤΩΝΒΑΦΕΩΝ

Fig. 3.4. Inscription on heroon raised by the association of the dyers at Hierapolis. Author's photo.

There is no mention of the honorand who, in statue form, may have previously reclined on the top of the heroon. While the recipient is now disconnected from his honor, the association of dyers are well preserved for their investment.

The inscriptions and monuments honoring leading individuals via associations of the textile trade not only indicate the size of this industry in the area but also the raising of the profile of the industry. One further inscription of Publius Aelius Glykon, also noted by Huttner, mentions both purple-dyers and carpet weavers. The inscription lists funds left to the presidency of the purple-dyers (πορφυροβάφεις), which should produce sufficient interest for participation in the festival of the Unleavened Bread,

---

33. Ascough, Harland, and Kloppenborg, *Associations in the Greco-Roman World*, 97–98.

Fig. 3.5. Heroon at Hierapolis crowned by the association of dyers. Author's photo. Located not far before the Frontinus Gate, 2016.

plus further funds whose interest would provide for the carpet weavers to distribute revenue during Kalends and Pentecost festivals.[34] Even though dated to the third century CE, we gain some insight into the continuance of festivals of differing religious groups, here Jewish, and the integration of religious life and textile production. Huttner dispels any case for Glykon as a Jewish Christian.[35] Glykon's presence does imply the strength of the connection between the trade and religious practice. Should we assume that these associations were only for Jewish purple-dyers and carpet weavers? What consequences would there then be for Christ followers who might separate themselves within a broader community?

Recent work by Richard Ascough has shown that evidence of associations and collegia is not a consistent pattern across locality or time.[36] One consistency that needs to be noted is the lack of any inscriptional evidence of associations for spinning. This can be surmised to be a gender issue as women were spinners. At this point let us move from the structures to the people of the many strands of the textile industry and trade.

---

34. Ascough, Harland, and Kloppenborg, *Associations in the Greco-Roman World*, 95–97; Huttner, *Early Christianity in the Lycus Valley*, 251–53.

35. Huttner, *Early Christianity in the Lycus Valley*, 252–23.

36. Richard Ascough presented a paper at Annual Meeting of the Society of Biblical Literature, Baltimore in 2013.

The People and the Industry

Here I am keen to recover something of the wider group of people in the city of Colossae and the Lycus Valley and their identity relationship with the industry in which they participated. Huttner notes an inscription from Laodikeia where fullers (γναφεῖς) and "simple workers" (ἁπλουργοί) traded.[37] Huttner considers these ἁπλουργοί to be engaged in the initial preparation of the wool for dyeing alongside the fullers.[38] Perhaps their designation reflects their work with unwashed wool. These workers along with weavers, wool workers, dye workers, purple dyers, and textile dyers are all inscribed in the record even if not in the same location.

As noted earlier, there appear to be no associations for spinners. Spinning and weaving of wool in the domestic arena is the activity of women. In Rome wool and wool-work are part of a young girl's education and preparation for womanhood and household management. Symbols of distaff, wool, and wool basket often appear on stelae and funerary reliefs as indication of the virtue of women. Elite women are noted with such symbols as they illustrate their virtue rather than their practice of this work. In Terrace House 2 in Ephesus, decorated distaffs were discovered and are believed to have been displayed in the public area of the house as testament to the virtue of the *matrona* or women of the house therein.[39]

The Denizli Archaeological Museum displays spindle whorls from the Middle Bronze Age (1900–1450 BCE) discovered at Beysesultan, less than one hundred kilometres north east of the Lycus Valley.[40] The existence of these indicates the advance in the technology of spinning in this area, so that spinning was more consistent, efficient, and faster than hand spinning.

---

37. Huttner, *Early Christianity in the Lycus Valley*, 168.

38. Huttner refers to the inscription listed in Corsten, *Die Inschriften von Laodikeia am Lykos*, 102–4, no. 50. See Huttner, *Early Christianity in the Lycus Valley*, 168.

39. Elisabeth Trinkl, "Artifacts Related to Preparation of Wool and Textile Processing Found inside the Terrace Houses of Ephesus, Turkey," in *Ancient Textiles: Production, Craft and Society*, ed. Carole Gillis and Marie-Louise B. Nosch (Oxford: Oxbow, 2007), 85.

40. Very similar examples of pottery from the Middle Bronze Age were found in both Beycesultan and Colossae. See Bahardır Duman and Erim Konakçi, "The Silent Witness of the Mound of Colossae: Pottery Remains," in Cadwallader, *Colossae in Space and Time*, 259.

Fig. 3.6. Symbols of wool working on a stela in Boğazköy Museum Garden. Author's photo.

There still appears, though, no consensus of opinion on how the workers were organized. An often-made argument is that production for markets beyond the local city and region required professional workers and production centers.[41] These centers were primarily located near the raw material. The Lycus Valley had both raw material and resources to produce a variety of qualities of wool product for local, regional, and overseas markets. Beyond this there was potential for related products such as leather goods, lanolin, rope, webbing, and more. The people who worked in these centers were a significant part of the industry but not the full picture. The diversity of work allied to the textile industry brings me to consider that a majority of people in the valley were connected in some way, whether in administration of trade or water, in production of garments and wool, in dyeing, as traders, graziers and shepherds, or engaged in associations or religious practices or festivals connected to the industry. The identity of the people in Colossae and the Lycus Valley was connected to their work and what brought status and prestige to their area.

---

41. Jeroen Poblome, "Comparing Ordinary Craft Production: Textile and Pottery Production in Roman Asia Minor," *Journal of the Economic and Social History of the Orient* 47.4 (2004): 492–94.

Fig. 3.7. Spindle whorls from Middle Bronze Age (1900–1450 BCE). Beycesultan, Denizli Archaeological Museum. Author's photo.

For example, at Philadelphia, in Asia Minor, in 138 CE the wool-weavers association has twelve members.[44] Huttner draws our attention to the concrete evidence of a dyers workshop that was discovered in Laodikeia in 2007.[45] Dated to the fifth century CE,[46] this workshop also revealed the presence of grinding stones, presses and containers, terracotta and limestone strainers, and a metal cauldron for heating the dye and dyeing the textile.[47] Of itself, this dyers workshop can only show that in the fifth century CE this was a form of organization in the dye trade in Laodikeia.

It simply is not clear how the production of textiles and clothing was organized in the Lycus Valley. The stages of production from growing wool, shearing, dyeing the fleece, carding, spinning, and weaving to the end product have quite gendered roles. If this industry was household-based, then centers of production may have had familial and religious links. Within the Lycus

---

42. Hartmut Waetzoldt, "The Use of Wool for the Production of Strings, Ropes, Braided Mats and Similar Fabrics," in *Ancient Textiles: Production, Craft and Society*, ed. Carole Gillis and Marie-Louise B. Nosch (Oxford: Oxbow, 2007), 113.

43. Poblome, "Comparing Ordinary Craft Production," 499.

44. Poblome, "Comparing Ordinary Craft Production," 499.

45. Huttner, *Early Christianity in the Lycus Valley*, 21.

46. This was discovered by Celal Şimşek as Director of the Pamukkale Archaeology Department and the Director of the excavation. See Huttner, *Early Christianity in the Lycus Valley*, 12; Celal Şimşek, "Laodikeia'da Tekstíl ve Üretím Atölyerí/Textile and Production Ateliers in Laodikeia," *Home Textile* 86 (2015): 142–44.

47. Isabella Benda-Weber, "Textile Production Centers, Products and Merchants in the Roman Province of Asia," in *Making Textiles in Pre-Roman and Roman Times: People, Places and Identities*, ed. Margarita Gleba and Judit Pásztókai-Szeöke, Ancient Textiles Series 13 (Oxford: Oxbow, 2013), 178. See also Şimşek, "Laodikeia'da Tekstíl," 142–44.

Valley it would also seem there was a segmentation between cities. What is clear is that all these stages of production were completed in order to make the fine cloth for which Laodikeia and the Lycus Valley became famous.

Social and Cultural Texture and Intertexture

Huttner indicates that the identities listed in Col 3:11 are social and cultural barriers and suggests that the Greek/Jew, circumcision/uncircumcision, and slave/free pairs in Col 3:11 are antitheses.[48] He joins a plethora of scholars who are perplexed by the insertion of Scythian and barbarian. So much ink has been spilled trying to work out whether the barbarians and Scythians were represented in the Lycus Valley and how they fit in this listing. I agree with Huttner that, whatever the relationships of these divisions, there is now only one center of belonging: Christ. In clothing oneself with Christ, the prime identity is as a member of the body of Christ regardless of any other affiliations. Huttner also suggests that the equality afforded Greeks and barbarians in the Isis cult may have assisted the crossing of barriers.[49] If we think of these as layers of identity rather than barriers, it may be possible to see something of the acculturation or integration that occurs as people live and work in communities together. Importantly in the Letter to the Colossians, male and female do not feature among the list of identities as in Gal 3:28, where there is "neither male nor female" among those who are baptized and clothed with Christ. This also points for me to the cities and their involvement in the textile industry as the place of dialogue between text and image and text and the surrounding world.

The adapted sociorhetorical diagram below assists in understanding the interaction between the text and the world of the text.[50] Within this model, particularly the social and cultural texture and the intertexture show transfer between the represented world of the text and information from the Greco-Roman world and between the verbal signs in the text and language of the world. This interpretive approach has allowed significant

---

48. Huttner, *Early Christianity in the Lycus Valley*, 135–37.
49. Huttner, *Early Christianity in the Lycus Valley*, 136.
50. This diagram is adapted from that originally created by Vernon Robbins. See Vernon Robbins, "Social-Scientific Criticism and Literary Studies," in *Modelling Early Christianity: Social-Scientific Studies of the New Testament in Its Context*, ed. Philip Esler (London: Routledge, 1995), 279.

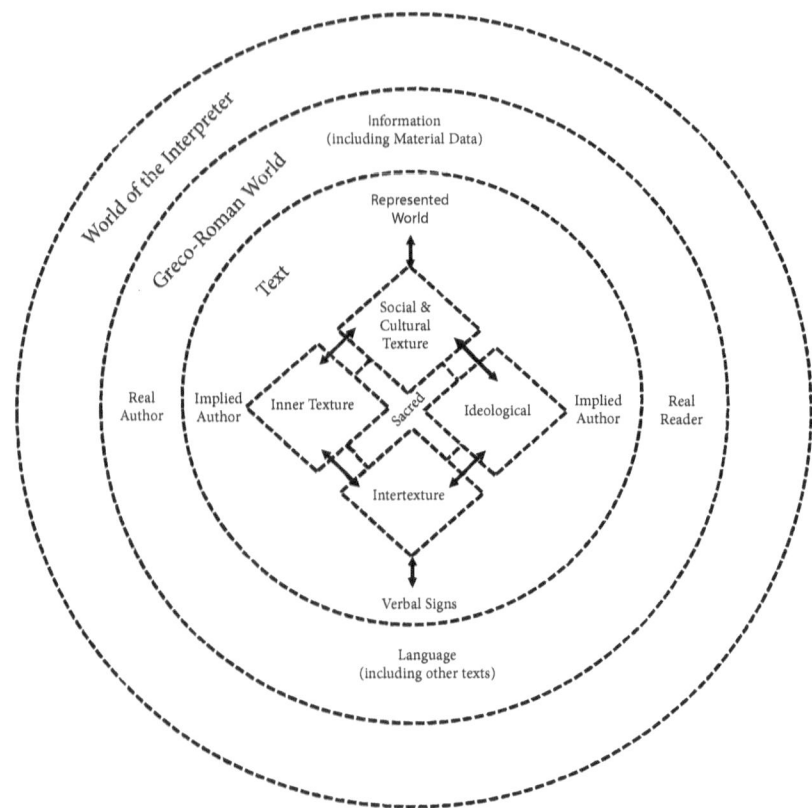

Fig. 3.8. Sociorhetorical Analytic

breadth of investigation particularly in relation to image and text and the discussion of visual exegesis.[51]

Indeed, I propose that the sociorhetorical analytic is a profitable tool to bring together the findings of a historically based investigation such as Huttner's with the biblical text and allow each to illuminate the other. I have determinedly focused on information and language in the world of the text (specifically the Lycus Valley) that interact with the social and cultural texture and intertexture of the Letter to the Colossians. In this focus we have observed evidence of how the cities and communities functioned. We have a complex tapestry of religious, political, cultural, ethnic, and

---

51. The recommendation of the use of visual exegesis for the interpretation of biblical text is made and demonstrated in Canavan, *Clothing the Body of Christ*.

civic threads that serve as identity and power, inclusion and exclusion. Many of these aspects are represented in the major industry of the valley: textile production. Zeus, who in the Greek pantheon reigned supreme, is manifest in this region as god of the sheep and shepherds. In the Roman regime, Zeus Ktesis Patrios's woolen garb does not compete with the power of the cuirassed and toga-draped heads of the world. The quality of the wool and garments, the dye, and the cloth provide the means of trade, prosperity, and status not only in the locality but in the wider world, a world governed from Rome. All power and authority in this realm belongs to the emperors who would be gods themselves, clothing themselves in the highest of virtues and managing an uneasy peace born of conquest and oppression. In nearby Aphrodisias, the Sebasteion provided a three-story stone pictogram carving of the order of power. How can the followers of Christ find and maintain their new identity and location within this?

In the Letter to the Colossians, there is a reordering of the cosmos from the beginning of the letter. The faithful ones share in "the inheritance of the saints in the light" (Col 1:12), having been rescued from the power of darkness and transferred to the reign of God's beloved son (Col 1:13). Christ is the head of the body, the *ekklēsia*, in direct opposition to Roman rule where the emperor, definitively Nero, was the head of the body of Rome and the head of the world, the cosmos.[52] This new body, the *ekklēsia*, needs to be clothed in a recognizable way that identifies as Christ. The members having clothed themselves in this "new self" (Col 3:10) are, as God's chosen and beloved (Col 3:12), to clothe themselves in virtues that emanate Christ. The intricacies of clothing that is the lifeblood of the region becomes the metaphor of their new life, a growing in wisdom and becoming as Christ, being formed as Christ's body, identified through clothing in the virtues of God.

The focus is on Christ as the identity of the members of the body of Christ: the community of believers. The author is exhorting the members to conform to this body by being clothed in virtues and love which will hold them together despite any other allegiances or belonging. It is not the clothing spun, woven, and dyed in their neighborhood but symbolic, metaphorical clothing with virtues and love, providing an outward sign of their belonging and of recognizing each other in Christ. It is these

---

52. Lucius Annaeus Seneca, *Clem.* 2.2.1. For further discussion of the body of the emperor, see Canavan, *Clothing the Body of Christ*, 121–23.

metaphorical images of clothing, body, and virtue that have the propensity to interact with the plethora of propaganda in the form of idealized clothing, body, and virtues of the Roman emperors, their families, and officials expounded in carved statues, reliefs, coins, and funerary monuments. It is the juxtaposition of standing victorious naked hero figures of emperors above crouched naked female personifications of conquered nations that gives rise to a strident discourse between what it is to belong to Christ and be identified in Christ in contrast to being a member of the Roman regime.

Among the list of virtues, Huttner notes "meekness," which he interprets as "meek friendliness" (πραΰτης), as appropriate to a person in authority.[53] Paul refers to this meekness as a quality of Christ in 2 Cor 10:1, characterizing it as the way he relates to them while with them. Paul is a master teacher by example and exhorts his communities to imitate him in imitating Christ (1 Cor 4:16, 11:1; 1 Thess 1:6, 2:14). Putting on the same clothes, clothing in the virtue of Christ makes the followers identifiable in Christ. This same term and virtue is listed as a fruit of the Spirit in Gal 5:23 and translated as "gentleness." In this way the meek friendship or gentleness is further identified with God, like Christ and the bounty of the Spirit. This meek friendliness (πραΰτης) fits well also with χρηστότες, which is usually translated as "kindness" (Col 3:12). Yet this word also extends in meaning through the range from goodness, excellence, honesty, and uprightness to goodness of heart.[54] In terms of intertexture, χρηστότες accompanies virtue in relation to the friendship that, in the civic sense, builds a state of good citizens.[55] Such kindness and integrity clothes the members of the body of Christ in the means of belonging and holding together.

Engaging Huttner's diligent research, the inscriptional evidence, images of the gods, trade symbols, and all that we can glean and imagine from the historic record, we have a picture of the significance of the clothing industry. I set out to see the propensity of this industry to be a source of vivid imagery to the Letter to the Colossians. It is fair to say that the clothing industry is instrumental in a network of images. For the emerging faith communities in the Lycus Valley, the imagery of clothing and body

---

53. Huttner, *Early Christianity in the Lycus Valley*, 134.

54. LSJ, s.v. "χρηστότες."

55. For Cicero, virtue comes first but friendship is "the greatest of all things." See Cicero, *Amic.* 27.71.

Unraveling the Threads of Identity

Fig. 3.9. Nero standing above naked female personification of Armenia, white marble relief circa first century CE, Aphrodisias Archaeological Museum, Geyre, Turkey.

assists the development of identity, which may be enhanced by the intensity of engagement with cloth and clothing in this area.

We see in the text of the letter traces of the world in which it was written: the named identities, the reference to festivals, new moon, and Sabbath, and the references to the worship of angels and dwelling on visions. All of these would elicit vivid pictures in the minds of the hearers. The issues of influence of other philosophy and the engaging in festivals, new moon, and Sabbath indicate something of the identity of the inhabitants of Colossae and the cities of the Lycus Valley and the competing claims on belonging. In chapter 2 the believers are warned against being held captive through philosophy and empty deceit (2:8) according to both human and elemental spirits rather than Christ. The persuasion is then reiterated three times using "in him":

- *In him* the whole fullness of the deity dwells bodily. (2:9)
- You have come to fullness *in him*. (2:10)

- *In him* also you were circumcised with a spiritual circumcision. (2:11)

Each of these usages points to the identity framework for Christ followers, marking them off for Christ and etching the difference of "us" and "them" with the connection to God, through Christ with no outward identifying sign. The new locus of this community is embraced in the cosmos where "God rescued us from the power of darkness and transferred us into the kingdom of his beloved son" (1:13). The reconfiguration of the cosmic realm reorders all the other allegiances.

Having elucidated this framework, there is a further exhortation not to be condemned in regard to matters of food and drink and observing festivals, new moon, and Sabbaths. Each of these matters are easily recognizable as adherence to Jewish practice and law. Yet they also intersect with local religious practice in relation to Mên, Zeus (especially the Ktesis Patrios representation), Athena, and other deities worshipped in the Lycus Valley. These activities are not required for those belonging to the body of Christ (2:17). The alignment of identity to the head, Christ (1:18), facilitates the new cosmic order that is not presided over by the pantheon of Greek and Roman gods nor ruled by the emperor of Rome.

The tour de force of how to be "us" in Christ is the clothing of this body. The rhetorical force of the clothing imagery is delivered through the blending of the rhetography of the cosmos where God reigns in heaven and on earth and his son is head of the body, the *ekklēsia*, of God's chosen and beloved in the Letter to the Colossians with the reality of the Roman Empire, best illustrated in physical architecture and statuary at the three-story Aphrodisian Sebasteion: the top story being devoted to the pantheon of gods, the second the imagery of the emperors as heroes and victors making the way for the reign of peace over subjugated peoples and citizens.[56] Through this blending there is a transformation of the discourse of the Christ followers that builds their identity in collective terms in Christ. The clothing that they are to put on or clothe themselves with is the new self (3:10), one that is conforming to Christ, one that is not complete but

---

56. *Rhetography* is defined as "the progressive, sensory-aesthetic, and/or argumentative texture of a text (rhetology) that invites a hearer/reader to create a graphic image or picture in the mind that implies a certain kind of truth and/or reality." See Vernon Robbins, *The Invention of Christian Discourse*, RRA 1 (Blandford Forum: Deo, 2009), xxvii.

still being renewed in knowledge according to its creator (3:10). Furthermore, they are to clothe themselves with the heart of compassion, kindness, humility, gentleness, and patience (3:12). Upon all love that is the bond of maturity (3:14). These community members from all differing identities can relate to clothing that covers over the usual identification markers. What they are putting on are threads of virtue, ways to weave unity in the body, "holding fast to the head" and "nourished and held together by its ligaments and sinews" so that it "grows with a growth that is from God:" (Col 2:19). These clothing and body metaphors create a contrast to the body of Rome whose head is the emperor, in this case Nero.[57] The identity of those living in the Lycus Valley is embedded in their Greco-Roman cities, which operate as members of the empire. These cities are renowned for their clothing industry. The focus of their status and their daily work becomes the metaphor the Christ followers engage for the understanding of their identity in Christ. Such a strong immersion in the clothing industry suggests the propensity for it to provide a rich source of vivid imagery. While the hearer or reader in the Lycus Valley may have an enhanced view of the clothing imagery, clothing is specifically linked with virtue and identity drawing a new collective of diverse identities into the body of Christ. The clothing in virtues is distinctive just as the *trimitos* cloth is in its weave. The list of virtues does not replicate common lists in the Greco-Roman world or those espoused by the Roman Empire but some of these are included in other New Testament writings. The clothing in the Letter to the Colossians is more easily broadly applied. The advantage within the community of believers in the Lycus Valley would be for subsequent local preaching and teaching to pick up on the threads and use them to advantage.

The use of clothing is paramount to setting the identity of the believers in Christ, not just between "us" and "them" but in a new cosmic order. The clothing that is not a barrier but a layer of virtue and relational cohesion is not just about membership of the body but also existence in all the warps and wefts.

---

57. It is Seneca who implements the term *corpus imperii*, the body of the empire, and adds Nero as the head of this body. Rome is the head of the world, *caput mundi*, so by implication Nero is the head of the world. See Seneca, *Clem.* 2.2.1. For further explanation of the body of the Roman Emperor, see Canavan, *Clothing the Body of Christ*, 121–23.

Conclusion

This response engages only a few threads of the thick-spun fabric of this magnificent volume by Huttner. I trust my little unravelling has shown the value of this work as well as offering persuasion that the context of the textile industry and trade provides vivid imagery for the hearers of the Letter to the Colossians in binding their identity in Christ.

Bibliography

"Ancient 'Water Law' Unearthed in Laodicea." *Hurriyet Daily News*, 21 August 2015.

Ascough, Richard S., Philip A. Harland, and John S. Kloppenborg. *Associations in the Greco-Roman World: A Sourcebook*. Waco, TX: Baylor University Press; Berlin: de Gruyter, 2012.

"Athena's Head Unearthed in Laodicea." *Hurriyet Daily News*, 15 August 2015.

Barber, E. J. W. *Prehistoric Textiles: The Development of Cloth in the Neolithic and Bronze Age with Special Reference to the Aegean*. Princeton: Princeton University Press, 1991.

Benda-Weber, Isabella. "Textile Production Centers, Products and Merchants in the Roman Province of Asia." Pages 171–91 in *Making Textiles in Pre-Roman and Roman Times: People, Places and Identities*. Edited by Margarita Gleba and Judit Pásztókai-Szeöke. Ancient Textiles Series 13. Oxford: Oxbow, 2013.

Cadwallader, Alan H. *Fragments of Colossae: Sifting through the Traces*. Hindmarsh: ATF Press, 2015.

Canavan, Rosemary. *Clothing the Body of Christ at Colossae: A Visual Construction of Identity*. WUNT 2/334. Tübingen: Mohr Siebeck, 2012.

———. "Texts, Houses and Public Offices: Investigation of Women in Leadership in Pauline Communities in Asia Minor in the First Century." BThHons thesis, Flinders University, 2006.

———. "Weaving Threads: Clothing in Colossae." Pages 111–33 in *Fragments of Colossae: Sifting through the Traces*. Edited by Alan H. Cadwallader. Hindmarsh: ATF Press, 2015.

Cleland, Liza, Glenys Davies, and Lloyd Llewellyn-Jones, eds. *Greek and Roman Dress from A to Z*. London: Routledge, 2012.

Corsten, Thomas. *Die Inschriften von Laodikeia am Lykos*. Bonn: Habelt, 1997.

Duman, Bahardır, and Erim Konakçi. "The Silent Witness of the Mound of Colossae: Pottery Remains." Pages 247–81 in *Colossae in Space and Time: Linking to an Ancient City*. Edited by Alan H. Cadwallader and Michael Trainor. Göttingen: Vandenhoek & Ruprecht, 2011.

Erdemir, Hatice. "Woollen Textiles: An International Trade Good in the Lycus Valley in Antiquity." Pages 104–29 in *Colossae in Space and Time: Linking to an Ancient City*. Edited by Alan H. Cadwallader and Michael Trainor. Göttingen: Vandenhoeck & Ruprecht, 2011.

Harland, Philip A. *Associations, Synagogues, and Congregations: Claiming a Place in Ancient Mediterranean Society*. 2nd rev. ed. Kitchener, ON: Philip A. Harland, 2013.

Huttner, Ulrich. *Early Christianity in the Lycus Valley*. Translated by David Green. AJEC 85; Early Christianity in Asia Minor 1. Leiden: Brill, 2013.

Kearsley, Rosalinde A. "Epigraphic Evidence for the Social Impact of Roman Government in Laodicea and Hierapolis." Pages 130–50 in *Colossae in Time and Space: Linking to an Ancient City*. Edited by Alan H. Cadwallader and Michael Trainor. Göttingen: Vandenhoeck & Ruprecht, 2011.

Lovén, Lena Larsson. "Wool Work as A Gender Symbol in Ancient Rome: Roman Textiles and Ancient Sources." Pages 229–38 in *Ancient Textiles: Production, Craft and Society*. Edited by Carole Gillis and Marie-Louise B. Nosch. Oxford: Oxbow, 2007.

Ormerod, H. A. "A Note on the Eastern Trade-Route in Asia Minor." *The Classical Review* 26.3 (1912): 76–77.

Poblome, Jeroen. "Comparing Ordinary Craft Production: Textile and Pottery Production in Roman Asia Minor." *Journal of the Economic and Social History of the Orient* 47 (2004): 491–506.

Ramsay, William M. *The Cities and Bishoprics of Phrygia*. 2 vols. Oxford: Clarendon, 1895.

Ritti, Tullia. *An Epigraphic Guide to Hierapolis (Pamukkale)*. Istanbul: Ege Yayinlari, 2006.

Robbins, Vernon. *The Invention of Christian Discourse*. RRA 1. Blandford Forum: Deo, 2009.

———. "Social-Scientific Criticism and Literary Studies." Pages 274–89 in *Modelling Early Christianity: Social-Acientific Studies of the New Testament in Its Context*. Edited by Philip Esler. London: Routledge, 1995.

Şimşek, Celal. "Laodikeia'da Tekstíl ve Üretim Atölyeleri/Textile and Production Ateliers in Laodikeia." *Home Textile* 86 (2015): 138–44.

Smith, R. R. R. "Cultural Choice and Political Identity in Honorific Portrait Statues in the Greek East in the Second Century AD." *JRS* 88 (1998): 56–93.

Smith, R. R. R., and Kenan T. Erim. *Aphrodisias Papers 2: The Theatre, a Sculptor's Workshop, Philosophers, and Coin-Types, Including the Papers Given at the Third International Aphrodisias Colloquium Held at New York University on 7 and 8 April, 1989.* Journal of Roman Archaeology Supplementary Series. University of Michigan, 1991.

Trinkl, Elisabeth. "Artifacts Related to Preparation of Wool and Textile Processing Found inside the Terrace Houses of Ephesus, Turkey." Pages 81–86 in *Ancient Textiles: Production, Craft and Society*. Edited by Carole Gillis and Marie-Louise B Nosch. Oxford: Oxbow, 2007.

Waetzoldt, Hartmut. "The Use of Wool for the Production of Strings, Ropes, Braided Mats and Similar Fabrics." Pages 112–21 in *Ancient Textiles: Production, Craft and Society*. Edited by Carole Gillis and Marie-Louise B. Nosch. Oxford: Oxbow, 2007.

On the Question of Comparative Method in Historical Research: Colossae and Chonai in Larger Frame

Alan H. Cadwallader

At the conclusion of an overview essay on the development of the city of Aphrodisias, Chris Ratté reflected that "archaeologists tend to vacillate between the extremes of seeing their sites as unique and as exemplars of general trends. All cities are both, and much historical research boils down to trying to distinguish between the typical and the exceptional ... of what cities had in common with each other and of how a particular city forged its own local identity."[1] Regional comparison can yield considerable insight, as, for example, in Rosalinde Kearsley's study of Latin and Greek bilingual inscriptions providing a measure of the chronology, societal level, geographic spread and degree of linguistic and cultural interaction across Asia.[2] Comparative archaeology and history can be turned to the

---

1. Christopher Ratté, "The Founding of Aphrodisias," in *Aphrodisias Papers 4: New Research on the City and Its Monuments*, ed. Christopher Ratté and R. R. R. Smith (Portsmouth: Journal of Roman Archaeology, 2008), 36.

2. IK 59. The collection includes one example from Hierapolis (IK 59.169) and four from Laodicea (IK 59.56, 57, 96, 170). Significantly perhaps, there is only one from Kibyra (IK 59.95), the city after which the *conventus* organizing Roman administration in the Lycus Valley, was named. See, however, from Kormasa, 80 km due northeast of Kibyra, a bilingual inscription not included by Kearsley, possibly because it fell into the province of Pisidia: N. P. Milner, *An Epigraphical Survey in the Kibyra-Olbasa Region*, RECAM 3 (London: BIAA, 1998), §152. Aphrodisias also has only one example (§128), significant because the city is the other contender for the assize center in the third century, according to some interpreters, on the basis of viewing Aphrodisias as the capital of the new province of Caria; see C. Roueché, *Aphrodisias in Late Antiquity: The Late Roman and Byzantine Inscriptions*, rev. 2nd ed. (London: King's College, 2004), 1.5, 1.9–10 (with qualifications).

highlighting of characteristics that mark out one city from another, for example. But they can also obfuscate distinctives that may characterize particular locations or even particular aggregations within a single location. Given the inheritance of competition between Greek *poleis* in Asia under Roman rule, and the interest of imperial authorities in cultivating contained rivalry as a mechanism for reinforcing imperial commitments,[3] a comparative approach, carefully directed, is clearly the way forward, even when narrowed to the investigation of an isolated site.

Michael Smith and Peter Peregrine have detailed nine dimensions for harnessing the value of comparative work. These are sample size (the number of cases compared), sample selection (what governs the cases brought into interpretative play), contextualization (the extent to which a context is provided for any particular artifact or text), scale (how vast is the societal focus), primary and secondary data, archaeological and historical data, synchronic and diachronic comparisons, the stage in the research trajectory at which the comparison is invoked, spatial and temporal domains.[4] All these factors are critical as a methodological hold on comparative research to provide a check on compression whereby overarching interpretations skim over local distinctives and a check on idiosyncracy, whereby the local (defined anywhere from infra-city to infra-region) is somehow hermetically sealed from outside influence.

When one's focus is turned to Colossae/Chonai, the comparative method becomes immensely attractive precisely because of the poverty of material and textual resources. Indeed, one might argue that the succeeding imperial sweep of Seleucid and Roman control cultivates a recognition of impact on everything from agriculture to architecture that emanates from a center located elsewhere. The *chora basilike* of the Seleucids, asserted through Asia (albeit with regular interruptions and challenges), did bring wide-ranging adjustments to human and religious settlement.[5]

---

3. See, generally, Anna Heller, *"Les bêtises des Grecs": Conflits et rivalités entre cites d'Asie et de Bithynie à l'époque romaine (129 a.C.–234 p.C.)* (Bordeaux: de Boccard, 2007).

4. See Michael E. Smith and Peter Peregrine, "Approaches to Comparative Analysis in Archaeology," in *The Comparative Archaeology of Complex Societies*, ed. Michael E. Smith (Cambridge: Cambridge University Press, 2011), 4, 9–15.

5. See Christian Mileta, *Der König und sein Land: Untersuchungen zur Herrschaft der hellenistischen Monarchen über das königliche Gebiet Kleinasiens und seine Bevölkerung* (Berlin: Akademie Verlag, 2008).

One need only point to the Seleucid penchant for colonization that so comprehensively made use of royal landholdings (as well as existing cities on occasion) to recognize the flow-on effects in linguistic change, appropriation of myths and cultural expression, let alone economic infrastructure.[6] A significant hint that Colossae was caught into this almost-programmatic Hellenization may be late in appearing, but it is clear both numismatically and onomastically.[7] The Treaty of Apameia of 188 BCE established the independence of the Attalid kingdom, but many of the cultural markers fostered by the Seleucids remained intact. Indeed, the devolving shift in Attalid benefaction and support allowed a greater parade of self-identification by cities even as Attalid control was enhanced.[8]

The earliest known coins of Colossae are thought to come from the mid-second to early first century, that is, in the period of Attalid rule characterized numismatically by "a patchwork of types, denominations and weight-standards produced in different places at different times."[9] Three types are known, though only one has gained formal catalogue publication and analysis.[10]

---

6. See Bezalel Bar-Kochva, *The Seleucid Army: Organization and Tactics in the Great Campaigns* (Cambridge: Cambridge University Press, 1976), 26; Richard A. Billows, *Kings and Colonists: Aspects of Macedonian Imperialism* (Leiden: Brill, 1995), 146; see generally, Getzel M. Cohen, *The Seleucid Colonies: Studies in Founding, Administration and Organization* (Wiesbaden: Steiner, 1978); Frank Daubner, "Seleukidische und attalidische in Westkleinasien—Datierung, Funktion und Status," in *Militärsiedlungen und Territorialherrschaft in der Antike*, ed. Frank Daubner (Berlin: de Gruyter, 2011), 41–63.

7. Nicholas Wright ("Seleucid Royal Cult, Indigenous Religious Tradition and Radiate Crowns: The Numismatic Evidence," *Med Arch* 18 [2005]: 71) sees the coinage especially as stressing "the Greek character of the empire." Compare the nuanced assessment of Rolf Strootman: "in the course of time a supranational imperial culture came into existence based on the Hellenic culture of the court"; Rolf Strootman, "Seleucids," in *The Encyclopedia of Ancient History*, ed. Roger Bagnall et al. (Malden: Wiley-Blackwell, 2012), 6122.

8. See Peter Thonemann, "The Attalid State, 188–133 BC," in *Attalid Asia Minor: Money, International Relations and the State*, ed. Peter Thonemann (Oxford: Oxford University Press, 2013), 38, 47.

9. Andrew Meadows, "The Closed Currency System of the Attalid Kingdom," in Thonemann, *Attalid Asia Minor*, 195.

10. Hans von Aulock, *Münzen und Städte Phrygiens*, 2 vols., IstMitt 25, 27 (Tübingen: Wasmuth, 1980–1987), 2.43–46. Additional examples may be found at https://gallica.bnf.fr/ark:/12148/btv1b103235058 and https://tinyurl.com/SBL4218a1. A fourth

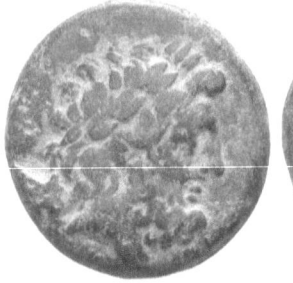

Fig. 4.1. Hellenistic coin of Colossae, probably mid-second century BCE. Zeus and his thunderbolt. From a private collection, used by permission.

The published coin has an obverse with the laureate head of Zeus facing right and a reverse of a winged thunderbolt contained in parallel by the legend ΚΟΛΟΣ | ΣΗΝΩΝ.[11] The stock interpretative approach to such numismatic evidence is reductive—simply asserting the presence of a cult of Zeus at Colossae.[12] Occasionally the combination of images expands the name to Zeus Bronton. Such an atomistic sampling of artefacts may succeed as a reasonable commentary, *if* diachronic corroboration is gathered from the prevalence of Zeus on Colossae's imperial coinage and/or other remains.[13] But a comparative approach

---

type was suggested by an auction house for a coin that came onto the market in 2012, but the coin is so worn as to defy confidence, even though it appears to display late Hellenistic iconography (obverse: laureate head of Zeus; reverse: standing Demeter holding sheaves in her right hand and a scepter in her left). See https://tinyurl.com/SBL4218d.

11. The inscription uses a four-bar sigma which disappears when Colossae's mint reemerges early in the reign of Hadrian, to be replaced by a lunate style.

12. For examples of this practice, see Markus Barth and Helmut Blanke, *Colossians*, trans. Astrid B. Beck, AB 34B (New York: Doubleday, 1994), 11; Clinton E. Arnold, *The Colossian Syncretism: The Interface between Christianity and Folk Belief at Colossae* (Grand Rapids: Baker, 1996), 107–8; Lukas Bormann, *Der Brief des Paulus an die Kolosser*, THKNT 10.1 (Leipzig: Evangelische Verlagsanstalt, 2012), 22. For a caution against a too-ready equation, see Barbara Levick, *Roman Colonies in Southern Asia Minor* (Oxford: Clarendon, 1967), 130–32. Compare Barclay Head's comments that, in spite of the variety of types in the Colossian catalogue, he considers them to be like medallions, issued only for "religious festivals and games" (*BMC Phrygia*, pp. l–li). The sheer variety of weights and sizes—exactly as one would expect for different values—renders this most unlikely. That Colossae's coins were part of currency exchange is clear from a recently-surfaced Geta-Artemis Ephesiaca coin with a Sardis countermark (CAPB) designating a value of two assaria: see http://www.vcoins.com/ancient/tomvossen/store/searchitem.asp.

13. Von Aulock, *Münzen und Städte Phrygiens* 2.458–60 (Nikephoros); 470 (laureate head); 471–482, 534–536, 546–547, 580, 588, and 590 (Aetophoros). Note that

affords greater sophistication in results. The iconography of both faces in fact closely imitates some coinage of the royal Seleucid mints. Other cities did the same,[14] albeit, like Colossae, confirming their own cultural inheritance from the appropriated representation. Although civic bronzes of the late Seleucid, Attalid, and Roman republic times often began to exert their own creativity,[15] Colossae was quite restrained. But of particular significance, given Colossae's pre-Greek eminence (see Xenophon, *Anab.* 1.2.6; Herodotus, *Hist.* 7.30; Diodoros Siculus, *Bib. hist.* 14.80.8; Polyaenus, *Strateg.* 7.16), is that the chosen representation is drawn from bronzes (not gold or silver) of mints further east, *not* the Seleucid coinage of the western Mediterranean sea-board.[16] In other

---

occasionally Zeus Aetophoros is dubbed Zeus Laodikensis on the basis of the frequency of this representation at Laodicea—this is misleading; so Christopher Howgego, *Greek Imperial Countermarks: Studies in the Provincial Coinage of the Roman Empire* (London: Royal Numismatic Society, 1985), 157. Some have identified a blend between mediate Serapis and Zeus on other coins from Colossae—this invites further enquiry; compare David Magie, "Egyptian Deities in Asia Minor in Inscriptions and on Coins," *AJA* 57.3 (1953): 163–87; James Walters, "Egyptian Religions in Ephesos," in *Ephesos: Metropolis of Asia: An Interdisciplinary Approach to its Archaeology, Religion, and Culture*, ed. Helmut Koester, HTS 41 (Valley Forge: Trinity Press International, 1995), 281–309, who however, omits numismatic evidence.

14. See, for example, the very similar Zeus-thunderbolt coin from Abbaitis in eastern Phrygia, distinguished only by a wreath circling the thunderbolt: *BMC Phrygia* 1.1–7, plate 2.1. The addition of the wreath is found on coins issued by the mint of Seleuceia Pieria in the first century BCE.

15. S. Psoma, "War or Trade? Attic-Weight Tetradrachms in Seleukid Syria," in Thonemann, *Attalid Asia Minor*, 294.

16. Edward T. Newell, *The Coinage of the Western Seleucid Mints: From Seleucus I to Antiochus III, with a Summary of Recent Scholarship by Otto Mørkholm* (New York: American Numismatic Society, 1977), 86–87 §894, 896, 898, 899 [with split placename] and plate 15.2, 6, 8, 10 (Seleucia Pieria; Seleucus I); 107 §§949–951 and plate 19.8–14 (Antioch; Seleucus I, some with monogram and additional symbols); see also in an addendum to Newell's volume on "Eastern Seleucid Mints," plate 1.17 (Seleucia on the Tigris; Antiochus II). See also Robert H. McDowell, *Stamped and Inscribed Objects from Seleucia on the Tigris* (Ann Arbor: University of Michigan Press, 1935), 115 who noted the Greek association of the thunderbolt with fertility (n. 6). Newell considers that the die-cutters, or at least their styles, for the mints on the eastern Mediterranean seaboard came from Seleucia on the Tigris (*Coinage of the Western Seleucid Mints*, 97). Newell's observations in this instance have been substantially confirmed by Arthur Houghton and Catharine C. Lorber, *Seleucid Coins: A Comprehensive Catalogue*, 2 vols. (New York: American Numismatic Society, 2002, 2008), even

words, Colossae—on the basis of this Hellenistic coin—is continuing to look toward the Achmaenid east of its past hey-days,[17] albeit through the lens of Seleucid preferences combined with the advantages to be gained from the new Attalid realities. Attalid rule, following the Peace of Apameia, probably devolved to Colossae the ability to mint *and name* its own bronze coinage. The recognition of additional Attalid favorites, such as Athena and Dionysos, and the dynastic hero-founder, Heracles, has only begun to be evidenced for Colossae's Hellenistic coins, with a single small bronze featuring Artemis on the obverse with the lion pelt and club of Heracles on the reverse.[18] This coin must await further analysis.

However, another significant coin-type suggests that Colossae had deliberately adopted the second of the two favored Seleucid gods, Zeus and Apollo.[19] The royal romance propaganda lauded Apollo as providing the paternity for Seleucus I; accordingly, the blood-line of the Seleucids was set.[20] This coin again involves Colossae's selection from the narrow range of bronze coin imagery, accenting a radiate Apollo with the choice

though this generally improved catalogue does not distinguish between "plain" and "winged" thunderbolts: 1.32–33 (Seleucus I); 1.343–344, 1.355–356 (Antiochus I); 1.625–626, 1.638 (Antiochus II). It does however note what it calls "thundering Zeus" iconography, that is, an advancing Zeus brandishing a thunderbolt (see, for example, 1.635–637. I recognize that my use of *eastern* may be confusing here. For the Seleucid Empire, *east* is generally understood as indicating Mesopotamia, Bactria, and beyond, with *west* encompassing Levantine cities such as Antioch on the Orontes as well as the more familiar area of Asia Minor. Even so, for Colossae, regardless of the origins of most of the early iconographic features (see next note), these cities to her east, rather than the output from Sardis and other western mints, appear to have provided the template.

17. This east-bearing compass is implicit in the early testimonia of Colossae and is reflected on the ground with the stylistic parallels to various strata of pottery; see my "The Historical Sweep of the Life of Colossae," in *Epigraphical Evidence Illustrating Paul's Letter to the Colossians*, ed. Joseph Verheyden, Markus Öhler, and Thomas Corsten, WUNT 411 (Tübingen: Mohr Siebeck, 2018), 25–67.

18. Kairos Numismatik sold via eBay May 21st 2017; 13 mm, 2.15 g. See also Robert Parker, *Greek Gods Abroad: Names, Natures and Transformations* (Berkeley: University of California Press, 2017), 219–20.

19. Hendrik Jan Willem Drijvers, *Cults and Beliefs at Edessa* (Leiden: Brill, 1980), 70–72. Drijvers has followed the lead of Newell, *Coinage of the Western Seleucid Mints*, 96, but added further nonnumismatic evidence. The privileging of Zeus and Apollo is seen in respective temples to each in Babakome and Kiddioukome, villages governed by Laodicea: ILaodikeia 1.

20. Paul J. Kosmin, *The Land of the Elephant Kings: Space, Territory, and Ideology*

Fig. 4.2. Hellenistic coin of Colossae, slightly off-center strike, of radiate and laureate Apollo on the obverse and his four-string kithara on the reverse. Some coins show only a three-stringed lyre, indicating different die-lots and therefore significant output from the Colossian mint. From a private collection, used by permission.

of symbol, a lyre.[21] The lyre was not the dominant symbol in Seleucid Apollonian coinage from the eastern Mediterranean (the preference is for omphalos or tripod), but Colossae joins with Ionian and Lycian coinage.[22]

The obverse radiate head is found on Seleucid royal coinage only from around 173–170 BCE and applied only to the kings' portraits not Apollo.[23] A bust of radiate Helios does occur as a small symbol in various sectors of the reverse field, additional to the representation of Zeus Aetophoros (seated), standing Nike, or Athena in an elephant-drawn biga on some gold

---

in the *Seleucid Empire* (Cambridge: Harvard University Press, 2014), 95–98; see Justin, *Epit.* 15.4.3–9.

21. Newell, *Coinage of the Western Seleucid Mints*, 96 §922, plate 17.5, 6 (Seleucus I; laureate Apollo on obverse, kithara on reverse; from Antioch on the Orontes); Houghton and Lorber, *Seleucid Coins*, 1. 20 (Seleucus I); 1.418, 1.424, 1.443 (Antiochus I); 1.528–529 (Antiochus II).

22. See Jodi Magness, "Some Observations on the Roman Temple at Kedesh," *IEJ* 40 (1990): 179, who takes the lyre and tripod as the key attributes for Apollo on Seleucid coins. See also J. Grafton Milne, *Kolophon and Its Coinage: A Study* (New York: American Numismatic Society, 1941), plates I–V. The kithara is also known on Ptolemaic coinage, also in bronze, from the same period: Otto Mørkholm, Philip Grierson, and Ulla Westermark, *Early Hellenistic Coinage from the Accession of Alexander to the Peace of Apamea (336–186 BC)* (Cambridge: Cambridge University Press, 1991), 70.

23. See Wright, "Seleucid Royal Cult," 74, for the variety of dating options. Occasionally in the late Greek west, radiate crowns for gods are known on coins, such as the third century coin from Leontinoi in Sicily featuring a radiate Demeter or Tyche: *BMC Sicily* 62. Radiate crowned heads appear on coins of Macedonia often with thunderbolts on the reverse.

and silver coins of Seleucus I.[24] Arthur Houghton and Catharine Lorber interpret this as likely an official mint-mark for identifying production output, so its significance for Seleucid iconography is minimal.[25] By contrast, the political importance of Rhodes in the Attalid kingdom almost certainly can be traced in its coin output;[26] here the emphasis on radiate Helios is pertinent. This may be an aid to the dating of this Colossian coin. The image tenaciously revived on Colossae's Roman-imperial-period coins. But on these coins, the radiate crown was not conferred upon the imperial head. Rather, it has been designated as Helios, possibility on the basis of the radiate driver of a quadriga that appears on other coins.[27] If this is the case, there appears less diachronic numismatic support for a sanctuary of Apollo at Colossae, compared with the previous coin. However, if the Hierapolitan coins of Apollo Lairbenos in the imperial period are indicative of the region, it seems clear that Apollo was quite capable of becoming radiate[28]—the falling curled locks on these coins of Hierapolis seem to me to be a characteristic of Apollo rather than Helios, even though inscriptions can combine the names.[29] The radiate heads of Colossae's imperial coinage lack this feature and therefore confirm the identification

---

24. Houghton and Lorber, *Seleucid Coins*, 1.162.2, 1.173.16, 1.174.9 (standing Nike, some with trophy); 1.165.1, 1.169 (seated Zeus Aetophorus); 1.177.1, 1.179 (Athena in biga).

25. Houghton and Lorber, *Seleucid Coins*, 1.xxi–xxii, 2.223.

26. See Richard Ashton, "The Use of the Cistaphoric Weight-Standard outside the Pergamene Kingdom," in Thonemann, *Attalid Asia Minor*, 257–58.

27. Von Aulock, *Münzen und Städte Phrygiens*, 2.448–452, 458–460, 483, 515–517 (radiate head designated Helios); see also 487–493, 496–506, 546 (Helios in quadriga); 564 (Apollo as child, with Artemis, of Leto). Of the radiate "Helios" coins, all in von Aulock's collection face right; however, one coin has emerged in the auctions with the head facing left; see now *RPC* 3.2313A online: https://rpc.ashmus.ox.ac.uk/search/browse?q=2313A.

28. *RPC* 4.2070, 4.9991–3; these coins follow Head in avoiding Helios in the description: BMC Phrygia 54–66 plate XXX.6.

29. On locks as a characteristic of Apollo rather than Heliosote, see Houghton and Lorber, *Seleucid Coins*, 1.188. For inscriptions that combine the names, see *MAMA* 4.269, 270, 275A, 275B, roughly the same time as the coins. These form the basis for Ulrich Huttner's accent on a Heliotic Apollo: *Early Christianity in the Lycus Valley*, trans. David Green, AJEC 85; Early Christianity in Asia Minor 1 (Leiden: Brill, 2013), 48–49. But it should be noted that the ascription of Helios is not present in all dedications to Apollo Lairbenos. Inscriptions dated earlier and contemporary appear to be lacking this epithet: see *MAMA* 4.277A (I) with commentary (p. 102), 282; M. Ricl,

as Helios. The off-centered strike of the fine examples of the coin do not allow an assessment of whether there were trailing locks. One very worn example does not appear to have this feature,[30] so it would suggest that a control symbol on Seleucid mints has grown in importance.

The debate over the Seleucid obverses is whether the radiate crown indicates a Heliotic or even an oriental association rather than an Apollo connection.[31] The option may be of minimal importance for Colossae itself; the city doubtless invested something of its own cultural commitments into the choice. But more significant than an early inventory of Colossian gods is the self-positioning of Colossae that these coins indicate. Given the Seleucid establishment of Laodicea and Hierapolis as preferred cities,[32] Colossae's *polis*-pride, probably at least in relation to its neighbors, asserted itself through a display of distinctive iconography. It needs to be borne in mind that the Hellenistic coins of Colossae thus far known portray the very gods claimed as the patrons of Laodicea and Hierapolis (respectively, Zeus and Apollo), *but the attributes and/or style of presentation differ markedly*. Moreover, Houghton and Lorber consider that Laodicea at the end of the third century BCE began to have some involvement in royal coin production.[33] This continued under the Attalids. Colossae's choice of symbols and attributes for its Hellenistic coinage appears to eschew that which emanated from the Laodicean mint. Perhaps, by stylistic affinities with early Seleucid iconography, Colossae may have subtly paraded its far greater antiquity.

A similar pattern of negotiation of the larger imperial realities impacting a local context can be discerned in the revival of the Colossian mint at the beginning of the reign of Hadrian.[34] For whatever reason Colossae's

---

"Les ΚΑΤΑΓΡΑΦΑΙ du sanctuaire d'Apollon Lairbenos," *Arkeoloji Dergisi* 3 (1995): 179 §30.

30. See https://tinyurl.com/SBL4218a4.

31. Wright, "Seleucid Royal Cult," 72, 77–82.

32. Hierapolis in early scholarship was thought to have been an Attalid flowering. However, the tribal names in the city, such as Seleukis, Antiochis, and Laodikis, clearly indicate a Seleucid foundation, even if Laodicea remained the leading city into the early Roman imperial period; see F. Kolb, "Zur Geschichte der Stadt Hierapolis in Phrygien: Die Phyleninschriften im Theater," *ZPE* 15 (1974): 269–70.

33. Houghton and Lorber, *Seleucid Coins*, 1.900–903 (Antiochus Hierax; Apollo on omphalos with bow); 989–998 (Antiochus III; Apollo on omphalos with arrow and bow).

34. See my "Wealthy, Widowed, Astute and Beneficent: Claudia Eugenetoriane and the Second Century Revival of the Colossian Mint," *NewDocs* 12 (forthcoming).

Fig. 4.3. Small civic coin minted under the auspices of Claudia Eugenetoriane, probably in 117/118 CE. From a private collection, used by permission.

mint had fallen into abeyance.[35] In a rare occurrence, a woman took responsibility for reinvigorating the mint.[36] Claudia Eugenetoriane timed her munificence to perfection, launching the coinage with a type that acknowledged Hadrian as Caesar, exactly what was contested immediately after the death of Trajan (117 CE).[37] A second coin-type has recently surfaced with two examples.[38] It also carries her name, though without an imperial

---

35. One suggestion is that it was the result of a Roman restriction imposed on Colossae at the end of the First Mithradatic War for its (forced?) compliance with Mithradates VI's seige of Laodicea in 89 BCE in the rebel's hunt for the Roman general Oppius. Laodicea had sycophanted its way back into Roman favor (*CIL* 1.2 728) and within a short time had restored prolific production of bronze coinage; see Ann Johnston, "Greek Imperial Statistics: A Commentary," *Révue numismatique* 26 (1984): 240–57. Under Hadrian, it even regained its early second-century (BCE) authority, for a brief period, to mint imperial cistaphoric coins; see William E. Metcalfe, *The Cistophori of Hadrian* (New York: American Numismatic Society, 1980), 64–71. Interestingly, the mint of Hierapolis does not appear to have been affected.

36. The coin credited to Caligula by von Aulock (*Münzen und Städte Phrygiens* 2.545) has been removed from consideration because it is a forgery: *RPC Supp.* 1 35.2891. Among the forty or so Colossian coins that have surfaced since von Aulock's catalogue was published, none have predated the time of Hadrian's reign. Laodicea also provides examples of women underwriting coin production: *RPC* 1.2924, 2925; 2.1273, 1275, 1277, 1279. A similar rarity is attested in the West as well: Peter Weiss, "The Cities and Their Money," in *Coinage and Identity in the Roman Provinces*, ed. Christopher Howgego, Volker Heuchert, and Andrew Burnett (Oxford: Oxford University Press, 2007), 63, 67.

37. Von Aulock, *Münzen und Städte Phrygiens*, 2.548. On the disputed credentials of Hadrian to succeed Trajan, see Hildegard Temporini, *Die Frauen am Hofe Trajans: Ein Beitrag zur Stellung der Augustae im Principat* (Berlin: de Gruyter, 1979), 123–24.

38. See https://tinyurl.com/SBL4218a2; and https://tinyurl.com/SBL4218a3.

obverse; it is a familiar-styled civic coin, but striking because of the unique designation in the reverse legend carrying her name. She is now "Claudia Eugenetoriane, widow" (ΚΛ•ΕΥΓΕΝΕΤΟΡΙΑΝΗ•ΧΗΡΗ).

A number of features point to a careful negotiation of Roman realities:

1. Even though the language of the legend is Greek, there are interpuncts on the reverse legend between the words on both coins, a feature of Roman inscriptions that had begun to interrupt Greek *scriptio continua* even in Athens.[39] It recurs on some later Colossian coins.[40]
2. The legend of the coin bearing Hadrian's portrait even adopts the Latin dative of dedication—ΚΛ•ΕΥΓΕΝΕΤΟΡΙΑΝΗ•ΚΟΛΟCCΗΝΟΙC—rather than the usual genitive, ΚΟΛΟC-CHNΩN, again a feature of Roman epigraphy, though also known occasionally on other coins accenting the euergetism.[41]
3. The woman is concerned to promenade her Roman citizenship on both coins. Later munificent underwriters of Colossian coinage were occasional in this display, including two who maybe her descendants in a family-dynastic, albeit partial, provision of coins for Colossae: (Tiberius) Claudius Sacerdos and, later, Claudius Priscus.[42] The adjustment in cognomens is significant—from the

---

39. Thomas N. Habinek, *The Colometry of Latin Prose* (Berkeley: University of California, 1985), 43; Leslie Threatte, *The Grammar of Attic Inscriptions* (Berlin: de Gruyter, 1980), 82. Of remaining interest is the use of the Ionic form, χήρη.

40. Von Aulock, *Münzen und Städte Phrygiens*, 2.518–519.

41. Kearsley, *Greeks and Romans in Imperial Asia*, 152–53. The dative occurs again on Colossian coinage under the reign of Antoninus Pius: von Aulock, *Münzen und Städte Phrygiens*, 2.455–457 and *RPC* 4.10833 (≠ *MSP*). The dative is common in Greek inscriptions when honors for the imperial family are in view, as at Colossae (*IGRR* 4.468, 469). See generally, Simon R. F. Price, "Gods and Emperors: The Greek Language of the Imperial Cult," *JHS* 104 (1984): 79–95. See, on the example of the provision at Smyrna by the famous rhetorician Polemo, Dietrich O. A. Klose, *Die Münzprägung von Smyrna in der römischen Kaiserzeit* (Berlin: de Gruyter, 1987), 68–69, 248–49, 250–54.

42. Von Aulock, *Münzen und Städte Phrygiens*, 2.471–482, 559–653. On family dynasties exercising significant input into a city's coin production, see Peter Weiß, "Euergesie oder römische Pragegenehmigung? Aitesamenou-Formular auf Städtmünzen der Provinz Asia, Roman Provincial Coinage (*RPC*) II und persönliche Aufwendungen im Münzwesen," *Chiron* 30 (2000): 237–38, 250–51.

Greek Eugenetoriane to the transliterated conversion of an office, Sacerdos, to the Latin name Priscus.
4. The symbolism is extremely carefully chosen. Athena is particularly apt for Hadrian, given his Attic service, credentials and display.[43] The choice of Demeter on the second coin, especially in combination with the self-designation "widow," is deliberate mimesis of the imperial widows, Marciana and Plotina, respectively sister and wife of Trajan, both supporters of Hadrian.[44] The combination of legend and iconography makes for a quite different communication than the later striking of Demeter by male magistrates.[45]

Eugenetoriane has exuded exemplary wisdom in her negotiation of Roman imperial realities and turned these realities to serve Colossae's interests, at least according to the lights of a wealthy, widowed leader in society at Colossae.

This lengthy, mainly numismatic example of the reality of Colossae's place in larger geopolitical movements has served as a warrant for the use of the comparative method in interpreting the city's life. Regardless of the surveys and excavations that one hopes will attend the site in the future, the necessity of the method is clear. In bringing the comparative method to bear in the course of this demonstration, the impact of political realities on coin production at Colossae has been demonstrated as well as the hints of Colossian self-definition in its chosen (and modified) iconography, opening up far more interpretative possibilities than a simple identification of deities as a register of cultic activity at Colossae. The connections of Colossae that strengthen the case for reference to a

---

43. Compare P. Karanastasi, "Hadrian im Panzer: Kaiserstatuen zwischen Realpolitik und Philhellenismus," *Jahrbuch des Deutschen Archäologischen Instituts* 127–128 (2012–2013): 323–91.

44. See *RIC* 2.750. The city layout of Antinoopolis contained the district of Matidia among the ten phylai. Matidia was the name of Trajan's niece. Of particular interest are the names of the five demoi within the designation: Demetrieus, Thesmophorios—both recalling the keys of the Eleusinian mysteries—then Kalliteknios and then Markianios and Plotinios, recalling the deified widows. The association is clear: see Anthony R. Birley, *Hadrian: The Restless Emperor* (London: Routledge, 1997), 254–55. He interprets *kalliteknios* as a reference to Sabina; it is worth noting however that there was a cult of *Kalliteknia* for the deified Julia (*SEG* 43.711; *AÉ* 1993.1521).

45. Von Aulock, *Münzen und Städte Phrygiens*, 2.447 = *RPC* 3.2316.

wider frame for interpretation, could be expanded beyond the limits of this chapter.[46]

But, even as wider parallels have brought assistance, so also some distinctive elements of Colossae's life have surfaced, not least the question of a distanced relationship between Colossae and its immediate Lycus Valley neighbors, Laodicea and Hierapolis. The two examples that follow address this question and are designed to demonstrate, firstly, that the comparative method, especially in the context of the hold of empire upon the mind of the Lycus Valley, can generate new insights; and secondly, that the comparative method must be sensitive to the particular distinctives that any one site may suggest. For the first, I will explore the critical impact of the immediate post-Julian years for interpreting one of Colossae's key surviving texts, The Miracle of the Archangel Michael at Chonai, in the light of the antagonism expressed in the text towards Laodicea. For the second, I will return to the thorny problem of the nature, extent and location of Jewish settlement in Phrygia and argue that the evidence for a *significant* Jewish population at Colossae is lacking.

The Miracle of Michael

A crucial but too-often forgotten informant of history and archaeology is the geographical setting that embeds text and artefact alike. As Kevin Walsh accents, "We need to consider why people chose to settle and establish settlements in particular topographic situations."[47] The story of Michael of Chonai is replete with references to a multitude of geographical features that are given religious, narratival even onomastic significance (the monolith, the chasm, rock formations, the rivers and most of all, the spring). These became key visual markers for pilgrims to Chonai, of old called Colossae, in later Byzantine times both guiding the journey and confirming the story (Constantine Porphyrogenitus, *Them.* 1.3).[48] They were also imbued with

---

46. See my *Fragments of Colossae: Sifting through the Traces*, 2nd rev and exp. ed. (Hindmarsh: ATF Press, forthcoming), ch. 10.

47. Kevin Walsh, *The Archaeology of Mediterranean Landscapes: Human-Environment Interaction from the Neolithic to the Roman Period* (Cambridge: Cambridge University Press, 2014), 5.

48. The issue of the relationship between Colossae and Chonai cannot be explored here. See, briefly, my "Refuting an Axiom of Scholarship on Colossae: Fresh Insights from New and Old Inscriptions," in *Colossae in Space and Time: Linking to an*

unfolding theological significance, especially in the iconoclast crises of the eighth and ninth centuries, just as they factored prominently in what was probably a pagan story of an epiphany of rescue.[49] Accordingly, distances, whether by crow-flight or by negotiating Roman roads and local tracks, only give a snatch of the story. The features of an area shape consciousness and carve associations by which a city, its people and surrounds become known: mountains, springs, rivers, caves along with peculiar formations such as monoliths and travertine mouldings. Roman land surveys tended to use natural features to form their judgments.[50]

The influence of local conditions was held, for example, to lie behind the area's famous textile manufacture, even though Laodicea as the prime center in the Lycus had begun to stamp its name on the regional production as a whole, not merely to its own city's output.[51] The recognition that the heavily urbanized areas often made recourse to rural religious centers, as at the site of the sanctuary of Apollo Lairbenos, and harnessed indigenous expressions that were linked to landscape,[52] shows how important

---

Ancient City, ed. Alan H. Cadwallader and Michael Trainor (Göttingen: Vandenhoeck & Ruprecht, 2011), 160–61. See also Glenn Peers, *Subtle Bodies: Representing Angels in Byzantium* (Berkeley: University of California Press, 2001), 151.

49. See Alan H. Cadwallader, "The Inversion of Slavery: The Ascetic and the Archistrategos at Chonai," in *Prayer and Spirituality in the Early Church V: Poverty and Riches*, ed. Geoffrey D. Dunn, David Luckensmeyer, and Lawrence Cross (Strathfield, NSW: Saint Pauls Publications; Virginia, Qld: Centre for Early Christian Studies, 2009), 215–36; Cadwallader, "Epiphanies and Religious Conflict: The Contests over the Hagiasma of Chonai," in *Reconceiving Religious Conflict: New Views from the Formative Centuries of Christianity*, ed. Chris de Wet and Wendy Mayer (London: Routledge, 2017), 110–35.

50. See, for example, *SEG* 24.1109. This was recognized among the jurists on disputes over land: see J. B. Campbell, *The Writings of the Roman Land Surveyors* (London: Society for the Promotion of Roman Studies, 2000), 61.

51. See especially Huttner, *Early Christianity in the Lycus Valley*, 20–22, 166–70; see also his "Die Färber von Laodikeia und Hierapolis: Eine Nachricht aus dem Corpus der Alchemisten," *MBAH* 26 (2009): 139–57; Peter Thonemann, *The Maeander Valley: A Historical Geography from Antiquity to Byzantium* (Cambridge: Cambridge University Press, 2011), 187–8; see generally Rosemary Canavan, "Weaving Threads: Clothing in Colossae," in Cadwallader, *Fragments of Colossae*, 111–33.

52. Tullia Ritti, Celal Şimşek, and H. Yıldız, "Dediche e καταγραφαί dal santuario frigio di Apollo Lairbenos," *EA* 32 (2000): 3. Note the express connection between Hierapolis and the sanctuary in *MAMA* 4.276A (I) (dedication of Apollonios the Hierapolitan), 276A (III) (dedication of Aphphia the Hierapolitan), 276B (dedication of Dion the Motellan; Motella a town under Hierapolis's orbit); see also 277A

topography can be in the formation of identity and behaviors. The gods frequented the high places especially, even though known in the depths and the waters, and recourse to them—a "going up" (ἀναβαίνω) from city or village as expressed in some devotions to Apollo Lairbenos—appears to have been invaluable for status, confession, manumission and the like.[53]

Of course, difficulties attend the handling of the materials, especially textual materials that have survived. References to topography in hagiographies, foundation stories, or epiphanies may be useful for locating the sites that such stories were intended to support. The issue comes when one attempts to derive historical information from these stories. Occasionally one sees a privileging of, for example, the Acts of the Apostles over such hagiographies, which, while justified to some extent, can cultivate a default surface acceptance of the canonical book.[54] The loose appreciation of the difference between rhetoric and history, say in Luke's hyperbolic sweeps referencing Phrygia (Acts 2:10, 16:6 with its dissonance between Asia and Phrygia, 18:23), forges greater historical weight for Paul's missionary activity into a back-reading of Colossians.[55] "Paul's defining role for early Christianity in Asia Minor is undisputed"[56] may be true as a general observation, but the application of this affirmation to the Lycus

---

(II) (dedication of Charixenos the Dionysopolitan), 281 (dedication of Apellas from Blaundos, about 50 kilometres north of Hierapolis). One inscription also provides a connection with Laodicea (and Erriza): Ritti, Şimşek, and Yıldız, "Dediche," 34 §K44.

53. See, for example, Georg Petzl, *Die Beichtinschriften Westkleinasiens* (Bonn: Habelt, 1994), 128–30 §110; *MAMA* 4.279, 283, 289.

54. As, for example, the acceptance of three missionary journeys: Huttner, *Early Christianity in the Lycus Valley*, 82–83. Paul's own recall of multiple shipwrecks (2 Cor 11:25) compared to only one in Acts (27:39–44) urges caution. Compare also Huttner, *Early Christianity in the Lycus Valley*, 99 who takes the designation of Paul as a πρεσβύτης in Phlm 9 as an indication of age rather than as part of Paul's rhetorical self-positioning in relation to Philemon. See Ronald F. Hock, "A Support for His Old Age: Paul's Plea on Behalf of Onesimus," in *The Social World of the First Christians*, ed. L. Michael White and O. Larry Yarbrough (Minneapolis: Fortress, 1995), 67–81. On the importance of the elder in social relations, see the character of the father in Plutarch's *Table Talk* (*Quaest. conv.* 1.2.2 [615f–616b]). Note also that a senator from Xanthus is designated, *inter alia*, as a πρεσβύτης Ἀσίας an honorific title designating a legate or envoy with no necessary correlation with age: Michel Christol and Thomas Drew-Bear, "Un sénateur de Xanthos," *Journal des savants* 3 (1991): 197, 203–6; see also *IGRR* 3.174, 175.

55. Huttner, *Early Christianity in the Lycus Valley*, 123.

56. Huttner, *Early Christianity in the Lycus Valley*, 82; see also Paul Trebilco, *The*

Valley may be an example of the compression occasionally charged against comparative history and archaeology. It certainly does not cohere with the interpretation of those scholars who accept the pseudonymity of Colossians. Thus, in my view, it is unconvincing to combine Acts 18:23 with Col 2:1 to produce a meaning that Paul did not meet all Christians in the Lycus Valley, having skipped Hierapolis in the course of a Lycus Valley visit.[57]

The problem here is that in the aftermath of the Pauline mission, the memory of Paul did not credit him with a defining role, at least for the Lycus Valley.[58] The Acts of John, Acts of Philip, Michael of Chonai, and an array of martyrologies are notably scant in mentions of Paul's impact; they rather esteem other apostles with a decisive shaping on the Lycus Valley. The cultivated Christian memory did not reiterate Lukan remembrance, nor indeed much of Colossians and Philemon. Rather, John is the key apostle along with Philip, even though both John and Philip are figures coalesced in amalgams of the evangelist and the author of Revelation, on the one hand, and the gospel apostle and the Acts evangelist/deacon/father of prophets on the other.[59] Ulrich Huttner certainly tracks the formation of these apostolic figures in the Lycus Valley texts. But the implication of this for the legacy of Paul is left muted.[60]

Paul is briefly revived in the martyr stories of Philemon, Archippus, and Apphia in the Synaxarion of Constantinople, sometimes known as the Menologion of Basil, but that is eleventh century and hardly reliable for historical reconstruction.[61] Its patchwork précis seems to owe some

---

Early Christians in Ephesus from Paul to Ignatius, WUNT 166 (Tübingen: Mohr Siebeck, 2004), 145–46.

57. Huttner, *Early Christianity in the Lycus Valley*, 123. The argument of Paul's familiarity with the Christian communities in the Lycus Valley on the basis of names shared in Colossians and Philemon (Huttner, *Early Christianity in the Lycus Valley*, 83) is not sufficient to substantiate a visit—Rom 16 shows the distinction between knowing people and having been "on the ground."

58. The assessment of Pauline influence in the Lycus Valley clearly depends on the time-frame one adopts; see Paul Trebilco, "Christians in the Lycus Valley: The View from Ephesus and from Western Asia Minor," in Cadwallader and Trainor, *Colossae in Space and Time*, 196–97.

59. Huttner, *Early Christianity in the Lycus Valley*, 185–90 (John), 190–95 (Philip).

60. Compare Trebilco "Christians in the Lycus Valley" (193–208) who seeks to establish for the apostolic and subapostolic period a compatibility/complementarity even if separateness in Pauline and Johannine influence.

61. The Menologion of Basil II as it is commonly (though incorrectly) called

material to the opening chapter of the Michael of Chonai narrative, which privileges John and Philip, and a little to the pagan foundation story for the city of Ephesos in the naming of the governor as Androcles, a quite typical mid-Byzantine conceit of compacting multiple Christian and pagan allusions.[62] But overall, the Pauline tradition in the Lycus Valley, outside of canonical and subapostolic transmission of epistolary texts, is somewhat like the figure of Paul in the Acts of Thecla—known more by his absence than his presence! Paul Veyne's caution is pertinent here: "by no means what the historians call event is seized directly and entirely; it is always completely and laterally ... should we say, through the *tekmeria*,

---

is usually dated to the eleventh century, though clearly drawing on prior traditions. See Nancy Patterson Ševčenko, "The Walters 'Imperial' Menologion," *Journal of the Walters Art Gallery* 51 (1993): 43–64; F. D'Aiuto, *El "Menologio de Basilo II": Città de estudios con occasion de la edición facsímil* (Vatican: Biblioteca Apostolica Vaticana; Athens: Diaconía Apostólica de la Iglesia de Grecia; Madrid: Testimonio Compania Editorial, 2008), 6. It should be noted that this synaxarion does not represent an already-established stable tradition of the November martyrs. The tenth–eleventh century Codex Leimonos 48 (a menologion), for example, does not include the lives of Philemon, Apphia, and Archippos in its collection; see Athanasios Papadopoulos-Kerameus, Μαυρογορδάτειος Βιβλιοθήκη [The Mavrogordati Collection], 2 vols., (Constantinople: Boutura, 1884), 1:57–58. It is also omitted in the BL Add MS 24372 and elsewhere. Other manuscripts include the martyrology on different days, for example, November 22 in BL Add MS 11870, fol 325v; elsewhere the feast-day is February 21; see Basilius Latyšev, *Menologii anonymi byzantine saeculi X quae super sunt* (Petropoli: 1911). There was a late Byzantine church of Philemon, Archippos, and Onesimos in Constantinople, notably substituting Onesimos for Apphia; see N. A. Beê, Τα χειρόγραφα των Μετεώρων: Κατάλογος περιγραφικός των χειρογράφων κωδίκων των αποκειμένων εἰς τὰς Μονάς των Μετεώρων [Meteōrōn manuscripts: A descriptive list of manuscript codices belonging to the Meteōrōn Monastery], 4 vols. (Athens: Akadēmia Athēnōn, 1967–1993), 3:771. But, despite Theodoret of Cyrrhus referring to a pilgrim site of Philemon's house (*Interpretatio Epistolae ad Philemonem* [PG 82.871–72A]), no church under such patronage is recorded: see my "The Reverend Doctor John Luke and the Churches of Chonai," *GBRS* 48.3 (2008): 319–38.

62. So, for example, the reference to Greeks, idolaters, Artemis, an attack, and an overpowering. These are stock features in hagiographies. The use of the term σιτοφύλαξ as Androcles's office may be a deliberate reminisce of Strabo's association of Androcles's descendants with control of the sacrifices for Demeter (Strabo, *Geogr.* 14.1.3). The specific term σιτοφύλαξ is not found in any surviving materials from Ephesos; however, the renowned Salutaris is known, among many offices, for being an ἀρχώνης σίτου (IEph 36D). On the importance of the name of Androcles in connection with Ephesos well into the Common Era, see Pausanias, *Descr.* 7.2.8–9, Ephorus *apud* Stephanus, *Ethn.* 2.68; Suda, s.v. "Ἰωνία" (1.494).

the vestiges."[63] Acts, in this sense, is itself a vestige for us, as well as displaying its own perspective on retrieved vestiges, and needs to be handled as such. Its difference from later Lives and Acts, outside of its canonical status, is one of degree rather than kind.

The question of how such stories might yield up their historical value is well illustrated by Johan Leemans's close analysis of Gregory of Nyssa's 380 CE encomium on Holy Theodore the Recruit.[64] At the surface level, the setting is the reign of the Emperor Galerius (305–311), during which time Theodore is alleged to have been martyred (Gregory of Nyssa, *De sancto Theodoro* [PG 46.741B]).[65] But Leemans shows that this earliest panegyric of Theodore is an opportunity for Gregory to mount a scathing critique of the period of Julian the Apostate (361–363). Even though that emperor is never explicitly named, the allusions are patent.[66] The history to be derived from this constructed memory therefore hangs below the surface level.[67] It speaks of the struggles of the church to reform its identity in the aftermath of the catastrophes and collusions of the Julian period,

---

63. Paul Veyne, *Comment on écrit l'histoire: Essai d'épistémologie* (Paris: Seuil, 1987), 14.

64. Johan Leemans, "Gregory of Nyssa: A Homily on Theodore the Recruit," in *'Let Us Die That We May Live': Greek Homilies on Christian Martyrs from Asia Minor, Palestine and Syria (c. AD 350–AD 450)*, ed. Johan Leemans et al. (London: Routledge, 2003), 82–90; see also his "A Preacher-Audience Oriented Analysis of Gregory of Nyssa's Homily on Theodore the Recruit," *StPatr* 37 (2001): 140–46.

65. The emperor is known here under the name Maximian.

66. Leemans, "Gregory of Nyssa," 83. It is worth noting that there is a specific reference not only to the mother of the gods (*De sancto Theodoro* [PG 46.741D], i.e., Cybele), one of the focal devotions of Julian, but also a reference to her temple at Amasea (PG 46.744A) and special attention to the pagan (high) priesthood ([PG 46.744D–745A])—all concerns of Julian: see *Or.* 3; *Or.* 5; *Fragmentum epistolae*. Moreover, Theodore is related as impugning emperors (plural), especially those assuming the title of high priest and becoming "cooks" aka "butchers" (*De sancto Theodoro* [PG 46.745A])—a clear indication of Julian's revival of and personal involvement in sacrifices, even though the plural could be taken as a reference to the rule of the three: Constantius I, Diocletian, and Maximian (209–305 CE). More direct homiletic criticisms did come, *inter alia*, from Asterius of Amasea, from a city renowned for its cult of the Great Mother: see Asterius of Amasea, *Hom.* 3, 4, and 10; and see Johan Leemans, "Christian Diversity in Amaseia: A Bishop's View," *Adamantius* 13 (2007): 247–57.

67. Christopher Walter simply observes that the period between a saint's martyrdom and the textual remembrance in a life or homily reduces the reliability of the text, for the martyr and her/his martyrdom—but this is not the only historical value in

particularly through a redirection of church building (with an accent on martyrions), the lavish painting designed to instruct the faithful, the ritual reiteration of the faith and its exemplars,[68] and, what Gregory does not mention, the weeding out of apostates (Asterius, *Hom.* 4.9).

This has particular relevance for the popular version of the story of Michael of Chonai. The narrative lampoons Laodicea as "the city of the lawless mob"[69] in a deliberate distortion of the etymology of its name. Laodicea becomes a staging point for idolatrous villains bent on the destruction of the Michael healing spring, its hagiasma and custodian.[70] The story's own chronological indicators, admittedly imprecise, point to the third century or fourth century.[71] The portrayal of Laodicea is quite tendentious. The city is unremittingly pagan; even the father of the healed daughter is introduced as living in Laodicea as a "godless idolater" (ἀσεβὴς καὶ εἰδωλοθύτης) who, himself, is violently opposed to the healing spring as a Christian center.[72] This Colossian/Chonian story completely ignores Laodicea's history—

---

such accounts. Christopher Walter, *The Warrior Saints in Byzantine Art and Tradition* (Aldershot: Ashgate, 2003), 292.

68. See Vasiliki M. Limberis, *Architects of Piety: The Cappadocian Fathers and the Cult of Martyrs* (Oxford: Oxford University Press, 2011), 55–62.

69. Michael of Chonai 7.4 (Bonnet 11.10). In the references to the Story of St Michael of Chonai, the first reference is to the chapter and section breakdown of my English translation in "The Story of the Archistrategos, St Michael of Chonai," in Cadwallader and Trainor, *Colossae in Space and Time*, 323–30. The second reference is to the Greek edition of Max Bonnet, *Narratio de Miraculo a Michaele Archangelo Chonis Patrato* (Paris: Librairie Hachette, 1890), by page and line number.

70. Michael of Chonai 3.6 (Bonnet 5.3–5); Michael of Chonai 5.2–4 (Bonnet 8.13–9.11); Michael of Chonai 7.3–4 (Bonnet 11.5–12.4); Michael of Chonai 8.2–3 (Bonnet 12.8–13.2); Michael of Chonai 10.1–3 (Bonnet 13.16–14.7).

71. The apostolic period (Michael of Chonai 1–2 [Bonnet 1.5–3.7]); a period of "many years" after that (Michael of Chonai 3.1 [Bonnet 3.8–10]), the global fame of the spring (Michael of Chonai 3.1 [Bonnet 3.11–12]); then the coming of a Laodicean pagan for his daughter's healing following a vision (Michael of Chonai 3.2–4 [Bonnet 3.14–5.3]); the building of a εὐκτήριον in honor of Saint Michael following the healing (Michael of Chonai 3.5 [Bonnet 4.17]); the coming of the first custodian, Archippos, some ninety years after that (Michael of Chonai 4.1 [Bonnet 5.6]), for a period of seventy years (Michael of Chonai 4.2 [Bonnet 5.10]). If one takes the end of the apostolic period as about 100 CE and "many years" as a half-century, we arrive at the second half of the third century into the first half of the fourth. Of course, in such stories, time allocations are notoriously loose.

72. Michael of Chonai 3.2 (Bonnet 3.15, 17–19). This is overlooked by Huttner (*Early Christianity in Lycus Valley*, 374). It should also be noted that the baptized

Laodicea is neither Johannine (as from Revelation and the Acts of John) nor Pauline (as from Col 4:13–16); rather it is heathen. The story arrogates John to itself and to Hierapolis and completely ignores any Pauline reference or, as far as I can tell, any allusion to a Pauline text.[73] Any stories of Christian presence in that city that clearly fall within the time-frame envisaged by the Michael narrative simply do not appear: not the Acts of John, not the martyrdom of Bishop Sagaris or Artemon[74] and, significantly, not the Pauline witness. By contrast, Hierapolis is noteworthy for its Christian presence, not only harnessing the legends of Philip and even a visitation from the apostle John to its credentials but also providing from its numbers, the foundational custodian, Archippos, for the hagiasma near Colossae.[75] Clearly, this is a distortion of the historical record; consequently, a surface reading of the text cannot be allowed. But it does raise the historical question of the rationale behind such a blatant misrepresentation.

The clue is to be found in elements that remain a constant in the relations between Greek *poleis* in Roman times.[76] Huttner, rightly in my view, understands that part of the dynamic behind the hagiographies of the Acts of John and the Acts of Philip is a tense competition between Laodicea and Hierapolis for preeminence and accord.[77] But this tension is not confined to ecclesiastical jockeying for position. It is evident also in relationships between the two cities under Rome (such as the claim on the title "metropolis," the maneuvering for the award of "neokoros"), no doubt exacerbated by the Roman tendency to collate the two cities.[78]

---

father and healed daughter are never said to return to Laodicea. They simply depart, glorifying God: Michael of Chonai 3.5 (Bonnet 5.2–3).

73. By contrast, the description of the devil as ἀνθρωποκτόνος seems to be an allusion to John 8:44 (Michael of Chonai 8.2 [Bonnet 12.13]). There are multiple Old Testament allusions and a lengthy quotation from Ps 92/93: 2–5 (Michael of Chonai 11.1 [Bonnet 14.11–15]). In illuminated Psalters, the story of Saint Michael of Chonai came to be used as the illustration for this psalm. See BL Add Ms 19.352, fol 125r.

74. See Huttner, *Early Christianity in the Lycus Valley*, 250–51, 334–35.

75. Significantly, Archippos, even though ten years old when he becomes the προσμονάριος of the εὐκτήριον is noted as sprung from Christian parentage—from Hierapolis (Michael of Chonai 4.1 [Bonnet 5.6–9]). One can perhaps hear echoes of the *katagraphai* inscriptions at Apollo Lairbenos here, some of which explicitly name parents dedicating their child as from Hierapolis (e.g., *MAMA* 4.276A [III]).

76. See generally, Heller, *"Les bêtises des Grecs."*

77. Huttner, *Early Christianity in the Lycus Valley*, 25, 189, 265, 365.

78. Huttner, *Early Christianity in the Lycus Valley*, 278–79. As in a certain sena-

Hagiography is but an example in a more long-standing strain in the relation between the two cities.

This is where the application of the comparative method must be mindful of the impact of imperial policies on the relations between neighbors in a confined region. This means more than the intense activity engendering civic projects that preface the visits of dignitaries—Hadrian's pan-hellenic tour, for example, clearly fostered mintings, inscriptions and building in the main cities of the Lycus in preparation for the 129 visit, including at Colossae.[79] Rather, it pertains to the constant attentiveness to imperial shifts that local authorities trained themselves to refine for direct dealings with the central authorities; more importantly, these factors fired these authorities in how to position themselves in relation to central government by asserting themselves over neighbors who were likewise attentive to the same realities.[80]

The key to Michael of Chonai, in my view, is the aftermath of the Julian years, where already-existing tensions became inflamed as cities sought to establish their credentials positively in relation to imperial and, in this case, ecclesiastical centers. In fact, it appears to have been a policy of Julian to cultivate ecclesial conflict.[81] It is no coincidence that the story appears to side with Hierapolis over Laodicea, the one cleansed and Christian, the other under the stranglehold of the devil; here a tacit alliance is signaled. The incendiary action and reaction can be sheeted home, I would suggest, to the Synod of Laodicea. It is a general observation that those dioceses subjected to criticism at synods rarely are found in attendance, so it is unlikely that Colossae and probably Hierapolis were among the small number gathered.[82] What is not noted in regard to this

---

tor, honored by a monument at Xanthos. Among other honors, he is designated an οἰκιστὴς Λα[ο]δικέων καὶ Ἱεραπολειτῶν; see Christol and Drew-Bear, "Un sénateur de Xanthos," 197 at lines B.3–4 of the inscription.

79. See *IGRR* 4.869; von Aulock, *Münzen und Städte Phrygiens*, 2.547.

80. See Alan H. Cadwallader, "Inter-City Conflict in the Story of St Michael of Chonai," in *Religious Conflict from Early Christianity to the Rise of Islam*, ed. Wendy Mayer and Bronwen Neil (Berlin: de Gruyter, 2013), 109–27.

81. "No wild beasts are so hostile to men as are Christian sects in general to one another" was Ammianus Marcellinus distillation of Julian's approach: Res gest. divi Aug. 22.5.4, translation from John J. Norwich, *Byzantium: The Early Centuries* (London: Penguin, 1990), 92.

82. See Huttner, *Early Christianity in the Lycus Valley*, 291–92 for one attempt to calculate the number of attendees. The total is disputed.

council is that Constantinople at this time (ca. 365 though Huttner places it later, at 380 CE)[83] is still under Arian-derivative control and would remain so until 380 with the death of Bishop Demophilos. Even though the Synod of Laodicea is replete with denunciations of heresies,[84] there is no mention of Arianism or its successor variants nor is there the avowal of Nicene orthodoxy so familiar from the opening of other synod texts.[85] The Council of Nicea had prescribed two provincial Synod meetings each year (Canon 5), and this had been reiterated at the Council of Antioch in 338 (Canon 20), but Laodicea omits any reference to this authority for its gathering.[86] The mention of Photinian heretics in Canon 7 makes

---

83. In the face of other evidence, the use of the reference to an ambo (Canon 15) to help the dating of the Synod (Huttner, *Early Christianity in the Lycus Valley*, 296) is too fragile to sustain the weight put upon it. The word was already being extended in the first century BCE to refer to a construction of steps leading to a height (Apollonios Citiensis, *Hipp.* 1.7)—its movement into a church setting is probably a natural development, with the Synod canon noting a preexistent reality (especially in a city with already established substantial church buildings). What is clear is that the church defined in terms of building is set off against the place to which those who worship angels retire, according to Canon 35: ἐγκαταλείπειν τὴν ἐκκλησίαν καὶ ἀπιέναι καὶ ἀγγέλους ὀνομάζειν καὶ συνάξεις ποιεῖν.

84. Synod of Laodicea 7–8, 11, 32–34. The council is called the Synod "against Montanus and other heresies" in a mosaic in a twelfth-century church at Bethlehem (*CIG* 8953). Only Canon 8 actually refers to "the heresy of the so-called Phrygians" but see Canon 11 and the reference to female leadership that Stephen Mitchell takes as a mark of Christian Phrygia rather than Montanism *per se*: S. Mitchell, "An Epigraphic Probe into the Origins of Montanism," in *Roman Phrygia: Culture and Society*, ed. Peter Thonemann (Cambridge: Cambridge University Press, 2013), 196–97; see also Huttner, *Early Christianity in the Lycus Valley*, 311–12. William Tabbernee overrates the number of canons (59 or 60) as indicating the importance of the Synod of Laodicea: *Fake Prophecy and Polluted Sacraments: Ecclesiastical and Imperial Reactions to Montanism* (Leiden: Brill, 2007), 301–2.

85. For example, the denunciation of the Photinians at the Council of Constantinople in 381 (§1) was on the basis of a lack of conformity with Nicea; this was *not* the basis of the Laodicean canon (§7) where the Photinians are simply numbered with the Novations and the Quartodecimans (now deemed a heresy) on the issue of reception of heretics.

86. Huttner, *Early Christianity in the Lycus Valley*, 291 is slightly misleading in implying that Laodicea was specifically mentioned by the Nicean canon, rather than provinces in general. It should be noted, on the one hand, that Canon 5 was by a lack of observance and, on the other, canon lists credited to one Synod are often a compilation of a succession of recommendations/decisions of smaller gatherings.

no reference to the Nicean settlement and advises reception without rebaptism,[87] even though it was precisely the Trinitarian formula that was at issue elsewhere. Significantly, the absence of the Laodicean metropolitan from the Council of Constantinople in 381 is usually explained on the basis that Laodicea was still unready to relinquish an Arian remnant in its theology.[88] It is only the after-reach of the orthodox church that has made Laodicea Nicean. There is no question, however, that the Laodicean synod, if it can be characterized under a single summation, is concerned to assert control and direction under a central authority.[89] The very form under which the Synod canons survive carries the atmosphere of legislative rescript.[90]

The story of Michael of Chonai by contrast emphasizes the Trinitarian formula, especially in the context of baptism.[91] Moreover, in designating Laodicea as idolatrous and the forces "gathered" there, it takes the specific language of Canon 35 (εἰδωλατρία, συνάξεις ποιεῖν) and turns it against its authoritarianism. Indeed, the slightly quizzical use of ἀγγέλους ὀνομάζειν in the canon (usually translated "worship," as from Col 2:18 θρησκεία)[92] finds

---

See Christopher W. B. Stephens, *Canon Law and Episcopal Authority: The Canons of Antioch and Serdica* (Oxford: Oxford University Press, 2015), 86–89.

87. The lack of reference to the Nicean settlement is unlike the Synods of Antioch 1, Sardica (*apud* Socrates, *Hist. eccl.* 2.20.7–11), and Constantinople 1, among others. The reception without rebaptism was "whether they are among the catechumens or *among the faithful*." Arguments for the deletion of "Photinians" as a later accretion on the basis of the conflict with "the mainstream view of the Trinity" (Huttner, *Early Christianity in the Lycus Valley*, 296 n. 128) become unnecessary once Laodicea's own Trinitarian heterodoxy is admitted.

88. J. B. Lightfoot, *Saint Paul's Epistles to the Colossians and to Philemon*, 9th ed. (London: Macmillan, 1890), 62. See, for example, Theodoret, *Hist. eccl.* 4.7.

89. The prohibition against bishops for country or villages (§57) is but a focused demonstration of the point.

90. Huttner, *Early Christianity in the Lycus Valley*, 297 calls them "lapidary summaries."

91. Michael of Chonai 3.1 (Bonnet 3.14); Michael of Chonai 3.3 (Bonnet 4.9–10); Michael of Chonai 4.4 (Bonnet 4.16–17); Michael of Chonai 12.4 (Bonnet 18.13–14).

92. So Theodoret of Cyrrhus, *Interpretatio epistulae ad Colossenses* (PG 82.613, 620D). The word can certainly bear the sense of worship (see Clement of Alexandria, *Protr.* 2.32–41 [GCS 12.17–31]) but could also be narrowed to onomastics—the very sophistic sleight-of-hand that later councils relished in order to restore the veneration of angels, as in the Letter of the Second Synod of Nicea: Erich Lamberz and Johannes B. Uphus, "Concilium Nicaenum II, 787," in *The Oecumenical Councils from Nicaea I*

a direct parallel in the Michael narrative with an emphasis on the *name* of Michael: "Mark my name" (in direct imitation of an oath "by Zeus")[93] and in the dedication of the εὐκτήριον.[94] Given that the period of Julian, on the one hand, and of Arianism on the other, are both dubbed "idolatry," it is little wonder that cities sought to elevate their own standing by demeaning their neighbors in such terms.[95] Laodicea deflected unwanted attention about its own embroilment in Arian and probably Julian alignments[96] by denigrating Colossae, suggesting perhaps through the reference to "hidden idolatry" (κεκρυμμένη εἰδωλατρία), the exact imitation of Julian's deception—"crypto-paganism" is Huttner's apt description.[97]

Colossae returned the favor, not by Synodal decision, given that it was in no position to call a council but by appeal to the populace and to the country where many ordinary people, far below the ethereal spheres of elite ecclesiastical battles, lived.[98] The story intimates that Laodicea's idolatry was characterized by devotion to the very female gods cleansed from Hierapolis and the ones given such favor by Julian: Artemis, Echidna, and

---

to Nicaea II (325–787), vol. 1 of *Conciliorum oecumenicorum generaliumque decreta: Editio critica*, ed. Giuseppe Alberigo et al. (Turnhout: Brepols, 2006), 314; see also Charlemagne, *Capitularia Admonitio Generalis* 16 (ca. 789 CE) (Alfred Boretius and Victor Krause, eds., *Capitularia Regum Francorum* (Hanover: Hahn, 1960).

93. See Alan H. Cadwallader, "St Michael of Chonai and the Tenacity of Paganism," in *Intercultural Transmission throughout the Medieval Mediterranean: 100–1600 CE*, ed. David W. Kim and Stephanie L. Hathaway (London: Continuum, 2012), 37–59.

94. Michael of Chonai 3.5 (Bonnet 4.5), see also Michael of Chonai 12.4 (Bonnet 18.14–15) where the name of God and of Michael are both to be esteemed.

95. For Julian, see Sozomen, *Hist. eccl.* 5.19 (GCS NF 4.226); Theodoret, *Hist. eccl.* 3.14 (GCS NF 5.190–92); for Arians, see Severus of Antioch *Ep.* 5.6. For fuller analysis, see the previously cited articles.

96. The accent on "Greeks" Ἕλληνες (Michael of Chonai 5.4 [Bonnet 9.9–10]) in addition to "the godless" ἀσεβεῖς (Michael of Chonai 7.4 [Bonnet 11.12]) probably reflects Julian's Hellenic and polytheistic campaign. See Theodoret, *Hist. eccl.* 3 (GCS NF 5.177–206 passim); Socrates, *Hist. eccl.* 3.1 (GCS NF 1.187–93); Zonaras, *Hist* 13.12. John Malalas, *Chron.* 13.19, tied Julian's soubriquet to his becoming "a Hellene." See Shaun Tougher, *Julian the Apostate* (Edinburgh: Edinburgh University Press, 2007), 48–62.

97. Huttner, *Early Christianity in the Lycus Valley*, 302. Allusions to the time and figure of Julian quickly developed as the typology of the false Christian. See Severus Letter 3 to Sergius.

98. In the story it is the country, not the city, that is privileged as the place of Michael's beneficence and protection.

especially the Great Mother. Colossae has reacted against the thinly-veiled attacks on its own privileged pilgrimage site by constructing Laodicea as thoroughly Julian—"Idolian," as Gregory of Nazianzus punned the name and the period (Gregory of Nazianzus, *Or.* 4.77)—and completely failing to live up to its high-aspiring name: unjust, *not* just in any fashion. One can hardly see the Laodicean metropolitan church being impressed, though the story's claim to fame for the spring indicates a turning to popular acclaim and devotion as a means to resist synodal decree.[99] Huttner is right in asserting that such stories as Michael of Chonai and the Acts of Philip show "how history was constructed and identities were created in the churches of the Lycus Valley";[100] even more, however, it can be asserted that such stories were constructed over against neighboring rival claims. The spurning of Colossae in favor of Laodicea by Antiochus II in the mid-third century BCE had bequeathed a long-standing virulent strain into ancient poliadic competition.[101]

This analysis demonstrates how a widening of the range of comparison to embrace imperial upheavals can be used to illuminate the particularities of local texts, in this case in relation to each other. It also has implications for how apologetic texts are interpreted, most particularly in assessing whether such texts, like the Acts of the Pagan Martyrs, were ever intended for an imperial audience or were cast in such terms as a means of shaping the identity of a local group.[102] The great world, specially when undergoing regime change, inevitably has massive ripple effects on regions

---

99. Compare Slater's reading of the Acts of Philip as a resistant document: R. N. Slater, "An Inquiry into the Relationship between Community and Text: The Apocryphal Acts of Philip 1 and the Encratites of Asia Minor," in *The Apocryphal Acts of the Apostles*, ed. François Bovon, Ann Graham Brock, and Christopher R. Matthews, Harvard Divinity School Studies, Religions of the World (Cambridge, MA: Harvard University Press, 1999), 295–96.

100. Huttner, *Early Christianity in the Lycus Valley*, 4.

101. See my "When You Say Concord You Mean Competition: Numismatic Witness to Colossae's Conflict with Laodicea" (paper presented at the Australasian Society for Classical Studies Conference, Adelaide, 28 January 2015). This conflict may add a quite different dimension to the sharing of resources implied in Col 4:16.

102. See Huttner, *Early Christianity in the Lycus Valley*, 231, 239–40. I find it far more likely that the Apology of Apollinarius, as other second century apologies, were written for internal consumption (as Huttner acknowledges on 236 and 241), especially in a context where there were highly fraught relations with imperial powers.

and localities, but these effects rarely are directly fed back to the source.[103] Rather they generate lateral renegotiations of positions, power, and access to resources.[104]

Jews at Colossae?

The converse side of the application of comparative archaeology and history, that is, the need for caution in compressing local particularities into subjection to generalized statements, develops from a striking omission in the Michael of Chonai story. The Synod of Laodicea dedicated a number of its canons to issues that have been categorized under the heading of Jewish practices (Canons 29, 37, 38, and perhaps 16). The seeming reference to Jewish practices in Col 2 has led some commentators to assume that the "worship of angels" was a Jewish practice, in both the New Testament text (Col 2:18) and in the later synod canon (Canon 35), again a compression of the evidence. More expansive is Severian of Gabala's interpretation of Colossians as addressed to a Jewish *and* a Greek audience, with different results in the meaning of the text for each group.[105] Moreover, Thomas Kraabel has alerted us to the rhetorical use of such terms as *Jewish* to foment identity formation rather than necessarily have a specific group presence in mind.[106] The supercessionism of a recent artifact unearthed at Laodicea

---

103. See Huttner, *Early Christianity in the Lycus Valley*, 286. Johannes Nollé sees occasional entrepreneurial efforts at direct dealing with central authorities but this is rare and, in fact, not encouraged in the Roman hierarchical construction of the world. See Johannes Nollé, "Marktrechte außerhalb der Stadt: Lokale Autonomie zwischen Statthalter und Zentralort," in *Lokale Autonomie und römische Ordnungsmacht in den kaiserzeitlichen Provinzen vom 1. Bis 3. Jahrhundert*, ed. Werner Eck and Elisabeth Müller-Luckner (Munich: Oldenbourg, 1999), 92–113.

104. Daniel N. Posner, "Regime Change and Ethnic Cleavages in Africa," *Comparative Political Studies* 40 (2007): 1307–9.

105. John A. Cramer, ed., *Catenae Graecorum Patrum in Novum Testamentum* (Oxford: Academic Typographer, 1844), 6:292; Karl Staab, *Die Pauluskommentare aus der griechischen Kirche* (Münster: Aschendorff, 1933), 315.

106. A. Thomas Kraabel, "*Synagoga Caeca*: Systematic Distortion in Gentile Interpretations of Evidence for Judaism in the Early Christian Period," in *"To See Ourselves as Others See Us": Christians, Jews, "Others" in Late Antiquity*, ed. Jacob Neusner and Ernest S. Frerichs, Scholars Press Studies in the Humanities (Chico, CA: Scholars Press, 1985), 236–41. Compare the historicist reading of Paul Trebilco, *Jewish Communities in Asia Minor*, SNTMS 69 (Cambridge: Cambridge University Press, 1991), 101–3.

suggests that there may be some on-the-ground religious conflict occurring along with the rhetorical positioning of church pronouncements.[107]

What is absent in the Michael narrative is any mention of Jews. This is all the more remarkable given that one particular text appears to contribute two key episodes to the story (namely, apostolic exorcism of snake-filled Hierapolis by Philip and John and the encratitism of the ascetic practice of a leading character, the shrine-custodian Archippos). That text is the Acts of Philip (including the appended Martyrion of Philip). The Philip collection is far from reserved in its inclusion of Jews in the narrative, even attempting to reproduce the sound of Hebrew (Acts Phil. 2.18; Mart. Phil. [15.]26; see also 9, 21, 26). But the Michael of Chonai story has no reference to Jews whatsoever.[108] This must raise the question of whether Jews were present at all at Colossae and, if so, in what way (an ethnohistorical question) and, if not, in what way did Jews function in the letter (a sociorhetorical question). One could readily see how the figure of the Jew could have been brought into service as the dangerous Other against which to be defined. Indeed, this can be amply demonstrated in Julian's own manipulations of Jews and consciousness of Jews (*Frag. ep.* 295C–D; *Gal.* 96C–E). But the Jew is clearly not the enemy in the story; that indictment fixes upon Laodicea.

The direct evidence for Jews at Colossae is in fact remarkably thin. Of the approximate 250 identified Jewish inscriptions in Asia Minor, 48 of which are from Phrygia, none are found at Colossae (and a large number of other cities as well, despite Philo's hyperbole).[109] Even the references to

---

107. A column drum, dated to the late fifth century, bears a menorah, palm branch, and shofar, over and above which has been heavily carved a cross. See Celal Şimşek, *Laodikeia (Laodikeia ad Lycum)* (Istanbul: Ege, 2007), 148–49, Steven Fine, "The Menorah and the Cross: Historiographical Reflections on a Recent Discovery from Laodicea on the Lycus," in *New Perspectives on Jewish-Christian Relations: In Honor of David Berger*, ed. Elisheva Carlebach and Jacob J. Schacter (Leiden: Brill, 2012), 31–50. The contrast with earlier practice is seen in Theophanes, *Chron.* 62 where Christians are reported as celebrating Pesach with Jews.

108. The reference to Moses (Michael of Chonai 12.3 [Bonnet 17.13–14]) and the allusions to and quotations of the Septuagint (Michael of Chonai 3.3 [Bonnet 4.2] [Gen 46:2, Dan 7:13]; Michael of Chonai 11.1 [Bonnet 14.11–15] [Ps 93:2–5]) hardly count given that the Greek Old Testament is largely the province of Christians by this period.

109. Walter Ameling, "The Epigraphic Habit and the Jewish Diasporas of Asia Minor and Syria," in *From Hellenism to Islam: Cultural and Linguistic Change in the Roman Near East*, ed. Hannah M. Cotton et al. (Cambridge: Cambridge University

Jew or those "of the circumcision" in the Letter to the Colossians generate a sense of a marked diminution of significance.[110] On the one hand, Colossians departs decisively and uniquely in the New Testament by inverting the salvation-historical succession of "Jew (first) and (then) Greek" (Col 3:11).[111] On the other hand, the greeter named Jesus is identified by the more familiar gentile homonym "Justus," as well as being singled out with Barnabas, Mark, and perhaps Aristarchos,[112] by an ethnic identifier (circumcision), again unique in the greetings lists in the Pauline corpus. Moreover, these Jews are extracommunal brothers. It raises the question of whether the pressure alluded to in Col 2:16 originates within the Colossian Christ-community/ies at all.

Outside the letter, the only further evidence for Jews in Colossae comes from a brief reference to Metropolitan Nicetas of Chonai resisting the presence of Jews in the city (*Chron.* 88). There is simply no evidence of Jews at Colossae between the first and twelfth century. And if the references to Jewish practices (new moon, Sabbath) are combined with the suggestion of little significant demographic presence, then such references take on more of a rhetorical than historical construction in Colossae in the second half of the first century or even that the reference alludes to pressure from Jews or Jewish-influenced Christ-followers outside the city of Colossae.

The usual means of populating Colossae with Jews is by referral to Josephus's record of the forced/enticed movement of Jews from Mesopotamia and Babylonia to Phrygia (Josephus, *A.J.* 12.148–153), sometimes combined with the hyperbolic references to Jews through Phrygia/Asia

---

Press, 2009), 203; Pieter W. van der Horst, "The Jews of Ancient Phrygia," *EJJS* 2.2 (2009): 285.

110. I develop this argument at length in "Greeks in Colossae: Shifting Allegiances in the Letter to the Colossians and Its Context," in *Attitudes to Gentiles in Ancient Judaism and Early Christianity*, ed. David C. Sim and James S. McLaren (London: Bloomsbury, 2013), 224–41.

111. Precisely here one would expect a scribal correction conforming the reading to the Pauline order (fourteen times in the Pauline corpus; nine times elsewhere in the New Testament suggesting a more-than-Pauline adherence). But only one Greek minuscule (17) makes the adjustment. It would appear that a gentile-dominant church was happy with the recognition this text afforded.

112. See Margaret MacDonald, *Colossians and Ephesians*, SP 17 (Collegeville: Liturgical Press, 2000), 181; James D. G. Dunn, *The Epistles to the Colossians and to Philemon*, NIGTC (Grand Rapids: Eerdmans, 1996), 278.

in Philo and Acts (Philo, *Legat.* 45, 281, 311; see also 214, 216; *Flacc.* 46; Acts 2:10) and a perhaps-tendentious extrapolation from Cicero's defense of the former governor of Asia, Valerius Flaccus (Cicero, *Flac.* 67–69).[113] The regional identification of Jews with Phrygia was a marker prepared to be worn by some Jews even in Israel, above or at least alongside a *polis* connection, so the ancient connection did carry some meaningful weight.[114] According to Josephus, Jews were sent to Phrygia and Lydia as oil on troubled waters adversely impacting Seleucid interests. Neither the details nor the authenticity need detain us here.[115] This action of moving peoples through the empire is well-attested among the Seleucids. Babylonians had been transferred to Seleucia on the Tigris under Antiochus I, primarily as a means of advancing agricultural production in a time of dearth.[116] The Iranian tribe of the Kardakes were shifted to create a settlement in Lycia near Telmessus and were given land allotments and tax exemptions.[117] So the settlement was, in the scheme of things, "scarcely [a] major development."[118] What is significant is that the demographic profile

---

113. See especially, Anthony J. Marshall, "Flaccus and the Jews of Asia (Cicero 'Pro Flacco' 28.67–69," *Phoenix* 29.2 (1975): 139–54.

114. *IJO* 2.184: ἀρχησυνάγωγος Φρύγιος, as minimally reconstructed. The city is harder to reconstruct and may be Dorylaion or Dokimeion. Less sure is Pieter van den Horst's identification (on the basis of similar phrasing) of a Phrygian Jew in Rome (*JIWE* 2.360): "Jews of Ancient Phrygia," 289. This marker would illustrate that the famous denunciation of the impact of Phrygia (especially the wine and baths) on Jewish practice reflects the hyperbole of infra-Jewish contests.

115. Against authenticity: Jörg-Dieter Gauger, *Beiträge zur jüdischen Apologetik: Untersuchungen zur Authentizität von Urkunden bei Flavius Josephus und im I. Makkabäerbuch* (Bonn: Hannstein, 1977); for (qualified) authenticity, Philippe Gauthier, *Nouvelles Inscriptions de Sardes II* (Geneva: Droz, 1989) 41–42. For appraisals, see Huttner, *Early Christianity in the Lycus Valley*, 67–79; Lester L. Grabbe, *A History of the Jews and Judaism in the Second Temple Period*, 2 vols. (London: T&T Clark, 2006, 2008), 2:324–26; John M. G. Barclay, *Jews of the Mediterranean Diaspora: From Alexander to Trajan (323 BCE–117 CE)* (Berkeley: University of California Press, 1996), 261–63; John Ma, *Antiochos III and the Cities of Western Asia Minor* (Oxford: Oxford University Press, 1999), 267.

116. See McDowell, *Stamped and Inscribed Objects*, 202–6.

117. M. Segre, "Iscrizioni di Licia I: Tolomeo di Telmesso," *Clara Rhodos* 9 (1928): 179–208. Compare *OGIS* 229 where a force of Persian cavalry under Omanes is supported by local estates at Palaimagnesia near Smyrna.

118. J. D. Grainger, *The Seleukid Empire of Antiochus III: 223–187 BC* (South Yorkshire: Pen & Sword, 2015), 83.

of the settlers was not the usual Greek or Macedonian.[119] This supply had largely been exhausted.[120] The move of Jews nevertheless appears to have been accompanied by a range of privileges (land, tax exemption, family groups) that were a familiar strategy of Seleucid colonization. The military component may have been minimal (see 1 Macc 10:36–37; 13:40).[121] Supply and stabilization of city life were crucial issues for Antiochus III at the time and military service may have been occasional rather than continuous.[122] Josephus's text of the rescript accents agriculture and subordinate service (*A.J.* 12.152). The choice may have been facilitated by the experience that Antiochus III and his viceroy Zeuxis had gained in dealing with expatriate Jews when both were in Babylon at an earlier time before Zeuxis's promotion (see 2 Macc 8:20). That experience may well lie behind the text of Josephus, where Antiochus states "I am persuaded that they have the disposition to be protectors of our interests" (πέπεισμαι ... εὔνους αὐτοὺς ἔσεσθαι τῶν ἡμετέρων φύλακας; *A.J.* 12.150; see also 152–153, where an incentive to safeguarding imperial interests is provided). Admittedly, this is not quite the lavish praise of loyalty that Antiochus in another letter to Zeuxis (209 BCE), his viceroy in Asia, credited to Nicanor (τῆς αὐτοῦ πίστεως καὶ εὐνοίας ll. 23–24),[123] justifying his appointment as high priest of all the temples "beyond the Taurus" (ἐν τῆι

---

119. See T. Boiy, *Late Achaemenid and Hellenistic Babylon* (Leuven: Peeters, 2004), 288. For an example of a Macedonian settlement near Philadelphia, see *TAM* 5.1:221.

120. Daubner, "Seleukidische und attalidische in Westkleinasien," 41–63.

121. Abraham Schalit, in my opinion, overstates the military aspect: "The Letter of Antiochus III to Zeuxis regarding the Establishment of Jewish Colonies in Phrygia and Lydia," *JQR* 50.4 (1960): 289–318; see also Barry F. Parker, "'Works of the Law' and the Jewish Settlement in Asia Minor," *JGRChJ* 9 (2013): 46–47. The use of mercenaries was an established Seleucid practice, stemming from Alexander, and would have been sufficient to meet Antiochus's objectives if military instability was the only or even primary concern. The appointment of Nicanor as high priest over a swathe of temples in 209 BCE in support of the dynastic cult (see the following) and with significant bureaucratic responsibilities (including contracts), indicates that Antiochus was advancing on a well-constructed plan of economic and political stabilization. See H. Malay, "A Copy of the Letter of Antiochos III to Zeuxis (209 BC)," in *Ad Fontes! Festschrift für Gerhard Dobesch*, ed. Herbert Hefner and Kurt Tomaschitz (Vienna: Phoibos, 2004), 407–13. Moreover, land grants were generally consequent upon military service (Arrian, *Anab.* 4.4.1; see also *SEG* 32.1252 [Attalid practice]).

122. See Ma, *Antiochos III*, 117, following Jeanne and Louis Robert's assessment that the essential character of these settlements was rural and nonstrategic (n. 39).

123. Compare the language in Josephus, *A.J.* 12.402 of a later Nicanor.

ἐπέκεινα τοῦ Ταύρου ll. 29–30), but the coincidence of the cognates in each letter (εὔνοος ~ εὔνοια) is striking.[124] Indeed, the valorization of this virtue is replicated in inscriptions from the period (e.g., *OGIS* 238). Josephus is at pains to accent the support of Antiochus III in a number of ways (*A.J.* 12.137–153), but his apologetic does not override complete historical probability: there is a hint in the rescript's admission that the transfer was not without problems—"even though removing them will be onerous" (καίπερ ἐργώδους ὄντος τούτους μεταγαγεῖν). Josephus's main concern is to accent that Jews throughout the diaspora were a recognized blessing to empire (*A.J.* 4.115–116)[125] in large part *because* they were permitted to observe their own customs (πάτριοι/ἴδιοι νόμοι). Yet from what we know of Seleucid movements of people, this was not the accent. The letter's use of ὑπηρέτης—subordinate service (*A.J.* 12.152)[126]—is in keeping with Seleucid understanding of these colonies. The extant inscribed honors for Seleucid leaders demonstrate that the settlers met the expectations of reinforcing Seleucid power relationships and civic administration.[127]

Crucial is the recognition that the action of relocating two thousand Jewish households in Phrygia and Lydia comes at the instigation of the Seleucid King, Antiochus III. Given that there were both stabilizing and agricultural-supply motivations behind the decision, it would be wise execution of the initiative to ensure connection with and preservation of Seleucid interests, that is, of the foundations that the Seleucids had made. This probably lies behind Josephus's reference to "garrisons and indispensable places" (εἰς τὰ φρούρια καὶ τοὺς ἀναγκαιοτάτους τόπους; *A.J.* 12.149), which indicates that the settlements of Jews were to be attached to preexisting habitations that had garrison facilities.[128] "Colonies" in this sense were frequently attachments to a preexisting city rather than independent settlements. John Grainger points out that founding or refounding cities

---

124. H. Malay, "Letter of Antiochos III to Zeuxis with Two Covering Letters (209 BC)," *EA* 10 (1987): 8; Compare Tullia Ritti et al., *Museo Archaeologico di Denizli-Hierapolis Catalogo delle iscrizioni greche e latine* (Naples: Liguori, 2008), 42 §3 l.8.

125. Josephus makes a significant extension of the Balaam oracle (Num 21:35).

126. Occasionally the word can have a military sense (LSJ, s.v. "ὑπηρέτης"), but this is a derivative connotation.

127. *SEG* 20.411; M. Wörrle, "Antiochos I, Achaios der Ältere und die Galater. Eine neue Inscrhift in Denizli," *Chiron* 5 (1975): 59–87.

128. So, Walter Ameling, "Die jüdischen Gemeinden im antiken Kleinasien," in *Jüdische Gemeinden und Organisationsformen von der Antike bis zur Gegenwart*, ed. Robert Jütte and Abraham P. Kustermann (Vienna: Böhlau, 1998), 33.

was not the contribution of Antiochus III.[129] Significantly, Christopher Tuplin considers that Colossae was not even an Achmaenid garrison-city, precisely because it was a capital in the satrapic organization.[130] Accordingly, it is likely that Colossae was reduced to part of the supply chain (a "billeting station") for these newly founded and fortified "indispensable places."[131] The loss of its privileged *and* strategic place as a "ducal" capital in the Phrygian satrapy[132] appears to be a deliberate objective in the foundation of Laodicea and, to a lesser extent, Hierapolis. With the rapid expansion of population brought by the movement of Jews into the region, it seems to me highly likely that Seleucid-founded cities would be the ones to receive Jewish settlers into their ambit of control (whether in the city itself, on land connected with a temple or in the villages and countryside connected with the cities).[133] That these two cities remained collated in the Roman administrative conception has been noted already.[134] The same pairing of these cities of the Lycus Valley occurs in another inscription honoring a Xanthian citizen, again in the context of Roman benefaction.[135] It clearly shows that, in the Roman mind, Laodicea and Hierapolis held an eminent standing, even being thought of *together* as recipients of formal Roman attention. It is likely that this Roman framing derived from the Seleucid privileging. For example, when a dispute over temple lands erupted at Aezani in northern Phrygia during Hadrian's time, the action was settled by reference to what could be found from the time of the Seleucid kings.[136]

---

129. Grainger, *The Seleukid Empire of Antiochus III*, 83.

130. Christopher Tuplin, "Xenophon and the Garrisons of the Achmaenid Empire," *Archäologische Mitteilungen aus Iran* 20 (1987): 183, 236.

131. Gerassimos George Aperghis, *The Seleukid Royal Economy: The Finances and Financial Adminsitration of the Sleukid Empire* (Cambridge: Cambridge University Press, 2004), 200.

132. Nicholas Sekunda, "Changing Patterns of Land-Holding in the South-Western Border Lands of Greater Phrygia in the Achaemenid and Hellenistic Periods," in *Colossae in Space and Time*, 56–57.

133. Some of these villages we know of, such as Heleinokapria (*CIG* 3954, tied to Laodicea) and Mamakome (*MAMA* 4.276A III for Hierapolis), Masakome (Ritti, "Dediche," 28 §K28, for Hierapolis).

134. Christol and Drew-Bear, "Un sénateur de Xanthos," 213–16.

135. *TAM* 2.1:194 IIa.

136. So critical was the exchange of letters that they were made part of inscribed temple fabric: *MAMA* 9.xxxvi–xliii; see also *MAMA* 9.9. Compare the practice of

One particular inscription from Hierapolis ties the Jews to the ancient settlement mentioned in general terms by Josephus. These "colonies" were designated κατοικίαι[137] regardless of whether they were independent of a city (Kardakon Kome), near a city (Dura Europos), or established as part of a city (Smyrna).[138] They might, at a later date, obtain *polis* status.[139] The settlers might be granted citizenship at the time of colonization or acquire it later or look to their successors to gain the grant, perhaps as individuals.[140] It is the terminology of the Seleucid placement of settlers (κατοικία) that is emphasized in the inscription. I give the inscription in full:

ἡ σορὸς καὶ ὁ περὶ αὐτὴν τόπος Αὐρ(ηλίας) Αὐγούστας Σω-
τικοῦ ἐν ᾗ κηδευθήσεται αὐτὴ καὶ ὁ ἀνὴρ <αὐ>τῆς Γλυκωνιανὸς
ὁ καὶ Ἅγνος καὶ τὰ τέκνα αὐτῶν· εἰ δὲ {ΕΤΕ} ἕτερος κηδεύσει, δ-
ώσει τῇ κατοικίᾳ τῶν ἐν Ἱεραπόλει κατοικούντων Ἰουδαί-
ων προστείμου (δηνάρια) τ' καὶ τῷ ἐκζητήσαντι (δηνάρια) ρ'. ἀντίγραφον
ἀπετέθη ἐν τῷ ἀρχίῳ τῶν Ἰουδαίων.

This grave and the surrounding place belong to Aurelia Augusta, daughter of Zotikos. In it she, her husband, who is called Glykonianos, also known as Hagnos, and their children will be buried. But if anyone else is buried here, the violator will pay a fine of 300 denaria to the settlement

---

inscribing decisions impacting the life of a temple, known elsewhere; see *OGIS* 669 (El-Khargeh, Egypt); IMagnesia 115; see a similarly based decision of Trajan: *AÉ* 1913.2.

137. See Bar-Kochva, *Seleucid Army*, 26 for a list.

138. Kardakon Kome: Compare also the village of Parloai where the villagers are called κάτοικοι: H. Malay and C. Tanriver, "The Cult of Apollo Syrmaios and the Village of Parloai near Saittai, North-Eastern Lydia," in *Between Tarhuntas and Zeus Polieus: Cultural Crossroads in the Temples and Cults of Graeco-Roman Anatolia*, ed. María Paz de Hoz, Juan Pablo Sánchez Hernández, and Carlos Molina Valero (Leuven: Peeters, 2016), 172–73. Dura Europos: See Charles Bradford Welles, Robert O. Fink, and Johnson Frank Gilliam, *The Parchments and the Papyri*, Excavations at Dura Europos 5.1 (New Haven: Yale University Press, 1959), 77. Smyrna: *OGIS* 229; see Getzel M. Cohen, "*Katoikiai, Katoikoi* and Macedonians in Asia Minor," *AncSoc* 22 (1991): 41–50.

139. *SEG* 47.1745. The opening of the inscribed letter illustrates the official designation: Βασιλεὺς Εὐμένης Τοριαιτῶν τοῖς κατοικοῦσι χαιρεῖν (ll. 2–3).

140. There is no necessary equation between settler and citizen; see IMylasa 306; IStratonikeia 186, 256. For citizenship at a later date, see ISmyrna 573. For citizenship for successors, see *SEG* 42.1791 and commentary. For individual citizenship, see, as an example, the citizenship gained by Menestratos of Phokaia (*BE* 1984.421) "under the reign of Antiochus the Great" in 201 BCE.

of the Judeans who are settled in Hierapolis and 100 denaria to the one who found out about the violation. A copy of this inscription was placed in the archives of the Judeans.[141]

It should be noted that this inscription is one of twenty-three identified as Jewish in the most recent collection.[142] Although these inscriptions date from the second century CE, the number demonstrably points to a sizable and long-standing Jewish population. This is confirmed by the reference in the inscription (l. 6) to archives maintained by the Jews in Hierapolis.[143] Secondly, we have seen that the records from the period of "the kings" in Asia were often maintained as part of the memory and securing of position, privilege and history well into the second century Roman empire. This means, thirdly, that the deliberate analepsis of κατοικ- in line 4 is more likely, in my view, to be tapping into a time-honored, officially recognized position of the Jews in the city of Hierapolis. That is, this inscription recalls that Jews were part of the Seleucid resettlement of Jews noted in the rescript of Antiochus III provided by Josephus. This resettlement into "Phrygia and Lydia" included the city of Hierapolis. Accordingly, the recalling of a Hellenistic technical term, as Tessa Rajak admits is evident here, is not, as she and others argue, to draw some ancient warrant into a synonym for a Jewish συναγωγή or λαός,[144] which to date would be a

---

141. *IGRR* 4.834 = *CIJ* 2.775 = Miranda §16 (E. Miranda, "La comunità giudaica di Hierapolis di Frigia," *EA* 31 [1999]: 109–56) = *IJO* 2.205. Translation from Philip A. Harland, *Dynamics of Identity in the World of the Early Christians* (London: Bloomsbury, 2009), 127.

142. *IJO* 2.

143. Other identifiably Jewish inscriptions refer in general to "the archives." Given the citizen status of the deceased, this is likely to mean the city archives: Miranda §10; see also §14a (= *IJO* 191A) where, after the reference to the archives (εἰς τὸ ἀρχεῖον), is added a seemingly free-standing Ἰουδαηκή. Elena Miranda takes this as referring to the grave (ἡ σορός l.1), though admits it may refer to one of the interred (Apphia); to this might be added the possibility that it is a classification within the archives (again, tied to ἡ σορός or to an understood ἡ ἐπιγραφή).

144. Tessa Rajak, "Synagogue and Community in the Graeco-Roman Diaspora," in *Jews in the Hellenistic and Roman Cities*, ed. John R. Bartlett (London: Routledge, 2002), 32. The explanation of the term λαός is almost always tied to its ubiquity in the First Testament. However, it should be considered that it was a semi-technical term in settlement language of the Hellenistic period in Asia Minor. See Fanoula Papazoglou, *Laoi et Paroikoi: Recherches sur la structure de la société hellénistique* (Beograd: Université de Belgrade, 1997); this invites further research.

unique application. Rather, it indicates the authority that the Jews of Hierapolis wanted to and could claim from antiquity in that city.¹⁴⁵ Philip A. Harland takes the κατοικία as a term used by ethnically based associations but has to admit that the repetition in line 4 involves "migration either in this generation *or some previous generation*."¹⁴⁶ This established position may help to explain not only why the inscribed protection on a number of epitaphs includes reference to the city archives but also, in a number of cases, of the payment of fines for grave disturbance to civic not only religious authorities.¹⁴⁷

Hierapolis's relatively rich supply of identifiably Jewish inscriptions overshadows those from Laodicea, though one eagerly awaits the publication of new inscriptions from recent excavations. However, some are present.¹⁴⁸ Of course, this may easily fall into the standard assessment of Colossae's lack of importance.¹⁴⁹ Comments are replete about how Laodi-

---

145. So Margaret H. Williams, "Semitic Name-Use by Jews in Roman Asia Minor and the Dating of the Aphrodisias *Stele* Inscriptions," in *Old and New Worlds in Greek Onomastics*, ed. Elaine Matthews (Oxford: Oxford University Press, 2007), 177-78; *contra* Ameling, "Die jüdischen Gemeinden," 34 (who does not take into account the survival of Seleucid records/identity fragments into the Roman imperial period). Whether or not this implied a Jewish quarter, as van der Horst suggests, must remain moot ("Jews of Ancient Phrygia," 286).

146. Harland, *Dynamics of Identity*, 127 (my emphasis). Used, for example, by Romans at Apameia (*MAMA* 6.177). Compare, however, Ameling (*IJO* 2:433-35), who is more cautious about both the equation with an association and in the synonymity proposed by Rajak.

147. City archives: *IJO* 2.189 (reconstructed), 192-193. Presumably these are the same archives as mentioned in other epitaphs not identifiably Jewish; see, for example, Fabrizio A. Pennacchietti, "Nuove iscrizioni di Hierapolis Frigia," *AAT* 101 (1966-1967): 297 §7. Payment of fines: *IJO* 2.198. Unlike van der Horst ("Jews of Ancient Phrygia," 286), I do not read a reference to "the most holy treasury" (e.g., *IJO* 2.199, 207) as indicating a Jewish agency, given that the same expression occurs in numerous inscriptions with no indication of a Jewish connection: Pennacchietti, "Nuove iscrizioni di Hierapolis Frigia," §22, l.4; Walther Judeich, "Inschriften," in Altertümer von Hierapolis, ed. Carl Humann (Berlin: Reimer, 1898), nos. 169/170, 195, 216, etc., as well as in a number of places beyond Hierapolis. See David Noy, *The City of Rome*, vol. 2 of *Jewish Inscriptions of Western Europe* (Cambridge: Cambridge University Press, 1995), 306.

148. *IJO* 2.212, 213.

149. Huttner's reappraisal of the honor for Zenon, twice successful in the "New Olympics" (*MAMA* 6.40) takes Ἀπολλωνίηα as a dedication to Apollo (*Early Christianity in the Lycus Valley*, 45) rather than as a place-name (= Tripolis, according to

cea eclipsed Colossae's size and status. But what is not considered in such assessments is that this is likely to be reflected in the Jewish component in Colossae's demography. It makes sense that not every city or city environs in Phrygia or Lydia received Jewish settlers.[150] Walter Ameling's collation for Phrygia lists fourteen cities; a brief glance at the *Barrington Atlas* (with Thomas Drew-Bear's list) demonstrates that this is a small, if significant, proportion of the total number.[151] Antiochus III did not engage in a scatter-gun approach to the movement of populations, especially given the careful advisor he had in his viceroy friend, Zeuxis. It also makes sense, I would suggest, that Colossae was not one of those cities considered for Jewish settlement. Accordingly, even though one may admit that there was a "high percentage of Jews in the overall population of the Lycus Valley," this does not require that such numbers be evenly distributed through the cities of the Lycus (including those in the high country such as Attouda, Trapezopolis, and Mossyna).[152] The absence of Jewish inscriptions from these places, as well as from Colossae, may, of course, be reversed in subsequent years. But, given the existing evidence and the probabilities deduced from the analysis of the Seleucid period, the eventuality appears unlikely. This may well cohere, as I have suggested above, with that decidedly non-Pauline word-order "Greeks and Jews" in Colossians (Col 3:11) and may explain how Jews do not figure in later texts such as the manifold versions of Michael of Chonai or the letters of Elias the monk (eleventh century),[153]

Buckler and Calder in *MAMA* 6). This would suggest that Colossae had a stadium, a claim on status and wealth that not even Hierapolis possessed. However, Tripolis did construct its own stadium in the third century, the date assigned to the Colossian inscription: compare C. Tanriver, "Three New Inscriptions from Tripolis," *EA* 42 (2009): 81–86.

150. Aizanoi, Akmoneia, Amorion, Apameia, Apollonia, Appia, Diokleia, Dokimeion, Dorylaion, Eumeneia, Hierapolis, Kotiaeion, Laodicea, Synnada.

151. It must be admitted that many of the cities are Roman foundations (or recognized through Roman remains); but this does not particularly affect the argument.

152. Huttner, *Early Christianity in the Lycus Valley*, 122. One inscription from Hierapolis, names the deceased as from Tripolis (*IJO* 2.191B). This invites speculation about a Jewish community at Tripolis but could equally conjure a move (*and* burial) to Hierapolis to link with an established Jewish community. Compare Pennacchietti, "Nuove iscrizioni di Hierapolis Frigia," 304 §22.

153. See George T. Dennis, "Elias the Monk, Friend of Psellos," in *Byzantine Authors: Texts and Translations Dedicated to the Memory of Nicolas Oikonomides*, ed. Nicolas Oikonomides and John W. Nesbitt (Leiden: Brill, 2003), 43–62.

even after Laodicea has effectively ceased operating. In such a scenario, the differences between Laodicea (Hierapolis) and Colossae become more pronounced and more pronounced with respect to demography than simply volume. A concerted inquiry has therefore illustrated that the tendency to compression of the evidence to generalize about Colossae's Jewish population is ill-founded.

Conclusion

Comparative archaeological and historical method has been demonstrated to be invaluable for the task of interpretation, especially in the case of a place where the material and textual evidence is limited. The foundation was laid by setting Colossae into the context of successive imperial realities, the Seleucids, Attalids, and the Romans. A handful of coins, once put into this context, yielded considerably more insight than has traditionally been achieved and it laid the *prima facie* case for the use of the method. This was then applied so as to demonstrate the need for a careful negotiation of the path between idiosyncracy and compression. For the former, this meant avoiding treating Colossae in isolation or only in terms of its biblically attested neighbors. The story of Michael of Chonai was shown not only to be a resistant text to the weight of authority imposed by its metropolitical neighbor, Laodicea, but to be part of both cities' renegotiation of their position in the face of rapidly changing imperial realities in the aftermath of the rule of Julian II. For the latter, this meant a cautionary approach to taking evidence of Jews found in other centers, notably Laodicea and Hierapolis, and holding that this was representative for other cities in the region such as Colossae. But the method for negotiating both extremes that have been charged against the comparative method, has been shown to lie in a careful application of the method. Throughout, my dialogue partner has been Ulrich Huttner, and I am grateful to him in his research for providing the impulse for the questions addressed here.

Bibliography

Ameling, Walter. "Die jüdischen Gemeinden im antiken Kleinasien." Pages 29–55 in *Jüdische Gemeinden und Organisationsformen von der Antike bis zur Gegenwart*. Edited by Robert Jütte and Abraham P. Kustermann; Vienna: Böhlau, 1998.

———. "The Epigraphic Habit and the Jewish Diasporas of Asia Minor and Syria." Pages 203–34 in *From Hellenism to Islam: Cultural and Linguistic Change in the Roman Near East*. Edited by Hannah M. Cotton, Robert G. Hoyland, Jonathan J. Price, and David J. Wasserstein. Cambridge: Cambridge University Press, 2009.

Aperghis, Gerassimos George. *The Seleukid Royal Economy: The Finances and Financial Adminsitration of the Sleukid Empire*. Cambridge: Cambridge University Press, 2004.

Arnold, Clinton E. *The Colossian Syncretism: The Interface between Christianity and Folk Belief at Colossae*. Grand Rapids: Baker, 1996.

Ashton, Richard. "The Use of the Cistaphoric Weight-Standard outside the Pergamene Kingdom." Pages 245–64 in *Attalid Asia Minor: Money, International Relations and the State*. Edited by Peter Thonemann. Oxford: Oxford University Press, 2013.

Aulock, Hans von. *Münzen und Städte Phrygiens*. 2 vols. IstMitt 25, 27. Tübingen: Wasmuth, 1980–1987.

Barclay, John M. G. *Jews of the Mediterranean Diaspora: From Alexander to Trajan (323 BCE–117 CE)*. Berkeley: University of California Press, 1996.

Bar-Kochva, Bezalel. *The Seleucid Army: Organization and Tactics in the Great Campaigns*. Cambridge: Cambridge University Press, 1976.

Barth, Markus, and Helmut Blanke. *Colossians*. Translated by Astrid B. Beck. AB 34B. New York: Doubleday, 1994.

Beê, N. A. *Τα χειρόγραφα των Μετεώρων: Κατάλογος περιγραφικός των χειρογράφων κωδίκων των αποκειμένων εἰς τὰς Μονάς των Μετεώρων* [Meteōrōn manuscripts: A descriptive list of manuscript codices belonging to the Meteōrōn Monastery]. 4 vols. Athens: Akadēmia Athēnōn, 1967–1993.

Billows, Richard A. *Kings and Colonists: Aspects of Macedonian Imperialism*. Leiden: Brill, 1995.

Birley, Anthony R. *Hadrian: The Restless Emperor*. London: Routledge, 1997.

Boiy, T. *Late Achaemenid and Hellenistic Babylon*. Leuven: Peeters, 2004.

Bonnet, Max. *Narratio de Miraculo a Michaele Archangelo Chonis Patrato*. Paris: Librairie Hachette, 1890.

Bormann, Lukas. *Der Brief des Paulus an die Kolosser*. THKNT 10.1. Leipzig: Evangelische Verlagsanstalt, 2012.

Boretius, Alfred, and Victor Krause. *Capitularia regum Francorum*. Hannover: Hahn, 1960.

Cadwallader, Alan H. "Epiphanies and Religious Conflict: The Contests over the Hagiasma of Chonai." Pages 110–35 in *Reconceiving Religious Conflict: New Views from the Formative Centuries of Christianity*. Edited by Chris de Wet and Wendy Mayer. London: Routledge, 2017.

———. *Fragments of Colossae: Sifting through the Traces*. 2nd rev. and exp. ed. Hindmarsh: ATF Press, forthcoming.

———. "Greeks in Colossae: Shifting Allegiances in the Letter to the Colossians and Its Context." Pages 224–41 in *Attitudes to Gentiles in Ancient Judaism and Early Christianity*. Edited by David C. Sim and James S. McLaren. London: Bloomsbury, 2013.

———. "The Historical Sweep of the Life of Colossae." Pages 25–67 in *Epigraphical Evidence Illustrating Paul's Letter to the Colossians*. Edited by Joseph Verheyden, Markus Öhler, and Thomas Corsten. WUNT 411. Tübingen: Mohr Siebeck, 2018.

———. "Inter-City Conflict in the Story of St Michael of Chonai." Pages 109–27 in *Religious Conflict from Early Christianity to the Rise of Islam*. Edited by Wendy Mayer and Bronwen Neil. Berlin: de Gruyter, 2013.

———. "The Inversion of Slavery: The Ascetic and the Archistrategos at Chonai." Pages 215–36 in *Prayer and Spirituality in the Early Church V: Poverty and Riches*. Edited by Geoffrey D. Dunn, David Luckensmeyer, and Lawrence Cross. Strathfield, NSW: Saint Pauls Publications; Virginia, Qld: Centre for Early Christian Studies, 2009.

———. "Refuting an Axiom of Scholarship on Colossae: Fresh Insights from New and Old Inscriptions." Pages 151–79 in *Colossae in Space and Time: Linking to an Ancient City*. Edited by Alan H. Cadwallader and Michael Trainor. Göttingen: Vandenhoeck & Ruprecht, 2011.

———. "The Reverend Doctor John Luke and the Churches of Chonai." *GBRS* 48.3 (2008): 319–38.

———. "The Story of the Archistrategos, St Michael of Chonai." Pages 323–30 in *Colossae in Space and Time: Linking to an Ancient City*. Edited by Alan H. Cadwallader and Michael Trainor. Göttingen: Vandenhoeck & Ruprecht, 2011.

———. "St Michael of Chonai and the Tenacity of Paganism." Pages 37–59 in *Intercultural Transmission throughout the Medieval Mediterranean: 100–1600 CE*. Edited by David W. Kim and Stephanie L. Hathaway. London: Continuum, 2012.

———. "Wealthy, Widowed, Astute and Beneficent: Claudia Eugenetoriane and the Second Century Revival of the Colossian Mint." *NewDocs* 12 (forthcoming).

———. "When You Say Concord You Mean Competition: Numismatic Witness to Colossae's Conflict with Laodicea." Paper presented at the Australasian Society for Classical Studies Conference. Adelaide, 28 January 2015.
Campbell, J. B. *The Writings of the Roman Land Surveyors*. London: Society for the Promotion of Roman Studies, 2000.
Canavan, Rosemary. "Weaving Threads: Clothing in Colossae." Pages 111–33 in *Fragments of Colossae: Sifting through the Traces*. Edited by Alan H. Cadwallader. Adelaide: ATF Press, 2015.
Christol, Michel, and Thomas Drew-Bear. "Un sénateur de Xanthos." *Journal des savants* 3 (1991): 195–226.
Cohen, Getzel M. "*Katoikiai, Katoikoi* and Macedonians in Asia Minor." *AncSoc* 22 (1991): 41–50.
———. *The Seleucid Colonies: Studies in Founding, Administration and Organization*. Wiesbaden: Steiner, 1978.
Cramer, John A., ed. *Catenae Graecorum Patrum in Novum Testamentum*. Oxford: Academic Typographer, 1844.
D'Aiuto, F. *El "Menologio de Basilo II": Città de estudios con occasion de la edición facsimile*. Vatican: Biblioteca Apostolica Vaticana; Athens: Diaconía Apostólica de la Iglesia de Grecia; Madrid: Testimonio Compania Editorial, 2008.
Daubner, Frank. "Seleukidische und attalidische in Westkleinasien—Datierung, Funktion und Status." Pages 41–63 in *Militärsiedlungen und Territorialherrschaft in der Antike*. Edited by F. Daubner. Berlin: de Gruyter, 2011.
Dennis, George T. "Elias the Monk, Friend of Psellos." Pages 43–62 in *Byzantine Authors: Texts and Translations Dedicated to the Memory of Nicolas Oikonomides*. Edited by Nicolas Oikonomides and John W. Nesbitt. Leiden: Brill, 2003.
Drijvers, Hendrik Jan Willem. *Cults and Beliefs at Edessa*. Leiden: Brill, 1980.
Dunn, James D. G. *The Epistles to the Colossians and to Philemon*. NIGTC. Grand Rapids: Eerdmans, 1996.
Fine, Steven. "The Menorah and the Cross: Historiographical Reflections on a Recent Discovery from Laodicea on the Lycus." Pages 31–50 in *New Perspectives on Jewish-Christian Relations: In Honor of David Berger*. Edited by Elisheva Carlebach and Jacob J. Schacter. Leiden: Brill, 2012.

Gauger, Jörg-Dieter. *Beiträge zur jüdischen Apologetik: Untersuchungen zur Authentizität von Urkunden bei Flavius Josephus und im I. Makkabäerbuch.* Bonn: Hannstein, 1977.

Gauthier, Philippe. *Nouvelles Inscriptions de Sardes II.* Geneva: Droz, 1989.

Grabbe, Lester L. *A History of the Jews and Judaism in the Second Temple Period.* 2 vols. London: T&T Clark, 2006, 2008.

Grainger, J. D. *The Seleukid Empire of Antiochus III: 223–187 BC.* South Yorkshire: Pen & Sword, 2015.

Habinek, Thomas N. *The Colometry of Latin Prose.* Berkeley: University of California, 1985.

Harland, Philip A. *Dynamics of Identity in the World of the Early Christians.* London: Bloomsbury, 2009.

Heller, Anna. *"Les bêtises des Grecs": Conflits et rivalités entre cites d'Asie et de Bithynie à l'époque romaine (129 a.C.–234 p.C.).* Bordeaux: de Boccard, 2007.

Hock, Ronald F. "A Support for His Old Age: Paul's Plea on Behalf of Onesimus." Pages 67–81 in *The Social World of the First Christians.* Edited by L. Michael White and O. Larry Yarbrough. Minneapolis: Fortress, 1995.

Horst, Pieter W. van der. "The Jews of Ancient Phrygia." *EJJS* 2.2 (2009): 283–92.

Houghton, Arthur, and Catharine C. Lorber. *Seleucid Coins: A Comprehensive Catalogue.* 2 vols. New York: American Numismatic Society, 2002, 2008.

Howgego, Christopher. *Greek Imperial Countermarks: Studies in the Provincial Coinage of the Roman Empire.* London: Royal Numismatic Society, 1985.

Huttner, Ulrich. "Die Färber von Laodikeia und Hierapolis: Eine Nachricht aus dem Corpus der Alchemisten." *MBAH* 26 (2009): 139–57.

———. *Early Christianity in the Lycus Valley.* Translated by David Green. AJEC 85; Early Christianity in Asia Minor 1. Leiden: Brill, 2013.

Johnston, Ann. "Greek Imperial Statistics: A Commentary." *Révue numismatique* 26 (1984): 240–57.

Judeich, Walther. "Inschriften." Pages 67–179 in *Altertümer von Hierapolis.* Edited by Carl Humann. Berlin: Reimer, 1898.

Karanastasi, P. "Hadrian im Panzer: Kaiserstatuen zwischen Realpolitik und Philhellenismus." *Jahrbuch des Deutschen Archäologischen Instituts* 127–128 (2012–2013): 323–91.

Kearsley, Rosalinde A. *Greeks and Romans in Imperial Asia*. IK 59. Bonn: Habelt, 2001.
Klose, Dietrich O. A. *Die Münzprägung von Smyrna in der römischen Kaiserzeit*. Berlin: de Gruyter, 1987.
Kolb, F. "Zur Geschichte der Stadt Hierapolis in Phrygien: Die Phyleninschriften im Theater." ZPE 15 (1974): 255–77.
Kosmin, Paul J. *The Land of the Elephant Kings: Space, Territory, and Ideology in the Seleucid Empire*. Cambridge: Harvard University Press, 2014.
Kraabel, A. Thomas. "*Synagoga Caeca*: Systematic Distortion in Gentile Interpretations of Evidence for Judaism in the Early Christian Period." Pages 219–46 in *"To See Ourselves as Others See Us": Christians, Jews, "Others" in Late Antiquity*. Edited by Jacob Neusner and Ernest S. Frerichs. Scholars Press Studies in the Humanities. Chico, CA: Scholars Press, 1985.
Lamberz, Erich, and Johannes B. Uphus. "Concilium Nicaenum II, 787." Pages 295–345 in *The Oecumenical Councils from Nicaea I to Nicaea II (325–787)*. Vol. 1 of Conciliorum oecumenicorum generaliumque decreta: Editio critica. Edited by Giuseppe Alberigo et al. Turnhout: Brepols, 2006.
Latyšev, Basilius. *Menologii anonymi byzantine saeculi X quae super sunt*. Petropoli: 1911.
Leemans, Johan. "Christian Diversity in Amaseia: A Bishop's View." *Adamantius* 13 (2007): 247–57.
———. "Gregory of Nyssa: A Homily on Theodore the Recruit." Pages 82–90 in *'Let us die that we may live': Greek Homilies on Christian Martyrs from Asia Minor, Palestine and Syria (c. AD 350–AD 450)* edited by Johan Leemans, Wendy Mayer, Pauline Allen, and Boudewijn Dehandschutter. London: Routledge, 2003.
———. "A Preacher-Audience Oriented Analysis of Gregory of Nyssa's Homily on Theodore the Recruit." *StPatr* 37 (2001): 140–46.
Levick, Barbara. *Roman Colonies in Southern Asia Minor*. Oxford: Clarendon, 1967.
Lightfoot, J. B. *Saint Paul's Epistles to the Colossians and to Philemon*. 9th ed. London: Macmillan, 1890.
Limberis, Vasiliki M. *Architects of Piety: The Cappadocian Fathers and the Cult of Martyrs*. Oxford: Oxford University Press, 2011.
Ma, John. *Antiochos III and the Cities of Western Asia Minor*. Oxford: Oxford University Press, 1999.

MacDonald, Margaret. *Colossians and Ephesians*. SP 17. Collegeville: Liturgical Press, 2000.
McDowell, Robert H. *Stamped and Inscribed Objects from Seleucia on the Tigris*. Ann Arbor: University of Michigan Press, 1935.
Magie, David. "Egyptian Deities in Asia Minor in Inscriptions and on Coins." *AJA* 57.3 (1953): 163–87.
Magness, Jodi. "Some Observations on the Roman Temple at Kedesh." *IEJ* 40 (1990): 173–81.
Malay, H. "A Copy of the Letter of Antiochos III to Zeuxis (209 BC)." Pages 407–13 in *Ad Fontes! Festschrift für Gerhard Dobesch*. Edited by Herbert Hefner and Kurt Tomaschitz. Vienna: Phoibos, 2004.
———. "Letter of Antiochos III to Zeuxis with Two Covering Letters (209 B.C.)." *EA* 10 (1987): 7–15.
Malay, H., and C. Tanriver. "The Cult of Apollo Syrmaios and the Village of Parloai near Saittai, North-Eastern Lydia." Pages 171–84 in *Between Tarhuntas and Zeus Polieus: Cultural Crossroads in the Temples and Cults of Graeco-Roman Anatolia*. Edited by Maria Paz de Hoz, Juan Pablo Sánchez Hernández, and Carlos Molina Valero. Leuven: Peeters, 2016.
Marshall, Anthony J. "Flaccus and the Jews of Asia (Cicero 'Pro Flacco' 28.67–69)." *Phoenix* 29.2 (1975): 139–54.
McDowell, Robert H. *Stamped and Inscribed Objects from Seleucia on the Tigris*. Ann Arbor: University of Michigan Press, 1935.
Meadows, Andrew. "The Closed Currency System of the Attalid Kingdom." Pages 149–205 in *Attalid Asia Minor: Money, International Relations and the State*. Edited by Peter Thonemann. Oxford: Oxford University Press, 2013.
Metcalfe, William E. *The Cistophori of Hadrian*. New York: American Numismatic Society, 1980.
Mileta, Christia. *Der König und sein Land: Untersuchungen zur Herrschaft der hellenistischen Monarchen über das königliche Gebiet Kleinasiens und seine Bevölkerung*. Berlin: Akademie Verlag, 2008.
Milne, J. Grafton. *Kolophon and Its Coinage: A Study*. New York: American Numismatic Society, 1941.
Milner, N. P. *An Epigraphical Survey in the Kibyra-Olbasa Region*. RECAM 3. London: BIAA, 1998.
Mitchell, Stephen. "An Epigraphic Probe into the Origins of Montanism." Pages 168–97 in *Roman Phrygia: Culture and Society*. Edited by Peter Thonemann. Cambridge: Cambridge University Press, 2013.

Mørkholm, Otto, Philip Grierson, and Ulla Westermark. *Early Hellenistic Coinage from the Accession of Alexander to the Peace of Apamea (336–186 BC)*. Cambridge: Cambridge University Press, 1991.

Newell, Edward T. *The Coinage of the Western Seleucid Mints: From Seleucus I to Antiochus III, with a Summary of Recent Scholarship by Otto Mørkholm*. New York: American Numismatic Society, 1977.

Nollé, Johannes. "Marktrechte außerhalb der Stadt: Lokale Autonomie zwischen Statthalter und Zentralort." Pages 92–113 in *Lokale Autonomie und römische Ordnungsmacht in den kaiserzeitlichen Provinzen vom 1. Bis 3. Jahrhundert*. Edited by Werner Eck and Elisabeth Müller-Luckner. Munich: Oldenbourg, 1999.

Norwich, John J. *Byzantium: The Early Centuries*. London: Penguin, 1990.

Noy, David. *The City of Rome*. Vol. 2 of *Jewish Inscriptions of Western Europe*. Cambridge: Cambridge University Press, 1995.

Papadopoulos-Kerameus, A. Μαυρογορδάτειος Βιβλιοθήκη [The Mavrogordati Collection]. 2 vols. Constantinople: Boutura, 1884.

Papazoglou, Fanoula. *Laoi et Paroikoi: Recherches sur la structure de la société hellénistique*. Beograd: Université de Belgrade, 1997.

Parker, Barry F. "'Works of the Law' and the Jewish Settlement in Asia Minor." *JGRChJ* 9 (2013): 42–96.

Parker, Robert. *Greek Gods Abroad: Names, Natures and Transformations*. Berkeley: University of California Press, 2017.

Peers, Glenn. *Subtle Bodies: Representing Angels in Byzantium*. Berkeley: University of California Press, 2001.

Pennacchietti, Fabrizio A. "Nuove iscrizioni di Hierapolis Frigia." *AAT* 101 (1966–1967): 287–328.

Petzl, Georg. *Die Beichtinschriften Westkleinasiens*. Bonn: Habelt, 1994.

Posner, Daniel N. "Regime Change and Ethnic Cleavages in Africa." *Comparative Political Studies* 40 (2007): 1307–9.

Price, Simon R. F. "Gods and Emperors: The Greek Language of the Imperial Cult." *JHS* 104 (1984): 79–95.

Psoma, S. "War or Trade? Attic-Weight Tetradrachms in Seleukid Syria." Pages 265–96 in *Attalid Asia Minor: Money, International Relations and the State*. Edited by Peter Thonemann. Oxford: Oxford University Press, 2013.

Rajak, Tessa. "Synagogue and Community in the Graeco-Roman Diaspora." Pages 22–38 in *Jews in the Hellenistic and Roman Cities*. Edited by John R. Bartlett. London: Routledge, 2002.

Ratté, Christopher. "The Founding of Aphrodisias." Pages 7–36 in *Aphrodisias Papers 4: New Research on the City and Its Monuments*. Edited by C. Ratté and R. R. R. Smith. Portsmouth: Journal of Roman Archaeology, 2008.
Ricl, M. "Les ΚΑΤΑΓΡΑΦΑΙ du sanctuaire d'Apollon Lairbenos." *Arkeoloji Dergisi* 3 (1995): 167–95.
Ritti, Tullia, Celal Şimşek, and H. Yıldız. "Dediche e καταγραφαί dal santuario frigio di Apollo Lairbenos." *EA* 32 (2000): 1–88.
Ritti, Tullia, H. Hüseyin Baysal, Elena Miranda, and Francesco Guizzi, eds. *Museo Archaeologico di Denizli-Hierapolis Catalogo delle iscrizioni greche e latine*. Naples: Liguori, 2008.
Roueché, Charlotte. *Aphrodisias in Late Antiquity: The Late Roman and Byzantine Inscriptions*. Rev. 2nd ed. London: King's College, 2004.
Schalit, Abraham. "The Letter of Antiochus III to Zeuxis regarding the Establishment of Jewish Colonies in Phrygia and Lydia." *JQR* 50.4 (1960): 289–318.
Segre, M. "Iscrizioni di Licia I: Tolomeo di Telmesso." *Clara Rhodos* 9 (1928): 179–208.
Sekunda, Nicholas. "Changing Patterns of Land-Holding in the South-Western Border Lands of Greater Phrygia in the Achaemenid and Hellenistic Periods." Pages 48–76 in *Colossae in Space and Time: Linking to an Ancient City*. Edited by Alan H. Cadwallader and Michael Trainor. Göttingen: Vandenhoeck & Ruprecht, 2011.
Ševčenko, Nancy Patterson. "The Walters 'Imperial' Menologion." *Journal of the Walters Art Gallery* 51 (1993): 43–64.
Şimşek, Celal. *Laodikeia (Laodikeia ad Lycum)*. Istanbul: Ege, 2007.
Slater, Richard N. "An Inquiry into the Relationship between Community and Text: The Apocryphal Acts of Philip 1 and the Encratites of Asia Minor." Pages 281–306 in *The Apocryphal Acts of the Apostles*. Edited by François Bovon, Ann Graham Brock and Christopher R. Matthews. Harvard Divinity School Studies, Religions of the World. Cambridge: Harvard University Press, 1999.
Smith, Michael E., and Peter Peregrine. "Approaches to Comparative Analysis in Archaeology." Pages 4–20 in *The Comparative Archaeology of Complex Societies*. Edited by M. E. Smith. Cambridge: Cambridge University Press, 2011.
Staab, Karl. *Die Pauluskommentare aus der griechischen Kirche*. Münster: Aschendorff, 1933.

Stephens, Christopher W. B. *Canon Law and Episcopal Authority: The Canons of Antioch and Serdica.* Oxford: Oxford University Press, 2015.

Strootman, Rolf. "Seleucids." Pages 6119–25 in *The Encyclopedia of Ancient History.* Edited by Roger Bagnall et al. Malden: Wiley-Blackwell, 2012.

Tabbernee, William. *Fake Prophecy and Polluted Sacraments: Ecclesiastical and Imperial Reactions to Montanism.* Leiden: Brill, 2007.

Tanriver, C. "Three New Inscriptions from Tripolis." *EA* 42 (2009): 81–6.

Temporini, Hildegard. *Die Frauen am Hofe Trajans: Ein Beitrag zur Stellung der Augustae im Principat.* Berlin: de Gruyter, 1979.

Thonemann, Peter. "The Attalid State, 188–133 BC." Pages 1–47 in *Attalid Asia Minor: Money, International Relations and the State.* Edited by Peter Thonemann. Oxford: Oxford University Press, 2013.

———. *The Maeander Valley: A Historical Geography from Antiquity to Byzantium.* Cambridge: Cambridge University Press, 2011.

Tougher, Shaun. *Julian the Apostate.* Edinburgh: Edinburgh University Press, 2007.

Threatte, Leslie. *The Grammar of Attic Inscriptions.* Berlin: de Gruyter, 1980.

Trebilco, Paul. "Christians in the Lycus Valley: The View from Ephesus and from Western Asia Minor." Pages 180–211 in *Colossae in Space and Time: Linking to an Ancient City.* Edited by Alan H. Cadwallader and Michael Trainor. Göttingen: Vandenhoeck & Ruprecht, 2011.

———. *The Early Christians in Ephesus from Paul to Ignatius.* WUNT 166. Tübingen: Mohr Siebeck, 2004.

———. *Jewish Communities in Asia Minor.* SNTMS 69. Cambridge: Cambridge University Press, 1991.

Tuplin, Christopher. "Xenophon and the Garrisons of the Achmaenid Empire." *Archäologische Mitteilungen aus Iran* 20 (1987): 167–245.

Veyne, Paul. *Comment on écrit l'histoire: Essai d'épistémologie.* Paris: Seuil, 1987.

Walsh, Kevin. *The Archaeology of Mediterranean Landscapes: Human-Environment Interaction from the Neolithic to the Roman Period.* Cambridge: Cambridge University Press, 2014.

Walter, Christopher. *The Warrior Saints in Byzantine Art and Tradition.* Aldershot: Ashgate, 2003.

Walters, James. "Egyptian Religions in Ephesos." Pages 281–309 in *Ephesos: Metropolis of Asia; An Interdisciplinary Approach to Its Archaeology, Religion, and Culture.* Edited by Helmut Koester. HTS 41. Valley Forge: Trinity Press International, 1995.

Weiss, Peter. "The Cities and Their Money." Pages 57–68 in *Coinage and Identity in the Roman Provinces*. Edited by Christopher Howgego, Volker Heuchert, and Andrew Burnett. Oxford: Oxford University Press, 2007.

———. "Euergesie oder römische Pragegenehmigung? Aitesamenou-Formular auf Städtmünzen der Provinz Asia, Roman Provincial Coinage (*RPC*) II und persönliche Aufwendungen im Münzwesen." *Chiron* 30 (2000): 235–54.

Welles, Charles Bradford, Robert O. Fink, and Johnson Frank Gilliam, *The Parchments and the Papyri*. Excavations at Dura Europos 5.1. New Haven: Yale University Press, 1959.

Williams, Margaret H. "Semitic Name-Use by Jews in Roman Asia Minor and the Dating of the Aphrodisias *Stele* Inscriptions." Pages 173–97 in *Old and New Worlds in Greek Onomastics*. Edited by Elaine Matthews. Oxford: Oxford University Press, 2007.

Wörrle, M. "Antiochos I, Achaios der Ältere und die Galater. Eine neue Inscrhift in Denizli." *Chiron* 5 (1975): 59–87.

Wright, Nicholas. "Seleucid Royal Cult, Indigenous Religious Tradition and Radiate Crowns: The Numismatic Evidence." *Med Arch* 18 (2005): 67–82.

Salience, Multiple Affiliation, and Christ Belief in the Lycus Valley: A Conversation with Ulrich Huttner's *Early Christianity in the Lycus Valley*

Harry O. Maier

It would not be an overstatement to suggest that Ulrich Huttner's *Early Christianity in the Lycus Valley* is a watershed in the study of Christ religion in Phrygian Asia Minor.[1] The book is a monument of gathered and sifted evidence, analysis of primary literary data and material culture, and bibliographical resources. It is a meticulous, state-of-the-art work that no future research on the development of Christianity in central Asia Minor will be able to ignore. Dedicated studies to Pauline literature, Phrygian religious movements, and differing moments in the unfolding of Christianity in the first four centuries can easily suffer from the peril of microhistorical study, namely, a precise focus that ignores a wider swath of evidence and thus fails to see the forest for the trees. But a clear strength of *Early Christianity in the Lycus Valley* is that it takes a long and wide view of the topic under consideration. Long, because it seeks to chart out the topography of an emerging Christian tradition from the first through to the fifth century, and wide, because it seeks to analyze it with the help of known data that includes epigraphical and archaeological data as we know it from each of the decades and centuries under consideration. In doing so it aims to fulfill a chief objective of the Ancient Judaism and Early Christianity series and its subseries, Early Christianity in Asia Minor, in which the monograph finds its place, namely, as the volume's frontispiece indicates, to "focus on the rise and expansion of Christianity in a specific geographic region of Asia Minor up to the Council of Chalcedon in AD 451."

---

1. Ulrich Huttner, *Early Christianity in the Lycus Valley*, trans. David Green, AJEC 85, Early Christianity in Asia Minor 1 (Leiden: Brill, 2013).

What lies behind the series in general is the goal of revisiting Adolf von Harnack's *Mission and Expansion of Early Christianity*, with a view to bringing to bear on the topic new data that has emerged for our understanding of the emergence of Christianity in the ancient world.[2] *Early Christianity in the Lycus Valley* is the first volume to appear in the subseries, and at the time of press another one was anticipated on Lycaonian Christianity.[3] Huttner has set the bar very high. He extends far beyond Harnack's discussion of Christianity in the Lycus Valley, if only because Harnack dedicated barely a paragraph to the topic, constrained as he was by the available evidence at the time.[4] Further, Harnack ended his analysis with the Council of Nicaea; the Early Christianity in Asia Minor series has Chalcedon as its terminus. Nevertheless, in its overall orientation, the hermeneutical focus of the book remains that of Harnack, namely, to explain how Christianity expanded in the Lycus Valley and what factors contributed to its growth. In that sense, Huttner's, like Harnack's, is a teleologically driven account. Unlike, Harnack, however, Huttner does not describe the expansion of Christianity as a tragic decline of the Christian gospel as represented by the church but a movement toward institutionalization and centralization of the Christian message. We might speak then not so much of a narrative that betrays the acute Hellenization of the Christian message and thus a fall from gospel to philosophy (Harnack), so much as the steady growth of Christianity in the Lycus Valley until it became recognized by the state as a legitimate and finally official religion. At the same time, Huttner is interested in how Christian community (*Gemeinschaft*) was embedded in a larger society (*Gesellschaft*) and how lines between the two were often blurred as so-called Christians moved back and forth between so-called pagan society as well between other groups.[5]

My interest in what follows is largely hermeneutical and historiographical in orientation. To put it simply, what do we mean when we

---

2. Adolf von Harnack, *Die Mission und Ausbreitung des Christentums in den ersten drei Jahrhunderten*, 4th ed. (Leipzig: Hinrichs, 1924). The two-volume English translation (most recently reissued in 1972) is of the enlarged and second edition of 1908, *The Mission and Expansion of Christianity in the First Three Centuries*, trans. James Moffatt (London: Williams & Norgate, 1908). The first German edition was published in 1902.

3. Editor note: The volume has appeared since the time of the composition of Maier's response.

4. Huttner, *Early Christianity in the Lycus Valley*, 1–2.

5. Huttner, *Early Christianity in the Lycus Valley*, 5–7, 388–93.

speak of Christianity in the Lycus Valley, and what tools should we use to measure it? I aim to describe how Huttner answers those questions, and then I will furnish my own response to them. *Early Christianity in the Lycus Valley* presents, I will argue, a too static way of answering them. My proposal will be to champion a more dynamic response. To begin with, I will survey Huttner's historiographical methods and the way he builds and develops conclusions about data based on his survey of a wide array of data. My own perspective in what follows is guided, like Huttner's, in the social geographical study of space, and, after some other observations, this is where I will present a different kind of spatial approach to the kind that *Early Christianity in the Lycus Valley* presents.

Spatiality furnishes the center point of discussion because the series and subseries where Huttner's study is lodged arises out of the Excellence Cluster Topoi, a German federal and state funded programme that started in 2005 and concluded in 2017. Huttner's monograph arises from cooperation with a team at the Humboldt University of Berlin under the oversight of Cilliers Breytenbach. The subtitle of the project is "The Formation and Transformation of Space and Knowledge in Ancient Civilizations." The description of the project repays attention for its sophistication in presenting a spatial approach to a host of cultural phenomena that extend far beyond the study of emergent Christianity.[6] The website reveals a well-formulated and ambitious research prospectus divided into four overarching foci listed from A to D: (A) Spatial and Environment and Conceptual Design; (B) Constructing Historical Space; (C) Perception and Representation; and (D) Theory and Science. Each theme is further subdivided into four to six categories, with a host of dedicated teams leading projects in each subgroup. This is a rich complement comprised of a variety of aspects of the study of space ranging from the biological cognitive to the historical symbolic. *Early Christianity in the Lycus Valley* is the fruit the second of the four foci, namely, "Constructing Historical Space," specifically "Research Group B-4": "Space—Identity—Locality: The Construction of Knowledge Related Identity Spaces." The website represents the theoretical orientation of the research group. The prospectus warrants quotation at some length because it will steer the comments that follow:

---

6. "Excellence Cluster Topoi: The Formation and Transformation of Space and Knowledge in Ancient Civilization," www.topoi.org.

> Our conceptions of space, knowledge and cultural players, as well as of their interaction, have changed dramatically in recent decades; in the course of the already ancient processes of globalization and universalization, what role is played by distinctions that emerge as a result of contrary tendencies such as regionalization, particularization and/or "localization"? And what connections to possible concepts of identity shared by the bearers of these bodies of knowledge do such distinctions indicate? These issues are explored through the analysis of diverse, interdependent bodies of knowledge and their respective media (e.g. literary and religious texts, paintings, inscriptions, archaeological artifacts, rituals and performances), which on the one hand are connected with space to varying degrees, and yet on the other hand are also concretely situated in space. Space, knowledge and identity are understood here as interdependent social constructs; consequently, factual or fictional self-assignations play just as important a role as the hotly disputed topics of remembrance and collective memory.... The research group focuses on knowledge-based spaces of identity, whose founders, designers and addressees create, modify and materialize spatial arrangements and knowledge, and are thus essential for the production of relational space and bodies of knowledge. This becomes clear, e.g. in place- and space-oriented narratives, through spatially referenced material culture, in the form of discourses on memory, and in the course of cultural transformation within the scope of spatial mobility and cultural contact situations.[7]

The goals of the project express well what is the promise of spatial study in the investigation of Christian origins even as they point to a neglected area in the existing state of affairs. In other words, the spatial turn is yet to be undertaken in the disciplines of New Testament and early Christian studies despite the fact that it has long been made in ancient Near Eastern, Old Testament / Hebrew Bible, and classical studies.[8] *Early Christianity in the Lycus Valley* offers an avenue into this more spatially oriented study.

From the quotation just cited two statements deserve further exploration to address the hermeneutical and historiographical analysis this essay intends: "Space, knowledge and identity are understood here as interdependent social constructs; consequently, factual or fictional self-assignations play just as important a role as the hotly disputed topics of remembrance

---

7. "Space—Identity—Locality: The Construction of Knowledge Related Identity Spaces. Research Group B-4," http://www.topoi.org/group/b-4/.

8. For a general overview, Eric C. Stewart, "New Testament Space/Spatiality," *BTB* 42 (2012): 139–50.

and collective memory." "The research group focuses on knowledge-based spaces of identity, whose founders, designers and addressees create, modify and materialize spatial arrangements and knowledge, and are thus essential for the production of relational space and bodies of knowledge." In other words, space is a social product as much as it is a material phenomenon. Spatial study involves the ways in which people in engagement with one another produce relational spaces around them, and how physical space creates types of social relations. These include the ways in which the practitioners of space view the actors around them and the histories of the spaces to which they belong. Historians are also entailed in this production, of course, since the way they describe ancient actors and their spaces results in a constructed past made more or less persuasive depending on their perspective and analysis and presentation of data. Historians are, even as are their sources, entangled in the complexities of the material under investigation.[9]

With all of this orientation behind us, then, there are two things the aforementioned quotation furnishes as a point for critique of *Early Christianity in the Lycus Valley*. The first is *early Christianity* and the second is *the Lycus Valley*. Both phrases reveal critical hermeneutical decisions and reflect an orientation rather closer to that of the historical positivism of Harnack than I think it should be over a century after his work.

It will hardly come as a surprise that in the second half of the second decade of the twenty-first century a North American biblical scholar should challenge usage of the phrase "early Christianity" as a concept whose content, from a historical point of view, is self-evident. The pendulum has swung very far in the direction of contesting straightforward designations like this. The presence of the phrase in the title of the monograph is an easy target, but my intention is to do more than invoke a reigning fashion in the historical study of an emergent religious movement we today call Christianity. My interests are rather more precise and pointedly hermeneutical. As *Early Christianity in the Lycus Valley* unfolds, there appears to be two Christianities in a hermeneutical tug-of-war with one another. On the one hand, as already indicated, one of the chief interests of the book is to describe the process by which a collection of believers became a self-

---

9. For a hermeneutical engagement with entangled historiography within the framework of "histoire croisée," a phrase coined by its authors, see M. Werner and B. Zimmerman, "Beyond Comparison: *Histoire Croisée* and the Challenge of Reflexivity," *History and Theory* 45 (2006): 30–50.

defined institution—a *Gemeinschaft* with a particular standpoint within a *Gesellschaft*. I will query that linear model directly. First, I want to remark how insightful I think it is that Huttner names the concluding chapter of his book: "Communitization and the Search for a Standpoint." He remarks, "Two aspects of [the everyday world of the average Christian] can be illuminated through the diverse facets of the source material: community formation and the search for a defining position, a standpoint."[10] As the conclusions unfold, he notes how standpoints were not always shared, a point amply attested by the canons of the fourth century synod of Laodicea (ca. 363–364 CE). They represent a highly diverse set of beliefs and practices among Christ believers at a time when an imperially sponsored cult close to the capital was seeking to eliminate diversity in favor of a sanctioned unity. Among other things, the decrees condemn the worship of angels, attendance by Christ believers at synagogues, observation of the Jewish Sabbath rather than Sunday as the Lord's Day, women holding clerical titles and perhaps presiding at eucharistic celebration, the observation of Easter on the wrong date, and so on. So it is that Huttner writes, "When we address the question of who determined the boundaries and assigned the Christians their proper place, we see the dependence of the churches on the authorities."[11] I pause here to ask of this quotation: What does "their proper place" mean? Is this a native category or one brought in from the outside? The issue becomes more pronounced when on the next page he writes, "The Lycus Valley presents us with an interesting constellation precisely because ideas and practices of Christians *outside the churches* emerged and left sufficient traces of, especially in the context of pagan cults, to allow comparisons."[12] These include offices, prophecies, penitential inscriptions, prophets, and cultic singing in so-called pagan cults. This he argues resulted in what he describes as the emergence of "divided identities."[13] "On account of their common tradition, the many Jews of the Lycus Valley were much closer to the Christian than the pagans: however often the Christian spokesmen urged distance, it was a long time before Jews and Christians went their separate ways."[14] I whole-heartedly agree with this assessment of things on the ground and how it must have

---

10. Huttner, *Early Christianity in the Lycus Valley*, 385.
11. Huttner, *Early Christianity in the Lycus Valley*, 389.
12. Huttner, *Early Christianity in the Lycus Valley*, 390, emphasis added.
13. Huttner, *Early Christianity in the Lycus Valley*, 391.
14. Huttner, *Early Christianity in the Lycus Valley*, 391.

collided with clear demarcations dividing Christ followers from Jews and adherents of Greco-Roman religion that certain leaders wanted. Yet, as the book proceeds, Huttner appears unconsciously to have taken on the point of view that such leaders advanced against those with divided loyalties.

The long arch of the book's discussion of evidence from the first through to the fifth century includes a host of normative statements such as the ones that follow, cited in a more fulsome manner in order to make explicit the counter-argument being advanced in what follows. The red thread that runs through Huttner's patient distilling and description of evidence relevant to the emergence of Christ belief in the Lycus Valley is comprised of statements such as these: The author of the Colossians was opposing "a competing concept, primarily of Jewish origin, circulating in the guise of a philosophy, reduced to *crude* angel worship, *pointless* self-mortification, and *pedantic* observation of rules," three adjectives that the Colossian polemicist nowhere deploys.[15] "The lukewarmness of the Laodiceans [in Rev 3:16–17] finds expression in unthinking self-righteousness."[16] Philip's daughters [Acts 21:9] offered prophecies that "appear not to have overstepped the boundary of what was generally accepted by the Christian churches: their inspiration was obviously not accompanied by irritating phenomena, such as symptoms of ecstasy"; they were free from "the loss of control of [Montanist] pseudo-prophets, whose appearances regularly culminated in frenzy."[17] It is difficult to know when exactly but "the hierarchalization of the clergy was moving forward and the monarchic episcopate was becoming standard in western Asia Minor, as Ignatius attests for a series of churches."[18] "With his treatise Πρὸς Ἰουδαίους, Apollinaris takes his place in a process of emancipation that was soon to reach the Latin West with Tertullian's *Adversus Iudaeos*."[19] The light is diffuse that "blurs the lines between Christians and Jews on the fringes of cultic communities at the time of Apollinarius."[20] "Apollinarius had every reason to speak out against the suspect ecstatics [i.e., Montanists]."[21] An anonymous anti-Montanist author "contrasts the ecstatic prattling of Montanus

---

15. Huttner, *Early Christianity in the Lycus Valley*, 131, emphasis added.
16. Huttner, *Early Christianity in the Lycus Valley*, 158.
17. Huttner, *Early Christianity in the Lycus Valley*, 199.
18. Huttner, *Early Christianity in the Lycus Valley*, 214.
19. Huttner, *Early Christianity in the Lycus Valley*, 246.
20. Huttner, *Early Christianity in the Lycus Valley*, 247.
21. Huttner, *Early Christianity in the Lycus Valley*, 261.

with the messages of true prophets actually transported by the Spirit."²² "The inscriptions therefore do not constitute an independent witness that might help us describe the influence of the Montanists on the Christian church of Hierapolis in greater detail."²³ In the fourth century "members of the mainstream church thus occasionally found spiritual fulfillment at the cultic sites of sectarians."²⁴ The canons of Laodicea show that "this was not the first time that conflict with heretics flared up in the Lycus Valley."²⁵ "Though the pagans might be classed together [by the Synod of Laodicea] with Jews and heretics, the danger that they presented and the potential for conflict with them was smaller: they had little in common, and hence there were only a few bridges that might tempt Christians to cross over to them."²⁶ "The dubious activities of the Montanists and their prophetesses along with the integration of women into the clergy within that heresy, which likewise sought to appeal to local traditions, may have led the bishops assembled at Laodicea to eliminate the Presbytides [i.e., female clergy officiants]."²⁷ Flavian deposed "the scheming Dioscorus," "increasing institutionalization beginning in the [second] century offered the churches of the Lycus Valley a basis for participating in the structures of the universal church."²⁸

Huttner can hardly be faulted for quoting his sources, but not all—indeed few—of his evaluative descriptions can be found there, however much one may assume many of the champions of what would emerge as a mainstream of Christ belief from the second century onward might have agreed. Tertullian, for example, had far more strident things to say about those opposed to what he conceived as a predetermined set of beliefs handed down from Christ to the apostles than anything found in *Early Christianity in the Lycus Valley*. And it is possible that Huttner's original German text that was subsequently translated and then published in English used the first rather than second subjunctive, namely, the grammatical construction one uses in German to recount the point of view of one's quoted source to distinguish a reporter's own perspective from

---

22. Huttner, *Early Christianity in the Lycus Valley*, 261.
23. Huttner, *Early Christianity in the Lycus Valley*, 265.
24. Huttner, *Early Christianity in the Lycus Valley*, 299.
25. Huttner, *Early Christianity in the Lycus Valley*, 299.
26. Huttner, *Early Christianity in the Lycus Valley*, 305.
27. Huttner, *Early Christianity in the Lycus Valley*, 312.
28. Huttner, *Early Christianity in the Lycus Valley*, 318, 329.

the one cited. That grammatical possibility notwithstanding, the overall impression nevertheless stands: Huttner is telling us a story about Lycus Valley Christianity that came to espouse a Christian orthodoxy and the developments of that Christianity are ultimately measured in the light of it. How otherwise can one explain such evaluative phrases one finds in this long list of citations? When we read that some believers had not overstepped the boundaries of what was generally accepted Christian teaching in the second century, a number of assumptions are being made that should be challenged. What was accepted Christian teaching in the second century? What was Christianity in the second century for that matter? The search for a standpoint seems, despite Huttner's statement of its inchoate nature, to have already been present. The hermeneutical basis of that position is implied by the assertion of a normative acceptable Christianity. The description of the search for a standpoint is hardly aided by the use of adjectives and concepts such as "unthinking self-righteousness," "dubious activities," "pseudo-prophet," "emancipation from Jews," "scheming," "ecstatic prattling," and "universal church." Again, it is, of course, the case that some representatives of what would ultimately emerge as a state-endorsed Christianity and who represented themselves as the spokespersons of the universal church would wholeheartedly have endorsed such evaluative commentary. It is hard to imagine the followers of Montanus and Marcion not deploying the same invective against those opposed to them, yet nowhere do we find adjectives used by opponents of an emergent mainstream set of beliefs and practices to describe the normative form of Christ belief that represents, in Huttner's scheme, the Christianity of *Early Christianity in the Lycus Valley*. This is because, at least if one is to take seriously the adjectives deployed to describe them, they either simply were not Christians or they promoted retrograde versions of right belief.

It is worth pausing to take up by way of illustration a more detailed reading of the emergence of a monepiscopate and finally monarchical episcopate in Asia Minor. It is a commonplace to see Ignatius invoked as evidence of an advanced level of institutionalized Christ belief and organization in Asia Minor because the bishop from Antioch can single out a single individual as a bishop of a church in each of the cities to which he addresses his respective letters. Consistent with this line of argumentation, Huttner writes of Ignatius of Antioch already evidencing the institutionalization of the Asia Minor church by his ability to name a monarchical bishop separate from the rest of the so-called clergy. But to speak of deacons, presbyters and bishops as clergy is already problematic, since Ignatius himself is starting to construct the category by calling offside any eucharistic celebration not conducted by a bishop or someone he (the bishop) designates (Ignatius, *Smyrn.* 8.1, 2; 9.1; Ignatius, *Magn.* 4.1; Ignatius, *Tral.* 2.2; 3.1; Ignatius, *Phld.* 8.2). And it is not the case that Ignatius treats these as discrete orders; indeed, he portrays them as a collective, and their legitimate leadership is assigned by their being treated as such (for example, Ignatius, *Eph.* 4.1–2; Ignatius, *Magn.* 2.1; 7.1; 13.1–2; Ignatius, *Trall.* 3.1; 7.1–2; Ignatius, *Phld.* inscrip.; 4.1; 7.1; 10.1; Ignatius, *Smyrn.* 12.2; Ignatius, *Pol.* 6.1).

Further, it is not so straightforward that Ignatius is evidence of an achieved institutionalization; he is in a battle with Christ followers who seem to enjoy integration within certain Asia Minor churches, and it is arguable that they were surprised to hear themselves singled out as followers inimical to the Christian witness (Ignatius, *Eph.* 7.1; Ignatius, *Magn.* 3.2; 4.1; Ignatius, *Phld.* 7.2). In Ignatius, *Phld.* 7.1–2, Ignatius records the suspicion of his opponents that he was able to detect their presence in an assembly he personally addressed.[29] He defends himself against an accusation that someone tipped him off by appealing to a divine gift of spiritual discernment. It is a curious passage a full discussion of which lies outside the confines of the topic taken up here. It is sufficient to indicate the very real possibility that some in the assembly at Philadelphia found no reason

---

29. Εἰ γὰρ καὶ κατὰ σάρκα μέ τινες ἠθέλησαν πλανῆσαι, ἀλλὰ τὸ πνεῦμα οὐ πλανᾶται, ἀπὸ θεοῦ ὄν· οἶδεν γὰρ πόθεν ἔρχεται καὶ ποῦ ὑπάγει, καὶ τὰ κρυπτὰ ἐλέγχει. ἐκραύγασα μεταξὺ ὤν, ἐλάλουν μεγάλῃ φωνῇ, θεοῦ φωνῇ· Τῷ ἐπισκόπῳ προσέχετε καὶ τῷ πρεσβυτερίῳ καὶ διακόνοις. οἱ ὑποπτεύσαντές με ὡς προειδότα τὸν μερισμόν τινων λέγειν ταῦτα. μάρτυς δέ μοι ἐν ᾧ δέδεμαι, ὅτι ἀπὸ σαρκὸς ἀνθρωπίνης οὐκ ἔγνων. τὸ δὲ πνεῦμα ἐκήρυσσεν, λέγον τάδε· Χωρὶς τοῦ ἐπισκόπου μηδὲν ποιεῖτε· τὴν σάρκα ὑμῶν ὡς ναὸν θεοῦ τηρεῖτε· τὴν ἕνωσιν ἀγαπᾶτε· τοὺς μερισμοὺς φεύγετε· μιμηταὶ γίνεσθε Ἰησοῦ Χριστοῦ, ὡς καὶ αὐτὸς τοῦ πατρὸς αὐτοῦ. "For even though certain people wanted to deceive me, humanly speaking, nevertheless the Spirit is not deceived, because it is from God; for it knows from where it comes and where it is going, and exposes the hidden things. I called out when I was with you; I was speaking with a loud voice, God's voice: 'Pay attention to the bishop, the council of presbyters, and the deacons.' To be sure, there were those who suspected that I said these things because I knew in advance about the division caused by certain people. But the one for whose sake I am in chains is my witness that I did not learn this from any human being. No, the Spirit itself was preaching, saying these words: 'Do nothing without the bishop. Guard your bodies as the temple of God. Love unity. Flee from divisions. Become imitators of Jesus Christ, just as he is of his Father'" (trans. Holmes).

for marking internal boundaries of belief before Ignatius came through Asia Minor and tried to draw them. To put it differently, there is no reason to suppose that they would have had any reason *not* to be present. It is, in other words, Ignatius marking distinctions that were not definitive in the way Ignatius thought they should be before he travelled through the area. The fact that he can name people as bishops is not proof of a monarchical or even monepiscopate, only that he has found someone to represent his own interests. The letter of Polycarp to the Philippians in which Polycarp treats himself as a copresbyter and not a bishop of Smyrna is, I think, testimony to a more general state of affairs (Polycarp, *Phil.* inscrip.).[30] It is thus that I find Huttner's notion of a search for a standpoint the most credible way of treating the evidence which honors the data without asking it to conform to categories some Christ believers were bringing to the world around them for often polemical reasons. But I query his own standpoint vis-à-vis the evidence. One of the goals of the Excellence Cluster Topoi project is "to conduct a—likewise thoroughly (self) critical—inquiry into the contribution made by our own research practices to the constituting of contemporary identities."[31] In other words, the ways we are entangled with our sources are as critical to take note of as it is to recognize the fraught nature of traditional taxonomic constructions of boundaries in the analysis of ancient Christianity.

This leads to a second observation that focuses on the issue of linear developments. As the epigraphic evidence of some Jews living in the Lycus Valley suggests and Huttner himself concludes from it, we are dealing in the religious world of Jews and Christ followers with complex patterns of affiliation. He points, for example, to some funerary data that shows Lucius Nonios Glykon, probably a Jew, setting forth instructions for the dispersion of funds to his association of fellow weavers at the feast of Kalends and the festival of Passover to set a wreath on his grave and likewise to an association of purple-dyers to do the same on the feast of unleavened bread.[32] The conclusion to be drawn from this is that Glykon has no trouble seeing

---

30. Πολύκαρπος καὶ οἱ σὺν αὐτῷ πρεσβύτεροι τῇ ἐκκλησίᾳ τοῦ θεοῦ τῇ παροικούσῃ Φιλίππους· ἔλεος ὑμῖν καὶ εἰρήνη παρὰ θεοῦ παντοκράτορος καὶ Ἰησοῦ Χριστοῦ τοῦ σωτῆρος ἡμῶν πληθυνθείη. "Polycarp and the presbyters with him, to the church of God that sojourns at Philippi: may mercy and peace from God Almighty and Jesus Christ our Savior be yours in abundance" (trans. Holmes).

31. "Space—Identity—Locality," www.topoi.org/group/b-4/.

32. Huttner, *Early Christianity in the Lycus Valley*, 251.

himself as occupying two social groups that from a strict ideological point of view should have been kept separate. We can see this reflected as well in the canons of the Synod of Laodicea that forbid Christians from keeping Jewish Sabbath, attending synagogue, angel worship, and so on. This is but the extension of what we discover already in the canon, in the Letter to the Colossians where the author exhorts Christ followers of the Lycus Valley to avoid new moons and Sabbaths, ascetical disciplines, and the worship of angels (Col 2:16–19). Huttner describes this as "a competing concept," which is true, but it is too easy from there to reify such beliefs into the fault lines of competing communities and make one Christian and the other not. We may say that if there was a search for *a* standpoint, there was competition that involved *several* standpoints. Like Ignatius with respect to the so-called docetists, could it not rather be that our author is making a line rather than describing one? Surely Colossians itself attests to a complex affiliation of one view with other ones, the former given a rhetorical seal of approval by associating it with Paul's name.

Eric Rebillard offers a promising avenue into a discussion of the social complexity of multiple affiliation.[33] In his work on identity and Christianity in North Africa he contests the picture presented by Tertullian of the call to more fervent discipleship through refusing to go to the games, meeting with Jews, opposing pagans, and so on. Drawing on the ethnographical studies of Rogers Brubaker, he uses the term *groupism* to describe "the tendency to take discrete, sharply differentiated, internally homogeneous and externally bounded groups as basic constituents of social life, chief protagonists of social conflicts, and fundamental units of social analysis."[34] In place of groupism, again following Brubaker, he asks that we focus instead on "the processes through which categories are used by individuals to make sense of their social world." In favor of groupism, he uses the term *groupness* to describe how identity as a process refers to "a type of contingent *event*."[35] Groupness, he argues, depends on shifting points of salience. *Salience* refers to how identities are marked and acted upon in differing situations: "The 'salience' of an identity is its probability of being active in a situation, and 'activation' refers to the conditions

---

33. Éric Rebillard, *Christians and Their Many Identities in Late Antiquity: North Africa, 200–450 CE* (Ithaca, NY: Cornell University Press, 2012).

34. Rebillard, *Christians and Their Many Identities*, 2, quoting Rogers Brubaker, "Ethnicity without Groups," *Archives européennes de sociologie* 43.2 (2002): 163–69.

35. Rebilliard, *Christians and Their Many Identities*, 2.

in which an identity is actively engaged, as opposed to being latent and inactive."[36] Salience is what determines how one can be in one group at one time and another group at another time while the two groups promote values and practices that taken as a whole are from a groupism perspective antagonistic to one another. If we apply these insights concerning groupism to the Lycus Valley, we arrive at a picture different from Huttner's and one that contests the linearity of the model of the so-called rise and expansion of Christianity.

Rather than a linear model, we should imagine a model of overlapping circles and a series of rhetorical moves to create groupism from shifting events of groupness. Such moves often occasioned a rhetorical attempt to advance one point of salience over another. For some Christ followers, there is no conflict between angel and Christ worship, because what counts as salience and group identification belongs somewhere else than cosmic devotion to a singular deity. This does not mean that angel worship was crude, self-mortification pointless, and observation of rules pedantic: instead it means that such practices were events of affiliation, an affiliation Colossians seeks, through a rhetorical performance of the Pauline voice, to end through the assertion of groupism. The search then is not so much for a standpoint, but there is rather a conflict of competing standpoints, with the result that ideological considerations come into play that include the uses of rhetoric to malign a rejected position and set of practices. Nor can we speak straightforwardly of *Gemeinschaft* embedded in *Gesellschaft* since either category reifies shifting, colliding, and recombinant social allegiances. Ultimately in the Lycus Valley the state endorsed one set of positions and not the other, but even then salience changed as debates over so-called Arianism and then the pro-Alexandrian christology of Eutyches made their way through the Lycus Valley. Even so, people continued to do their own thing—if the canons of Laodicea are anything to go by—in practices that could not be confined to one circle or another. We will then not speak, like Harnack, of a rise and expansion of Christianity but rather of the creation of circles and their delimitation and strategies for control. Nor will we speak in a simple way of Christianity; rather, we will refer to strategies such as those undertaken by figures such Ignatius, Apollinarius, or the formulators of the canons of Laodicea to create something normative out of diverse practices and

---

36. Rebilliard, *Christians and Their Many Identities*, 3.

commitments. The question is then not a battle for Christianity per se but over what counts as salience and the rhetorical means of affirming groupism in the face of an inchoate groupness.

The second challenge to Huttner's formulation of the evidence is his study's use of the phrase *Lycus Valley*. Again, there are two valleys, as it were, that emerge in *Early Christianity in the Lycus Valley*. There are the geographical empirical boundaries of the valley, and then there are the social networks that form a web of relations both by those within and outside it. To focus too strictly on the valley as a limit for the consideration of data becomes problematic in some cases. For example, in his treatment of the message to the Laodiceans in Rev 3:15–22, Huttner invites us to consider the valuable material evidence of a thriving textile industry at the city. He then takes up each of the phrases of the admonitions and exhortations of the message (3:17–18) and shows how they can find an analogue in Laodicean material culture: eye salve, gold, white clothing, wealth. However, the message to the Laodiceans is one of seven messages, and one must ask how valid it is to seek to interpret the message without reference to the other six messages. It is true that none of the other cities addressed are in the Lycus Valley, but it is arguable that the messages are to be taken as a rhetorically constructed whole so that those Christ followers living in the Lycus Valley receive the references to the other cities as well. The difference this makes is, again, that we discover a contest over salience. It falls outside the confines of this essay to discuss in detail the scholarship that argues that John's messages reveal a contest over the kinds of economic practices and involvement Christ followers should have in imperial Asia Minor.[37] Arguably some—perhaps like believers in Corinth (1 Cor 8:10)—were inviting a much more relaxed attitude and did not limit them from meeting with colleagues in temple dining rooms where sacrificed food was consumed; John stridently opposes this. We cannot see this if we take up the message to the Laodiceans alone. The broader view allows us again to witness a battle over salience and the limits of affiliation. While some in Laodicea practice a groupness with

---

37. For example, Paul B. Duff, *Who Rides the Beast? Prophetic Rivalry and the Rhetoric of Crisis in the Churches of the Apocalypse* (Oxford: Oxford University Press, 2001), and Leonard L. Thompson, *The Book of Revelation: Apocalypse and Empire* (Oxford: Oxford University Press, 1990), furnish two studies that take up competing interpretations among Christ believers regarding believers' participation in the Roman imperial economy.

more porous boundaries, John under the rhetorical form of an apocalypse seeks a much more defined set of markers.

This then brings me to my third and final point, that of social geography and the social construction of space and identity. There is, of course, a physical Lycus Valley, and then there is an imagined and practiced one. Edward Soja, developing the categories of Henri Lefebvre outlined in his *The Production of Space*, distinguishes between first, second, and thirdspace.[38] Applying these concepts to the topic discussed here: firstspace is the topography and material geography and geology of the Lycus Valley as a set of earth coordinates; secondspace is the human design of firstspace for particular activities (the creation of cities, roads, trade routes, housing blocks, temples, and so on); thirdspace designates the idiosyncratic ways in which the inhabitants of the Lycus Valley lived first and secondspace. It is at the third level that the Excellence Cluster Topoi project is for me the most exciting: namely, we may describe thirdspace as the ways in which inhabitants of the valley used religious imagination and ideological strategies to live and delimit the living of space. The Lycus Valley under this aspect is an imaginary world with protagonists and antagonists, mythic narratives, socially constructed memory, and a set of rhetorically charged incentives to live space in one way rather than another. Here polemic and apologetic find their place as what people do when they meet are taken up in overarching narratives and places are populated with heroes and villains. It is this imaginary world where we can legitimately use a host of adjectives to describe differing accounts of Christian practices. But we do so knowing that we are engaging in the creation of a kind of noumenal or imagined Lycus Valley. Perhaps that particular chapter has yet to be written about the Lycus Valley—the imaginary valley made up of destructive and constructive religious forces and their chief characters with their corresponding virtues and vices. It is this imagined Paul who addresses this imagined set of Christ followers in the Lycus Valley in a letter alleging to come from him. It is a world where the Colossians Christ followers are part of a grand narrative that like the imperial gospel is growing and taking the world by storm (Col 1:6) in which angel worshipers only reveal that they have fallen prey to a villainous philosophy (2:8).

---

38. Edward Soja, *Thirdspace: Journeys to Los Angeles and Other Real-and-Imagined Places* (Oxford: Blackwell, 1996); Henri Lefebvre, *The Production of Space*, trans. Donald Nicholson-Smith (Oxford: Blackwell, 1991).

Such an imagined valley is central to the establishment of competing standpoints and overlapping circles I have discussed. Groupness springs forth from imaginary fields of belonging. Salience appears and disappears as some practices and beliefs become the focus of one imaginary or another. These do not continue statically but rather are made and remade in different kinds of encounters. On such an account religion in the Lycus Valley is a dynamic lived phenomenon, even as its intersections with the poleis of the region unfold in differing constellations of actors with shifting interests and objectives. Historians by virtue of hindsight have the capacity to furnish a kind of freeze frame perspective on one moment or another, a particular set of actors, and on material spaces and identities. In doing so they also inhabit their own spatial imaginaries, sometimes consciously and often unconsciously.

Bibliography

Brubaker, Rogers. "Ethnicity without Groups." *Archives européennes de sociologie* 43.2 (2002): 163–69.

Duff, Paul B. *Who Rides the Beast? Prophetic Rivalry and the Rhetoric of Crisis in the Churches of the Apocalypse*. Oxford: Oxford University Press, 2001.

Harnack, Adolf von. *Die Mission und Ausbreitung des Christentums in den ersten drei Jahrhunderten*. 4th ed. Leipzig: Hinrichs, 1924.

———. *The Mission and Expansion of Christianity in the First Three Centuries*. Translated by James Moffatt. London: Williams & Norgate, 1908.

Holmes, Michael, trans. *The Apostolic Fathers: Greek Texts and English Translations*. 3rd ed. Grand Rapids: Baker Academic, 2007.

Huttner, Ulrich. *Early Christianity in the Lycus Valley*. Translated by David Green. AJEC 85; Early Christianity in Asia Minor 1. Leiden: Brill, 2013.

Lefebvre, Henri. *The Production of Space*. Translated by Donald Nicholson-Smith. Oxford: Blackwell, 1991.

Rebillard, Éric. *Christians and Their Many Identities in Late Antiquity: North Africa, 200–450 CE*. Ithaca, NY: Cornell University Press, 2012.

Soja, Edward. *Thirdspace: Journeys to Los Angeles and Other Real-and-Imagined Places*. Oxford: Blackwell, 1996.

Stewart, Eric C. "New Testament Space/Spatiality." *BTB* 42 (2012): 139–50.

Thompson, Leonard L. *The Book of Revelation: Apocalypse and Empire*. Oxford: Oxford University Press, 1990.

Werner, M., and B. Zimmerman. "Beyond Comparison: *Histoire Croisée* and the Challenge of Reflexivity." *History and Theory* 45 (2006): 30–50.

Part 3
Thematic Essays on the Lycus Valley

Initiation, Vision, and Spiritual Power: The Hellenistic Dimensions of the Problem at Colossae

Clinton E. Arnold

The precise nature of the problem at Colossae has been an insoluble riddle in biblical scholarship. We are no closer to a consensus solution now than we were thirty years ago when I began puzzling over this conundrum.[1] So why not join the mounting chorus of voices that claim that there is no more to be said on this issue? Precisely because there is more to be said— actually a lot more. There are new texts and new vantage points on familiar texts. Our understanding of the depth and complexities of Judaism at this time has been greatly expanded by both the publication of new texts and insights into what these texts reveal about life in these diaspora communities. It is simply no longer adequate to conclude that the source of the competing teaching in the church at Colossae was some sort of Jewish influence and leave it at that. We need to ask: What kind of Judaism?

We have also learned more about the local religions, particularly the Apollo cult, arguably the most important local god in the Lycus Valley. Our knowledge of the nature and function of the Apollo oracle sanctuaries in western Asia Minor has increased through ongoing excavations, especially at Claros.

Perhaps most importantly, over the past thirty years we have learned a great deal more about Roman-era interest in ritual power. How does one gain access to spiritual power for personal well-being and the good of the community? This was a practical concern for matters of daily life. How do I keep my livestock from dying? How do I protect my kids from the ravages of fever? How do I avert the evil eye or a curse placed on

---

1. See my *The Colossian Syncretism: The Interface between Christianity and Folk Belief at Colossae*, WUNT 2/77 (Tübingen: Mohr Siebeck, 1995).

me by my disgruntled neighbor? Interest in ritual power is a phenomenon that crossed all religious lines and was exceedingly important to common people.

Interpreting the Colossian problem as some form of syncretism has actually been the consensus view until recently. For many scholars, Martin Dibelius's important 1917 essay, "The Isis Initiation in Apuleius and Related Initiatory Rites," confirmed that the teaching was syncretistic.[2] Dibelius appeared to provide proof positive that the Colossian teaching was informed by mystery initiation ritual through the discovery of the Colossian catchword ἐμβατεύω in a series of oracular inscriptions in the Apollo temple at Claros. This view held sway until Fred Francis wrote two highly influential essays attempting to refute Dibelius's claims and locating the problem squarely in Judaism.[3] His two major lines of contribution were in seeking to establish (1) that ἐμβατεύω from Col 2:18 was not a technical term of the mysteries and that it could be used simply in the sense of entering, especially entering into possession of property, and (2) that "the worship of angels" could and should be taken as a subjective genitive meaning that the angels were not the objects of worship but were the ones doing the worshipping. Thus, Francis argued, the author of Colossians was concerned about Jewish ascent to heaven visionary experiences and the Colossian believers were seeking to worship with the angels around the heavenly throne. This view made it possible for Francis, and many subsequent interpreters, to deny any kind of Hellenistic or local religious influence on the problematic teaching at Colossae. Consequently, James Dunn and others could contend that the issue is simply the persistent influence of the synagogue down the road and that the problem is much like the one looming in the background of Galatians[4] (never mind that the word "law" never appears in Colossians, much less "works of the law").

---

2. Martin Dibelius, "The Isis Initiation in Apuleius and Related Initiatory Rites" in *Conflict at Colossae*, ed. Fred O. Francis and Wayne A. Meeks, SBLSBS 4 (Missoula, MT: Scholars Press, 1973), 61–121.

3. Fred O. Francis, "Humility and Angelic Worship in Col 2:18," in Francis and Meeks, *Conflict at Colossae*, 163–95, and Francis, "The Background of EMBATEUEIN (Col 2:18) in Legal Papyri and Oracle Inscriptions," in *Conflict at Colossae*, 197–207.

4. James D. G. Dunn, *The Epistles to the Colossians and to Philemon*, NIGTC (Grand Rapids: Eerdmans, 1996), 23–35, esp. 33–35. See also his "The Colossian Philosophy: A Confident Jewish Apologia," *Bib* 76 (1995): 153–81.

Advocates of this perspective, in my view, have certainly been correct in affirming that there are Jewish elements to the Colossian philosophy. Dibelius and Lohse went much too far in denying this.[5] "Festivals, new moons, and sabbaths" is clearly a Jewish contribution. But, again, what kind of Judaism are we talking about? And has the trend to resist seeing any form of Hellenistic or local religious influence neglected important data?

Initiation

The achilles heel to a purely Jewish view of the Colossian problem has been the presence of the term ἐμβατεύω in Col 2:18 as part of the author's polemical description of the variant teaching. If this is a technical term from mystery initiation ritual and is reflective of the experience of the rival teacher at Colossae, then the problem at Colossae truly is a mixing of religious traditions. Joachim Gnilka has rightly characterized the expression, ἃ ἑόρακεν ἐμβατεύων, as the most puzzling clause of the entire letter.[6] Was ἐμβατεύω a technical term of the higher stage of initiation ritual (parallel to the ἐποπτεία at Elesusis), or was it a simple equivalent of εἰσέρχομαι? More important, had the ringleader of the competing teaching at Colossae undergone ritual initiation as the basis for his knowledge and claims? There are many reasons for maintaining that it was indeed a technical term of ritual initiation and that its presence in Colossians implies that initiation had something to do with the Colossian problem.

In spite of Francis's claim that ἐμβατεύω was a well-known term and "was the common property of any man on the street," the evidence proves otherwise. Whereas εἰσέρχομαι appears 710 times in the LXX and 194 times in the New Testament, ἐμβατεύω never appears in the New Testament (outside of Colossians) and only seven times in the LXX. It never appears in the Greek pseudepigrapha, nor does it ever appear in the Apostolic Fathers. Even Philo never makes use of the term. It is also quite rare in all other ancient literature. Thus, the fact that it appears four times in oracle inscriptions at an

---

5. Martin Dibelius and Heinrich Greeven, *An die Kolosser, Epheser, an Philemon*, HNT 12, 3rd ed. (Tübingen: Mohr Siebeck, 1953), 38–40; Eduard Lohse, *Colossians and Philemon*, Hermeneia (Philadelphia: Fortress, 1971), 116: "The 'philosophy; made use of terms which stemmed from Jewish tradition, but which had been transformed in the crucible of syncretism to be subject to the service of 'the elements of the universe.'"

6. Joachim Gnilka, *Der Kolosserbrief*, HThKNT 10.1 (Freiburg: Herder, 1980), 150.

oracle center for Apollo just north of Ephesus where delegations came from the Lycus Valley could be rather relevant to our inquiry.[7] Francis does recognize the unusual concentration of the term's usage at Claros, but he contends that its use there probably spurred the popular nontechnical use.[8] He has no answer to the question of *why* it was used so frequently there.

Francis and others who have embraced his conclusions regarding ἐμβατεύω have sought to argue that the term had no technical significance at Claros. Yet three of the four occurrences are preceded by a widely recognized technical expression of the mysteries as a dependent adverbial participle—μυηθέντες (μυέω), to be initiated into the mysteries.[9] The fourth is a different but equally technical expression of the mysteries, "having received the mysteries" (παραλαβὼν τὰ μυστήρια).[10] Although it could be argued that the μύησις, or "receiving the mysteries," was the initiation proper and that experience was the prelude to entering the oracle chamber, that argument would accomplish nothing since the climax of the whole ritual was yet to come with the entering. It is in the entering when the prophet would receive his mantic inspiration and convey the oracle as well as the occasion when the god himself would make an appearance. It is precisely in this second stage where the visionary experience would occur. The unique and rare term ἐμβατεύω is, in fact, the technical term for conveying the climax of the ritual initiation.

We now know much more about the sanctuary of Apollo at Claros thanks to the excavations over the past couple of decades by a French delegation led by Juliette de Genière and now under the direction of Professor Nuran Sahin. There was, in fact, a labyrinth-like subterranean level underneath the temple structure.[11] This was built around the sacred spring—the

---

7. See the collected inscriptions with English translation and discussion in my *Colossian Syncretism*, 109–13.

8. Francis, "Background of EMBATEUEIN," 203.

9. The first three inscriptions were originally published by Theodore Macridy in "Altertümer von Notion," *JÖAI* 8 (1905): 165 (= §2.2), 170 (= §5.4); see also *OGIS* 530 (192–97); *IGRR* 4.1586 (521), and in Macridy, "Antiquités de Notion II," *JÖAI* 15 (1912): 46, no. 1.1.

10. This inscription was originally published by Charles Picard, "Un Oracle d'Apollon Clarios a Pergame," *BCH* 46 (1922): 190–97. See also *CIG* 2.3538; Reinhold Merkelbach, *Philologica: Ausgewählte Kleine Schriften*, ed. Wolfgang Blümel et al. (Stuttgart: Teubner, 1997), 162–67 (= no. 2).

11. Fritz Graf, *Apollo*, Gods and Heroes of the Ancient World (New York: Routledge, 2009), 72.

source of the water from which the priest would drink for prophetic inspiration. The term ἐμβατεύω gave expression to the action of going down the steps of the sanctuary leading to this underground area and entering the room where vision and revelation would take place. Only three ancient writers provide written testimony to how the oracle operated (Tacitus, *Ann.* 2.54; Pliny, *Nat.* 2.232; Iamblichus, *Myst.* 3.11). Iamblichus gives us the most detail:

> It is agreed by everyone that the oracle at Colophon [the Clarian Apollo] prophesies by means of water. There is a spring in a subterranean chamber, and from it the prophet drinks on certain appointed nights, after performing many preliminary ceremonies, and after drinking, he delivers his oracles, no longer seen by the spectators present.... Still, not every inspiration that the water gives is from the god, but this only bestows the receptivity and purification of the luminous spirit in us through which we are able to receive the god. But the presence of the god is different from and prior to this, and flashes like lightning from above. This holds aloof from no one who, through a kindred nature, is in union with it; but it is immediately present and uses the prophet as an instrument while he is neither himself nor has any consciousness of what he says or where on the earth he is, so that even after prophesying, he sometimes scarcely gets control of himself. Even before drinking, he fasts the whole day and night, and after becoming divinely inspired, he withdraws by himself to sacred, inaccessible places, and by this withdrawal and separation from human affairs, he purifies himself for receiving the god; and through these means, he has the inspiration of god illuminating the pure sanctuary of his own soul, and providing for it an unhindered divine possession, and a perfect and unimpeded presence. (Iamblichus, *Myst.* 3.11)

Although Iamblichus writes later than the first century, he likely conveys an accurate framework for how the oracle at Claros operated in the first century and before.

Archaeological evidence and comparison with what happened at the Apollo sanctuaries at Didyma and Delphi can bring further clarification. Celeste Guichard describes it in this way:

> The cult officials accompanied the *mantis* in his descent. The entire group first walked through a small doorway at the back of the porch and the left of the large, central door. After crossing the threshold, the officials turned right, descended the staircase and followed a corridor to the first of two subterranean rooms—all of the cult officials, except the *mantis*, remained in the first room. The *mantis* continued alone into

the next, hypaethral chamber and drank from the sacred spring, which enabled him to communicate with Apollo.[12]

As Guichard contends, because the *mantis* received inspiration in the hypaethral chamber, the oracular inspiration took place in a portion of the temple open to the sky, thus lending an astrological flavor to the entire experience. "The hypaethral spaces at Didyma and at Klaros enabled the *mantis* to be in contact with the cosmos as it exists above, below, and all around."[13] This would also fit with the experience of Apuleius who witnessed the cosmic powers in his initiation in the Isis sanctuary at Cenchrae (Apuleius, *Metam.* 11.23).

So why did members of delegations consulting the Clarian Apollo seek initiation? Fritz Graf describes the initiation experience at Claros in this way:

> Not everybody, however, was allowed to come so close: in order to "go down" [*embateuein*], one had to undergo an initiation, a presumably costly privilege offered only to the select few. Throughout Greece, initiations were a ritual means of entering into close and often personal contact with a divinity.[14]

The experience of initiation provided one with direct contact with the divine. It was a source of spiritual power and imparted wisdom into spiritual matters. It was often a foundational and prerequisite experience for becoming a community healer and wise man, a role anthropologists refer to as a shaman.[15] As Guichard notes, "initiates received the arcane knowledge that elevated them above the unenlightened masses."[16] This arcane knowledge would likely be closely related to the major areas of Apollo's contributions to a community. He is not only an oracular god who can advise on the future or reveal what is behind a situation (like the reason for a plague), but he is a healing god.[17] He is also the "Averter of Evil"

---

12. Celeste L. Guichard, "Travels and Traversals in the Hellenistic Oracular Temples at Klaros and Didyma" (PhD diss., Columbia University, 2005), 89.

13. Guichard, "Hellenistic Oracular Temples," 102.

14. Graf, *Apollo*, 59.

15. On the topic of shamanism, see Thomas A. DuBois, *An Introduction to Shamanism* (Cambridge: Cambridge University Press, 2009). See especially chapter 5, "The Shamanic Calling," 56–81.

16. Guichard, "Hellenistic Oracular Temples," 97.

17. See Graf, *Apollo*, 79–102 (= chapter 4: "Apollo, God of Healing").

(*Alexikakos*) and the "Guardian of the Gates" (*Propylaioi*).[18] Healing and protection from evil were the concerns of every rural community and would certainly have been a concern for individuals within the Christian community at Colossae.

How, then, is the Apollo temple at Claros relevant to people living in the Lycus Valley? Of the twenty-seven epigraphic oracles extant from Claros dating between the first and third centuries, nineteen were delivered to cities, and two of these cities included Laodicea and Hierapolis. Cities of the Lycus Valley were not only familiar with the oracle, but sometimes they sent embassies to seek a response from the god. Hierapolis was, in fact, one of five cities where Clarian epigraphic oracles survive outside of Claros.[19] Hierapolis was also home to two local forms of the god Apollo: Apollo Kareios (the epithet could mean "Carian") and Apollo Archegetes. The most well-known embassy from Hierapolis took place in 160 CE to seek the god's input about the problem of a plague after the Parthian campaign of Lucius Verus (see Cassius Dio, *Hist. rom.* 71.2.4; Aelius Aristides, *Or.* 33.6, 48.38–39, 51.25).[20] Laodicea also consulted the Clarian Apollo with great frequency.[21] Thus, there was a direct connection between the Lycus Valley and Claros, which can explain how the vocabulary of the cult would be familiar to people living in Colossae.

This evidence does not prove that the use of ἐμβατεύω in Colossians must be derived from its technical use in the language of mystery initiation practices associated with the Apollo temple at Claros.[22] But it definitely

---

18. Graf, *Apollo*, 93.

19. Zsuzsanna Várhelyi, "Magic, Religion, and Syncretism at the Oracle at Claros," in *Between Magic and Religion: Interdisciplinary Studies in Ancient Mediterranean Religion and Society*, ed. Sulochana R. Asirvatham, Stephen Harrison, and Jaś Elsner (New York: Rowman & Littlefield, 2001), 15.

20. Várhelyi, "Oracle at Claros," 15; the text is translated by Ian Rutherford, "Trouble in Snake-Town: Interpreting an Oracle from Hierapolis-Pamukkale," in *Severan Culture*, ed. Simon Swain et al. (Cambridge: Cambridge University Press, 2007), 450–51.

21. Louis Robert and Jeanne Robert, *Claros I: Décrets Hellénistiques* (Paris: Éditions Recherche sur les Civilisations, 1989), 5.

22. During the discussion period of the "Polis and Ekklesia: Investigations of Urban Christianity" section of the Society of Biblical Literature on November 21, 2015 where I presented this paper, Angela Standhartinger objected to the relevance of these inscriptions for Colossians by observing that the Clarian inscriptions relate to embassies and not individuals (like a shaman). Yet we know that individuals did consult the

enhances the plausibility. And, of course, if the Colossian philosophy has something to do with mystery initiation ritual, then it is clearly syncretistic. But does the idea of ritual initiation fit with the other indicators that we have from the text of Colossians on what this rival teaching and practice was advocating?

Vision

The immediate context for the occurrence of ἐμβατεύω in Colossians is the relative clause ἃ ἑόρακεν, "what he has seen" (2:18). The neuter accusative plural relative pronoun could refer to the immediately preceding "humility" and "the worship of angels" as the objects of entering. But this creates an awkward picture, for how does one see humility? Francis tried to escape this difficulty by arguing that ταπεινοφροσύνη should be understood here as "instruction in humility for the purpose of obtaining visions," that is, angelic instruction is the object of the vision."[23] But such an explanation grossly overinterprets ταπεινοφροσύνη. Many of the followers of Francis do not sense this difficulty.

The more likely interpretation is that the relative clause, "what he has seen," is the object of ἐμβατεύω, thus giving the result, "entering what he has seen." This would fit with the idea of entering into the oracle grotto or entering into the visionary experience that is associated with this culminating experience of initiation. The priest would have led the initiate through ecstatic visionary experiences—perhaps including descent to the underworld and ascent to heaven—ultimately culminating in a vision of the god. "What he has seen" thus sums up the totality of the visionary experience as part of the second stage of the mystery initiation following the μύησις.

All interpreters of Colossians agree that the clause "what he has seen" signals visionary experience of some sort. The key question remains: Was this a Jewish visionary ascent to heaven experience, such as we see, for instance, in the Qumran Songs of the Sabbath Sacrifice? There the

---

oracle as we can see in the example of Germanicus who travelled to Claros to consult the oracle shortly after he was made consul for the second time (Tacitus, *Ann.* 2.54). The inscriptions set up to honor the oracle god appear only to be necessary for the groups who came and received the oracle. The fact that individuals were not put under this obligation may relate to the expense.

23. Francis, "Humility and Angel Worship," 195–98.

mystic observes angels "enter through the gates of glory … the gates of the entrance" and sees even the gates "blessing and praising all the spirits of God in the exits and in the entrances through the gates of holiness" (4Q405 23 I, 8–10). Or was this visionary experience something that the Colossian teacher experienced in a pagan ritual initiation?

Markus Barth asks the right question when he says, "From the context, which points to visionary experiences, we could deduce that 'naturally' heaven was meant where the worship of angels was observed. But still we need to ask why *embateuein* was even put here when it cannot explain the context, but rather must be explained from within it."[24] This, of course, could be easily explained if ἐμβατεύω were a catchword of the opponents related to ritual initiation. There is still no evidence of ἐμβατεύω ever used to speak of entry to heaven in a visionary way in Jewish texts.[25] But we do have it used multiple times to speak of entry into the oracle grotto as the higher stage of an initiation ritual in the Klaros inscriptions.

Spiritual Power

There has been strong resistance to seeing the problem at Colossae as having some kind of meaningful connection with local religions or Hellenistic religious thought. Thus, Witherington says that my case "underplays the Jewishness of what Paul is dealing with here."[26] So also, Bevere, who notes, "Arnold's position ultimately does not take seriously the Jewishness of the philosophy.… He and others who want to propose some sort of syncretistic thesis fail to take seriously the Jewishness of the practices of the philosophy."[27]

But the question needs to be posed to them: What kind of Judaism? One of the lessons of the last thirty years is that there is a dimension of Judaism that can be described as a Judaism of ritual practices to gain power

---

24. Markus Barth and Helmut Blanke, *Colossians*, trans. Astrid B. Beck, AB 34B (New York: Doubleday, 1994), 348.

25. Contra Michael Bird, *Colossians and Philemon*, New Covenant Commentary Series (Eugene, OR: Cascade Books, 2009), 86 n. 38, who erroneously claims that "the word was frequent in Jewish apocalyptic literature in reference to visionary ascents."

26. Ben Witherington III, *The Letters to Philemon, the Colossians, and the Ephesians: A Socio-rhetorical Commentary on the Captivity Epistles* (Grand Rapids: Eerdmans, 2007), 162.

27. Allan R. Bevere, *Sharing in the Inheritance: Identity and Moral Life in Colossians*, JSNTSup 226 (New York: Sheffield Academic, 2003), 113.

for the well-being of the community.²⁸ This is precisely the kind of Judaism that is reflected in a figure such as Sceva in Acts 19—an itinerant Jewish exorcist who styled himself as a high priest. This is the Judaism of folk piety that was interested in exorcism, healing, counteracting curses, and insuring prosperity. This is actually a substructure to Judaism that could cross a variety of other group boundary markers within Judaism.

It is also a form of Judaism where we can expect to see some of the highest levels of assimilation to the beliefs and practices of local religions. As John Barclay notes in his important volume on *Jews in the Mediterranean Diaspora*, this is a facet of Judaism where there was a strong tendency toward syncretism.²⁹ We have learned much about this dimension of Judaism through the study of texts like the Hekhalot literature, Sepher Harazim, the eighteenth chapter of the Testament of Solomon, newly published sectarian texts from Qumran, amulets, curse tablets, magical bowls, and even Jewish texts embedded in the Greek Magical Papyri (such as the Eighth Book of Moses). All of these texts show a level of syncretism that goes beyond what we find in any other Jewish texts. Those involved in these arts were far more concerned about power than orthodoxy or piety. This is why Helios is invoked in Sepher Harazim, why Apollo is invoked alongside Jewish angels in *PGM* 1.296–300, and why the god Aion/Helios is called upon in the Eighth Book of Moses.

Although there is little evidence for Jewish involvement in pagan ritual initiation, there is some—precisely in the realm of magic and folk belief. The initiation experience is central in the so-called Eighth Book of Moses, a handbook for magic/religious ritual that serves as an important "witness to the rich interpenetration of Judaism and paganism in late antiquity."³⁰ This syncretistic text contains a variety of ritual preparations that are essential to being filled prior to the initiation proper.³¹ This includes seven days

---

28. See Rebecca M. Lesses, *Ritual Practices to Gain Power: Angels, Incantations, and Revelation in Early Jewish Mysticism*, HTS (Harrisburg, PA: Trinity Press International, 1998). See also James R. Davila, *Descenders to the Chariot: The People behind the Hekhalot Literature*, JSJSup 70 (Leiden: Brill, 2001).

29. John M. G. Barclay, *Jews in the Mediterranean Diaspora: From Alexander to Trajan (323 BCE–117 CE)* (Berkeley: University of California Press, 1996), 121.

30. Todd E. Klutz, "The Eighth Book of Moses," *MOTP* 1:189.

31. This text was ultimately pagan, but it is infused with a number of Jewish elements reflecting the kind of Jewish magic and shamanistic practices of the Roman era. Bert Jan Lietaert Peerbolte, "The *Eighth Book of Moses* (PLeid. J 395): Hellenistic Jewish Influence in a Pagan Magical Papyrus," in *A Kind of Magic: Understanding*

of purification (involving various taboos) and a set of rituals that begin with the new moon. This particular initiation is closely associated with the god Apollo. The book is replete with invocations of spirits and gods. The end result is that the initiate is endowed with wisdom and spiritual power that enables him to serve the community such as in providing healing for assorted ailments and casting demons away from people.

There is no doubt that there were Jewish elements in the Colossian philosophy. The real issue is how these Jewish elements fit with all of the other features of the teaching that we can identify. I have argued elsewhere that θρησκεία τῶν ἀγγέλων, "the worship of angels," in Col 2:18 is the letter writer's reference to the tendency to invoke and call upon angels in the practice of the Colossian philosophy.[32] The genitive τῶν ἀγγέλων is thus an objective genitive. θρησκεία is not the normal word for "worship" in the biblical texts; those would normally be προσκυνέω or λατρεύω. In fact, θρησκεία never appears in the Greek Old Testament and only four times in the New Testament. Bauer characterizes it as an "expression of devotion to transcendent beings, esp. as it expresses itself in cultic rites, *worship*, the being who is worshiped is given in the obj. gen."[33] Thus, Wis 4:27 says, "For the worship of idols [εἰδώλων θρησκεία] not to be named is the beginning and cause and end of every evil." The sense in Colossians is that the rival teachers were advocating rituals directed at angels. This would encompass invoking angels, the use of charms and amulets to solicit their help, and rituals designed to obtain their assistance.

There are numerous Jewish texts that illustrate this kind of an approach to angels, and I have documented these elsewhere. Archaeologists have recently uncovered an important text of this type in very close proximity to Colossae that has now been published in *Epigraphica Anatolica*.[34] In the necropolis just north of Hierapolis, excavators found a bronze scroll in a silver tube in a tomb. The text reads: "I adjure you by God who founded

---

Magic in the New Testament and Its Religious Environment, ed. Bert Jan Lietaert Peerbolte and Michael Labahn, LNTS 306 (London: T&T Clark, 2007), 192, notes, "Next to the mention of the temple in Jerusalem, there are more Jewish elements in *Moses VIII* that are difficult to account for if not by postulating some kind of interaction between Jewish and pagan sorcerers."

32. Arnold, *Colossian Syncretism*, 90–102.
33. BDAG, *s.v.* "θρησκεία."
34. Murat Aydaş, "New Inscriptions from Asia Minor," *Epigraphica Anatolica* 37 (2004): 124.

the earth and the heavens; I adjure you by the angels, Cherubim, the harmony above, Michael, Raphael, Abrasax [at this point the text breaks away and no other names are legible] to be averted from injury."

Conclusion

My contention is that the ringleader behind the spiritual practices advocated at Colossae is a Jewish (now Christian) shaman-like figure that bears a resemblance to Sceva in Acts 19. He is someone of stature within the community and known for his wisdom, knowledge, and expertise regarding spiritual power. He is the go-to person in the community for matters related to healing, exorcism, and protection from evil. In continuity with the tradition of spiritual healers and shamans in the past, he performs an important function in the community.

The various identifiable features of the Colossian philosophy cohere well in this kind of figure. Ritual initiation and visionary experience serve as a basis for his wisdom and arcane knowledge. This knowledge extends to the operations of spirits and powers. Because he has knowledge of their ways, he can function as a healer and can prescribe measures to counteract curses and provide protection from spirits. Asceticism, including fasting and taboos, are important aspects of preparation in rituals of power.

The author of Colossians takes strong exception to this person and his ritual methods for the community. In the author's view, this rival leader is full of pride and his arrogance is leading him to exploit the church. Although he claims to be spiritual, the leader is not in a close connection with Christ, according to the letter writer. The letter therefore admonishes the Colossian Christians to reject this person's leadership and teaching. Rather, they should hold on tight to Christ, immerse themselves in the Word about Christ, and grow in the knowledge of who Jesus is and who they are in him.

Bibliography

Arnold, Clinton E. *The Colossian Syncretism: The Interface between Christianity and Folk Belief at Colossae.* WUNT 2/77. Tübingen: Mohr Siebeck, 1995.

Aydaş, Murat. "New Inscriptions from Asia Minor." *Epigraphica Anatolica* 37 (2004): 121–25.

Barclay, John M. G. *Jews in the Mediterranean Diaspora: From Alexander to Trajan (323 BCE–117 CE)*. Berkeley: University of California Press, 1996.

Barth, Markus, and Helmut Blanke. Translated by Astrid B. Beck. AB 34B. New York: Doubleday, 1994.

Bevere, Allan R. *Sharing in the Inheritance: Identity and Moral Life in Colossians*. JSNTSup 226. New York: Sheffield Academic, 2003.

Bird, Michael. *Colossians and Philemon*. New Covenant Commentary Series. Eugene, OR: Cascade, 2009.

Davila, James R. *Descenders to the Chariot: The People behind the Hekhalot Literature*. JSJSup 70. Leiden: Brill, 2001.

Dibelius, Martin. "The Isis Initiation in Apuleius and Related Initiatory Rites." Pages 61–121 in *Conflict at Colossae*. Edited by Fred O. Francis and Wayne A. Meeks. SBLSBS 4. Missoula, MT: Scholars Press, 1973.

Dibelius, Martin, and Heinrich Greeven. *An die Kolosser, Epheser, an Philemon*. HNT 12. 3rd ed. Tübingen: Mohr Siebeck, 1953.

DuBois, Thomas A. *An Introduction to Shamanism*. Cambridge: Cambridge University Press, 2009.

Dunn, James D. G. *The Epistles to the Colossians and to Philemon*. NIGTC. Grand Rapids: Eerdmans, 1996.

———. The Colossian Philosophy: A Confident Jewish Apologia." *Bib* 76 (1995): 153–81.

Francis, Fred O. "The Background of EMBATEUEIN (Col 2:18) in Legal Papyri and Oracle Inscriptions." Pages 197–207 in *Conflict at Colossae*. Edited by Fred O. Francis and Wayne A. Meeks. SBLSBS 4. Missoula, MT: Scholars Press, 1973.

———. "Humility and Angelic Worship in Col 2:18." Pages 163–95 in *Conflict at Colossae*. Edited by Fred O. Francis and Wayne A. Meeks. SBLSBS 4. Missoula, MT: Scholars Press, 1973.

Gnilka, Joachim. *Der Kolosserbrief*. HThKNT 10.1. Freiburg: Herder, 1980.

Guichard, Celeste L. "Travels and Traversals in the Hellenistic Oracular Temples at Klaros and Didyma." PhD diss., Columbia University, 2005.

Graf, Fritz. *Apollo*. Gods and Heroes of the Ancient World. New York: Routledge, 2009.

Klutz Todd E. "The Eighth Book of Moses." *MOTP* 1:189–235.

Lesses, Rebecca M. *Ritual Practices to Gain Power: Angels, Incantations, and Revelation in Early Jewish Mysticism*. HTS. Harrisburg, PA: Trinity Press International, 1998.

Lohse, Eduard. *Colossians and Philemon*. Hermeneia. Philadelphia: Fortress, 1971.
Macridy, Theodore. "Altertümer von Notion." *JÖAI* 8 (1905): 155–73.
———. "Antiquités de Notion II." *JÖAI* 15 (1912): 36–67.
Merkelbach, Reinhold. *Philologica: Ausgewählte Kleine Schriften.* Edited by Wolfgang Blümel et al. Stuttgart: Teubner, 1997.
Peerbolte, Bert Jan Lietaert. "The *Eighth Book of Moses* (PLeid. J 395): Hellenistic Jewish Influence in a Pagan Magical Papyrus." Pages 184–94 in *A Kind of Magic: Understanding Magic in the New Testament and Its Religious Environment.* Edited by Bert Jan Lietaert Peerbolte and Michael Labahn. LNTS 306. London: T&T Clark, 2007.
Picard, Charles. "Un Oracle d'Apollon Clarios a Pergame." *BCH* 46 (1922): 190–97.
Robert, Louis, and Jeanne Robert. *Claros I: Décrets Hellénistiques.* Paris: Éditions Recherche sur les Civilisations, 1989.
Rutherford, Ian. "Trouble in Snake-Town: Interpreting an Oracle from Hierapolis-Pamukkale." Pages 449–57 in *Severan Culture.* Edited by Simon Swain et al. Cambridge: Cambridge University Press, 2007.
Várhelyi, Zsuzsanna. "Magic, Religion, and Syncretism at the Oracle at Claros." Pages 13–31 in *Between Magic and Religion: Interdisciplinary Studies in Ancient Mediterranean Religion and Society.* Edited by Sulochana R. Asirvatham, Stephen Harrison, and Jaś Elsner. New York: Rowman & Littlefield, 2001.
Witherington, Ben, III. *The Letters to Philemon, the Colossians, and the Ephesians: A Socio-rhetorical Commentary on the Captivity Epistles.* Grand Rapids: Eerdmans, 2007.

Everyday Life in a Roman Town Like Colossae: The Papyrological Evidence

Peter Arzt-Grabner

A recently published ostracon (O.Did. 412), inscribed before the year 140 CE in Didymoi in the Eastern desert of Egypt, preserves a letter addressed to Ammonios from a sender whose name is lost and who—among other things—asks Ammonios to bring him a jar of filtered Laodicean wine, if he comes and has a donkey.[1] Alas, this ostracon does not provide evidence that Laodicea in the Lycus Valley exported wine to Egypt but rather that this wine had been transported from the famous port Laodicea in Syria,[2] south to Egypt. The Syrian port is also mentioned in a register of merchant ships that was drawn up in Alexandria in second century CE (P.Bingen 77 with *BL* 12:36), registering ships bringing into Alexandria different goods from different ports, among them a ship[3] from Laodicea bringing wine (ll. 17–18). Several days later—we are informed by the register—a ship from

---

1. See lines 7–9: ἐὰν ἔρχῃ καὶ ὄνον | ἔχῃς καὶ δύνῃ ἡμεῖν τῆς τειμῆς [.] ὑλισ|τὸν ἐνένκαι (read ἐνεγκεῖν) Λαδικηνοῦ (read Λαοδικηνοῦ), καλῶς ποιήσις (the ed. translates: "if you come, and if you have a donkey, please, if you can, bring a jar of filtered Laodicean wine—you will be reimbursed").

2. Or does λαδικηνόν in line 9 refer to a type of jar? On the discussion see the references and bibliography given by A. Bülow-Jacobsen in "Private Letters," in *Les textes*, vol. 2 of *Didymoi: Une garnison romaine dans le désert oriental d'Égypte*, ed. Hélène Cuvigny, FIFAO 67 (Cairo: Institut français d'archéologie orientale, 2012), 347; and Hans-Joachim Drexhage and Kai Ruffing, "P. Bingen 77 und der Handel zwischen Asia Minor und Ägypten," in *Vom Euphrat bis zum Bosporus: Kleinasien in der Antike; Festschrift für Elmar Schwertheim zum 65. Geburtstag*, ed. Engelbert Winter, Asia Minor Studien 65 (Bonn: Habelt, 2008), 154 note 5. P.Bingen 77.17–18 (see below) refers to a cargo of wine brought into Alexandria from Laodicea in Syria.

3. Of the ship's name only the first part ("Hope," Ἐλπίς) is preserved in line 17, the cargo of wine is mentioned in line 18.

Side in Asia Minor named "Hope (and) Ourania" (Ἐλπὶς Οὐρανία), owned by the Roman citizen Gaius Ulpius Iason, arrived after twenty days at sea bringing in wood, and 216 half-jars (about 700 liters) of oil from Aspendos (ll. 21–23).[4]

In the year 142 CE, a certain Pamphilos aka Kanopos was traveling the same route from Side to Alexandria. He was an Alexandrian slave dealer carrying with him the ten-year-old slave girl Abaskantis who was of Galatian origin and whom he had just bought at the slave market in Side.[5] We learn this from the slave sale contract P.Turner 22 (with *BL* 12:284),[6] which was written by the city scribe of Side in the forum of that very city. The slave dealer carried the contract with him to Alexandria where he obviously sold the slave girl to an Egyptian who was living in the Chora where the papyrus was found in modern times. The structure, formulae, contents, and details of this contract as well as of two other contracts from Asia Minor[7] are well comparable with other slave sale contracts from different places throughout the Roman Empire: with contracts from Syria, Dacia Superior (modern

---

4. See Drexhage and Ruffing, "P. Bingen 77"; Peter Herz, "Beiträge zur Organisation der Getreideversorgung Roms," in *Ad fontes! Festschrift für Gerhard Dobesch zum fünfundsechzigsten Geburtstag am 15. September 2004 dargebracht von Kollegen, Schülern und Freunden*, ed. Herbert Heftner and Kurt Tomaschitz (Wien: Eigenverlag der Herausgeber, 2004), 612–13; on the trade between Side and Egypt, see also Hans-Joachim Drexhage, "Die Kontakte zwischen Side, Alexandria und Ägypten in der römischen Kaiserzeit (1.–3. Jh. n. Chr.)," in *Studien zum antiken Kleinasien: Friedrich Karl Dörner zum 80. Geburtstag gewidmet*, ed. Anke Schütte, Daniela Pohl, and Jutta Teichmann, Asia Minor Studien 3 (Bonn: Habelt, 1991), 75–90

5. On the archaeological, literary, epigraphic, and papyrological record concerning Side, including its port and commerce, see Johannes Nollé, *Geographie-Geschichte–Testimonia–Griechische und lateinische Inschriften (1–4)*, vol. 1 of *Side im Altertum: Geschichte und Zeugnisse*, IGSK 43 (Bonn: Habelt, 1993); Nollé, *Griechische und lateinische Inschriften (5–16)–Papyri–Inschriften in sidetischer Schrift und Sprache–Ergänzungen und Berichtigungen–Konkordanzen–Epigraphische Indices*, vol. 2 of *Side im Altertum: Geschichte und Zeugnisse*, IGSK 44 (Bonn: Habelt, 2001); Peter R. Franke, et. al., *Side: Münzprägung, Inschriften und Geschichte einer antiken Stadt in der Türkei; Beiträge zu einer Ausstellung in Saarbrücken, Homburg, München, Kiel, Wien, Augsburg und Aalen*. 2nd ed. Saarbrücken: Landesbank Saar Girozentrale; Institut für Alte Geschichte der Universität des Saarlandes, 1989.

6. See the new edition by Nollé, *Griechische und lateinische Inschriften (5–16)*, 613–17.

7. BGU 3.887 (with *BL* 1:77, 350; 3:15; 7:16; 8:36; Side/Pamphylia; July 8, 151 CE) and BGU 3.913 (with *BL* 1:82; 4:6; Myra/Lycia; June 12, 206 CE).

Romania), Italy, Rhodes, and, of course, Egypt. Most of these contracts are preserved on papyrus, some on waxed tablets.[8]

They all give clear evidence that Egypt can no longer be seen as a "Sonderfall"—a special case—within ancient studies but that the papyri from Egypt provide us with a more or less accurate view of private, business, and administrational life that should be valid throughout the empire. Egypt has ceased to be the only *locus* of papyri and other perishable documents from the Roman Empire, although about 98 percent of the edited documents still come from Egypt. About 2 percent have been excavated outside Egypt: in Israel and Jordan, Syria, Afghanistan, Iran, Libya, Crete, Romania, Italy, Switzerland, Great Britain, and Spain.[9] Additionally, documents that

---

8. The references for slave sale contracts from outside Egypt are given in the following notes.

9. The most recent list published is still Hannah M. Cotton, Walter E. H. Cockle, and Fergus G. B. Millar, "The Papyrology of the Roman Near East: A Survey," *JRS* 95 (1995): 214–35 (listing 609 papyrus documents from outside Egypt). Several more can be added meanwhile: Israel and Jordan: P.Murabba'ât (most of them second century CE), P.Masada (Papyri and Ostraca, most of them 66–73/74 CE), P.Yadin 1 and 2, P.Hever (archives of two Jewish women, Babatha and Salome Komaïse, daughter of Levi; documents written in Maḥoza/Roman province Arabia; the women brought these archives with them when moving to En Gedi during the Jewish revolt under the leadership of Bar Kochba; both early second century CE), P.Jud.Des.Misc. (Jericho) 4–6; 16–19; (Naḥal Ḥever) 4; (Naḥal Mishmar) 2; (Naḥal Şe'elim) 4 und 5, P.Petra (152 carbonized papyri found in a room near byzantine basilica; sixth century CE). Syria: P.Dura (from Dura Europos; second–third centuries CE), P.Euphrates (documents from Roman province Syria Coele, especially from Beth Phuraia, on papyrus or leather; 232–256 CE [no. 1–5 = SB 22.15496–15500]), Palmyra (ca. sixty unpublished papyrus fragments in Greek and Palmyrene, found in the tower of Kitot, built in 40 CE; according to the writing dating to second–third centuries CE). Afghanistan: SB 22.15765: tax receipt on leather from Bactria; second century BCE. Iran: Two deeds on parchment from Avroman (Kopanis): Jur.Pap. 36 (October 20–November 18, 88 BCE); *JHS* 35 (1915): 22–65, no. 2 (ed. Ellis H. Minns; 22–21 BCE). Libya: O.BuNjem: Latin ostraca; third century CE. Rodney Ast, to mention only one recently started project, is about to edit and reedit all ostraca from Northern Africa outside Egypt that have been found so far, among them ostraca from Gigthi in Libya and Carthage in modern Tunisia. Crete: O.Cret.Chers.: Greek ostraca from Chersonesos (second century CE). Romania: T.Dacia: wax tablets from Alburnus Maior/Dacia Superior; second century CE; two slave sale contracts (tablets 6 and 7) reprinted as *CIL* 3.6 (139 CE); 3.7 (142 CE). Italy: Tablets from Pompeji: T.Jucundus and T.Sulpicii (written in Puteoli; no. 42 and 43 are slave sale contracts), wax tablets from Herculaneum: T.Hercul. (no. 60 and 62 are slave sale contracts), Ravenna: Ch.L.A. 12.547 (after Feb-

had been written in Asia Minor, Syria, Rhodes, or Italy were sent or brought to Egypt in antiquity and preserved there until the nineteenth or twentieth century.[10] Thus, the material from Egypt can now be collated with similar material originating from elsewhere.[11]

---

ruary 22, 433 CE) and P.Rain.Cent. 166 (sixth–seventh centuries CE). Switzerland: T.Vind. (= C.Epist.Lat. 16–71): wax tablets; first half of first century CE. Great Britain: Vindolanda (Hadrian's Wall): T.Vindol. (wooden tablets, late first/early second century CE), Luguval(l)ium (Carlisle): C.Epist.Lat. 3.88bis.1–43 (wooden tablet, Flavian time), Londinium: C.Epist.Lat. 1.87–88. The discovery of more than four hundred Roman waxed tablets from Londinium was announced in 2016 by the Museum of London Archaeology; the tablets are written in Latin and can be dated to the second half of the first century CE, among them notes, bills, and contracts. Spain: Christian tablets on stone (fifth–seventh centuries CE), edited by Isabel Velázquez Soriano: *Las Pizarras Visigodas (Entre el latín y su disgregación: La lengua hablada en Hispania, siglos VI–VIII)*, Colección Beltenebros 8 (Madrid: Real Academia Española; Brugos: Instituto Castellano y Leonés de la Lengua, 2004).

10. Asia Minor: As already mentioned, from Side/Pamphylia: P.Turner 22 (with *BL* 12:284; 142 CE; sale of slave), and BGU 3.887 (with *BL* 1:77, 350; 3:15; 7:16, and 8:36; July 8, 151 CE; sale of slave); from Myra/Lycia: BGU 3.913 (with *BL* 1:82 and 4:6; June 12, 206 CE; sale of slave); further from Bithynia: P.Münch. 3.63 (May 8, 248 CE; fragment with date of Philippus Arabs and Philippus II), Pompeiopolis/Paphlagonia: P.Mich. 9.546 (with *BL* 7:113 and 9:162; 207 CE; copy of sale of slave, original drawn up in Pompeiopolis), Caria: especially three letters to Zenon: P.Cair.Zen. 1.59037 (after June 12, 258 BCE; business letter); 59036 (with *BL* 3:37; February 1, 257 BCE; letter); 59056 (March 14, 257 BCE; private letter), Cappadocia(?): Ch.L.A. 11.477 (first–third centuries CE; letter[?] of a veteran in Latin), Mysia–Kyzikos(?): SB 3.6260 (with *BL* 8:324; before June 13, 230 CE; administrational[?] letter). Syria: P.Lond. 2.229 (p. XXI) (Seleucia Pieria; May 24, 166 CE; sale of slave). Rhodes: P.Oxy. 50.3593 (238–244 CE; sale of slave); 3594 (prob. 238–244 CE; subject not clear). Italy: Rome: P.Mich. 8.487, 491 and 501 (all second century CE; private letters); BGU 1.27 (with *BL* 12:10; second–third centuries CE; private letter); P.Mich. 8.490 (Portus Ostia; second century CE; private letter); SB 6.9557 (with *BL* 6:155; Rome; 264–282 CE; business letter by a Christian), Misenum: BGU 2.423 (with *BL* 8:27 and 9:20) and probably 632 (with *BL* 1:58; both second century CE; private letter), Puteoli: P.Oxy. 18.2191 (with *BL* 5:81; second century CE; private letter), Nea Polis: P.Lond. 3.1178 (p. 214) (with *BL* 1:290; 3:96; 8:186 and 9:141; 200–212 CE; diploma), Ravenna: SB 3.6304 (wax tablet; ca. 151 CE; sale of slave).

11. About 102,500 clay impressions of seals were found in the Agora Archives in the rescue excavations at Zeugma in 1998–2000; some of them have papyrus or leather traces preserved on the reverse side, thus confirming the use of papyrus for documents filed in Zeugma and, moreover, the cultural interrelations between Egypt and other provinces as several clay impressions carry the images of Sarapis or Isis; see

Concerning the Lycus Valley, none of the three major cities (Hierapolis, Laodicea, Colossae) is mentioned in any documentary papyrus or ostracon of the Ptolemaic or Roman period, yet it is worth mentioning that the region of Phrygia is attested in two papyri: the other slave sale contract from Side, besides P.Turner 22, deals with the purchase of the twelve-year-old slave girl Sambatis who is of Phrygian origin (cf. BGU 3.887.3–4 and 14–15 with *BL* 3:15 [July 8, 151 CE]).[12] SB 22.15538 (with *BL* 11:238; Alexandria; March 27–April 25, 13 BCE) is a contract by Gaius Iulius Philios who is apprenticing his slave Narcissus to Gaius Iulius Eros to learn to play with several kinds of flutes, among them also with "Phrygian flutes" (l. 4: Φρυγ[ιαυλίοις]), which are thus attested to have been well-known in Egypt.[13] Only in a Byzantine anonymous letter from Oxyrhynchus, PSI 4.311 (first half of the fourth century CE), we find the note that there are two Laodiceas, one in Phrygia (i.e., in the Lycus Valley) and one in Syria.[14]

Due to the ever-increasing evidence from papyri, ostraca, and tablets from outside Egypt, we learn more and more, and the information obtained from the Egyptian material serves also to illuminate various aspects of Roman government and society elsewhere in the Roman Empire. Of course, we can find regional and local differences already between Egyptian nomes and villages, and the more detailed something is, the more different it might be locally or regionally. But the basics of life are, nevertheless, the same everywhere: people were born, and if a child survived the first five years, she or he had a good chance to live thirty, forty, or fifty

---

Mehmet Önal, "Deities and Cultures Meet on the Seal Impressions in Zeugma," *Bolletino di archeologia online* 1 (2010): 25–53.

12. See also the new edition by Nollé, *Griechische und lateinische Inschriften (5–16)*, 617–22 (concerning the name Sambatis and its attestation, see pp. 621–22; in the note on lines 3 and 14 in *BL* 12:16, Σαμβτίς has to be corrected to Σαμβατίς).

13. On this contract, see Annie Bélis and Daniel Delattre, "À propos d'un contrat d'apprentissage d'aule ète (Alexandrie; an 17 d'Auguste = 13ª)," *PapyLup* 2 (1993): 103–62; Angela Bellia, "Una regione e la sua musica: Il caso della Caria," *Bollettino dell'Associazione Iasos di Caria* 19 (2013): 25–26.

14. The context of this note are orders to deliver a letter (this letter?) to Theodotos, the bishop of Laodicea in Syria. Se AnneMarie Luijendijk, *Greetings in the Lord: Early Christians and the Oxyrhynchus Papyri*, HTS 60 (Cambridge: Harvard University Press, 2008), 81 n. 1; see also the new edition of this letter by Lincoln H. Blumell, "*PSI* 4.311: Early Evidence for 'Arianism' at Oxyrhynchus?," *BASP* 49 (2012): 277–96; Blumell, *Lettered Christians: Christians, Letters, and Late Antique Oxyrhynchus*, NTTSD 39 (Leiden: Brill, 2012), 139–49.

years, some even up to their seventies, eighties, and nineties. Perhaps the son or daughter received some education, maybe some training in a craft, or a son joined the army or navy. Several years later they probably married and founded a family, ran a business, paid taxes, suffered from diseases or the difficulties of life, joined an association, took part in a cult group, made a career in the Roman administration or in their business affairs, and finally died.

In the following I will present the papyrological evidence of three major events in the life of an average family: the birth of a child, the census, and marriage. After concluding what the papyri from Egypt may teach us about birth, census, and marriage in Colossae, I will briefly deal with the issue[15] of the place of Philemon's household, before presenting the papyrological evidence on two topics that are well represented in both letters: slavery and textile industry (in particular the weaver's craft).

Birth Returns

The first papyrus document that we may encounter at the beginning of the life of a Greco-Egyptian relates to his or her birth.[16] Most recently, the documents in question have been called "birth returns," but in former days also the terms "declarations of birth," "birth certificates," or "applications to register a child" had been in use.[17] There is no specific term that

---

15. To comment on all possible details of Philrmon and Colossians that could be illuminated by documentary papyri, ostraca, and tablets would by far exceed the length of this article. Concerning Philemon, see Peter Arzt-Grabner, *Philemon*, PKNT 1 (Göttingen: Vandenhoeck & Ruprecht, 2003); the Colossians volume of the series Papyrologische Kommentare zum neuen Testament will be published in due time by its newly appointed author.

16. In this short overview, I will not include a different type of birth returns that is covered by Latin documents of which some are explicitly submitted by Roman citizens (an early example is P.Mich. 3, p. 154–56 [wax tablet; Alexandria; July 23, 62 CE]).

17. On the discussion, see Carlos Sánchez-Moreno Ellart, "Ὑπομνήματα ἐπιγεννήσεως: The Greco-Egyptian Birth Returns in Roman Egypt and the Case of P.Petaus 1–2," *APF* 56 (2010): 94 (with bibliographical references in n. 8), who uses the term *birth returns*. The designation "application to register a child in a privileged order" was first brought forward by Bo Frid in his edition of P.Ups.Frid. 6 (see also Andrea Jördens using the term "Registrierungsgesuch" for P.Bingen 105); the term explains best the function of the Oxyrhynchus documents. On the administrative procedure concerning birth returns, see also especially Thomas Kruse, *Der Königliche Schreiber und die Gauverwaltung: Untersuchungen zur Verwaltungsgeschichte Ägyptens*

is applicable to all sorts of these documents as they differ in some details from one nome to the other nome of Egypt.[18] What is common to all of them is the fact that they are typically Roman, the earliest are dating back to the mid-first century CE.

By submitting P.Tebt. 2.299 (with *BL* 11:278) to the village scribe (κωμογραμματεύς) of Tebtynis in the Arsinoite nome, the priest Psyphis registered the birth of his son Pakebkis, born in the tenth year of Claudius (i.e., 49–50 CE). The text reads:

   Ἀρείωι Λυσιμά[χου κωμο-]
   γραμματεῖ Τεβ[τύνεως]
   παρὰ Ψύφιος[19] το[ῦ Ἁρπο-]
   κρᾶ τοῦ Πακή[βκιος μη-]
 5 τρὸς Θενμαρσ[ισούχου]
   τῆς Ψύφιος μη[τρὸς Κελ-]
   λαύθιος τῶν ἀ[πὸ τῆς κώ-]
   μης πέμπτη[ς φυλῆς]
   ἱερέος[20] τῶν ἐν [τῇ κώμῃ]
 10 θεῶν Κρόνου [θεοῦ μεγίστ(ου(?))]
   καὶ Εἴσιδος[21] κα[ὶ Σαράπιδος]
   θεῶν μεγάλ[ων ἀπολυσί-]
   μ[ο]υ ἀπὸ ἀνδ[ρῶν πεντή-]
   κοντα. ἀπογρ[άφομαι]
 15 τὸν γεγονώτ[α[22] μοι υἱὸν]
   Πακῆβκιν μ[ητρὸς(?) Τα(?)-]
   ασιείους τῆς [...]
   μητρὸς Ταώ[πεως τῶι]

---

in der Zeit von Augustus bis Philippus Arabs (30 v.Chr.–245 n.Chr.), 2 vols, APF Series 11.1–2 (Munich: Saur, 2002), 171–76 (with bibliography on 171 n. 326).

18. For complete lists, see tables 1–3 in Peter Arzt-Grabner, "Census Declarations, Birth Returns, and Marriage Contracts on Papyrus and Paul's Ideas on These Matters," in *Second Annual Meeting of Bertinoro (1–4 October 2015)*, vol. 2 of *Texts, Practices and Groups: Multidisciplinary Approaches to Jesus and the History of His Followers in the First Two Centuries*, ed. Adriana Destro and Mauro Pesce with Andrea Annese (Turnhout: Brepols, 2019); see also nn. 24, 30, and 37 below. On the different features, see Sánchez-Moreno Ellart, "Ὑπομνήματα ἐπιγεννήσεως," 98–114; on different remarks made by public officials in the birth returns, see 128.

19. Read Ψοίφιος here and in line 6.
20. ἱερεος *corr. ex* αιρεος, read ἱερέως.
21. Read Ἴσιδος.
22. Read γεγονότ[α].

```
            δεκάτωι ἔτ[ει Τιβερίου]
    20   Κλαυδίου Κα[ίσαρος]
            Σεβαστοῦ Γε[ρμανικοῦ]
            Αὐτοκράτορ[ος, καὶ ἀξιῶ]
            ταγῆναι τὸ [τοῦ προκει-]
            μένου μο[υ υἱοῦ Πακήβ-]
    25   κιος ὄνομα [ἐν — ]
            - - - - - - - - -
```

To Areios, son of Lysimachos, village scribe of Tebtynis, from Psyphis, son of Harpokras, the son of Pakebkis, his mother being Thenmarsisouchos, daughter of Psyphis and Kellauthis, inhabitants of the village, priest of the fifth tribe of the gods at the village, Kronos the most great god, and Isis and Sarapis, the great gods, and one of the fifty exempted persons.[23] I register Pakebkis, the son born to me and Taasies daughter of N.N. her mother being Taopis in the tenth year of Tiberius Claudius Caesar Augustus Germanicus Imperator, and request that the name of my aforesaid son Pakebkis be entered on the list [here the papyrus breaks off].

Unfortunately, this earliest preserved birth return breaks off before we get the date of the document, which makes it impossible to learn about the age of the boy at the time he was registered. So far, seventeen birth returns from the Arsinoite nome have been edited,[24] and they all follow, more or less, the same pattern. Most documents are submitted by both parents, only a few either by the father or the mother of the child who—at the time

---

23. Fifty priests at the temple of Sokneptynis were exempt from ordinary taxes, especially the poll-tax (see also P.Tebt. 2.298.11 and 292.6).

24. Besides the document from Tebtynis, we can list: from the Arsinoite nome without any further (preserved) specification: P.Warr. 2 (July 11, 72 CE) and BGU 11.2020 (with *BL* 6:19–20; December 24, 124 CE); from Nilopolis and Soknopaiou Nesos: SPP 22.37 (with *BL* 11:268; February 25, 184 CE); from Ptolemais Euergetis: CPR 15.24 (with *BL* 11:72; 119 CE); BGU 1.110 (with *BL* 1:21; 138–139 CE); 111, col. 2 (with *BL* 1:21; after October 1, 138 CE); P.Gen. 4.162 (138–143 CE); 1^2.33 (September 9, 155 CE); SB 26.16803 (second century CE); from Ptolemais Hormu: P.Petaus 1 and 2 (February 14, 185 CE); from Soknopaiou Nesos: SPP 22.100 (with *BL* 11:268 and 12:279; 147–148 or 170–171 CE); 18 (with *BL* 2.2:116, 8:479, and 11:268; April 14, 149 CE); 38 (with *BL* 8:481; September 3, 155 CE); P.Berl.Cohen 12 (= SB 26.16074; 178–179 or 210–211 CE); BGU 1.28 (with *BL* 1:9 and 6:10; October 11, 183 CE); from Theadelphia: P.Fay. 28 (150–151 CE). See also table 1 in Arzt-Grabner, "Census Declarations."

of the birth return—is between one and eight years of age. The description of the parents follows the usual form how a person is generally identified, giving the person's name, the names of parents and grandfathers, the age of the person, and if this person had scars or marks on his or her body. The birth returns from the Arsinoites are addressed to the responsible local official: in Ptolemais Euergetis and Theadelphia to the scribes of the metropolis, in Soknopaiou Nesos, Ptolemais Hormu and Tebtynis to the village scribe, and in one case that cannot be attributed to a particular village or city (P.Warr. 2) to the *amphodarch*, the head of a quarter. Until mid-third century CE, the documents are more or less clearly related to the house-to-house census (κατ' οἰκίαν ἀπογραφή, see below),[25] thus being used to update the census records. But as there are several birth returns that register daughters[26] and, thus, testify that fiscal privileges were not the only issue of those applications (as females were generally exempted from the poll tax, see below). Also because almost all preserved birth returns are filed by privileged people, these documents most probably also intended to register the privileges for the child.[27] What privileges or rights were addressed in these cases is not clear.[28]

---

25. A clear reference to the census is, e.g., preserved in BGU 1.111, col. 2.12–15 (Ptolemais Euergetis; after October 1, 138 CE): ἀπογραφόμεθα [τ]οὺς γεννηθ(έντας) ἡμεῖν | με[τ]ὰ τὴν τοῦ ις (ἔτους) θεοῦ Ἀδ[ρι]ανοῦ | κατ οἰκ(ίαν) [ἀπο]γραφὴν ἐξ ἀλλήλ(ων) υἱοὺς | τῷ μὲν κ (ἔτει) θεοῦ Ἀδριανοῦ ("we register the sons, who were born to us jointly after the house-to-house registration of the 16th year of the God Hadrianus in the 20th year of the God Hadrianus").

26. See two documents from Soknopaiou Nesos (P.Berl.Cohen 12 [178–179 or 210–211]; BGU 1.28 [with *BL* 1:9 and 6:10; October 11, 183 CE]), and one from Ptolemais Hormu (P.Petaus 1–2 [February 14, 185 CE]); another document from the Arsinoites, BGU 11.2020 (with *BL* 6:19–20; December 24, 124 CE), returns the births of two sons and of twins, one male and one female.

27. From P.Mich. 11.603 (Ptolemais Euergetis; February 4, 134 CE) we learn that scribes were not only drawing up the registration from the census but also lists of *katoikoi*, lists of minors, and of those excluded from the tax estimate (l. 6–10: συν|θεῖναι μόνα ἀντίγραφα λαογραφιῶν | [κ]ατ' ἄνδρα καὶ λόγους κατοίκων καὶ | ἀπολογισμοὺς ἀφηλίκων καὶ ἐκτὸς | συνόψεως). See Roger S. Bagnall and Bruce W. Frier, *The Demography of Roman Egypt*, Cambridge Studies in Population, Economy and Society in Past Time 23 (Cambridge: Cambridge University Press, 1994), 102–4.

28. John R. Rea (in P.Oxy. 43, p. 109) refers to girls who were often required to prove their privileged status before marriage, or parents could have been interested in registering the child's legitimate status (see, e.g., Kruse, *Der Königliche Schreiber*, 173); we know that a girl of a priestly family had special rights in the temple, which could

An important contribution to our knowledge was the edition of two documents from Ptolemais Hormu, P.Petaus 1 and 2 (February 14, 185 CE). Both papyri preserve two copies of the registration of the girl Taesis, who was already eight years old at the time of the application, and this birth return also informs us that Taesis's parents were not privileged as they are identified as "fatherless" (i.e., their father was not known) and, therefore, could not prove their paternal ancestors. One of the two copies is addressed to the village scribe of Ptolemais Hormu as the local official that relates this document to the other birth returns from the Arsinoite nome, but P.Petaus 2 is addressed to the royal scribe (βασιλικὸς γραμματεύς) of the Heracleides part of the Arsinoite nome. Moreover, it contains an order by this scribe, written below the birth return and addressed to the village scribe of Ptolemais Hormu, "to follow the usual procedure" (cf. ll. 13–14). According to Thomas Kruse, it is probable that P.Petaus 1 and 2 do not cover an exception but the usual procedure, at least in the Arsinoite nome: that the declarant(s) had to submit two copies of a birth return, one to the local official and one to the royal scribe who added his order to the subordinate in the local administration and had this copy sent to him. After fulfilling his duties, the local official stored both copies in his archive as, again, becomes evident from P.Petaus 1 and 2: both documents were found in the archive of the village scribe Petaus.[29]

The preserved documents from Oxyrhynchus[30] differ from those from the Arsinoites in several details. The earliest of these "applications to register

---

explain the existence of BGU 1.28 (with *BL* 1:9 and 6:10; October 11, 183 CE), a birth return concerning the daughter of a local priest in Soknopaiou Nesos. Another option is supposed by Sánchez-Moreno Ellart, "Ὑπομνήματα ἐπιγεννήσεως," 120: "We should also take into account again that the census did not exclude women, despite their non-liability from the poll tax."

29. See Kruse, *Der Königliche Schreiber*, 175–76; Sánchez-Moreno Ellart, "Ὑπομνήματα ἐπιγεννήσεως," 126–29.

30. These are twenty-two documents so far: P.Oxy. 38.2858 (August 23, 171 CE); P.Bingen 105 (201–202 CE); P.Oxy. 10.1267 (January 5, 209 CE); 12.1552 (with *BL* 8:247; 214–215 CE); PSI 12.1257 (249–250 CE); P.Col. 8.231 (249–261 CE); P.Oxy. 74.4993 (253–254 CE?); 4994 (May 26 or June 24, 254 CE); 4995 (January 6, 254 CE); P.Köln 2.87 (with *BL* 7:73; June 25–July 24?, 271 CE); P.Ups.Frid. 6 (July 25–August 28, 273 CE); P.Oxy. 66.3295 (August 24–28, 285 CE); PSI 3.164 (with *BL* 1:391 and 8:393; May 10, 287 CE); P.Corn. 18 (cf. *BL* 2.2:49 and 8:90; July 24, 291 CE); P.Oxy. 38.2855 (April 4, 291 CE); 43.3136 (June 21, 292 CE); 44.3183 (July 26, 292 CE); 74.4999 (August 12, 292); 43.3137 (July 4, 295 CE); P.FuadUniv. 13 (with *BL* 3:61 and 4:32;

a child" was submitted by the parents of the child and by the female owner of the house in which the family lived (P.Oxy. 38.2858 [August 23, 171 CE]).[31] Within the next one hundred years following this document, all applications are submitted by the owner(s) of the house in which the child had been born.[32] From the end of the third century CE onward, it seems that the applications have to be submitted by a man who is in some way responsible for the family, be it the father, grandfather, an uncle, or a friend.[33] Two applications are submitted (also) for daughters (P.Corn. 18 [July 24, 291 CE] concerning two sons and two daughters; P.Oxy. 43.3136 [June 21, 292 CE] for one daughter). Up to mid-third century CE, the child is between one and six years old at the time of the application's submission; later on, starting with 254 CE, the given age increases to six to seventeen years. The authorities to whom the applications are submitted differ from time to time. During the fourteen-years cycle of the census declarations, the applications are more or less clearly related to the census system;[34] that people continued to file such applications also afterwards seems to confirm that they also had their privileges registered for their children by doing so.[35] Maybe it is no coincidence that the applications for girls in Oxyrhynchus "appear precisely at this moment, i.e. after the end of the fourteen-years cycle."[36]

297–298 CE); P.Oxy. 65.4489 (August 5, 297 CE); 54.3754 (320 CE). See also table 2 in Arzt-Grabner, "Census Declarations."

31. It is not impossible that earlier birth returns from Oxyrhynchus were submitted by the father or by both parents, like in the Arsinoite nome, and that P.Oxy. 38.2858 was written at a time when it had already become important to have a child registered at a particular place within the city for which the personal confirmation of the owner of that accommodation was compulsory. Unfortunately, we do not have birth returns from Oxyrhynchus from the first or early second century CE. But maybe it is important to observe that the owner's personal confirmation is part of the birth returns only up to some time before 285 CE.

32. In several cases, the owner was identical with the father: P.Bingen 105 (201–202 CE); P.Oxy. 10.1267 (January 5, 209 CE); 74.4995 (January 6, 254 CE); P.Köln 2.87 (with BL 7:73; June 25–July 24?, 271 CE); in two cases the owners can be identified with both parents: P.Oxy. 74.4994 (May 26 or June 24, 254 CE) and P.Ups.Frid 6 (July 25–August 28, 273 CE; the parents are divorced).

33. P.Oxy. 66.4489 (August 5, 297) is submitted by the child's mother.

34. See Sánchez-Moreno Ellart, "Ὑπομνήματα ἐπιγεννήσεως," 104–8.

35. On the privileged classes from Oxyrhynchus, see Sánchez-Moreno Ellart, "Ὑπομνήματα ἐπιγεννήσεως," 106–9.

36. Sánchez-Moreno Ellart, "Ὑπομνήματα ἐπιγεννήσεως," 109.

Birth returns from Antinoopolis are thus far preserved from the second and the first half of the third centuries CE,[37] the earliest was written on May 5, 133 CE (P.Fam.Tebt. 30 with *BL* 8:198), that is, soon after Hadrian had founded the city in commemoration of his deified lover Antinous. All the documents are related to the so-called *fundationes alimentariae*, special alimentary programs installed by Hadrian for the maintenance of children as proclaimed by the *praefectus Aegypti* Petronius Mamertinus that, to receive the benefits, it was obligatory to enroll a child within thirty days after birth, to prove the citizenship of the parents, and to present an ἀπαρχή (that is by which the declaration was called) to the βουλή of the city.[38] The declaration had to be confirmed by three witnesses. All preserved birth returns from Antinoopolis concern sons. It seems that the procedure consisted of two steps: (1) submission of an application for enrolment by the father or both parents, and (2) issue of a certificate containing the core of the application, confirmed a few days later and signed by the responsible official.[39] Actually, the requirement to submit an application within thirty days after the child's birth was only complied with in three cases out of ten.[40]

---

37. P.Fam.Tebt. 30 (May 5, 133 CE); 33 (February 9, 151 CE; cf. P.Fam.Tebt. 34); SB 12.11103 (June 3, 155 CE); 16.12742 (September 28, 157 CE; cf. SB 16.12743); P.Diog. 2 (after 197 CE); P.Stras. 7.634 (with *BL* 8:427; 206–211 CE); P.Ant. 1.37 (with *BL* 3:6, 4:2 and 8:9; 208–209 CE); P.Diog. 3 (October 17, 209 CE); 4 (212–217 CE); P.Vind.Bosw. 2 (with *BL* 3:101, 6:66 and 7:93; 247–248 CE).

38. This fund is explicitly mentioned in P.Fam.Tebt. 33.3–6 (February 9, 151 CE) and SB 16.12742.6–10 (September 28, 157 CE).

39. In two cases, both documents are preserved: P.Fam.Tebt. 33 (February 9, 151 CE) is the application for enrolment of the twenty-days-old son Heracleides aka Valerius, and P.Fam.Tebt. 34 is the certificate (issued on February 24 of the same year, i.e. fifteen days later); SB 16.12742 (September 28, 157 CE) is the application for enrolment of the twenty-five-days-old son Philantinoos aka Isidoros, and 12743 is the certificate (issued on October 27 of the same year, i.e. almost a month later). Of the other documents, P.Stras. 7.634 (with *BL* 8:427), P.Ant. 1.37 (with *BL* 3:6, 4:2, and 8:9), and P.Vind.Bosw. 2 (with *BL* 3:101, 6:66, and 7:93; on doubts that this is an ἀπαρχή, see Andrea Jördens in P.Bingen, p. 391) seem to be applications, whereas P.Fam.Tebt. 30 (with *BL* 8:198), SB 12.11103 and P.Diog. 2–4 are obviously certificates.

40. P.Fam.Tebt. 33 (February 9, 151 CE) within twenty days, SB 16.12742 (September 28, 157 CE) and P.Vind.Bosw. 2 (with *BL* 3:101, 6:66 and 7:93) within twenty-five days. The other applications were submitted within about a year after the child's birth, except the earliest document P.Fam.Tebt. 30 (with *BL* 8:198), which was

Besides the birth returns from the Arsinoite nome, from Oxyrhynchus, and from Antinoopolis, we should mention an ostracon from Thebes (O.Brux. 14 [38–39 or 42–43 CE]), which was a formulary for scribes in Thebes to write a birth return in copying the text and filling in the personal names. The ostracon reads as follows:[41]

    Σαραπίωνι βασιλ(ικῷ) γρα(μματεῖ) Κοπ(τίτου) καὶ Περὶ Θ(ήβας)
    παρὰ ὁ δῆν(α) τοῦ δῆ(νος)[42] ⟦α ... ⟧ τῶν
    ἀπὸ Δ(ιοσπόλεως) τῆς μεγάλη(ς). ἀπογρά(φομαι) εἰς τὸ γ (ἔτος)
    τοὺς γεγενημένους μου παῖδα(ς)
5   μετὰ τὴν ἐπίκρισιν τοῦ κ (ἔτους), ὧν
    ὁ δῆ(να) τοῦ δῆ(νος)[43] ὡς (ἐτῶν)·
    Σποδῆς κομογρα(μματεύς).[44]

To Sarapion, the basilikos grammateus (royal scribe) of Kopites and Peri Thebas, from N.N., son of N.N. ... of those from the great city Diospolis. I register for the 3rd year my children[45] who have been born after the epicrisis of the 20th year, of whom N.N., son of N.N., about ... years of age. Spodes, village scribe.

Carlos Sánchez-Moreno Ellart argues, following Thomas Kruse, that μετὰ τὴν ἐπίκρισιν in line 5 of the formulary refers to the house-to-house census and "possibly alludes to the census of AD 33/34."[46] So far, we do not have any preserved birth returns following exactly this formulary, but we do not have any birth returns from Upper Egypt either. Presumably, we have here

---

submitted when one of the two children to be registered was already seven years of age (the other one was one year old).
    41. According to Sánchez-Moreno Ellart, "Ὑπομνήματα ἐπιγεννήσεως," 126.
    42. Read παρὰ τοῦ δεῖν(ος) τοῦ δεῖ(νος).
    43. Read ὁ δεῖ(να) τοῦ δεῖ(νος).
    44. Read κωμογρα(μματεύς).
    45. The male form τοὺς γεγενημένους μου παῖδα(ς) probably refers only to sons, but as this document is a formulary, i.e., a genre that uses male forms throughout (see P.Turner 22 with *BL* 12:284, the slave sale contract from Side where we find *male* forms although they refer to a slave *girl*), a male form can refer to anyone.
    46. Sánchez-Moreno Ellart, "Ὑπομνήματα ἐπιγεννήσεως," 127; see also Kruse, *Der Königliche Schreiber*, 174. Indeed, a reference to a previous κατ' οἰκίαν ἀπογραφή with a μετά clause can be found in two birth returns from Ptolemais Euergetis/Arsinoites, in BGU 1.111, col. 2.12–14 (after October 1, 138 CE) and P.Gen. 4.162.9–12 (138–143 CE).

evidence for an early birth return from Upper Egypt, even earlier than all other birth returns so far but in a form similar to that of the Arsinoites. As it is addressed to the royal scribe, a similar administrational procedure as in P.Petaus 2 (see above) seems to have been usual also in other nomes besides the Arsinoites and, presumably, from the earliest birth returns onwards. As a summary, Sánchez-Moreno Ellart writes: "this document makes one contribution to our knowledge, that the practice might have been more widespread than we can deduce from the documents filed by privileged people in the capitals of the nomes."[47] Together with P.Petaus 1–2, we have two references that hint in the direction of a widespread and compulsory practice of submitting birth returns.

What does this mean for the probable filing of birth returns in other Roman provinces, and particularly in a city like Colossae during the first century CE? We have no idea what a comparable formulary in the Lycus Valley may have *exactly* looked like, if it was similar to that of the Arsinoite nome and the formulary from Thebes or that of Oxyrhynchus. A similarity with the one of Antinoopolis, which is related to alimenta programs, is the least probable as this program was installed by Hadrian after he had founded the city in 130 CE. And a comparison with the birth returns from Oxyrhynchus is problematic as we do not have documents earlier than 171 CE (P.Oxy. 38.2858). It is not impossible that earlier birth returns from Oxyrhynchus were submitted by the father or by both parents, like in the Arsinoite nome, and that P.Oxy. 38.2858 was written at a time when it had already become important to have a child registered at a particular place within the city for which the personal confirmation of the owner of that accommodation was compulsory, but so far, we do not have birth returns from Oxyrhynchus from the first or early second century CE. Maybe it is, nevertheless, important to observe that the owner's personal confirmation is part of the birth returns only up to sometime before 285 CE.

Concerning Colossae, we can only assume that also the people of that city were interested to file birth returns in order to have their privileges registered for their children or that they were obliged to do so, so that the local authorities could update the census records. According to the earliest

---

47. Sánchez-Moreno Ellart, "Ὑπομνήματα ἐπιγεννήσεως," 127; see also Kruse, *Der Königliche Schreiber*, 174: "Dass bisher keine weiteren an den Königlichen Schreiber adressierten Geburtsanzeigen bekannt geworden sind, ist wohl lediglich auf den Zufall der Überlieferung zurückzuführen, denn offenbar war es auch in anderen Gauen üblich, solche Anzeigen an den βασιλικὸς γραμματεύς zu richten."

documents from Egypt, those from the Arsinoite nome and from Thebes, it is probable that during the first century CE it was the responsibility of the father or of both parents to file a birth return. What all preserved birth returns from different Egyptian nomes, cities, and villages have in common is the fact that people clearly tended to submit them only at a later time after the birth of a child (even the applications from Antinoopolis show this tendency). Obviously due to high infant mortality, an earlier submission was not at all advisable—in Egypt and elsewhere.

The Census System

As any other government, the Roman government had to collect taxes. The Romans taxed more or less everything they could, but the main tax was the *poll tax* that had to be paid annually for every male (including slaves) who did not have any fiscal privileges (e.g., Roman citizenship) and who was between the ages of fourteen and sixty. Therefore, the Romans set out to know exactly who the men were, who were between the ages of fourteen and sixteen. The Roman *census* system served exactly that purpose and was carried out—not accidentally—every fourteen years, so that nobody would ever escape.

With the help of the papyri and ostraca from Egypt we are able to reconstruct the whole process that was connected with the census.[48] We know that the first census in Egypt was taken under Augustus in 11/10

---

48. See especially Ulrich Wilcken, *Historischer Teil: Grundzüge*, vol. 1.1 of *Grundzüge und Chrestomathie der Papyruskunde*, by Ludwig Mitteis and Ulrich Wilcken (repr. Hildesheim: Olms, 1963), 192–96; Sherman L. Wallace, *Taxation in Egypt from Augustus to Diocletian* (repr. New York: Greenwood Press, 1969), 96–115; Rafael Taubenschlag, *The Law of Greco-Roman Egypt in the Light of the Papyri 332B.C.– 640A.D.*, 2nd ed. (repr. Milan: Cisalpino-Goliardica, 1972), 611–13; Orsolina Montevecchi, "Il censimento romano d'Egitto: Precisazioni," *Aev* 50 (1976): 72–84; Marcel Hombert and Claire Préaux, *Recherches sur le recensement dans l'Égypte romaine*, Papyrologica Lugduno-Batava 5 (Leiden: Brill, 1952); Roger S. Bagnall, "The Beginning of the Roman Census in Egypt," *GRBS* 32 (1991): 255–65; Bagnall and Frier, *Demography of Roman Egypt*; Bernhard Palme, "Die ägyptische κατ' οἰκίαν ἀπογραφή und Lk 2,1–5," *PzB* 2 (1993): 1–24; Palme, "Neues zum ägyptischen Provinzialzensus: Ein Nachtrag zum Artikel PzB 2 (1993) 1–24," *PzB* 3 (1994): 1–7; Walter Scheidel, *Measuring Sex, Age and Death in the Roman Empire: Explorations in Ancient Demography*, JRASup 21 (Ann Arbor, MI: Journal of Roman Archaeology, 1996).

BCE.[49] In the early times of the Roman census we find a seven-years cycle, but from 19/20 CE[50] onwards and until mid-third century CE a fourteen-years cycle is attested for Egypt. The process of a single census started with the edict of the Roman governor, like the one preserved in P.Lond. 3.904, col. 2 (p. 125) (with BL 3:94, 5:54, and 11:112; Alexandria; June 25–July 24, 104 CE). In this document, C. Vibius Maximus, the prefect of Egypt, declares that—the house-by-house census (ἡ κατ' οἰκίαν ἀπογραφή) having begun—it is necessary that all persons, who for any reason whatsoever are absent from their home districts, be alerted to return to their place of origin so that they may complete the customary formalities of registration and apply themselves to the farming for which they are responsible. Only those people from the countryside, who show their presence in Alexandria to be necessary, shall receive signed permits to stay, but all others are to return home within thirty days.[51] From the Egyptian papyri we also learn

---

49. According to SB 20.14440 (Theadelphia/Arsinoites; January 22[?], 12 CE), the declarations had to be submitted in 11/10 BCE for the first time; the registrations took place in 10/9 BCE. From then onwards we find a seven-years cycle of declarations and registrations until 19/20 CE, i.e., declaration in 4/3 BCE and registration in 3/2 BCE, declaration in 4/5 CE and registration in 5/6 CE, declaration in 11/12 CE and registration in 12/13 CE. See Bagnall, "Beginning of the Roman Census"; Palme, "Neues zum ägyptischen Provinzialzensus," 5–6. The first census in 11/10 BCE is also confirmed by a recently published census declaration from Theadelphia (P.Mich. inv. 4406a; January 26–February 24, 3 BCE; ed. W. Graham Claytor and Roger S. Bagnall, "The Beginnings of the Roman Provincial Census: A New Declaration from 3 BCE," *GRBS* 55 [2015]: 637–53).

50. See P.Oxy. 2.254 (with BL 10:137–38 and 11:143; ca. 13–26 CE).

51. See Adolf Deissmann, *Light from the Ancient East: The New Testament Illustrated by Recently Discovered Texts of the Graeco-Roman World*, trans. Lionel R. M. Strachan (repr., Peabody, MA: Hendrickson, 1995), 271. See also P.Gen. 1².16 (October 12, 207 CE) with a reference to the edict of Subatianus Aquila in lines 18–21; on this edict P. Schubert and I. Jornot comment in P.Gen. 1², p. 72: "Dans notre document (17–21), les paysans font référence aux ordres du préfet Subatianus Aquila les enjoignant de rester dans leur ἰδία, c'est-à-dire vraisemblablement le village où ils étaient enregistrés pour le recensement. L'édit dont il est question ici, attribué aux empereurs Septime Sévère et Caracalla dans SB 14284 (207 ap. J.-C.), ne fait malheureusement pas partie de ceux qui nous ont été conservés. Les édits renvoyant les gens dans leur ἰδία étaient généralement promulgués en vue d'un recensement, comme par exemple P.Lond. 3.904 (p. 125; = *W.Chr.* 202; 104 ap. J.-C.), ou à la suite de troubles, comme BGU 2.372 (= *W.Chr.* 19; 154 ap. J.-C.). U. Wilcken, dans l'introduction de *W.Chr.* 354, a rapproché 16 du recensement de 201/2. Comme notre document (18–21) fait allusion à l'édit du préfet Subatianus Aquila, lequel est en fonction entre 206 et

that—contrary to Luke 2:1-3—the Roman census was not exacted at the same time throughout the empire but in different years in particular provinces: the census in Syria, for example, was conducted one year later than the census in Egypt.

The census declarations[52] themselves hold an enormous treasure of information: we learn who the people were, who completed them, where they lived, what type of property they lived in, and who was in the household. We learn about the head of the household, if he had a wife, or sometimes the head of the household was a woman who was divorced or widowed or simply living by herself. We discover if there were children, whether there were grandparents, aunts, uncles, slaves, or others taken in as lodgers, and just about anyone else who might have lived with them. We find out as well, where the people had scars or marks on their bodies and how old they were, and we read about their occupation or if they were unemployed. The papyri also evidence that the same tax rate had to be paid per person, no matter if the people were rich or poor, if they earned a high salary or were unemployed.[53] It happened quite often that whole families or even a large part of a village preferred fleeing to another nome, where the general rate of the poll tax was lower, to losing everything and dying of starvation.

SB 1.5661 (with *BL* 2.2:120 and 9:243-44) is a census declaration by a woman submitted to the responsible authorities (the so-called λαογράφοι and the village scribe) of Philadelphia in the Arsinoite nome on June 13,

---

211, il faut considérer que l'édit est promulgué non pas en vue du recensement, mais après le recensement."

52. See Bagnall and Frier, *Demography of Roman Egypt*, 179-312; additions in Amphilochios Papathomas, "Drei unveröffentlichte Papyri aus der Sammlung der Griechischen Papyrologischen Gesellschaft," *APF* 42 (1996): 201; see also, e.g., P.Col. 10.262 (60 CE); 269 (second-third centuries CE).

53. A dramatic example is *SPP* 20.11 (with *BL* 3:236, 8:461 and 10:269; July 23, 175 CE): Peteamunis, son of Peteamunis and Tamasis, seventy-five years of age, grave digger in the village Moithymis in the Memphite nome, registers himself and his family, including his daughters-in-law and grandchildren, as homeless; also his three sons are grave diggers (so altogether four grave diggers in the small village Moithymis), and all their wives are currently unemployed. Nevertheless, the three sons are obliged to pay the poll tax. See Peter Arzt-Grabner, "Christlicher Alltag anhand der Papyri aus dem 2. Jahrhundert," in *Das ägyptische Christentum im 2. Jahrhundert*, ed. Wilhelm Pratscher, Markus Öhler, and Markus Lang, SNTSU 2/6 (Vienna: LIT, 2008), 107-9.

34 CE. Below the woman's declaration, we find a registration note by one of the officials and finally the notification by the village scribe. The document reads:

```
    Εἰρηναίῳ καὶ Μάρωνι καὶ Ἡρακλείδῃ
    καὶ Ἀμμωνίῳ καὶ Πετεσούχωι λαο-
    γράφοις καὶ Ἡρακλείδῃ κωμογραμ-
    ματε[ῖ] Φιλαδελφείας
 5  παρὰ Τατυβύγχιος τῆς Μαρήους
    τῶν ἀπὸ τῆς αὐτῆς κώμης
    μετὰ κυρίου τοῦ ἐματῆς⁵⁴ συγ-
    γενοῦς Πατουάμτιος τοῦ Πτόλ-
    λιδος. ἀπογράφομαι εἰς τὸ ἐν[εσ-]
10  τὸς κ (ἔτος) Τιβερίου Καίσαρος Σεβαστοῦ
    τὸν υἱόν⁵⁵ μου Πανετβεῦειν Κεφά-
    λωνος καταγινόμενον ἐν τῇ εἰ-
    δίᾳ⁵⁶ οἰκίᾳ,
    καὶ ἔστι[ν] ὁ προγεγραμμένος μου
15  υἱειὸς⁵⁷ {π}
    Πανετβεῦεις Κεφάλωνος ὡς (ἐτῶν) ε,
    καὶ ἐματὴν⁵⁸ Τατυβύγχιν Μαρήους
    ὡς (ἐτῶν) λε οὐλὴ ὑπ' ἀντίχιρα⁵⁹
    δεξιόν,
20  μετὰ κυρίου τοῦ προγεγραμμένου
    Πατουάμτιος τοῦ Πτόλλιδος
    ὡς (ἐτῶν) λϛ οὐλὴ ὑπ' ὀφρὺν δεξιόν.
    (ἔτους) κ Τιβερίου Καίσαρος Σεβαστοῦ, Παῦνι ιθ.
    (hand 2) κατακ(εχώρισται) (ἔτους) κ Τιβερίου Καίσαρος Σεβαστοῦ,
    Παῦνι ιθ.
25  (hand 3) Ἡρακλείδ(ης) κωμογρ(αμματεὺς) σεσημείομ(αι).⁶⁰
```

To Eirenaios and Maron and Herakleides and Ammonios and Petesouchos, laographoi, and to Herakleides, village scribe of Philadelphia, from Tatybynchis, daughter of Mareis, of the same village, with my rela-

---

54. Read ἐμαυτῆς.
55. Read υἱόν.
56. Read ἰ|δίᾳ.
57. Read υἱός.
58. Read ἐμαυτὴν.
59. Read ἀντίχειρα.
60. Read σεσημείωμ(αι).

tive Patouamtis, son of Ptollis, as guardian. I register for the present 20th year of Tiberius Caesar Augustus my son Panetbeveis, son of Kephalon, who lives in my own house, and my abovementioned son Panetbeveis, son of Kephalon, is (about)[61] 5 years of age, and myself, Tatybynchis, daughter of Mareis, (about) 35 years old, with a scar/mark on my right thumb, together with the guardian, the abovementioned Patouamtis, son of Ptollis, (about) 36 years of age, with a scar/mark below his right brow. In year 20 of Tiberius Caesar Augustus, Payni 19.
(2nd hand) Registered in year 20 of Tiberius Caesar Augustus, Payni 19.
(3rd hand) I, Herakleides, village scribe, have noted it.

From census registers we learn that the declarations were taken seriously by the authorities. To build the registers, the collected declarations were arranged according to the particular districts or streets of a place, and then glued together.[62] A special evidence for the authorities' accuracy is preserved in P.Lond. 2.324 (p. 63) (with *BL* 1:245 and 10:98; Prosopite nome): the papyrus contains copies of two extracts from census registers, the first one referring to the census of year 131–132 CE and the second one referring to the follow up census of year 145–146 CE; both declarations evidence that a certain Anikos and one Thamistis are siblings of the same mother and father, but in his cover letter, which follows below the two copies (ll. 28–34) and is dated to March 24, 161 CE, Anikos informs his sister that they are only brother and sister from the same mother and that she is ἀπάτωρ (i.e., her father is not known).[63]

The only *papyrological* evidence for the census outside Egypt so far is preserved in a document of the famous archive of Babatha, a woman from Maḥoza in the Roman province Arabia, who refers to "an evaluation of the province that is conducted by Titus Aninius Sextius Florentinus," the provincial governor (P.Yadin 1.16.11–13 [Rabbath-Moab/Arabia; after

---

61. Many age numbers in the papyri are preceded by ὡς (maybe the majority); therefore, ὡς in this context rather means "as exactly as possible" than just "about."

62. BGU 13.2228 (with *BL* 8:55; Soknopaiou Nesos/Arsinoites; 175–188 CE) is the extract of such a census register. Similar documents are, e.g., BGU 1.124 (with *BL* 1:22, 8:19, and 10:12; Ptolemais Euergetis/Arsinoites; after 187–188 CE); P.Amh. 2.76 (with *BL* 1:2; Hermopolis; second–third centuries CE).

63. Concerning reasons for this change, see Myrto Malouta, "Fatherless Persons," in *Law and Legal Practice in Egypt from Alexander to the Arab Conquest: A Selection of Papyrological Sources in Translation, with Introductions and Commentary*, ed. James G. Keenan, Joseph G. Manning, and Uri Yiftach-Firanko (Cambridge: Cambridge University Press, 2014), 198–200.

December 4, 127 CE]: ἀποτιμήσεως | Ἀραβίας ἀγομένης ὑπὸ Τίτου Ἀνεινίου Σεξ{σ}τίου Φλωρεντείνου | πρεσβευτοῦ Σεβαστοῦ ἀντιστρατήγου). According to Hannah M. Cotton, this was the first census of the province, conducted shortly after it became part of the Roman Empire.[64] The narrative of the nativity in Luke's Gospel, although problematic in several details and not in consistency with Luke's own chronology concerning Jesus of Nazareth, is, according to Graham Claytor and Roger Bagnall, "important evidence for the provincial impression of the census as universal and stemming from the direct command of the emperor"[65] (see Luke 2:1). And Claytor and Bagnall add, what is also relevant for Colossae and the Lycus Valley:

> The census reinforced imperial ideals, strengthening the notion that the emperor could "see everything and hear everything," even when ruling from the Palace in Rome. It also of course aided imperial interests, such as the collection of revenue and the maintenance of social hierarchy. For most provincials, on the other hand, the census and the closely-related poll tax were simply facts of life and burdens from which there was little chance of escape; for some, the imposition of a poll tax and regular censuses could have become "a potent symbol of subjection to Roman rule."[66] In short, the census was a common feature of the imperial experience and a key component of Rome's control over provincial society.[67]

Marriage Contracts

From marriage contracts we learn that marriage, in general and before the time of Diocletian, was a private matter and not regulated by any public, administrative, or religious authority; occasionally contracts were filed in a notary's office and registered in the record office or grapheion.[68] Marriages without a written contract (ἄγραφος γάμος) shared

---

64. See Hannah M. Cotton, "Ἡ νέα Ἀραβία: The New Province of Arabia in the Papyri from the Judaean Desert," *ZPE* 116 (1997): 206; see also Claytor and Bagnall, "Beginnings of the Roman Provincial Census," 645.

65. Claytor and Bagnall, "Beginnings of the Roman Provincial Census," 637–38.

66. Quotation from Dominic W. Rathbone, "Egypt, Augustus and Roman Taxation," *Cahiers du Centre Gustave Glotz* 4 (1993): 86.

67. Claytor and Bagnall, "Beginnings of the Roman Provincial Census," 638. For a survey of literary and legal sources as well as inscriptions related to the provincial census see Peter A. Brunt, "The Revenues of Rome," in *Roman Imperial Themes* (Oxford: Clarendon, 1990), 329–35 (with tables on 345–46).

68. See Hans Julius Wolff, *Organisation und Kontrolle des privaten Rechtsverkehrs*,

the same value or status with marriages with a written contract (ἔγγραφος γάμος).⁶⁹ Actually, there is no particular type of document that could just be called a "marriage contract." According to the papyrological record, Uri Yiftach-Firanko distinguishes between *Ekdosis* Documents (widely used in Greco-Roman societies, containing a clause about the "giving away" of one's daughter for the purpose of marriage), Marriage *Sunchoreseis* (from Augustan Alexandria, filed by bridegroom and bride declaring "to have come together"), Dowry Receipts, Loan Contracts (from Oxyrhynchus), *Paratheke* Documents (deeds of deposit with a list of objects "deposited" on the occasion of marriage), Dowry Inventories, several unique documents, and unclear cases.⁷⁰ In addition to these various

---

vol. 2 of *Das Recht der griechischen Papyri Ägyptens in der Zeit der Ptolemäer und des Prinzipats*, Handbuch der Altertumswissenschaft 10.5.2 (Munich: Beck, 1978), 136–37 n. 2, 177–78. In the grapheion, the contracts could also be stamped in order to attach complete legal validity (such a stamp is preserved, e.g., on P.Dime 3.39 [Soknopaiou Nesos/Arsinoites; 11–10 BCE]; see Katelijn Vandorpe in P.Dime 3, p. 437).

69. P.Ryl. 2.154 (with *BL* 3:160; Bakchias/Arsinoites; October 19, 66 CE) is filed between a certain Chairemon and his father-in-law, from whom he receives the dowry for Taisarion who is described as προούση[ι] κ[αὶ] συνούσηι τοῦ Χα[ιρήμονος] γυναικί (line 4: "being already before and being together with him as Chairemon's wife"). Contracts that transform an ἄγραφος γάμος into an ἔγγραφος γάμος, are often filed between husband and wife, cf. PSI 1.36a (with *BL* 1:390, 6:172, and 12:248; Oxyrhynchus or Arsinoites; October 29–November 27, 11 CE, or October 28–November 26, 12 or 13 CE); BGU 1.183 (with *BL* 1:24–25, 5:10, 7:10, 8:20, and 12:11; Soknopaiou Nesos/Arsinoites; April 26, 85 CE); P.Oxy. 2.265 (with *BL* 1:319, 2:94, 6:96, and 9:179; Oxyrhynchus; 81–96 CE); BGU 1.252 (Ptolemais Euergetis/Arsinoites; December 24, 98 CE); 232 (Arsinoites; October 28–November 26, 108 CE): this contract explicitly states that the wife "has been before and is together with him as his wife according to the laws" (l. 3–4: τῇ προούσῃ κ[αὶ συν]ούσῃ αὐτῷ κατὰ | νόμους γυναικεί).

70. Uri Yiftach-Firanko, *Marriage and Marital Arrangements: A History of the Greek Marriage Document in Egypt; Fourth Century BCE–Fourth Century CE*, MBPF 93 (Munich: Beck, 2003), 14–20 (for an inventory of marriage documents by provenance, including documents from outside Egypt, see 27–32; on the formulaic features, see table 1 on 271–72). On marriage and marriage documents in documentary papyri, see also Orsolina Montevecchi, "Ricerche di sociologia nei documenti dell' Egitto greco-romano, II. I contratti di matrimonio e gli atti di divorzio," *Aeg* 16 (1936): 3–83; Ilias Arnaoutoglou, "Marital Disputes in Greco-Roman Egypt," *JJP* 25 (1995): 11–28; David Instone-Brewer, *Marriage and Divorce Papyri of the Ancient Greek, Roman and Jewish World: A Collection of Papyri from Fourth C BCE to Fourth C CE.* 2000. http://www.tyndalearchive.com/Brewer/MarriagePapyri/Index.html; Ruth E. Kritzer in Peter Arzt-Grabner et al., *1. Korinther*, PKNT 2 (Göttingen: Vandenhoeck

documents dealing with marriage, we find a broad variety of clauses and arrangements within one and the same document type.[71] What they all have in common is—as Hans Julius Wolff and Uri Yiftach-Firanko have observed—"that marriage documents were composed not for recording the formation of marriage, but rather for documenting property arrangements connected with marriage, whenever, in the course of joint life, these arrangements became sufficiently important to be committed to writing."[72] The contracts focus most of all (if not exclusively) on the dowry, the *parapherna* (consisting of the woman's personal chattels), and the *prosphora* (consisting of land and slaves):[73] what and how it was handed over to the bride groom, in which way he was allowed to use it, and how and in which time frame he had to hand it back in the case of divorce. It is, therefore, understandable that many couples did not file a marriage contract at all. If there was no dowry that was worth mentioning, there was no reason for a contract.

A rather small portion of the contracts is dedicated to moral issues, the so-called terms of joint life:[74] that the couple should live together blamelessly, that the husband should supply to his wife and to their children whatever is necessary according to his means, that he must not set up a house different from the home which he is sharing with his wife, not have children from another wife, and not introduce another wife into the joint house. These prohibitions had two objectives: "protecting the family resources from embezzlement and guarding the exclusivity of the union."[75] The wife, on the other hand, was not allowed to have sex with another

& Ruprecht, 2006), 247–53. The most complete list of marriage documents has been compiled by Yiftach-Firanko, *Marriage and Marital Arrangements*, 9–13. On Latin marriage documents see, e.g., Martti Leiwo and Hilla Halla-Aho, "A Marriage Contract: Aspects of Latin-Greek Language Contact (*P. Mich.* VII 434 and *P. Ryl.* IV 612 = *ChLA* IV 249)," *Mnemosyne* 55 (2002): 560–80.

71. See below on the different arrangements in case of divorce.

72. Hans Julius Wolff, *Written and Unwritten Marriages in Hellenistic and Postclassical Roman Law*, Philological Monographs 9 (Lancaster: Lancaster Press, 1939); Yiftach-Firanko, *Marriage and Marital Arrangements* (quote from 104; see the full discussion 81–104).

73. On the papyrological evidence of the dotal system in the Roman period, see Yiftach-Firanko, *Marriage and Marital Arrangements*, 129–82 (and tables 3–11 on 276–311).

74. See Yiftach-Firanko, *Marriage and Marital Arrangements*, 182–95.

75. Yiftach-Firanko, *Marriage and Marital Arrangements*, 190.

man, to cause any shame to her husband, or to ruin the common home, which "probably means a ruin caused by lax moral conduct."[76] The terms concerning the wife also established her "active participation in the management of the family estate throughout the marriage," but also instructed her "to abide by, and show obedience to, her husband."[77] The documents themselves show a broad variety of forms and a remarkable individuality in the selection of obligations to be included in a contract.[78]

Many marriage documents already address the case of a possible divorce.[79] We find different forms in different nomes, and several times the scribes who draw up the contracts seem to use variants of their own devising. The contracts of the Arsnoite nome show a great variety of options even within one and the same city or village and at about the same time. Some people distinguished between the husband's sending away his wife and the wife's voluntary withdrawal, in the latter case granting the husband a time frame of thirty or sixty days to hand back the dowry and *parapherna*,[80] whereas in case of the husband's divorce they should be

---

76. Yiftach-Firanko, *Marriage and Marital Arrangements*, 191.

77. Yiftach-Firanko, *Marriage and Marital Arrangements*, 191.

78. A good evidence for this is given in table 12 of Yiftach-Firanko, *Marriage and Marital Arrangements*, 312–17, covering every single contract. Regarding divorce, it has to be underscored that—somewhat similar to marriages (becoming valid with or without a written contract)—"spouses who wished to dissolve their marriage were offered routine procedures for doing so by the marriage documents. Yet these procedures were by no means obligatory" Uri Yiftach, "Was There a 'Divorce Procedure' among Greeks in Early Roman Egypt?," in *Atti del XXII Congresso Internazionale di Papirologia, Firenze, 23–29 agosto 1998*, ed. Isabella Andorlini et al., vol. 2 (Florence: Istituto Papirologico "G. Vitelli," 2001), 1338.

79. On the papyrological evidence for the Roman period, see especially Yiftach-Firanko, *Marriage and Marital Arrangements*, 205–19.

80. The thirty-days variant is preserved, e.g., in P.Ryl. 2.154.24–30 (Bakchias/Arsinoites; October 19, 66 CE): ἐὰν δὲ διαφορᾶς αὐτοῖς γεναμένης | [χ]ωρίζονται (read χωρίζωνται) ἀπ' ἀλλήλων, ἤτοι τοῦ Χαιρήμονος ἀποπέμποντος τ[ὴ]ν Θαισάριον ἢ καὶ αὐτῆς ἑκουσίω[ς | ἀ]παλλασσομέν[η]ς [ἀ]π' αὐτοῦ, ἔστω{ι} τοῦ τῆ[ς] Θα[ι]σαρ[ί]ου πατρὸς Σισόιτος, ἐὰ[ν] δὲ [ο]ὗτος μὴ περιῆι, αὐ[τῆς] Θ[α]ισαρί[ου | ὁ] σημαινόμενο[ς κλῆρ]ος τῶν ἀρουρῶν δ[έκα] ἡμίσους τετάρτου καθὼ[ς] πρόκειται· ἔτι δὲ καὶ προ[σα]πο|δώσ<ε>ιν αὐτῆι ὁ Χ[αιρ]ήμων καὶ τὴν προγ[εγρα]μμένην φερνὴν καὶ τὰ παράφερνα οἷα ἐὰν ἐκ τῆς τρί[ψ]εως ἐγβῆι (read ἐκβῆι), ἐπ[ὶ μὲν] τῆς ἀποπομπῆς πα[ραχρῆ]μα, ἐπὶ δὲ {του}τῆς ἑκουσ[ίο]υ ἀπαλλαγῆς ἐν ἡμέρα[ι]ς τριά|[κο]ντα ἀφ' ἧς ἐὰ[ν ἀπαι]τηθῆι ("but if any difference arises between them and they separate the one from the other, either Chairemon divorcing Thaisarion or Thaisarion withdrawing of her own free will, then the before-mentioned holding of ten [and] a half [and] a quarter [= 10¾] aruras shall

handed back at once. Other couples did not distinguish between the two cases, some of them granting the husband a time frame of thirty or sixty days, others obliging him to hand back dowry and *parapherna* at once.[81] In the contracts from Oxyrhynchus that show a smaller variety of options, we find two main groups: either people did not distinguish between the husband's sending away his wife and the wife's voluntary withdrawal (but wrote about the couple's "separation"), or they included a clause in the contract that explicitly mentioned the wife's decision to withdraw and, in this case, allowing the husband a sixty-day time frame for handing back the dowry, which seems to be the standard time frame also if the contract contains only a clause about the couple's possible separation.[82] Some of the preserved contracts have been crossed out, which is a clear hint that the respective contract was cancelled, that is, the marriage ended in divorce and the dowry had been handed back.[83]

All these aspects concerning marriage in the Roman Empire, some of them quite different from marriages in modern societies, must be kept in mind also when interpreting ancient literary or New Testament texts about marriage or divorce. Particularly concerning New Testament texts,

---

belong to Thaisarion's father Sisois, or, if he be no longer living, to Thaisarion herself; and Chairemon shall also restore the dowry aforesaid and the *parapherna* as they emerge from wear and tear, in the case of divorce at once, and in the case of voluntary withdrawal within thirty days from the day on which he is demanded to do so").

81. See table 4 in Arzt-Grabner, "Census Declarations" (with some differences compared to, and some updates to the data given by, Yiftach-Firanko, *Marriage and Marital Arrangements*, 207 [incl. nn. 40 and 41]). In *SPP* 20.15.16–20 (with *BL* 8:461; Ptolemais Euergetis; before October 27, 189 CE), the parties made a distinction only regarding the dowry (at once / thirty days), but they did not regarding the *parapherna* that should be handed back at once in any case.

82. For contracts that do not distinguish, see, e.g., P.Oxy. 49.3491.18–20 (Oxyrhynchus; 157–158 CE), and P.Oxy. 6.905.11–14 (Psobthis/Oxyrhynchites; March 14, 170 CE); both contracts distinguish between handing back the *parapherna* (at once), and the dowry (within sixty days). For contracts that explicitly mention of wife's decision to withdraw, see e.g., P.Oxy. 3.497.4–6 (Oxyrhynchus; early second century CE). For contracts that contain only a clause about the couple's possible separation, see table 5 in Arzt-Grabner, "Census Declarations" (with some differences compared to, and some updates to the data given by, Yiftach-Firanko, *Marriage and Marital Arrangements*, 209 [incl. notes 45–47]).

83. See, e.g., the demotic and greek "Ehefrauenurkunde" P.Dime 3.40 (Soknopaiou Nesos/Arsinoites; August 15, 28 CE?); P.Choix 10 (Tebtynis/Arsinoites; June 25–July 24, 162 CE).

it is worth noticing that we do not find anything about the dowry or the *parapherna*, that is, about the central issue of a marriage document, but solely terms of joint life that were more or less freely arranged in marriage documents or not even mentioned. Even those are sometimes very short and of a general character in New Testament texts, as in Col 3:18–19: wives should be subject to their husbands, and husbands should love their wives and never treat them harshly. However, we find nothing in New Testament texts concerning marriage that would be inconsistent with arrangements expressed in marriage documents, even the possibility of divorce, which, also according to marriage documents, should not but may happen (see 1 Cor 7:11).[84] On the other hand, everything could be more or less well represented in a marriage document filed by members of an early Christ group. If it is true that the majority of the members of early Christian communities did not belong to the privileged classes and were not very wealthy, we have to assume that only few couples filed a contract when entering into marriage. Perhaps, someone like Apphia's father or her parents were wealthy enough to make arrangements for a dowry in a written document with Philemon and hand it over to him on the occasion of the couple's marriage (or sometime after that event took place)—if the first two addressees of Paul's Letter to Philemon (see Phlm 1–2) were husband and wife.

The Place of Philemon's Household

Recent New Testament scholarship has situated Philemon's house (see Phlm 1–2) either in Colossae or in Rome (or nearby). One of the more important arguments for the Colossian hypothesis is Col 4:9 where a certain Onesimus is referred to as ὅς ἐστιν ἐξ ὑμῶν, that is, who is one of the Colossian community.[85] Thus, it has been argued, Paul's prison while writing Philemon must have been in the vicinity of Colossae, most probably in Ephesus. Other scholars have opted for Rome and have argued that the

---

84. There is a difference between New Testament texts regarding divorce and explicit documents of divorce where the couple agrees upon that—contrary to 1 Cor 7:11 (cf. Matt 5:31–32; 19:9)—each one is legally free to marry another partner without either of them being liable (cf., e.g., BGU 4.1103.22–25 [Alexandria; March 28, 13 BCE]).

85. See, e.g., Dietrich-Alex Koch, *Geschichte des Urchristentums: Ein Lehrbuch* (Göttingen: Vandenhoeck & Ruprecht, 2013), 572.

supposed imprisonment in Ephesus would, according to a chronology derived from Paul's letters, have been too short[86] to write Philippians and Philemon from there. Consequently, it has been suggested that Paul was imprisoned in Rome, and that also Philemon's household has to be settled in Rome or nearby.[87] In support of the Roman hypothesis it has been underscored that Apphia and Philemon are not mentioned in Colossians, which should have been the case if they were living in Colossae, and it has been argued that Col 4:9 does not necessarily mean that Onesimus's master was also from Colossae, but that only his slave originated from there *before* becoming Philemon's slave.[88]

From a papyrological perspective, none of these suggestions can be decisively confirmed. Even the identification of the Onesimus of Col 4:9 with the slave of Philemon is not absolutely certain,[89] although plausible. It is true that, if the origin of a slave is mentioned (most of all in slave sale contracts, i.e., as a legal issue mentioned in legal documents),[90] this notice usually refers to the place or region where the respective slave was born (and raised) and is introduced because slaves of special origin were known for special abilities. Of course, and it almost goes without saying, a slave's place of origin was not necessarily identical with the site where she or he

---

86. According to Marlis Gielen, "Paulus—Gefangener in Ephesus?," *BN* 2/131 (2006): 79–103; 133 (2007): 63–77, esp. 71, it lasted only about two weeks.

87. See Gielen, "Paulus—Gefangener in Ephesus?"; Vicky Balabanski, "Where Is Philemon? The Case for a Logical Fallacy in the Correlation of the Data in Philemon and Colossians 1.1–2; 4.7–18," *JSNT* 38 (2015): 141–43, 145–48.

88. See Balabanski, "Where Is Philemon?," especially 134, 139–40.

89. *Onesimus* is a very common and widely attested slave name; see Heikki Solin, *Griechische Namen*, vol. 2 of *Die stadtrömischen Sklavennamen: Ein Namenbuch*, Forschungen zur antiken Sklaverei 2 (Stuttgart: Franz Steiner, 1996), 465–68: 185 references for *Onesimus*, 18 for *Onesime*, 1 for *Onesimio(n)*, 2 for *Onesi*[—]. For inscriptions from Attica, see Charilaos Fragiadakis, "Die attischen Sklavennamen von der spätarchaischen Epoche bis in die römische Kaiserzeit: Eine historische und soziologische Untersuchung" (Diss., Universität Mannheim, 1986), 52 no. 23–25; 54 no. 3; 364 no. 584–587. Also a figure of Menander's *Epitrepontes* is a slave called Onesimus. Concerning papyri from Egypt see, e.g., SB 16.12764, col. II 17 (Oxyrhynchus; first–second centuries CE), and P.Lond. 2.208, recto a 3–5 (with *BL* 10:97; Ptolemais Euergetis/Arsinoites; June 25–July 24, 138 CE).

90. See, e.g., P.Turner 22.3 and 16–17 (Side; 142 CE) where the ten-year-old slave girl Abaskantis, who is ppurchased at the forum in Side by an Egyptian slave dealer, is described as being Galatian according to her origin (γένει Γαλάτιν).

currently served,⁹¹ which was very important to know in (private or business) relationships; there it was not to be neglected whose property a slave was or to which household she or he belonged. If the Onesimus of Col 4:9 has to be identified with Philemon's slave, I have, therefore, strong doubts that ὅς ἐστιν ἐξ ὑμῶν refers to his geographical or ethnic origin⁹² because, moreover, this phrase is neither an established way of referring to a slave's geographic or ethnic origin, nor does it, in Col 4:9, refer to a particular village, city, or region, but to a group of people, thus describing Onesimus as a current (ἐστιν!) member of the Christ group in Colossae.

That a certain Apphia, a name well attested in inscriptions from western Asia Minor (CIG 4380, k³,1 [3:1168] is from Colossae), is addressed in Phlm 2 does not prove that this woman has to be located there, since she, or even one of her ancestors, could have left the place of origin and traveled to another province (or, e.g., to Rome) in earlier days, without leaving any traces in the inscriptions.⁹³ Philemon itself suggests that, if the letter was addressed to a house church in Rome and written during Paul's

---

91. See Jean A. Straus, "Le pays d'origine des esclaves de l'Égypte romaine," *CdE* 46 (1971): 363–66; Iza Bieżuńska-Małowist, *Période romaine*, vol. 2 of *L'esclavage dans l'Égypte gréco-romaine*, Archiwum Filologiczne 35 (Wrocław: Zakład Narodowy imienia Ossolińskich; Warsaw: Wydawnictwo Polskiej Akademii Nauk, 1977), 13–42; Jean A. Straus, *L'achat et la vente des esclaves dans l'Egypte romaine: Contribution papyrologique à l'étude de l'esclavage dans une province orientale de l'Empire romain*, APF Series 14 (Munich: Saur, 2004), 276–83 (with a list of references).

92. It is also possible that Philemon's slave Onesimus was a house-born slave (οἰκογένης). On the different options of Onesimus' origin, see Arzt-Grabner, *Philemon*, 87–96.

93. See the references in Arzt-Grabner, *Philemon*, 82–83, and especially Arzt-Grabner, "Die Auswertung inschriftlicher Zeugnisse für die neutestamentliche Exegese: Erfahrungen, Chancen und Herausforderungen," in *Epigraphik und Neues Testament*, ed. Thomas Corsten, Markus Öhler and Joseph Verheyden, WUNT 365 (Tübingen: Mohr Siebeck, 2016), 36–37. So far, the name is not attested in papyri or ostraca. See p. 37 concerning the epigraphic record of Apphia: "Insgesamt ist also die Beleglage hier für West-Kleinasien, bes. Lydien, hervorragend, während Inschriften aus Rom und Italien erst aus späterer Zeit stammen. Es erscheint nicht unmöglich, dass Trägerinnen des Namens Apphia in Rom zur Zeit des Paulus noch nicht vertreten waren, doch sicher ist dies keineswegs: zum Einen findet sich ja nicht jede Person auf einer Inschrift, zum Anderen besagt der Befund nur, dass bisher keine Apphia vor dem 3. Jh. n.Chr. für Rom nachweisbar ist. Die Apphia des Phlm könnte nach Rom eingewandert sein, ohne dort Spuren zu hinterlassen. Der epigraphische Befund lässt also auch hier kein eindeutiges Urteil zu."

Roman imprisonment, it must have been written a certain amount of time, maybe several months, after Paul's arrival in Rome as he already shares a close relationship with Philemon, Apphia, Archippus, and the Christ group meeting in Philemon's house. On the other hand, and based on the conventions of ancient letter writing in general and those concerned with people who are in jail in particular,[94] a short letter like Philemon could easily have been written within a day, especially while being forced to stay in a prison cell. That Paul was in detention several times before being arrested in Caesarea and eventually sent to Rome is evidenced by Paul himself in 2 Cor 6:5 and 11:23, which also suggests that one or the other of the respective arrests took place in the province of Asia. Philemon could easily have been written during any of these imprisonments; moreover, there is no absolute certainty that Philippians and Philemon were composed and written during one and the same imprisonment. Of course, this does not mean that Philemon was definitely written in Ephesus or nearby, but that, as a location of Paul's prison while writing Philemon, Ephesus remains at least as plausible as Rome and that Colossae is still a good option for the location of Philemon's household.

Paul's reference to his old age in Phlm 9 does not necessarily evidence a Roman origin of Philemon, as πρεσβύτης sometimes refers to people who are over sixty, but in other cases to persons who are still in their fifties.[95]

The fact that Apphia and Philemon are not mentioned in Col does not mean that they are not living (or do not live anymore) in Colossae. It is a common feature in ancient letter writing that a sender of several letters, addressed to one and the same person or group, does not always address or greet every single member of the household or family (even the major figures of a household are no exception to that). For example, within the correspondence of a certain Athenodoros, who lived during the time of the emperor Augustus, we find two letters that were sent by a certain Tryphas to Athenodoros. Both letters are preserved completely, and they were written and found in the Herakleopolite nome; moreover, as

---

94. On the papyrological record concerning prisons and the bad conditions therein as well as concerning detentions before trial, see Arzt-Grabner et al., *2. Korinther*, PKNT 4 (Göttingen: Vandenhoeck & Ruprecht, 2014), 207–10.

95. See Arzt-Grabner, *Philemon*, 76–77 (with literary and documentary references); Michael Wolter, *Der Brief an die Kolosser: Der Brief an Philemon*, ÖTK 12, Gütersloher Taschenbücher Siebenstern 519 (Gütersloh: Mohn; Würzburg: Echter, 1993), 260.

both are exactly dated, we know that they were written within only about two months. BGU 16.2618 was written on May 10, 7 BCE, and addressed to Athenodoros, the son,[96] and Artemis, the daughter, whereas via BGU 16.2617, written on July 11 of the same year and addressed to Athenodoros, Tryphas sends greetings to her "ladies and daughters" Tryphas and Artemis. Daughter Tryphas is mentioned only in one of the two letters, the later one (2617). On the other hand, only the earlier letter (2618) also contains greetings by Nardos, Neikas, and all the others in the house (see ll. 22–24). Besides the option that the author of Colossians simply did not have in mind to mention Philemon and Apphia explicitly, papyrus letters also offer another convincing and simple solution to the question why he did not do so: Philemon and Apphia may have died after Philemon and before Colossians was written, and Archippus may have been the new patron of the household. A good example for a comparable situation is, according to the unanimous interpretation, attested by two letters of the Roman soldier Apion aka Antonius Maximus who is of Egyptian origin but garrisoned at Misenum. Both letters were written during the second century CE, the earlier one (BGU 2.423 with *BL* 1:45, 8:27, and 9:20), addressed to his father in Philadelphia (Arsinoite nome), and mentioning already in the letter opening his brother and his sister together with her daughter. In the letter corpus, Apion informs his father that he safely arrived in Misenum and received some journey-money (l. 9 βιάτικον = *viaticum*) from the Caesar. After sending greetings to a certain Capito, to his siblings, to a certain Serenilla and to his friends, he certifies that he had already sent his father an image of himself and that his name in the imperial fleet is now Antonius Maximus. BGU 2.632 (with *BL* 1:58) is clearly the later one of the two letters, as Apion now uses only his Roman name Antonius Maximus and makes clear that he has started a family several years ago (he sends greetings from his spouse Aufidia, his son Maximus, and his daughters Elpis and Fortunata). But what is most important in comparison with Colossians is this: he does not mention his father but addresses the letter to his sister Sabina and sends greetings to a certain Maximus ("probably the sister's son, who would then be named after his

---

96. It is not certain if Tryphas was Athenodoros's mother as in BGU 16.2615.1–2 (ca. 21 BCE–5 CE); the couple Menelaos and Herakleia address Athenodoros also as "son"; one of the two "mothers" must have addressed Athenodoros as "son" in a metaphorical way.

uncle") and to Copres "the lord" (probably his brother-in-law).⁹⁷ Epimachos, his father, has most probably died some time before, which is also suggested by the soldier's confirmation that he on every occasion does not delay to write to his sister who has become the main "link between her brother and his old home" (see ll. 11–14).⁹⁸ Concerning Colossians, it is also worth noticing that Archippus is the only person mentioned by name who is currently in Colossae. The term διακονία in Col 4:17 is probably referring to his care for the local Christ group that is still intending to meet in his house.⁹⁹ And, probably, one of the main purposes of Colossians was to remind Archippus of his important function as patron of the Colossian community, a function inherited from Philemon some time before.

Two topics, extensively represented in documentary papyri, are referred to in both letters, Philemon and Colossians: First, slavery is the main issue of Philemon, and slaves are—more extensively than other groups—addressed in Col 3:22–25 (masters in 4:1). Second, the textile industry and its regulations and conventions are an important background of Col 3:9–14, and a particular clause in several contracts of apprenticeship to a weaver is paralleled in Phlm 13 and provides some fresh information about Paul's own craft and his position in it. Both letters, therefore, must have been written to communities where slavery and textile industry were an important fact, well-known among the inhabitants and generally known by people from outside, including Paul of Tarsus and the author of Colossians. This does not prove that both letters were written to the same Christian community, but, and in combination with the arguments discussed above, it is most probable that we have to think of the same city, but at different times, when dealing with the addressees of Philemon and Colossians. Concerning Rome, slavery and textile production was not worth mentioning as anything special or known as particularly Roman, whereas Colossae and Laodicea were well-known centers of producing

---

97. Deissmann, *Light from the Ancient East*, 185 nn. 7–8.
98. Deissmann, *Light from the Ancient East*, 186. On the interpretation of both letters, see also Reinhold Scholl and Margit Homann, "Antike Briefkultur unter Familienmitgliedern," in *Papyrologie und Exegese: Die Auslegung des Neuen Testaments im Licht der Papyri*, ed. Jens Herzer, WUNT 2/341 (Tübingen: Mohr Siebeck, 2012), 80–85.
99. Notice also that 1 Cor 16:15 is the only passage where Paul himself uses this term to attribute it to a known person other than himself, namely, to Stephanas, the head of a Corinthian household. In Phlm 5–6, Paul writes about Philemon's ἀγάπη and πίστις that he has for the local Christian community.

special textiles (also with many slaves working in this industrial branch) and making a fortune by exporting them. This observation may point to Colossae rather than to Rome as the place of Philemon's household and the Christ group meeting there, addressed again in Colossians.

Slavery

Among the many aspects of ancient slavery about which we get extensive information from documentary papyri, ostraca, and tablets, I would like to focus, in a first step, on slave sale contracts. Besides house-born slaves for whom a slaveholder could file a declaration of οἰκογένεια to register the slave's status as such,[100] the best option to get slaves for one's household or branch of business was to buy them on the slave market, and Side, one of the biggest and most important slave markets in antiquity, was connected with the Lycus Valley by a Roman road that started in Pergamum and ran via Thyateira, Sardis, Philadelphia, Hierapolis, Laodicea, Colossae, Takina, Attalia, and Perga into Side.[101] In general, the slave market was regulated by the Edict of the Curule Aediles,[102] a large part of which has been pre-

---

100. Like birth returns for one's legal offspring, these declarations were not filed immediately after a slave's birth, but when the slave boy or girl was already two, three, or even seven years old. See PSI 6.690 (with *BL* 2:141; Arsinoites; first–second centuries CE) for the seven-year-old slave girl Iulia, SB 3.6995 (Tenis/Memphites; April 26, 124 CE) for the three-year-old slave boy Phoineikas (a later copy of this document is preserved in SB 3.6996, col. I [Tenis/Memphites; April 3, 127 CE]), and 6996, col. 2, for the two-year-old slave boy Zosimos; the declarations for both boys were submitted by the female slaveholder Baibia Rufilla, the mother of both boys was her slave Tyche who had been bought at the slave market. See also SB 16.12950 (Ptolemais Euergetis/Arsinoites; 230–231 CE), a declaration filed by Aurelia Kyrilla regarding two slaves (names and ages not preserved), who had been born by Kyrilla's slave Techosous aka Isidora.

101. A bilingual milestone (in Latin and Greek) from Side, which can be dated to 129–126 BCE (*SEG* 41.1336), reads: M.' · Aquillius ·M.' · f ·| (vacat) cos · CCCXXXI | Μάνιος Ἀκύλλιος Μανίου, | (vacat) ὕπατος Ῥωμαίων· | τλα' ("M. Aquillius, son of Manius, consul of the Romans. 331 [miles]"). According to the first editor, the distance of 331 miles suggests the described route (see David H. French, "Sites and Inscriptions from Phrygia, Pisidia and Pamphylia," *Epigraphica Anatolica* 17 [1991]: 53–54 no. 3). See also Nollé, *Griechische und lateinische Inschriften (5–16)*, 497 no. 175; Nollé, *Geographie–Geschichte–Testimonia–Griechische*, 23.

102. On this edict, and especially on its clauses concerning the guarantee for slaves, see especially Éva Jakab, *Praedicere und cavere beim Marktkauf: Sachmän-*

served in book 21 of Justinian's Digest. The aim of the edict was to protect the purchaser from false information about a slave by the vendor, ordering the vendor to provide clear and public information about any diseases or defects of the slaves, if they had ever run away, or proved to be truants, or had not been released from liability for damage that they had committed. If nothing of that kind was true, the vendor was not obliged to provide any information at all. On the other hand, the edict clearly forced the vendor to keep all the promises he made, which means: the vendor was liable for all that he said or promised (*dictum promissumve*) at the time of the sale.[103]

---

gel im griechischen und römischen Recht, MBPF 87 (Munich: Beck, 1997); Berthold Kupisch, "Römische Sachmängelhaftung: Ein Beispiel für die 'ökonomische Analyse des Rechts'?," *Legal History Review* 70 (2002): 21–54; Peter Arzt-Grabner, "'Neither a Truant nor a Fugitive': Some Remarks on the Sale of Slaves in Roman Egypt and Other Provinces," in *Proceedings of the Twenty-Fifth International Congress of Papyrology, Ann Arbor, July 29–August 4, 2007*, ed. Traianos Gagos and Adam Hyatt, American Studies in Papyrology Special Edition (Ann Arbor: The University of Michigan Library, Scholarly Publishing Office, 2010), 21–32. On the guarantee clauses in papyrus contracts, see also Hans-Albert Rupprecht, "Die Eviktionshaftung in der Kautelarpraxis der graeco-ägyptischen Papyri," in *Studi in onore di Arnaldo Biscardi*, ed. Franco Pastori and Mariagrazia Bianchini, vol. 3 (Milan: La Goliardica, 1982), 463–79; Straus, *L'achat et la vente des esclaves*, 152–57; Giuseppe Camodeca in T.Sulpicii, pp. 115–16; Camodeca, *L'archivio Puteolano dei Sulpicii*, vol. 1, Pubblicazioni del Dipartimento di Diritto Romano e Storia della Scienza Romanistica dell'Università degli Studi die Napoli "Federico II" 4 (Naples: Jovene, 1992); Camodeca, "Tabulae Herculanenses: Riedizione delle emptiones di schiavi (TH 59–62)," in *Quaestiones Iuris: Festschrift für Joseph Georg Wolf zum 70. Geburtstag*, ed. Ulrich Manthe and Christoph Krampe, Freiburger rechtsgeschichtliche Abhandlungen 2/36 (Berlin: Duncker & Humblot, 2000), 74–76 (the documents are cited as T.Hercul.); Otto Eger, "Eine Wachstafel aus Ravenna aus dem zweiten Jahrhundert nach Chr," *ZSS Romanistische Abteilung* 42 (1921): 456–58.

103. See Dig. 21.1.1.1 (Ulpianus 1 ad ed. aedil. curul.): *qui mancipia vendunt certiores faciant emptores, quid morbi vitiive cuique sit, quis fugitivus errove sit noxave solutus non sit: eademque omnia, cum ea mancipia venibunt, palam recte pronuntianto. quodsi mancipium adversus ea venisset, sive adversus quod dictum promissumve fuerit cum veniret, fuisset, quod eius praestari oportere dicetur: emptori omnibusque ad quos ea res pertinet iudicium dabimus, ut id mancipium redhibeatur. [...] item si quas accessiones ipse praestiterit, ut recipiat. item si quod mancipium capitalem fraudem admiserit, mortis consciendae sibi causa quid fecerit, inve harenam depugnandi causa ad bestias intromissus fuerit, ea omnia in venditione pronuntianto: ex his enim causis iudicium dabimus. hoc amplius si quis adversus ea sciens dolo malo vendidisse dicetur, iudicium dabimus.* (For an English translation by S. P. Scott, see http://www.constitution.org/sps/sps05.htm).

In the exegetical discussion that has been generated by scholars, trying to illuminate Paul's description of the case of Onesimos in Philemon by referring to Roman jurists, it has been argued that "it is quite unclear to what extent the categories of the Roman jurists might be relevant to the dialogue between Paul and Philemon."[104] But slave sale contracts preserved on papyri and waxed tablets, and from different Roman provinces, suggest that such doubts are not justified. Several documents explicitly refer to the edict: documents from Egypt, from Puteoli and Herculaneum in Italy, from Syria, and—most relevant for Colossae—two contracts from Side.[105] Most of the preserved slave sale contracts do not give any information about diseases or defects but provide promises that none of these is relevant; many vendors confirm the slave's healthy condition, whereas some exclude a guarantee concerning epilepsy and leprosy and others refuse to guarantee that the slave is neither a truant nor a fugitive; comparably few slave dealers include such a guarantee in the contracts.[106] Only recently,

---

104. Ulrich Huttner, *Early Christianity in the Lycus Valley*, trans. David Green, AJEC 85, Early Christianity in Asia Minor 1 (Leiden: Brill, 2013), 106. See also Peter Lampe, "Keine 'Sklavenflucht' des Onesimus," *ZNW* 76 (1985): 135–37; J. Albert Harrill, *Slaves in the New Testament: Literary, Social, and Moral Dimensions* (Minneapolis: Augsburg Fortress, 2006), 8–11; John G. Nordling, "Onesimus Fugitivus: A Defense of the Runaway Slave Hypothesis in Philemon," *JSNT* 41 (1991): 114–17.

105. Egypt: P.Hamb. 1.63 (with *BL* 7:66; Thebais?; 125–126 CE); see Wolff, *Organisation und Kontrolle*, 167–68. Puteoli: T.Sulpicii 43 (August 21, 38 CE; cf. T.Sulpicii 42 [March 18, 26 CE?]; 44). Herculaneum: T.Hercul. 60 (before 63/64 CE; cf. T.Hercul. 62 [November 30, 47 CE]). Syria: P.Lond. 1.229 (p. xxi) (Seleucia Pieria; May 24, 166 CE). Side: P.Turner 22 (with *BL* 12:284; 142 CE), and BGU 3.887 (with *BL* 1:77, 350; 3:15; 7:16, and 8:36; July 8, 151 CE). In addition, also the clause *bonis condicionibus*, signifying that the sale took place "under good conditions" is a reference to the conditions explained in the edict (see Jakab, *Praedicere und cavere*, 187–90); it is attested in a contract from Ravenna (SB 3.6304 [117–161 CE]). A contract from Seleucia Pieria (P.Lond. 1.229 [p. xxi] [May 24, 166 CE]) contains both clauses. Probably, the clause καλῇ αἱρέσει can be identified as the Greek equivalent to *bonis condicionibus*; it is attested in several contracts from Egypt and one from Ascalon/Phoenicia (SB 5.8007.5 [Hermoupolis?; first half of the fourth century CE]; P.Abinn. 64.15 [Alexandria or Philadelpha; 337–350 CE]; P.Cair.Masp. 1.67120.5 [but see *BL* 3:34; Aphrodites Kome/ Antaiopolites; ca. 567–568 CE]; BGU 1.316.5 [Ascalon/Phoenicia; 359 CE]; see Jakab, *Praedicere und cavere*, 208–9). It is also important to notice that the contracts from Side, Ravenna, Seleucia, and Ascalon were brought to Egypt, obviously together with the purchased slaves, and found there.

106. For references see Arzt-Grabner, "'Neither a Truant nor a Fugitive,'" 25–30; Arzt-Grabner, "How to Deal with Onesimus? Paul's Solution within the Frame of

the first documentary evidence of a vendor, who explicitly informed the buyer about any disease or defect of the slave, has been edited: P.Oxy. 78.5166 (Oxyrhynchus; 29–20 BCE) offers at least an indirect hint to the fact that the vendor of the female slave Thermuthion, about thirty years old, had clearly informed the buyer, a certain Philiscus, that the slave was a runaway. The document is an instruction to the banker Apollophanes to receive from Philiscus the tax on the sale of the slave.[107] The female slave is literally described as "a runaway, whom Philiscus will track down and bring back for himself" (ll. 5–6: οὔσης ἐν δρασμῶι, ἣν ἀναζητήσας | ὁ Φιλ[ί]σκος ἑαυτῶι ἀνάξει). Obviously, Thermuthion *is* not only a slave who ran away once, but she is still on the run at the time when the contract is filed and the tax on the sale is paid.[108]

If someone from Colossae wanted to make a good decision when intending to buy a slave, he almost certainly went to Side, which could be reached within about ten days when traveling on foot but in five days when using a fast carriage.[109] In both contracts originating from there, the vendors provide information about the slaves age, origin, and body

---

Ancient Legal and Documentary Sources," in *Philemon in Perspective: Interpreting a Pauline Letter*, ed. D. Francois Tolmie, BZNW 169 (Berlin: de Gruyter, 2010), 126–33.

107. As stated in line 8, the price for the slave was "10 talents, 3,000 drachmas in bronze"; the tax, which Philiscus paid, is calculated as "2 talents, 693 drachmas and 3½ obols in bronze (converted) to silver." Thus, this document gives clear evidence for a sales tax of 20 percent on slaves and not 10 percent as has sometimes been assumed on the analogy of the rate on other sales (already questioned by Wallace, *Taxation in Egypt*, 230, and Straus, *L'achat et la vente des esclaves*, 76–77). On the rate of 20 percent sales tax on slaves from the early Ptolemaic period see P.Col. 1.inv. 480 (Arsinoites; ca. 198–197 BCE) and P.Sijp. 45 (Arsinoites or Herakleopolites; January 7, 197 BCE); see also Reinhold Scholl in C.Ptol.Sklav., p. 62. On the prices paid for slaves, see Kai Ruffing and Hans-Joachim Drexhage, "Antike Sklavenpreise," in *Antike Lebenswelten: Konstanz–Wandel–Wirkungsmacht; Festschrift für Ingomar Weiler zum 70. Geburtstag*, ed. Peter Mauritsch et al., Philippika, Marburger altertumskundliche Abhandlungen 25 (Wiesbaden: Harrassowitz, 2008), 321–51.

108. An interesting document is also P.Cair.Preis. 1 (2nd ed.), the report of proceedings about a fugitive slave girl, possibly written in Oxyrhynchus between 147 and 150 CE. The case of the anonymous plaintiff is all the more dramatic as the slave girl Eutychia, whom he had purchased from a certain Sarapion, has not only taken "much of his belongings" but also "her sales contracts" (line 6 τάς τε ἀσφαλείας τὰ<ς> τῆς πράσεως ἑα[υτῆς]) so that he is no longer able to prove whether the contract contained a guarantee against flight or not.

109. The calculations were executed by using http://orbis.stanford.edu.

marks, but also that they are free of any claim by anyone else, neither truants nor fugitives (μήτε ῥέμβον μήτε δραπετικόν),[110] and not suffering from epilepsy. The distinction between a truant and a fugitive (also preserved in other contracts),[111] which is also important for the interpretation of Philemon, is in coincidence with a juridical discussion that is again preserved in Justinian's Digest. Ulpian, who died in 223 CE in Rome, argued that the truant slave roams about with no reason but returns home to his master at a late hour.[112] The same idea is expressed—earlier than Ulpian—by Paul in Phlm 15 when he argues that Onesimus "went away for only a while," so that Philemon might "have him back forever."[113] We do not know for sure what was really going on with Onesimus before he visited Paul in prison;

---

110. See P.Turner 22.4 and 20–21 (142 CE) and BGU 3.887.5 and 16–17 (July 8, 151 CE).

111. See, in addition to the contracts from Side: T.Sulpicii 43 (Puteoli/Italy; August 21, 38 CE); T.Hercul. 62 (Herculaneum/Italy; Nov. 30, 47 CE); 60 (before 63/64 CE); T.Dacia 6 (Alburnus Maior/Dacia; March 17, 139 CE); 7 (May 16, 142 CE). The contracts that were written in Egypt, either state that the slave is faithful and not (given to) running away (πιστὸς καὶ ἄδραστος, see SB 3.6016.26 [Alexandria; March 28, 154 CE]; 5.8007.5 [Hermoupolis?; first half of fourth century CE]; P.Abinn. 64.14 [Alexandria or Philadelphia; 337–350 CE]; see also, from Ascalon/Phoenicia, BGU 1.316.29 [359 CE]), or they exclude a guarantee concerning a later(!) flight (the earliest reference, BGU 4.1059.17–18 [Alexandria; reign of Augustus], expresses this by δρασμὸς δὲ καὶ θάνατος τῆς δούλης ἀπὸ τοῦ νῦν οὐκ ἔσται πρὸς τὴν | Λαοδίκην ["but flight and death of the slave are from now on not in the responsibility of Laodike," the vendor] whereas later contracts from the Arsinoite nome guarantee the sale with every guarantee, except against flight, πλὴν δρασμοῦ: BGU 3.987.7–9.22–23 [with BL 4:6 and 10:18; Arsinoites; 19 or 45 CE]; P.Mich. 5.278 and 279.5–6 [Tebtynis; ca. 30 CE; the duplicate nr. 279 ed. by Straus, L'achat et la vente des esclaves, 327–28]; 264.11–14.24 and 265.6 [Tebtynis; February 7, 37 CE; the duplicate nr. 265 ed. by Straus, L'achat et la vente des esclaves, 328–30]; 281.6 [Tebtynis; ca. 48 CE]; P.Stras. 6.505.23–26 [Tebtynis; 107–115 CE; on line 14 cf. Straus, L'achat et la vente des esclaves, 356]; BGU 3.859.11–13 [with BL 1:74, 3:15 and 8:35; Arsinoites; 161–163 CE]; on this interpretation see Arzt-Grabner, "'Neither a Truant nor a Fugitive,'" 28, contrary to Jakab, Praedicere und cavere, 205–6).

112. See Dig. 21.1.17.14: *sed proprie erronem sic definimus: qui non quidem fugit, sed frequenter sine causa vagatur et temporibus in res nugatorias consumptis serius domum redit.*

113. In literary as well as in documentary sources, a passive form of χωρίζω is always used in the active sense "to go away," when expressed about a person; see Arzt-Grabner, Philemon, 103–5; Arzt-Grabner, "Onesimus erro: Zur Vorgeschichte des Philemonbriefes," ZNW 95.1–2 (2004): 136–39.

at least, Paul does not picture Onesimus as a fugitive but as a slave who was just roaming about, as he had done before.[114] We are not able to know, and we never will be, whether Paul was downplaying a much more dramatic situation or providing a more or less authentic description of the facts. But in drawing this particular picture of Onesimus as truant, not as fugitive, Paul also—in addition to slave sale contracts—offers good evidence that at least the basic ideas and intentions of the edict were generally shared and that they should have been known also to the Christ group meeting in Philemon's house.

As mentioned above, no other group is more extensively addressed in Colossians than slaves (see 3:22–25). Some points of the author's appeals in this section can be illuminated by documentary papyri. According to verse 22, slaves should obey their masters in everything, not to please them (ἀνθρωπάρεσκοι), but wholeheartedly (ἐν ἁπλότητι καρδίας). Neither the rare adjective ἀνθρωπάρεσκος[115] nor the clause ἐν ἁπλότητι καρδίας are attested in documentary papyri so far, but BGU 4.1141.24 evidences that it was a slave's usual behavior to please her or his master. The papyrus preserves a private letter, or more probably a draft of it, written on the verso of the sheet, presumably in Alexandria between August 30, 14 BCE, and August 28, 13 BCE.[116] If, as I assume, the *recto* has been inscribed before the *verso*, this letter draft must have been written after April 9, 13 BCE. The author of the letter is probably a freedman addressing his patron, a certain Erotes.[117] The text refers to a previous letter, which obviously contained a great deal of information that we are missing for a clearer understanding of the whole situation. Now, the anonymous author reproaches his addressee for mistrusting him, and he also expresses fundamental thoughts about the behavior of a slave toward his master in lines 23–25: οὐδὲ γὰρ ἐφιλίασά

---

114. See Arzt-Grabner, "Onesimus erro"; Arzt-Grabner, *Philemon*, 101–108; Arzt-Grabner, "How to Deal with Onesimus?," esp. 133–35.

115. LSJ, s.v. "ἀνθρωπάρεσκος," refers only to biblical texts (besides Col 3:22 only Ps 52:6 LXX and Eph 6:6), *DEG*, s.v. "ἀνθρωπάρεσκος" also to 2 Clem. 13.1 and later Christian literature.

116. See Berliner Papyrusdatenbank, berlpap.smb.museum/00523/. See there also for a digital image. Concerning the Greek text (and German translation), see, in addition to the *editio princeps* by Wilhelm Schubart, Bror Olsson, *Papyrusbriefe aus der frühesten Römerzeit* (Uppsala: Almquist & Wiksells, 1925), no. 9; *BL* 3:17; 8:42; 11:25; Amphilochios Papathomas, "Textkritische Bemerkungen zu Berliner Papyrusbriefen," *APF* 53 (2007): 188; Arzt-Grabner et al., *2. Korinther*, 62–66.

117. See *BL* 11:25.

σοι εἰς τὸ ἀφαρπάσαι τι, ἀλλὰ ἡ | σὴ ψυχὴ ἐπίσταται, ὅτι ὡς δοῦλος ἐπ' ἐλευθερίᾳ θέλει ἀρέσαι οὕτω | κἀγὼ τη⟦ς⟧\ν/ φιλίαν σου ⟦θέλω{ι}⟧ \θέλων/ ἄμεμπτ[ον] ἐμα<υ>τὸν ἐτήρησα ("for I have not become a friend to you to steal anything from you, but your soul knows that like a slave in the hope of manumission wants to please, I too, wanting your friendship, behaved blamelessly"). The author describes the relation between a pleasant slave and his master as it is and without glossing over it: a slave wants to please the master because he or she hopes to get manumitted one day. Moreover, he himself confesses that, similarly, he behaved blamelessly because he wanted his (former) master's friendship. It seems that the author's intention is not to manipulate his patron with sweet words but to underscore that everything that he writes is true and without any personal exaggeration. His words are as true and honest as possible and might have served him well in his intention to gain his patron's trust and friendship (again).[118]

It is possible that the author of Col 3:22 had a similar connection in mind (to please one's master in order to get manumitted) and that he rejects this attitude. But in comparison with BGU 4.1141.23–25, it is more probable that he appeals to slaves to behave truthfully and honestly, with their whole heart—or blamelessly (ἄμεμπτος) as the author of the papyrus letter confirms, with whatever intention in mind. As the papyrological record shows, there was—it almost goes without saying—nothing wrong with slaves who hoped for manumission. That blameless slaves with goodwill and long-lasting affection toward their masters had some reason to do so and that masters sometimes really manumitted them because of their attitude and behavior is (in addition to BGU 4.1141) attested by two wills that are preserved on two papyri from the first or second century CE: According to P.Scholl 5.3 (Tholthis/Oxyrhynchites; first–second centuries CE), the testator is manumitting several slaves "on account of their goodwill and affection" ([— κατ' εὔνοιαν κα]ὶ φιλοστοργίαν δουλικὰ σώματ[α —]). The same clause is attested by P.Col. 10.267.5 (Oxyrhynchus; 180–192 CE).

In Col 3:23, slaves are told to do everything "out of [their] soul" (ἐκ ψυχῆς ἐργάζεσθε, NRSV translates: "whatever your task, put yourselves into it"). Documentary papyri or ostraca do not attest a similar appeal so far, but, nevertheless, it is worth having a closer look at SB 24.16257. In

---

118. See also Peter Arzt-Grabner, "Wisdom in Non-Christian Papyrus Letters from Roman Egypt," in *Tra pratiche e credenze: Traiettorie antropologiche e storiche; Un omaggio ad Adriana Destro*, ed Claudio Gianotto and Francesca Sbardella (Brescia: Morcelliana, 2017), 197–216.

col. I, the papyrus preserves a petition, written after October 18, 123 CE, and submitted to Eudemos, the strategos of the Herakleides division of the Arsinoite nome. Two priests of Soknopaiou Nesos claim that another priest, Harpagathes, had deluded and abducted two of their slaves, named Horion and Soteris, after the slaves had also stolen some of their masters' belongings. Afterward Harpagathes had written to them by means of an officially registered document, with the surety of his wife and another Harpagathes, in which he had promised to return the slaves within thirty days or to pay a sum to be adjudicated. But Harpagathes did not keep his promises. On the contrary, the priests claim, he disappeared together with his wife and the other Harpagathes.[119] In connection with Col 3:23, line 5 of the petition is of special interest where the priests claim that Harpagathes "deluded" the two slaves: [ψ]υχαγωγήσας δουλικὰ σώματα δύο. If we are allowed to take the phrase literally, it means that slaves have a soul that can be (mis)guided to do something in particular. In this context, Col 3:23 includes the notion that the slaves of the Christian community should have control over their own souls, never let anyone mislead them to act against their masters, but always act in accordance with their inner selves.

As brief and simple as the appeal to the slave masters in Col 4:1 may seem, as strange it must have sounded to them, a master might have treated his slaves in a just way, but not all of them equally. The differences between slaves concerning their duties and opportunities were huge, not only if we look at the whole spectrum of ancient slavery, where we find all types of slaves from those miserable fellows who were forced to work in the mines or on the galleys up to stewards and physicians, but also within a household, where a messenger or steward was entrusted with much higher responsibilities[120] than one working in the fields or in the kitchen. Needless to say, the opportunities to earn and save less or more money of

---

119. See Ann E. Hanson, "A Petition and Court Proceedings: P. Michigan inv. 6060," *ZPE* 111 (1996): 175–79.

120. A steward, e.g., could be entrusted with "filing of tax-returns, loans, suretyship, hiring of service or work to be done, accepting or receipting of payments, management of estates" (Taubenschlag, *Law of Greco-Roman Egypt*, 90–91); on the papyrological record of slaves working in the Roman administration, see Bieżuńska-Małowist, "Les esclaves imperiaux dans l'Egypte romaine"; concerning the papyrological evidence of the great variety of the duties and occupations of slaves, see also Jean A. Straus, "L'esclavage dans l'Egypte romaine," *ANRW* 10.1:867–876 (with bibliography p. 867 n. 141); Straus, "Quelques activités exercées par les esclaves d'après les papyrus de l'Égypte romaine," *Historia* 26 (1977): 74–88; Bieżuńska-Małowist,

the so-called *peculium*¹²¹ were also different. On special occasions, a slave could even be in higher esteem than a freeborn or freedman, which is attested, for example, by an ostracon from Didymoi in the Eastern desert of Egypt (O.Did. 438 [before about 110–115 CE]) whose addressee is asked to "recommend [someone] to your slave since he is inexperienced" (ll. 6–8: συνστῆσαι τῷ παι|δαρίῳ σου ἐπειδὴ αὐτὸς ἰδιώτης | ἐστίν). This letter represents just another example of a slave who was a trained craftsman or steward with some experience so that other slaves or—as most probably in this case—even inexperienced freeborn persons or freedmen would be entrusted to him to take care of them.¹²² Paul of Tarsus attests that he had something similar in mind when he asked the slave-holder Philemon to take his slave Onesimus as his partner (κοινωνός, see Phlm 17).

Weaving Industry

The Lycus Valley was well known for its produce of cloth and clothes, well known beyond the Lycus Valley.¹²³ It makes perfect sense that Col 3:9–14

Période romaine, 73–108; Arzt-Grabner, "How to Deal with Onesimus?," 116–19, 122–23.

121. The ostracon P.Scholl 9 (Memnoneia [Thebes west]; after? September 12, 131 or 152 or 175 CE) probably confirms that already child slaves could earn some money. It is an account, listing the wages for workers on an estate between 12th and 15th Toth of year 16. The workers are listed in groups of ἄνδρες ("men"), ὀνηλάται ("donkey drivers"), and παιδ( ), who are—most probably—to be interpreted as παιδ(ία) ("child slaves") as they are paid less: they get only 1 chalkine (= 1 bronze drachma) whereas men and donkey drivers receive at least 1 drachma and 1 obol, except the one donkey driver mentioned in line 4 who also receives just 1 chalkine and, therefore, most probably was a slave, too. If the interpretation for slave children is correct, they were hired from a slaveholder. On the value of the χαλκίνη, see Fabian Reiter, "Unerkannte Bronzedrachmen," in *Honi soit qui mal y pense: Studien zum pharaonischen, griechisch-römischen und spätantiken Ägypten zu Ehren von Heinz-Josef Thissen*, ed. Hermann Knuf, Christian Leitz, and Daniel von Recklinghausen, OLA 194 (Leuven: Peeters, 2010), 419–23.

122. For other examples, see Arzt-Grabner, *Philemon*, 96–101, 230–34; Arzt-Grabner, "How to Deal with Onesimus?," 137–39.

123. See Hatice Erdemir, "Woollen Textiles: An International Trade Good in the Lycus Valley in Antiquity," in *Colossae in Space and Time: Linking to an Ancient City*, ed. Alan H. Cadwallader and Michael Trainor, NTOA–SUNT 94 (Göttingen: Vandenhoeck & Ruprecht, 2011), 104–29; Rosemary Canavan, "Weaving Threads: Clothing in Colossae," in *Fragments of Colossae*, 111–33. Similarly, also Paul's hometown, Tarsus,

reflects metaphorically how convenient it was in a town such as Colossae to buy new garments and dress oneself nicely. Documentary papyri and ostraca broadly illumine all the steps from sheep rearing and producing wool to fulling, dyeing, and especially weaving. Most excitingly, a particular clause in some contracts of apprenticeship to a weaver is paralleled in Phlm 13.

Contracts of apprenticeship of the first century CE are preserved from the Arsinoite nome and from Oxyrhynchus.[124] An adult relative (in most cases a father or mother or the master of a slave) apprentices a boy or girl to a master weaver to learn the weaver's craft. Such a contract usually contains a clause by which the apprenticing party confirms that the apprentice will do everything that is ordered by the master weaver according to his craft.[125] Among the contracts from the first century CE, we have three

---

was known for a special type of weaving, and *tarsikarioi*, who were familiar with it, are to be found also among weavers in Egypt from the third century CE onwards (the earliest references are P.Oxy. 14.1765.2, 21, 30 [Oxyrhynchus; third century CE]; P.Laur. 3.79.3 [Oxyrhynchus; third–early fourth centuries CE]; see John Peter Wild, "The Tarsikarios, a Roman Linen-Weaver in Egypt," in *Hommages à Marcel Renard*, ed. Jacqueline Bibauw, vol. 2, Collection Latomus 102 [Bruxelles: Latomus, 1969] 810–19; concerning the references cf. Arzt-Grabner, *Philemon*, 65 n. 26).

124. The earliest one on a larger scale is P.Tebt. 2.384 (with *BL* 3:242, 6:198, and 9:356; Oxyrhyncha/Arsinoites; August 9, 10 CE). On apprentice contracts in general, see William L. Westermann, "Apprentice Contracts and the Apprentice System in Roman Egypt," *CP* 9 (1914): 295–315; Joachim Hengstl, *Private Arbeitsverhältnisse freier Personen in den hellenistischen Papyri bis Diokletian* (Bonn: Habelt, 1972), 83–97; Marco Bergamasco, "Le διδασκαλικαί nella ricerca attuale," *Aeg* 75 (1995): 95–167; Peter van Minnen, "Urban Craftsmen in Roman Egypt," *Münsterische Beiträge zur antiken Handelsgeschichte* 6 (1987): 31–88; Angela Zambon, "Διδασκαλικαί," *Aeg* 15 (1935): 3–66; Orsolina Montevecchi, *I contratti di lavoro e di servizio nell'Egitto greco romano e bizantino* (Milan: Vita e pensiero, 1950); Johannes Herrmann, "Vertragsinhalt und Rechtsnatur der διδασκαλικαί," *JJP* 11–12 (1957–1958): 119–39; for references, see further R. A. Coles in P.Oxy. 41, p. 72, and Marco Bergamasco, "Una petizione per violazione di un contratto di tirocinio: P. Kell. G. 19.a," *Aeg* 77 (1997): 7–26 (including Bergamasco, "P.Kell. G. 19.A, Appendix," *ZPE* 119 [1997]: 193–96).

125. E.g., P.Tebt. 2.384.23–25 (Oxyrhyncha/Arsinoites; August 9, 10 CE): [ἐ]ργαζόμενον [κατὰ τὴν] | γερδιακὴν τέχνην καὶ ποιοῦντα τὰ ἐπ[ιταχθη]|σόμε[να] πάντα (he will "work according to the weaver's craft and do everything that is ordered"); P.Mich. 5.355.2–3 (Tebtynis/Arsinoites; ca. 48–56 CE; duplicate PSI 8.902.3–4): διατρίβοντα καὶ ποιοῦντα πάντα | τὰ ἐπιτασσόμενα (a certain Harmiysis apprentices himself to a master weaver and promises that he will "work and do everything that is ordered"); P.Oxy.Hels. 29,12–15 (September 8, 54 CE): ποιοῦντα π[άντα τ]ὰ

documents that were filed between weavers, that is, a member of a family of weavers apprenticed one's son to another master weaver. In these three contracts, all from Oxyrhynchus, the clause just mentioned is preceded by the confirmation that the apprentice will also "serve" (διακονέω) the master weaver.

In the earliest reference, SB 10.10236 (with *BL* 7:216–17; September 25, 36 CE), a certain Thamounion apprentices her son Onophris to the weaver Abaros, son of Didymos; lines 13–15 read: διακονοῦν|τα κ[αὶ] ποιοῦντ[α τὰ] ἔργα πάντα τὰ ἐπι|τα[σσ]όμενα α[ὐτῷ] ὑπὸ τοῦ Ἀβάρου | κατὰ τὴν γερδιακ[ὴ]ν τέχνην (Onophris will "serve and do all the works ordered to him by Abaros according to the weaver's craft"). This papyrus is part of an archive, the protagonist of which is the weaver Tryphon, son of Dionysios.[126] In this contract Tryphon himself acts as guardian (κύριος) of his mother Thamounion whose husband Dionysios, the father of Tryphon and Onophris, is obviously no longer alive.[127] The taxation account P.Oxy. 2.288 (with *BL* 1:320 and 7:129), written in Oxyrhynchus after July 22, 25 CE, contains the copy of an *epicrisis* extract of the year 11–12 CE (ll. 35–40 with *BL* 7:129) from which we learn that Tryphon's grandfather was a weaver; in 11–12 CE this Tryphon, son of Didymos, was the head of the household, and sixty-four years old. From the same list we learn that also Tryphon's father Dionysios (in 11–12 CE, thirty-two years old) and his two uncles, Didymos (thirty-seven years old) and Thoonis (twenty-one years old), were weavers.[128] The taxation account itself proves that our Tryphon paid the weaver's tax (see P.Oxy. 2.288.1–34 with *BL* 1:320), thus confirming that he had been a weaver himself for several years when he acted as guardian for his mother Thamounion at the time when she apprenticed her other son Onophris to the weaver Abaros.

In 66 CE, Tryphon himself apprentices his own son Thoonis to the weaver Ptolemaios, son of Pausirion, and both weavers file a contract of apprenticeship on September 18, 66 CE (P.Oxy. 2.275 with *BL* 9:179).

ἐπιτασσόμενα αὐτῶι | ὑπὸ τοῦ Ἡρᾶ[τος] κατὰ τὴν γερδιακὴν | τέχνην ἥνπερ καὶ αὐτὸς ἐκδιδάξει | τοῦ\τον/ καθὼς ἐπίστατα[ι] (he will "do everything that he is ordered by Heras according to the weaver's craft which also he himself will teach as he knows it").

126. See Trismegistos Archives: www.trismegistos.org/archive/249.

127. See Maria Valentina Biscottini, "L'archivio di Tryphon, tessitore di Oxyrhynchos," *Aeg* 46 (1966): 209.

128. See also SB 10.10220 (with *BL* 7:216; Oxyrhynchus; after July 25, 22 CE).

The respective clause in lines 10–13 is almost identical: διακονοῦ(ν)|τα καὶ ποιο[ῦ]ντα πάντα τὰ ἐπιτασσόμε|να αὐτῷ ὑπὸ τοῦ Πτολεμαίου κατὰ τὴν | γερδιακὴν τέχνην πᾶσαν (Thoonis will "serve and do everything ordered to him by Ptolemaios according to the entire[129] weaver's craft").

The third example, P.Wisc. 1.4 (with *BL* 6:69; August 29–September 27, 53 CE), is part of another weaver's archive, of Pausiris, son of Ammonios:[130] We know that several years earlier, in 49 CE, the same weaver Pausiris, son of Ammonios, wished to apprentice his son Ammonios to the master weaver Apollonios, son of Apollonios, and that on September 16 of that year, he applied to the *topogrammateis* and *komogrammateis* of Oxyrhynchus, Apollonios and Didymos, to register his son in the list of apprentices (see P.Mich. 3.170 with *BL* 3:109). The contract of apprenticeship is not preserved in this case, but P.Wisc. 1.4 (August 29–September 27, 53 CE) deals with another son of Pausiris, Dioskous, who is now apprenticed by his father to the same master weaver as before, again to Apollonios, son of Apollonios. The respective clause is shorter than the other two but starts identically; lines 9–10 read: διακονοῦντα καὶ ποιοῦντα π[άντα τὰ] | ἐπιτασσόμενα αὐτῶι (Dioskous will "serve and do everything ordered to him"). Nine years later, Pausiris wishes to apprentice a third son, Pausiris, to the master weaver Epinikos, son of Theon, and he applies to the tax-farmer of the weaver's tax, Theon, that his son be registered in the list of apprentices (see P.Mich. 3.172 [Oxyrhynchus, October 20, 62 CE]). The contract of apprenticeship itself is, unfortunately, not preserved, but we see that the weaver Pausiris apprenticed his three sons, one after the other, to another master weaver in Oxyrhynchus. A similar document as P.Mich. 3.170 and 172 is P.Mich. 3.171 (Oxyrhynchus, September 26, 58 CE) which is also connected with Pausiris, but this time he is the master weaver to whom Helene, daughter of Horion, and her husband Epinikos, son of Theon, the weaver to whom Pausiris will apprentice his son Pausiris four years later (see P.Mich. 3.172 above), wish to apprentice her nephew Amoitas, son of Helene's deceased brother Pasion.

The intention of this procedure, followed by Tryphon's family, by Pausiris, and by Epinikos and his wife Helene, was most probably that a master weaver not only wanted his son(s) or, as in the case of Epinikos, his nephew to learn the weaver's craft solely in one's own workshop but

---

129. B. P. Grenfell and A. S. Hunt translate "in respect of the weaver's art in all its branches" (P.Oxy. 2, p. 264).

130. See Trismegistos Archives: www.trismegistos.org/archive/176.

to improve the weaver's art and perhaps even learn a technique different from his own.[131]

The clause that the apprentice will serve and do all the works ordered to him by the master weaver according to the weaver's craft can be fully restored in yet another contract from Oxyrhynchus, SB 24.16253,[132] written during the reign of the Roman emperor Trajan (98–103 CE). The two parties filing the contract were brothers, Hermas and Papontos, both the sons of Hermas, but we know only of Papontos that he was a weaver.[133] Yet, διακο[νοῦντα] in line 7 suggests that we have here a situation similar to those in the other three contracts of apprenticeship where we find this form: that in this case both brothers were weavers, presumably running separate workshops, so that the weaver Hermas apprenticed his son Hermes to his brother Papontos.

Why do we find the clause, that the apprentice will not only do everything ordered by the master weaver but also serve him, only in contracts filed between two weavers or the heads of two weaving workshops? Perhaps because the apprentice has already been serving his own father or uncle in the family workshop, and it is, therefore, clarified that from now on he is to serve another master weaver. Whatever the reason may have been, it is fascinating that Paul of Tarsus, who had been trained in the weaver's craft in his hometown, perhaps even ran his father's workshop for some time,[134] and who claimed that he still worked as a craftsman (see

---

131. See O. M. Pearl and V. B. Schuman in P.Mich. 3, p. 164, who, alternatively, think of "a tax law or trade regulation, unknown to us, which forbade that a son be apprenticed to his father" (this theory had been suggested earlier by John G. Winter, *Life and Letters in the Papyri: The Jerome Lectures* (Ann Arbor: University of Michigan Press, 1933), 71.

132. The respective clause is preserved, and partly restored, in lines 7–9: διακο[νοῦντα καὶ ποιοῦντα τὰ ἔργα] | πάντα τὰ ἐπιτασσ[όμενα αὐτῷ ὑπὸ τοῦ αὐτοῦ] | Παποντῶτος κατ[ὰ τὴν γερδιακὴν τέχνην πᾶσαν (?)].

133. Concerning his reconstruction of γέρδιος in line 1, the editor writes: "Γέρδιος habe ich zwar lediglich *exempli gratia* ergänzt, weil der weitaus überwiegende Teil der mir bekannten Lehrlingsverträge das Weberhandwerk betrifft, jedoch scheinen mir auch alle anderen in Frage kommenden Berufsbezeichnungen für den in der Zeile zur Verfügung stehenden Platz zu lang zu sein" (Thomas Kruse, "Eine Neuedition von SB XII 10946," *ZPE* 111 [1996]: 151).

134. Joachim Hengstl, "Zum Erfahrungsprofil des Apostels Paulus aus rechtshistorischer Sicht," in *Light from the East: Papyrologische Kommentare zum Neuen Testament; Akten des internationalen Symposions vom 3.–4. Dezember 2009 am Fachbereich Bibelwissenschaft und Kirchengeschichte der Universität Salzburg*, ed. Peter Arzt-Grabner and

1 Cor 4:12; 9:6; 1 Thess 2:9), mentioned the same obligation in Philemon, this time attributing it to the slave Onesimus and his mission of preaching the εὐαγγέλιον: in Phlm 13, Paul writes that he wanted to keep Onesimus with him, so that the slave might serve him in Philemon's place during his imprisonment for the gospel (ὃν ἐγὼ ἐβουλόμην πρὸς ἐμαυτὸν κατέχειν, ἵνα ὑπὲρ σοῦ μοι διακονῇ ἐν τοῖς δεσμοῖς τοῦ εὐαγγελίου). Thus, Paul's expression may hint at his familiarity with the relevant feature in apprentice contracts of weavers, and it may also attest that the clause was known also outside Egypt. It is not necessary that Philemon was familiar with this background of verse 13; its meaning was understandable by itself. But it would have made perfect sense if also Philemon was running a weaving workshop because, in that case, he would have understood exactly that Paul was talking about him, Philemon, potentially apprenticing his slave to Paul, the master, and that Paul would have taught Onesimus everything that he himself knew about the important task of his mission. There are, at least, two more hints in Paul's letter that Philemon could have been a weaver himself. First, in verse 17, Paul calls himself a κοινωνός of his addressee, which in the papyri most of all has the meaning of a business partner.[135] Although there is certainly a connection between Philemon's κοινωνία τῆς πίστεως in Phlm 6 and κοινωνός in verse 17, which attributes to κοινωνός an equivalent metaphorical meaning, the choice of that term was certainly intentional so that Philemon would immediately get its principal meaning and agree to it. Second, already in the introductory greeting of the letter, Paul addresses Philemon as his and Timothy's coworker (συνεργός).[136] Also Paul's idea of a συνεργός originates most probably from his craft, as two out of only three clear papyrological refer-

---

Christina M. Kreinecker, Philippika–Marburger altertumskundliche Abhandlungen 39 (Wiesbaden: Harrassowitz, 2010), 77–79, argues that Paul must have been an entrepreneur who filed apprentice contracts himself; see also Giovanni Bazzana, "New Testament Studies and Documentary Papyri: Interactions and New Perspectives," *PapyLup* 22 (2013): 23.

135. See Arzt-Grabner, *Philemon*, 226–29; Alan H. Cadwallader, "Name Punning and Social Stereotyping: Re-inscribing Slavery in the Letter to Philemon," *ABR* 61 (2013): 52; Julien M. Ogereau, *Paul's Koinonia with the Philippians: A Socio-historical Investigation of a Pauline Economic Partnership*, WUNT 2/377 (Tübingen: Mohr Siebeck, 2014), passim.

136. Besides Philemon, only Titus is called κοινωνός and συνεργός by Paul (see 2 Cor 8:23).

ences for συνεργός in a positive sense[137] deal with a coworker or partner of a weaver.

Bibliography

Arnaoutoglou, Ilias. "Marital Disputes in Greco-Roman Egypt." *JJP* 25 (1995): 11–28.

Arzt-Grabner, Peter. "Census Declarations, Birth Returns, and Marriage Contracts on Papyrus and Paul's Ideas on These Matters." Pages 335–72 in *Second Annual Meeting of Bertinoro (1–4 October 2015)*. Vol. 2 of *Texts, Practices and Groups: Multidisciplinary Approaches to Jesus and the History of His Followers in the First Two Centuries*. Edited by Adriana Destro and Mauro Pesce with Andrea Annese. Turnhout: Brepols, 2019.

———. "Christlicher Alltag anhand der Papyri aus dem 2. Jahrhundert." Pages 101–23 in *Das ägyptische Christentum im 2. Jahrhundert*. Edited by Wilhelm Pratscher, Markus Öhler, and Markus Lang. SNTSU 2/6. Vienna: LIT, 2008.

———. "Die Auswertung inschriftlicher Zeugnisse für die neutestamentliche Exegese: Erfahrungen, Chancen und Herausforderungen." Pages 27–44 in *Epigraphik und Neues Testament*. Edited by Thomas Corsten, Markus Öhler and Joseph Verheyden. WUNT 365. Tübingen: Mohr Siebeck, 2016.

———. "How to Deal with Onesimus? Paul's Solution within the Frame of Ancient Legal and Documentary Sources." Pages 113–42 in *Philemon in Perspective: Interpreting a Pauline Letter*. Edited by D Francois Tolmie. BZNW 169. Berlin: de Gruyter, 2010.

———. "'Neither a Truant nor a Fugitive': Some Remarks on the Sale of Slaves in Roman Egypt and Other Provinces." Pages 21–32 in *Pro-*

---

137. BGU 15.2471 (with *BL* 8:61; Ptolemais Euergetis/Arsinoites; ca. 158 CE) is an official letter by which the linen-weaver (line 2a λινούφο[ς]) Dioskoros is notifying the authorities that he has formerly claimed a certain Maron as his coworker but is now claiming Heraklides as coworker instead (see ll. 7–11). In some minutes of judicial proceedings, a certain Paulos is mentioned as coworker of a linen-weaver (P.Ryl. 4.654.4 [Oxyrhynchites; ca. 302–309 CE?]). The third example, P.Michael. 30,4–5 (Oxyrhynchus; fourth century CE?), refers to an *exactor* as coworker of a certain Silvanus. The earliest reference for συνεργός in the positive sense of "coworker" is P.Cair. Zen. 4.59758.8 (Philadelphia/Arsinoites; 254–250 BCE), but there is no information about the coworkers' occupation. See Arzt-Grabner, *Philemon*, 159–60.

ceedings of the Twenty-Fifth International Congress of Papyrology, Ann Arbor, July 29–August 4, 2007. Edited by Traianos Gagos and Adam Hyatt. American Studies in Papyrology Special Edition. Ann Arbor: The University of Michigan Library, Scholarly Publishing Office, 2010.

———. "Onesimus erro: Zur Vorgeschichte des Philemonbriefes." *ZNW* 95.1–2 (2004): 131–43.

———. *Philemon*. PKNT 1. Göttingen: Vandenhoeck & Ruprecht, 2003.

———. "Wisdom in Non-Christian Papyrus Letters from Roman Egypt." Pages 197–216 in *Tra pratiche e credenze: Traiettorie antropologiche e storiche; Un omaggio ad Adriana Destro*. Edited by Claudio Gianotto and Francesca Sbardella. Brescia: Morcelliana, 2017.

Arzt-Grabner, Peter, et al. *1. Korinther*. PKNT 2. Göttingen: Vandenhoeck & Ruprecht, 2006.

———. *2. Korinther*. PKNT 4. Göttingen: Vandenhoeck & Ruprecht, 2014.

Bagnall, Roger S. "The Beginning of the Roman Census in Egypt." *GRBS* 32 (1991): 255–65.

Bagnall, Roger S., and Bruce W. Frier. *The Demography of Roman Egypt*. Cambridge Studies in Population, Economy and Society in Past Time 23. Cambridge: Cambridge University Press, 1994.

Balabanski, Vicky. "Where Is Philemon? The Case for a Logical Fallacy in the Correlation of the Data in Philemon and Colossians 1.1–2; 4.7–18." *JSNT* 38 (2015): 131–50.

Bazzana, Giovanni. "New Testament Studies and Documentary Papyri: Interactions and New Perspectives." *PapyLup* 22 (2013): 5–34.

Bélis, Annie, and Daniel Delattre. "À propos d'un contrat d'apprentissage d'aule ète (Alexandrie; an 17 d'Auguste = 13ᵃ)." *PapyLup* 2 (1993): 103–62.

Bellia, Angela. "Una regione e la sua musica: Il caso della Caria." *Bollettino dell'Associazione Iasos di Caria* 19 (2013): 24–29.

Bergamasco, Marco. "Le διδασκαλικαί nella ricerca attuale." *Aeg* 75 (1995): 95–167.

———. "P.Kell. G. 19.A, Appendix." *ZPE* 119 (1997): 193–96.

———. "Una petizione per violazione di un contratto di tirocinio: P. Kell. G. 19.a." *Aeg* 77 (1997): 7–26.

Bieżuńska-Małowist, Iza. "Les esclaves imperiaux dans l'Egypte romaine." Pages 175–83 in *Schiavitù, manomissione e classi dipendenti nel mondo antico: Atti del Colloquio Imternazionale di Bressanone, 25–27 novembre 1976*. Edited by Maria Capozza. Università degli Studi di

Padova–Pubblicazioni dell'Istituto di Storia Antica 13. Rome: L'Erma di Bretschneider, 1979.

———. *Période romaine*. Vol. 2 of *L'esclavage dans l'Égypte gréco-romaine*. Archiwum Filologiczne 35. Wrocław: Zakład Narodowy imienia Ossolińskich; Warsaw: Wydawnictwo Polskiej Akademii Nauk, 1977.

Biscottini, Maria Valentina. "L'archivio di Tryphon, tessitore di Oxyrhynchos." *Aeg* 46 (1966): 60–90, 186–292.

Blumell, Lincoln H. *Lettered Christians: Christians, Letters, and Late Antique Oxyrhynchus*. NTTSD 39. Leiden: Brill, 2012.

———. "*PSI* 4.311: Early Evidence for 'Arianism' at Oxyrhynchus?" *BASP* 49 (2012): 277–96.

Brunt, Peter A. "The Revenues of Rome." Pages 324–46 in *Roman Imperial Themes*. Oxford: Clarendon, 1990.

Cadwallader, Alan H. "Name Punning and Social Stereotyping: Reinscribing Slavery in the Letter to Philemon." *ABR* 61 (2013): 44–60.

Camodeca, Giuseppe. *L'archivio Puteolano dei Sulpicii*. Vol. 1. Pubblicazioni del Dipartimento di Diritto Romano e Storia della Scienza Romanistica dell'Università degli Studi die Napoli "Federico II" 4. Naples: Jovene, 1992.

———. "Tabulae Herculanenses: Riedizione delle emptiones di schiavi (TH 59–62)." Pages 53–76 in *Quaestiones Iuris: Festschrift für Joseph Georg Wolf zum 70. Geburtstag*. Edited by Ulrich Manthe and Christoph Krampe. Freiburger rechtsgeschichtliche Abhandlungen 2/36. Berlin: Duncker & Humblot, 2000.

Canavan, Rosemary. "Weaving Threads: Clothing in Colossae." Pages 111–33 in *Fragments of Colossae: Sifting through the Traces*. Edited by Alan H. Cadwallader. Hindmarsh: ATF Press, 2015.

Claytor, W. Graham, and Roger S. Bagnall. "The Beginnings of the Roman Provincial Census: A New Declaration from 3 BCE." *GRBS* 55 (2015): 637–53.

Cotton, Hannah M. "Ἡ νέα Ἀραβία: The New Province of Arabia in the Papyri from the Judaean Desert." *ZPE* 116 (1997): 204–8.

Cotton, Hannah M., Walter E. H. Cockle, and Fergus G. B. Millar. "The Papyrology of the Roman Near East: A Survey." *JRS* 95 (1995): 214–35.

Deissmann, Adolf. *Light from the Ancient East: The New Testament Illustrated by Recently Discovered Texts of the Graeco-Roman World*. Translated by Lionel R. M. Strachan. Repr., Peabody, MA: Hendrickson, 1995.

Drexhage, Hans-Joachim. "Die Kontakte zwischen Side, Alexandria und Ägypten in der römischen Kaiserzeit (1.–3. Jh. n. Chr.)." Pages 75–90 in *Studien zum antiken Kleinasien: Friedrich Karl Dörner zum 80. Geburtstag gewidmet*. Edited by Anke Schütte, Daniela Pohl, and Jutta Teichmann. Asia Minor Studien 3. Bonn: Habelt, 1991.

Drexhage, Hans-Joachim, and Kai Ruffing. "P. Bingen 77 und der Handel zwischen Asia Minor und Ägypten." Pages 153–65 in *Vom Euphrat bis zum Bosporus: Kleinasien in der Antike; Festschrift für Elmar Schwertheim zum 65. Geburtstag*. Edited by Engelbert Winter. Asia Minor Studien 65. Bonn: Habelt, 2008.

Eger, Otto. "Eine Wachstafel aus Ravenna aus dem zweiten Jahrhundert nach Chr." *ZSS Romanistische Abteilung* 42 (1921): 452–68.

Erdemir, Hatice. "Woollen Textiles: An International Trade Good in the Lycus Valley in Antiquity." Pages 104–29 in *Colossae in Space and Time: Linking to an Ancient City*. Edited by Alan H. Cadwallader and Michael Trainor. NTOA–SUNT 94. Göttingen: Vandenhoeck & Ruprecht, 2011.

Fragiadakis, Charilaos. "Die attischen Sklavennamen von der spätarchaischen Epoche bis in die römische Kaiserzeit: Eine historische und soziologische Untersuchung." Diss., Universität Mannheim, 1986.

Franke, Peter R., Wolfgang Leschhorn, Brigitte Müller, and Johannes Nollé. *Side: Münzprägung, Inschriften und Geschichte einer antiken Stadt in der Türkei; Beiträge zu einer Ausstellung in Saarbrücken, Homburg, München, Kiel, Wien, Augsburg und Aalen*. 2nd ed. Saarbrücken: Landesbank Saar Girozentrale; Institut für Alte Geschichte der Universität des Saarlandes, 1989.

French, David H. "Sites and Inscriptions from Phrygia, Pisidia and Pamphylia." *Epigraphica Anatolica* 17 (1991): 51–68.

Gielen, Marlis. "Paulus—Gefangener in Ephesus?" *BN* 2/131 (2006): 79–103; 133 (2007): 63–77.

Hanson, Ann E. "A Petition and Court Proceedings: P. Michigan inv. 6060." *ZPE* 111 (1996): 175–82.

Harrill, J. Albert. *Slaves in the New Testament: Literary, Social, and Moral Dimensions*. Minneapolis: Augsburg Fortress, 2006.

Hengstl, Joachim. *Private Arbeitsverhältnisse freier Personen in den hellenistischen Papyri bis Diokletian*. Bonn: Habelt, 1972.

———. "Zum Erfahrungsprofil des Apostels Paulus aus rechtshistorischer Sicht." Pages 71–89 in *Light from the East: Papyrologische Kommentare zum Neuen Testament; Akten des internationalen Symposions vom*

3.–4. Dezember 2009 am Fachbereich Bibelwissenschaft und Kirchengeschichte der Universität Salzburg. Edited by Peter Arzt-Grabner and Christina M. Kreinecker. Philippika–Marburger altertumskundliche Abhandlungen 39. Wiesbaden: Harrassowitz, 2010.

Herrmann, Johannes. "Vertragsinhalt und Rechtsnatur der διδασκαλικαί." *JJP* 11–12 (1957–1958): 119–39.

Herz, Peter. "Beiträge zur Organisation der Getreideversorgung Roms." Pages 609–18 in *Ad fontes! Festschrift für Gerhard Dobesch zum fünfundsechzigsten Geburtstag am 15. September 2004 dargebracht von Kollegen, Schülern und Freunden*. Edited by Herbert Heftner and Kurt Tomaschitz. Wien: Eigenverlag der Herausgeber, 2004.

Hombert, Marcel, and Claire Préaux. *Recherches sur le recensement dans l'Égypte romaine*. Papyrologica Lugduno-Batava 5. Leiden: Brill, 1952.

Huttner, Ulrich. *Early Christianity in the Lycus Valley*. Translated by David Green. AJEC 85; Early Christianity in Asia Minor 1. Leiden: Brill, 2013.

Instone-Brewer, David. *Marriage and Divorce Papyri of the Ancient Greek, Roman and Jewish World: A Collection of Papyri from Fourth C BCE to Fourth C CE*. 2000. http://www.tyndalearchive.com/Brewer/MarriagePapyri/Index.html.

Jakab, Éva. *Praedicere und cavere beim Marktkauf: Sachmängel im griechischen und römischen Recht*. MBPF 87. Munich: Beck, 1997.

Koch, Dietrich-Alex. *Geschichte des Urchristentums: Ein Lehrbuch*. Göttingen: Vandenhoeck & Ruprecht, 2013.

Kruse, Thomas. *Der Königliche Schreiber und die Gauverwaltung: Untersuchungen zur Verwaltungsgeschichte Ägyptens in der Zeit von Augustus bis Philippus Arabs (30 v.Chr.–245 n.Chr.)*. 2 vols. APF Series 11.1–2. Munich: Saur, 2002.

———. "Eine Neuedition von SB XII 10946." *ZPE* 111 (1996): 149–58.

Kupisch, Berthold. "Römische Sachmängelhaftung: Ein Beispiel für die 'ökonomische Analyse des Rechts'?" *Legal History Review* 70 (2002): 21–54.

Lampe, Peter. "Keine 'Sklavenflucht' des Onesimus." *ZNW* 76 (1985): 135–37.

Leiwo, Martti, and Hilla Halla-Aho. "A Marriage Contract: Aspects of Latin-Greek Language Contact (*P. Mich.* VII 434 and *P. Ryl.* IV 612 = ChLA IV 249)." *Mnemosyne* 55 (2002): 560–80.

Luijendijk, AnneMarie. *Greetings in the Lord: Early Christians and the Oxyrhynchus Papyri*. HTS 60. Cambridge: Harvard University Press, 2008.

Malouta, Myrto. "Fatherless Persons." Pages 191–202 in *Law and Legal Practice in Egypt from Alexander to the Arab Conquest: A Selection of Papyrological Sources in Translation, with Introductions and Commentary*. Edited by James G. Keenan, Joseph G. Manning, and Uri Yiftach-Firanko. Cambridge: Cambridge University Press, 2014.

Minnen, Peter van. "Urban Craftsmen in Roman Egypt." *Münsterische Beiträge zur antiken Handelsgeschichte* 6 (1987): 31–88.

Montevecchi, Orsolina. *I contratti di lavoro e di servizio nell'Egitto greco romano e bizantino*. Milan: Vita e pensiero, 1950.

———. "Il censimento romano d'Egitto: Precisazioni." *Aev* 50 (1976): 72–84.

———. "Ricerche di sociologia nei documenti dell' Egitto greco-romano, II. I contratti di matrimonio e gli atti di divorzio." *Aeg* 16 (1936): 3–83.

Nollé, Johannes. *Geographie–Geschichte–Testimonia–Griechische und lateinische Inschriften (1–4)*. Vol. 1 of *Side im Altertum: Geschichte und Zeugnisse*. IGSK 43. Bonn: Habelt, 1993.

———. *Griechische und lateinische Inschriften (5–16)–Papyri–Inschriften in sidetischer Schrift und Sprache–Ergänzungen und Berichtigungen–Konkordanzen–Epigraphische Indices*. Vol. 2 of *Side im Altertum: Geschichte und Zeugnisse*. IGSK 44. Bonn: Habelt, 2001.

Nordling, John G. "Onesimus Fugitivus: A Defense of the Runaway Slave Hypothesis in Philemon." *JSNT* 41 (1991): 97–119.

Ogereau, Julien M. *Paul's* Koinonia *with the Philippians: A Socio-historical Investigation of a Pauline Economic Partnership*. WUNT 2/377. Tübingen: Mohr Siebeck, 2014.

Olsson, Bror. *Papyrusbriefe aus der frühesten Römerzeit*. Uppsala: Almquist & Wiksells, 1925.

Önal, Mehmet. "Deities and Cultures Meet on the Seal Impressions in Zeugma." *Bolletino di archeologia online* 1 (2010): 25–53.

Palme, Bernhard. "Die ägyptische κατ' οἰκίαν ἀπογραφή und Lk 2,1–5." *PzB* 2 (1993): 1–24.

———. "Neues zum ägyptischen Provinzialzensus: Ein Nachtrag zum Artikel PzB 2 (1993) 1–24." *PzB* 3 (1994): 1–7.

Papathomas, Amphilochios. "Drei unveröffentlichte Papyri aus der Sammlung der Griechischen Papyrologischen Gesellschaft." *APF* 42 (1996): 179–207.

———. "Textkritische Bemerkungen zu Berliner Papyrusbriefen." *APF* 53 (2007): 182–200.

Rathbone, Dominic W. "Egypt, Augustus and Roman Taxation." *Cahiers du Centre Gustave Glotz* 4 (1993): 81–112.
Reiter, Fabian. "Unerkannte Bronzedrachmen." Pages 419–23 in *Honi soit qui mal y pense: Studien zum pharaonischen, griechisch-römischen und spätantiken Ägypten zu Ehren von Heinz-Josef Thissen*. Edited by Hermann Knuf, Christian Leitz, and Daniel von Recklinghausen. OLA 194. Leuven: Peeters, 2010.
Ruffing, Kai, and Hans-Joachim Drexhage. "Antike Sklavenpreise." Pages 321–51 in *Antike Lebenswelten: Konstanz–Wandel–Wirkungsmacht; Festschrift für Ingomar Weiler zum 70. Geburtstag*. Edited by Peter Mauritsch et al. Philippika. Marburger altertumskundliche Abhandlungen 25. Wiesbaden: Harrassowitz, 2008.
Rupprecht, Hans-Albert. "Die Eviktionshaftung in der Kautelarpraxis der graeco-ägyptischen Papyri." Pages 463–79 in *Studi in onore di Arnaldo Biscardi*. Edited by Franco Pastori and Mariagrazia Bianchini. Vol. 3. Milan: La Goliardica, 1982.
Sánchez-Moreno Ellart, Carlos. "Ὑπομνήματα ἐπιγεννήσεως: The Greco-Egyptian Birth Returns in Roman Egypt and the Case of P.Petaus 1–2." *APF* 56 (2010): 91–129.
Scheidel, Walter. *Measuring Sex, Age and Death in the Roman Empire: Explorations in Ancient Demography*. JRASup 21. Ann Arbor, MI: Journal of Roman Archaeology, 1996.
Scholl, Reinhold, and Margit Homann. "Antike Briefkultur unter Familienmitgliedern." Pages 47–126 in *Papyrologie und Exegese: Die Auslegung des Neuen Testaments im Licht der Papyri*. Edited by Jens Herzer. WUNT 2/341. Tübingen: Mohr Siebeck, 2012.
Solin, Heikki. *Griechische Namen*. Vol. 2 of *Die stadtrömischen Sklavennamen: Ein Namenbuch*. Forschungen zur antiken Sklaverei 2. Stuttgart: Franz Steiner, 1996.
Straus, Jean A. *L'achat et la vente des esclaves dans l'Egypte romaine: Contribution papyrologique à l'étude de l'esclavage dans une province orientale de l'Empire romain*. APF Series 14. Munich: Saur, 2004.
———. "L'esclavage dans l'Egypte romaine." *ANRW* 10.1:841–911.
———. "Le pays d'origine des esclaves de l'Égypte romaine." *CdE* 46 (1971): 363–66.
———. "Quelques activités exercées par les esclaves d'après les papyrus de l'Égypte romaine." *Historia* 26 (1977): 74–88.

Taubenschlag, Rafael. *The Law of Greco-Roman Egypt in the Light of the Papyri 332B.C.–640A.D.* 2nd ed. Repr. Milan: Cisalpino-Goliardica, 1972.

Velázquez Soriano, Isabel. *Las Pizarras Visigodas (Entre el latín y su disgregación: La lengua hablada en Hispania, siglos VI–VIII).* Colección Beltenebros 8. Madrid: Real Academia Española; Brugos: Instituto Castellano y Leonés de la Lengua, 2004.

Wallace, Sherman L. *Taxation in Egypt from Augustus to Diocletian.* Repr. New York: Greenwood Press, 1969.

Westermann, William L. "Apprentice Contracts and the Apprentice System in Roman Egypt." *CP* 9 (1914): 295–315.

Wilcken, Ulrich. *Historischer Teil: Grundzüge.* Vol. 1.1 of *Grundzüge und Chrestomathie der Papyruskunde.* By Ludwig Mitteis and Ulrich Wilcken. Repr. Hildesheim: Olms, 1963.

Wild, John Peter. "The *Tarsikarios*, a Roman Linen-Weaver in Egypt." Pages 810–19 in *Hommages à Marcel Renard.* Edited by Jacqueline Bibauw. Vol. 2. Collection Latomus 102. Bruxelles: Latomus, 1969.

Winter, John G. *Life and Letters in the Papyri: The Jerome Lectures.* Ann Arbor: University of Michigan Press, 1933.

Wolff, Hans Julius. *Organisation und Kontrolle des privaten Rechtsverkehrs.* Vol. 2 of *Das Recht der griechischen Papyri Ägyptens in der Zeit der Ptolemäer und des Prinzipats.* Handbuch der Altertumswissenschaft 10.5.2. Munich: Beck, 1978.

———. *Written and Unwritten Marriages in Hellenistic and Postclassical Roman Law.* Philological Monographs 9. Lancaster: Lancaster Press, 1939.

Wolter, Michael. *Der Brief an die Kolosser: Der Brief an Philemon.* ÖTK 12; Gütersloher Taschenbücher Siebenstern 519. Gütersloh: Mohn; Würzburg: Echter, 1993.

Yiftach, Uri. "Was There a 'Divorce Procedure' among Greeks in Early Roman Egypt?" Pages 1331–39 in *Atti del XXII Congresso Internazionale di Papirologia, Firenze, 23–29 agosto 1998.* Edited by Isabella Andorlini et al. Vol. 2. Florence: Istituto Papirologico "G. Vitelli," 2001.

Yiftach-Firanko, Uri. *Marriage and Marital Arrangements: A History of the Greek Marriage Document in Egypt; Fourth Century BCE–Fourth Century CE.* MBPF 93. Munich: Beck, 2003.

Zambon, Angela. "Διδασκαλικαί." *Aeg* 15 (1935): 3–66.

A City with a Message: Colossae and Colossians

Angela Standhartinger

Although Acts has Paul wandering through Phrygia twice and even "strengthening all the disciples" there, we have no evidence that he ever visited Colossae.[1] Nor does the Letter to the Colossians make this claim. Rather, Colossians insinuates that it was Paul's coworker, or more literally "coservant" (σύνδουλος), Epaphras, who brought the gospel to Colossae (Col 1:7; cf. 4:12). Later, Epaphras met Paul at an unnamed place of imprisonment, from which Paul and Timothy wrote to the congregation in the Lycus valley.

Yet, Colossians was most likely not written by Paul. By means of his detailed comparison of the language and style of Colossians to the seven letters generally accepted as having been authored by Paul, Walter Bujard convinced most scholars, including myself, that Colossians was written not by Paul himself but rather by one or more of Paul's friends and companions, most likely after Paul's death, which occurred sometime after 65 CE.[2] This observation raises the question of why the author—or as I prefer to assume, the group of authors—chose to address their letter to a city about 170 km east of Ephesus, where there was no documented history of any Pauline congregation. What did they know about this city in the Lycos valley on the western border of Phrygia? Was Colossians prompted by pressing questions emerging at a concrete historic location and Pauline *ekklesia*, or is its address part of the message the letter intends to convey? In the following I will argue for the latter option. But first I shall summa-

---

1. See Acts 16:6; 18:23. It is not explained where the μαθηταί of Acts 18:23 came from.

2. Walter Bujard, *Stilanalytische Untersuchungen zum Kolosserbrief als Beitrag zur Methodik von Sprachvergleichen*, STUNT 11 (Göttingen: Vandenhoeck & Ruprecht, 1973).

rize what modern historians know about ancient Colossae in the first two centuries of our era.

Ancient Colossae

The ruins of Colossae have never been excavated. Information about the city and its history can only be gleaned from the writings of ancient historians and geographers, coins, eighteenth–twentieth-century travel accounts, and the few archaeological surface finds collected in the vicinity of the remaining *höyük* (mound). Alan H. Cadwallader and his team from Flinders University in Australia are to be thanked for the most recent finds and observations.[3] Current excavations of the neighboring cities of Hierapolis and Laodicea as well as of some smaller villages in Phrygia have changed our picture of the region and of its development in the early Roman Empire.[4] Any statements we might make about ancient Colossae must remain provisional until the city is excavated, hopefully in the not so distant future.

Pottery finds testify to a more or less continuous settlement from the Late Chalcolithic (4000–3000 BCE) to the Byzantine period.[5] In literature, Colossae is first mentioned in Persian times, when it was referred to as the most important city in the Lycos valley. Herodotus reports that Xerxes rested in this "large city" (πόλις μεγάλη) in 480 BCE on his way to the Phrygian interior (*Hist.* 7.30). Xenophon recounts that eighty years later the Persian king Cyros stopped at Colossae, a "large, prosperous and cosmopolitan city" (πόλις οἰκουμένη καὶ εὐδαίμονα καὶ μεγάλη) on his march with the famed "ten thousand" Greek mercenaries. Later he arrived at the even more important city of Kelainai/Apamea in central Phrygia, where

---

3. See Alan H. Cadwallader, and Michael Trainor, eds., *Colossae in Space and Time: Linking to an Ancient City*, NTOA-STUNT 94 (Göttingen: Vandenhoeck & Ruprecht, 2011) and most recently Cadwallader, *Fragments of Colossae. Sifting through the Traces* (Adelaide: ATF, 2015).

4. See for instance Axel Filges, *Blaundos: Berichte zur Erforschung einer Kleinstadt im lydisch-phrygischen Grenzgebiet*, IstForsch 48 (Tübingen: Wasmuth, 2006). Peter J. Thonemann, "Phrygia: An Anarchist History, 950 BC–AD 100," in *Roman Phrygia: Culture and Society*, ed. Peter Thonemann (Cambridge: Cambridge University Press, 2013), 1–40.

5. Bahadir Duman and Erim Konakçi, "The Silent Witness of the Mound of Colossae: Pottery Remains," in Cadwallader and Trainor, *Colossae in Space and Time*, 247–81.

Kyros himself owned a παράδεισος μέγας, a palace with hunting grounds (Xenophon, *Anab.* 1.2.7). In 396 we hear of a Persian satrap having been appointed to Colossae, a further indication of its status and importance.[6]

However, when the Macedonians appeared on the scene, Colossae declined in influence. From the Hellenistic and early Roman times, our evidence is limited to four similar coins dated to the second or first century BCE, featuring on one side the head of Zeus with a laurel wreath and on the reverse, a winged thunderbolt.[7] Hence, while there must have been a town there in Hellenistic and early Roman times, it was certainly a small one. The dimensions of the biconical *höyük*, which is approximately 30 m high and 280 m by 330 m broad/long, testify to this. Still visible is the *cavea* (seating sections) of a theater with twelve–fifteen rows, which could seat about nine hundred people.[8] At the turn of the era, Strabo refers to Colossae as merely a πόλισμα (*Geogr.* 12.8.13). By the first century CE, the honor of being called an *urbs celeberrima* (famous city) was transferred to Laodicea,[9] located about 15 km downriver (Pliny the Elder, *Nat.* 5.29).

Laodicea was founded by Antiochos II Theos around 250 BCE on a private estate belonging to one of his generals and named after his wife.[10] The *höyük* of Laodicea is about 5km in size. On the basis of its successful wool and textile industry, which boasted a distribution network that extended throughout the empire, Laodicea prospered greatly between the first and third centuries CE. Under Tiberius, the city first applied for the privilege to house a temple to Roma and Caesar but was judged at that time to be too small (Tacitus, *Ann.* 4.55). It received the *neocorate* recognition only at the end of the second century under Commodus and two decades later again, under Caracalla. Reliefs indicate that in the

---

6. The satrap Arisaios summoned by a letter to murder Ataxerxes military commander Tissaphernes. See Diodorus Siculus, *Bib. hist.* 14.80.7–8; Polyaenus, *Strateg.* 7.16.

7. Hans von Aulock, *Münzen und Städte Phrygiens*, 2 vols., IstMitt 25, 27 (Tübingen: Wasmuth, 1987), 2:83 and table 14, no. 443–46.

8. Georg Bean, *Jenseits des Mäander: Karien mit dem Vilayet Mugla* (Stuttgart: Kohlhammer, 1985), 268–70.

9. In *Nat.* 5.41, Pliny calls Colossae an *oppida celeberrima* (famous town) but uses an older list. This list still names Apamea Celaenae.

10. Thomas Corsten, "Laodikeia by the Lykos," *Encyclopedia of Ancient History* 7:3905–6.

intervening period, the Laodiceans worshipped Zeus Laodiceus, Hera, and Athena in imitation of the Capitoline Triad.[11]

Some 19 km to the north of Colossae, on the road between Sardis and Apamea, the Seleucids also founded the city of Hierapolis. Hierapolis was famous not only for its thermal springs and hard water but also for its temple to Apollo Kareios with a cave, the *Plutonion*, which emitted lethal gases and in which one could consult with an oracle.[12] Inscriptions indicate that this city was home to associations of wool-washers, carpet-weavers, and dyers.[13] Foremost among them were the purple-dyers, who, aided by the area's calcium-rich water, earned their fortune by imitating the purple of sea-snails with plants called *Anchusa tinctoria* and *Rubia Tinctorum* (Strabo, *Georg.* 12.8.16).[14] One of them was a wealthy benefactor who funded the celebration of the Festival of the Unleavened Bread.[15] There was at least one synagogue at Hierapolis and

---

11. Zeus = Jupiter, Hera = Juno; Athena represents Minerva. Those coins appear from Domitian onwards. See Andrea J. Armstrong, "Roman Phrygia: Cities and Their Coinage" (PhD Diss., London, 1998), 167–78.

12. For the history of the city and recent excavation, see Francesco D'Andria, "Hierapolis of Phrygia: Its Evolution in Hellenistic and Roman Times," in *Urbanism in Western Asia Minor: New Studies on Aphrodisias, Ephesos, Hierapolis, Pergamon, Perge and Xanthos*, ed. David Parrish, JRASup 45 (Portsmouth, RI: Journal of Roman Archaeology, 2001), 96–115.

13. See Imogen Dittmann-Schöne, *Berufsvereine in den Städten des kaiserzeitlichen Kleinasiens* (Regensburg: S. Roderer Verlag, 2001), 219–31.

14. See Ulrich Huttner, "Die Färber von Laodikeia und Hierapolis: Eine Nachricht aus dem Corpus der Alchemisten," in *MBAH* 26 (2008): 139–57. For associations of textile workers in Hierapolis, see Heinrich-Wilhelm Drexhage, *Wirtschaftspolitik und Wirtschaft in der römischen Provinz Asia in der Zeit von Augustus bis zum Regierungsantritt Diokletians*, Asia Minor Studies 59 (Bonn: Habelt, 2007), 172–73, 338–39. Isabella Benda-Weber, "Textile Production Centers, Products and Merchants in the Roman Province of Asia," in *Making Textiles in Pre-Roman and Roman Times: People, Places, Identities*, ed. Margarita Gleba and Judit Pásztókai-Szeoke, Ancient Textiles Series 13 (Oxford: Oxbow, 2013), 171–91.

15. Walter Ameling, *Kleinasien*, vol. 2 of *Inscriptiones Iudaicae Orientis* (Tübingen: Mohr Siebeck, 2004), 308–448, nos. 187–209, 414–422, no. 196.n; see also Philip A. Harland, *North Coast of the Black Sea, Asia Minor*, vol. 1 of *Greco-Roman Associations: Texts, Translations, and Commentary*, BZNW 204 (Berlin: de Gruyter, 2014), no. 116. The deceased Publious Aelius Glykon Zeuxianos Aelianus mandates not only that the purple-dyers should commemorate his death at the festival of Unleavened Bread but also that the carpet-weavers should commemorate it at the (Roman) festival of the Kalends. Therefore, his religious identity is much debated. See Philip A. Harland,

more than twenty gravestones on which the deceased is referred to as a Ἰουδαῖος.¹⁶ The archaeological record points strongly to the integration of Jews within the city of Hierapolis.¹⁷ In addition, there is evidence of a Jewish presence at Laodicea as well as in twenty-three other towns in Phrygia, confirming the extensive Jewish presence in the region referred to by Cicero and Josephus.¹⁸

Laodicea and Hierapolis enjoyed such prosperity that they were able to bounce back from the five documented earthquakes that shook the region between 20 BCE and the early third century CE.¹⁹ Tacitus reports that in 60 CE, "the famous Asiatic city" of Laodicea was laid to ruin but recovered through its own resources (*Ann.* 14.27).²⁰ The fourth-century Christian authors, Eusebius and Orosius, report that Colossae was also destroyed by the earthquake of 60 CE (Eusebius, *Chron.* 2.154. Orosius, *Adv. pag.* 7.12). For Bo Reike, this indicates that the Letter to the Colossians must have been written before 60 CE and therefore by Paul himself.²¹ Andreas Lindemann has advanced the opposite argument, that the devastation of Colossae allowed the author(s) to get away with the pseudepigraphon because the authenticity of a letter to a city that no longer existed could not be verified.²²

"Interaction and Integration. Judean Families and Guilds at Hierapolis," in *Dynamics of Identity in the World of the Early Christians: Associations, Judeans, and Cultural Minorities* (New York: T&T Clark, 2009), 123–42.

16. See Ameling, *Kleinasien*, 308–448, nos. 187–209. For the synagogue, see 406, no 191.

17. Tullia Ritti, *An Epigraphic Guide to Hierapolis (Pamukkale)* (Istanbul: Ege Yayinlari, 2006), 196.

18. Ameling, *Kleinasien*, 443–447 nos. 212–213. See Cicero, *Flac.* 28.68–9. In *A.J.* 12.148–153, Josephus cites a (fictive) letter from Antiochos III (223–287) in which he orders two thousand Jewish families from Babylon to settle in Phrygia. In *A.J.* 14.241–243 he quotes a letter from the "*Archontes*" of Laodicea to the consul of the province Asia of 45 BCE guaranteeing the right to life according to the laws of their fathers for the Jews of the city.

19. T. R. S. Broughton, "Roman Asia Minor," in *An Economic Survey of Ancient Rome IV*, ed. Frank Tenney (Paterson, NJ: Pageant, 1959), 601–2.

20. The date is disputed in ancient sources. For the evidence see Ulrich Huttner, *Early Christianity in the Lycus Valley*, trans. David Green, AJEC 85; Early Christianity in Asia Minor 1 (Leiden: Brill, 2013), 100–3.

21. Bo Reike, "The Historical Setting of Colossians," *RevExp* 70 (1973): 429–38.

22. Andreas Lindemann, "Die Gemeinde von 'Kolossä': Erwägungen zum 'Sitz im Leben' eines pseudopaulinischen Briefes," *WD* 16 (1981): 111–34. See recently,

But Colossae did not cease to exist.²³ Between Hadrian's reign and the middle of the third century CE, Colossae resumed minting pseudo-autonomous copper coins.²⁴ The likely inducement was a visit to the Lycos valley by Hadrian, which is documented at least for Hierapolis as having taken place in the year 129 CE.²⁵ Strikingly, the coins no longer feature the images of Zeus and the thunderbolt. Instead many of the 157 coins of 55 different types minted from the time of Hadrian till the time of Gallienus bear images previously used by the Laodiceans and therefore belong to the Laodicean stylistic group.²⁶ These include Zeus Laodiceans, the reclining river god Lykos, and Artemis of Ephesus.²⁷ Two images peculiar to the Colossian coins are those of the god Helios, with or without his *quadriga* (four-horse chariot), and Artemis as a huntress. Helios is represented on Phrygian gravestones as the highest godhead, while depictions of Artemis hunting might refer either to the good hunting conditions in the region or to her significance as a fighter of illness.²⁸ Thus it remains to be seen how these coins represent the cults and temples of the city. Unfortunately, neither architecture nor temples are featured on Colossian coins.

Colossian coins were sometimes authorized by the δῆμος ("citizens"), but more often by one of its officers, such as the ἄρχων (leader), the

---

Vincent A. Pizzuto, *A Cosmic Leap of Faith: An Authorial, Structural, and Theological Investigation of the Cosmic Christology in Col 1:15–20* (Leuven: Peeters, 2006), 817.

23. See also Alan H. Cadwallader, "Refuting an Axiom of Scholarship on Colossae: Fresh Insights from New and Old Inscriptions," in Cadwallader and Trainor, *Colossae in Space and Time*, 151–79.

24. The coin *BMC* 2891, earlier dated to the time of Caligula, must be deleted.

25. Francesco D'Andria, *Hierapolis in Phrygien (Pamukkale): Ein Archäologischer Führer* (Istanbul: Ege Yayinlari, 2010), 10.

26. See Andrew Burnett, Michael Amandry and Pere Pau Ripollès, *Roman Provincial Coinage*, vol. 1 (London: British Museum Press, 1998), 375–76.

27. Amstrong, "Roman Phrygia," 350 (von Aulock, *Münzen und Städte Phrygiens*, 2.551–552), 351 no. 12 (Marcus Aurelius, von Aulock, *Münzen und Städte Phrygiens*, 2.565); 355 no. 8 (von Aulock, *Münzen und Städte Phrygiens*, 2.458); 256 no. 17 (von Aulock, *Münzen und Städte Phrygiens*, 2.495–498, 507–512).

28. See Reinhold Merkelbach and Josef Stauber, "Die Orakel des Apollon von Klaros," *EA* 27 (1996): 1–53. The oracle of Apollon of Claros no. 2 to Pergamon orders songs also to Artemis against pestilence; the oracle to Kallipolis no. 9 orders statues of Apollon with an arrow at each town gate to fight a pestilence and an oracle to Phrygian place orders an altar to Apollon-Helios (no. 20).

γραμματεύς (town clerk), or στεφανηφόρος (magistrate).[29] Some coins also bear the name of the elite benefactor who financed its minting. One of those benefactors was a lady called Eugenetoriane.[30] The approximately thirty inscriptions from Colossae that have thus far been recorded and published have broadened our knowledge of the city's authorities. In one of the oldest inscriptions, the council and the people of Colossae honor M(arcus) Larcius Crispinus, the son of M(arcus) Larcius Papias, who was the caretaker of the "honor" (most likely a statue) of Asinius Epaphrodius. The two Larcii, whose Roman citizenship is shown by their *tria nomina* (combination of praenomen, nomen, and cognomen), were of Italian origin. Asinius Epaphrodius were probably relatives of Caius Asinus Pollio, who was proconsul of Asia at the beginning of the first century CE.[31] Another Roman is referred to in an inscription as a benefactor of the city.[32] Thus the city seems to honor Roman officials. In a further inscription, we hear about the priestess Apphia who dedicated something, perhaps a statue, to Trajan; we also learn of a χε[ι]λίαρχο[ς] (commander) perhaps named Lukios the Macedonian and another priestess named Apphia, each of whom dedicated a statue to the emperor Hadrian.[33] Another townsperson, perhaps a former soldier, is represented on his gravestone with his weaponry.[34] This might suggest the presence of some Roman veterans

---

29. For the coins see Armstrong, "Roman Phrygia," 349–58; von Aulock, *Münzen und Städte Phrygiens*, 2.83–94 and plates 15–19. Two coins from the Time of Gallienus show the figure of the "senate" (von Aulock, *Münzen und Städte Phrygiens*, 2.543 and 542, see also Armstrong, "Roman Phrygia," 357 no. 28). For the number of coins see Cadwallader, "Refuting an Axiom of Scholarship on Colossae," 162–63.

30. Von Aulock, *Münzen und Städte Phrygiens*, 2.548.

31. *MAMA* 6.39 = Tullia Ritti et al., *Museo Archeologico di Denizli-Hierapolis: Catalogo delle iscrizione greche e latine* (Napoli: Liguori Editore, 2008), no. 59.

32. Klaudius Menander Flavianus; Michel Armand Clerc, "Inscriptions de la vallée du Méandre: Tralles, Nysa, Attuda, Laodicée et Colosses," *BCH* 11 (1887): 353.5, no. 10.

33. *IGRR* 4.868–869. But the name of the χειλίαρχος is not well preserved, being reduced to Λ. Μα[. For the bearer of this, Lucius, see Lukas Bormann, *Der Brief des Paulus an die Kolosser*, THKNT 10.1 (Leipzig: Evangelische Verlagsanstalt, 2012), 25. To whom Apphia was a priestess is debated. Some argue to Zeus's son Herakles, but this would be unusual. Louis Robert, "Inscriptions," in *Laodicée du Lycos: Le Nymphée; Campagnes 1961–1963*, ed. Jean des Gagniers, Pierre Devambez, Lilly Kahil, and René Ginouvès (Québec: Presses de l'Université Laval, 1969), 279, argues that the name of the husband is Herakles Diosoride but loses the identification of god by this reconstruction.

34. *IGRR* 4.869 = J. G. C. Anderson, "A Summer in Phrygia II," *JHS* 18 (1898): 90,

among the citizenry. An unnamed member of the city's elite, who had accumulated a long list municipal offices, traveled as an ambassador to the Emperor and made a sacrifice (συνθύσας) with him at the second temple of Caesar, most likely at Ephesus.[35] In addition, a patriot called Korumbos financed the repair of a bath that had been damaged, probably during of the era's major earthquakes. For this, he was honored by a *bomos* (altar) financed by twenty-nine of his fellow Colossians.[36] Yet another townsman went to study philology at Smyrna.[37] Two further inscriptions refer to a sporting event called Nea Olympia and a local boxer, respectively.[38]

Yet most Colossians appear to have been farmers. The relief on the aforementioned *bomos* for Korumbos includes the image of a hunting dog. On gravestones, people from Colossae are represent variously with a herd of pigs, a goose, a sheepdog, and agricultural products.[39] One gravestone mentions a leatherworker.[40] Perhaps the *hetairoi* (calvary) of Glykonas were wool-workers, judging by the striking coats of the two figures represented on the stone.[41] As Strabo tells us at the beginning of the first century CE, Colossae was famous for its wool; indeed, a particular color of wool was named after the city (*Geogr.* 12.8.16; see also Pliny the Elder,

---

no. 25; Ernst Pfuhl and Hans Möbius, *Die Ostgriechischen Grabreliefs*, 4 vols. (Mainz: Zabern, 1977–1979), no. 1607 (late imperial times).

35. *IGRR* 4.870 = Robert, "Inscriptions," 278–79.

36. Alan H. Cadwallader, "Honouring the Repairer of the Baths: A New Inscription from Kolossai," *Antichthon* 46 (2012): 150–83.

37. ISmyrna 440.

38. *BCH* 11 (1887): 353–54 n. 11 = *MAMA* 6.40 (after 212 CE); Anderson, "Summer in Phrygia," 90 no. 26 = Reinhold Merkelbach and Josef Stauber, *Die Westküste Kleinasiens von Knidos bis Ilion*, vol. 1 of *Steinepigramme aus dem griechischen Osten* (Stuttgart: Teubner), no 199802/15/01.

39. Pigs: Pfuhl and Möbius, *Grabreliefs*, no. 1165 (around 200) = *MAMA* 6.50; Ritti et al., *Museo Acheologico di Denizli-Hierapolis*, no 80. Goose: Pfuhl and Möblius, *Grabreliefs*, no. 1974; *MAMA* 6.48 tav. 10; Ritti et al., *Museo Acheologico di Denizli-Hierapolis*, no. 73 (second–third centuries CE). Sheepdog: Pfuhl and Möbius, *Grabreliefs*, no. 236 (late imperial times); no. 1635 (late imperial time); no 1973 (late imperial times); no. 2005 (late imperial times). Agricultural products: Pfuhl and Möbius, *Grabreliefs*, no. 1665b (200 BCE); no. 1920 (third century CE); no. 1973 (late imperial times); no. 2005 (late imperial times).

40. Alan H. Cadwallader, "A New Inscription, a Correction and a Confirmed Sighting from Colossae," *EA* 40 (2007): 111, no. 2; *SEG* 57.1385.

41. Pfuhl and Möbius, *Grabreliefs*, no. 594 (third century CE); *MAMA* 6.47 and plate 10; Ritti et al., *Museo Acheologico di Denizli-Hierapolis*, no. 113.

Nat. 21.27.51). Pliny the Elder tells us that the water at Colossae was also extremely chalky, which would have made it well suited for dying (*Nat.* 31.21.29).

In sum, the famous Persian city of Colossae had an afterlife during Hellenistic and Roman times and never, or at least not in the first and second centuries CE, ceased to exist. Located in a prosperous region, Colossae remained or was reestablished as a *polis* with institutionalized offices in early imperial times. The wealth of its benefactors originated from agriculture and especially wool and textile production. Some Romans and veterans settled there, among the Greco-Phrygian farmers. Proud of their city, the wealthy elite promoted it by means of coins, buildings and dedications, or diplomatic missions to the emperors. However, compared to its flourishing neighbors, Laodicea and Hierapolis, Colossae remained small and much less developed. For example, only one coin celebrating *homonoia* (unity) with Aphrodisias, dating from the end of the second century, is known.[42]

Colossae and Colossians

How much is the specific context of ancient Colossae reflected in the letter? Some scholars point to the so-called Colossian philosophy or opponents, others to the clothing metaphors in the paraenetic section or to the multi-ethnic environment of Phrygia reflected in the addition of Barbarians and Scythians to the baptismal formula in Colossians (3:11).

Clinton E. Arnold and more recently Ulrich Huttner find a parallel to Phrygian cult practice in the admonishment in Col 2:18: "Let no one keep defrauding you of your prize by delighting in self-abasement and the worship of the angels, taking his stand on visions he has seen" (NASB). Following William M. Ramsey and Martin Dibelius, they explain the relative clause ἃ ἑόρακεν ἐμβατεύων in Col 2:18 as a reference to a mystery cult at the oracle sanctuary of Apollo at Claros, which was visited by people from Hierapolis and Laodicea seeking answers on behalf of their cities.[43]

---

42. David MacDonald, "The Homonoia of Colossae and Aphrodisias," *JNG* 33 (1984): 25–27 and plate 9.2.

43. Clinton E. Arnold, *The Colossian Syncretism: The Interface between Christianity and Folk Belief at Colossae*, WUNT 2/77 (Tübingen: Mohr Siebeck, 1995), esp. 108–27; see also Huttner, *Early Christianity in the Lycus Valley*, 131. See also William M. Ramsay, "The Relation of St. Paul to the Greek Mysteries," in *The Teaching of*

Hierapolis and Laodicea recorded in stone such official visits to the oracle sanctuary on the Ionian coast, which featured boys and girls singing hymns to the god at Claros. Two inscriptions mention that the leader of such a delegation "received mysteries" as they entered (μυηθέντες ἐνεβάτευσαν). Yet, this does not mean that they were initiated into a mystery cult. Rather, at Claros some kind of staging of their worthiness took place by allowing them to enter the subterranean rooms beneath the temple where the priest delivered answers from Apollo in metrical verse.[44] Although the fourth-century CE Christian synod of Laodicea forbade the idolatry of angels (*angelos idolatriam*), we have no other evidence of cultic worship of angels, nor of any other mystery religion, for that region before the eight century CE.[45] Of course, apocalypticism and other forms of mysticism cannot be ruled out among the large Jewish population of the region. However, it remains difficult to identify the message of the opponents in Colossians with Jewish apocalypticists, gnostics, followers of a cult of angles, Platonists, Stoics, Epicureans, or adherents to Cynic philosophy and the like, because the authors refer to those with whom they disagree only in vague terms.[46] The letter argues against not one specific heresy but contains a

---

Paul in Terms of the Present Day: The Deems Lectures in New York University, 2nd ed. (London: Hodder & Stoughton, 1914) 281–305; Martin Dibelius, "Die Isisweihe bei Apuleius und verwandte Initationsriten," in *Botschaft und Geschichte II* (Tübingen: Mohr, 1956), 30–79, 55–65.

44. Theodore Macridy, "Altertümer von Notion," *JÖAI* 8 (1905): 168, no. 4/5.4: θεοπρόποι (meet for a god) ἦλθο[ν] Κρίσπος Τρύφωνος καὶ Π(όπλιος) Πούπιος Καλλικλῆς οἵτινες μυηθέντες ἐνεβάτευσαν. Macridy, "Anitquités de Notion II," *JÖAI* 15 (1912): 46, no. 2: θεοπρόπος Ἀνδρικὸς Ἀλεξάνδρου παραλαβὼν τὰ μυστήρια ἐνεβάτευσεν. See also Merkelbach and Stauber, "Die Orakel des Apollon von Klaros," 6, no. 2[2]: οἵτινες μυ]ηθέντες καὶ ἐμβα[τεύσαντες ἐχρήσαντο καὶ ἀπέδωκαν τ]ὸν ὑπογεγραμμένον [τοῦ Κλαρίου Ἀπόλλωνος ἀκέρ]αιον χρησμόν. See also Jean-Louis Ferrary, "Le Sanctuaire de Claros à l'époque hellénistique et Romaine," in *Colloque Les Sanctuaires et Leur Rayonnement dans le Monde Méditerranéen de l'Antiquité à l'Époque Moderne*, ed. Juliette de La Genière (Paris: de Boccard, 2010), 111–14.

45. Council of Laodicea, canon 35. See also Glenn Peers, *Subtle Bodies: Representing Angels in Byzantium* (Berkeley: University of California Press, 2001), 143–93. Theodoret's *Commentary on Colossians* (PG 82.613 A–B) concludes this from the council of Laodicea as he admits himself. Pace Huttner, *Early Christianity in the Lycus Valley*, 128.

46. See most recently George H. van Kooten, *Cosmic Christology in Paul and the Pauline School: Colossians and Ephesians in the Context of Graeco-Roman Cosmology, with a New Synopsis of the Greek* Texts, WUNT 2/171 (Tübingen: Mohr Siebeck, 2003).

cluster of general warnings that point to many philosophical schools, religious groups, and syncretistic movements.[47]

While they are not unique to it, clothing metaphors play a strikingly prominent role in the letter's rhetoric.[48] For Rosemary Canavan, this reflects the importance of the local clothing and wool industry.[49] The letter builds on this specific local environment to discuss Christian identity. Yet, while Colossian farmers, leatherworkers, weavers, and woolworkers were likely proud of their products, the metaphorical language of Colossians—the "putting off" of vices and "putting on" of virtue—does not so much refer to cloth production as to the change in status symbolized by one's clothing.

To Cadwallader and Lukas Bormann, the insertion of Scythians in the baptismal creed of Col 3:11 reflects the multicultural environment of the region in which the city functioned as a mediator between the major cities in the Lycos valley and the Phrygian hinterland. A newly found inscription "Markos, son of Markus, chief interpreter and translator [...]" seems to indicate a multicultural environment in which indigenous languages like Phrygian and Scythian had to be translated.[50] However, it is under debate if and how far Phrygian were still spoken at this time.[51] Markus might also have been an interpreter of the revelations of Apollo at Hierapolis or elsewhere.[52] On the *bomos* that honors Korumbos for repairing

---

47. Angela Standhartinger, *Studien zur Entstehungsgeschichte und Intention des Kolosserbriefes*, NovTSup 94 (Leiden: Brill, 1999), 16–27.

48. For this imagery, see Col 3:8; 10; 12.

49. Rosemary Canavan, *Clothing the Body of Christ at Colossae: A Visual Construction of Identity*, WUNT 2/334 (Tübingen: Mohr Siebeck, 2012), 67–177.

50. *SEG* 57.1382. Cadwallader, "New Inscription," 109–18, nos. 3112–3118. See also Bormann, *Brief des Paulus*, 26–28.

51. Rick Strelan, "The Languages of the Lycus Valley," in Cadwallader and Trainor, *Colossae in Space and Time*, 77–103, argues by analogy from Australia for multiple indigenous languages still in use. Claude Brixhe, "Interactions between Greek and Phrygian under the Roman Empire," in *Bilingualism in Ancient Society: Language Contact and the Written Text*, ed. J. N. Adams, Mark Janse, and Simon Swain (Oxford: Oxford University Press, 2002), 246–66, sees traces of Phrygian language in Greek inscriptions. More critical to the existence of spoken Phrygian in Phrygia is Ute Kelp, "Grave Monuments and Local Identities in Roman Phrygia," in *Roman Phrygia: Culture and* Society, ed. Peter Thonemann (Cambridge: Cambridge University Press, 2013), 92–93.

52. Angelos Chaniotis, "Epigraphic Bulletin of Greek Religion 2007," *Kernos* 23 (2010), 285–86.

the bath at Colossae, two Thracian and one likely Scythian name appear among sixty Greek names.[53] Yet the non-Greek names all belong to the generation of the grandfathers.

Until a full picture of the city emerges when excavations finally take place, none of these local contextualizations can be ruled out. However, in my view, the address "to the saints and faithful siblings in Christ in Colossae" (1:1) sends a more open message to its readers. It is telling that no mention is made of an *ekklesia* in this city. The only geographically specific *ekklesia* referred to in the letter is said to gather in the house of Nympha at Laodicea, a place we hear of again at the end of the first century in Revelation (Col 4:16; Rev 3:14–21). Colossae itself is part of the worldwide *ekklesia*, a body of which Christ is the head (Col 1:18; 1:24; 2:19). From the very beginning of the letter, Colossae symbolizes the worldwide spread of the gospel even to this far-flung corner of Asia Minor, a small polis at the edge of the Lycos valley (see Col 1:6; 10).[54]

The letter implies a lot of contact between Paul and the congregation at Colossae. Not only has the gospel reached them through Epaphras, their missionary, but they have also received some instructions regarding "Mark, the cousin of Barnabas." Onesimos, "the faithful and beloved brother" (4:8), came from Colossae to Paul's place of imprisonment. Yet of the twelve names appearing in Colossians and the Letter to Philemon, ten are identical. As Eduard Lohse showed long ago, this concurrence is due to literary dependence.[55] We do not know where the house of Philemon once

---

53. Alan H. Cadwallader, "Greeks in Colossae: Shifting Allegiances in the Letter to the Colossians and Its Context," in *Attitudes to Gentiles in Ancient Judaism and Early Christianity*, ed. David Sim and James S. McLaren (London: T&T Clark, 2013), 224–41. One Latin name, Likinios, might be a slave because he bears no *gentile* name.

54. There is almost no afterlife of the community at Colossae. John Chrysostomus, *Hom. Col.* 3.1 knows nothing and had to conclude from his knowledge of Laodicea that Colossae was placed in the Lycus valley. Theodoret, *Interpretatio in xiv epistulas sancti Pauli* (PG 82.628.4) claims that one can see the house of Philemon still there, but this is a standard formulation and does not hint to local information. Pace Huttner, *Early Christianity in the Lycus Valley*, 111.

55. Eduard Lohse, "Die Mitarbeiter des Apostels Paulus im Kolosserbrief," in *Verborum Veritas: Festschrift für Gustav Stählin zum 70. Geburtstag*, ed. Otto Böcher and Klaus Haacker (Wuppertal: Brockhaus, 1970), 189–94; see also Lohse, *Der Brief an die Kolosser und an Philemon*, KEK 9.2 (Göttingen: Vandenhoeck & Ruprecht, 1968), 247. See Standhartinger, *Studien*, 81–85; Angela Standhartinger, "Colossians and the Pauline School," *NTS* 50 (2004): 572–93.

stood. And the information provided in Colossians beyond that which we learn from the Letter to Philemon regarding those around Paul only embellishes the story of the imprisoned Paul, who is preparing himself to die.[56] In Colossians, Paul is on his way to "completing what is lacking in Christ's afflictions" (1:24 NRSV), an expression most likely hinting at the recent death and martyrdom of the Apostle. Therefore, it is not for Paul's release but for the release of the Word that the congregation should pray (4:3–4). Some information contradicts what is said in the Letter to Philemon. While in the latter, Epaphras sends greetings to those in Philemon's house as Paul's "fellow-prisoner," in Colossians he is referred to as a member of the local congregation (see Phlm 23 with Col 1:7–8; 4:12–13). The information given in Colossians regarding Aristarchus and Markus—that they are "the only ones of the circumcision among my co-workers for the kingdom of God, and they have been a comfort to me" (4:11 NRSV)—evokes the impression that the righteous one, Paul, has been forsaken by almost everybody and especially by the Jews. Yet, a mostly non-Jewish congregation is unlikely to have existed in the historical Lycus Valley (see Col 1:21; 2:11). "A beloved physician" such as Luke is definitely needed by somebody who is languishing in Roman imprisonment. Thus, in my view, the additional information beyond the names already mentioned in the Letter to Philemon strengthens the impression of Paul's approaching martyrdom but does not provide details about historical personalities known to the authors.

Some local information is given, however. Although I am not sure that the authors ever saw Colossae in person—they might have picked up the name from the name of a well-known kind of colored wool—one piece of information about the city seem most important to them: that it was located in the Lycos valley. They knew that Colossae was close enough to Laodicea that a letter could easily be exchanged (4:16) between the two cities. Paul fights not only for Colossae but also, if secondarily, for Laodicea (2:1). At the end of the letter, Epaphras's work at Hierapolis is mentioned as well (4:13). Yet, it is not the famous and prosperous Laodicea, nor the equally wealthy Hierapolis, that receives the honor of a letter from Paul, but rather this small and modest city at the edge of the Lycos valley. What addressing the letter to Colossae does most in effect is to redraw the map that most inhabitants of Asia and the Roman world would have in mind

---

56. Pace Huttner, *Early Christianity in the Lycus Valley*, 111.

when they thought about this region. The focus is shifted from the important and prosperous cities to the rural hinterlands to which the gospel has spread and where it has already born fruit. It is this small and unimportant city, known only for its sheep and colored wool that is honored by a letter documenting steadfastness and praising the spiritual life of its faithful congregation.

The address "to the holy and faithful siblings at Colossae" is in itself a message. The message is that is not the powerful, nor the many, nor those of noble birth but rather the foolish, the weak, and the lowly that God has chosen as most fitting for the message of the faithful crucified Christ.

Bibliography

Anderson, J. G. C. "A Summer in Phrygia II." *JHS* 18 (1898): 81–128, 340–44.

Arnold, Clinton E. *The Colossian Syncretism: The Interface between Christianity and Folk Belief at Colossae*. WUNT 2/77. Tübingen: Mohr Siebeck, 1995.

Ameling, Walter. *Kleinasien*. Vol. 2 of *Inscriptiones Iudaicae Orientis*. TSAJ 99. Tübingen: Mohr Siebeck, 2004.

Armstrong, Andrea J. "Roman Phrygia: Cities and Their Coinage." PhD diss., University of London, 1998.

Bean, Georg. *Jenseits des Mäander: Karien mit dem Vilayet Mugla*. Stuttgart: Kohlhammer, 1985.

Benda-Weber, Isabella. "Textile Production Centers, Products and Merchants in the Roman Province of Asia." Pages 171–91 in *Making Textiles in Pre-Roman and Roman Times: People, Places, Identities*. Edited by Margarita Gleba and Judit Pásztókai-Szeoke. Ancient Textiles Series 13. Oxford: Oxbow, 2013.

Bormann, Lukas. *Der Brief des Paulus an die Kolosser*. THKNT 10.1. Leipzig: Evangelische Verlagsanstalt, 2012.

Brixhe, Claude. "Interactions between Greek and Phrygian under the Roman Empire." Pages 246–66 in *Bilingualism in Ancient Society: Language Contact and the Written Text*. Edited by J. N. Adams, Mark Janse, and Simon Swain. Oxford: Oxford University Press, 2002.

Broughton, T. R. S. "Roman Asia Minor." Pages 601–2 in *An Economic Survey of Ancient Rome IV*. Edited by Frank Tenney. Paterson, NJ: Pageant, 1959.

Bujard, Walter. *Stilanalytische Untersuchungen zum Kolosserbrief als Beitrag zur Methodik von Sprachvergleichen.* SUNT 11. Göttingen: Vandenhoeck & Ruprecht, 1973.
Burnett, Andrew, Michael Amandry, and Pere Pau Ripollès. *Roman Provincal Coinage.* Vol. 1. London: British Museum Press, 1998.
Cadwallader, Alan H. "A New Inscription, a Correction and a Confirmed Sighting from Colossae." *EA* 40 (2007): 109–18.
———. *Fragments of Colossae: Sifting through the Traces.* Adelaide: ATF, 2015.
———. "Greeks in Colossae: Shifting Allegiances in the Letter to the Colossians and Its Context." Pages 224–41 in *Attitudes to Gentiles in Ancient Judaism and Early Christianity.* Edited by David Sim and James S. McLaren. London: T&T Clark, 2013.
———. "Honouring the Repairer of the Baths: A New Inscription from Kolossai." *Antichthon* 46 (2012): 150–83.
———. "Refuting an Axiom of Scholarship on Colossae: Fresh Insights from New and Old Inscriptions." Pages 151–79 in *Colossae in Space and Time: Linking to an Ancient City.* Edited by Alan H. Cadwallader and Michael Trainor. NTOA–SUNT 94. Göttingen: Vandenhoeck & Ruprecht, 2011.
Cadwallader, Alan H., and Michael Trainor, eds. *Colossae in Space and Time: Linking to an Ancient City.* NTOA–SUNT 94. Göttingen: Vandenhoeck & Ruprecht, 2011.
Canavan, Rosemary. *Clothing the Body of Christ at Colossae: A Visual Construction of Identity.* WUNT 2/334. Tübingen: Mohr Siebeck, 2012.
Chaniotis, Angelos. "Epigraphic Bulletin of Greek Religion 2007." *Kernos* 23 (2010): 271–327.
Clerc, Michel Armand. "Inscriptions de la vallée du Méandre: Tralles, Nysa, Attuda, Laodicée et Colosses." *BCH* 11 (1887): 346–54.
Corsten, Thomas. "Laodikeia by the Lykos." *Encyclopedia of Ancient History* 7:3905–6.
D'Andria, Francesco. "Hierapolis of Phrygia: Its Evolution in Hellenistic and Roman Times." Pages 96–115 in *Urbanism in Western Asia Minor: New Studies on Aphrodisias, Ephesos, Hierapolis, Pergamon, Perge and Xanthos.* Edited by David Parrish. JRASup 45. Portsmouth, RI: Journal of Roman Archaeology, 2001.
———. *Hierapolis in Phrygien (Pamukkale): Ein Archäologischer Führer.* Istanbul: Ege Yayinlari, 2010.

Dibelius, Martin. "Die Isisweihe bei Apuleius und verwandte Initationsriten." Pages 30–79 in *Botschaft und Geschichte II*. Tübingen: Mohr, 1956.

Dittmann-Schöne, Imogen. *Berufsvereine in den Städten des kaiserzeitlichen Kleinasiens*. Regensburg: S. Roderer Verlag, 2001.

Drexhage, Heinrich-Wilhelm. *Wirtschaftspolitik und Wirtschaft in der römischen Provinz Asia in der Zeit von Augustus bis zum Regierungsantritt Diokletians*. Asia Minor Studies 59. Bonn: Habelt, 2007.

Duman, Bahadir, and Erim Konakçi. "The Silent Witness of the Mound of Colossae: Pottery Remains." Pages 247–81 in *Colossae in Space and Time: Linking to an Ancient City*. Edited by Alan H. Cadwallader and Michael Trainor. NTOA-SUNT 94. Göttingen: Vandenhoeck & Ruprecht, 2011.

Ferrary, Jean-Louis. "Le Sanctuaire de Claros a L'époque hellénistique et Romaine." Pages 91–114 in *Colloque Les Sanctuaires et Leur Rayonnement dans le Monde Méditerranéen de l'Antiquité à l'Époque Moderne*. Edited by Juliette de La Genière. Paris: De Boccard, 2010.

Filges, Axel. *Blaundos: Berichte zur Erforschung einer Kleinstadt im lydisch-phrygischen Grenzgebiet*. IstForsch 48. Tübingen: Wasmuth, 2006.

Harland, Philip A. "Interaction and Integration: Judean Families and Guilds at Hierapolis." Pages 123–42 in *Dynamics of Identity in the World of the Early Christians: Associations, Judeans, and Cultural Minorities*. New York: T&T Clark, 2009.

———. *North Coast of the Black Sea, Asia Minor*. Vol. 1 of *Greco-Roman Associations: Texts, Translations, and Commentary*. BZNW 204. Berlin: de Gruyter, 2014.

Huttner, Ulrich. "Die Färber von Laodikeia und Hierapolis: Eine Nachricht aus dem Corpus der Alchemisten." *MBAH* 26 (2008): 139–57.

———. *Early Christianity in the Lycus Valley*. Translated by David Green. AJEC 85; Early Christianity in Asia Minor 1. Leiden: Brill, 2013.

Kelp, Ute. "Grave Monuments and Local Identities in Roman Phrygia." Pages 70–94 in *Roman Phrygia. Culture and Society*. Edited by Peter Thonemann. Cambridge: Cambridge University Press, 2013.

Kooten, George H. van. *Cosmic Christology in Paul and the Pauline School: Colossians and Ephesians in the Context of Graeco-Roman Cosmology, with a New Synopsis of the Greek Texts*. WUNT 2/171. Tübingen: Mohr Siebeck, 2003.

Lindemann, Andreas. "Die Gemeinde von 'Kolossä': Erwägungen zum 'Sitz im Leben' eines pseudopaulinischen Briefes." *WD* 16 (1981): 111–34.
Lohse, Eduard. *Die Briefe an die Kolosser und an Philemon*. KEK 9.2. Göttingen: Vandenhoeck & Ruprecht, 1977.
———. "Die Mitarbeiter des Apostels Paulus im Kolosserbrief." Pages 189–94 in *Verborum Veritas: Festschrift für Gustav Stählin zum 70. Geburtstag*. Edited by Otto Böcher and Klaus Haacker. Wuppertal: Brockhaus, 1970.
MacDonald, David. "The Homonoia of Colossae and Aphrodisias." *JNG* 33 (1984): 25–27 and plate 9.2.
Macridy, Theodore. "Altertümer von Notion." *JÖAI* 8 (1905): 155–73.
———. "Anitquités de Notion II." *JÖAI* 15 (1912): 36–67.
Merkelbach, Reinhold, and Josef Stauber. "Die Orakel des Apollon von Klaros." *EA* 27 (1996): 1–53.
———. *Die Westküste Kleinasiens von Knidos bis Ilion*. Vol. 1 of *Steinepigramme aus dem griechischen Osten*. Stuttgart: Teubner. 1998.
Peers, Glenn. *Subtle Bodies: Representing Angels in Byzantium*. Berkeley: University of California Press, 2001.
Pfuhl, Ernst, and Hans Möbius. *Die Ostgriechischen Grabreliefs*. 4 vols. Mainz: Zabern, 1977–1979.
Pizzuto, Vincent A. *A Cosmic Leap of Faith: An Authorial, Structural, and Theological Investigation of the Cosmic Christology in Col 1:15–20*. Leuven: Peeters, 2006.
Ramsay, William M. "The Relation of St. Paul to the Greek Mysteries." Pages 281–305 in *The Teaching of Paul in Terms of the Present Day: The Deems Lectures in New York University*. 2nd ed. London: Toronto: Hodder & Stoughton, 1914.
Reike, Bo. "The Historical Setting of Colossians." *RevExp* 70 (1973): 429–38.
Ritti, Tullia. *An Epigraphic Guide to Hierapolis (Pamukkale)*. Istanbul: Ege Yayinlari, 2006.
Ritti, Tullia, H. Hüseyin Baysal, Elena Miranda, and Francesco Guizzi, eds. *Museo Archeologico di Denizli-Hierapolis: Catalogo delle iscrizione greche e latine*. Napoli: Liguori Editore, 2008.
Robert, Louis. "Inscriptions." Pages 248–364 in *Laodicée du Lycos: Le Nymphée; Campagnes 1961–1963*. Edited by Jean des Gagniers, Pierre Devambez, Lilly Kahil, and René Ginouvès. Québec: Presses de l'Université Laval, 1969.

Standhartinger, Angela. "Colossians and the Pauline School." *NTS* 50 (2004): 572–93.

———. *Studien zur Entstehungsgeschichte und Intention des Kolosserbriefes.* NovTSup 94. Leiden: Brill, 1999.

Strelan, Rick. "The Languages of the Lycus Valley." Pages 77–103 in *Colossae in Space and Time: Linking to an Ancient City.* Edited by Alan H. Cadwallader and Michael Trainor. NTOA–SUNT 94. Göttingen: Vandenhoeck & Ruprecht, 2011.

Thonemann, Peter J. "Phrygia: An Anarchist History, 950 BC–AD 100." Pages 1–40 in *Roman Phrygia: Culture and Society.* Edited by Peter Thonemann. Cambridge: Cambridge University Press, 2013.

Von Aulock, Hans. *Münzen und Städte Phrygiens.* 2 vols. IstMitt 25, 27. Tübingen: Wasmuth, 1980, 1987.

Employing Numismatic Evidence in Discussions of Early Christianity in the Lycus Valley: A Case Study from Laodicea

Michael P. Theophilos

1. Introduction

This paper offers an analysis of the significance of numismatic material for our understanding of early Christianity in the Lycus Valley. Attention will also be given to methodological issues pertaining to employing numismatic evidence in linguistic, historical, and theological perspectives in Asia Minor. Cognizant that the geographical demarcation of the Lycus Valley is a modern and relatively artificial boundary and that trade, commercial relations, and other interactions were more geographically fluid, we will investigate a case study related to Laodicea. This study could easily, and methodologically more plausibly, be expanded to include coinage of the immediate locale (Cibyra, Colossae, Laodicea, Hierapolis, Hydrela) and the broader region of Phrygia (Cadi, Aezani, Synaus, Ancyra, Dionysopolis, Apamea, Fulvia/Eumenea, Sebaste, Eucarpia, Sibilia, Acmonea, Synnada, Iulia, Prymnessus, Docimeum, Appia, Cotiaeum, Midaeum, Amorium, Philomelium). Konrad Kraft, for example, has identified connections between so-called coin workshops through a network of obverse die-links throughout Asia Minor.[1] Kraft estimates that there were approximately twelve workshops servicing over two hundred cities minting coins

---

1. Konrad Kraft, *Das System der kaiserzeitlichen Münzprägung in Kleinasien: Materialien und Entwürfe* (Berlin: Mann, 1972); Ann Johnston, "Die Sharing in Asia Minor: The View from Sardis," *Israel Numismatic Journal* 6–7 (1982–1983): 59–78; Johnston, "Greek Imperial Statistics: A Commentary," *Review Numismatique* 26 (1984): 240–57.

pre-Septimius (193 CE), that one workshop could service more than ten cities simultaneously, and that the variety and output of new types seem linked to the availability of an engraver (in Phrygia, for example, the Apameia workshop in 200–205 CE and the Sardis workshop in 242–247 CE).[2]

2. Previous Research

First-century CE Roman provincial coinage of Asia Minor, as a distinct area of study, has regularly drawn attention from classical and Roman historians.[3] On the basis of Hans von Aulock's index volume, Wolfgang Leschhorn provided an analysis of the numismatic evidence in his article entitled, "Le monnayage impérial d'Asie Mineure et la statistique," in which he detailed the distribution pattern of coinage in Asia Minor from Augustus to Tacitus (276 CE), focusing especially on numbers of cities issuing coins.[4] Ann Johnson, however, highlights one important methodological difficulty in this process by noting that true frequency is obscured "because we do not know how many issues per reign there were, or when precisely they were struck; we can only note the existence or absence of coins for a given emperor."[5] Indeed, the variation in length of rule of individual emperors further obscures, or perhaps, should nuance, any analysis

---

2. Kraft, *Das System*, 6, 13.

3. Clemens Bosch, "Kleinasiatischen Münzen der römischen Kaiserzeit," *Jahrbuch des Deutschen Archäologischen Instituts* 46 (1931): 424–56; Tom B. Jones, "A Numismatic Riddle: The So-Called Greek Imperials," *Proceedings of the American Philosophical Society* 107 (1963): 308–47; Jones, "Greek Imperial Coins," *The Voice of the Turtle: North American Journal of Numismatics* 4 (1965): 295–308; Ursula Kampmann, "*Homonoia* Politics in Asia Minor: The Example of Pergamon," in *Pergamon, Citadel of the Gods: Archaeological Record, Literary Description, and Religious Development*, ed. Helmut Koester (Harrisburg: Trinity Press International, 1998), 373–93; V. M. da Costa, "Five Roman Empresses: Chronology and Style in the Roman Provincial Coin Issues of Asia Minor," in *Notes of the First International Numismatic Symposium of the Turkish Numismatic Society* (Istanbul: Turkish Numismatic Society, 1999), 1–27; Ann Johnston, *Greek Imperial Denominations, ca. 200–275: A Study of Roman Provincial Bronze Coinages of Asia Minor* (London: Royal Numismatic Society, 2007).

4. Peter R. Franke and Wolfgang Leschhorn, *Index to Sylloge Nummorum Graecorum Deutschland: Sammlung H. von Aulock* (Berlin: Mann, 1981); Wolfgang Leschhorn, "Le monnayage impérial d'Asie Mineure et la statistique" *PACT: Revue de groupe européen d'études sur les techniques physiques, chimiques et mathematiques appliquées à l'archéologie* 5 (1981): 252–66.

5. Johnston, "Greek Imperial Statistics," 241.

of the distribution of coinage and mints in first century Asia Minor.[6] Furthermore, Michael Grant notes the additional factor of coin types being struck posthumously, a figure that he places at more than one hundred types for Augustus.[7] Many of the cities in Asia Minor had been producing civic issues during the Roman Republic, so it is not surprising that they continued to do so during the reign of Augustus. That being said, perhaps one sustainable observation from Leschhorn's analysis is the distinct increase in the number of cities issuing coins in first-century Asia Minor, a figure which effectively doubles from Augustus (ca. one hundred cities) to Trajan (ca. two hundred cities).[8]

Regional differences within Asia Minor are also apparent.[9] Coinage in Phrygia was not limited to main cities but is also attested in population centers that more closely resemble a village. Victor Schultze's three volume, four-part, work on Christianity in Asia Minor devotes a total of eighty-one pages to Phrygia and forty-one pages to the cities of the Lycus Valley.[10] Despite regular reference to the numismatic material (more than forty times), Schultze typically engages the material in a tangential and relatively superficial manner. Similarly, William Ramsay, renowned for his pioneering work on the Lycus Valley, included both the epigraphic sources and close attention to considerations of historical geography[11] but rarely incorporated relevant numismatic material. Ramsay does however acknowledge that his incorporation of all relevant sources for the Lycus

---

6. As noted by Johnston, "Greek Imperial Statistics," 242, if one does plot the length of reigns alongside Leschhorn's "mints in operation," the two are in almost perfect synchronization.

7. Michael Grant, *From Imperium to Auctoritas* (Cambridge: Cambridge University Press, 1946), appendix 7.

8. Leschhorn, "Le monnayage," 256.

9. William E. Metcalf, "Regionalism in the Coinage of Asia Minor," in *Regionalism in Hellenistic and Roman Asia Minor*, ed. Hugh Elton and Gary Reger (Pessac: Ausonius, 2007), 147–59.

10. Victor Schultze, *Konstantinopel*, vol. 1 of *Altchristliche Städte und Landschaften* (Leipzig: Gütersloh, 1913); Schultze, *Kleinasien*, vol. 2 of *Altchristliche Städte und Landschaften*, 2 parts (Leipzig: Gütersloh, 1922–1926); Schultze, *Antiocheia*, vol. 3 of *Altchristliche Städte und Landschaften* (Leipzig: Gütersloh, 1930). For Phrygia, see *Kleinasien*, 1:397–477. For the Lycus Valley, see *Kleinasien* 1:410–50.

11. William M. Ramsay, *The Letters to the Seven Churches of Asia and Their Place in the Plan of the Apocalypse* (London: Hodder & Stoughton, 1904), 413–30; Ramsay, *The Lycos Valley and South-Western Phrygia*, vol. 1 of *The Cities and Bishoprics of Phrygia* (Oxford: Clarendon, 1895).

Valley was "the least satisfactory and the least complete."[12] While Ramsay's work in historical geography was furthered by his student J. G. C. Anderson and the epigraphic survey of the region was carried further by W. M. Calder and W. H. Buckler, "who consciously followed in the tradition of Ramsay," little attention has been paid to the numismatic material in its relation to early Christianity.[13]

3. Methodological Considerations

The incorporation of coins as a distinct form of evidence for understanding nascent Christianity in the Roman world raises a range of methodological questions. This section will address a selection of the most important issues including, (1) the propagandistic nature of coinage and whether coins are a valid source of evidence given this potential bias? (2) addressing the question of whether coinage, both image and inscription, was noticed by the populace? and (3) does the (elite) social origin of coinage lessen its importance, impact, or relevance for the question under discussion? This, by no means, is an exhaustive analysis of the full range of concerns that may be relevant to our enquiry. We will not, for example, closely examine the methodological issues of applying visual phenomena in hermeneutics, although it is readily acknowledged that coin iconography and coin inscription are to be mutually interpreted.[14]

---

12. William M. Ramsay, *Impressions of Turkey during Twelve Years' Wanderings* (London: Hodder & Stoughton, 1897), 88.

13. J. G. C. Anderson, "A Summer in Phrygia I," *JHS* 17 (1897): 396–424; Anderson, "A Summer in Phrygia II," *JHS* 18 (1898): 81–128, 340–44; Ulrich Huttner, *Early Christianity in the Lycus Valley*, trans. David Green, AJEC 85, Early Christianity in Asia Minor 1 (Leiden: Brill, 2013), 9. There are some notable exceptions to the dearth of numismatic investigation, which will be engaged with and acknowledged below.

14. For a discussion of this issue Annette Weissenrieder and Friederike Wendt, "Images as Communication: The Methods of Iconography," in *Picturing the New Testament: Studies in Ancient Visual Images*, ed. Annette Weissenrieder, Friederike Wendt, and P. von Gemünden (Tübingen: Mohr Siebeck, 2005), 3–49. Erika Manders (*Coining Images of Power: Patterns in the Representation of Roman Emperors on Imperial Coinage, AD 193–284* [Leiden: Brill, 2012], 30) notes, "on many coins the image either presents a visualization of the legend or the legend forms a textual rendering of the image. This cooperation between text and image facilitated not only illiterates' understanding of the messages present on coins, it also reduced the various possibilities of how Romans could interpret a message." The *Lexicon Iconographicum Numismatica* is an effort to categorize visual types into a systematized catalogue, including the "cre-

The first consideration is whether coinage is a legitimate source of historical information given its propagandistic tendencies. Harold Mattingly has noted the relationship of coins and forms of propaganda in the Roman world: "coin types are constantly changing, and constantly emphasising definite events and policies, and, as they change move in close agreement with the political changes of the time."[15] He continues by stating, "the possible influence of such coinage on public opinion could not possibly be overlooked or minimized by the Emperor. He must ... have censored, if not inspired it."[16] In similar regard, Warren Carter states that "coins demonstrated Roman sovereignty ... [and] symbolized Roman accomplishments and the blessings of the gods which the emperor mediated to the people. There was no escaping Roman presence even in daily transactions."[17] In first-century Mediterranean village life, K. Dyer suggests that the circulation of coinage operated as one of the most efficient and concrete forms of communication.[18]

The various media available in this effort of persuasion in the ancient Roman world reinforced Roman ideals. Everything from architecture and inscriptions to the provision of "conveniences" (*commoda*) such as public leisure (baths), mass entertainment (chariot racing, gladiatorial games), and processions (*triumphi*), contributed to a well-defined Roman cultural narrative. Coins distinctly contribute to our understanding of these phenomena due to their ubiquity, distribution, and continuous use. J. Rufas

---

ation of a coin iconographic lexicon. See related DIANA project website here: http://ww2.unime.it/diana/, and further M. Caccamo Caltabiano, L. Campagna, and A. Pinzone, eds., *Nuove prospsettive della ricerca sulla Sicilia del III sec. a.C.: Archeologia, numismatica, storia* (Messina: Dipartimento di Scienze dell' Antichita dell'Università degli Studi di Messina, 2004); Marianna Spinelli, "The 'Soma' of the God: Subtypes as Qualification of the Corporal Gestures of the Main Subject on the Kaulonia Coins," in *Identity and Connectivity: Proceedings of the Sixteenth Symposium on Mediterranean Archaeology*, ed. Luca Bombardieri et al. (Oxford: Aracheopress, 2013), 793.

15. Harold Mattingly, *Coins of the Roman Empire in the British Museum*, 6 vols. (London: British Museum, 1936), 3:xlv.

16. Mattingly, *Coins of the Roman Empire*, 3:xlv.

17. Warren Carter, *Matthew and the Margins* (Sheffield: Sheffield Academic, 2000), 38.

18. K. D. Dyer, "'But Concerning that Day ...' (Mark 13:32): 'Prophetic' and 'Apocalyptic' Eschatology in Mark 13," in *Society of Biblical Literature 1999 Seminar Papers*, SBLSP 38 (Atlanta: Society of Biblical Literature, 1999), 112; see also Michael H. Crawford, "Money and Exchange in the Roman World," *JRS* 60 (1970): 40–46.

Fears suggests that the numismatic material is preferable to any other evidence in the discernment of imperial ideology,

> The literary sources are secondary sources; at their best, they are idiosyncratic, and at their worst they consciously distort the deeds and intentions of individual emperors. Thus, we will never know much of what 'really' transpired under Trajan, and nothing at all of his actual intentions. Through the coinage, however, we know an inordinate amount about what the Roman government wanted its citizens and subjects to believe happened and how it wished the person and deeds of Trajan to be perceived by those citizens and subjects. The coinage was a medium of propaganda. Its purpose was the creation and propagation of a belief. It is the medium by which we can best approach the ideology of the imperial system.[19]

Although literary sources may never reveal the *historical* intentions of the ruling elite, be they in Rome or in the provinces, coinage reveals, at a minimum, an objective perspective of how rulers wanted their subjects to perceive their political activity. Edwin A. Judge alludes to a similar phenomenon of the treatment of history by ancient writers: "in the case of Roman history, we typically mean by 'documents' the coins, inscriptions, and papyri that survive directly from the time, as distinct from the treatment of the history by ancient writers."[20] While ancient coins were certainly not ideologically neutral, they do accurately depict a real picture of how the emperor wanted to be perceived. In this respect, the image and text can profitably be employed for historical purposes, be they linguistic, iconographic, or social and cultural windows into the Roman world.[21] But did people pay attention or notice the inscribed imagery of coinage?

---

19. J. Rufus Fears, "The Cult of Virtues and Roman Imperial Ideology," *ANRW* 17.2:945.

20. Edwin A. Judge, "Setting the Record Straight: Alternative Documents of a Protest in the Roman Army of Egypt," in *The First Christians in the Roman World: Augustan and New Testament Essays*, ed. James R. Harrison (Tübingen: Mohr Siebeck, 2008), 378.

21. Peter Brennan, Michael Turner, and Nicholas L. Wright's comment resonate deeply at this point: the coins "are a true reflection of their time—of a 'face of power's' perception of what he had done, what he was going to do, what he was going to get others to do, or what others were going to get him or her to do." Peter Brennan, Michael Turner, and Nicholas L. Wright, *Faces of Power: Imperial Portraiture on Roman Coins* (Sydney: Nicholson Museum, 2007), 5.

The second methodological question emerges out of a pragmatic concern for the effectiveness of the so-called propaganda noted above. Literary and other evidence suggests that ancient people did pay attention to and were aware of the images, symbols, and inscriptions on the coinage that was handled on a daily basis. The Stoic philosopher Epictetus, writing toward the end of the first century or beginning of the second century CE, notes that, "the imprints which he brought with him in his mind, such as we look for also upon coins, and, if we find them, we accept the coins, but if we do not find them, we throw the coins away. 'Whose imprint does this sestertius bear? Trajan's? Give it to me. Nero's? Throw it out, it will not pass, it is rotten'" (τοὺς χαρακτῆρας, οὓς ἔχων ἐν τῇ διανοίᾳ ἐλήλυθεν, οἵους καὶ ἐπὶ τῶν νομισμάτων ζητοῦντες, ἂν μὲν εὕρωμεν, δοκιμάζομεν, ἂν δὲ μὴ εὕρωμεν, ῥιπτοῦμεν. τίνος ἔχει τὸν χαρακτῆρα τοῦτο τὸ τετράσσαρον; Τραιανοῦ; φέρε. Νέρωνος; ῥῖψον ἔξω, ἀδόκιμόν ἐστιν, σαπρόν; Epictetus, *Disc.* 4.5.16–17).[22] While the images and symbols on the coins were the most noticeable and prominent features, coin inscriptions were often used to explain or clarify the potentially complex imagery that might then be further extended for a particular purpose.[23] The famous incident concerning Jesus in the temple when asked about paying taxes to Caesar also appeals to the hearers' knowledge of the imagery on a denarius, "Whose image is this? And whose inscription?" (τίνος ἡ εἰκὼν αὕτη καὶ ἡ ἐπιγραφή; Matt 22:20; see also Matt 22:15–22; Mark 12:13–17; Luke 20:20–26). These and

---

22. W. A. Oldfather, trans. *Epictetus. Discourses, Books 3–4; Fragments; The Encheiridion*, LCL (Cambridge: Harvard University Press, 1928), 336–37. An important distinction is to be acknowledged between Roman coins and their Greek predecessors. Although "designs on Greek coins typically remained unchanged for decades or even centuries, varying only in style or detail over time" (Jonathan Williams, "Religion and Roman Coins," in *A Companion to Roman Religion*, ed. Jörg Rüpke [Oxford: Blackwell, 2007], 143), Roman coinage exhibited both continuity and discontinuity in its iconography stamped on coinage. It is true that "it was the usual practice in the ancient world to imitate existing types that were current locally, in order to secure greater confidence in and prestige for a new coin minted by a recently established authority" (Ya'akov Meshorer, *Jewish Coins of the Second Temple Period* [Tel-Aviv: Am Hassefer, 1967], 58), but it is also apparent that Roman coinage was much more dynamic and adaptable to new images and environments.

23. Michael H. Crawford, "Roman Imperial Coin Types and the Formation of Public Opinion," in *Studies in Numismatic Method Presented to Philip Grierson*, ed. C. Brooke, B. Steward, J. Pollard, and T. Volk (Cambridge: Cambridge University Press, 1983), 54–57; Christopher Howgego, *Ancient History from Coins* (London: Routledge, 1995), 75.

other incidents,²⁴ in both the Republican and Imperial periods, provide some literary evidence that the images and inscriptions on coinage were noticed and often elicited a vivid response.

In addition to the literary evidence, Tonio Hölscher and Paul Zanker have developed a theory by which imperial imagery became embedded in private contexts from Augustus onwards.²⁵ Zanker notes that numismatic imagery appears on "jewelry and utensils, furniture, textiles, walls and stuccoed ceilings, door jambs, clay facings, roof tiles, and even on tomb monuments and marble ash urns."²⁶ It is thus evident that numismatic imagery was one way in which imperial symbols and ideas came to be present in private Roman life. This implies that people did not only notice what was on coinage, but they were demonstrably influenced by them in their personal lives, explicitly through active response and implicitly through culture adaptation.

The third specific methodological area of concern for the use of coinage is the social origin of the coins and the way in which this influences our historical or linguistic reconstruction. Historians have frequently noted that coins are issued by the narrow, upper stratum of society, and thus forming a historical picture based only on numismatic evidence is not only methodological suspicious but may in many circumstances be outright misleading. This admission of a limitation seems obvious. However, rather than one's response to be dismissal of numismatic evidence *en toto*, a more plausible solution is to simply acknowledge that the distillation of historical, social, and philological reconstruction on coinage does not represent the full spectrum of the contemporary social world. However, this does not discount the potential for valid contribution of the evidence, albeit of a relatively narrow section of elite social life. This being said, there are several significant contributions that do pertain to the larger social milieu, as will be discussed in the various case studies below.

---

24. For further evidence that imagery on coins was noticed, especially in the eastern Roman Empire, see Linda-Marie Hans, "Der Kaiser mit dem Schwert," *JNG* 33 (1983): 57–66, esp. 63–64 and n. 21.

25. Paul Zanker, *The Power of Images in the Age of Augustus*, trans. Alan Shapiro (Ann Arbor: University of Michigan Press, 1988), 265–95; T. Hölscher, *Staatsdenkmal und Publikum: Vom Untergang der Republik bis zur Festigung des Kaisertums in Rom*, Konstanzer althistorische Vorträge und Forschungen 9 (Konstanz: Universitätsverlag Konstanz, 1984), 20–32.

26. Zanker, *Power of Images*, 266.

Related to this is whether the extant numismatic record is representative, by ratio, of numbers of ancient coinage minted and circulated in antiquity. An illuminating study by Christopher Howgego found that the absolute number of coins retrieved from an archaeological site was heavily dependent on local factors.[27] Elsewhere he notes that "the hoards left in the ground are the ones that were not recovered in antiquity. Concentrations of coin hoards tend to reflect not prosperity or heavily monetized contexts, but rather the insecurity (particularly warfare) which resulted in owners not recovering their treasure."[28] Hoards, which mainly consist of the more precious metals, may then give a skewed picture of the circulation of coinage, excluding bronze coinage and lower denominations.[29] It is also a relatively crude and obvious fact that we possess only a fraction of a fraction of a fraction of numismatic material that originally circulated in antiquity. Edwin Yamauchi astutely notes the severely limited view that archaeological excavation affords in this regard: only a fraction of what is made or what is written survives, only a fraction of that material is preserved in archaeological sites that have been surveyed, only a fraction of the surveyed sites have been excavated, only a fraction of any excavated site is actually examined, and only a fraction of materials are actually published.[30] Numismatic material that is published generally consists of the large and prestigious museum collections, which naturally marginalizes poor-quality or illegible coins that do not find their way into those collections. There is also the problem of unprovenanced coins that appear in private collections and auction catalogues. Problems abound with inaccurate attribution or failure to recognize inauthentic examples, especially so in the older collections. These can and have misled scholars in the recent past on the very topic under consideration. We therefore will

---

27. Christopher Howgego, "The Supply and Use of Money in the Roman World 200 B.C. to A.D. 300," *JRS* 82 (1992): 1–31.

28. Howgego, *Ancient History from Coins*, 88. See also Richard Duncan-Jones, *Money and Government in the Roman Empire* (Cambridge: Cambridge University Press, 1994), 85.

29. For example, Galba's silver and gold coinage focused on garnering provincial support while bronze coins focused on rallying the urban citizens and featured urban symbols. See Olivier Hekster, "Coins and Messages: Audience Targeting on Coins of Different Denominations?," in *Representation and Perception of Roman Imperial Power*, ed. Paul Erdkamp et al. (Leiden: Brill, 2003), 26.

30. Edwin Yamauchi, *The Stones and the Scriptures* (New York: Holman, 1972), 146–54.

limit our discussion to those numismatic examples that have appeared in peer-reviewed publication outlets and carefully weigh, where necessary, questions of authenticity.

Despite these potential limitations, there are also several methodological strengths of numismatic evidence. First is the relative ubiquity of coinage in archaeological sites and throughout the Mediterranean. The broad geographic distribution of evidence is particularly helpful for lexicography of the New Testament. The composition, dissemination, and reception of the New Testament is not confined to the Levant. Indeed, early Christian missionary interactions span the entire scope of the Mediterranean world. The extant record of contemporaneous coinage that circulated in the geographical areas inhabited by the recipients of Paul's epistles, for example, provide ideal linguistic evidence for comparison. Coinage in these provincial areas of the Roman Empire varied in value, shape, and size as much as they did in type, depiction, and linguistic value. Paul's movement "from city to city and region to region from the years spanning the mid-30s to the mid-50s, exposed him to an extraordinary maze of small change,"[31] examples of which are mostly accessible in the publication of numismatic holdings in main museum collections. This geographical specificity is invaluable for consideration of localized communication in the provinces or cities, particularly in relation to civic rivalries. Furthermore, unlike literary texts, coins can often be precisely dated or at the very least be assigned limited ranges, which allow a clear demarcation for their introduction and circulation.

4. Numismatic Evidence from Laodicea

Phrygia already had a long history of minting coins by the first century CE. Otto Mørkholm traces the silver cistophoros (κιστοφόρος) in Phrygia back into the early to mid-second century BCE, most probably introduced in the years between 175 and 160 BCE as a substitute for Seleucid coins and the tetradrachms of Philetairos.[32] Peter Thonemann also notes that

---

31. Peter Lewis and Ron Bolden, *The Pocket Guide to Saint Paul: Coins Encountered by the Apostle on His Travels* (Kent Town: Wakefield Press, 2002), vii.

32. Otto Mørkholm, *Early Hellenistic Coinage: From the Accession of Alexander to the Peace of Apamaea (336–188 BC)* (Cambridge: Cambridge University Press), 9–10. See also Fred S. Kleiner and Sydney P. Noe, *The Early Cistophoric* (New York: The American Numismatic Society, 1977), 86–89.

the first half of the first century BCE witnessed "a sudden leap in the numbers of communities in Phrygia minting bronze coins in their own name."[33] Leschhorn identifies at least twenty communities producing bronze and brass coinage in Phrygia by the middle of the first century BCE.[34] Despite this apparent abundance, Stephen Mitchell has documented that there was, in fact, a significant shortage of coinage in Asia Minor from the first century BCE and that it was this shortage that catalyzed the allowance for payment of taxes in kind rather than cash.[35] William Metcalf suggests that the increase in mint activities during this period "was clearly to put money into circulation ... and to ensure the functioning of a cash economy."[36] The manner in which this increased production of coinage enhanced the economic circumstances was through encouraging community trade through this so-called small-change monetization of Phrygia.[37]

The geographical positioning of the city contributed significantly to its prosperity. Laodicea was situated on a plateau of the Lycus River Valley at the junction of the north-south road from Pergamum to the Mediterranean and east-west road from Ephesus to the interior of an Asia Minor. As many commentators have noted, the location of the city at a key intersection of major routes enhanced the trade and commercial opportunities of the city. Indeed, the thriving and prosperous city of Laodicea is amply demonstrated in both inscriptional and literary sources of the period. ILaodikeia 48 and 82.1 attest to both Greek and Roman inhabitants of Laodicea involved in business enterprises. Additionally, Strabo attributes the initial growth of Laodicea and its ability to recover after invasion or disaster to the fertility of the region and prosperity of the inhabitants and also notes that one of the benefactors, Polemon son of Zeno, was so impressive that he was appointed as a client king of the region by the Romans (*Geogr.* 12.8.16).[38] In terms of specific business enterprises, Strabo notes the pro-

---

33. Peter Thonemann, "Phrygia: An Anarchist History, 950 BC–AD 100," in *Roman Phrgia*, ed. Peter Thonnemann (Cambridge: Cambridge University Press, 2013), 28.

34. Leschhorn, "Le monnayage," 254.

35. Stephen Mitchell, *Anatolia: Land, Men and Gods in Asia Minor*, 2 vols. (Oxford: Clarendon, 1993), 1:247–50, 256–57.

36. Metcalf, "Regionalism in the Coinage of Asia Minor," 159.

37. Thonemann, "Phrygia," 28.

38. Strabo, *Geogr.* 12.8.16: "Laodiceia, though formerly small, grew large in our time and in that of our fathers, even though it had been damaged by siege in the time of Mithridates Eupator. However, it was the fertility of its territory and the prosper-

duction of the high-quality and desirable black wool, which was a very lucrative local enterprise (Strabo, *Geogr.* 12.8.16),[39] a Laodicean characteristic echoed in both Vitruvius (*Arch.* 8.3.14) and Pliny the Elder (*Nat.* 8.73.190). The only perceived detriment of Laodicea that Strabo highlights is that the region is prone to earthquakes, a phenomenon he attributes to the subterranean rivers (Strabo, *Geogr.* 12.8.16).[40]

---

ity of certain of its citizens that made it great" (Ἡ δὲ Λαοδίκεια, μικρὰ πρότερον οὖσα, αὔξησιν ἔλαβεν ἐφ' ἡμῶν καὶ τῶν ἡμετέρων πατέρων, καίτοι κακωθεῖσα ἐκ πολιορκίας ἐπὶ Μιθριδάτου τοῦ Εὐπάτορος· ἀλλ' ἡ τῆς χώρας ἀρετὴ καὶ τῶν πολιτῶν τινὲς εὐτυχήσαντες μεγάλην ἐποίησαν αὐτήν); "At first Hieron, who left to the people an inheritance of more than two thousand talents and adorned the city with many dedicated offerings, and later Zeno the rhetorician and his son Polemon, the latter of whom, because of his bravery and honesty, was thought worthy even of a kingdom, at first by Antony and later by Augustus" (Ἱέρων μὲν πρότερον, ὃς πλειόνων ἢ δισχιλίων ταλάντων κληρονομίαν κατέλιπε τῷ δήμῳ πολλοῖς τ' ἀναθήμασιν ἐκόσμησε τὴν πόλιν, Ζήνων δὲ ὁ ῥήτωρ ὕστερον καὶ ὁ υἱὸς αὐτοῦ Πολέμων, ὃς καὶ βασιλείας ἠξιώθη διὰ τὰς ἀνδραγαθίας ὑπ' Ἀντωνίου μὲν πρότερον, ὑπὸ Καίσαρος δὲ τοῦ Σεβαστοῦ μετὰ ταῦτα). Translations from Strabo, *Books 10–12*, vol. 5 of *Geography*, trans. Horace Leonard Jones, LCL (Cambridge: Harvard University Press, 1928), 510–11.

39. Strabo, *Geogr.* 12.8.16: "The country round Laodiceia produces sheep that are excellent, not only for the softness of their wool, in which they surpass even the Milesian wool, but also for its raven-black colour, so that the Laodiceians derive splendid revenue from it, as do also the neighbouring Colosseni from the colour which bears the same name" (φέρει δ' ὁ περὶ τὴν Λαοδίκειαν τόπος προβάτων ἀρετὰς οὐκ εἰς μαλακότητα μόνον τῶν ἐρίων, ᾗ καὶ τῶν Μιλησίων διαφέρει, ἀλλὰ καὶ εἰς τὴν κοραξὴν χρόαν, ὥστε καὶ προσοδεύονται λαμπρῶς ἀπ' αὐτῶν· ὥσπερ καὶ οἱ Κολοσσηνοὶ ἀπὸ τοῦ ὁμωνύμου χρώματος πλησίον οἰκοῦντες; trans. Jones). See also ILaodikeia 50, which attests to the association of textile and garment industries.

40. Strabo, *Geogr.* 12.8.16: "And here the Caprus River joins the Maeander, as does also the Lycus, a river of good size, after which the city is called the 'Laodiceia near Lycus. Above the city lies Mt. Cadmus, whence the Lycus flows, as does also another river of the same name as the mountain. But the Lycus flows underground for the most part, and then, after emerging to the surface, unites with the other rivers, thus indicating that the country is full of holes and subject to earthquakes; for if any other country is subject to earthquakes, Laodiceia is, and so is Carura in the neighbouring country" (ἐνταῦθα δὲ καὶ ὁ Κάπρος καὶ ὁ Λύκος συμβάλλει τῷ Μαιάνδρῳ ποταμῷ, ποταμὸς εὐμεγέθης, ἀφ' οὗ καὶ ἡ πρὸς τῷ Λύκῳ Λαοδίκεια λέγεται. ὑπέρκειται δὲ τῆς πόλεως ὄρος Κάδμος, ἐξ οὗ καὶ ὁ Λύκος ῥεῖ, καὶ ἄλλος ὁμώνυμος τῷ ὄρει. τὸ πλέον δ' οὗτος ὑπὸ γῆς ῥυείς, εἶτ' ἀνακύψας συνέπεσεν εἰς ταὐτὸ τοῖς ἄλλοις ποταμοῖς, ἐμφαίνων ἅμα καὶ τὸ πολύτρητον τῆς χώρας καὶ τὸ εὔσειστον· εἰ γάρ τις ἄλλη, καὶ ἡ Λαοδίκεια εὔσειστος, καὶ τῆς πλησιοχώρου δὲ Κάρουρα; trans. Jones). Strabo indicates in 12.8.18 that the city received Roman support for earthquake damage in 20 BCE (see Seuto-

The mint at Laodicea, both in the late Republican and early Imperial period, was notably active, producing coinage with imperial portraiture as well as pseudo-autonomous issues.[41] There are at least 70 provincial coin types from first-century Laodicea presently attested in 538 extant specimens catalogued in *Roman Provincial Coinage* and its supplements.[42] Adding to this diverse image is Andrew Burnett, Michel Amandry, and Ian Carradice's consideration of the possibility that Laodicea was the home base for a numismatic die engraver who serviced the upper Maeander valley and southern Phrygia.[43] In sum, the picture, in Phrygia generally, and at Laodicea in particular, is that of a diverse and extensive program of minting and circulation. Our following case study analysis will seek to elucidate themes significantly informed by the numismatic record and relate these to concerns that are particularly relevant for New Testament studies. Although a somewhat artificial division, we will pursue these concerns along the following lines: (1) Laodicea's relationship with Rome and its cultivation of imperial relations, (2) the polyvalent religious identities in

---

nius, *Tib.* 8). Tacitus (*Ann.* 14.27) notes that on another occasion (60 CE) Laodicea declined Roman support for repairs preferring to recover through recourse to its own resources; remarkable attestation of the wealth of the city. For further discussion, see section 4.3 below.

41. *Pseudo-autonomous* is the typical nomenclature for provincial coins without the depiction of the emperor's portrait on the obverse.

42. Coinage produced under Augustus (*RPC* 1.2892, seven examples [Seitalkas]; *RPC* 1.2893–2895, forty-two examples [Zeuxis philalethes]; *RPC* 1.2896–2897, twenty-three examples [Sosthenes]; *RPC* 1.2898–2900, thirty-six examples [Anto Polemon philopatris]); Tiberius (*RPC* 1.2901–2005, fifty-five examples [Pythes Pythou]; *RPC* 1.2906–2907, thirty-seven examples [Dioskourides]; *RPC* 1.2908–2910, twenty-nine examples [Pythes Pythou II]; *RPC* 1.2911, thirteen examples [Dioskourides II]); Claudius (*RPC* 1.2912–2916 [inclusive of 2912A in *RPC Supp.* 4, 37, and S-2913A in *RPC Supp.* 1–3, 127, details of which see below], sixty-three examples [Anto Polemon, son of Zenon, priest for the fourth time]); Nero (*RPC* 1.2917–2918, twenty-six examples [Gaios Postomos]; *RPC* 1.2919, nine examples [Krateros nomothetes]; *RPC* 1.2920–2925, sixty-nine examples [Ioulios Andronikos euergetes and Ioulia Zenonis]; *RPC* 1.2926–2927, twenty-five examples [Aineias]; *RPC* 1.2928, eighteen examples [Anto Zenon, son of Zenon]), Vespasian (*RPC* 2.1268, three examples [no personal name]; *RPC* 2.1269–1270, five examples [Ioulios Andronikos euergetes]; *RPC* 2.1271, four examples [Marcellus procus]); Titus (*RPC* 2.1272–1280, fifty-three examples [Gaios Ioulios Kotys and Klaudia Zeonis]); Domitian, seventy-five examples (*RPC* 2.1281–1296 [Kornelios Dioskourides]), and three further types that are possibly late first century CE attested in fifteen examples (*RPC* 2.1297–1299).

43. *RPC* 1, p. 376, 475.

Laodicea, and (3) other local traditions and difficulties in distilling a clear view of the issues.

4.1. Laodicea's Relationship with Rome and Its Cultivation of Imperial Relations

The mid-twentieth century witnessed the canvasing of a minority view that postulated that the expansion and development of the Roman Empire should be classified as defensive imperialism, accidental, and lacking any deliberate policy of expansion or intent by the Roman state.[44] The same has also been suggested of Rome's cultural approach to conquered territory and the process of Romanization. Martin Millett, for example, proposed that the native elite were responsible for initiating the change and setting new fashions,[45] which at very best obfuscates Rome's role in the cultivation of the elites' perpetuation of Roman ideals. Both these views of Roman passive expansion (Badien et al.) and passive Romanization (Millett et al.) have been tested throughout the last half of the twentieth century and been found to be wanting in several regards,[46] not least in its omission of serious consideration of numismatic material.

---

44. Ernst Badian, *Roman Imperialism in the Late Republic* (Oxford: Blackwell, 1968), 29–43; M. Cary, *A History of Rome down to the Reign of Constantine* (London: Macmillan, 1954), 143–45; Howard H. Scullard, *A History of the Roman World, 753–146 BC* (London: Methuen, 1951), 141–45; Paul Veyne, "Y a-t-il eu un Impérialisme Romain?," *Mélanges de l'Ecole française de Rome* 87 (1975): 793–855.

45. Martin Millett, *The Romanization of Britain: An Essay in Archaeological Interpretation* (Cambridge: Cambridge University Press, 1990), 99–101.

46. On the former see Peter A. Brunt, review of *Die Aussenpolitik des Augustus und die augusteische Dichtung*, by H. G. Meyer, *JRS* 53 (1963): 170–76; William V. Harris, *War and Imperialism in Republican Rome, 327–70 B.C.* (Oxford: Oxford University Press, 1985), 54–104; Benjamin Isaac, *The Limits of Empire: The Roman Army in the East* (Oxford: Oxford University Press, 1990), 19–53, 372–418; C. R. Whittaker, *Frontiers of the Roman Empire* (Baltimore: John Hopkins Press, 1994), 31–59. On the latter, see Francis H. Haverfield, *The Romanization of Roman Britain* (Oxford: Oxford University Press, 1915), 11–14; Peter A. Brunt, "The Romanization of the Local Ruling Classes in the Roman Empire," in *Assimilation et résistance à la culture gréco-romaine dans le monde ancien: Travaux du VIe Congrès international d'études classiques*, ed. D. M. Pippidi (Paris: Belles Lettres, 1974), 161–73; Peter Garnsey and Richard P. Saller, *The Roman Empire: Economy, Society and Culture* (Oakland: University of California Press, 1987), 186–95.

Asia Minor is certainly no exception in this regard. Among others, Bruce W. Winter has argued that Asia Minor displays civic obligation that is more consistent with Roman rather than Greek traditions.[47] Mitchell notes that the "diffusion of the cult of Augustus and of the other members of his family in Asia Minor and the Greek East from the beginning of the empire was rapid, indeed almost instantaneous."[48] The aspirations and manner of governance of many cities in western Asia Minor in the first century CE were defined by interest in/and allegiance to Rome.[49] This is demonstrably visible on multiple levels including governance where the Greek ideals of independent city-state had been supplanted by Roman civic obedience and duty. This commitment to and association with Rome included (both real and perceived) benefits to the local community. Barbara Levick has gone so far as to suggest that the wellbeing of the citizens in Asia Minor primarily depended on participating in the Roman system of imperial expectations and relations.[50]

Laodicea's aspiration to demonstrate her positive standing with Rome is celebrated on the so-called Ὁμόνοια (lit. "oneness of mind") coinage. The Roman ideal of *homonoia* contrasts sharply with historic Greek civil unrest, from whence the term ὁμόνοια derived.[51] A. R. R. Sheppard notes the central role Concordia performed in administering this dimension of Roman life during the Imperial period, and H. L. Wilson highlights the importance of the cult of Concordia in its relation to the imperial family.[52] It is certainly unproblematic to document widespread attestation of this connection in both epigraphic (*CIL* 2.3349; 3.14195; 4.91–94;

---

47. Bruce W. Winter, *Seek the Welfare of the City: Christians as Benefactors and Citizens* (Grand Rapids: Eerdmans, 1994), 124–43.

48. Mitchell, *Anatolia*, 1:100.

49. Theodor Mommsen argues for the intensified Romanization of Phrygia during this period, see Theodor Mommsen, *The Provinces of the Roman Empire: The European Provinces* (Chicago: University of Chicago Press, 1968).

50. Barbara Levick, *Roman Colonies in Southern Asia Minor* (Oxford: Clarendon, 1967), 104–5.

51. Peter Funke, *Homonoia und Arche: Athen und die griechische Staatenwelt vom Ende des Peloponnesischen Krieges bis zum Königfrieden (404/3–287/6 v. Chr.)* (Wiesbaden: Steiner, 1980); Andrés Rosler, *Political Authority and Obligation in Aristotle* (Oxford: Oxford University Press, 2005), 210–14.

52. A. R. R. Sheppard, "Homonoia in the Greek Cities of the Roman Empire," *Ancient Society* 15–17 (1984–1986): 229–52; H. L. Wilson, "A New Collegium at Rome," *American Journal of Archaeology* 16.1 (1912): 94–96.

8.15447) and numismatic (Augustus *RIC* 1.72; Tiberius 1.55; Nero 1.48; Galba 1.35) evidence.

Turning to provincial coinage at Laodicea, we note the following. *RPC* 1.2912 is an issue under Claudius (50–54 CE). The obverse reads ΔΗΜΟΣ ΛΑΟΔΙΚΕΩΝ ΚΑΙ ΖΜΥΡΝΑΙΩΝ ("people of Laodicea and Smyrna") with the appropriate accompanying laureate head of the Demos of Laodicea facing the laureate head of the Demos of Smyrna. The obverse has ΕΠΙ ΙΕΡΕΩΣ ΑΝΤΩΝΙΟΥ ΠΟ ΥΙΟΥ ΖΗΝΩΝΟΣ ("at the time of the priest Antonios Polemon, son of Zenon")[53] with a depiction of Zeus Laodiceus standing facing left with eagle and staff. A similar *homonoia* issue under Nero, *RPC* 1.2928 has ΝΕΡΩΝ ΣΕΒΑΣΤΟΣ ("Nero Augustus") with laureate head on the obverse facing right. The reverse depicts the Demoi of Laodicea and Smyrna clasping hands and holding scepters and inscribes the names of the two magistrates on the perimeter, ΑΝΤΩ[ΝΙΟΣ] ΖΗΝΩΝΟΣ ΖΗΝΩΝ ΥΙΟΣ ΛΑΟΔΙΚΕΩΝ ΖΜΥΡΝΑΙΩΝ ("Antonios, son of Zenon and Zenon"), with ΟΜΗΡΟΣ ("harmony") between the figures. A third example of *homonoia* coinage appears during the reign of Vespasian under the Magistrate Marcellus procos. *RPC* 2.1271 inscribes ΔΗΜΟ ΛΑΟΔΙΚΕΩΝ ("people of Laodicea") with the laureate head of Demos facing right. The reverse has ΟΜΟΝΟΙΑ ΕΠΙ ΜΑΡΚΕΛΛΟΥ ΑΝΘΥ(ΠΑΤΟΣ) ("concord at the time of Marcellus, proconsul") in five lines in a laurel wreath. In 70–73 CE Titus Clodius Eprius Marcellus held the proconsul, and it seems entirely probably that *RPC* 2.1271 was issued after a period of civil strife in Asia in order to ease tensions in the region.[54]

Peter R. Franke and D. A. O. Klose agree that there does not appear to be an overall explanation for the *homonoia* coinage, and Burnett et al. suggest that they are "a single manifestation of many different sets of circumstances (rivalry between cities, political or religious links, bound-

---

53. *RPC* 1.2914 indicates Antonios Polemon was priest for the fourth time during this period.

54. Peter J. Thonemann, *The Menander Valley: A Historical Geography from Antiquity to Byzantium* (Cambridge: Cambridge University Press, 2011), 152. For other *homonoia* coinage from the broader region during the reign of Domitian see *RPC* 2.920 (Pergamum and Ephesus), *RPC* 2.1079–1093 (Ephesus and Smyrna), *RPC* 2.1332 (Philadelphia and Ephesus), *RPC* 2.1317 (Sardis and Smyrna), and *RPC* 2.1369 (Aezani and Cadi).

ary disputes)."[55] Examples in the Julio-Claudian period (such as *RPC* 1.1553 [Thessalonica and Rome], *RPC* 1.2143 [Amisus and Rome stand facing], *RPC* 1.2988 [Pergamum and Sardis under Augustus], *RPC* 1.5445 [Hypaepa and Sardis under Tiberius], *RPC* 1.5446 [Hypaepa and Sardis], *RPC* 1.2912 [Laodicea and Smyrna under Claudius] noted above, *RPC* 1.2928 [Laodicea and Smyrna under Nero] noted above) indicate that alliance coinages had not yet been standardized. For instance, the word OMONOIA does not always occur, rather two cities can simply be listed (*RPC* 1.1553, *RPC* 1.2143), joined by καί (1.2912), or even have a variant of OMONOIA, see also OMHPOΣ (1.2928)—which may refer to the person responsible for the issue rather than the relationship per se, but it is evident that the phraseology is not standardized. So much more is the case when one includes the "hundred different issues of homonoia ('concord') coinages, recording concord between two or more cities ... [made] over seventy cities under the empire."[56]

Although there may not have been a homogenous catalyst for these *homonoia* issues, it was a distinct mechanism by which "the coin issues served as symbols that mediated the power within regional alliances, bolstered the prestige of the divine realm in human activity and provided the glue that bound together the political and the cosmic spheres."[57] It is readily apparent that the pronouncement of harmonious relationships between two cities on coinage was a meaningful cultural symbol, which implemented a local structure and enhanced civic identity, and an opportunity for the urban elite to operate as a "cultural conveyor and construct of Roman imperialism,"[58] precisely where the Roman ideal of *pax* was embodied and eagerly embraced.

---

55. Peter R. Franke, "Zu den Homonoia-Münzen Kleinasiens," in *Stuttgarter Kolloquium zur Historische Geographie des Altertums I, 1980*, ed. Eckart Olshausen (Bonn: Habelt, 1987), 81–102; Dietrich O. A. Klose, *Die Münzprägung von Smyrna in der römischen Kaiserzeit* (Berlin: de Gruyter, 1987), 44–63; *RPC* 1, 48.

56. Simon R. F. Price, *Rituals and Power: The Roman Imperial Cult in Asia Minor* (Cambridge: Cambridge University Press, 1985), 126. On distribution and frequency see Dietmar Kienast, "Die Homonoiaverträge in der romischen Kaiserzeit," *JNG* 14 (1964): 51–64; Jean Pierre Callu, *La Politique Monetaire Desempereurs Romains de 238 à 311* (Paris: de Boccard, 1969), 29–33.

57. Douglas R. Edwards, "Defining the Web of Power in Asia Minor: The Novelist Chariton and His City Aphrodisias," *JAAR* 63.3 (1994): 710.

58. C. R. Whittaker, "Imperialism and Culture: The Roman Initiative," in *Dialogues in Roman Imperialism: Power, Discourse and Discrepant Experience in the*

Laodicea, like the other cities mentioned in Rev 2-3, was deeply rooted in the Roman administrative, commercial, and religious systems represented by the *homonoia* coinage. The early Christian community in Asia Minor generally, and Laodicea in particular, would have been under considerable pressure to participate in and support notions of imperial identity. Arjan Zuiderhoek and Wouter Vanacker parse this identity as "belonging to, and identification with, the *Imperium Romanum* ... [namely,] ideological notions, ideas, institutions and practices produced by the centre of power and/or its representatives."[59] In Laodicea the *Imperium Romanum* took many forms, including an impressive stadium (280 m x 70 m) dedicated by Titus in 79 CE, decorative city gates, two theaters (the latter one built under Hadrian), baths, agora, temples, and a sophisticated sanitation system that was masterfully engineered.[60] Several of these architectural features are accented in the iconography and inscriptions on first century Laodicean coinage.

According to the most up to date record of coinage from Laodicea,[61] Domitian issued sixteen coin-types during his reign, preserved in seventy-five extant coins as published in *RPC* 2.1281-1296. Almost 40 percent of the Domitian types (six out of sixteen) variously depict, on the reverse, an imperial temple as either a tetrastyle (four column, *RPC* 2.1284, 2.1286, 2.1287, 2.1290), or hexastyle (six column, *RPC* 2.1281, 2.1291) façade rising above a flight of three or four steps.[62] S. J. Friesen suggests that the

---

Roman Empire, ed. David J. Mattingly (Ann Arbor: Cushing-Malloy, 1997), 145. Whittaker also notes that the "instruments of power to realize this imperial ideology were the army and the city.... [The] ideology of cities coupled them to the moral order of society as a whole and to the *securitas* of empire" (144).

59. Arjan Zuiderhoek and Wouter Vanacker, "Introduction: Imperial Identities in the Roman World," in *Imperial Identities in the Roman World*, ed. Wouter Vanacker and Arjun Zuiderhoek (London: Routledge, 2017), 2. See further Andrew Lintott, *Imperium Romanum: Politics and Administration* (London: Routledge, 1993).

60. Stadium: ILaodikeia 15; Gates: C. Şimşek, *Laodikeia (Laodikeia ad Lycum)* (Istanbul: Yayinlari, 2007), 92-102; Theatres: Şimşek, *Laodikeia*, 207-20; Baths: ILaodikeia 14; Agora: Şimşek, *Laodikeia*, 221-24. On temple, see further below; On sanitation: ILoad 13-14; Gerald L. Stevens, *Revelation: The Past and Future of John's Apocalypse* (Eugene, OR: Pickwick, 2014), 351.

61. *RPC* 1 and *RPC* 2, read together with supplementary material in *RPC Supp.* 1-3, *RPC Supp.* 4, and *RPC Supp.* 5.

62. Thus far the imperial sacral structure has not been located, presumably because only a limited area of the city has been excavated. 1991 was the first time modern methods of archaeology were applied to Laodicea. Attention was directed

omission of the two columns in tetrastyle depiction is deliberate in order to provide space for the engraver to include images of statues.[63] However, this cannot be consistently applied to even this very short series of Domitian, as *RPC* 2.1290 and 2.1291 have only four columns and no depiction of figures between. Nonetheless, the obverses of the series depict Domitian (*RPC* 2.1286, 2.1287), Domitia (2.1281, 2.1290, 2.1291), or both Domitian and Domitia (2.1284).

Of particular interest is *RPC* 2.1284, which in addition to the facing busts of the imperial couple, has the inscription ΔΟΜΙΤΙΑΝΟC ΚΑΙCΑΡ CΕΒΑCΤΟC ΓΕΡΜΑΝΙΚΟC ΔΟΜΙΤΙΑ CΕΒΑCΤΗ ("Domitian Caesar Augustus Germanicus, Domitia Augusta"). The title Germanicus would imply that the coin was struck subsequent to Domitian's victory over the Chatti (83 CE), where he assumed that title.[64] This is reinforced through other military themes that are evident on this particular coin, including the cuirassed bust of Domitian on the obverse, and the inscription ΕΠΙΝΕΙΚΙΟC ("of victory" or "triumphal") on the architrave of the four-column temple on the reverse. The male and female figures (Domitian and Domitia) are enclosed within the temple also support this military picture with a victory trophy of Nike held between them. Domitian is also cuirassed and holds a spear in his left hand, while Domitia holds a scepter in her right.

The obverse of *RPC* 2.1281 depicts the draped bust of Domitia facing right, with accompanying inscription ΔΟΜΙΤΙΑ CΕΒΑCΤΗ. The reverse has the name of the magistrate, ΔΙΑ ΚΟΡ(ΝΕΛΙΟC) ΔΙΟCΚΟΥΡΙΔΟΥ, an ethnic identification, ΛΑΟΔΙΚΕΩΝ, and the aforementioned impressive hexastyle imperial temple. Although the emperor cult was officially introduced to Asia Minor at Pergamum in 29 BCE through the construction of a temple to Roma and Augustus,[65] it

---

primarily toward the Severan-era nymphaeum, the results of which were published in Jean des Gagniers et al., *Laodicée du Lycos: Le Nymphée, Campagnes 1961–1963* (Paris: de Boccard, 1969).

63. Steven J. Friesen, *Imperial Cults and the Apocalypse of John: Reading Revelation in the Ruins* (Oxford: Oxford University Press, 2001), 61–62.

64. Huttner, *Early Christianity in the Lycus Valley*, 180; Peter Kneissl, *Die Siegestitulatur der römischen Kaiser* (Göttingen: Vandenhoeck & Ruprecht, 1969), 43–48.

65. Christian Habicht, "Die augusteische Zeit und das erste Jahrhundert nach Christi Geburt," in *Les Culte Des Souverains Dans L'Empire Romain: 7 Exposés Suivis de Discussions*, ed. W. den Boer (Geneva: Fondation Hardt pour l'étude de l'antiquité classique, 1973), 55.

was eagerly embraced by cities of the Lycus Valley. Inscriptions and other sources from the region indicate that the influential Antonii Zenones/ Polemones family was a significant part of advancing the emperor cult at Laodicea and a role that Ulrich Huttner describes as introducing initiatives that "support ... [the] cultic veneration of the imperial house."[66] Allegiance to the imperial cult, as demonstrated on coinage of Laodicea surveyed above, is consistent with the epigraphic evidence. In an honorary inscription on a marble slab found at Attouda (*MAMA* 6.66), Livia, the wife of Augustus, is identified as Λιβίαν θεάν, γυν[αῖκα αὐτοκράτορος] | Καίσαρος θεοῦ [υἱοῦ θεοῦ Σεβαστοῦ].[67]

A frequently overlooked dimension of this theme at Laodicea is the physical placement of the image of the emperor on a provincial coin. Typical for a standard provincial Roman coin of Laodicea is to depict the emperor's bust on the obverse and an image of a deity (typically Zeus but other gods are also copiously attested) on the reverse. This phenomenon is clearly apparent in Laodicea under Augustus (e.g., *RPC* 1.2893, 2894), Tiberius (e.g., *RPC* 1.2901, 2908), Claudius (e.g., *RPC* 1.2913, 2916), Nero (e.g., *RPC* 1.2917, 2919), Vespasian (e.g., *RPC* 2.1268, 1269), Titus (e.g., *RPC* 2.1273), and Domitian (e.g., *RPC* 2.1282, 1283). This strategic positioning of portraits functioned on various levels to emphasize the connection between divinity and emperor. The obverse of coins, which hitherto had carried an image of the head of gods, now displayed a youthful Augustus and subsequently other emperors. Ramsay highlights the significance of the subtle but profound iconographic shift when he notes, "there was nothing else to hold the province together in a unity except the enthusiastic loyalty which all felt to the Roman imperial government."[68] This theme is particularly evident in *RPC* 2.1295, a coin from Laodicea under Domitian, which depicts a helmeted and draped bust of Roma with the ethnic inscription ΛΑΟΔΙΚΕΩΝ on the obverse, and then, quite remarkably, depicts the celebrated image of Rome's founding of the wolf and twins on the reverse. *RPC* 2.1293 and 1294 have a similar bust

---

66. Huttner, *Early Christianity in the Lycus Valley*, 180. See also ILaodikeia 53; Peter J. Thonemann, "Polemo, Son of Polemo (Dio, 59.12.2)," *EA* 37 (2004): 144–50.

67. Compare the dedication to Zeus Soter and the divine emperors (ΘΕΟΙ ΣΕΒΑΣΤΟΙ), T. Ritti, H. H. Baysal, E. Miranda, F. Guizzi, *Catalogo delle iscrizioni latine e greche, Museo archeologico di Denizli-Pamukkale* (Naples: Università degli Studi, 2008), 94, §29.

68. Ramsay, *Letters to the Seven Churches*, 84.

of Roma on the obverse. The composite picture at Laodicea is one of the aristocracy's imperial indebtedness, political commitment, and ideological allegiance to Rome.

In this light the narratives of the New Testament that intersect with the immediate region or city of Laodicea (Col 2:1; 4:13, 15, 16; Rev 1:11; 3:14) would have ostensibly been, at the very least, in ideological tension with the competing claims for allegiance between the *Imperium Romanum*, which demanded the loyalty of its subjects, and the distinct claims of the early Christians regarding the superiority of their κύριος over the imperial κύριος. This is distinctly highlighted in the broader context of the apocalyptic proclamation to Laodicea (cf. Rev 1:8; 22:21 [κύριος]; 3:14 [ἀμήν]; 19:16 [κύριος κυρίων]) and the rhetoric of empire in Colossians (Col 2:15 [τὰς ἀρχὰς καὶ τὰς ἐξουσίας]), among many other examples that have been investigated.[69]

4.2. Polyvalent Religious Identities in Laodicea

The imperial cult (noted above) was not the only expression of communal identity in Laodicea. Indeed, there were a great variety of temples and diversity of gods and goddesses in and around the city. No less than a dozen deities, a significant portion of the Greco-Roman pantheon, were current throughout the first century. This diversity of tradition and local interest is well represented on the coinage of the city and provides a distinct window into the religious, socioeconomic, and political matrix of Laodicea.

By far the most popular divinity at Laodicea was Zeus. The triple Syrian Gate dedicated by Vespasian in 79 CE has an inscription (84–85 CE) that associates Zeus and Domitian Διὶ Μεγίστωι Σωτῆρι καὶ Αὐτοκράτορι [Δομιτιανῶι] Καίσαρι ("for Zeus the greatest saviour and Imperator Domitian").[70] It is thus no surprise to see Zeus feature prominently on the iconography of coinage in Laodicea, including several examples under Augustus (*RPC* 1.2893, 2894, 2896, 3898), Tiberius (1.2901, 2906, 2908),

---

69. Among other good works are Richard A. Horsley, ed., *Paul and Empire: Religion and Power in Roman Imperial Society* (Harrisburg: Trinity Press International), 1997, and Horsley, ed., *In the Shadow of Empire: Reclaiming the Bible as a History of Faithful Resistance* (Louisville: Westminster John Knox, 2008).

70. ILaodikeia 24b. See des Gagniers's discussion of earlier traditions of Zeus in the region based on Pliny, *Nat.* 5.105 in Gagniers et al., *Laodicée du Lycos*, 1.

Claudius (1.2912, 2913, 2914), Nero (1.2917, 2919, 2920, 2921, 2922, 2923, 2926), Vespasian (2.1268, 1269, 1270), and Domitian (2.1282, 1288, 1292).

Just outside the urban center of Laodicea, on the road toward Carura, Strabo, *Geogr.* 12.8.20 records that "between Laodiceia and Carura is a temple of Mên Carus, as it is called, which is held in remarkable veneration. In my own time a great Herophileian school of medicine has been established by Zeuxis, and afterwards carried on by Alexander Philalethes" (Μεταξὺ δὲ τῆς Λαοδικείας καὶ τῶν Καρούρων ἱερόν ἐστι Μηνὸς Κάρου καλούμενον, τιμώμενον ἀξιολόγως. συνέστηκε δὲ καθ' ἡμᾶς διδασκαλεῖον Ἡροφιλείων ἰατρῶν μέγα ὑπὸ Ζεύξιδος, καὶ μετὰ ταῦτα Ἀλεξάνδρου τοῦ Φιλαλήθους; trans. Jones). Representations of the god Men wearing a Phrygian cap are fairly common for the period and are attested in Laodicea. *RPC* 1.2907 is a small bronze issue of Dioskourides under Tiberius which depicts a bust of Men, wearing a Phrygian cap facing right on the obverse with ethnic ΛΑΟΔΙΚΕΩΝ. Similar iconography of Men with a cap occurs on *RPC* 1.2927, also from Laodicea, by Aineias under Nero. Cognizant that Huttner cautions against automatically assuming syncretism with Asclepius, which E. Lane notes is rare in the ancient world,[71] we note with cautious optimism that Zeuxis Philalethes, the director of the medical center under Augustus, also minted coins as magistrate at Laodicea in ca. 15 BC with the rod of Asclepius, the god of healing, on the reverse. *RPC* 1.2895 is a leaded bronze issue that has, on the obverse, a laureate head facing right with *lituus* (curved augural staff) in right field and ΣΕΒΑΣΤΟΣ inscribed in left. The obverse has ΖΕΥΞΙΣ ΘΙΛΑΛΗΘΗΣ in two horizontal lines above a serpent-entwined staff, with ΛΑΟΔΙΚΕΩΝ below. The connection with and interest in Asclepius, the god of healing, given Zeuxis's role is particularly appropriate.

Although there is no recorded oracle of Apollo in Laodicea, the appeal of Apollo was fervent. Louis Robert records a series of twenty-five inscriptions at the shrine of Apollo in Clarus (17 km northwest of Ephesus), which record a cultic delegation from Laodicea traveling over 200 km to consult the oracle of Apollo every year at its height.[72] This interest in Apollo is also reflected in the coinage of Laodicea. *RPC* 1.2903 displays, on the obverse, the laureate bust of Apollo facing lyre to right, with ethnic inscription to

---

71. Huttner, *Early Christianity in the Lycus Valley*, 180; Eugene Lane, *Interpretations and Testimonia*, vol. 3 of *Corpus Monumentorum Religionis dei Menis* (Leiden: Brill, 1976), 84.

72. Louis Robert, "Les inscriptions," in Gagniers et al., *Laodicée du Lycos*, 299–303.

left, ΛΑΟΔΙΚΕΩΝ. The reverse has the name of the magistrate ΠΥΘΗΣ ΠΥΘΟΥ ("Pythes, son of Pythes") in two vertical lines upwards to left and right of a serpent-entwined altar, which is surmounted by headdress of Isis. *RPC* 1.2905 and 1.2909 similarly have, on the obverse, the laureate head of Apollo facing right, but *RPC* 1.2905 has lyre to left and monogram to right, whereas 1.2909 has lyre to the right and ΛΑΟΔΙΚΕΩΝ to the left. Both *RPC* 1.2905 and 1.2909 depict the headdress of Isis on the reverse, but *RPC* 1.2909 has the headdress surmounted on an altar with the name of the magistrate ΠΥΘΗΣ ΠΥΘΟΥ ΔΙΣ ("Pythes, son of Pythes, the second"), rather than ΛΑΟΔΙΚΕΩΝ as per *RPC* 1.2905. The sustained interest in representing Apollo on the coinage of Laodicea throughout the breadth of the first century, including issues under Augustus (*RPC* 1.2903), Tiberius (1.2905, 1.2909), and Domitian (2.1294) is testament to the appeal of Apollo to the inhabitants of the city.

Depictions of and references to other gods are also evidenced on the first century coinage of Laodicea, albeit less regularly than those surveyed above. They are nonetheless important in providing a more accurate picture of the breadth of numismatic themes. Deities attested include Aphrodite (*RPC* 1.2904, 1.2910, 1.2924, 1.2925), Isis (1.2903, 1.2905, 1.2909; 2.1278), Hera (2.1282), and Roma (2.1279, 2.1280, 2.1293, 2.1294, 2.1295, 2.1297).

4.3. Other Local Traditions and Comparative Statistics of Production

There are several other motifs that emerge from the coinage of Laodicea throughout the first century, two of which warrant brief further comment. First, a consistent theme in literary, epigraphic, and also numismatic sources is that of the abundant wealth of the city and region. As was highlighted in the survey of literary and epigraphic sources for the history and background of the city, the geographical positioning of the city contributed significantly to its prosperity (Strabo, *Geogr.* 12.8.16), as did its thriving economy (Vitruvius, *Arch.* 8.3.14; Pliny the Elder, *Nat.* 8.73.190). This picture of economic prosperity in Laodicea, which even Cicero acknowledges and recommends as a place for financial services (Cicero, *Fam.* 3.5.4, *Att.* 5.15.2), is celebrated in the iconography of the coinage. *RPC* 1.2897, a leaded bronze minted by the magistrate Sosthenes under Augustus, depicts a capricorn with cornucopia on the obverse facing right, along with the inscription ΣΕΒΑΣΤΟΣ. The reverse has three ears of corn and accompanying ethnic and magistrate identification, ΛΑΟΔΙΚΕΩΝ

ΣΩΣΘΕΝΗΣ. Similarly, an issue under Titus by Klaudia Zenonis has the helmeted bust of Roma facing right on the obverse and on the reverse has the ethnic and cornucopia. These symbols of abundance and nourishment, irrespective of its Greek or Roman aetiological account,[73] provides a vivid symbol for a city to proclaim its prosperous status.

Similar displays of wealth and status are evident in the titles of Laodicean magistrates. RPC 1.2920 is a large bronze depicting a veiled bust of Boule facing the laureate head of Demos with accompanying inscription on the obverse, ΒΟΥΛΗ ΔΗΜΟΣ ΛΑΟΔΙΚΕΩΝ. The reverse has Zeus standing left with a staff and eagle with the name of the magistrate and title, ΙΟΥΛΙΟΣ ΑΝΔΡΟΝΙΚΟΣ ΕΥΕΡΓΕΤΗΣ ΛΑΟΔΙΚΕΩΝ ("Ioulios Andronikos, benefactor, of the Laodiceans"). It is significant that this issue accenting benefaction is dated to 62 CE, a period shortly following the earthquake of 60 CE and Laodicea's sufficiency to rebuild without Roman funds or monetary assistance. Tacitus records that "In the same year, Laodicea, one of the famous Asiatic cities, was laid in ruins by an earthquake, but recovered by its own resources, without assistance from ourselves" (*Eodem anno ex inlustribus Asiae urbibus Laodicea tremore terrae prolapsa, nullo a nobis remedio, propriis opibus revaluit*; *Ann.* 14.27).[74] RPC 2.1269 has the laureate head of Vespasian facing right on the obverse with inscription ΟΥΕΣΠΑΣΙΑΝΟΣ ΚΑΙΣΑΡ ΣΕΒΑΣΤΟΣ, and Zeus standing facing left on the reverse, with the name and then title of the magistrate, ΕΥΕΡΓΕΤΗΣ ("benefactor"), accompanied by the ethnic, ΛΑΟΔΙΚΕΩΝ. These examples of numismatic displays of benefaction are not surprising, given the quantity and admiration of benefaction in the city in its recent past. Strabo, for instance, notes that an individual of extraordinary wealth gave 2,000 talents to the city of Laodicea in the first century BCE, in addition to the civic improvements donated for public benefit (*Geogr.* 12.8.16).

The second theme that relates to coinage that deserves further consideration is the volume of coinage minted by the city of Laodicea in the first century and how this might compare with other locales. We noted above (§2) Leschhorn's landmark study, nuanced by Ann Johnston's com-

---

73. Greek: David Leeming, *The Oxford Companion to World Mythology* (Oxford: Oxford University Press, 2005), 13; Roman: Fears, "Cult of Virtues and Roman Imperial Ideology," 827–948.

74. Translation from Tacitus, *Annals: Books 13–16*, trans. John Jackson, LCL (Cambridge: Harvard University Press, 1937), 150–51.

ments, on the distribution and pattern of coinage in Asia Minor where his focus was primarily on the number of cities issuing coins.[75] However, our question at this point is sharpened considerably. How does the output of coinage at Laodicea, in terms of the numerical volume of coins minted, as well as their great variety of type, compare with the volume and type in other cities in Asia Minor and beyond? There are several models of die estimation formulae, in both absolute and relative terms, that have been proposed and contested over the last thirty years.[76] It is rare to have a full record of the output of ancient coinage and to be able to compare it directly with coin issues, such as with the Amphictionic coinage of Delphi.[77] Preferably numismatists attempt to develop statistical methods to calculate output at a < 95 percent confidence interval. Typically this involves, (1) an estimate of the number of dies used through detailed die studies which catalogue and link the slight variations of letter forms or relative placement of features of the coin in the hand cut dies, multiplied by, (2) an estimate of how many coins were struck per die. The difficulty in this process is the potential for methodological issues such as sample size, random selection of samples, assumptions regarding the consistent number of coin-strikes per die, et cetera ... any of which has the potential to render the estimation wildly inaccurate. Warren W. Esty has admirably attempted to preempt and minimize these biases in his own model, but no one model has emerged as the scholarly consensus among numismatists.[78]

Let us now return to the question of coinage in Asia Minor more broadly and Laodicea in particular. Although some preliminary work has been carried out on die studies of the cistophoric coinage of Asia Minor

---

75. Leschhorn, "Le monnayage"; see also Johnston, "Greek Imperial Statistics."

76. Christopher Howgego, "Coin Circulation and the Integration of the Roman Economy," *JRA* 7 (1994): 5–21; T. V. Buttrey, "Calculating Ancient Coin Production: Facts and Fantasies," *NumC* 153 (1993): 338–45; Buttrey, "Calculating Ancient Coin Production 2: Why It Cannot Be Done," *NumC* 154 (1999): 342–52; Buttrey, "The Content and Meaning of Coin Hoards," *JRA* 12 (1999): 526–32.

77. Philip Kinns, "The Amphictionic Coinage Reconsidered," *NumC* 143 (1983): 1–22.

78. Warren W. Esty, "Estimating the Size of a Coinage," *NumC* 144 (1984): 180–83; Esty, "Estimation of the Size of a Coinage: A Survey and Comparison of Methods," *NumC* 146 (1986): 185–215. See the critique of Esty in C. S. S. Lyon, "Die Estimation: Some Experiments with Simulated Samples of a Coinage," *British Numismatic Journal* 59 (1989): 1–12.

during the Republic,[79] a detailed die study of the Laodicean coinage in conjunction with a comprehensive hoard analysis remains a desideratum for numismatic studies. In part, the difficulty is highlighted by William E. Metcalf who notes that, "in theory, with a large enough sample, it would be possible to document the entire history of a coinage based on the history of its dies."[80] But he willingly concedes that for many samples that are large, a "study by die is a practical impossibility."[81] Therefore in the current absence of either a detailed die study or agreed upon formula for a "die to coin production ratio," we must appropriately nuance our view on the matter. However, if we were tempted to offer a crude summative statement on Laodicea's output, with the ready admission of its rudimentary and premature computation, one could note that within Asia Minor, Phrygia does seem to have the largest number of mints in operation during the first century,[82] with an average of eleven mints per emperor from Augustus to Domitian. By similar analysis, most other regions of Asia Minor are dwarfed by Phrygia's activity.[83] One could thus tentatively agree with Huttner, subject to the provisional nature of the impression that emerges, that, "during the imperial period ... only a few cities in Asia Minor minted as much local money as Laodicea; the variety of coin types from Laodicea is extraordinary."[84]

5. Coins of Laodicea and New Testament Studies

Laodicea is mentioned seven times in the New Testament, four times in relation to Colossae (Col 2:1; 4:15, 16 [2x]), once in relation to Hierapolis (Col 4:13), and twice directly in reference to the Laodicean church in Revelation (Rev 1:11; 3:14). The significance of the Roman provincial coinage of Laodicea for helping understand elements of early Christianity in the

---

79. William E. Metcalf, *The Silver Coinage of Cappadocia, Vespasian–Commodus* (New York: American Numismatic Society, 1996).

80. William E. Metcalf, introduction to *The Oxford Handbook of Greek and Roman Coinage*, ed. William E. Metcalf (Oxford: Oxford University Press, 2012), 5.

81. Metcalf, introduction, 5–6.

82. Leschhorn, "Le monnayage," 254.

83. Troas, two; Mysia, five; Ionia, seven; Lydia, nine; Caria, ten; Pontus, one; Bithynia, five; Lycia, one. A similar picture emerges on the raw calculation of coin catalogue numbers representing coin types for each region as listed in *RPC* 1.2201–3248 and *RPC* 2.801–1425.

84. Huttner, *Early Christianity in the Lycus Valley*, 162.

Lycus Valley is at least fivefold. First, the *homonoia* coinage at Laodicea regarding their alliance with Smyrna under Claudius (*RPC* 1.2912), and again with Smyrna under Nero (1.2928), and a third example of concord at the time of Marcellus (2.1271) firmly establishes the eager willingness of the city to actively display loyalty to the program of *Imperium Romanum*. Roman cultural assimilation of the church at Laodicea has caused complete misappropriation of allegiance and alliance so that the church can brashly declare, "I need nothing" ("οὐδὲν χρείαν ἔχω"; Rev 3:17) without any realization of their deprivation. Roman maintenance of power within the empire relied on mechanisms like the *homonoia* coinage to mediate power, especially so in the provinces, where Roman identity was harder for the empire to foster. It is this identity that Jesus, speaking to the church, seeks to redeem. Even now, despite the complete absence of any positive words to the church in Laodicea, there is hope offered to respond to the love of Jesus in repentance (Rev 3:19).

Second, the prominent display of the imperial temple on almost half of Domitian's coins, in either tetrastyle (*RPC* 2.1284, 1286, 1287, 1290) or hexastyle form (2.1281, 2.1291), highlights the genuine threat that the state religion posed to the young church in Laodicea. The posthumous deification of Julius Caesar in 42 BCE effectively set in motion the series of events which by the 80's CE saw Domitian issue demands to be referred to as "Lord and God" (Suetonius, *Dom.* 13). There are several indications throughout the book of Revelation that the early Christians were being pressured into emperor worship (Rev 13:4, 14–17; 14:9; 15:2; 16:2; 19:20; 20:4). The theme of the deified emperor in the coinage of Laodicea is seen in the placement of the emperor's image on the obverse and deity on the reverse, which serves to emphasize the connection between the two. There is a striking contrast between *RPC* 2.1284, with its militaristic titles (Germanicus, ΕΠΙΝΕΙΚΙΟC), dress (cuirass), and imagery (spear and victory trophy),[85] and Jesus's promise to give a heavenly reward to the one who can resist the lure and threat of Rome in Laodicea, "I will give the victor the right to sit with me on my throne" (Ο νικῶν δώσω αὐτῷ καθίσαι μετ' ἐμοῦ ἐν τῷ θρόνῳ μου; Rev 3:21).

Third, the thoroughly polytheistic context of the Lycus Valley is reflected in the coinage at Laodicea. That is not to say the inhabitants are presented with a generic one-size-fits-all version of the Greco-Roman gods. The indi-

---

85. See further Price, *Rituals and Power*, 183.

vidual gods are chosen, presented, and modified to suit the local Laodicean context. In a relief of Zeus (ILaodikeia 49), the god is shown wearing a sheep's skin coat, which is otherwise unknown. This was presumably motivated by a contextual connection to the thriving wool industry at Laodicea surveyed above. The adaptation of the gods is frequently detectable on coinage also. Zeus becomes Zeus Laodiceus (*RPC* 1.2898, 1.2096), Tyche become Tyche of Laodicea with turreted bust (1.2925), and Laodicea is presented with turreted bust (2.1299). Amid this polytheistic context, two divinities stand out in light of the stated spirit of the church in Rev 3:17. The combination of the god Men and associated sanctuary (*RPC* 1.2907 and 1.2927), Asclepius (1.2895), and Zeuxis Philalethes, the director of the medical center under Augustus, provides an illuminating and deeply ironic background to the accusation in 3:17, "blind" (τυφλὸς). The reference to being blind could also have the connotation of spiritual blindness and not understanding their true condition, hence the disjuncture between what they say, and what corresponds to reality.

Fourth, we briefly explored above the economic prosperity of the land and inhabitants of Laodicea. The overall picture we have of the inhabitants of the city is one of financial strength, agricultural stability, and a thriving economy. The threefold claim, "I am rich > I have prospered > I have no need" (Rev 3:17a) builds together as a climax, the first naming the fact, the second describing the process, and the third stating the result. Their prosperity was celebrated on coinage with symbols of abundance and nourishment (*RPC* 1.2897) as well as commemorating the regular benefaction that has defined the city's recent past (1.2920; 2.1269). However, despite the confidence of the church that they are self-sufficient (3:17a), they are informed of their true fivefold state (3:17b), "wretched, pitiful, poor, blind, and naked" (ταλαίπωρος καὶ ἐλεεινὸς καὶ πτωχὸς καὶ τυφλὸς καὶ γυμνός).

Finally, Jesus invites the church at Laodicea to purchase from him "gold refined by fire" (χρυσίον πεπυρωμένον ἐκ πυρός). Importantly, the verb used, συμβουλεύω (Rev 3:18), connotes thoughtfulness, mutual participation, and considered advice rather that stern command. Although gold coinage had been introduced by Caesar from 46 BCE, it was relatively rare. Augustus only permitted gold for his own coinage issues, but no other gold coins were officially minted. There were some Bosporan gold coins minted, but they were exclusively for Bosporan kings (*RPC* 1.1842–1863, 1.1937–1938), but there had not been any gold coins in Laodicea for centuries. Every coin produced by Laodicean mints in the first century was bronze. The reference to gold could have also brought back a vivid recollection of the confiscation of twenty talents of gold from the sizeable Jewish community by L. Valerius Flaccus in 61–60 BCE (Cicero, *Flac.* 28.68). Nonetheless, the emphasis of the biblical passage is that they require something that their wealth could never purchase. Herein lies the challenge to the ancient Christian church at Laodicea: they perceive their physical reality (wealth, security, and self-sufficiency) as reflective of their spiritual reality, yet they are spiritually destitute and are required to acknowledge that the very thing they lack or need, in this case gold, their city has never produced and is not available to them.

6. Conclusion

Robert Grant's words are as valid today as when they were penned in 1968, where he advocated a tactile engagement with the material and upon the "concrete actuality of the ancient historians, of papyri, inscriptions, coins and other archaeological remains."[86] Our analysis in this chapter has sought to illuminate aspects of the New Testament's interaction with Laodicea in light of the provincial numismatic record for the purposes of enhancing our understanding of nascent Christianity in the Lycus Valley. The above numismatic analysis sought (1) to offer a case study on Laodicea but suggest one could more plausibly expand subsequent studies to include coinages of the broader region, (2) to contextualize previous research on the use of coins for this purpose, (3) to clarify methodological considerations in the use of numismatic material, specifically addressing the question of why the propagandistic character, noticeability, and social origin of coinage does not disqualify the source material from inclusion in scholarly consideration, (4) to focus attention on significant numismatic themes at Laodicea, including representation of the city's relationship with Rome and active cultivation of the *Imperium Romanum*, the polyvalent religious identities in Laodicea, and assessment of the local realities which informed life in the city, and (5) in sum, to demonstrate that the numismatic evidence from Laodicea directly supports "the contention that the symbolism of the letters [Rev 2–3] was forcibly applicable to the original readers."[87]

---

86. Robert Grant, "American New Testament Study," *JBL* 87 (1968): 48.
87. Colin J. Hemer, *The Letters of the Seven Churches of Asia in Their Local Setting* (Sheffield: Sheffield Academic, 1986), 210.

Bibliography

Anderson, J. G. C. "A Summer in Phrygia I." *JHS* 17 (1897): 396–424.
———. "A Summer in Phrygia II." *JHS* 18 (1898): 81–128, 340–44.
Badian, Ernst. *Roman Imperialism in the Late Republic*. Oxford: Blackwell, 1968.
Bosch, Clemens. "Kleinasiatischen Münzen der römischen Kaiserzeit." *Jahrbuch des Deutschen Archäologischen Instituts* 46 (1931): 424–56.
Brennan, Peter, Michael Turner, and Nicholas L. Wright. *Faces of Power: Imperial Portraiture on Roman Coins*. Sydney: Nicholson Museum, 2007.
Brunt, Peter A. Review of *Die Aussenpolitik des Augustus und die augusteische Dichtung*, by H. G. Meyer. *JRS* 53 (1963): 170–76.
———. "The Romanization of the Local Ruling Classes in the Roman Empire." Pages 161–73 in *Assimilation et résistance à la culture gréco-romaine dans le monde ancien: Travaux du VIe Congrès international d'études classiques*. Edited by D. M. Pippidi. Paris: Belles Lettres, 1974.
Buttrey, T. V. "Calculating Ancient Coin Production: Facts and Fantasies." *NumC* 153 (1993): 338–45.
———. "Calculating Ancient Coin Production 2: Why It Cannot Be Done." *NumC* 154 (1999): 342–52.
———. "The Content and Meaning of Coin Hoards." *JRA* 12 (1999): 526–32.
Callu, Jean Pierre. *La Politique Monetaire Desempereurs Romains de 238 à 311*. Paris: de Boccard, 1969.
Caltabiano, M. Caccamo, L. Campagna, and A. Pinzone, eds. *Nuove prospsettive della ricerca sulla Sicilia del III sec. a.C.: Archeologia, numismatica, storia*. Messina: Dipartimento di Scienze dell' Antichita dell'Università degli Studi di Messina, 2004.
Carter, Warren. *Matthew and the Margins*. Sheffield: Sheffield Academic, 2000.
Cary, M. *A History of Rome down to the Reign of Constantine*. London: Macmillan, 1954.
Costa, V. M. da. "Five Roman Empresses: Chronology and Style in the Roman Provincial Coin Issues of Asia Minor." Pages 1–29 in *Notes of the First International Numismatic Symposium of the Turkish Numismatic Society*. Istanbul: Turkish Numismatic Society, 1999.
Crawford, Michael H. "Money and Exchange in the Roman World." *JRS* 60 (1970): 40–46.

———. "Roman Imperial Coin Types and the Formation of Public Opinion." Pages 47–64 in *Studies in Numismatic Method Presented to Philip Grierson*. Edited by C. Brooke, B. Steward, J. Pollard, and T. Volk. Cambridge: Cambridge University Press, 1983.

Duncan-Jones, Richard. *Money and Government in the Roman Empire*. Cambridge: Cambridge University Press, 1994.

Dyer, K. D. "'But Concerning that Day …' (Mark 13:32): 'Prophetic' and 'Apocalyptic' Eschatology in Mark 13." Pages 104–22 in *Society of Biblical Literature 1999 Seminar Papers*. SBLSP 38. Atlanta: Society of Biblical Literature, 1999.

Edwards, Douglas R. "Defining the Web of Power in Asia Minor: The Novelist Chariton and His City Aphrodisias." *JAAR* 63.3 (1994): 699–718.

Esty, Warren W. "Estimating the Size of a Coinage." *NumC* 144 (1984): 180–83.

———. "Estimation of the Size of a Coinage: A Survey and Comparison of Methods." *NumC* 146 (1986): 185–215.

Fears, J. Rufus. "The Cult of Virtues and Roman Imperial Ideology." *ANRW* 17.2: 827–948.

Franke, Peter R. "Zu den Homonoia-Münzen Kleinasiens." Pages 81–102 in *Stuttgarter Kolloquium zur Historische Geographie des Altertums I, 1980*. Edited by Eckart Olshausen. Bonn: Habelt, 1987.

Franke, Peter R., and Wolfgang Leschhorn. *Index to Sylloge Nummorum Graecorum Deutschland: Sammlung H. von Aulock*. Berlin: Mann, 1981.

Friesen, Steven J. *Imperial Cults and the Apocalypse of John: Reading Revelation in the Ruins*. Oxford: Oxford University Press, 2001.

Funke, Peter. *Homonoia und Arche: Athen und die griechische Staatenwelt vom Ende des Peloponnesischen Krieges bis zum Königfrieden (404/3–287/6 v. Chr.)*. Wiesbaden: Steiner, 1980.

Gagniers, Jean des, Pierre Devambez, Lilly Kahil, and René Ginouvès. *Laodicée du Lycos: Le Nymphée, Campagnes 1961–1963*. Paris: de Boccard, 1969.

Garnsey, Peter, and Richard P. Saller. *The Roman Empire: Economy, Society and Culture*. Oakland: University of California Press, 1987.

Grant, Michael. *From Imperium to Auctoritas*. Cambridge: Cambridge University Press, 1946.

Grant, Robert. "American New Testament Study." *JBL* 87 (1968): 42–50.

Habicht, Christian. "Die augusteische Zeit und das erste Jahrhundert nach Christi Geburt." Pages 41-88 in *Le Culte Des Souverains Dans L'Empire*

Romain: 7 Exposés Suivis de Discussions. Edited by W. den Boer. Geneva: Fondation Hardt pour l'étude de l'antiquité classique, 1973.

Hans, Linda-Marie. "Der Kaiser mit dem Schwert." *JNG* 33 (1983): 57–66.

Harris, William V. *War and Imperialism in Republican Rome, 327–70 B.C.* Oxford: Oxford University Press, 1985.

Haverfield, Francis H. *The Romanization of Roman Britain*. Oxford: Oxford University Press, 1915.

Hekster, Olivier. "Coins and Messages: Audience Targeting on Coins of Different Denominations?" Pages 20–35 in *Representation and Perception of Roman Imperial Power*. Edited by Paul Erdkamp, O. Hekster, G. de Kleijn, Stephan T. A. M. Mols, and Lukas de Blois. Leiden: Brill, 2003.

Hemer, Colin J. *The Letters of the Seven Churches of Asia in Their Local Setting*. Sheffield: Sheffield Academic, 1986.

Hölscher, Tonio. *Staatsdenkmal und Publikum: Vom Untergang der Republik bis zur Festigung des Kaisertums in Rom*. Konstanzer althistorische Vorträge und Forschungen 9. Konstanz: Universitätsverlag Konstanz, 1984.

Horsley, Richard A., ed. *In the Shadow of Empire: Reclaiming the Bible as a History of Faithful Resistance*. Louisville: Westminster John Knox, 2008.

———. *Paul and Empire: Religion and Power in Roman Imperial Society*. Harrisburg: Trinity Press International, 1997.

Howgego, Christopher. *Ancient History from Coins*. London: Routledge, 1995.

———. "Coin Circulation and the Integration of the Roman Economy." *JRA* 7 (1994): 5–21.

———. "The Supply and Use of Money in the Roman World 200 B.C. to A.D. 300." *JRS* 82 (1992): 1–31.

Huttner, Ulrich. *Early Christianity in the Lycus Valley*. Translated by David Green. AJEC 85; Early Christianity in Asia Minor 1. Leiden: Brill, 2013.

Isaac, Benjamin. *The Limits of Empire: The Roman Army in the East*. Oxford: Oxford University Press, 1990.

Johnston, Ann. "Die Sharing in Asia Minor: The View from Sardis." *Israel Numismatic Journal* 6–7 (1982–1983): 59–78.

———. *Greek Imperial Denominations, ca 200–275: A Study of Roman Provincial Bronze Coinages of Asia Minor*. London: Royal Numismatic Society, 2007.

———. "Greek Imperial Statistics: A Commentary." *Review Numismatique* 26 (1984): 240–57.
Jones, Tom B. "Greek Imperial Coins." *The Voice of the Turtle: North American Journal of Numismatics* 4 (1965): 295–308.
———. "A Numismatic Riddle: The So-Called Greek Imperials." *Proceedings of the American Philosophical Society* 107 (1963): 308–47.
Judge, Edwin A. "Setting the Record Straight: Alternative Documents of a Protest in the Roman Army of Egypt." Pages 378–84 in *The First Christians in the Roman World: Augustan and New Testament Essays*. Edited by James R. Harrison. Tübingen: Mohr Siebeck, 2008.
Kampmann, Ursula. "*Homonoia* Politics in Asia Minor: The Example of Pergamon." Pages 373–93 in *Pergamon, Citadel of the Gods: Archaeological Record, Literary Description, and Religious Development*. Edited by Helmut Koester. Harrisburg: Trinity Press International, 1998.
Kienast, Dietmar. "Die Homonoiaverträge in der romischen Kaiserzeit." *JNG* 14 (1964): 51–64.
Kinns, Philip. "The Amphictionic Coinage Reconsidered." *NumC* 143 (1983): 1–22.
Kleiner, Fred S., and Sydney P. Noe. *The Early Cistophoric*. New York: The American Numismatic Society, 1977.
Klose, Dietrich O. A. *Die Münzprägung von Smyrna in der römischen Kaiserzeit*. Berlin: de Gruyter, 1987.
Kneissl, Peter. *Die Siegestitulatur der römischen Kaiser*. Göttingen: Vandenhoeck & Ruprecht, 1969.
Kraft, Konrad. *Das System der kaiserzeitlichen Münzprägung in Kleinasien: Materialien und Entwürfe*. Berlin: Mann, 1972.
Lane, Eugene. *Interpretations and Testimonia*. Vol. 3 of *Corpus Monumentorum Religionis dei Menis 3*. Leiden: Brill, 1976.
Leeming, David. *The Oxford Companion to World Mythology*. Oxford: Oxford University Press, 2005.
Leschhorn, Wolfgang. "Le monnayage impérial d'Asie Mineure et la statistique." *PACT: Revue de groupe européen d'études sur les techniques physiques, chimiques et mathematiques appliquées à l'archéologie* 5 (1981): 252–66.
Levick, Barbara. *Roman Colonies in Southern Asia Minor*. Oxford: Clarendon, 1967.
Lewis, Peter, and Ron Bolden. *The Pocket Guide to Saint Paul: Coins Encountered by the Apostle on His Travels*. Kent Town: Wakefield Press, 2002.

Lintott, Andrew. *Imperium Romanum: Politics and Administration.* London: Routledge, 1993.

Lyon, C. S. S. "Die Estimation: Some Experiments with Simulated Samples of a Coinage." *British Numismatic Journal* 59 (1989): 1–12.

Manders, Erika. *Coining Images of Power: Patterns in the Representation of Roman Emperors on Imperial Coinage, AD 193–284.* Leiden: Brill, 2012.

Mattingly, Harold. *Coins of the Roman Empire in the British Museum.* 6 vols. London: British Museum, 1923–1976.

Meshorer, Ya'akov. *Jewish Coins of the Second Temple Period.* Tel-Aviv: Am Hassefer, 1967.

Metcalf, William E. Introduction to *The Oxford Handbook of Greek and Roman Coinage.* Edited by William E. Metcalf. Oxford: Oxford University Press, 2012.

———. "Regionalism in the Coinage of Asia Minor." Pages 147–59 in *Regionalism in Hellenistic and Roman Asia Minor.* Edited by Hugh Elton and Gary Reger. Pessac: Ausonius, 2007.

———. *The Silver Coinage of Cappadocia, Vespasian–Commodus.* New York: American Numismatic Society, 1996.

Millett, Martin. *The Romanization of Britain: An Essay in Archaeological Interpretation.* Cambridge: Cambridge University Press, 1990.

Mitchell, Stephen. *Anatolia: Land, Men and Gods in Asia Minor.* 2 vols. Oxford: Clarendon, 1993.

Mommsen, Theodor. *The Provinces of the Roman Empire: The European Provinces.* Chicago: University of Chicago Press, 1968.

Mørkholm, Otto. *Early Hellenistic Coinage: From the Accession of Alexander to the Peace of Apamea (336–188 B.C.).* Cambridge: Cambridge University Press, 1991.

Oldfather, W. A. trans. *Epictetus: Discourses, Books 3–4; Fragments; The Encheiridion.* LCL. Cambridge: Harvard University Press, 1928.

Price, Simon R. F. *Rituals and Power: The Roman Imperial Cult in Asia Minor.* Cambridge: Cambridge University Press, 1985.

Ramsay, William M. *The Lycos Valley and South-Western Phrygia.* Vol. 1 of *The Cities and Bishoprics of Phrygia.* Oxford: Clarendon, 1895.

———. *Impressions of Turkey during Twelve Years' Wanderings.* London: Hodder & Stoughton, 1897.

———. *The Letters to the Seven Churches of Asia and Their Place in the Plan of the Apocalypse.* London: Hodder & Stoughton, 1904.

Ritti, T., H. H. Baysal, E. Miranda, and F. Guizzi. *Catalogo delle iscrizioni latine e greche, Museo archeologico di Denizli-Pamukkale*. Naples: Università degli Studi, 2008.
Robert, Louis. "Les inscriptions." Pages 248–389 in *Laodicée du Lycos: Le Nymphée, Campagnes 1961–1963*. Edited by Jean des Gagniers, Pierre Devambez, Lilly Kahil, and René Ginouvès. Paris: E. de Boccard, 1969.
Rosler, Andrés. *Political Authority and Obligation in Aristotle*. Oxford: Oxford University Press, 2005.
Schultze, Victor. *Antiocheia*. Vol. 3 of *Altchristliche Städte und Landschaften*. Leipzig: Gütersloh, 1930.
———. *Kleinasien*. Vol. 2 of *Altchristliche Städte und Landschaften*. 2 parts. Leipzig: Gütersloh, 1922–1926.
———. *Konstantinope*. Vol. 1 of *Altchristliche Städte und Landschaften*. Leipzig: Gütersloh, 1913.
Scullard, Howard H. *A History of the Roman World, 753–146 BC*. London: Methuen, 1951.
Sheppard, A. R. R. "Homonoia in the Greek Cities of the Roman Empire." *Ancient Society* 15–17 (1984–1986): 229–52.
Şimşek, C. *Laodikeia (Laodikeia ad Lycum)*. Istanbul: Yayinlari, 2007.
Spinelli, Marianna. "The 'Soma' of the God: Subtypes as Qualification of the Corporal Gestures of the Main Subject on the Kaulonia Coins." Pages 793–800 in *Identity and Connectivity: Proceedings of the Sixteenth Symposium on Mediterranean Archaeology*. Edited by Luca Bombardieri, Anacleto D'Agostino, Guido Guarducci, Valentina Orsi, and Stefano Valentini. Oxford: Aracheopress, 2013.
Stevens, Gerald L. *Revelation: The Past and Future of John's Apocalypse*. Eugene, OR: Pickwick, 2014.
Strabo. *Books 10–12*. Vol. 5 of *Geography*. Translated by Horace Leonard Jones. LCL. Cambridge: Harvard University Press, 1928.
Tacitus. *Annals: Books 13–16*. Translated by John Jackson. LCL. Cambridge: Harvard University Press, 1937.
Thonemann, Peter J. "Polemo, Son of Polemo (Dio, 59.12.2)." *EA* 37 (2004): 144–50.
———. *The Menander Valley: A Historical Geography from Antiquity to Byzantium*. Cambridge: Cambridge University Press, 2011.
———. "Phrygia: An Anarchist History, 950 BC–AD 100." Pages 1–40 in *Roman Phrgia*. Edited by Peter Thonemann. Cambridge: Cambridge University Press, 2013.

Veyne, Paul. "Y a-t-il eu un Impérialisme Romain?" *Mélanges de l'Ecole française de Rome* 87 (1975): 793–855.
Weissenrieder, Annette, and Friederike Wendt. "Images as Communication: The Methods of Iconography." Pages 3–49 in *Picturing the New Testament: Studies in Ancient Visual Images*. Edited by Annette Weissenrieder, Friederike Wendt, and P. von Gemünden. Tübingen: Mohr Siebeck, 2005.
Williams, Jonathan. "Religion and Roman Coins." Pages 143–63 in *A Companion to Roman Religion*. Edited by Jörg Rüpke. Oxford: Blackwell, 2007.
Whittaker, C. R. *Frontiers of the Roman Empire*. Baltimore: John Hopkins Press, 1994.
———. "Imperialism and Culture: The Roman Initiative." Pages 143–65 in *Dialogues in Roman Imperialism: Power, Discourse and Discrepant Experience in the Roman Empire*. Edited by David J. Mattingly. Ann Arbor: Cushing-Malloy, 1997.
Wilson, H. L. "A New Collegium at Rome." *American Journal of Archaeology* 16.1 (1912): 94–96.
Winter, Bruce W. *Seek the Welfare of the City: Christians as Benefactors and Citizens*. Grand Rapid, MIs: Eerdmans, 1994.
Yamauchi, Edwin. *The Stones and the Scriptures*. New York: Holman, 1972.
Zanker, Paul. *The Power of Images in the Age of Augustus*. Translated by Alan Shapiro. Ann Arbor: University of Michigan Press, 1988.
Zuiderhoek, Arjan, and Wouter Vanacker. "Introduction: Imperial Identities in the Roman World." Pages 1–15 in *Imperial Identities in the Roman World*. Edited by Wouter Vanacker and Arjun Zuiderhoek. London: Routledge, 2017.

Rome's Market Economy in the Lycus Valley: Soundings from Laodicea and Colossae

Michael Trainor

The Mediterranean world of the first century was Roman. Imperial Rome imposed its presence throughout this world, especially through its armies and local administrators—notwithstanding indigenous regional and local cultures that perdured and moderated Rome's influence. Rome's market economy, an essential characteristic of Roman influence, pervaded the world, shaping values and determining relationships. Its economic reach also spread into Asia Minor, though geographically distant and distinct from Italy. Its market economy affected those living in western Anatolia's Lycus Valley in the mid-to-late first century CE. Its economy impacted Philemon, a *paterfamilias* of a Jesus household, and other Jesus followers in Colossae, Laodicea, and Hierapolis, the three principal networked cities of the valley.

My aim in what follows is to offer some insights into these writings through the lens of Rome's pervasive market economy, appropriating perspectives from Peter Temin's recent monograph on the issue.[1] Economics is a useful methodological approach, though not the only one, for providing insights into the ancient world.[2] It was embedded within

---

1. Peter Temin's *The Roman Market Economy* (Princeton: Princeton University Press, 2012) and Ulrich Huttner's *Early Christianity in the Lycus Valley*, trans. David Green, AJEC 85, Early Christianity in Asia Minor 1 (Leiden: Brill, 2013) are valuable sources for understanding the economic interactions that occurred among the Jesus followers in the Lycus Valley with significant theological consequences, as we shall see.

2. Temin, *Roman Market Economy*, 2. For New Testament scholarship on the issue, see Thomas R. Blanton IV and Raymond Pickett, eds., *Paul and Economics: A Handbook* (Minneapolis: Fortress, 2017). For scholarship on the ancient Roman economy, reflecting a variety of methodologies, see A. H. M. Jones, *The Roman*

everything that constituted Roman society. I will suggest that a picture of the socioeconomic realities of Jesus followers living in the Lycus Valley in the early empire period can be gleaned from the writings addressed to them. This picture was one of relative wealth and social stability shaped by a market economy, that is, an economy "where many resources are allocated by prices that are free to move in response to changes in underlying conditions."[3] An identification of these resources and the conditions in

---

Economy: Studies in Ancient Economic and Administrative History, ed. P. A. Brunt (Oxford: Blackwell, 1974); Richard Duncan-Jones, *The Economy of the Roman Empire: Quantitative Studies*, 2nd rev. ed. (Cambridge: Cambridge University Press, 1982); Duncan-Jones, *Money and Government in the Roman Empire* (Cambridge: Cambridge University Press, 1994); Willem Jongman, *The Economy and Society of Pompeii* (Amsterdam: Gieben, 1988); Jongman, "The Rise and Fall of the Roman Economy: Population, Rents and Entitlement," in *Ancient Economies, Modern Methodologies: Archaeology, Comparative History, Models and Institutions*, ed. Peter F. Bang, Mamoru Ikeguchi, and Harmut G. Ziche (Bari: Edipuglia, 2006), 237–54; Jongman, "Gibbon Was Right: The Decline and Fall of the Roman Economy," in *Crises and the Roman Empire: Proceedings of the Seventh Workshop of the International Network Impact of Empire (Nijmegen, June 20–24, 2006)*, ed. Olivier Hekster, Gerda de Kleijn, and Danielle Slootjes (Leiden: Brill, 2007), 183–99; Roger S. Bagnall and Bruce W. Frier, *The Demography of Roman Egypt*, Cambridge Studies in Population, Economy and Society in Past Time 23 (Cambridge: Cambridge University Press, 1994); Walter Scheidel, Ian Morris, and Richard Saller, *The Cambridge Economic History of the Greco-Roman World* (Cambridge: Cambridge University Press, 2007); Dennis P. Kehoe, *Law and the Rural Economy in the Roman Empire* (Michigan: University of Michigan Press, 2007); P. F. Bang, *The Roman Bazaar: A Comparative Study of Trade and Markets in a Tributary Empire* (Cambridge: Cambridge University Press, 2008); Walter Scheidel and Steven J. Friesen, "The Size of the Economy and the Distribution of Income in the Roman Empire," *JRS* 99 (2009): 61–91; Keith Hopkins, "The Political Economy in the Roman Empire," in *The Dynamics of Ancient Empires: State Power from Assyria to Byzantium*, ed. Ian Morris and Walter Scheidel (Oxford: Oxford University Press, 2009), 178–204; Koenraad Verboven, "City and Reciprocity: The Rome of Cultural Beliefs in the Roman Economy," *Annales* 67.4 (2012): 597–627. See, too, The Oxford Roman Economy Project, publishing the series Oxford Studies on the Roman Economy, currently listing fourteen publications, with further volumes projected. See http://oxrep.classics.ox.ac.uk/oxford_studies_on_the_roman_economy/.

3. Temin, *Roman Market Economy*, 6. Temin's analysis of the Roman market economy is in reaction to the analysis of Moses I. Finley (*The Ancient Economy* [Berkeley: University of California Press, 1999], 22), who argues that "ancient society did not have an economic system which was an enormous conglomeration of interdependent markets." Temin's work, however, is not without limitations. See the insightful critique of the monograph offered by Paul Erdkamp, "How Modern Was the Market Economy

which they exist will assist us in interpreting the domestic relationships found in Philemon and Colossians. It will further help spotlight the real issue that lies behind the concern of the seer John in his prophetic letter to the Jesus *domus* of Laodiceans (Rev 3:14–21) in the book of Revelation.[4]

The Roman Market Economy

Economics today affects what we do and how we do it. It is embedded in everything. The accumulation of wealth provides security, comfort, and the possibility of a defined future. What concerns and affects us today has its parallel with the peoples of ancient Rome and its provinces. While some have judged Rome's economic structure as a "conglomeration of interdependent markets," the Roman world was a huge market localized in provinces and towns.[5] This economic strategy determined a trade system of supply and demand that provided an economy knit together, resilient, and secure. The local context in which the Roman market and its economics operated was also influential and adjusted the dominance of the imperial system. We shall see this below, when we look at the Phrygian context and its industries.

The early Roman Empire, the time in which the three New Testament Lycus Valley writings appear, was a period of economic security and growth, perhaps in a way that was unique before the industrial revolution. It was, overall, a period of wealth with ordinary people living within interactive networks designed to assist the exchange and transfer of goods and services.[6] At the same time, a social pattern of wealth and poverty existed

---

of the Roman World?" *Œconomia* 4.2 (2014): http://journals.openedition.org/oeconomia/399.

4. I take for granted that Paul wrote the Letter to Philemon sometime in the mid-50s CE and that one evangelized by Paul (possibly Epaphras) wrote the Letter to the Colossians within at least one or two generations after Paul died—or certainly while Paul's historical ministry was within living memory. I date Revelation after Colossians. I am convinced that all three writings emerge from the Lycus Valley, contra Vicky Balabanski, "Where Is Philemon? The Case for a Logical Fallacy in the Correlation of the Data in Philemon and Colossians 1:1–2; 4:7–8," *JSNT* 38 (2015): 131–50, who argues for Italy, possibly Rome, as the provenance for Philemon. See also Michael Trainor, *Epaphras: Paul's Educator at Colossae* (Collegeville, MN: Liturgical Press, 2008), 2–5.

5. Finley, *Ancient Economy*, 22–23.

6. Temin, *Roman Market economy*, 4. Temin (6–7) further expands Polyani's original analysis of ancient economic exchange ("reciprocity," "redistribution," and

in cities throughout the empire. This pattern decided people's socioeconomic status located within a hierarchy in which most people (about 90 percent) lived at or near subsistence,[7] while 3 percent could be classified as the super elite, and 7 percent were artisans, skilled merchants, and small property owners. These owners maintained their status in the sociopolitical hierarchy through rents and slave ownership who could manage and skillfully run workshops that addressed different urban demands. Rome's artisans, merchants, and landlords were insulated from the factors that would have compromised their subsistence, unlike the majority caught up in and victimized by the Roman economic system.[8]

In other words, the economic situation of people in the empire was not a simple division between two groups, the haves and have nots, or the rich and the poor. It was multifaceted. Urban inhabitants and rural workers belonging to Jesus households in Rome or Asia Minor, including the Lycus Valley, reflected this complex socioeconomic reality. However, as I shall suggest, the principal though not exclusive addressees of the Lycus Valley Second Testament writings belonged to the middle strata of the economic hierarchy, though inscriptions pertinent to the valley suggest economic variations. The valley's inhabitants, like everyone else in this stratum, benefited from the financial stability and economic growth throughout the Roman world in this early period of the empire. Although, as we shall see, the socioeconomic status of Lycus-Valley Jesus followers was variegated, reflecting local Phrygian flavor and indigenous economic activity, and certainly not monochromatic.

Temin suggests two factors among many others for Rome's economic development. The first was the availability of food, particularly wheat. Rome was the largest urban center in an ancient world that was 10 percent urbanized with a population of seventy million.[9] Rome's population of

---

"exchange") in adopting Pryor's economic transactional analysis (market or reciprocal "exchanges"; centric and noncentric "transfers"; customary, command, and instrumental "behaviour").

7. Katherine Bain, *Women's Socioeconomic Status and Religious Leadership in Asia Minor in the Frist Two Centuries CE* (Minneapolis: Fortress, 2014), 17, borrowing from the research of Steven Friesen, "Poverty in Pauline Studies: Beyond the So-called New Consensus," *JSNT* 26 (2004): 323–61. However, see the reworked percentages of Bruce W. Longenecker (*Remember the Poor: Paul, Poverty, and the Greco-Roman World* [Grand Rapids: Eerdmans, 2010], 44–53).

8. Bain, *Women's Socioeconomic Status*, 17.

9. Temin, *Roman Market Economy*, 252.

approximately a million people required feeding on a diet mainly of wine, oil, dry legumes, and especially wheat. This grain was most popular in the Roman diet and was universally sought after.[10] One measure of wealth in Roman society was its availability. Italy itself could not supply all the wheat and other consumption needs for Roman citizens. Rome's merchant providers drew heavily on the food resources that came from the empire's provinces. A ship sailing to Rome's harbor, Ostia, could carry an average of 6,700 metric tons of wheat. Two thousand ships a year berthed at Ostia.[11]

The access to such a vast quantity of the grain in a balanced Mediterranean market economy, in which wheat prices in one far-off province reflected those in Rome with relative consistency, indicated economic prosperity. The need for grain and its value as an economic commodity is well illustrated in the Lycus Valley. Colossae and Laodicea could boast of a purchaser of wheat or corn (a *sitones*).[12] This meant that the presence of the office of a *sitones* for Colossae and Laodicea implied the necessity of such an office to deal with the quantity of grain available for sale. It is not known for whom the *sitones* was purchasing the grain, but it would be conceivable that the transactions were conducted on behalf of a grain transporter with an eye to the Roman international market.

The demand for wheat and other grains made agriculture the most important economic activity in the Roman world. Improved agricultural technology and farming techniques enhanced wheat's quality and quantity available for purchase by the *sitones* and offered material well-being and prosperity.

A second factor that led to Rome's economic prosperity was due to the *Pax Romana*, the political stability across the empire that began with the reign of Augustus (27 BCE–14 CE) and flagged earlier, in 67 BCE, by Pompey ensuring the safe passage of ships across the Mediterranean Sea unhindered by piracy. Shipping transportation became safer and economically more effective. It further allowed for a greater quantity and variety of foodstuffs (fruits and vegetables, hitherto unknown in Rome) to arrive at Ostia.[13] Meat, the food of the elite, was more consumed. This, in turn,

---

10. Temin, *Roman Market Economy*, 30.

11. Temin, *Roman Market Economy*, 40.

12. The *sitones* in Colossae is mentioned in *IGRR* 4.870, and, in the case of Laodicea, in I.Laodikeia 47.6.

13. Temin, *Roman Market Economy*, 225. The centrality of Ostia as a receiver and distributor of food is illustrated by its epigraphic and archaeological evidence.

reflected the rise in income per capita and real wages around the empire.¹⁴ Overall, living standards seemed to increase throughout the empire.¹⁵

Economic growth in the Roman world, formed by its intricately linked market economy, partly mirrored the economic status of some of those from the middle economic strata living in the Lycus Valley in Colossae, Laodicea, and Hierapolis and was influenced by the Phrygian cultural, social, and economic context of this part of Asia Minor.¹⁶ We do have hints of the diverse local economic and market situations in which the valley's inhabitants lived.

An example of an indigenous commercial activity that generated some wealth is seen in the third-century CE funerary inscription dedicated to M. Aur. Ammianos, from Hierapolis. Ammianos invented a water-powered twin saw for cutting stones for civic building projects. The inscription reads,

> M. Aur. Ammianos, citizen of Hierapolis, skilful as Daedalus in wheel-working (?), made (the represented mechanism) with Daedalean craft (or: "with the skill of Daedalus"), and now I'll stay here.¹⁷

Stone masonry was an important industry of the area and would have provided Ammianos and his household with some economic security. However, the limestone nature of the inscription, rather than marble, would suggest that he was not a person of wealth or high social standing.¹⁸

Inscriptions mention a prefect/chief of the grain supply (L. Bourke van der Meer, *Ostia: Inscriptions, Buildings and Spaces in Rome's Main Port* [Leuven: Peeters, 2012], 29, 54), an office of grain traders (36), six superintendants of the granary (70), and a guild of grain measurers (71). The archaeological remains of the granary of Hortenius also exist in the port city (107–8). Note, too, the archaeological remains of fishmonger shops (90–91), mosaics of fish in the House of Fish (94–97) and, in a shop, a mosaic of a fisherman standing in a ship, holding two fish in his right hand (103). There is also mention of the *macellum* ("meat market," 92) in another inscription.

14. Temin, *Roman Market Economy*, 225–31.
15. Temin, *Roman Market Economy*, 196.
16. Sheidel and Friesen ("Size of the Economy," 62) argue that "middling groups" (craftsmen, merchants) only comprised 10 percent of the Roman Empire.
17. Tullia Ritti, Klaus Grewe, and Paul Kessner, "A Relief of a Water-Powered Stone Saw Mill on a Sarcophagus at Hierapolis and Its Implications," *JRA* 20 (2007): 139. More generally, see Ben Russell, *The Economics of the Roman Stone Trade* (Oxford: Oxford University Press, 2013).
18. Ritti, "Relief of a Water-Powered Stone Saw Mill," 139. For an example of

The stone-cutting machines that Ammianos and, presumably, other colleagues constructed were important in an area where water mills operated. A second funerary inscription from the same period gives further weight to the presence and popularity of water-millers:

> [This sarcophagus and the (surrounding) area] belong to Mar. Aur. Apollodotos Kalliklia(nos); Apollodotos shall be buried in it, and also his wife Aur. Tertia, their children and their son-in-law Aur. Tatianos; burying and being buried in it is not permitted to others, except if Apollodotos will give his consent; anybody transgressing shall pay to the most holy *ficus 500 denarii*, and the water-millers association *300 denarii*. A copy of this inscription has been registered in the archives.

The penalty incurred by transgressing the restrictions engraved on the inscription was paid to the *association* of water-millers. That they were able to form an association indicated their number and influence. They would have formed one of the more numerous guilds in competition with other guilds, like the purple dyers, discussed below. The millers would have been necessary to ensure the good working of their machinery used by fullers and bakers.[19] The relationship between all these, and epigraphical evidence of other guilds, gardeners, grocer, cattle breeders, metal, and textile workers,[20] suggest a complex economic industrial environment that impinged on the valley's village-domestic network.

This economic network would particularly affect the addressees of Philemon, Colossians, and the Letter to the Laodiceans in the book of Revelation (Rev 3:14–22). The addressees were Jesus followers living within domestic contexts. The recognition of the household context adds a further level of economic implication and status. Metaphors drawn from the market economy of Rome and Phrygia would also infiltrate Colossians and the Letter to the Laodiceans. They shape the theological insights

---

the building costs and the labor force required for a marble stoa at Hierapolis, see Dominik Maschek, "The Marble Stoa at Hierapolis: Materials, Labour Force and Building Costs," in *Ancient Quarries and Building Sites in Asia Minor: Research on Hierapolis in Phrygia and Other Cities in South-Western Anatolia; Archaeology, Archaeometry, Conservation*, ed. Tommaso Ismaelli and Giuseppe Scardozzi (Bari: Edipuglia, 2016), 393–402.

19. Ritti, "Relief of a Water-Powered Stone Saw Mill," 145.
20. Ritti, "Relief of a Water-Powered Stone Saw Mill," 144.

which their respective writers offer their Phrygian audiences. To these contexts and the respective economic imagery, I now turn.

Paul's Letter to Philemon addresses a Jesus household in general and its *paterfamilias* in particular. A similar domestic context lies behind Colossians. The explicit identification of the Roman *domus* in both writings implies an economic institution. The household was "the most important ancient economic institution in which economic behaviour was embedded."[21] It was a residence for a large group of people (parents, children, and slaves) and also a manufacturing or production unit within the other business and agricultural institutions, *collegia*, and associations of the Lycus Valley.[22] The *domus* linked to the market place of the nearby city, of the indigenous Phrygian economic context indicated above, and Rome's larger Mediterranean market composed of an intricate industrial and familial network. Whether the domestic contexts presumed in Philemon and Colossians was urban or rural is a moot point.

We know from the Roman situation that wealthy landowners had two villas, one in the country and the other in the city. The urban setting provided the opportunity for the *paterfamilias* to display his grandiose wealth to the passers-by who would venture into the outer courtyard and therefore heap upon him honor and prestige as they awaited benefits to fall upon them from their acts of adulation.[23] The urban villa would be supplied by products that came from the country estate. While south eastern Asia Minor was a long way from Italy, there is no reason to suggest that this same situation did not apply in the Lycus Valley and the *domus* context, explicit in Philemon and Colossians, albeit with local indigenous

---

21. Ekkehard W. Stegemann and Wolfgang Stegemann, *The Jesus Movement: A Social History of Its First Century* (Minneapolis Fortress, 1999), 18.

22. The interlocking nature of ancient Roman houses as residential and workplace spaces is confirmed by archaeological research on houses and the locale in Pergamon and Pompeii. See the summary of this in Bain, *Women's Socioeconomic Status*, 83–84. The economic value and agricultural richness of Colossae throughout history, especially evidenced in its inscriptions and coins, is described in Alan H. Cadwallader, *Fragments of Colossae: Sifting through the Traces* (Hindmarsh: ATF Press, 2015). On the nature of associations in the Lycus Valley, see Huttner, *Early Christianity in the Lycus Valley*, 30.

23. On the visibility of elite households, see Kate Cooper, "Closely Watched Households: Visibility, Exposure and Private Power in the Roman 'Domus,'" *Past and Present* 197 (2007): 3–33.

Phrygian variations and competitive interests as the following inscription from the village of Kaygetteia illustrates.[24]

Kaygetteia is far from Hierapolis but within its ambit of influence and locale. The inscription concerns the actions which vineyard owners can take if their vineyards are damaged:

> ... from all the vineyards, [it being permitted] to the owners alone to cut them down or, on the pretext of lack of substance, to engage in any [...]. If anyone acts contrary to this, [it is permitted] to the owners of the vineyards, and likewise to [anyone of their household] to whom they have entrusted their affairs, [to seize] all of the cattle or sheep in their vineyards, to carry them off and keep them in recompense for the harm, [doing with them] whatever they wish. (The vineyard-owner) may have the shepherds whipped, if they are slaves, once they have been reported to those appointed *paraphylakes* for the year, in that they may refrain from persistent [theft?]. As for the masters of the flocks, and free shepherds, and [headmen?] of the villages who do not prevent shepherds from herding their sheep into vineyards and breaking off vine-branches, (the vineyard-owner) is permitted to make exactions from their other property, and to take sureties from them ... exacting from them ... Apollo *archegetes* ... any inhabitant of the place ... slave or shepherd.[25]

There are several things about this inscription that are noteworthy. Like many others identified in the area around Hierapolis, this inscription dates from the third century CE, well after Philemon, Colossians, and the Letter to the Laodiceans were written to the valley's Jesus followers. However, it might well reflect the tense relations that existed between agriculturalists, herdsmen, and viticulturalists over centuries. Whatever this possibility, the inscription illustrates the rights and authority that the vineyard owner and the members of the vineyard household had over their property and its produce. In the event of crop or vine damage, their authority was clearly defined. They could confiscate the animals, the sheep or cattle, that belonged to others. This confiscation would continue until the vineyard

---

24. In regard to the competitive interests between the poleis of the Lycus valley, note the inscription revealing a fishing dispute between Hierapolis and Tripolis with Laodicea: Tullia Ritti, *Hierapolis di Frigia IX: Storia e istituzioni di Hierapolis* (Istanbul: Ege, 2017), 388–95.

25. *MAMA* 4.297; trans. Peter Thonemann, *The Maeander Valley: A Historical Geography from Antiquity to Byzantium* (Cambridge: Cambridge University Press, 2011), 194.

owner was compensated for the damage done. The shepherds could also be punished for theft from the vineyard. Further, vineyard owners could also exact compensation from the property of the actual flock owners, the shepherds who grazed freely on the land, and village leaders.

The inscription illustrates the local issues that created tension within a smaller village economic network and vineyard household. Whether this issue concerned a larger elite household or a smaller village-domestic unit involved with wine production is not clear. However, the relationships and tensions described in the inscription from a situation geographically related to Hierapolis, and thus to the Jesus followers of the Lycus Valley, though from a later era, might possibly reflect similar problems that occurred in much earlier times, involving households from another part of the Lycus Valley and perhaps the addressees of the three letters. If this was the case, then the inscription might shed light on the affirmation the author of Colossians gives to the ministry of Epaphras, "who has worked hard for you [Colossians] and for those in Laodicea and Hierapolis" (Col 4:13). Epaphras's role might not just be about the proclamation of the gospel, but also involve acting as intermediary when tensions arose among the villagers, herdsmen, viticulturalists, stone workers, agriculturalists, or any of the other workers in industries known to operate in the Lycus Valley. The ministry of those "entrusted with the ministry of reconciliation" was one accentuated by Paul in 2 Cor 5:19. The focus of this ministry concerned reconciliation with God, but it would have practical implications for reconciliation among Jesus followers who might have been at blows with each other over what might seem simple things such as grazing activities, vineyard care, and grape production.

No matter how speculative this reconciling aspect of Epaphras's ministry from Colossians might be, the inscription does indicate the relational and economic complexity that existed in village-urban economic life. This complexity would moderate the impression that the Roman *domus* integral model offered a uniform template for urban-village domestic life and production all over the empire.[26] The vineyard owners and wine producers of Kaygetteia would hold a different opinion.

---

26. See also Peter Thonemann, "Households and Families," in *Roman Phrygia: Culture and Society*, ed. Peter Thonemann (Cambridge: Cambridge University Press, 2013), 124–42, who argues for distinctions between family life in the *domus* at Rome and at Phrygia.

This reflection from the Phrygian Kaygetteia inscription would further temper the way the Roman urban-rural relationship was perceived. One contemporary commentator describes that relationship this way:

> Our image of a city of antiquity, however, would be very different according to our status. If we were a member of the Roman elite, for instance, we would leave our country house—spacious, centrally heated, with a swimming bath, library, works of art, etc.—and estate, and drive, ride or be carried in a litter to the city. We would pass the tombs of the great along the highway nearer to the city. Our entourage would make a way for us through the teeming city streets. We would thus make our way through the city centre, past splendid theatres, amphitheatres, public halls and baths and parks. Eventually we would be welcomed by yet more attendants in our town house, which would be almost as elegant as our country house—and largely supplied with foodstuffs by our country estate. There our clients would be waiting to dance attendance upon us.[27]

This analysis describes the world of the Roman elite, not the middle strata of the household owners envisaged in the Lycus Valley context or the relationship that would have existed been sheep and vineyard owners. However, the description is helpful from another point of view. It reflects the patterned and interlocking network between the rural and urban contexts, with the urban domestic center acting as a collecting node for grain and other products harvested and manufactured in the surrounding countryside.

A rural or urban location of the *domus* of Philemon or the Colossians would, in a sense, not matter, given the symbiotic relationship between rural producers and urban residences. The *domus* would still be the setting for produce collection and cottage industries with its symbiotic and intertwining relationship within the wider Roman market economy and reflective of the local economy and industries. The relative proximity of Hierapolis, Colossae, and Laodicea to one another would further underscore the economic symbiosis that existed in the valley, though not without its tensions and competition, as we have seen. Every *domus* in the valley would also be economically attached and aligned to these cities. This would apply to the households envisaged in Philemon, Colossians,

---

27. T. F. Carney, *The Shape of the Past: Models and Antiquity* (Lawrence: Coronado Press, 1975), 85.

and the Letter to the Laodiceans and the cities and villages associated with them. These would be the locations for local business transactions and the gathering of food stuffs, especially grain, for distribution and transportation to Rome's market abroad.[28]

This trading relationship between the Lycus Valley cities and Rome is evident in an inscription concerning the merchant, Titus Flavius Zeuxis, a citizen of Hierapolis:

> Titus Flavius Zeuxis, merchant, who navigated around Cape Maleas towards Italy during seventy-two sailings, built the monument for

---

28. See the instructive study of Jésus Bermejo Triado, "*Domus* and Household Production. Towards a New Model for the Study of Roman Economy; The Case of the House of Bachus Ariadne (*Thuburbo Maius*)," in *L'Africa Romana XVIII: I luoghi e le forme dei mestieri e della produzione nelle province africane atti del XVIII convegno di studio, Olbia, 11–14 dicembre 2008*, ed. Marco Milanese, Paolo Ruggeri, and Cinzia Vismara (Roma: Carocci, 2010), 851–62. In an investigation of the *domus* of Bachus and Ariadne in the Romano-African city of *Thuburbo Maius* (the former province of *Africa Proconsularis*), Triado demonstrates how the household moved beyond a "self-sufficiency economy" to a much higher level of household production than that which was required, based entirely around the products of its olive mill press. In sum, the rates of production showed a complexity of economic activity that was clearly "aimed at the market, at intraregional levels" (858). On household estates in Asia Minor, see Thomas Corsten, "Estates in Roman Asia Minor: The Case of Kibyratis," in *Patterns in the Economy of Roman Asia Minor*, ed. Stephen Mitchell and Constantina Katsari (Swansea: Classical Press of Wales, 2005), 1–51. In the case of the Lycus valley, any assessment of the urban *domi* of Colossae (Col 1:1: ἐν Κολοσσαῖς) is totally stymied by the fact that the site remains unexcavated. The inner-city evidence of nearby Laodicea is ambiguous, with *insulae* predominating in House A Alley and elsewhere there are two-story peristyle houses (Celal Şimşek, "Urban Planning of Laodikeia on the Lykos in the Light of New Evidence," in *Landscape and History in the Lykos Valley: Laodikeia and Hierapolis in Phrygia*, ed. Celal Şimşek and Francesco D'Andria [Newcastle upon Tyne: Cambridge Scholars, 2017], 13–14, 18–19). But the most impressive candidate for a Lycus valley *domus* of the kind discussed in this chapter is the Southern Roman Villa outside of Laodicea, though, significantly, it postdates the New Testament period. Şimşek ("Urban Planning of Laodikeia," 18) summarizes the archaeological finds there with these words: "The owners of the villa are believed to have not only cultivated the land but also to have manufactured and marketed things such as glass, wine and olive-oil, during the Late Roman Imperial period (third century to the first quarter of the fifth century AD). Coins of Attouda and Hierapolis, as well as lead seals, demonstrate commercial relations with these cities. Thus, this villa is a complex that was intended for agricultural and industrial production" (18).

himself and his sons Flavius Theodoros and Flavius Theudas, and for whoever shall obtain the concession for them.[29]

Titus's mausoleum inscription indicates that he made a significant number of trips, seventy-two around Cape Maleas towards Italy and, presumably, Rome. We do not know what he was trading, perhaps valley cloth or dyes that would have been commercially and internationally popular.[30] Nevertheless, the inscription affirms the profitable commerce with Rome and the importance of the Roman connection for the citizens of Hierapolis and those in other parts of the valley (see Rev 18:15–17).

The *Domus* in Philemon

In Paul's letter addressed to Philemon, the addressee is clearly the owner of a house that gathers an association of Jesus followers. This is the *ekklesia* that Paul identifies and salutes. It is a gathering place which has economic implications.

After greeting Philemon, Paul next addresses Apphia, whom he calls "sister" (a significant title to which I shall return shortly); then, before finally greeting the whole *ekklesia* in Philemon's house, he hails Archippus, whom he describes as a "fellow-soldier." This military designation that Paul gives to Archippus reflects, in Paul's imminent eschatology, the nature of those committed in a gospel ministry that involves an eschatological battle preparing for the final coming of the Christ. Nevertheless, these three, Philemon, Apphia, and Archippus, represent part of the membership of a wider community that form the *ekklesia* of a larger (and wealthy) household.

The fact of Apphia's mention immediately after the letter's addressee and before the male, Archippus, in a social context of male hierarchy is not without its significance. It would suggest something of Apphia's status in the *ekklesia* gathering. Paul calls her "sister" (Phlm 2). The only other female that Paul explicitly addresses with this title is Phoebe, the female deacon of the *ekklesia* at Cenchreae, the harbor town of Corinth (Rom

---

29. *IGRR* 4.841. Translated by Tullia Ritti, *Epigraphic Guide to Hierapolis (Pamukkale)*, tran. P. Arthur (Istanbul: Italian Archaeological Mission at Hierapolis, 2006), 68. Ritti speculates: "We may suppose that Zeuxis exported loads of cloths or clothes, in particular those coloured with the local vegetal dye" (70).

30. Ritti, *Epigraphic Guide to Hierapolis*, 70.

16:1). Paul conceivably entrusts her with his Letter to the Romans. She will carry it to Rome, read it the Jesus followers there, and prepare them for his intended visit. Her task in Rome is quite delicate, given the competing jealousies and tensions that seem to exist among the leaders of the Jewish and gentile Jesus households there.

Paul's use of "our sister" in relationship to Phoebe, therefore, implies status within the network of Jesus households. It affirms her colleagueship with Paul in his mission and her authority to represent him in a very complex and difficult situation. Paul's designation of her as "sister" precedes the other qualifiers that confirm her status. She is a *diakonos* at Cenchreae (Rom 16:1b), a formal title that designates her as an entrusted communicator of an important (and in this case with Paul's letter, divine) message.[31] She is also named *prostasis* (Rom 16:2c), suggesting that she is a woman of wealth, Paul's benefactor.[32] This woman's high socioeconomic status and leadership at Cenchreae, flagged by the preeminent address that Paul gives her—"sister"—would not be unknown among women in the Roman world, as numismatic evidence testifies.[33]

A similar understanding might conceivably apply in Paul's address to Apphia in Philemon. She is a woman of at least equal rank and leadership with Philemon in the *ekklesia* that meets in his *domus*, irrespective of her marital status and relationship to Philemon. From the perspective of the Rome's market world, if she were his spouse, then Apphia, whose Anatolian name is frequently associated with wealth, would also share his socioeconomic status like a Roman matron.[34] Though Paul greets Philemon first

---

31. Bain, *Women's Socioeconomic Status*, 108.

32. See Rosalinde A. Kearsley, "Women in Public Life in the Roman East: Iunia Theodora, Claudia Metrodora and Phoebe, Benefactress of Paul," *TynBul* 50 (1999): 189–211.

33. There is numismatic evidence of a Colossian female benefactor, Claudia Eugenetoriane. She minted two bronze Colossian coins, one featuring Hadrian on the obverse, the other with Helios on the obverse. Claudia's name is clearly present as the minter on both. On the smaller of the two coins she identifies herself very unusually as XHPH ("widow"). See, Alan Cadwallader, "Wealthy, Widowed, Astute and Beneficent: Claudia Eugenetoriane and the Second Century Revival of the Colossian Mint," *NewDocs* 12 (forthcoming).

34. On the Anatolian association of Apphia's name with wealth, see Huttner, *Early Christianity in the Lycus Valley*, 85. For the name Aphia/Apphia at Hierapolis, see *MAMA* 4.276; *SEG* 33.1128, 54.1330; IDenizli 126; *IJO* 2.193 (of a Jew). There are two inscriptions where the name Aphia/Apphia is related to Colossae, one a priest-

and Apphia second, this order reflects the conventional patriarchal precedence given to the *paterfamilias* of a household. Philemon would also be greeted first because he is also the one to whom Paul directs his appeal on behalf of Onesimus who has fled the household and Philemon's authority.

If Apphia were his wife, she held a position of authority within the *domestic* context parallel to the authority exercised by Philemon in the *public* arena. Within the specific domestic setting, she would exercise religious leadership in the Jesus household, especially as it gathered for the Lord's Supper, as we have seen with Phoebe, not unusual in the Pauline households. From a socioeconomic viewpoint, her influence would also extend over those responsible for the manufacturing aspects and marketing production of the *domus*, albeit under the supervision of Philemon as *paterfamilias* who exercised authority over the slaves and the freed workers, of which Onesimus was one. A final point about Apphia is worth noting. The Phrygian origin of her name suggests that she is local. This indigenous recognition adds further weight to the regional provenance of Philemon's *domus* situated in the Lycus Valley, and given the duplication of names between Philemon and Colossians (with Timothy, Epaphras, Aristarchus, Onesimus, Luke, and Archippus) in or close to Colossae, though—with the network and urban symbiosis between Colossae, Hierapolis, and Laodicea—not necessarily.

The size and style of this agricultural and manufacturing unit are further hinted at by two further facts: its architecture and the explicit identification of Onesimus.

- Philemon's house includes a guest room (Phlm 22), not unusual in a Roman styled villa. It existed within an intimate social and familial network upon which rested the security and stability of the province and the Roman Empire. Set against Rome's economic backdrop, what distinguishes Philemon's house from many others in the valley is the affiliation of its members to Jesus. One resident was Onesimus.
- We know from Paul's letter that Onesimus has absconded from Philemon's authority, for reasons that are not at first apparent,

---

ess (*IGRR* 4.868). There is also one example from Laodicea: Jean-Louis Ferrary, *Les mémoriaux de délégations du sanctuaire oraculaire de Claros, d'après la documentation conserve dans le Fonds Louis Robert*, Des inscriptions et belles-lettres Tome 40 (Paris: Mémoires de l'Académie, 2014), 1.31.20.

though become clearer when we apply Rome's economic grid over the situation envisaged in Philemon. Onesimus comes to Paul to request that he broker a renewed relationship with Philemon. The letter is Paul's response to this request. But the status and name of Onesimus are most interesting.

Some scholars have suggested that Onesimus is Philemon's sibling who has come to grief in the close-knit domestic relationship of Philemon's household. Many more commentators are convinced the Onesimus is a runaway slave seeking to be restored to his master.[35] I am convinced by Ulrich Huttner's argument that Onesimus is a freedman or manumitted slave. He would not be the only other person in a household that would accommodate other slaves and free men and women. Their presence would reinforce the fiscal value and status of the house and bring greater honor to Philemon.

Further, a person's name in the ancient world communicated identity, status, and relationships. It symbolized the slave's occupational and economic value and the tribal and social network to which the person belonged. This is reflected in Onesimus's name. Its meaning, "useful" or "beneficial," reflects an industrial, pecuniary, and social status in Philemon's household.[36]

---

35. Though most commentators consider Onesimus a runaway slave, there are some who hold for the sibling relationship between Onesimus and Philemon. See Allen Dwight Callaghan, "Paul's Epistle to Philemon: Toward and Alternative Argumentum," *HTR* 86 (1993): 357–76; Margaret M. Mitchell, "John Chrysostom on Philemon: A Second Look," *HTR* 88 (1995): 135–48. For challenges to the runaway-slave theory, see John Knox, *Philemon among the Letters of Paul* (New York: Abingdon, 1935); Sarah Winter, "Paul's Letter to Philemon," *NTS* 33 (1987): 1–15; Peter Lampe, "Keine 'Sklavenflucht' des Onesimus," *ZNW* 76 (1985): 135–37; Peter Arzt-Grabner, "Onesimus erro: Zur Vorgeschichte des Philemonbriefes," *ZNW* 95 (2004): 131–43; Arzt-Grabner, "How to Deal with Onesimus? Paul's Solution within the Frame of Ancient Legal and Documentary Sources," in *Philemon in Perspective: Interpreting a Pauline Letter*, ed. D. Francois Tolmie, BZNW 169 (Berlin: de Gruyter, 2010), 113–42. For a summary of scholarship on the letter's occasion, see Bonnie Beattie Thurston and Judith M. Ryan, *Philippians and Philemon* (Collegeville, MN: Liturgical Press, 2005), 181–82; Joseph A. Fitzmyer, *The Letter to Philemon* (New York: Doubleday, 2000), 17–19.

36. The name Onesimus was typical of a slave. Of the 150 Onesimus-names identified from north and west Asia Minor, several were free-born, and some had higher social status (Huttner, *Early Christianity in the Lycus Valley*, 86–87).

It is not inconceivable that Onesimus may have been a freed slave, manumitted by Philemon himself.[37] Perhaps he could have even been an imperial freed slave valued highly, in economic terms, by his previous owners. There is inscriptional evidence, for example, of imperial freed slaves in the Lycus Valley.[38] In one inscription from Laodicea we note,

> Tiberius Claudius Tryphon, freedman of the emperor, donated the towers and the triple gateway, the proconsul Sextus Iulius Frontinus dedicated the whole construction.[39]

It is clear from this that the freed imperial slave, Tryphon, had wealth enough to donate money for the construction of towers and a processional entrance to the city. This may not have been Onesimus's situation, but the high economic regard he is held in could well explain the reason that he first fled from Philemon's influence and later wanted to return to the household but under different conditions brokered by Paul. Paul redefines Onesimus's economic worth, "benefit" or "use." He is now "useful" in a different, non-economic sense within the Jesus household defined by his baptismal status rather than his market value (Phlm 11). Paul affirms Onesimus's new status. He challenges the hierarchically prescribed and economically determined social conventions that would have shaped the network of relations that operated in Philemon's house. Paul judges Onesimus's departure from Philemon as an opportunity of reminding him about the essential truth upon which every Jesus household is grounded: its relationship to the risen Jesus:

> Perhaps this is why he was parted from you for a while, that you might have him back for ever, no longer as a slave but more than a slave, as a beloved brother, especially to me but how much more to you, both in the flesh and in the Lord. (Phlm 15–16)

Paul reminds Philemon that Onesimus is no longer to be regarded as an economically viewed domestic possession. Rather as a "beloved brother" he will have similar status, authority, and leadership as Paul's "sister,"

---

37. Huttner, *Early Christianity in the Lycus Valley*, 104–7.
38. Rosalinde Kearsley, "Epigraphic Evidence for the Social Impact of Roman Government in Laodicea and Hierapolis," in *Colossae in Space and Time: Linking to an Ancient City*, ed. Alan H. Cadwallader and Michael Trainor, NTOA-SUNT 94 (Gottingen: Vandenhoek & Ruprecht, 2011), 130–50.
39. I.Laodikeia 24b; Kearsley, "Epigraphic Evidence for Social Impact," 134.

Apphia, greeted in the beginning of the letter. Finally, as the letter comes to its concluding verses, Paul reminds Philemon that he plans to visit (Phlm 22). Paul's reminder to Philemon implies that he will check out what kind of treatment Onesimus will receive from Philemon when he returns.

In summary, there is nothing unusual about Philemon's household. Like other houses in the early period of the Roman Empire occupied and owned by those of the middle economic social strata, it forms part of an integrated industrial and production complex within a network of marketable goods well-known in the Lycus Valley. The nature of these goods we shall discuss below. However, Philemon's household would be similar to other Jesus households in the valley, including those addressed, one to two generations later, by the pseudepigraphic Letter to the Colossians. An economic lens placed over these dwellings highlights the issues with which their inhabitants have to contend—relationships, material wealth, and social approval. All these surface in the writings from Jesus followers that emerge out of first-century CE Lycus Valley.

The *Domus* in the Letter to the Colossians

While the household context of Philemon is clear enough, unearthing the domestic setting for Colossians requires a little more excavation. The letter addresses "the saints and faithful brothers and sisters [*adelphoi*] in Christ at Colossae" (Col 1:2). The physical context in which they gather as Christ followers is not explicit, at least not at the beginning of the letter as the writer moves to applaud the ministry of Epaphras. He is the faithful conduit of Paul's teaching for a new time. He carries the memory of Paul's gospel teaching as his authorized representative and link to the wider Pauline "school" (Col 1:3–8). But there are two indicators towards the letter's end in which the domestic setting becomes more explicit.

The first is the household code of Col 3:18–4:1. Commentators have written much about the nature and purpose of this code—the writer's adoption of a classical topos that designates prescribed lines of domestic authority to reinforce social stability, cultural harmony, and provincial security.[40] Jesus followers are part of, and not sectarian disputants in, the social landscape in which they live. The theological twist that the writer

---

40. See, for example, Angela Standhartinger, "The Origin and Intention of the Household Code in the Letter to the Colossians," *JSNT* 79 (2000): 117–30.

gives the code softens its hierarchal reinforcement and makes Christ the ultimate authority to whom all within the household are subject. Before him all will be judged. The subject matter of the code with its designated lines of authority reinforce the status of those addressed and their interrelationship. This is not a small domestic dwelling occupied by people of lower social status. The code gives greatest attention to slaves. They are the most singled-out group among all the members of a household.[41]

Three reasons, all economically related, suggest themselves for this extra attention: the commercial value of slaves, the free status of Epaphras, and the discouragement given to slave resistance or revolt that would compromise the potential for the Colossian Jesus households to become a marketing cooperative or association.

First, slaves were a prominent social group in the Lycus Valley Jesus households. Within the early Roman Empire, they represented at least 10 to 20 or 30 percent of the population and formed a distinctive institution upon which the Roman economy depended.[42] They were the most economically exploited group in Roman society.[43]

The institution of chattel slavery is one of the most striking features of Roman society. Slaves were an almost totally malleable product: they could be used to display the wealth of their owner or for the most specialized purposes, such as being virtual talking books. The Roman upper classes were aware of this reliance and not uncommonly expressed concern at this dependence on those beneath them. The demand for slave labor was supplied by domestically bred slaves and also by the purchase of considerable numbers of imported slaves, some from outside the empire but most from within the area of Roman rule.[44]

---

41. In the Greek text, forty-two words describe the conventional familial relationships (wives—husbands, children—parents, fathers—children). Masters receive twenty-three. The code's address to the slaves occupies fifty-six Greek words.

42. See Temin, *Roman Market Economy*, 31, who estimates that slaves were 10 percent of the Roman population. Other sources make them 20 to 30 percent (at least in Roman Italy, 1–1.5 million in an overall population of 5–6 million). See also Tim G. Parkin and Arthur Pomeroy, *Roman Social History: A Sourcebook* (London: Routledge, 2007), 157, 357; Leonhard Schumacher, "Slaves in Roman Society," in *The Oxford Handbook of Social Relations in the Roman World*, ed. Michael Peachin (Oxford: Oxford University Press, 2011), 509–608.

43. Schumacher, "Slaves in Roman Society," 509.

44. Parkin and Pomeroy, *Roman Social History*, 154.

In other words, slaves represented wealth and symbolized economic prestige for the household to which they belonged.

A second consideration comes from an appreciation of the background of Epaphras and his status among the Jesus followers of the Lycus Valley. Epaphras is a shorted form of Epaphroditus, derived from the Greek name for the goddess Aphrodite. This connection suggests that he was a Hellenized Jewish Jesus follower who moved away from the earlier religious practices of his parents, who had chosen to name him after the goddess of love. Inscriptional evidence gleaned from around the Mediterranean locates his name in Macedonia, Achaia, Magna Graecia (southern Italy), and Sicily. It is associated with a variety of backgrounds and occupations, with benefactors, slaves, freedmen, and, in one inscription from the imperial cult at Ephesus, a priest. The majority of Magna Graecia references associate the name with conquered males from other countries forced into slavery.[45]

On balance then, it seems possible that Epaphras came from a servile background, not necessarily from the poorer fringes of society, given that some slaves were the trophies of elite households. At the time of the writing of Colossians, his availability to move freely about the Lycus Valley to Laodicea and Hierapolis (Col 4:13) suggests that he is now a freedman. If this is true, then Epaphras would take not a little interest in the slaves of the Lycus Valley Jesus households with whom he would identify. He would also be able to exercise considerable influence among them, especially if he was the one who brought Paul's gospel to the valley, if not the actual writer of Colossians at which some commentators have hinted.[46]

Third, this recognition of the prominence and market value of slaves at Colossae makes sense to the opening injunction in the household code (that slaves "obey in everything those who are earthly masters," Col 3.22). This reinforces their status quo. In Roman society slave resistance, rebellion, and desertion was more common than previously thought.[47] The code's injunction counterbalances a perception easily derived from Col

---

45. For more on Epaphras, see Trainor, *Epaphras*, 6–10.

46. Ephaphras as the author to the Letter to the Colossians is not a new suggestion. It first appeared in the nineteenth century with Albert Klöpper, *Der Brief an die Colosser: Kritisch untersucht und in seinem Verhältnisse zum paulinischem Lehrbegriff exegetisch und biblisch-theologisch erortet* (Berlin: Reimer, 1882). See also Mark Christopher Kiley, *Colossians as Pseudepigraphy* (Sheffield: JSOT Press, 1986).

47. Allen Dwight Callahan and Richard A. Horsley, "Slave Resistance in Classical Antiquity," *Semeia* 83 (1998): 133–51.

3:11 that there is "no Greek and Jew, circumcised and uncircumcised, barbarian, Scythian, slave, free, but Christ is all, and in all." If this text were interpreted literally and acted out socially, the removal of any distinction between slave and free would lead to revolt or the growing demand for manumission. Social anarchy and economic upheaval would follow. However, the content of the code's address to slaves beyond its opening injunction offers a counter balance more aligned to Paul's gospel. The code subtly but carefully redefines the true social status of slaves in terms of their relationship to the Lord, rather than their earthly masters, in a way that honors the spirit of Col 3:11.

The author addresses the members of the household in the plural (wives, husbands, children, slaves, and masters). This number would be part of the conventional inheritance carried over from the expected address already present in the code. The plurality of children and slaves addressed would not be surprising.

On the other hand, those addressed are members of the one household of Jesus in Colossae. The plurality of spouses ("wives" and "husbands") indicates that those addressed by the letter do not form only *one* household (as envisaged in Philemon). There exist a number of households in which the husbands were also slave masters. All the members of these various *domi* would form a domestic collective and an interrelated marketing cooperative that would gather in one structure, a larger *domus*, in order to celebrate the Lord's Supper, remember the story of Jesus, and receive Pauline instruction (as, say, by the Letter to the Colossians). It would not take much to imagine how Colossians and its code would be heard and comprehended with everyone, from different social classes, attentive at the same time and in the same place. This liturgical setting would be a concrete expression and demonstration of Col 3:11.

Nympha's House

The Colossians author envisages several households. However, the writer identifies explicitly one house and greets it in words that echo Philemon: "Give my greetings to the brothers and sisters at Laodicea, and to Nympha and the *ekklesia* in her house" (Col 4:15). The fact that no other male is mentioned in regard to this household clearly indicates that Nympha is a woman of elevated social and economic status. "As owner of the central assembly place," asserts Huttner,

Nympha did serve as one of the prominent pillars of her community. Clearly she came from a relatively wealthy family and was among the women—by no means rare in Asia Minor—who had more or less extensive assets at their disposal more or less independently.[48]

She hosts and leads her household when the *ekklesia* gathers and conceivably presides at the Lord's Supper. Nympha is also a widow in the classical understanding of the word: one who did not live with a male or an elite woman who survived her older husband.[49] In later history, as Jesus households become more male dominated and female household leadership discouraged and suppressed, her name was changed to the masculine in the New Testament text![50] In fact, Nympha's position, description, and status meant that she, like Apphia and Philemon and the other households envisaged in the Colossian household code, was responsible for a *domus* in Laodicea with all the economic connections this implied. It was a production and economic unit within the interrelated commercial symbiosis of the Lycus Valley with its marketing and economic wealth from the products that we know were produced there.

The Wealth of the Lycus Valley

From inscriptions and steles discovered in the valley, this wealth could have come from the raising of pigs; the production of wine; the harvesting of wheat, other grains, fruits, and vegetables; and the production of additional marketable goods, especially dyed wool.[51] Inscriptions found on tombstones, reliefs, and agricultural equipment from the first and second centuries testify to the variety and quality of the goods produced and manufactured in the Lycus Valley. Huttner offers a helpful summary of the agricultural wealth of the region in which the houses of Philemon

---

48. Huttner, *Early Christianity in the Lycus Valley*, 96.

49. Bain, *Women's Socioeconomic Status*, 69.

50. Huttner, *Early Christianity in the Lycus Valley*, 95. However, see the recent proposal of Thomas Corsten ("Man oder Frau: Nympha oder Nymphas in Laodikeia?," in *Epigraphical Evidence Illustrating Paul's Letter to the Colossians*, ed. Joseph Verheyden, Markus Öhler, and Thomas Corsten, WUNT 411 [Tübingen: Mohr Siebeck, 2018], 215–19) who proposes that the name is indeed Νυμφᾶς and that the person is therefore a male.

51. For more on these goods, especially in ancient Colossae, see Cadwallader, *Fragments of Colossae*.

and those addressed by Colossians, including Nympha's (Col 4:15), were located. Huttner's summary reflects the archaeological and numismatic evidence gleaned from the Lycus Valley in recent years:

> The Lycus and its tributaries flow through a hilly alluvial landscape, including some ravines, that allows the cultivation of several crops. Where cotton is the primary crop today, followed increasingly by wine, in antiquity it is clear that grain flourished along with fruits and vegetables, which were naturally irreplaceable as fundamental foodstuffs, but also olive trees (probably mostly on the hillsides) and wine grapes, albeit without suggesting agricultural continuity. Vitruvius speaks in one place of the "gardens and vineyards" around Hierapolis. At higher elevations, especially on the hillsides to the north and south, we may assume that cattle and especially sheep were raised.[52]

Dried food, harvested grain, and locally produced wine, wool, and other material products that exceeded local demands could be easily transported along the main trade route, which was connected to Ephesus in the west and then shipped across the Mediterranean Sea to Rome. A tombstone relief from the Hierapolis necropolis witnesses to one involved in the transportation trade.

The Letter to the Laodiceans (Rev 3:14–22)

Before concluding, one final writing, the Letter to the Laodiceans in the book of Revelation (Rev 3:14–22), deserves brief attention. I have argued up until now for the Roman *domus* as the setting for Paul's Letter to Philemon and in the later pseudonymous letter to the Colossians. The *domus* provides an entrée into considering the economic context and status for the Jesus followers of the Lycus Valley, the addressees of the letters. I have suggested that they would represent a middle stratum of social status and wealth. In turning to the third of the writings addressed to Lycus Valley Jesus followers, John's Letter to the Laodiceans (Rev 3:14–22), a similar and more explicit economic picture emerges. This surfaces from a study of the writer's language and metaphors used of the addressees and a consideration of these in the light of the economic resources and material wealth that we know of the Laodiceans. The *domus* setting is also clearly present.

---

52. Huttner, *Early Christianity in the Lycus Valley*, 20–21.

The letter itself is part of a larger apocalyptic work designed to offer comfort and security to late first-century Jesus followers experiencing economic, civic, and social suppression from the civic authorities and those who enforce the *pax Romana*. After an initial heavenly vision in which the Lordship and universal reign of Christ is affirmed (Rev 1:1–8), the writer addresses seven churches: Ephesus (Rev 2:1–7), Smyrna (Rev 2:8–11), Pergamum (Rev 2:12–17), Thyatira (Rev 2:18–29), Sardis (Rev 3:1–6), Philadelphia (Rev 3:7–11), and Laodicea (Rev 1:9–3:22). Whether these churches accurately reflect the local historical, social, and theological situations of the various locales or whether they are symbolic of more universal ecclesial phenomena is debatable.[53] However, the background of the places addressed helps to understand the issues about which the writer is concerned for each Jesus household. John encourages the Jesus disciples in Smyrna in anticipation of the "tribulation" about to come upon them (Rev 2:10). The other six churches are also encouraged, but they are also critiqued for their failures in discipleship. This same pattern emerges in the address to Laodicea.

From the monetary perspective of Rome's market economy that influenced commercial production, manufacturing, economic transactions, and industry in the Lycus Valley, Laodicea was clearly a city of wealth. Its status emerged and bypassed ancient Colossae in the early imperial period. Its natural resources, gold, wool, water, production of dyes and eye salves, and its medical reputation helped its growth in economic prosperity, status recognition, and its capacity to rebuild itself without any outside support in the wake of the earthquake of 67 CE.[54] Of significance was Laodicea's access to gold.

Laodicea's natural resources and production prowess, while the source of wealth and economic power, also have spiritual consequences, which the writer of the book of Revelation names. Disciples do not live in a vacuum but are influenced by the economic realities that surround them.

---

53. See, for example, the summary comments offered by Leonard L. Thompson, *The Book of Revelation: Apocalypse and Empire* (New York: Oxford: Oxford University Press, 1997), 11–36. A celestial interpretation of the seven churches is offered in Bruce J. Malina, *Social-Science Commentary on the Book of Revelation* (Minneapolis: Fortress, 2000), 34.

54. On the importance of the natural resources of the Lycus Valley and its dye-works as a means to economic wealth, see Huttner, *Early Christianity in the Lycus Valley*, 119.

Their economic wealth and comfort lead them into a state of spiritual poverty, which the writer names, using metaphors drawn from the economic world so familiar to the Laodicean Jesus followers:

> For you say, "I am rich, I have prospered, and I need nothing." You do not realize that you are wretched, pitiable, poor, blind, and naked. Therefore I counsel you to buy from me gold refined by fire so that you may be rich; and white robes to clothe you and to keep the shame of your nakedness from being seen; and salve to anoint your eyes so that you may see. (Rev 3:17–18)

John, in his visionary ecstasy, echoes the voice of the risen, apocalyptic Christ in identifying the real issues that are affecting these Jesus followers. He encourages them to a spirit of repentance (Rev 3:19), converting their wealthy resources (refined gold, clothing, and eye salve) into theological symbols of this conversion that brings a refinement in their discipleship ("gold refined by fire") and a renewed baptismal commitment ("white robes," "salve to anoint your eyes"). The fruit of this repentance will be seen in their celebration of the communal meal of Lord's Supper. The explicit context for this is the Roman *domus*:

> Listen! I am standing at the door, knocking; if you hear my voice and open the door, I will come in to you and eat with you, and you with me. (Rev 3:20)

The Laodicean Jesus *domus* reflects the same qualities that we have seen in Philemon and Colossians. It is the domestic setting for the gathering of Jesus householders, who represent a cross-section of Western Anatolian-Phrygian-Roman society, weighted towards the more wealthy industrialists and merchants representative of the middle stratum, who have benefited from the prosperity gleaned from the Roman economic market. The seer John invites them to consider their wealthy situation and to return to the fundamentals of their discipleship: their relationship to the risen Christ and their relationship to each other.[55] These same truths echo what we have already seen in the households addressed by Philemon and Colossians.

---

55. Note especially John's critique of the merchants who were dependent upon the wealth of the (now fallen) Rome in Rev 18:15–17. See Richard Bauckham, "The Economic Critique of Rome in Revelation 18," in *The Climax of Prophecy: Studies on the Book of Revelation* (Edinburgh: T&T Clark, 1993), 373.

Conclusion

The Lycus Valley was an agriculturally rich and industrially successful region in south western Anatolia, situated within the wider matrix of Rome's market economy. Its regional wealth occurred because of the rich natural resources of the valley and the technical expertise of its inhabitants.[56] Access to its natural wealth and economic largesse influenced relationships within the Jesus households, which collectively would have formed a marketing cooperative, though, as we noted, competition was not unknown. As Huttner notes,

> The readiness of individuals to form associations was deeply rooted in the Lycus Valley, as is apparent from the epigraphic evidence, which documents a dense concentration of trade associations, cultic communities, family associations, and *hetairiai*.[57]

In this context, the Roman market economy was embedded in everything that affected its members, though Phrygian manufacturing and industrial practices indigenous to the valley moderated Rome's economic influence. My economic focus has been on the three New Testament Lycus Valley writings, Philemon, Colossians, and the Letter to the Loadiceans in the book of Revelation. In all three writings, the *domus* is clearly the context. These were commercial and industrial units, besides places of habitation. An economic dynamic operated within the Jesus households. A key consideration interprets the *domus*, not as a spiritual "cell" isolated from the social, commercial, and pecuniary interests of the valley in which it dwells but as a production and manufacturing unit within an integral economic network of the Lycus Valley, perhaps in an association of cottage industries formed through an alliance in their discipleship to Jesus.

My focus here has been to conjecture about the effects of the Roman market economy and its relative wealth upon the Jesus followers in the Lycus Valley, who represent the middle social stratum. However, I have also suggested that this was not a monochromatic picture. Local Phrygian industrial and agricultural industries shaped relationships and balanced out Rome's influence. More thought is needed about those Jesus followers who represent the lower, poorer stratum of Roman society, not explicitly

---

56. Huttner, *Early Christianity in the Lycus Valley*, 119.
57. Huttner, *Early Christianity in the Lycus Valley*, 30.

addressed by, but not excluded from the New Testament writings associated with the Lycus Valley.

I have suggested that using a Roman economic lens throws light on key issues in each of the writings. An appreciation of the nature of the Roman market economy, in a period of relative wealth and social stability for those representing the middle strata of the Roman economic ladder, illuminates the main concern in Philemon with Paul's advocacy of Onesimus in his changed status. Other inscriptional evidence from Phrygia relevant to our discussion has thrown further light on this. This provides us with a variegated economic lens with which to view the transactions and relationships.

With regard to Colossians, the main focus has been upon the explicit households addressed in Colossians through the *Haustafel* and Nympha's singled-out *domus*. However, the use of the Roman-Phrygian economic dynamic also assists us in appreciating the main theological issues with which Colossians is concerned: the author's reassertion of the cosmic authority of Christ among Jesus followers, who were beguiled by their attraction to indigenous Jewish ascetical practices and angelic worship in an effort to assuage the dominant "principalities and powers" (Col 2:13–23). These "principalities and powers" are pervasive political and economic forces that Christ has disarmed (Col 2:15a). The communion with the Christ that the Jesus followers have through baptism is the real power that will thwart and overcome any form of suppression (Col 3:1–3).

Finally, a brief study of the Letter to the Laodiceans affirms the embedded nature of economics within the Lycus Valley industrial, production, and manufacturing network. Rome's economic system did not entirely dominate. Laodicea's gold and clothing resources, its dyeing industry, and its medical practice account for its wealth. Economics are also embedded within the attitudes of the householders of the *domus* envisaged in Laodicea. They have been distracted by their access to gold, their prosperous clothing and dyeing industry, and their manufacture of medical goods. The seer John invites them to a renewal in their baptismal discipleship of the apocalyptic and risen Christ with eucharistic hospitality as central.

Bibliography

Arzt-Grabner, Peter. "How to Deal with Onesimus? Paul's Solution within the Frame of Ancient Legal and Documentary Sources." Pages 113–42 in *Philemon in Perspective: Interpreting a Pauline Letter*. Edited by D. Francois Tolmie. BZNW 169. Berlin: de Gruyter, 2010.

———. "Onesimus erro: Zur Vorgeschichte des Philemonbriefes." *ZNW* 95 (2004): 131–43.

Bain, Katherine. *Women's Socioeconomic Status and Religious Leadership in Asia Minor in the Frist Two Centuries CE*. Minneapolis: Fortress, 2014.

Bagnall, Roger S., and Bruce W. Frier. *The Demography of Roman Egypt*. Cambridge Studies in Population, Economy and Society in Past Time 23. Cambridge: Cambridge University Press, 1994.

Balabanski, Vicky. "Where Is Philemon? The Case for a Logical Fallacy in the Correlation of the Data in Philemon and Colossians 1:1–2; 4:7–8." *JSNT* 38 (2015): 131–50.

Bang, P. F. *The Roman Bazaar: A Comparative Study of Trade and Markets in a Tributary Empire*. Cambridge: Cambridge University Press, 2008.

Bauckham, Richard. "The Economic Critique of Rome in Revelation 18." Pages 338-83 in *The Climax of Prophecy: Studies on the Book of Revelation*. Edinburgh: T&T Clark, 1993.

Blanton, Thomas R., IV, and Raymond Pickett, eds. *Paul and Economics: A Handbook*. Minneapolis: Fortress, 2017.

Bourke van der Meer, L. *Ostia: Inscriptions, Buildings and Spaces in Rome's Main Port*. Leuven: Peeters, 2012.

Cadwallader, Alan H. *Fragments of Colossae: Sifting through the Traces*. Hindmarsh: ATF Press, 2015.

———. "Wealthy, Widowed, Astute and Beneficent: Claudia Eugenetoriane and the Second Century Revival of the Colossian Mint." *NewDocs* 12 (forthcoming).

Callaghan, Allen Dwight. "Paul's Epistle to Philemon: Toward and Alternative Argumentum." *HTR* 86 (1993): 357–76.

Callahan, Allen Dwight, and Richard A. Horsley. "Slave Resistance in Classical Antiquity." *Semeia* 83 (1998): 133–51.

Carney, T. F. *The Shape of the Past: Models and Antiquity*. Lawrence: Coronado Press, 1975.

Cooper, Kate. "Closely Watched Households: Visibility, Exposure and Private Power in the Roman 'Domus.'" *Past and Present* 197 (2007): 3–33.

Corsten, Thomas. "Estates in Roman Asia Minor: The Case of Kibyratis." Pages 1–51 in *Patterns in the Economy of Roman Asia Minor*. Edited by Stephen Mitchell and Constantina Katsari. Swansea: Classical Press of Wales, 2005.

———. "Man oder Frau: Nympha oder Nymphas in Laodikeia?" Pages 215–19 in *Epigraphical Evidence Illustrating Paul's Letter to the Colossians*. Edited by Joseph Verheyden, Markus Öhler, and Thomas Corsten. WUNT 411. Tübingen: Mohr Siebeck, 2018.

Duncan-Jones, Richard. *The Economy of the Roman Empire: Quantitative Studies*. 2nd rev. ed. Cambridge: Cambridge University Press, 1982.

———. *Money and Government in the Roman Empire*. Cambridge: Cambridge University Press, 1994.

Erdkamp, Paul. "How Modern Was the Market Economy of the Roman World?" *Œconomia* 4.2 (2014): http://journals.openedition.org/oeconomia/399.

Ferrary, Jean-Louis. *Les mémoriaux de délégations du sanctuaire oraculaire de Claros, d'après la documentation conserve dans le Fonds Louis Robert*. Vol. 1–2. Des inscriptions et belles-lettres Tome 40. Paris: Mémoires de l'Académie, 2014.

Finley, Moses I. *The Ancient Economy*. Berkeley: University of California Press, 1999.

Fitzmyer, Joseph A. *The Letter to Philemon*. New York: Doubleday, 2000.

Friesen, Steven. "Poverty in Pauline Studies: Beyond the So-Called New Consensus." *JSNT* 26 (2004): 323–61.

Hopkins, Keith. "The Political Economy in the Roman Empire." Pages 178–204 in *The Dynamics of Ancient Empires: State Power from Assyria to Byzantium*. Edited by Ian Morris and Walter Scheidel. Oxford: Oxford University Press, 2009.

Huttner, Ulrich. *Early Christianity in the Lycus Valley*. Translated by David Green. AJEC 85; Early Christianity in Asia Minor 1. Leiden: Brill, 2013.

Jones, A. H. M. *The Roman Economy: Studies in Ancient Economic and Administrative History*. Edited by P. A. Brunt. Oxford: Blackwell, 1974.

Jongman, Willem. *The Economy and Society of Pompeii*. Amsterdam: Gieben, 1988.

———. "Gibbon Was Right: The Decline and Fall of the Roman Economy." Pages 183–99 in *Crises and the Roman Empire: Proceedings of the Seventh Workshop of the International Network Impact of Empire (Nijmegen, June 20–24, 2006)*. Edited by Olivier Hekster, Gerda de Kleijn, and Danielle Slootjes. Leiden: Brill, 2007.

———. "The Rise and Fall of the Roman Economy: Population, Rents and Entitlement." Pages 237–54 in *Ancient Economies, Modern Methodologies: Archaeology, Comparative History, Models and Institutions*. Edited by Peter F. Bang, Mamoru Ikeguchi, and Harmut G. Ziche. Bari: Edipuglia, 2006.

Kearsley, Rosalinde A. "Epigraphic Evidence for the Social Impact of Roman Government in Laodicea and Hierapolis." Pages 130–50 in *Colossae in Space and Time: Linking to an Ancient City*. Edited by Alan H. Cadwallader and Michael Trainor. NTOA–SUNT 94. Göttingen: Vandenhoeck & Ruprecht, 2011.

———. "Women in Public Life in the Roman East: Iunia Theodora, Claudia Metrodora and Phoebe, Benefactress of Paul." *TynBul* 50 (1999): 189–211.

Kehoe, Dennis P. *Law and the Rural Economy in the Roman Empire*. Michigan: University of Michigan Press, 2007.

Kiley, Mark Christopher. *Colossians as Pseudepigraphy*. Sheffield: JSOT Press, 1986.

Klöpper, Albert. *Der Brief an die Colosser: Kritisch untersucht und in seinem Verhältnisse zum paulinischem Lehrbegriff exegetisch und biblisch-theologisch erortet*. Berlin: Reimer, 1882.

Knox, John. *Philemon among the Letters of Paul*. New York: Abingdon, 1935.

Lampe, Peter. "Keine 'Sklavenflucht' des Onesimus." *ZNW* 76 (1985): 135–37.

Longenecker, Bruce W. *Remember the Poor: Paul, Poverty, and the Greco-Roman World*. Grand Rapids: Eerdmans, 2010.

Malina, Bruce J. *Social-Science Commentary on the Book of Revelation*. Minneapolis: Fortress, 2000.

Maschek, Dominik. "The Marble Stoa at Hierapolis: Materials, Labour Force and Building Costs." Pages 393–402 in *Ancient Quarries and Building Sites in Asia Minor: Research on Hierapolis in Phrygia and Other Cities in South-Western Anatolia; Archaeology, Archaeometry, Conservation*. Edited by Tommaso Ismaelli and Giuseppe Scardozzi. Bari: Edipuglia, 2016.

Mitchell, Margaret M. "John Chrysostom on Philemon: A Second Look." *HTR* 88 (1995): 135–48.

Parkin, Tim G., and Arthur Pomeroy. *Roman Social History: A Sourcebook*. London: Routledge, 2007.

Ritti, Tullia. *Epigraphic Guide to Hierapolis (Pamukkale)*. Translated by P. Arthur. Istanbul: Italian Archaeological Mission at Hierapolis, 2006.

———. *Hierapolis di Frigia IX: Storia e istituzioni di Hierapolis*. Istanbul: Ege, 2017.

Ritti, Tullia, Klaus Grewe, and Paul Kessner. "A Relief of a Water-Powered Stone Saw Mill on a Sarcophagus at Hierapolis and Its Implications." *JRA* 20 (2007): 139–63.
Russell, Ben. *The Economics of the Roman Stone Trade*. Oxford: Oxford University Press, 2013.
Scheidel, Walter, Ian Morris, and Richard Saller. *The Cambridge Economic History of the Greco-Roman World*. Cambridge: Cambridge University Press, 2007.
Scheidel, Walter, and Steven J. Friesen. "The Size of the Economy and the Distribution of Income in the Roman Empire." *JRS* 99 (2009): 61–91.
Schumacher, Leonhard. "Slaves in Roman Society." Pages 509–608 in *The Oxford Handbook of Social Relations in the Roman World*. Edited by Michael Peachin. Oxford: Oxford University Press, 2011.
Şimşek, Celal. "Urban Planning of Laodikeia on the Lykos in the Light of New Evidence." Pages 1–51 in *Landscape and History in the Lykos Valley: Laodikeia and Hierapolis in Phrygia*. Edited by Celal Simsek and Francesco D'Andria. Newcastle upon Tyne: Cambridge Scholars, 2017.
Standhartinger, Angela. "The Origin and Intention of the Household Code in the Letter to the Colossians." *JSNT* 79 (2000): 117–30.
Stegemann, Ekkehard W. and Wolfgang Stegemann. *The Jesus Movement: A Social History of Its First Century*. Minneapolis: Fortress, 1999.
Temin, Peter. *The Roman Market Economy*. Princeton: Princeton University Press, 2012.
Thompson, Leonard L. *The Book of Revelation: Apocalypse and Empire*. New York: Oxford: Oxford University Press, 1997.
Thonemann, Peter. "Households and Families." Pages 124–42 in *Roman Phrygia: Culture and Society*. Edited by Peter Thonemann. Cambridge: Cambridge University Press, 2013.
———. *The Maeander Valley: A Historical Geography from Antiquity to Byzantium*. Cambridge: Cambridge University Press, 2011.
Thurston, Bonnie Beattie, and Judith M. Ryan, *Philippians and Philemon*. Collegeville, MN: Liturgical Press, 2005.
Trainor, Michael. *Epaphras: Paul's Educator at Colossae*. Collegeville, MN: Liturgical Press, 2008.
Triado, Jésus Bermejo. "*Domus* and Household Production: Towards a New Model for the Study of Roman Economy; The Case of the House of Bachus Ariadne (*Thuburbo Maius*)." Pages 851–62 in *L'Africa Romana XVIII: I luoghi e le forme dei mestieri e della produzione nelle province*

africane atti del XVIII convegno di studio, Olbia, 11–14 dicembre 2008. Edited by Marco Milanese, Paolo Ruggeri, and Cinzia Vismara. Roma: Carocci, 2010.

Verboven, Koenraad. "City and Reciprocity: The Rome of Cultural Beliefs in the Roman Economy." *Annales* 67.4 (2012): 597–627.

Winter, Sarah. "Paul's Letter to Philemon." *NTS* 33 (1987): 1–15.

Has the Vita Abercii Misled Epigraphists in the Reconstruction of the Inscription?

Allen Brent

This chapter seeks to show how the fourth-century Vita Abercii is a legend that has reshaped the original words and meaning of the Abercius inscription, an original portion of which is found on one side of one surviving fragment (subsequently broken in two) of a βωμός (altar) that capped a tomb. W. M. Ramsay and J. R. S. Sterrett's nineteenth-century discovery is now in the Vatican Museo Pio Christiano (plates 1 and 2). The legend represents the fourth-century Christianization, as Peter Thonemann argues, of the original Hellenistic culture of Hierapolis by giving a Christian interpretation of several of its originally pagan artifacts. If this is the case why, we shall ask, is *prima facie* Abercius's βωμός-shaped tomb to be excluded from that category? Why is it the one artifact that was always Christian and needed no reinterpretation from an original, pagan significance? Finally, what might its original significance have been if not Christian? Let us begin with a brief sketch of the details of the Vita Abercii.

1. The Vita Sancti Abercii

Abercius is bishop of Hierapolis and a contemporary of the emperors Marcus Aurelius and Lucius Verus. Publius Dolabella is governor of Phrygia Salutaris and implements the imperial command for a general sacrifice, in response to which Abercius provokes a riot (Vit. Aberc. 1–6).[1] The bishop preaches, heals three epileptics, and baptizes five hundred con-

---

1. All citations from the Vita Abercii are from Theodor Nissen, *S. Abercii Vita* (Leipzig: Teubner, 1912). All citations from the epitaph (*Grabschrift*) are from Willy Lüdtke and Theodor Nissen, *Die Grabschrift des Aberkios, Ihre Überlieferung und Ihr Text* (Leipzig: Teubner, 1910).

verts (Vit. Aberc. 9–11). Phrygella, the mother of Euxeinianus Pollio, who is to be the correspondent of the two emperors, is healed of her blindness along with three others (Vit. Aberc. 20–23; 33; 47–50).

Abercius miraculously creates a thermal spring that becomes the location of a bathhouse (Vit. Aberc. 65–66). The devil flees to Rome and takes possession of Lucilla, daughter of Marcus Aurelius, sixteen years of age and the intended bride of Lucius Verus his coemperor: they are to be married at Ephesus (Vit. Aberc. 36–43). Marcus takes the advice of the prefect Cornelianus and writes to Euxeinianus in order to summon bishop Abercius to Rome to exorcise Lucilla (Vit. Aberc. 45–49).

Valerius and Bassianus are the emperor's *agentes in rebus* (μαγιστριανοί, or messengers) and deliver the imperial letter to the governor Spintha who has replaced Dolabella in office (Vit. Aberc. 50–51). The μαγιστριανοί subsequently bring Abercius to the eparch Cornelius at Rome. Abercius expels Lucilla's daemon and commands it to pick up a marble altar and carry it to Hierapolis. Abercius's previous miracle in producing the hot springs at Agros is monumentalized by Faustina's gift of a bathhouse and a *frumentatio* (grain dole) of 3000 *modioi* for the poor of Hierapolis (Vit. Aberc. 52–56).

On his way to Rome, Trophimus joins Abercius and carries bread and wine, though when the former drinks from the wine-flask without the latter's consent, vinegar comes out instead (Vit. Aberc. 56). Abercius finally, before his death, builds a tomb for himself on top of which is the altar, brought by the daemon from Rome, where we read the full text of the epitaph (Vit. Aberc. 76–77).

From what historical sources if any was the Vita Abercii constructed? Were there any elements that might be true and a record of what was witnessed in the middle to late second century? We shall argue that there are various elements from secular history, put together in a somewhat garbled form, but no plausible details of Christianity at this time.

2. Vita Sancti Abercii: Possible Historical Sources

The Vita Abercii itself shows some historical details, a few accurate and others clearly anachronistic. These features complicate the question of possible sources for the legend: where did the author find the particular, true details from Hierapolis that he wove into his fiction?

There are a host of post-fourth-century details. The emperor Julian ended Faustina's *frumentatio*. The administrative divisions of Phrygia into

Pacatiana (Prima Maior) and Salutaris (Secunda Minor) were only made under the administrative reforms of Diocletian.[2] Valerius and Bassianus, imperial letter bearers, are described here as μαγιστριανοὺς τῶν θείων ὀφφικίων (*magistriani sacrorum officiorum*) but elsewhere as βερηδάριοι. But these titles did not exist before 326 CE.[3]

However, the letter purportedly written by Emperor Marcus Aurelius excites most of Thonemann's historical interest: its form as an imperial *epistola* can be paralleled with surviving epigraphs. It has two parts in the Vita Abercii, the first of which contains some remarkably accurate historical details, but the second, involving the fabulous life of Abercius, consists wholly of anachronisms (Vit. Aberc. 48–49).[4]

Thonemann established the accuracy of this first half of the imperial *epistula*. Euxeinianus Pollio, the wealthy individual to whom the emperor's letter is addressed, has a name that is also well attested epigraphically.[5] Claudius Pollio, as asiarch (161–169 CE), commemorated his office by minting coins of five types, with effigies of Marcus Aurelius, Lucius Verus, and Faustina that date them. Some of them abbreviated, they bear the legend ἐπιμεληθέντος Κλ. Πωλλίωνος ἀσιάρχου Ἱεροπολεῖτων.[6] Furthermore, we have an inscription from neighboring Acmonia where the city honors Κυ[ίντον] Κλαύδιον Πωλίων[α] Τιβερίου Κλα[υδ]ίου Εὐξένου υἱόν.[7]

The emperor's titles "Germanicus" and "Sarmaticus" were used between 175–178 CE when the deteriorating military situation led to their

---

2. Stephen Mitchell, *Anatolia: Land, Men, and Gods in Asia Minor*, (Oxford: Oxford University Press, 1993), 2:161.

3. Various forms of these title appear throughout as in Vit. Aberc. 47; 49 (μαγιστριανοὺς τῶν θείων ὀφφικίων); 50; 57. The same officials are called βερηδάριοι in 52; 54; 57; 60. Roland Delmaire, *Les institutions du bas-empire romain de Constantin à Justinien: Les institutions civiles palatines* (Paris: Cerf, 1995), 97–118; Mitchell, *Anatolia*, 1:129–32; Anna Avramea, "Land and Sea Communications, Fourth–Fifteenth Centuries," in *The Economic History of Byzantium*, ed. Angeliki E. Laiou, vol. 1, Dumbarton Oaks Studies 39 (Washington DC: Dumbarton Oaks, 2002), 58–64, 74–77.

4. For details see Peter Thonemann, "Abercius of Hierapolis: Christianisation and Social Memory in Late Antique Asia Minor," in *Historical and Religious Memory in the Ancient* World, ed. Beate Dignas and R. R. R. Smith (Oxford: Oxford University Press, 2012), 266–67.

5. Thonemann, "Abercius of Hierapolis," 269–73.

6. For full references see Thonemann, "Abercius of Hierapolis," 272 n. 30: "with Claudius Pollio, Asiarch of Hierapolis, taking responsibility."

7. Thonemann, "Abercius of Hierapolis," 269, fig. 12.2: "Quintus Claudius Pollio, son of Tiberius Claudius Euxenos."

demise. The name mentioned of "our procurator [ἐπίτροπος] Caecilius" seems likely to have been the M. Caecilius Numa, a *procurator Augusti*, who was a contemporary with Marcus Aurelius and was responsible for the construction of the *Trachon* that was a highway through a mountain between Ephesus and Magnesia.[8]

One last name to be mentioned in this context is that of Cornelianus, not mentioned in the text of the first half of the imperial *epistula* but introduced shortly before in the narrative as the "prefect" (ἔπαρχος) who commends Euxeinianus to the emperor as a good contact through whom to contact the wonder-working bishop. There is a Cornelianus with the office of *ab epistulis graecis* (the emperor's Greek secretary) recorded at Rome at the date claimed for the emperor's letter to Pollio (177–178 CE).[9] Thus the cluster of different names and titles, all contemporaneous with a date around the Smyrnaean earthquake also mentioned (177 CE), represents an island of fact among so many bewildering anachronisms.

But the first part of the *epistula* contains no Christian historical details: the emperor thanks Euxeinianus Pollio at Hierapolis for giving, at his command, material assistance to Smyrna following the earthquake there (Vit. Aberc. 48).[10] As such this part stands alone without any details about bishop Abercius: there is no mention of an order to summon Abercius the wonder-worker to heal the emperor's daughter. Euxeinianus's assistance was reported to the emperor by a procurator named Caecilius. The emperor included in his titles "Germanicus, Sarmaticus."

The names of the two unknown *magistrani*, Valerius and Bassianus, appear to be derived from the names of a single figure, Valerius Bassianus,

---

8. IEph 3157; IEph 1799; Jeanne Robert and Louis Robert, *Exploration, histoire, monnaies et inscriptions*, vol. 1 of *Fouilles d'Amyzon en Carie* (Paris: de Boccard 1983), 30–32; Carlo Franco, *Elio Aristide e Smirne* (Rome: Bardi 2005), 503; Thonemann, "Abercius of Hierapolis," 269 n. 27.

9. Werner Eck, "P. Aelius Apollonides, ab epistulis Graecis, und ein Brief des Cornelius Fronto," *ZPE* 91 (1992): 239–41; Reinhold Merkelbach, "Grabepigramm und Vita des Bischofs Aberkios von Hierapolis," *EA* 28 (1997): 135–36; Glen W. Bowersock, *Greek Sophists in the Roman Empire* (Oxford: Oxford University Press, 1969), 54–55.

10. περὶ ὧν κατ' ἐπιτροπὴν ἡμετέραν ἔναγχος διεπράξω κατὰ τὴν Σμυρνέων πόλιν ὡς ἐπικουφίσαι τοῖς ἐκεῖσε οἰκοῦσιν τὴν συμβᾶσαν αὐτοῖς συμφορὰν ἐκ τοῦ κλόνου τῆς γῆς ("I recently took action in accordance with our duty of care for these matters toward the city of Sirmium so as to relieve its inhabitants in the disaster that befell them from the earthquake").

who was executed late in the reign of Commodus (Hist. Aug., Comm. 7.7).[11] They deliver the eparch Cornelius's letter to the hegemon Spinther (Dolabella having left office by this point) (Vit. Aberc. 51).[12] There is no evidence of a hegemon Spinther in Asia in the second century, but in 44 BCE P. Cornelius Dolabella seized the province, adopting the title of imperator, and, after his departure for Syria, was succeeded by P. Cornelius Lentulus Spinther for a brief period in 43 BCE (Cicero, *Fam.* 12.14–15).[13] It is the second part of the alleged imperial rescript that includes the anachronistic titles of Valerius and Bassianus.

Thonemann sees the Vita Abercii therefore in the context of the lives of the saints that began to appear in the fourth century as part of the transformation of Graeco-Roman culture and its Christianization. The author had no earlier written source, but there were material artifacts. As Thonemann perceptively says, "The Life of Abercius should be understood as a biography, not of a man, but of a city. It aspires to provide a Christian history for a city whose real history was insistently, inconveniently, and all too visibly pagan."[14] We can therefore seek to follow the fourth-century Christian reconstruction of the pagan narrative of Hierapolis and its artifacts.

Thonemann's account undoubtedly represents a considerable advance on earlier attempts to regard the Vita Abercii as containing earlier second-century Christian elements and so valid historical grounds to give the title of a Christian bishop to the Abercius of the epitaph who uses no such title nor claims such status. Reinhold Merkelbach is the most recent representative of such a claim for a limited historical accuracy.[15] Despite the reference to Emperor Julian, Merkelbach insists that there is something of historical value behind the final edition and earlier version composed soon after the death of Abercius.[16] This necessity Merkelbach grounds

---

11. With Merkelbach, "Grabepigramm und Vita," 136.

12. [The Μαγιστριανοί] ἀπέδωκαν τὰ γράμματα Κορνηλιανοῦ τοῦ ἐπάρχου πρὸς τὸν ἡγέμονα Σπινθῆρα περὶ τούτου γραφέντα ("They handed over the document written by Cornelianus in reference to the matter at hand to Spinther the governor"). See also Vit. Aberc. 66: Σπινθῆρα τὸν κατ' ἐκεῖνου καιροῦ ἄρχοντα Φρυγίας μικρᾶς ("Spinther, who was the governor of Lesser Phrygia at that time").

13. For further references, see Thonemann, "Abercius of Hierapolis," 275 n. 39.

14. Thonemann, "Abercius of Hierapolis," 278.

15. Merkelbach, "Grabepigramm und Vita," 125–39.

16. Merkelbach, "Grabepigramm," 128: "bald nach 363 ein Geistlicher sich eine ältere Lebensbeschreibung des Aberkios vorgenommen und für seine Zweck herg-

in the "fullness of reports historically verifiable" or that refer to places in Hierapolis or its surroundings found in the Vita Abercii.[17]

But if we examine carefully such examples, we find that they are such as the absence of Marcus Aurelius with Lucius Verus for the Roman–Parthian War (161–166 CE) and the feast of the *Victoria Parthica* anachronistically recorded as attacked by Abercius in his preaching (Vit. Aberc. 2–8).[18] There are no accurate *Christian* references here. An analysis however of the text of Abercius's sermons on this occasion and later leads Merkelbach to postulate parallels with Justin Martyr, Pliny, Hippolytus on the Elchasites, and Melito of Sardis that show an earlier form of missionary catechesis that he argues died out come the fourth century.[19]

It would, however, be false to draw a contrast between the catechumenate of the fourth with that of the second century on the grounds that in the former preparation for baptism after the peace of the church was of long duration but was quickly executed in the second.[20] And apart from this feature, all other historical features of the Vita Abercii, even when surprisingly evoking original sources, have been better explained by Thonemann as a sometimes accurate, sometimes wildly inaccurate use of surviving public monuments given an *interpretatio christiana* from which to embroider a more detailed miracle tale.

The one exception is the general attempt to identify Abercius with an Avirkius Marcellus mentioned by Eusebius.[21] But the latter is simply the name of an otherwise unknown person to whom an anonymous writer dedicates his work against the so-called Phrygian heresy (Montanism) (Eusebius, *Hist. Eccl.* 5.16.3). This Avirkius himself has no direct connection with Hierapolis but is simply associated with Apolinaris of Hierapolis.

---

erichtet hat. Diese ältere Fassung müsste bald nach dem Tod des Aberkios niedergeschrieben worden sein."

17. Merkelbach, "Grabepigramm und Vita," 128: "den die Vita enthält eine solche Fülle von Nachrichten, die historisch verifizierbar sind oder sich auf Plätze in Hierapolis und seiner Umgebung beziehen."

18. Merkelbach, "Grabepigramm und Vita," 129, where nevertheless the actual destruction of pagan temples and statues are considered a later addition to the text.

19. Merkelbach, "Grabepigramm und Vita," 129–31. See Vit. Aberc. 13 and 36; Pliny, *Nat.* 10.96.7; Pseudo-Hippolytus, *Ref.* 9.15.67; Justin Martyr, *Dial.* 85.

20. Merkelbach, "Grabepigramm und Vita," 132.

21. Thonemann, "Abercius of Hierapolis," 258 n. 1 follows this general consensus with the unsubstantiated claim: "Abercius himself is almost certainly to be identified with Avircius Marcellus."

He is described neither as a native nor a bishop of that city. But this is the one early Christian, literary text to which Thonemann can appeal.

Thonemann's account has, in fact, critically undermined the case for any historical information contained in the Vita Abercii that can give documentary corroboration to the case for the Christianity of the epitaph. But, notwithstanding, Thonemann makes the ill-considered conclusion directly in the face of where his analysis has taken us that the inscription is "by far the longest and most explicit profession of Christian faith known to us from documentary sources of the period."[22] But despite this common opinion of the majority of scholars, I believe that the case for the Christianity of the epitaph can be shown to rest on nothing more than on a general acceptance of unexamined assumptions or at best a case like that of Merkelbach that is exposed by Thonemann's argument to rest upon somewhat flimsy grounds.

3. The Vita Abercii as an Inference from Surviving Fourth-Century Material Artifacts

The Vita Abercii, I submit, if constructed out of the author's speculation upon and reconfiguration of the material fabric of fourth-century Hierapolis, included speculation also on a βωμός-capped tomb with an epitaph, dedicated to a man named Abercius, that he interpreted as Christian, without any more grounds for doing so than other artifacts such as Faustina's bathhouse as a reward for a Christian exorcism. The author of the Vita Abercii had no episcopal list to support his bishop's title, nor were there any other details of the life of a Christian bishop that he could not have inferred from the words of the epitaph. Let us now attempt some reasonable inferences about how the author proceeded in embroidering so fabulously with a fourth-century Christian motif the artifacts that he observed.

The author of the Vita Abercii looked first at the bathhouse (βαλανεῖον) at Agros Thermôn and its dedication recording the beneficence of Empress Faustina with her *frumentatio* (σιτηρέσιον, food allowance) (Vit. Aberc. 66). The benefaction now in his Christian rewriting of the material fabric becomes a thanksgiving offering because the Christian Abercius of Hierapolis had exorcised a daemon from her daughter. The hot springs at

---

22. Thonemann, "Abercius of Hierapolis," 259.

Agros had been themselves the result of a miracle performed by Abercius, who had been concerned for the poor health of the poor (Vit. Aberc. 40).

The author's eyes now wandered around other artifacts. There was the imperial *epistula* of Marcus Aurelius that he found engraved on a pillar in the forum. Euxeinianus (and therefore the city) had been publically commended for the Smyrna relief with imperial mention of "our procurator Caecilius." The Christian hagiographer adds a second paragraph that brings in his legendary exorcist-bishop. The anachronistically described *magistriani sacrorum officiorum* derive their names from the epitaph or decree recording the execution of Valerius Basianus. A further as yet undiscovered inscription would have been from 43 BCE recording the names both of Dolabella and Spinther, whose date was not clear to the hagiographer but who afforded conveniently the names of the governors immediately past and present. Spinther is named the governor of Phrygia Minor (that did not exist as a separate entity at the time) with Dolabella. Thus the writer of the Vita Abercii can reorder the pagan material fabric of Hierapolis within the matrix of his Christian legend.

But amidst these artifacts, some with remains (the βαλανεῖον at Agros Thermôn) and others hypothesized from other remains but themselves having perished (e.g., the *stele* with the imperial *epistula*), there also stands the βωμός with the epitaph ascribed to, it is claimed, a Christian bishop, Abercius. But if, in fact, the βωμός was a Christian monument to a known and famous bishop Abercius, why are there no details in the Vita Abercii, following the failure of Merkelbach's argument, that cannot be inferred from the words of the epitaph itself? Surely the author of the Vita Abercii would have possessed additional Christian historical information with which to contextualize the words of the epitaph?

If the Vita Abercii reinterprets a number of pagan artifacts with a narrative that gives them a Christian expression, why should we assume that the epitaph on the βωμός was itself Christian and the one exception sticking out from his otherwise pagan landscape. Given the project of cultural transformation witnessed by the production of the Christian Vita Abercii, what are the grounds for identifying the βωμός as untouched by this fourth-century, Christianizing project?

I propose now examining the artifact as the author of the Vita Abercii viewed it, drawing on the actual way in which he interpreted it in a fourth-century context. Ramsay's artifact gives us only the surviving piece of an original inscription that itself is highly mutilated: the author of the Vita Abercii read a far more complete inscription, on which we are therefore dependent for the reconstruction of the whole text. But Ramsay's fragment will allow us to assess to what extent the Vita Abercii has refashioned the text of the epitaph itself. It will also invite us to ask if the artifact was already damaged in the fourth century in the form in which it is transcribed in the Vita Abercii.

4. The βωμός and Epitaph as the Author Saw Them

Margaret M. Mitchell has pointed out that the partially ruined βωμός that survives was only a section of the original artifact, like the monument of C. Etuvius Capreolus, at Aquileia, where we find an altar with epigraphy mounted on a tomb above five slabs, the top two of which are decorated with relief images. The top of the square-shaped altar is decorated ornately. Alternative decorations might have been acroteria and rosettes or even angula acroteria.[23] Given these general features of such funerary altars, we should not exclude the possibility that the lost, ruined top of the altar had contained apertures for libation offerings. We have from the cemetery of Ss Petrus and Marcellinus at Rome in the fourth century the sarcophagus lid of Justa decorated with a Constantinian monogram that Franz Joseph Dölger compared with that of Caecilius Fustus with its *Diis Manibus* formula: both contain a *piscina* with drilled holes for drink offerings (plate 3). Justa was arguably a Christian (she is called sanctissima, "most holy"), but of what form of Christianity? Could she not have been a pagan who adopted some Christian religious imagery?[24] We should remember that the Abercius epitaph ends with curses on violators of the tomb that are claimed as compatible with early Christian artifacts only somewhat implausibly.[25]

---

23. Margaret M. Mitchell, "Looking for Abercius: Reimagining Contexts of Interpretation of the Earliest Christian Inscription," in *Commemorating the Dead: Texts and Artifacts in Context; Studies of Roman, Jewish, and Christian Burials*, ed. Laurie Brink and Deborah Green (Berlin: de Gruyter 2008), 321–23 and her plate 9.5.

24. For references and discussion, see Allen Brent, "Methodological Perspectives in the Interpretation of Early Christian Artefacts," *StPatr* 73 (2014): 17–18.

25. *Grabschrift* 20–22: οὐ μέντοι τύμβῳ τις ἐμῷ ἕτερόν τινα θήσει. / εἰ δ' οὖν, Ῥωμαίων ταμείῳ θήσε[ι] δισχείλια [χ]ρῦσα / καὶ χρηστῇ πατρίδι Ἱεροπόλει χείλια χρυσά ("Let not, however, anyone place another person on my tomb. / If anyone does, he shall place 2,000 denarii in the Roman treasury and 1,000 denarii for my good homeland Hierapolis"). See, for example, Margherita Guarducci, "L'iscrizione di Abercio e La 'Vergine Casta,'" *Ancient Society* 4 (1973): 180–81, where she cites (n. 29) the third-century epitaph of Leo and the later of bishop Theophilus.

As Mitchell points out, such curses (mainly found in the fourth century), have been frequently used to counter Adolf von Harnack's original doubt that such a funeral monument could have been Christian. But if such examples had become simply conventional in the fourth century, this was unlikely to have been the case as early as the second century.[26] We need to once more focus on how the author of the Vita Abercii regarded this βωμός and not what significance isolated texts and artifacts might allow us to give to it. If the artifact had been at all plausibly Christian, then the Vita Abercii would not have needed to explain its use by a Christian bishop as a trophy in his victory over a daemon: he has constructed an aetiological legend explaining away the pagan character of the artifact: Abercius prepared his grave but arranged its placement under a pagan altar, a marble βωμός, that the daemon had at his instruction brought from Rome and placed at the gate of the harbor.

It was clearly a curiosity in the eyes of Christians in fourth-century Hierapolis, not considered normally Christian or even normally Hierapolitan rather than Roman. How could a square pagan stone altar have been erected over the burial place of the deceased whom they had clearly come to believe had been a Christian bishop, despite the inscription never claiming that title itself? It was not simply, therefore, taken for granted that a grave with a βωμός on top of it was a normal and unremarkable funeral monument for a Christian bishop.

The Vita Abercii's Christian interpretation in this case was as equally contrived as that for Faustina's βαλανεῖον and her σιτηρέσιον, or indeed Cornelius's imperial *epistula*. Historically, Faustina had simply contributed to Hierapolis a normal example of pagan imperial munificence and the *epistula* refered to Pollio's benefactions to Smyrna: neither example originally had anything to do with the request of a Christian bishop for his reward for exorcising the emperor's daughter, whose miraculous act in the first place had caused the warm springs to gush forth (Vit. Aberc. 39–40; 48–51; 65). The Christian claim to the βωμός was arguably equally contrived, and the fact of this contrivance shows that for the author it is not a commonplace

---

26. Adolf von Harnack, *Zur Abercius-Inschrift*, TU 12.4B (Leipzig: Hinrichs, 1895), 5; Joseph Wilpert, *Fractio Panis: Die älteste Darstellung des eucharistischen Opfers in der "cappella Greca"* (Freiburg im Breisgau: Herder, 1895), 105–6; Louis Duchesne, "L'épitaphe d'Abercius," *Mélanges d'archéologie et d'histoire* 15 (1895): 166. See also Mitchell, "Looking for Abercius," 320–21.

artifact usual for both Christian and pagan burials and as such unremarkable: it is one that cries out for urgent Christian reinterpretation.

When we come to the actual words of the epitaph, we find that these were equally strange to the fourth-century author. Mitchell has convincingly confirmed that a βωμός for a τύμβον ἰσοτετράγωνον ("a tomb with four equal sides") would have the full verses distributed over three sides, of which the Ramsay fragment would have represented the second side.[27] The Vita Abercii describes the epitaph engraved on the altar as a "divinely inspired inscription" (θεόπνευστον ἐπίγραμμα), intelligible "to those worthy of Christ and profitable" (τοῖς μὲν ἀξίοις τοῦ Χριστοῦ νοούμενον καὶ ὠφέλιμον) but "to the unbelievers not being able to be grasped" (τοῖς δὲ ἀπίστοις μὴ γινωσκόμενον ἔχον) (Vit. Aberc. 76).[28] The author now proceeds to interpret this mysterious language with a Christian meaning not immediately obvious to his contemporaries. We shall now see that his application of many of the terms to specifically Christian rites and practices is somewhat forced and that their more natural interpretation might be in a highly ambiguously Christian if not more clearly a pagan context.

References to Paul and πίστις (faith) seem to provide us with a secure Christian anchor around which to interpret an otherwise quite ambiguous set of images (Vit. Aberc. 77; *Grabschrift* 12).[29] But the manuscript tradition is highly confused in reading the two lines. I will argue that the manuscript tradition is evidence for a confusion that comes from alternative readings of these damaged words on the epitaph.

5. The Epitaph and the Manuscript Tradition: Paul and Πίστις as Game Changers

Once we use the Paul-πίστις anchor to argue a Christian interpretation of the epitaph, it will follow that the "Chaste Shepherd" (ποιμήν ἁγνός) of

---

27. Mitchell, "Looking for Abercius," 329–30 and nn. 77 and 78; Vit. Aberc. 76. For her criticism of the reconstruction in the Museo Pio Christiano where it appears in its entirety on the front face, see Mitchell, "Looking for Abercius," 331, criticizing Antonio Ferrua, "Nuove osserazioni sull'epitaffio di Abercio," *Rivista di Archelogia Cristiana* 20 (1943): 286; Margherita Guarducci, *Epigrafi sacre pagane e cristiane*, vol. 4 *Epigrafia Graeca* (Rome: Istituto Poligrafico dello Stato, Libreria dello Stato, 1978), 377.

28. Cited from Nissen's critical text from a passage whose form was to be abbreviated by the *textus receptus* of Symeon Metaphrastes.

29. Παῦλον δὲ ἔσωθεν Πίστις παντὶ προῆγε.

whom Abercius is a "disciple" (μαθητής) is Jesus Christ, who had taught him "the words of faith" (γράμματα πιστά) (*Grabschrift* 3, 6). At Rome Bishop Abercius saw the "empire" (βασιλεία), or perhaps a "princess" (βασίλεια), and a "queen" (βασίλισσα), which are personifications of the church and the Blessed Virgin Mary or perhaps of the Church of Rome and her primatial rule. He visited the Roman congregation marked with the seal of baptism (*Grabschrift* 7–9).[30] Wherever he stopped in Syria or in Nisibis beyond the Euphrates he found his fellow Christian believers, accompanied by the letters of the apostle Paul with his πίστις leading him everywhere.[31] Πίστις provided the fish that is Jesus, from the font of baptism, born of Mary the Holy Virgin, as eucharistic food, the wine mixed with water that was their common meal.[32]

The imagery of the Chaste Shepherd and Pure Virgin, the seal and the fish, the kingdom or princess and the queen were highly ambiguous and tended to fade into their pagan counterparts. But references to Paul and to πίστις seemed to clinch matters in support of Christianity. But first, as we shall now see, in the following section, the manuscript tradition has produced three different versions of the lines on Paul and πίστις, in the three different recensions of the Vita Abercii.

Second, we may query, following a close examination of the process by which Ramsay's fragment was brought to life, whether the author of the Vita Abercii had read and apparently faithfully transcribed an originally more perfect version of the mutilated stone? Was the mutilation earlier than the composition of the Vita Abercii, or was it later and connected with excavations at the time of Ramsay and Sterrett? If the former was the case then, the author of the Vita Abercii did not make a more perfect transcription than that afforded us by Ramsay's fragment.

---

30. εἰς Ῥώμη[ν ὃς ἔπεμψεν] ἐμὲν βασιλ[ηΐδ' ἀθρῆσαι] / καὶ βασίλισσ[αν ἰδεῖν χρυσό]στολον χρυ[σοπέδιλον.] / λαὸν δ'εἶδον ἐ[κεῖ λαμπρὰν] σφραγεῖδαν ἔ[χοντα] ("who sent me to Rome, to gaze upon a kingdom and to see a queen with golden robe and golden sandals, and I saw there a people who had a shining seal"). See also below below nn. 79, 80, and 81.

31. See below, nn. 37 and 42 and associated text.

32. See below, n. 35 and associated text.

6.1. The Manuscript Tradition of Paul and Πίστις

The author of the Vita Abercii read and transcribed Abercius's claim, according to a restoration of one of the three versions printed in Nissen's edition:

(1) Nissen's favored anonymous Recension I has, as its principal archetype, P 1540 (Codex Parisianus graecus).[33] Though he follows the Vita Abercii in creating a single line, Ramsay's fragment shows that these words were originally, like those of the rest of the entire epitaph, on different lines so that what the author saw or imagined that he saw was something like:

Παῦλον δὲ ἔσωθεν
Πίστις πάντῃ δὲ προῆγε κτλ ...

By running the two lines together, we can therefore construe the sense as "in every place I had my fellow assembly members, and Paul was within us. And Faith led us everywhere...."[34] The problem, however, is that the Russian version (R) related to this archetype omits πίστις on the epitaph. As a result, the Παῦλος as in Παῦλον δὲ ἔσωθεν would become the subject of πάντῃ δὲ προῆγε and the provider also of the τροφὴν πάντῃ ἰχθὺν ἀπὸ πηγῆς (R 11.12-13; see also 15.12). Otherwise, it will be the παρθένος ἁγνή who makes such provision in addition to catching the fish, since πίστις does not appear.[35]

---

33. Supported by R; H 27; M 379 (Codex Mosquensis).

34. Nissen, *S. Abercii Vita*, 53.17-18 (around Vit. Aberc. 77): Εὐφράτην διαβάς. πάντῃ δ' ἔσχον συνομηγύρους, Παῦλον δὲ ἔσωθεν. Πίστις παντὶ προῆγεν καὶ παρέθηκε τροφὴν κτλ. ("Having crossed the Euphrates, I had everywhere companions, and Paul was on the inside. Faith everywhere led the procession and provided nourishment..."). Amended readings for συνομηγύρους, with which all three versions agree, are: συνομήμος (H. Grégoire, "Bardesane et S. Abercius," *Byzantion* 25-27 [1955-1957]: 363-68; William M. Calder, "The Epitaph of Avircius Marcellus," *JRS* 29 [1939]: 1-4) and συνομαίμους (Wolfgang Wischmeyer, "Die Aberkiosinschrift als Grabepigramm," *JAC* 23 [1980]: 25).

35. Nissen, *S. Abercii Vita*, 53.18-54.1-3 (around Vit. Aberc. 77): καὶ παρέθηκε τροφὴν πάντῃ ἰχθὺν ἀπὸ πηγῆς πανμεγέθη καθαρόν, ὃν ἐδράξατο παρθένος ἁγνή, καὶ τοῦτον ἐπέδωκε φιλίοις ἐσθίειν διὰ παντός, οἶνον χρηστὸν ἔχουσα, κέρασμα διδοῦσα μετ' ἄρτου ("[Faith] provided me everywhere a fish from the fountain, a great and pure fish, that the [Holy Virgin or Faith] caught (or 'conceived'), and presented to the Friends to eat continually, giving it mixed with wine").

(2) Nissen's Recension II is also anonymous and relies on C (Codex Coislinianus 110).[36] Here the whole line on the epitaph is omitted (half the stanza line) so that there is no witness here to Παῦλον δὲ ἔσωθεν, although πίστις does appear in the following line. The originator of this manuscript tradition did not share, therefore, the confidence of the scribes of versions I and III in constructing the upper letters as originally having been Παῦλον. Without the line with Paul, the only object on which πίστις as the subject of the verb "led before me" (προῆγεν) can work is the preceding: "Faith led my fellow initiates forward ..."[37]

(3) Nissen's Recension III (Simeon Metaphrastes) has the full stanza line (which on the epitaph would have been in two, half-stanza lines) that read substantially that of Recension I (with the exception of R's omission of πίστις).[38]

We thus have a situation in which the whole line is omitted in one important manuscript (C), and even if version I is preferred, an important witness (R) to its manuscript tradition omits πίστις from the line.

It is therefore far more important than has been acknowledged to ask whether we have here an example of scribal speculation on an original mutilated text and also whether the great divergence between recent scholars in restoring these two lines on the stone are scarcely worth less than these manuscript attempts at restoration. We need to ask whether the great divergent manuscript readings for these lines is not, in fact, the creation of what were originally divergent observations of the words of Ramsay's mutilated epitaph that survived in that form from a time contemporary with the production of the Vita Abercii. The condition of the epitaph, found as part of a single fragment of a βωμός broken by its extraction from the bathhouse wall into two and reunited in 1892, reveals what I shall argue to be through its mutilation the source of the ambivalent manuscript reading of these lines.

---

36. Published originally by Jean Francois Boissonarde, *Anecdota Graeca* (Paris: Excusum in Regio Typographeo, 1829–1833), 462–88.

37. Nissen, *S. Abercii Vita*, 82.5–7 (around Vit. Aberc. 77): πάντη δ' ἔσχον συνομηγύρους, / Πίστις παντὶ προῆγε / καὶ παρέθηκε τροφὴν κτλ ...

38. Recension III is based upon Codex Parisiensis (A) 1480, (M) 1484, (C) 1495, (D) 1494, (E) 1501, (F) 1512, (G) 1503, Codex Coislinianus (H) 145.

6.2. Paul and Πίστις on the Stone in Comparison with Versions of the Vita Abercii

The words of two lines as they stand on the surviving epitaph are almost entirely obliterated with damage done to the lower part of the letters in the first and to the upper part in the second. What appears to us on the epitaph in a highly fragmented form in the first line is, as Ramsay in 1897 reproduces as the copy, presumably the squeeze that he and Sterrett had made:

ΠΑΥΛΟΝ⁻ΥϹΩΝΕΠΟ

Here we have no corroboration of versions I and III's difficult reading of Παῦλον δὲ ἔσωθεν that II (C) omitted entirely either due to carelessness or incomprehension or because originally the transcription of the viewed epitaph was so indecipherable. Π[ ]ŸΛΟΝ seems secure and sufficiently guaranteed by the half Π, a full Υ and half Λ, half Ο with Ν missing its right stroke. The absence of δὲ also concurs with the reading of one witness to the manuscript tradition of version I, namely, H (Codex Hierosolymitanus Sabaiticus 27), omits this particle, as does version III in all manuscripts. Thus we have simply Παῦλον ἔχων.

But what the final mutilated traces on this line of the epitaph now do establish is the complete impossibility of the ἔσωθεν of versions I and III of the Vita Abercii. ΕΠΟ clearly cannot lead to such a reconstruction but requires completion as something like ΕΠΟΜΗΝ, ΕΠΟΧΟΝ, ΕΠΟΧΩΝ, or ΕΠΟΧΩ. Wolfgang Wischmeyer (also Thonemann) favors ἐπ' ὄχῳ and thus sees Paul as "on the wagon (or chariot)" as his companion, though Adolphe Abel does reference some who restore these words as ἐπ'ὄχων.[39] Margherita Guarducci prefers ἔποχον as an adjective describing Paul as "mounted on my chariot" following Albrecht Dieterich.[40] Amongst others, Orazio Marucchi, Louis Duchesne, Gerhard Ficker, Vera Hirschmann, and Merkelbach have simply reproduced the text of the epitaph at this point with blank spaces.[41]

---

39. Wischmeyer, "Aberkiosinschrift als Grabepigramm," 25; Adolphe Abel, "Étude sur l'inscription d'Abercius," *Byzantion* 3.2 (1926): 339–40 nn, 1, 2, and 3 for further references.

40. Guarducci, *Epigrafi sacre pagane e cristiane*, 380, no. 4; Albrecht Dieterich, *Die Grabschrift des Aberkios* (Leipzig: Teubner, 1896), 9.

41. ΕΠΟ … ΙΣΤΙΣ: Orazio Marucchi, "Nuove osservazioni sulla iscrizione di

If the Vita Abercii had never existed and we had this epigraphic fragment alone, on what basis would we have concluded that a person named Paul who shared his chariot or wagon was, in fact, Paul the apostle? Ramsay's originally widely accepted restoration seemed to support this: the text support by the restored ἑπόμην meant, according to Ramsay, "everywhere I had companions—Paul in my hands and Faith guiding and feeding me."[42] But if we accept instead the ἐπ' ὄχῳ amendment (or versions of it, ἐπ' ὄχων, ἔποχον), it is by no means clear that these words refer metaphorically to texts of Paul's writings: they could equally apply to an otherwise unknown individual who accompanied Abercius on his journey.

It was Ramsay's ἑπόμην that had enabled πίστις to be thus securely anchored into a pattern of Pauline interpretation with a logic of "following-leading" (ἑπόμην-προῆγε). The author of the Vita Abercii as first reader of the epitaph as a Christian statement had introduced this interpretation that Ramsay and most observers were subsequently to follow. The former had used ἔσωθεν that was quite impossible to fit into the letters that have survived, yet we can be sure that he believed that Παῦλον was within his orthodox, non-Marcionite Christian community whose gatherings of his "fellow worshipers" (ΣΥΝΟ[μηγύρους]) he thinks to have been Christian.

If we add a reference from the Vita Abercii to the activity of Abercius in Syria after he has left Rome in resisting "the heresy of Marcion," we can regard Abercius here as claiming to be the true, anti-Marcionite follower

---

Abercio," *Nuovo Bulletino di archeologia Cristiana* 1 (1895): 23; EPO[ ]: Duchesne, "L'épitaphe d'Abercius," 157; Gerhard Ficker, "Der heidnische Charakter des Abercius-Inschrift," *Sitzungsberichte der Könlich Preußischen Akademie der Wissenschaften zu Berlin* (1894): 89; Vera Hirschmann, "Untersuchungen Zur Grabschrift Des Aberkios," *ZPE* 129 (2000): 109; Merkelbach, "Grabepigramm und Vita," 126.

42. Π[α]ῦλον ἔχων ἑπό[μην]·[Π]ίστις π[άντη δὲ προῆγε]. William M. Ramsay, "The Cities and Bishoprics of Phrygia," *JHS* 4 (1883): 427, translated more literally: "Faith went in front, and I followed with Paul." Ramsay was followed by George de Sanctis, "Die Grabschrift des Aberkios," *ZKT* 21.4 (1897): 674; Abel, "Étude sur l'inscription d'Abercius," 325; Frederick C. Conybeare, review of *Zur Abercius Inschrift*, by Adolf von Harnack, *Classical Review* 9 (1895): 296–97: "The stone is broken asunder in the middle of this twelfth line, and ten of the letters on it are uncertain, and thirteen altogether absent. The Armenian is very tantalizing. The words 'In all ways facing forward' answer to παντὶ δὲ προῆγε. 'Inwardly facing' echoes ἔσωθεν, a misreading by the Greek compiler of ἔχων ἐπ' or of ἔχων alone.... But the word *anci* which = 'I passed by (*or* over)' may answer to ἑπόμην."

of Paul the apostle (Vit. Aberc. 69).[43] Merkelbach recently has defended such a thesis, understandably from his standpoint that there are genuine historical facts embedded in the Vita Abercii about a bishop called Abercius.[44] But we have rejected such a possibility of reading the epitaph in the perspective of the Vita Abercii whose author knows nothing that we do not know: the author remains in the same position as ourselves attempting to make valid inferences from the words on the stone and has no independent Christian source.

Such considerations will also apply to the line that the Vita Abercii reads as πίστις παντὶ προῆγε and whose reconstruction assisted the Pauline association. If we proceed on the assumption that the author had the epitaph before him more or less in the mutilated condition in which Ramsay found it, then all that he had were the following letters on a single line:

ιΣιΣι

He, and we, have in other words ΠΣΙΙΣ^I, with a single half stroke to the right (I) that he and we have reconstructed as the πίστις of Pauline theology, with the half stroke the remains of an original Π[αντὶ]. But once we concede the absence of any Christian second-century source for the Vita Abercii, there are other, plausible reconstructions of the damaged inscription that do not rely on the phantasmagoric imagination of its fourth-century author.

If we are not simply controlled by the text of the Vita Abercii and accept that the author's reconstruction is as speculative as our own, we

---

43. πάνυ γὰρ ἐν τῷ χρόνῳ ἐκείνῳ ἡ αἵρεσις τοῦ Μαρκίωνος ἐθορύβησε τὰς τῶν Χριστανων ἐκκλησίας ("For at that time generally Marcion's heresy was creating tumult in Christian churches"). Abel, "Étude sur l'inscription d'Abercius," 366–67, went as far as to claim: "L'opinion général est qu'Abercius se recommendait de Paul dans ses voyages, Paul étant l'apôtre des gentils.... La conjecture ἐ ὄχων de Hirschfeld trouvera un excellent commentaire dans ce passage des Actes des Apôtres, VIII,27.... Abercius lisait Paul en voyage pour s'inspirer de son zèle apostolique et se servait comme d'un signe de reconnaissance envers les chrétiens orthodoxes de la Syrie." Unfortunately, the reference to the Aethiopian eunuch in Acts 8:27 refers to him as καθήμενος ἐπὶ τοῦ ἅρματος and not as ἐπ' ὄχων or ὄχῳ. See also David Bundy, "The Life of Abercius: Its Significance for Early Syrian Christianity," *Second Century* 7 (1989–1990): 169; Mitchell, "Looking for Abercius," 313, 335.

44. Reinhold Merkelbach and Josef Stauber, *Der "Ferne Osten" und das Landesinnere bis zum Tauros*, vol. 3 of *Steinepigramme aus dem griechischen Osten* (Munich: Saur, 2001), 182. See also nn. 7–9 above and associated text.

would have to concede that there were other ways of reconstructing the four vertical letters that stand as vertical strokes and that cannot all have been Is. If we examine the first two, rather than form a Π and be lacking a vowel, we might propose a T I and make the word T I Σ T I Σ reconstructing the second pair of vertical strokes identically (both I I = T I). Although Ficker was prepared "perhaps" (*wohl*) to see traces of the absence of a following I, he doubted such a reconstruction. Instead, he regarded the first I as having originally a vertical bar (T) and the damaged I between the two Σ-Σ being originally an H.[45] Thus Ficker concluded that ΤΙΣΗΣ was a name for Cybele of whose cult Abercius, priest of Attis, as the μαθητὴς ποιμένος ἁγνοῦ ("disciple of the Chaste Shepherd") was a devotee.[46]

Dieterich followed Ramsay in observing that the first I in the Vita Abercii πίστις appeared to be missing, if the author is to be followed, and the partial letters restored as Π Σ T I Σ. But using Marucchi's photographic reproduction, he looked again at the first pair (I I) and detected at the foot of the initial letter the traces of a stroke sloping left that was, in fact, the remains of an N (ᴺΙΣΙΙΣι). The second I was to be read as an H since in the Phrygian dialect an ι can sound like an η. Thus Dieterich arrived at his proposal that the word be reconstructed as the name of a river goddess, ΝΗΣΤΙΣ (plate 4).[47]

The proposals of Dieterich and of Ficker met with an initial response of nineteenth-century Catholic scholars that in many instances just about fell short of ridicule.[48] Duchesne regarded Ficker's work to be on a par

---

45. Ficker, "Der heidnische Charakter des Abercius-Inschrift," 110: "Das Facismile des Inschriftsfragments is der Lesung gar nicht günstig. Dort finden sich nämlich ... wohl die Spuren eines Π aber das darauf folgende I fehlt. Nach dem ersten Σ scheint nicht TI zu lesen zu sein, sondern zwischen dem ersten und dem zweiten Σ eher ein H."

46. Ficker, "Der heidnische Charakter des Abercius-Inschrift," 110: "Ich würde zunächst daran denken, dass hier irgend ein Name der von Abercius verehrten Cybele gestanden hätte, wenn nicht die aenigmatische Sprache der Inschrift es verböte.... Der Glaube an die Götter ging voran, war Führer. Er ist der Veranlasser der Reisen des Abercius gewesen."

47. Carl Maria Kaufmann, *Handbuch der Altchristlichen Epigraphik* (Freiburg im Breisgau: Herder, 1917), 177; Dieterich, *Die Grabschrift des Aberkios*, 9 n. 12.

48. Von Harnack, "Zur Abercius-Inschrift," 3: "Katholische Gelehrte haben sich bisher mit dem Versuch begnügt, sie lächerlich zu machen. Dieser Ton ist Leider zuerst im Bullet. critique 15. März angeschlagen worden, wie man hört von einem Gelehrten, dessen Ernst and Unparteilichkeit bisher über jedem Zweifel stand."

with someone who wanted to deny on historical grounds the existence of Christ or Napoleon or to argue that the corpus of Tacitus was a fifteenth-century forgery.[49] Marucchi equally vehemently attacked both the "false premises" and "false conclusions" of Ficker, claiming the support with Duchesne of the "fundamental principles" of Christian archaeologists (*i principi fondamentali della nostra scienza*), including Giovanni De Rossi, on the grounds of allegedly parallel other early Christian artifacts (the Autun inscription, those of Licinia Amias and Livia Primitiva, representations of the Good Shepherd, etc.) without pausing to consider whether their ambiguous claims might also be suspect.[50] But Marucchi's fundamental principles have not appeared to Catholic epigraphists in the late twentieth and early twenty-first centuries as unquestionable givens of a framework of scientific interpretation of early Christian artifacts. The use of images of the Good Shepherd, the Fish, and the anchor in particular, as clear criteria for a certain, "Christian" identification, have been seriously challenged by Theodore Klausner and, more recently, Carlo Carletti and Emanuele Castelli.[51]

Significantly, as Duchesne made clear, the basis for the Christian claim was also that, however fabulous, the fourth century Vita Abercii contained genuine earlier Christian elements that I have given grounds for denying.

Regarding someone who had anonymously supported him, von Harnack asked "ist—trotz Ficker—die katholische Christlichkeit der Inschrift so evident, dass ein ernster Gelehrter für seinen Ruf fürchten musste wenn er sie noch einmal bewies?" See also Abel, "Étude sur l'inscription d'Abercius," 340: "La lecture ΝΕΣΤΙΣ de Dieterich … n'est pas appuyée que sur le désir qu'avait l'auteur d'ajouter un argument a sa these."

49. Duchesne, "L'épitaphe d'Abercius," 161.

50. Marucchi, "Nuove osservazioni," 40: "Nulla aggiungerò per ora sulle altre false conclusioni che il Ficker deduce dalle sue false premesse intorno ad altri monumenti senza dubbio cristiani che egli vorrebbe giudicare pagani con critica veramente demolitrice ed irragionevole; come l'iscrizione di Autun, quella di Licinia Amias e di Livia Primitiva del Vaticano ed alcune rappresentanze del buon pastore. Di ciò si tratterà venendone l'occasione nei prossimi fascicoli del Bullettino per difendere i principi fondamentali della nostra scienza stabiliti dal De Rossi ed ora con tanta leggerezza impugnati."

51. Emanuele Castelli, "The Symbols of Anchor and Fish in the Most Ancient Parts of the Catacomb of Priscilla: Evidence and Questions," *StPatr* 59 (2013): 11–20; Carlo Carletti, "Origini cristiane ed epigrafa: Note di lettura a proposito di alcune iscrizioni (forse) 'protocristiane,'" *Annali di Storia dell'Esegesi* 31.1 (2014): 83–94; Theodor Klauser, "Studien zur Entstehungsgeschichte der christlichen Kunst I," *JAC* 1 (1958): 46–51.

Duchesne also made clear that it was generally believed that the testimony of the author of the Vita Abercii was founded on more than the words that he read on the stone.[52] Ficker, however, believed to the contrary and rejected the Vita Abercii's reading of these damaged lines that was the only putative Christian source available to him.[53] Thus there was always an unexamined assumption on the part of a Christian reading of this and other lines, used to trump Duchesne's view against Ficker's: the readings of the Vita Abercii are to be trusted over pagan readings of the epitaph since its author had a better view of the text than Ramsay's mutilated fragment.

But it could, of course, be argued that the transcription of the words of the epitaph in the Vita Abercii nevertheless represents a more perfect as well as complete copy of the epitaph, even though the author had no historically based Christian details. We depend on this author for the full text of the epitaph of which we only have Ramsay's fragmentary remains of one panel: the original text was spread across three sides as Mitchell has recently confirmed.[54] Could we not argue that the mutilation was later, perhaps even at the time of the nineteenth-century archaeological investigations and that therefore the Vita Abercii had access to a genuine reading that we do not have? But, as we have seen, the manuscript tradition is very confused and itself appears to be based upon a speculative reading of a damaged line. In other words, that tradition gives plausibility to the thesis that the epitaph was already in the damaged and mutilated form when the author of the Vita Abercii transcribed its words.

Nevertheless, I propose examining the possibility that the damaged line is more recent with some more detailed attention to the place and circumstances of Ramsay's discovery.

---

52. Duchesne, "L'épitaphe d'Abercius," 160–63: "Quoiqu'il en soit de la date, il est manifeste que le légendaire considère l'inscription comme chrétienne, qu'il y voit l'épitaphe d'un évêque du lieu, vénéré par les Hiéropolitains non seulement comme un saint quelconque, mais comme le saint local par excellence, l'apôtre, le fondateur de leur église. Que la légende ait incorporé çà et là quelques traditions altérées."

53. Ficker, "Der heidnische Charakter des Abercius-Inschrift," 110: "Jedenfalls darf man bis jetzt das Zeugnisse des alten Biographen nicht ins Feld führen, da schon zu seiner Zeit die Inschrift sich nicht mehr im besten Zustande befand."

54. See above, n. 27.

7. The Fissure and the Broken Line

The stone itself and the probable distribution of the lines of the epigram make it clear that the transliteration in the Vita Abercii epigram is missing a line between two separate lines on the stone that have been joined together as the one line, for example, line 12 in Willy Lüdtke and Theodor Nissen's edition or lines 11 and 12 in Ramsay's or Carl Robert's squeeze.[55] In the latter case, line 12 begins with the remains of the disputed ΤΙΣΗΣ-ΝΗΣΤΙΣ-ΠΣΤΙΣ reconstruction with the remaining words of the stanza obliterated. But the lost line is indicated by the bottom of letters of line 11 are partially lost, whereas in line 12 it is the top:

ΠΑΥΛΟΝ˜ΥϖΝΕΠΟ
ΙΙΣΙΙΣΙ

The emendations of Ramsay's implausible ἑπόμην challenged the logic of "following-leading" (ἑπόμην-προῆγε) and thus the identification of a Christian, Pauline pattern that was tied to πίστις.[56] But the failure of Ramsay's connection we have now established to be beyond all challenge, given that originally there was a lost line that clearly disengaged Paul and faith. The author of the Vita Abercii had not observed the lost line, even though it had been indicated by the bottom letters of the first line being damaged, in contrast with the damaged top letters of the second. So, in his ignorance he had run together two quite separate lines as one.

Thus the variant readings between the three versions of the Vita Abercii imply that its author would have read the epitaph in its present mutilated condition and been as puzzled as we are by the missing, mutilated line and damaged text above and below the fissure. Ramsay observed both from the meter and from the state of the epigraphy that "there is a gap in the traditional text where the words are far too few to fill the measure." The combination of lines 11 and 12 should produce one hexameter, which

---

55. So also in *Grabschrift* 36–43 each of the separate lines on the stone run into a single line so as to produce a text of nine lines (7–15) that thus fit in the place they occupy in the full twenty-two lines of the text on the stone, as represented by all three versions of the Vita Abercii. But on the stone they are separated as eighteen lines and numbered as such by Ramsay, "Cities and Bishoprics of Phyrgia," 424–26 no. 36. See also Ramsay, *The Cities and Bishoprics of Phrygia* (Oxford: Clarendon, 1897), 1.2:723–24 no. 657; Carl Robert, "Archaeologische Nachlese," *Hermes* 29.3 (1894): 422.

56. See above, n. 42 and associated text.

they fail metrically to do when they so appear combined together by the author of the Vita Abercii.

It thus follows that the reader and transcriber of the epitaph who was the author of the Vita Abercii had no information about the original text that we ourselves do not have with which to decipher the stone. Both we and the transcriber have inherited an inscription on which one line has been obliterated intentionally by an otherwise unknown hand. He, like us, when confronted by line 11 and the fragmentary letters (plate 5) may infer the words of line 11 in this way, but, as Wolfgang Wischmeyer records, "the letters are not clearly readable."[57] But another important consequence now follows.

Ramsay's Christian interpretation was founded upon a logic of "following-leading" suggested by the juxtaposition of line 11—Π[α]ῦλον ἑπόμενην Πίστις [πάντη δὲ ...]—that thus securely anchored the words and images of the epitaph into a pattern of Christian, Pauline interpretation. Quite apart from an ambiguous manuscript tradition and the emendation ἐπ'ὄχῳ that for reasons that I have pointed out also lessens the interpretative firmness of such a juxtaposition, the presence of a gap with a line deliberately obliterated thus breaks Ramsay's "following-leading" pattern of Christian and Pauline interpretation and exposes the contrived character of the reconstruction that the speculations of the Vita Abercii have produced from an already damaged artifact.

Even if therefore the excavated βῶμος had not revealed a damaged half line missing from the transcription of the Vita Abercii, the absence of sufficient words to fill the hexameter and the highly ambiguous and divergent manuscript readings would not have allowed us to proceed with confidence. But there can be no doubt that the fissure that appears in the fragment that now stands in the Museo Pio Christiano did not simply appear there when Ramsay in Scotland and Sultan Abdul-Hamid in Istanbul sent the two halves to the Vatican to be recombined. How then did these two halves become separated?

Sterrett and Ramsay had not found the fragmentary βῶμος in two halves as is sometimes assumed.[58] As Sterrett makes clear, they had dis-

---

57. Wischmeyer, "Die Aberkiosinschrift als Grabepigramm," 25; Thonemann, "Abercius of Hierapolis," 258.

58. As in Thonemann, "Abercius of Hierapolis," 258: "Ramsay was rewarded with the spectacular discovery of two large fragments of the tombstone of Abercius itself, built into a bath-house at the hot springs near Kochisar." Mitchell, "Looking for Aber-

covered the stone in the walls of the *apodyterium* (changing room) at the entrance of the baths in ancient Hierapolis.⁵⁹ In a letter in French to Salomon Reinach, Ramsay described the marble fragment with a small part of the epitaph of the Vita Abercii "*un petit morceau*" (a little piece) to which Sterrett had directed him and that was clearly the entire remains, lines 7–15.⁶⁰ It is clear that the marble fragment found in the wall from which Ramsay and Sterrett made their squeeze consisted of the whole fragment now reconstituted in the form in which it stands now in the Vatican, using to their obvious joy the warm water of the spring that the Vita Abercii claims as one of Abercius's miracles. That embedded fragment was whole but bore the mark of a chiseled-out, obliterated line. When Sterrett had therefore made reference to "the stone that had been broken into two parts," he was referring to one part that was the two sides of the βῶμος that survive as opposed to the other, lost section that originally bore the first and last parts of the full epitaph.⁶¹

Ramsay's object was not to excavate but, principally, to draw a map of Phrygia locating ancient sites and then to visit and record monuments and inscriptions that survived there.⁶² They found a half-fragment of a βῶμος not free-standing but embedded in the masonry wall of an *apo-*

---

cius," 307: "A scant two years later on a June morning after breakfast Ramsay and his companion, the American J. R. S. Sterrett, found two fragments of Abercius's own epitaph in the ruins of a bath house on the site they identified as ancient Hierapolis, in Phrygia Salutaris."

59. J. R. Sitlington Sterrett, *Leaflets from the Notebook of an Archeological Traveler in Asia Minor* (Austin: University of Texas, State Printing Office, 1889), 15.

60. Ramsay's letter from Ushak on 12 July 1883, in Salomon Reinach, "Chronique de Orient," *Revue Archéologique* 3.2 (1883): 194–95: "nous avons trouvé un fragment du tombeau de saint Abercius avec une partie des linges depuis ΕΙC ΡΩΜΗΝ jusqu'à ΕΔΡΑJΑΤΟΠΑΡΘΗ. Ce n'est qu'un petit morceau.... Le marbre est encastré dans le mur des bains, et ce n'est pas sans peine, à cause de l'humidité, que nous réussîmes à faire un estampage de l'inscription, avec la même eau thermal dont saint Abercius, suivant la tradition, a doté jadis ses concitoyens d'Otrous."

61. Sitlington Sterrett, *Leaflets*, 15: In the summer of 1883 "Mr. Ramsay and I not only located definitely the site of Hierapolis, but we actually found what remains of the marble block which bore the epitaph quoted in the Acta Sanctorum. The stone has been broken into two parts, of which we found one." See also William M. Ramsay, "The Utilisation of Old Epigraphic Copies," *JHS* 38 (1918): 191.

62. Ramsay, "Cities and Bishoprics of Phrygia," 370: "Our chief aim was to construct the map of ancient Phrygia, and our method was to examine each district thoroughly enough to be able to say, not only where there were, but also where there

dyterium at Otrous that was ancient Hierapolis, with the remains of the epitaph that they published from a squeeze that showed not the line of a broken stone but of an intentional eradication of some words of its text.[63] Both agreed on Ramsay's transliteration of the remains as one text and not two separate ones, as it is necessary to emphasize here in the light of Calder's later criticism.[64]

The inscription was cracked at lines 11–12, but the fragment embedded in the bathhouse wall not split in two. It was only at the point that the ruined stone was lifted by archaeologists from its cavity in the wall that it broke in two, along the absent line of which the chiseled fissure remained, with the upper section passing on to Istanbul and the lower section retained in Ramsay's possession and taken to Scotland. It was in this way that the one fragmentary artifact became two only to be rejoined and placed in the Lateran museum in 1892.[65]

Our discussion has therefore led us to the conclusion that the author of the Vita Abercii had the same view of an intentionally damaged epitaph that we have. He had, of course, viewed all three of the inscribed sides, so he could transcribe the words in their entirety, and we are very much dependent upon him for the complete text. But there was no other historical information available to him than there is to us. Our careful review of the work of Ficker and Dieterich has shown us that their epigraphical analysis was careful and scientific and unworthy of the ridicule that it received.[66]

The Vita Abercii itself, as Thonemann has shown, is a quite fabulous, *interpretatio Christiana* of a number of pagan artifacts at Hierapolis in the

---

were not, ancient sites. The discovery of monuments and inscriptions was a secondary object, and we did not aim at completeness in this regard."

63. Abel, "Étude sur l'inscription d'Abercius," 325: "L'inscription était fendue en son milieu, au même endroit où les manuscrits présentaient l'étrange leçon Παῦλον ἔσωθεν. On pouvait en conclure que la 'vie' avait été écrite et l'inscription copiée lorsqu' elle était déjà endommagée. Ramsay supposa d'abord un martelage de la pierre."

64. Ramsay, "Cities and Bishoprics of Phrygia," 424–25, no. 36; see also 370 n. 2: "Besides this I have impressions made by Mr. Sterrett of many of the inscriptions which he copied: in such case I still attach his initials to the text"; Sterrett, *Leaflets*, 14–15. For a discussion of Calder, see below, n. 75 and associated text.

65. Abel, "Étude sur l'inscription d'Abercius," 325: "Lorsqu' on enleva le fragment de son alvéole, il se brisa en deux à cet endroit. La partie supérieure passa à Constantinople, l'autre fut conservée par Ramsay."

66. See above nn. 48 and 49 and associated text.

fourth century undergoing a process of Christian, cultural transformation. What I have argued is that the Abercius inscription cannot be privileged as a Christian artifact that precedes such an *interpretatio Christiana* but stands alongside and as part of the material fabric of second-century Hierapolis, sharing the prevalent cultural and historical backcloth before its fourth-century, cultural transformation. Thus, in our own process of interpretation, we must not fall into the trap of a vicious circularity in which we interpret the epitaph in the light of the Vita Abercii since the latter is itself an interpretation of the former. And I have challenged the fourth-century, Christian interpretation as a rereading of a purposely obliterated line the motive for which is plausibly the removal of a pagan message that did not square with the fourth-century character of Abercius, saint and bishop.

Dieterich's restoration of the Vita Abercii's πίστις (ΠΙΣΤΙΣ) with ΝΗΣΤΙΣ, for example, becomes plausible, particularly in the light of the place of the inscription's discovery. Nestis was a river goddess mentioned in a fragment of Empedokles preserved by Pseudo-Hippolytus where he attacks Marcion as the representative of a pagan philosopher's two principles of love and strife. Water represents the fourth element after fire (Zeus), earth (Hera), and air (Adoneus). He calls the goddess of water Νῆστις and calls her "the chariot that brings nourishment" (ὄχημα τρόφης), since she is its "cause [αἴτιον], for all who are nourished [γιν(ό)μενον πᾶσι τοῖς τρεφομένοις]."[67] Given the highly allegorical character of the imagery of the epitaph, Nestis is the source of nourishment that provides in every place the "fish from the fountain" in a cultic meal. Thus we can read the

---

67. Dieterich, *Die Grabschrift des Aberkios*, 43–44; Pseudo-Hippolytus, *Ref.* 7.29.4-7: Τέσσαρα τῶν πάντων ῥιζώματα πρῶτον ἄκουε·/ Ζεὺς <αἰθὴρ> Ἥρη τε φερέσβιος ἠδ' Ἀϊδωνεὺς / Νῆστις θ' ἣ δακρύοις τέγγει κρούνωμα βρότειον/ Ζεύς ἐστι, <φησί> τὸ πῦρ, Ἥρη τε φερέσβιος ἡ γῆ, ἡ φέρουσα τοὺς πρὸς τὸν βίον καρπούς, Ἀϊδωνεὺς δὲ ὁ ἀήρ, ὅτι πάντα δι' αὐτοῦ βλέπο<ν>τες μόνον αὐτὸν οὐ καθορῶμεν, Νῆστις δὲ τὸ ὕδωρ· μόνον γὰρ τοῦτο «ὄχημα τρόφης», (τουτέστιν) αἴτιον, γιν(ό)μενον πᾶσι τοῖς τρεφομένοις, αὐτὸ τρέφειν οὐ δύναται τὰ τρεφόμενα ... διὰ τοῦτο <οὖν> Νῆστιν καλεῖ τὸ ὕδωρ, ὅτι τροφῆς αἴτιον γινόμενον, τρέφειν οὐκ εὐτονεῖ τὰ τρεφόμενα ("Hear the four roots of all that exist: Zeus the aether, Hera giver of life, and Adoneus, and Nestis who with her tears bedews the mortals' fountain. Zeus they say is fire, but Hera the life-giving earth that bears the fruits that sustain life, and Adoneus the air, because though seeing all things through him our eyes do not light on him himself. But Nestis is water because this is the basis of nourishment, its cause, becoming this to all things that are nourished.... on this account therefore water is called Nestis, because though it causes nourishment, it is not of itself to nourish what is being nourished"). See also, Diogenes Laertius, *Lives*, 8.76.

lines 12–16 as: Νῆστις παντὶ προῆγε καὶ παρέθηκε τροφὴν ἰχθὺν πανμεγέθη καθαρόν ὃν ἐδράξατο παρθένος ἁγνή ("Nestis everywhere led the procession and provided me everywhere a fish from the fountain, a great and pure fish, that the [Holy Virgin or Faith] caught [or 'conceived']").

It is important to recall in the context of such an interpretation the location in the masonry wall of the baths at which Ramsay and Sterrett made their squeeze of the epitaph. We possess from the theatre at Hierapolis above the middle section of the great area above the eighteenth row of seats an inscription celebrating one of the mountain streams that provided Hierapolis with warm waters an epigram asking "the mistress of the Nymphs" to send greetings "to the golden city, Hierapolis ... distinguished by her shining streams."[68] One of these streams is called Χρυσορόας who has become personified as a goddess with her image on Roman coins.

The second-century baths with the discovered masonry wall were found at Agros Thermôn, a little way to the south of Hierapolis, where the Vita Abercii claims Abercius's miracle and his successful petition to Faustina for a βαλανεῖον (Vit. Aberc. 39–40).[69] The author of the Vita Abercii saw the whole monument still intact so that only after the fourth century was it broken up and the fragmentary debris used for a masonry wall in the baths and presumably stood originally in the vicinity of where a broken fragment was thus used. The reading Nestis would have been congruent with the emphasis on water and water goddesses throughout Hierapolis and in particular in the location of the baths.

---

68. Reinhold Merkelbach and Josef Stauber, *Die Westküste Kleinasiens von Knidos bis Ilion*, vol. 1 of *Steinepigramme aus dem griechischen Osten* (Stuttgart: Teubner, 1998), 265: (1–3) Ἀσίδος εὐρείης | προσφέρεστατον | οὖδας ἁπάντων. | (4–6) Χαίροις, χρσόπο|λι, Ἱερὴ πόλι, πότνια | Νυμφῶν (6–7) Νάμασιν, | ἀγλαίῃσι κεκασμένη – – – – –.

69. As a reward for Abercius's exorcism of Lucilla, *Vita* 65: ᾔτησεν δὲ ἐφ' ᾧ πέμψαι αὐτὴν ἀρχιτέκτονα εἰς τὸ κτισθῆναι βαλανεῖον ἐν τῷ Ἀγρῷ λεγομένῳ παρὰ ποταμόν, ἔνθα κλίνας τὰ γόνατα ηὔξατο καὶ αἱ πηγαὶ τῶν θερμῶν ὑδάτων ἀνέβλυσαν, ἀπονεῖμαι δὲ σιτηρέσιον τοῖς πτωχοῖς τῆς πόλεως ("He requested that he might send an architect for this purpose, that a bathhouse might be built in the place that is called Agros, alongside a river where falling to his knees he prayed and springs of warm water gushed forth and that she allocate a food allowance for the poor of the city"). In 66 the place is officially named Agros Thermôn (Ἀγρὸς Θερμῶν ἐπωνομάσθη).

8. Conclusion

My chapter has focused on the discussion of the restoration of the text of the mutilated line, but as part of the observation that generally the conjectured restoration by the author of the Vita Abercii has no more historical basis than our own. Scholarly discussion of the restoration has largely ignored an important procedural principle, namely, that the fourth-century Vita Abercii must not be used as a serious commentary on the inscription but rather the inscription must speak independently for itself: the fourth-century legend is merely a fable that explains the ignorance rather than the knowledge of its author. But my concentration on these lines has a further purpose.

The reconstruction of the line with the creation of the Paul-πίστις, leading-following relationship that involved the ignoring of a lost line was also fundamental to identifying the epitaph as that of a second-century Christian. Only the name of the apostle Paul could identify his books "on the wagon" and thus the source of the γράμματα πιστά.[70] With Dieterich, and following his careful epigraphic analysis of the mutilated letters, we have seen that a reconstruction of the lines occurs, which gains in plausibility when the general background revealed in the material fabric of second-century Hierapolis is considered. The images of the fish and the fountain, of the sacred meal, and the celebration of a pagan myth of creation abound in that background in particular relationship to the iconography of the mistress of the nymphs and of the nymph Χρυσορόας, in association with whom Nestis clearly belongs.[71]

Once we concede the dubious validity of the reconstruction of the mutilated words and the lost line between them, then now additionally the imagery that without them becomes at least highly ambiguous now comes into question as genuinely Christian. The μαθητὴς ποιμένος ἁγνοῦ, the "Chaste Shepherd" (and not the "Good Shepherd") becomes plausibly a priest of Attis teaching his mysteries (γράμματα πιστά), who is described appropriately as a shepherd god (*Grabschrift* 4 and 6).[72] The language of the epitaph strongly implies a cult statue of Attis, who, in the Naasene

---

70. See n. 42 above and associated text.
71. See n. 67 above and associated text.
72. ὃς βόσκει προβάτων ἀγέλας ὄρεσι πεδίοις τε … οὗτος γὰρ μ' ἐδίδαξε – – γράμματα πιστά ("who grazes his flocks on the hills and the plains.… It is he who taught me … the words of faith").

Psalm of Pseudo-Hippolytus is described as the "shepherd of the white stars" (ποιμὴν λευκῶν ἄστρων) who is also "many eyed" (μυριόματος) in the Naasene Psalm.[73]

The mutilated form ΒΑΣΙΛ that Abercius is sent to Rome to see is rendered in Attic form by the editions of the Vita Abercii as either βασίλεια ("queen") or as βασιλεία ("kingdom"). Nissen's preferred version I supports the latter, as does the Metaphrastis, whilst edition II the former.[74] I submit that the reconstruction by the fourth-century Christian writer, before Greek accentuation, was the βασίλεια that he imposed upon Ionic letters and was shaped by the legend of bishop Abercius's visit to queen Faustina and princess Lucilla. The question of whether the original stone ended ΒΑΣΙΛΗ, as Ramsay maintained, or as ΒΑΣΙΛ as Calder maintained, is inconsequential for the discussion and should not have been given the weight that it has.[75]

The author of the Vita Abercii undoubtedly sought a βασίλεια-βασίλισσα juxtaposition in conformity with his legend of the visit to Lucilla and Faustina.[76] But in the light of this, and without the influence of the Vita Abercii legend compounded by the misleading later accentuation that produced βασιλεία, we would have expected a "king" with a "queen" and pondered supplying the lost ending as ΒΑΣΙΛ[ῆᾶ] ("king") reconstructed in the Vita Abercii as though it had read instead βασιληΐδα (to be duly atticized as βασίλεια) so as to provide Abercius with a visit to a princess.[77]

Consequently, both reconstructions of a mutilated ΒΑΣΙΛ require an Ionic continuation beginning with η. Thus both Ficker's more complicated quest for Zeus as king as part of the Attis cult or Dieterich's account of

---

73. Line 5: ὀφθαλμοὺς ὃς ἔχει μεγάλους πάντῃ καθορῶντας ("who has great eyes gazing around in all directions"); see also Pseudo-Hippolytus, *Ref.* 5.9.60.

74. Nissen, *S. Abercii Vita*, 53 adopts βασιλεία in I (77.7), but for version II (p. 82) he reads βασίλεια. For the titles of the three versions, see above, nn. 32, 36, 38 and associated text.

75. Ramsay, "Utilisation of Old Epigraphic Copies," 190; Calder, "Epitaph of Avircius Marcellus," 1–4.

76. See above, n. 27 and associated text.

77. Recently there has been a preference for βασίλεια (princess); see Merkelbach, "Grabepigramm und Vita," 126–27; Hirschmann, "Untersuchungen Zur Grabschrift Des Aberkios," 109–16, who gives: ... βασιληΐδ' ἀθρῆσαι καὶ βασίλισσαν ἰδεῖν (109) but does not translate into German but simply has "Basileia erblicken und die Basilissa zu sehen" (110). See also Ficker, "Der heidnische Charakter des Abercius-Inschrift," 89–90; ICUR 2.1 Proemium XV–XVII.

Abercius's witnessing (219 CE) the ἱερός γάμος of Elagabalus as king with the Vestal Virgin, Aquilia Severa, his queen, "with golden robe, with golden sandals" (χρυσόστολος, χρυσοπέδιλος).[78] Abercius also saw in Rome "the people having the shining seal," using the typically Christian word, λαός for the "people of God," who in baptism had received the σφραγίς (*Grabschrift* 9).[79] Once again, to read this line in a Christian light is to follow the legend of the Vita Abercii that on such a speculative basis can describe his saintly and episcopal subject describing his converts as having received "the seal of baptism" (τὴν σφραγεῖδαν τοῦ βαπτίσματος). (Vit. Aberc. 9).

While it is true that σφραγίς is used in 2 Clement and, as more recently documented, in the rediscovered work of Melito of Sardis, it was by no means a term unique to Christianity: it described an impress, or even a tattoo applied to initiants, although not generally, in some mystery cults.[80] Certainly, in some of those cults impresses on stone or metal were made into rings or amulets as objects of contemplation in secret or for apotropaic purposes. Whilst Ficker looked for the σφραγίς as mysterious image on metal or stone reverenced in private by a priest of the Attis cult, Dieterich rather saw it as the image impressed upon the sacred stone of Edessa at the center of Heliogabalus's attempt at a universal pagan monotheism. Dieterich, proposed to rewrite λαός as an ionic form of λᾶας, which means a "stone," and claimed that Abercius saw the σφραγίς on black stone of Elagabalus's supreme deity. Thus the term referred not to Christian baptism but the τύπον τοῦ ἐπιχωρίου θεοῦ added to the image of Elagabalus set up in the Senate.[81]

---

78. Dieterich, *Die Grabschrift des Aberkios*, 16, see also Ficker, "Der heidnische Charakter des Abercius-Inschrift," 97 and 101: "Im Tempel der Göttin zu Rom muss, wie im Tempel der Göttin im syrischen Hierapolis neben dem Standbilde der Göttin ein Standbild des Gottes gestanden haben. Vergegenwärtigen wir uns ferner, dass βασιλεύς und βασίλισσα sogar sehr häufig Titel für orientalische Gottheiten sind, so kann die Bezeichnung des Zeus und der Cybele als βασιλεύς und und βασίλισσα erst recht nicht auffallen." See also his reference to Julian, *Or.* 5.180.A.

79. λαὸν δ᾿εἶδον ἐ[κεῖ λαμπρὰν] σφραγεῖδαν ἔ[χοντα].

80. Margaret Mitchell, "The Poetics and Politics of Christian Baptism in the Abercius Monument," in *Ablution, Initiation, and Baptism in Early Judaism, Graeco-Roman Religion, and Early Christianity*, ed. David Hellholm (Berlin: de Gruyter, 2011): 1746–47; Clemens Romanus, *Cor.* 2.7.6: τῶν γὰρ μὴ τηρησάντων ... τὴν σφραγῖδα; Shepherd of Hermas, *Sim.* 93(9.16).4: ἡ σφραγίς οὖν τὸ ὕδωρ ἐστίν; Melito, *Pasch.* 67: "sealed our souls with his own spirit."

81. Ficker, "Der heidnische Charakter des Abercius-Inschrift," 98; Dieterich,

If we therefore factor out of the discussion the Christian reconstruction of the mutilated line in terms of Paul-πίστις and their leading-following relationship, σφραγίς as a reference to Christian baptism, though a possibility, becomes considerably lessened as a possibility. Though the Christian meaning of the term cannot by itself be excluded when measured against the general cultural backcloth of second-century Hierapolis, we nevertheless must ask whether the epitaph contains any further clues as to the kind of groups in which the σφραγίς might be found that would lessen considerable the ambiguity of the term.

The answer is that such terms are indicative not of a Christian assembly but of a pagan cult association. Abercius, aware that he is using the language of mystery only comprehensible to the initiated, invites the whole gathering that fathoms the meaning of his language to pray for him (*Grabschrift* 19).[82] But the prayer that is apparently sung for the "gathering" is rather a choir (συνῳδός). We find copious references to ὑμνῳδοί and συνυμνῳδοί particularly with reference to imperial mysteries commemorating an emperor's birthday, such as for example on a stone altar from the temple of Roma and Augustus at Pergamon.[83] It is within such

---

Die Grabschrift des Aberkios, 32–33; Apuleius, *Apol.*, 55: "Sacrorum pleraque initia in Graecia participaui. Eorum quaedam signa et monumenta tradita mihi a sacerdotibus sedulo conseruo ... uel unius Liberi patris patris mystae qui adestis scitis, quid conditum celetis et absque omnibus profanis tacite ueneremini. At ego, ut dixi, multiiuga sacra et plurimos ritus et uarias cerimonias studio ueri et officio erga deos didici" ("I have participated in various Greek mysteries. I carefully preserve some images and mementoes that have been handed on to me by their priests.... For example, you know who are present and initiants of our father Dionysius alone what you keep hidden, concealed under wraps, and you revere in silence apart from all removed from the rites. And I, as I have said, have learned many kinds of mysteries, very many rites and ceremonies, in my desire for truth and my duty toward the gods"); Cassius Dio, *Hist. rom.* 80.9–10; Herodian, *Hist.* 5. 5.6–7. See also Allen Brent, *The Imperial Cult and the Development of Church Order: Concepts and Images of Authority in Paganism and Early Christianity before the Age of Cyprian*, VCSup 45 (Leiden: Brill, 1999), 319–27.

82. ταῦ θ' ὁ νοῶν εὔξαιτο ὑπὲρ Ἀβερκίου πᾶς ὁ συνῳδός ("May all the cult who understand these words sing prayers on behalf of Abercius").

83. *IGRR* 4.353. For a full discussion, see Henri W. Pleket, "An Aspect of the Imperial Cult: Imperial Mysteries," *HTR* 58.4 (1965): 331–47; Brent, *Imperial Cult and the Development of Church Order*, 194–95. See also *IGRR* 4.1436.2–3, 15–18; *SEG* 37.961.6–11. Wischmeyer, "Die Aberkiosinschrift als Grabepigramm," 44, wrongly claims: "Jedenfalls fehlt dem Wort jeder Hinweis auf ein nur von Glaubensgenossen geteiltes Arcanum oder von Mysterienvereinen." Rather, συνῳδός is cognate with a host

a mystery cult that the concealed meaning of the σφραγίς whether of a mark tattooed on an initiate's flesh or as the impress on a sacred object can be understood.

But how then can the Virgin catching the "fish from the fountain ... a fish of great size and pure" now be understood (*Grabschrift* 13–16)?[84] Is the παρθένος ἁγνή the subject of καὶ παρέθηκε τροφὴν in the form of the fish that she catches, or is it Nestis, Dieterich's river goddess, or Ficker's Tises (ΤΙΣΗΣ), a name of Cybele? Once we have rejected the Paulus-πίστις (ἑπόμην-προῆγε) matrix, Christian interpretations can be disregarded, that variously see the Virgin as the church providing baptism or the church personified or even the Blessed Virgin Mary providing the Eucharist in all places.[85] The παρθένος ἁγνή and her catch of fish, provided by herself directly or by Nestis or Tises, must be located against a cultural backcloth of second-century Hierapolitan paganism.

Although since the nineteenth century there have been no absence of Christian interpretations of what is provided, either as baptism or as a meal, we should firstly note that although the author of the Vita Abercii could interpret the σφραγίς unequivocally as baptism, there is no embellishment of the fish and the fountain in the form of the Eucharist as an element in his legend of Abercius.

Rather, the Vita Abercii infers from the words of the epitaph a miracle performed by Abercius involving "a mixture of wine, oil and vinegar, with also a few loaves" (οἶνον καὶ ἔλαιον καὶ ὄξος μίξας ἑκάτερα καὶ ὀλίγους ἄρτους) (Vit. Aberc. 55). If Trophimion his companion drank from his flask with-

---

of terms that clearly are associated with mystery associations, such as ὑμνῳδοί and συνυμνῳδοί.

84. καὶ παρέθηκε [τροφὴν] πάντῃ ἰχθὺν [ἀπὸ πηγῆς] / πανμεγέθη καθ[αρόν, ὃν] ἐδράξατο παρθέ[νος ἁγνή,] / καὶ τοῦτον ἐπέ[δωκε φι]λίοις ἐσθε[ῖν διὰ παντός,] / [οἶνον χρηστὸν ἔχουσα, κέρασμα διδοῦσα μετ' ἄρτου.] /πανμεγέθη καθ[αρόν (for translation, see n. 35 above).

85. Tertullian, *Bapt.* 1.3. Ilaria Ramelli, "L'epitafio di Abercio: Uno *status quaestionis* ed alcune osservazioni," *Aevum* 74 (2000): 202; Georg Kretschmar, "Erfahrung der Kirche: Beobachtungen zur Aberkios-Inschrift," in *Communio Sanctorum: Mélanges offerts à Jean-Jaques von Allmen*, ed. Boris Bobrinskoy et al. (Neuchâtel: Université de Neuchâtel, Facultés de Théologie, 1982), 81. For a eucharistic interpretation, see Wilpert, *Fractio Panis*, 105–6. For the church symbolized by the Blessed Virgin Mary, see Franz Joseph Dölger, ΙΧΘΥΣ, *Das Fischsymbol in frühchristlicher Zeit* (Münster in Westfalen, 1910), 2:486–507. See also Guarducci, "L' inscrizione di Abercio e La 'Vergine Casta," 271–79.

out the saintly bishop's permission, only oil and vinegar came out. But if Abercius had given his consent, then the wine came out "pure" (καθαρόν). This was the limit to the sense that this fourth-century Christian could give to the οἶνον χρηστὸν ... κέρασμα διδοῦσα μετ' ἄρτου ἰχθὺν ἀπὸ πηγῆς with the ἰχθὺν ... καθαρόν (for translations, see n. 35 above; Vit. Aberc. 56; see also *Grabschrift* 14, 16).

If we wish to find images of bread, wine, olives, and vinegar we need to look not at images of the Eucharist in early Christian art but of funerary banquets whose depiction was well suited to an epitaph. We can identify the meal provided to Abercius by the παρθένος ἁγνή as a *refrigerium*, against which we can identify the social and religious milieu reflected in the epitaph. The features of the *refrigerium*, the "refreshment meal" for the dead, point to a popular religious culture in which an emerging, second-century Christianity would appear at best highly ambiguous and at worst almost invisible in public expressions of religious concepts and icons.

In the third and fourth centuries, we find forms of *refrigeria* that have come to develop out of that general culture a clearer Christian definition. What is at issue is whether that culture had assumed such a Christian definition in the second century and is witnessed as such in the Abercius epitaph. The figure of a female is frequently found prominently serving at such a meal. There was a fourth-century Constantinian celebration of such meals in some parts of the cemetery of Ss Petrus and Marcellinus, whose Christianity is vouchsafed in frescoes that personify the Christian virtues of Agape and Eirene (plates 5 and 6).[86] But at what point in the development of such a practice did these two figures replace the pagan representations of Psyche and Amor as part of a funerary motif: both these figures were still decorating one panel of a Christian sarcophagus, that of Junius Bassus, in 359 CE.[87]

In the cemetery of Ss Petrus and Marcellinus, we find some of the frescoes of the *refrigerium* banquet decorated with verbal inscriptions associated with the figures of Agape and Eirene. I interpret these as allegorical figures that represent the souls of departed individuals, often as husband and wife, as to the figures of Amor and Psyche in their pagan equivalents.[88] The verbal accompaniments to these figures are reminiscent

---

86. Brent, "Methodological Perspectives," 18–22, 27–34.

87. Elizabeth Struthers Malbon, *The Iconography of the Sarcophagus of Junius Bassus* (Princeton: Princeton University Press, 1990), 91–95 and figs. 31–32.

88. See Brent, "Methodological Perspectives," 28–29 and his plate 35 (Dölger,

of Abercius's οἶνον χρηστὸν ... κέρασμα διδοῦσα μετ' ἄρτου. Prominent in many of these *refrigeria* scenes is the image of a fish, and so we have, too, the ἰχθὺν ἀπὸ πηγῆς ("a fish from the fountain"). The κέρασμα theme is expressed by: AGAPE MISCE MI(hi) ("Agape mix for me (the wine)," or "IREN[E] MISCE" (plates 5 and 6) even though Abercius's παρθένος ἁγνή stands alone as the provider.[89]

But Agape and Irene only thus appear in the fourth century, when, as I have said, their pagan predecessors Amor and Psyche still appear on an artifact like the sarcophagus of Junius Bassus. In the second century a single divine figure, the παρθένος ἁγνή in a scene with a pitcher of wine or of oil or presenting a cup in her hand is more likely to be an image highly infused with the features of a pagan culture, even if a second figure is not introduced so as the set both figures in the context of the Amor-Psyche myth (see plate 7). We do have further examples of such meals at San Sebastiano, originally Ss Petrus et Paulus ad Catacombas, around 239 CE when the clay pits were filled in burying the tombs of Codius Hermes, the Innocentiores, and the so-called Axe.[90] Here was then constructed a Villa whose courtyard contained a Triclia or dining hall. On the east side of the portico was a stone bench behind which ran a wall decorated with many graffiti offering votive prayers to the apostles, Ss Petrus et Paulus, along with *refrigeria* meals from the Triclia. Typical is the graffito of Victor who invokes the intercessions of the two apostles or of one Tomius Caelius who records his *refrigerium* meal.[91]

But no Christian theological justification is given for such offerings for the dead apostles. We may then have here evidence of a form of Christianity far closer to pagan religious practice and perhaps on the part of some worshipers the pagan/Christian distinction was only indistinctly made. This is the culture in terms of which perhaps the epitaph of Abercius was composed.

We have, for example, those Christians criticized most harshly by Cyprian for their preparedness to participate in the emperor Decius's

---

ΙΧΘΥΣ, 3.53), where images of husband and wife are embellished with birds' wings (Amor) and butterfly wings (Psyche).

89. Brent, "Methodological Perspectives," 20, 31–33 and his plates 23, 40, 44, and 46. We have also SABINA MISCE where Psyche's allegorical veil appears to have slipped to reveal the real identity of the departed thus allegorized. See above, n. 81.

90. Brent, "Methodological Perspectives," 13–15.

91. Brent, "Methodological Perspectives," 14.

universally decreed *supplicatio* to the gods of the Roman state (249 CE). Cyprian regarded them as apostates who, incredibly for him, had thrown away in one act the new birth at their baptism. But they no doubt viewed their willing and eagerly desired participation in a pagan sacrament of imperial unity more positively.[92] Furthermore, bishop Basilides of Legio Asturica had invoked pagan gods on what he thought mistakenly was his death-bed, and bishop Martialis of Emerita, also in Spain, had celebrated pagan *refrigeria* at the interment of his sons in a pagan burial ground.[93] Both were deposed respectively from the Sees at the instigation of Cyprian but who were clearly part of a social culture that did not make the distinctions between Christianity and paganism that Cyprian was demanding.

If the Abercius epitaph is a witness to early Christianity at all, perhaps it was a witness to a highly ambiguous religious culture. Such a popular culture would have viewed more positively the association and assimilation rather than exclusive opposition of Christian and pagan images and ritual practices as witnessed by the iconography of the Good Shepherd and of Orpheus and the practice of commemorative funeral meals. We will find such a witness in a literary form that takes us beyond the speculation of the last paragraph. In the Naasene Psalm found in Pseudo-Hippolytus, *Ref.* 5.7.30–34, Hermes, the waker of souls from the dead, is equated with Christ in an allegorical interpretation of Odysseus and the suitors (Homer, *Od.* 24.6–8). But here also Hermes, the waker of souls from the dead, is equated with Christ who becomes part of the meaning of the allegory.[94]

Here we may discover the true world of the Abercius epitaph.

Bibliography

Abel, Adolphe. "Étude sur l'inscription d'Abercius." *Byzantion* 3.2 (1926): 321–411.
Avramea, Anna. "Land and Sea Communications, Fourth–Fifteenth Centuries." Pages 57–90 in vol. 1 of *The Economic History of Byzantium*. Edited by Angeliki E. Laiou. Dumbarton Oaks Studies 39. Washington DC: Dumbarton Oaks, 2002.

---

92. Brent, *Imperial Cult and the Development of Church Order*, 225–40.
93. Brent, *Imperial Cult and the Development of Church Order*, 15, 310–11.
94. Pseudo-Hippolytus also uses biblical references to Isa 28:16; Ps 117:22; Eph 3:16; 5:14, etc.

Boissonarde, Jean François. *Anecdota Graeca*. Paris: Excusum in Regio Typographeo, 1829–1833.

Bowersock, Glen W. *Greek Sophists in the Roman Empire*. Oxford: Oxford University Press, 1969.

Brent, Allen. *The Imperial Cult and the Development of Church Order: Concepts and Images of Authority in Paganism and Early Christianity before the Age of Cyprian*. VCSup 45. Leiden: Brill, 1999.

———. "Methodological Perspectives in the Interpretation of Early Christian Artefacts." *StPatr* 73 (2014): 1–38.

Bundy, David. "The Life of Abercius: Its Significance for Early Syrian Christianity." *Second Century* 7 (1989–1990): 163–76.

Calder, William M. "The Epitaph of Avircius Marcellus." *JRS* 29 (1939): 1–4.

Carletti, Carlo. "Origini cristiane ed epigrafa: Note di lettura a proposito di alcune iscrizioni (forse) 'protocristiane.'" *Annali di Storia dell'Esegesi* 31.1 (2014): 83–94.

Castelli, Emanuele. "The Symbols of Anchor and Fish in the Most Ancient Parts of the Catacomb of Priscilla: Evidence and Questions." *StPatr* 59 (2013): 11–20.

Conybeare, Frederick C. Review of *Zur Abercius Inschrift*, by Adolf von Harnack. *Classical Review* 9 (1895): 295–97.

De Sanctis, George. "Die Grabschrift des Aberkios." *ZKT* 21.4 (1897): 673–65.

Delmaire, Roland. *Les institutions du bas-empire romain de Constantin à Justinien: Les institutions civiles palatines*. Paris: Cerf, 1995.

Dieterich, Albrecht. *Die Grabschrift des Aberkios*. Leipzig: Teubner, 1896.

Dölger, Franz Joseph. ΙΧΘΥΣ, *Das Fischsymbol in frühchristlicher Zeit*. Vol. 2. Münster in Westfalen: Metzler, 1910.

Duchesne, Louis. "L'épitaphe d'Abercius." *Mélanges d'archéologie et d'histoire* 15 (1895): 155–82.

Eck, Werner. "P. Aelius Apollonides, ab epistulis Graecis, und ein Brief des Cornelius Fronto." *ZPE* 91 (1992): 236–42.

Ferrua, Antonio. "Nuove osserazioni sull'epitaffio di Abercio." *Rivista di Archelogia Cristiana* 20 (1943): 279–305.

Ficker, Gerhard. "Der heidnische Charakter des Abercius-Inschrift." *Sitzungsberichte der Könlich Preußischen Akademie der Wissenschaften zu Berlin* (1894): 87–112.

Franco, Carlo. *Elio Aristide e Smirne*. Rome: Bardi, 2005.

Grégoire, H. "Bardesane et S. Abercius." *Byzantion* 25–27 (1955–1957): 363–68.
Guarducci, Margherita. *Epigrafi sacre pagane e cristiane*. Vol. 4 of *Epigrafia Graeca*. Rome: Istituto Poligrafico dello Stato, Libreria dello Stato, 1978.
———. "L' inscrizione di Abercio e La 'Vergine Casta.'" *Ancient Society* 4 (1973): 271–79.
Harnack, Adolf von. *Zur Abercius-Inschrift*. TU 12.4B. Leipzig: Hinrichs, 1895.
Hirschmann, Vera. "Untersuchungen Zur Grabschrift Des Aberkios." *ZPE* 129 (2000): 109–16.
Kaufmann, Carl Maria. *Handbuch der Altchristlichen Epigraphik*. Freiburg im Breisgau: Herder, 1917.
Klauser, Theodor. "Studien zur Entstehungsgeschichte der christlichen Kunst I." *JAC* 1 (1958): 20–51.
Kretschmar, Georg. "Erfahrung der Kirche: Beobachtungen zur Aberkios-Inschrift." Pages 73–85 in *Communio Sanctorum: Mélanges offerts à Jean-Jaques von Allmen*. Edited by Boris Bobrinskoy et al. Neuchâtel: Université de Neuchâtel, Facultés de Théologie, 1982.
Lüdtke, Willy, and Theodor Nissen. *Die Grabschrift des Aberkios, Ihre Überlieferung und Ihr Text*. Leipzig: Teubner, 1910.
Malbon, Elizabeth Struthers. *The Iconography of the Sarcophagus of Junius Bassus*. Princeton: Princeton University Press, 1990.
Marucchi, Orazio. "Nuove osservazioni sulla iscrizione di Abercio." *Nuovo Bulletino di archeologia Cristiana* 1 (1895): 17–41.
Merkelbach, Reinhold. "Grabepigramm und Vita des Bischofs Aberkios von Hierapolis." *EA* 28 (1997): 125–39.
Merkelbach, Reinhold, and Josef Stauber. *Der "Ferne Osten" und das Landesinnere bis zum Tauros*. Vol. 3 of *Steinepigramme aus dem griechischen Osten*. Munich: Saur, 2001.
———. *Die Westküste Kleinasiens von Knidos bis Ilion*. Vol. 1 of *Steinepigramme aus dem griechischen Osten*. Stuttgart: Teubner, 1998.
Mitchell, Margaret M. "Looking for Abercius: Reimagining Contexts of Interpretation of the Earliest Christian Inscription." Pages 303–25 in *Commemorating the Dead: Texts and Artifacts in Context; Studies of Roman, Jewish, and Christian Burials*. Edited by Laurie Brink and Deborah Green. Berlin: de Gruyter, 2008.
———. "The Poetics and Politics of Christian Baptism in the Abercius Monument." Pages 1739–78 in *Ablution, Initiation, and Baptism in*

Early Judaism, Graeco-Roman Religion, and Early Christianity. Edited by David Hellholm. Berlin: de Gruyter, 2011.
Mitchell, Stephen. *Anatolia: Land, Men, and Gods in Asia Minor*. Vols. 1 and 2. Oxford: Oxford University Press, 1993.
Nissen, Theodor. *S. Abercii Vita*. Leipzig: Teubner, 1912.
Pleket, Henri W. "An Aspect of the Imperial Cult: Imperial Mysteries." *HTR* 58.4 (1965): 331–47.
Ramelli, Ilaria. "L'epitafio di Abercio: Uno *status quaestionis* ed alcune osservazioni." *Aevum* 74 (2000): 191–205.
Ramsay, William M. "The Cities and Bishoprics of Phrygia." *JHS* 4 (1883): 370–436.
———. *The Cities and Bishoprics of Phrygia*. Oxford: Clarendon, 1897.
———. "The Utilisation of Old Epigraphic Copies." *JHS* 38 (1918): 124–92.
Reinach, Salomon. "Chronique de Orient." *Revue Archéologique* 3.2 (1883): 192–95.
Robert, Carl. "Archaeologische Nachlese." *Hermes* 29.3 (1894): 417–35.
Robert, Jeanne, and Louis Robert. *Exploration, histoire, monnaies et inscriptions*. Vol. 1 of *Fouilles d'Amyzon en Carie*. Paris: de Boccard, 1983.
Sitlington Sterrett, J. R. *Leaflets from the Notebook of an Archeological Traveler in Asia Minor*. Austin: University of Texas, State Printing Office, 1889.
Thonemann, Peter. "Abercius of Hierapolis: Christianisation and Social Memory in Late Antique Asia Minor." Pages 252–82 in *Historical and Religious Memory in the Ancient World*. Edited by Beate Dignas and R. R. R. Smith. Oxford: Oxford University Press, 2012.
Wilpert, Joseph. *Fractio Panis: Die älteste Darstellung des eucharistischen Opfers in der "cappella Greca."* Freiburg im Breisgau: Herder, 1895.
Wischmeyer, Wolfgang. "Die Aberkiosinschrift als Grabepigramm." *JAC* 23 (1980): 22–47.

The Inscriptions and Oracular Prophecy in the Eastern Mediterranean Basin: Assessing the Book of Revelation in Its Greco-Roman Revelatory Context

James R. Harrison

1. Epigraphic Case Studies of Oracular Prophecy
in the Eastern Mediterranean

In the Second Sophistic period interest in the oracular revitalized and flourished once again across the Roman Empire in Greece and Asia Minor. This was reflected initially not only in the works of Plutarch (*On the Obsolescence of Oracles*) but also later in Lucian's *Alexander the False Prophet* and Aelius Aristides's *Sacred Tales*. The elites founded, financed, promoted, and maintained the oracular sites. Oracular responses from the god, delivered through a prophet in response to an enquiry, characterized the sites of Delphi and Dodona in Greece and Klaros and Didyma in Asia Minor, whereas the lot-oracle was used in southern Asia Minor.[1] Notably, the city

---

1. For oracular responses delivered through a prophet, see Samson Eitrim, *Orakel und Mysterien am Ausgang der Antike* (Zürich: Rhein, 1947); Joseph Fontenrose, *The Delphic Oracle: Its Responses and Operations* (Berkeley: University of California Press, 1978); Fontenrose, *Didyma: Apollo's Oracle, Cult, and Companions* (Berkeley: University of California Press, 1988); Thomas Lonzo Robinson, "Theological Oracles and the Sanctuaries of Claros and Didyma: A Thesis" (PhD diss., Harvard University, 1981); H. W. Parke, *The Oracles of Zeus: Dodona, Olympia, Ammon* (Oxford: Blackwell, 1967); Parke, *The Oracles of Apollo in Asia Minor* (London: Croom Helm, 1985); Parke, "The Temple of Apollo at Didyma: The Building and Its Function," *JHS* 106 (1986): 121–31; Reinhold Merkelbach and Josef Stauber, "Die Orakel des Apollon von Klaros," *EA* 27 (1997): 1–54; Aude Busine, *Paroles d'Apollon: Practiques et traditions oraculaiues dans l'Antiquité tardive (IIᵉ–VIᵉ siècles)*, RGRW 156 (Leiden: Brill, 2005), 18–86; Alexander Herda, *Der Apollon-Delphinios-Kult in Milet und die Neujahrsprozession nach Didyma: Ein neuer Kommentar der sog. Molpoi-Satzung* (Mainz: Philipp von Zabern, 2006),

of Laodicea in the Lycus Valley, one of the seven churches of Revelation to whom an oracle was addressed (Rev 3:14–22), is regularly mentioned in the delegations sent to the oracular site of Klaros. The powerful oracular mentality in many of the Asian cities confirmed the existence of the gods in the face of Epicurean skepticism, reaffirming not only traditional religious cultic belief but also offering guidance and redemption in times of personal and civic crisis, including outbreaks of plague or disease within the cities and in the surrounding countryside. Furthermore, in the case of an alphabetic oracle from Hierapolis, another Lycus Valley city mentioned in the New Testament (Col 4:15–16), the Apolline oracles provided ethical guidance for the urban elites in their civic life. Even in the case of the confession inscriptions, another epigraphic phenomenon of Lydia and Phrygia in the Second Sophistic, the gods occasionally urged propitiation and reconciliation in a time of moral and cultic crisis by means of oracular replies, an interesting variant on the routine propitiation oracles. A rarity, however, is the political oracle. Our sole epigraphic example from the early Julian period endorses the political status quo. This makes the prophecy of Revelation all the more unusual for its anti-imperial thrust.[2]

This chapter will propose that the oracular epigraphic corpus of Second Sophistic Asia Minor provides us new with insights into the rhetoric, intentions, and context of the prophecy of Revelation. Such a localized, documentary approach avoids the uncritical use of vastly differing genres

---

not sighted by me; Eric L'Hôte, *Les lamelles oraculaires de Dodone* (Geneva: Droz, 2006); Jean-Charles Moretti, "Le temple de l'oracle d'Apollon à Claros," in *Archéologies et espaces parcourus*, ed. Olivier Henry (Istanbul: Institut français d'études anatoliennes, 2012), 1–23; Moretti, "Le temple d'Apollon mis en chantier à Claros à la fin du ive s. av. J.-C.," in APXITEKTΩN: τιμητικός τόμος για τον καθηγητή Μανόλη Κορρέ, ed. Kostas Zambas et al. (Athènes: Melissa, 2016), 585–600; Antii Lampinem, "Θεῷ μεμελημένε Φοίβῳ—Oracular Functionaries at Claros and Didyma in the Imperial Period," in *Studies in Ancient Oracles and Divination*, ed. Mika Kajava, Direttore degli Acta Instituti Romani Finlandiae 40 (Rome: Instituti Romani Finlandiae, 2013), 50–88; Jean-Charles Moretti with Liliane Rabatel, eds., *Le sanctuaire de Claros et son oracle*, Maison de l'Orient et de la Méditerranée 65 (Lyon: Jean Poulloux, 2014). On the interaction of architecture in the Apolline sanctuaries of Klaros and Dodona, see Celeste L. Guichard, "Travels and Traversals in the Hellenistic Oracular Temples at Klaros and Didyma" (PhD diss., Columbia University, 2005). For lot-oracles, see Johannes Nollé, *Kleinasiatische Losorakel: Astragal- und Alpabetchresmologien der hochkaiserzeitlichen Orakelrenaissance* (Munch: Beck, 2007).

2. On the anti-imperial thrust of Revelation, see n. 124.

of evidence from diverse geographic backgrounds spanning hundreds of years in the reconstruction of the context of early Christian prophecy.[3] In the first half of this chapter the inscriptional evidence from oracular sites in Asia Minor, including several of the biblical cities, will be explored for the light that it throws on the prophecy of Revelation (προφητεία: 1:3; 22:7, 10, 18–19).[4] This will enable us to highlight how the motifs of the book of Revelation reflected local first-century Asian revelatory concerns and incipient oracular developments as much as the traditional rhetoric of Jewish prophecy and apocalyptic. At the outset, three observations about our approach are apposite.

First, an immediate issue is that the inscriptional evidence mostly postdates the New Testament, belonging to the Second Sophistic revival of the oracular in the Asian cities, whereas the book of Revelation, whether dated to 69 CE or the reign of Domitian or Trajan, is probably a late first-century composition or possibly an early second-century composition. The danger of anachronism is real. Further, the phenomenon of

---

3. The classic works on New Testament prophecy are Theodore M. Crone, *Early Christian Prophecy: A Study of Its Origin and Function* (Baltimore: Saint Mary's University Press, 1973); David Hill, *New Testament Prophecy* (London: Marshall, Morgan & Scott, 1979); Wayne A. Grudem, *The Gift of Prophecy in 1 Corinthians* (Lanham, MD: University of America Press, 1982); David E. Aune, *Prophecy in Early Christianity and the Ancient Mediterranean World* (Grand Rapids: Eerdmans, 1983); Antoinette Clark Wire, *The Corinthian Women Prophets: A Reconstruction through Paul's Rhetoric* (Minneapolis: Fortress, 1994); Thomas W. Gillespie, *The First Theologians: A Study in Early Christian Prophecy* (Grand Rapids: Eerdmans, 1994); Christopher Forbes, *Prophecy and Inspired Speech in Early Christianity and Its Hellenistic Environment* (Peabody, MA: Hendrickson, 1997); Max Turner, *Power from on High: The Spirit in Israel's Restoration and Witness in Luke-Acts* (Sheffield: Sheffield Academic, 2000); Laura Nasrallah, *An Ecstasy of Folly: Prophecy and Authority in Early Christianity* (Cambridge: Harvard University Press, 2004). Surprisingly, little on the topic has been written since.

4. This remains a relatively unexplored comparison. Pieter de Villiers ("Oracles and Prophecies in the Graeco-Roman World and the Book of Revelation in the New Testament," *APB* 8.1 [1997]: 79–86) largely ignores the inscriptional evidence, as does A. Kerkeslager ("Apollo, Graeco-Roman Prophecy, and the Rider on the White Horse in Rev. 6:2," *JBL* 112 [1992]: 116–21). However, James R. Edwards ("The Rider on the White Horse, the Thigh Inscription, and Apollo: Revelation 19:16," *JBL* 137 [2018]: 519–36) is a conspicuous and insightful exception. So far as I am aware, this article is the first study of the Second Sophistic oracular inscriptions from Asia Minor in relation to the prophecy of Revelation.

early Christian prophecy is markedly different from the prophecy practiced and experienced at the Asian (and Greek) oracular centers. The expression of early Christian prophecy is not confined to a particular geographical site; it is unsolicited inspiration rather than the technical and inductive oracular revelation of the Asian and Greek centers; it involves no priestly or prophetic hierarchies because of its emphasis on the pneumatic χαρίσματα (gifts); and, apart from προφήτης, the central terminology of Greco-Roman prophecy is not found in the New Testament documents.[5]

Nevertheless, despite the substantial differences,[6] such a comparison remains valuable. It may enable us to gain further insight into why the later Asian oracular sites such as Didyma issued anti-Christian oracles. The second-century revival of the oracular may embody incipient trends, social and religious, that were beginning to emerge in first-century Asia, with which the early Christians, if Revelation is sufficiently representative, were either competing, struggling, or opposing. There also remain sufficient first-century strands of evidence among this second to third century epigraphic corpus—certainly at Didyma and, by implication, at Klaros[7]—to warrant the investigation. Our geographically based study of the documentary evidence, site-by-site and case study-by-case study, adds

---

5. These contrasts may be gleaned from a close reading of Forbes, *Prophecy and Inspired Speech*.

6. The substantial differences should not be underestimated. Such an investigation is not just a matter of comparing apples with oranges, as I naively opined at the Annual Meeting of the Society of New Testament Studies in Pretoria in 2017, but it is in actuality, as Professor Judith Lieu acutely observed, more a case of comparing green apples with yellow tennis balls! I am very grateful to Professor John Kloppenborg and Professor Lieu, along with the other conference delegates attending the Society of New Testament Studies "Papyrology, Epigraphy and the New Testament" Session, for their generous and incisive responses to the original paper, now revised.

7. For evidence that prophecy at Didyma had revived by the late first century BCE and was in full swing again by the mid first century CE, see Mark Wilson, "The Rise of Christian Oracles in the Shadow of the Apollo Cults," *Ekklesiastikos Pharos* 90 (2008): 162–75. Note, too, the Didymean inscriptions in Fontenrose, *Didyma*, §§15, 17, 44, B2, B5, B8, spanning 100 BCE—100 CE. Since the earliest extant delegation inscription from Klaros is datable to the forty-sixth prytany of Apollo (ca. 105 CE: Jean-Louis Ferrary, *Les mémoriaux de délégations du sanctuaire oraculaire de Claros, d'après la documentation conserve dans le Fonds Louis Robert*, vol. 1–2, Des inscriptions et belles-lettres Tome 40 [Paris: Mémoires de l'Académie, 2014], §1), the oracular site was operating during the first century CE. See Robinson, *Theological Oracles*, 21.

depth to David E. Aune's discussion of the Greco-Roman oracular evidence, which is dominated by genre concerns.[8] We do not gain a strong historical understanding of what was occurring *locally* in Aune's approach, and it is hoped that by our exclusive focus on the Asian documentary evidence this lacuna will be filled.

Second, the *Apolline* basis of much revelatory activity at local oracular sites (Didyma, Klaros) is worthy of special consideration, given the centrality of Apollo in the early principate as Augustus's tutelary deity. This attachment to Apollo continued under his Julio-Claudian heirs. James R. Edwards, has recently argued that Revelation recalls prototypes and symbols of the Apolline cult in first-century Asia (Rev 12; 19:6) but presents them as perfected and fulfilled in Jesus Christ.[9] Furthermore, Andrew J. Coutras, after demonstrating the prominence of the Apolline cult and its propaganda throughout Asia Minor and in the Lycus Valley in particular,[10] proposes that John in Revelation peels away any positive association of Apollo in popular religion or imperial ideology. Instead, the seer depicts the revelatory cult as perpetrating chaos and destruction in the form of the Dragon (Rev 12).[11] What other allusions to Apollo might be present in Revelation and what function do they play in the apocalyptic work?[12] Do such Apolline motifs merely underline the importance of the cult to the Julio-Claudian rulers, subsumed under John's critique of empire, or do they point more widely to John's awareness of the revitalization of the oracular sites of Apollo at Klaros and Didyma at the time of writing?

Third, the recurrence of important motifs in the prophecy of Revelation and in the oracular inscriptions of Asia Minor could point to the possibility that each tradition draws independently upon familiar oracular conventions, some Greco-Roman and, in John's case, some drawn from

---

8. Aune, *Prophecy in Early Christianity*, 23–79.

9. Edwards, "Rider on the White Horse."

10. Andrew J. Coutras, *Chaos and Clairvoyance: Apollo in Asia Minor and in the Apocalypse* (PhD thesis, Asbury Theological Seminary, 2018), 75–113, 116–41. Note the excellent discussion of the Apolline coins and inscriptions at Hierapolis and Laodicea on 117–26, 126–35.

11. Coutras (*Chaos and Clairvoyance*, 7) states: "John's treatment of Apollo is one of inversion and recharacterization: the references to Apollo in Revelation move from portraying him simply as a rival to Christ to portraying him as an abyssal chaos monster who makes war upon the saints in the service of the Dragon."

12. See now the exhaustive discussion in Coutras, *Chaos and Clairvoyance*, 155–219.

the LXX and Second Temple Judaism. Alternatively, each tradition could be possibly based upon a more *localized common knowledge* from Asia Minor. In terms of common motifs, it will be argued that the references to famines and plagues fall into the former category, whereas the motif of oracular veracity and faithfulness is more likely to have localized reference. Other common motifs (e.g., honorific crowning and hymn-singing), we will propose, are polyvalent in John's case, but again they display the genuine possibility of localized knowledge.

In sum, there is enough evidence to indicate that the revival of oracular sites had already begun before the heyday of the Second Sophistic. In particular, the Apolline cult issued a serious challenge to the truth claims of Christian revelation because of the considerable social status that accrued to the cult personnel and delegations associated with the Asian sites of Didyma and Klaros. It will be argued that this clash of oracular traditions, underestimated in scholarship on Revelation, is an important clue to understanding neglected elements of John's prophecy. We turn now to an exploration of the oracular epigraphic evidence belonging to the Second Sophistic period.

1.1. Oracular Enquiries and Responses: Didyma, Klaros, and Hierapolis

1.1.1. Didyma

The extent of early Christian knowledge of the ancient oracular site of Didyma is uncertain. Paul spent several days at Miletus (Acts 20:17; see also 2 Tim 4:20) while his coastal boat docked, unloaded, and reloaded cargo, allowing the apostle sufficient time to invite the Ephesian elders to come to him for a final address (20:18–31).[13] Miletus was the nearby caretaker of the Apolline oracle of Didyma, with both sites being joined by a new road in Trajan's reign. The Milesian New Year festival, established in archaic times, saw the entire population of Miletus assemble in the agora and then move along the 18 km processional road to the sanctuary in

---

13. On the trip of the Ephesian elders to Miletus, see Mark Wilson, "The Ephesian Elders Come to Miletus: An Annaliste Reading of Acts 20:15–18a," *VeEc* 34.1 (2013): art. #744, pp. 1–9, http://dx.doi. org/10.4102/ve.v34i1.744. Wilson estimates that the trip of the elders from Ephesus to Miletus would take four long days of travel, spanning some 72 km by land and water (6).

Didyma, the oracular site of Apollo Didymeus.[14] Mark Wilson speculates that Paul may have seen some of the prominent inscriptions, mentioning Didymean prophets, that graced the beginning of the Sacred Way to Didyma at Miletus, even if he did not go to Didyma himself.[15] Thus, in the context of nearby oracular Didyma, it is significant that Luke's Paul is divinely equipped with the prophetic words of the Spirit in the city of Miletus before his impending journey to Jerusalem (Acts 20:23; see also 21:4, 10–12). This "portended a clash of prophetic voices" that would eventually lead to the Christian cult challenging the dominance of the Apolline cults as an oracular movement.[16] Two oracles, each from the Didyma shrine and reported by Augustine and Lactantius,[17] deride the gullible believers and mock Christ's crucifixion. It is worth pondering why this clash occurred. What was it about the early Christian understanding of prophecy that became so objectionable to their later Greco-Roman neighbors? Or was the clash unrelated to prophecy, congregating more around other issues?

---

14. See Herda, *Der Apollon-Delphinios-Kult*; Herda, "How to Run a State Cult: The Organisation of the Cult of Apollo Delphinios in Miletos," in *Current Approaches to Religion in Ancient Greece: Papers Presented at a Symposium at the Swedish Institute at Athens, 17–19 April 2008*, ed. Matthew Haysom and Jenny Wallensten (Stockholm: Swedish Institute at Athens, 2011), 73–74. For the Milesian regulations regarding the procession to Didyma, see the Molpoi decree (*LSAM* §50.27–31 (trans. Herda, "How to Run a State Cult," 82–86). Since there were still regulative insertions being made in this archaic decree at 200 BCE, the very strong likelihood is that the procession continued well into the New Testament era and beyond. The decree and its rituals were a pivotal expression of Milesian self-identity that spanned the centuries.

15. Wilson, "Rise of Christian Oracles," 4.

16. Wilson, "Ephesian Elders Come to Miletus," 7.

17. Augustine, *Civ.* 19.23: When inquiring at Didyma how his wife way might be persuaded way from her Christian conversion, the male enquirer was given this oracular response: "Let her continue as she wishes, persisting in her vain delusions, / and singing in lamentation for a god who died in delusions, / whom, condemned by judges who deliberated justly, / the most ignominious death, bound in iron, destroyed." Lactantius, *Epit.* 4.13.11: Milesian Apollo responded with this oracle in response to the question whether Christ was god or man: "He was a mortal according to the flesh, a wise man with portentous works, / but when he was seized by Chaldean judges, / nailed with stakes, he fulfilled a sharply bitter end." For Christian responses to these oracles, see Wilson, "Rise of Christian Oracles," 11–12; Pier Franco Beatrice, "Monophysite Christology in an Oracle of Apollo," *International Journal of the Classical Tradition* 4 (1997): 3–22.

First, in examining the oracular responses to the enquiries at Didyma, it is important to establish what portrait of the god/gods emerges.[18] An important motif in the oracular replies at Didyma is the need for devotion to ancestral custom ("it is right to do as your fathers"; "it is better to perform it according to ancestral custom").[19] Enquirers themselves are also closely attuned to the importance of ancestral custom, whether that is establishing an altar for "the most holy ancestral goddess Soteira Kore" or simply affirming the reliability of the ancestral gods in prefacing a question to the oracle.[20] Further, the *correct* gods, with their priests and heralds, must be consulted. Thus, in establishing a treaty with Herakleia under Latmos, the oracle advises that for an advantageous outcome to occur for both cities (1) appropriate sacrifices and processions of victims must be made to Apollo Didymeus, Apollo Delphinios, Artemis, Leto, Athena, and Zeus Soter, and (2) the priest and sacred heralds to Hestia Bûlaia should offer prayers.[21] The strategic propitiation of Aspheleos Soter Poseidon with ox-sacrifices—establishing a new cult in this instance—was designed to forestall the danger of earthquakes and water disasters to the city, given Poseidon's superintendence of each natural phenomenon.[22] A

---

18. The enquiries and responses to the oracle at Didyma are listed in Fontenrose, *Didyma*, 177–244. The more mundane issues of enquirers at the Apolline sanctuary of Didyma—e.g., harmony in government, establishing a crowned athletic festival at Didyma, various building projects (see Fontenrose, *Didyma*, §§9, 10, 18, 19)—will be bypassed. The famous hexametrical oracle of Klarian Apollos from city of Oenoanda will also not be examined. For discussion, see Louis Robert, "Un oracle grave à Oinoanda," *Comptes rendus des séances de l'Académie des Inscriptions et Belles-Lettres*, 115.3 (1971): 597–619; A. S. Hall, "The Klarian Oracle at Oenoanda," *ZPE* 32 (1978): 263–68.

19. Respectively, Fontenrose, *Didyma*, §2 (IDidyma 11 [sixth century BCE]); Fontenrose, *Didyma*, §28 (IDidyma 499 [third century CE]). Note, too, that the games at Didyma were to be celebrated "in accordance with ancestral custom for Apollo Didymeus"; Fontenrose, *Didyma*, §10 (SIG 530: Miletus [205–200 BCE]).

20. Fontenrose, *Didyma*, §31 (IMilet 1.7.205a [130 CE]); Fontenrose, *Didyma*, §20 (IDidyma 504 [285–305 CE]).

21. Fontenrose, *Didyma*, §12 (IMilet 1.3.150 [180 CE]).

22. Fontenrose, *Didyma*, §14 (IDidyma 132: late second century BCE): "ask him to come propitiously [ἵλαον] and to preserve the order of your city in stability, free from danger" (ll. 3–5). See also Fontenrose, *Didyma*, 191. For other oracles responses regarding the propitiation of specific gods, see the enquiry of Posidonius from Halikarnassus regarding his household piety in *LSAM* §72.6 (ἱλασκομένοις [300 BCE]). For two enquiries regarding good crops in Kaunos, see *SEG* 40.1109.9 (ἱλασκομένου

final example shows how the cultic omission of an altar of Soteira Kore in the altar circle of Apollo's temenos had deeply grieved a Didymian enquirer who was described as a "god-loving man." The response from Apollo Didymeus Helios was not unexpected: the new altar to Soteira Kore should be established immediately.[23] In sum, Apollo Didymeus is a powerful friend to those who carry out the cultic rituals to the gods prescribed in the oracular response and who also demonstrate respect for ancestral custom and divine honor at all times.[24] To act otherwise is to risk the very real danger of arousing the enmity of the gods. As it is, alternate forms of divine revelation such as dreams and visions run the risk of being true or false, as one fragmentary oracle involving Artemis reminds the enquirer:[25] so the importance of carrying out what Apollo says at Didyma about ritual is further reinforced.

Second, considerable attention is given to the cult officials at Didyma and the honors accorded to them. Tryphosa, whose grandmother was a prophetess, is duly appointed a prophetess.[26] The auspiciousness of the gods is particularly linked to the post of Alexandra, priestess of Demeter of Thesmophoros: "Since from the time when she assumed the office of priestess the gods have been so manifest through their appearances."[27] A priestess of Demeter, Alexandra, is praised for being "a seeker of the goal

---

[undated]); E. Bean, "Notes and Inscriptions from Caunus (Part 2)," *JHS* 74 (1954): 85–87, no. 2.9 (ἱλασκομένου [first century CE]).

23. Fontenrose, *Didyma*, §30 (IDidyma 504 [285–305 CE]). See also Fontenrose, *Didyma*, §29 (IDidyma 277), where the enquirer asks "where shall he place the holy table, honouring the god correctly?"

24. Note the paean of praise for the fruitful goddess Deo (Fontenrose, *Didyma*, §23 [IDidyma 496B [second century CE]). This goddess had brought an end to the hunter-gatherer existence of humankind by providing them crops, whereas before they had lived in beastlike savagery in mountain caves, only having "gluttonous fare in raw-meat-eating jaws." This goddess, therefore, had to be especially honoured for her civilising influence. See also Fontenrose, *Didyma*, 21 (IMilet. 1.7.205b).

25. Fontenrose, *Didyma*, §A6 (IDidyma 505 [200 CE]). Fontenrose, *Didyma*, §29 (IDidyma 277 [third century CE]) refers to the god "speaking to him in vision and now in oracle because of his piety."

26. Fontenrose, *Didyma*, §17 (first century CE). In response to a question whether Satornelia should be appointed priestess of Athena Polias, this woman, from a noble family, is eulogized in a most fulsome and extensive manner for the office (Fontenrose, *Didyma*, §25 [P. Herrmann, "Inscriptions of Miletos," *Chiron* 1 (1971): 292]).

27. Fontenrose, *Didyma*, §22 (IDidyma 496A [second century CE]).

of a principled course of life" and performing the rites of Eumolpos.²⁸ Of particular interest are the stratospheric accolades accorded the prophet and stephanephor, Philodemos, in an elegiac verse honoring him:

> Apollo himself is witness to a pious soul, having set the sacred crowns upon you in the same year. And lovely Miletos, renowned kingdom of Phoibos, has awarded you these thanks for good sense, that as the only person in the countryside called stephanephor and prophet you may shine equally with the celestials.²⁹

Equally intriguing is the high-status prophet whose profession is a doctor. Pollio has been chosen by the god: but there is an inherent ambiguity in the text. Has he been chosen to be a prophet at Miletus by the god in a manner unspecified? Or has Pollio been told by the god to be a doctor at Miletus? The text is set out below:

> Prophet [Προφήτης], Quintus Pomponius Pollio, pious, serving in the festival year, physician [ἰατρός], called by the god [κληθεὶς ὑπὸ θεοῦ]....³⁰

V. Nutton has argued that Pollio was connected to the elite senatorial circles at Rome, being a relative of the T. Pomponius Vitrasius Pollio, the proconsul of 167–168 CE.³¹ As a doctor, therefore, Pollio was a member of the Galenic circle at Rome. But he was summoned by the god to become a prophet at the oracular shrine of Didyma, and, upon settling at Miletus, he would have become part of the religious life of the city and its nearby sanctuary. Although there was considerable accrued status in that elite community, Pollio, as Nutton notes, nevertheless "forsook the life of a senator for the privilege and honour of attendance at a Hellenic oracle."³² The immortal nature of fame inherited by some prophets, symbolized by their many coronal awards, is also emphasized in the Didymean inscription below:

> I see, Posidonios, that by pious lots you have thrice won immortal crowns [στέμμασιν ἀθανάτοις], such a man as Apollo himself has welcomed as a

---

28. Fontenrose, *Didyma*, §23 (IDidyma 496B [second century CE]).
29. Fontenrose, *Didyma*, §B2 (IDidyma 229 [67/66 BCE]).
30. Fontenrose, *Didyma*, §B4 (IDidyma 280 [166–67 CE]).
31. V. Nutton, "The Doctor and the Oracle," *RBPH* 47 (1969): 37–48.
32. Nutton, "Doctor and the Oracle," 48.

prophet, approving judgment and your mother's piety. And time will not forget your fame [κλέος]: for he has picked a man not at all inferior to the ministers before him.[33]

Last, the social status of prophets at Didyma can be seen from the fact that they could reserve stadium seats for others and themselves during the tenure of their office in the city.[34] Not only are the personal ethics and cultic piety of the prophets to Apollo emphasized in the Didymean inscriptions, but also through this medium the elite hierarchies of the sanctuary flaunted their religious and familial prominence for all to see.

1.1.2. Klaros

From the second to the third century CE, the sanctuary and oracle of Klaros kept meticulous documentary records of the consultations of the oracle of Apollo made by the θεοπρόποι ("public messengers sent to enquire of an oracle") on behalf of their cities. However, these city delegations of pilgrims, which, in the case of Laodicea, routinely included a προφήτης in addition to the choirs of children, were memorialized in 427 extant inscriptions, now collected by Jean-Louis Ferrary.[35] This collection builds upon last century's excavations of T. Macridy, Charles Picard, and Louis Robert, among other scholars. In the case of the oracular site of Didyma, the inscriptions of the ὑδροφόροι ("water carriers"), who were attached to the cult of Artemis Pythia, recounted their responsibilities in celebrating the mysteries of the god. However, neither the mysteries of the cult nor its servants are the focus in the inscriptions of Klaros but rather the elite members of the various city delegations.[36] These comprised representatives from predominantly Asia Minor (including the biblical cities of Thyatira, Laodicea, Pisidian Antioch, Iconium), mainland Greece (Corinth), Macedonia, Thrace, and the islands (Crete). Significantly, Smyrna and Ephesus are absent, though

---

33. Fontenrose, *Didyma*, §B5 (IDidyma 282 [first century CE?]).
34. For discussion and translation of the Didymean stadium inscriptions, see Tamara Jones, "Seating and Spectacle in the Greco-Roman World" (PhD diss., McMaster University, 2008), 326–36.
35. Ferrary, *Les mémoriaux de délégations*. On the choirs of children, see 1:115–22.
36. Ferrary, *Les mémoriaux de délégations*, 1:129–30. For the full range of cities, their geographic spread, and discussion, see 133–82; see also Busine, *Paroles d'Apollon*, 55–69.

there is literary evidence of delegations for the latter.[37] Even though there is no record of a delegation inscription from Pergamum to Klaros extant in Ferrary's corpus, there is an oracle of Klarian Apollo, found at Pergamum and erected to avert a plague, which mentions the Pergameme leader of the delegation to the oracle (IPergamon 324).[38] The inscriptions, originating mainly from the second century CE, were publicly inscribed on the walls, columns, stelae, and steps of the buildings in the sacred site.

Ferrary has intensively studied the prosopography of the Klarian officials and of the various members of the delegations. In contrast to the life-long tenure of the priest (ἱερεύς) and *thespiodos* (θεσπιῳδός: "singer in prophetic strains"), those individuals who held the annual magistracy of prophet (προφήτης) and secretary (γραμματεύς) in the delegation inscriptions often went on to hold the same offices two or three times or transitioned from one office to the other.[39] Family dynasties in these offices were also established with fathers, son, and brothers holding the office of either secretary or prophet.[40] Clearly the municipal elites from Greek and Asian city states established significant pathways of honor through the delegations to Klarian Apollo.[41] One delegation inscription from Herakleia under Karian Salbake, erected on the Sacred Way, will suffice to illustrate the epigraphic genre and its ethos:

> (Delegation) of citizens from Heraklea under Salbake:
> when Apollo was *prytanis* for the seventy-ninth time [155/156 CE],
> Klaudios Roufos [= Claudius Rufus] was priest, Gnaios Ioulios [= Cn. Iulius]
> Rheginos Alexandros was *thespiodes*,

---

37. Ferrary, *Les mémoriaux de délégations*, 1:112–13.

38. Charles Picard, "Un Oracle d'Apollon Clarios à Pergame," *BCH* 46 (1922): 190–97. Ferrary (*Les mémoriaux de délégations*, 1:112 n. 80) cites another fragmentary honorific inscription from Pergamum referring to "a [pro]phet of [Ap]ollo, a counsellor of the most illustrious metropolis of the Pergamemes."

39. Ferrary, *Les mémoriaux de délégations*, 1:90–93. See Robinson, *Theological Oracles*, 22–23, on whether or not the office of *thespiodes* was created after 132 CE.

40. Ferrary, *Les mémoriaux de délégations*, 1:92.

41. Aude Busine ("Oracles and Civic Identity in Roman Asia Minor," in *Cults, Creeds, and Identities in the Greek City after the Classical Age*, ed. Richard Alston, Onno van Nijf, and Christiana Williamson [Leuven: Peeters, 2013], 179) writes: "Visiting the oracle seems to have allowed citizens to reinforce their familial status so that father, sons, daughters and cousins were gathered for the occasion and would subsequently have enjoyed the prestige that stemmed from their involvement."

Klaudios [= Claudius] Kritolaos was prophet, Gnaios Ioulios [= Cn. Iulius] Alkimos was secretary:
theopropos: Tatianos son of Apollonios; young choristers having sung in honour of the god: Apollonios son of Tatianos, priest of the children; Tatianos the second son of Apollonios; Dionysios son of Dionysios son of Philotas,
Apollonios the third son of Hipparchos; Apollonios son of Athenion; Tatianos son of Athenion; Tryphon son of Glykon son of Papias son of Trophimos,
Hermogenes the second; Dionysios son of Hermogenes, stone-cutter;
choregoi: Moschas and Diogenianos for the sixteenth time.[42]

The oracular personnel of the sanctuary at Klaros are set out at the beginning of the delegation inscription, dated by the prytanis of the god Apollo.[43] The conventional elite roll call of honor at the Klaros sanctuary includes the priest, *thespiodes*, prophet, and secretary.[44] As Aude Busine argues, it is likely that the actual oracle pronounced by the sanctuary prophet or the *thespiodes* was never inscribed at Klaros but was rather copied down by the secretary and the handed over to the consultants of Heraklea, who then took the copy back to their city to inscribe on a public stela or in the temple to Apollo.[45] This procedure is verified by the absence of oracular inscriptions at Klaros, but it is possible that there was an archive offsite.[46] In terms of the delegation to Klaros itself, the inscribing of the delegation stela—mostly on the surfaces of the propylaea or on the temple columns in the Klaros sanctuary—sometimes allows the city to vaunt its own importance by mentioning its honorific titles. This is not the case with the inscription of Heraklea under Salbake, cited above, but it is the case with Amesia, which introduces its delegation thus: "(Delegation) of the citizens of Amesia, metropolis and *neokoros* and first of Pontus."[47] The competition

---

42. Ferrary, *Les mémoriaux de délégations*, §136 (155/156 CE); trans. Busine, "Oracles and Civic Identity," 195.

43. Robinson (*Theological Oracles*, 21) writes: "the prytanis of Colophon was Apollo himself, that is, the financial responsibilities that a prytanis would have had to bear were paid out of the revenues of the temple."

44. Busine, *Paroles d'Apollon*, 50–51.

45. Busine, *Paroles d'Apollon*, 53. The extant twenty-eight Apolline oracles of Klaros, each of which inscribed in the consulting city and spanned the period of 50–250 CE, are found in Merkelbach and Stauber, "Die Orakel des Apollon von Klaros."

46. Busine, *Paroles d'Apollon*, 54–55. See Robinson, *Theological Oracles*, 18.

47. Ferrary, *Les mémoriaux de délégations*, §251; see also §168.

for oracular precedence at Klaros between the high-profile cities of Asia must have been immense.

In terms of the delegation proper from Heraklea under Salbake, the *theopropos* leads the delegation, accompanied by two *choregoi* (χοραγοί), each making the trip from Heraklea to Klaros for the sixteenth time and undoubtedly defraying the costs of the trip on each occasion. The mention of Dionysios the "stone cutter" or "mason" (λαοτύπος) is interesting in this context.[48] Is he involved in the preparation of the stela or indeed its inscribing back at Heraklea? Furthermore, is his presence for the delivery of the oracle at Klaros somehow necessary for the sanctity and verification of the stela, with its oracle, at Heraklea? Eight boys in the choir singing to the god Apollo are listed but without any mention of girls, an omission unusual for the delegation inscriptions. The boy designated ὁ ἱερεοὺς τῶν παίδων ("priest of the boys") seems to be an important position.[49] This could be, I suggest, because he is more experienced in the affairs of cult of Klarian Apollo, either because of his more advanced age than the other boys or due to his previous visits to the site, thus being able to mentor new members to the choir. Busine speculates that the boys perhaps belong to the same family, but the evidence is too tenuous for such a sweeping conclusion.[50] There is little doubt, however, that the boys are members of the aristocratic families of Heraklea, as the impressive career of another choir member from Heraklea, T. Statilius Solon, amply testifies during the reign of Hadrian.[51]

1.1.3. Hierapolis

The oracle of Apollo Klarius at Hierapolis is found in the sanctuary of Apollo in the central part of the city. While Apollo Archegetes was the protector of Hierapolis,[52] Apollo Kàreios, a local divinity, met the divina-

---

48. Busine translates "sculptor" (*Paroles d'Apollon*, 79; "Oracles and Civic Identity," 180), but Robert translates "stone cutter" (Jeanne Robert and Louis Robert, *Le plateau de Tabai et ses environs*, vol. 2 of *La Carie: Histoire et géographie historique avec le recueil des inscriptions antiques* [Paris: Librairie d'Amérique et d'Orient, Adrien-Maisonneuve, 1954], 210 §146).

49. Busine "Oracles and Civic Identity," 195.

50. Busine "Oracles and Civic Identity," 179, 195.

51. Ferrary, *Les mémoriaux de délégations*, §4, esp. 208–13; Busine, *Paroles d'Apollon*, 75.

52. Tullia Ritti, *Epigraphic Guide to Hierapolis (Pamukkale)*, trans. P. Arthur (Istanbul: Italian Archaeological Mission at Hierapolis, 2006), §16.

tory needs of enquirers in the sanctuary. A reused and re-sited oracular inscription (ca. 165–170) was found on the outside wall of the inner chamber of a small building. On the upper left side of the block, five lines of a fragmentary inscriptional text state that "[…]llianos, son of Th[…]eas, had the oracles incised at his own expense" by the "command of the god Archegetes Apollo."[53] On the right is displayed a thirty-line inscription setting out the oracular response of Apollo to the delegation from Hierapolis. The delegation had gone to Colophon in order to consult Apollo of Klaros at his famous oracular site.[54] Tullia Ritti correctly notes that Apollo Kàreios, the local divinity, would not have the capability to answer their question regarding the plague afflicting the town: "hit by the destructive miseries of the mortal pestilence, hard to heal … afflicted by the vindictive malevolence of the gods").[55] The reason was that the Apolline god Kàreios only provided revelation through brief predetermined alphabetic lot oracles.[56]

The answer given to the delegation was that (1) they should make the appropriate sacrifices and libations to the gods at Hierapolis upon their return; (2) they should also honor Apollos Kàreios and Mopsos, the founder of Hierapolis; (3) they should erect a statue of the bow-carrying Apollo Klarius in the city; (4) and, after Apollo Klarius's arrows have driven away the "insatiable malady," the delegation should return to Colophon and give thanks to Apollo Klarius, thereby fulfilling the demands of the reciprocity system in not forgetting their benefactors, human or divine. Here we see the soteriological power of Apollo wielded by Apollo Klarius, on behalf of Apollo Archegetes, the city's divine founder, when the power of the lot oracle of the local Apolline god Kàreios would not avail.

1.1.4. Laodicea and Smyrna

The inscriptions of Laodicea refer to a prophet, Lucius Antonius Aurelianus, in an honorific dedication (ILaodikeia 67 [141/142 CE]).[57] Although

---

53. Ritti, *Epigraphic Guide*, §16a.1–5. For another translation, see Robinson, *Theological Oracles*, C-17 296–301.
54. Ritti, *Epigraphic Guide*, §16b.22
55. Ritti, *Epigraphic Guide*, §16b.2–5.
56. Ritti, *Epigraphic Guide*, §38.
57. See the exhaustive discussion of Louis Robert, "Inscriptions," in *Laodicée du Lycos: Le nymphée. campagnes 1961–1963* (Paris: de Boccard, 1969), 289–312.

this is a rare occurrence in the Laodicean epigraphic corpus, many more references to prophets from the city occur in the Klaros delegation corpus, mentioned above. Among the twenty-five inscriptions discussed by Robert touching on the delegations of Laodicea to the oracular sanctuary of Apollo of Klaros, various prophets of Laodicea are also referred to among the delegations.[58] Robert argues that the prophets, whose tenure was annual, were either children or young men who had not yet reached puberty, mentioned along with the hymn singers to the god. The master of the choir also regularly features in Laodokeian inscriptions.[59] Normally there were six boys and six girls for the choir in these delegations, though occasionally the numbers varied (e.g., two boys, six girls).[60] Nevertheless, the Laodicean prophets conducted the delegations, accompanied by the choirs of children.[61] What was the precise role of the prophet other than leading the delegation is never specified in the delegation inscriptions: it may well have been a largely honorific function, depending upon the age of the office holder. Moreover, it was the father of the prepubescent boys, who, as the θεοπρόπος ("public messenger sent to enquire of a god"), consulted the oracle on the majority of occasions.[62] Robert rightly concludes that the epigraphic texts of Klarian Apollo show the great fidelity of Laodicea in sending delegations to consult the oracle at the site of the sanctuary and, while there, to sing hymns in praise of the god.[63]

However, the Laodicean delegation inscriptions also highlight the social status of those either conducting or participating in the procession to Klaros. In a unique inscription from the delegation corpus, two prophets, one representing Klarian Apollo and the other Pythian Apollo,

---

58. Robert, "Inscriptions," 299–303, §§1, 3, 4, 5, 8, 11, 12, 13, 14, 15, 18, 19, 21, 22, 23, 24. The expanded edition of the Laodicean delegation inscriptions, with full Greek texts and commentaries, are Ferrary, *Les mémoriaux de délégations*, vol. 1, §§27, 31, 32, 34, 37, 40, 43, 45, 50, 54, 63, 96, 101, 105, 107, 111, 134, 139, 200, 209, 223, 224, 247, 281, 283, 287, 289, 290, 341–52.

59. Ferrary, *Les mémoriaux de délégations*, §§34, 43, 45, 50, 139, 209. The wide-ranging terminology for this official not only varies across the Laodicean inscriptions but the Klaros delegation inscriptions per se (Busine, *Paroles d'Apollon*, 76–77).

60. E.g. Ferrary, *Les mémoriaux de délégations*, §§31, 34, 37, 139. By contrast, at Chios, the eponymous magistrate leads the procession (276 §42). For variation in numbers, see, e.g. Ferrary, *Les mémoriaux de délégations*, §45.

61. Ferrary, *Les mémoriaux de délégations*, §§31, 34.

62. Robert, "Inscriptions," 304.

63. Robert, "Inscriptions," 303.

honor their father, Chairemon, with a brief *elogium* at the end: "Chairemon, son of Aristides, the son (himself) of Herodes, having shown, in the exercise of magistracies and the more important liturgies, good will both from himself and towards his country."[64] No such other *elogium* exists in the delegation corpus, so we are witnessing here a calculated departure from epigraphic convention in order to enhance family honor. Elsewhere, in another unique inscription from the delegation corpus, a prophet of Apollo Pythia holds two prestigious positions simultaneously: priest of the children and *agōnothetēs* (ἀγωνοθέτης) of Deia Cleoxenia.[65] Another eponymous magistrate from Chios is a *choragus* (ὁ χοραγός), *gymnasiarchos* (γυμνασίαρχος), *nauarchos* (ναύαρχος), and *stephanēphoros* (στεφανηφόρος).[66] Another interesting individual in the Laodicean delegation is designated "marvellous poet for life [ποιητὴς παράδοξος ὁ διὰ βίου], teacher of hymns [διδάσκολος τῶν ὕμνων]."[67] Were some of the hymns sung to Klarian Apollo composed by this person? In conclusion, while Robert was correct in noting the faithfulness of Laodicea in sending such delegations to Klarian Apollo, another equally potent motivation animated the delegations: the opportunity for the Laodicean elites to display their civic status before the watching citizens of their own city and at nearby Klaros, as well as to exhibit their *personal* piety towards the god.

Last, a fragmentary oracle of a prophet of Klarian Apollo has been found at Laodicea (ILaodikeia 67 [141/142 CE]), as well as a fragmentary oracle of Klarian Apollo at Smyrna (ISmyrna 647.3-4 [second half of second century CE]), an Ionian city also addressed in Revelation (2:8–11): "those will be three-and-four times blessed who will live in the Pagos beyond the sacred Meles (rivers)." Notwithstanding the all-pervasive importance of the oracular at Sardis in Asia, there are nevertheless other revelatory phenomena that display the power of the gods in the city. For example, a dedication to the Nymphs at Sardis expresses its gratitude for the dream revelation associated with the healing cult of Asklepios. (I SardBR 1.89

---

64. Ferrary, *Les mémoriaux de délégations*, §289.20–26.
65. Ferrary, *Les mémoriaux de délégations*, §209. On other prophets of Apollo Pythia, see §§27, 32. On the *agōnothetēs*, see James R. Harrison, "Paul and the *Agōnothetai* at Corinth: Engaging the Civic Values of Antiquity," in *The First Urban Churches 2: Roman Corinth*, ed. James R. Harrison and L. L. Welborn (Atlanta: SBL Press, 2016), 271–326.
66. Ferrary, *Les mémoriaux de délégations*, §42.
67. Ferrary, *Les mémoriaux de délégations*, §222; see also §223.

[175–150 BCE]): "Eutychianos the barber because of a vision in his sleep dedicated to the Nymphs for his complete health a shrine [alternatively, an 'image'] to Asklepios, and I gave thanks."

1.2. The Lot Oracles of Southern Asia

Although the gods regularly dispensed favors and mercy to suppliants, the relations between the gods and their dependents were fraught with dangers and ambiguities and had to be approached carefully. A particularly valuable inscription in this regard is the dice oracle of Kremna in Central Pisidia, carved on all four sides of a tall rectangular pillar in the center of the west side of the forum.[68] The fifty-six responses of the oracle are secured in each case by five throws of the dice, the sum of which leads the inquirer to the particular oracle of the god after whom each throw is named.

Most of the lot oracles dispense a prosperity theology, with various qualifications punctuating the promises dispensed to the inquirer. In particular, one constant refrain is divine delivery from sickness and disease.[69] Little attention is given to the world of the enquirer outside of the oracular site: there is vague mention of judicial affairs, economic decisions, travel, and marriage,[70] but everything else is couched in predictable generalities. However, occasionally, there are clear limits to the unqualified grace of the god consulted. For example, the favor of Olympian Zeus is only available to those who "appease Aphrodite and the son of Maia."[71] Elsewhere, the

---

68. For our text, see G. H. R. Horsley and S. Mitchell, eds., *The Inscriptions of Central Pisidia: Including Texts from Kremna, Ariassos, Keraia, Hyia, Panemoteichos, the Sanctuary of Apollo of the Perminoundeis, Sia, Kocaaliler, and the Döşeme Boğazı* (Bonn: Habelt, 2000), §5 (117–138 CE). The inscription of Kremna is one of several editions of the same inscription found in several locations in Asia Minor, all collected and translated by Johannes Nollé, *Kleinasiatische Losorakel: Astragal- und Alphabetchresmologien der hochkaiserzeitlichen Orakelrenaissance*, Vestigia 57 (Munich: Beck, 2007), 31–221.

69. A.VIII; A.IX; C.XXXIV; C.XLIII; D. XLVII; D.LIV. The letters A, B, C, and D reference the four sides of the pillar, each of which faces (respectively) the direction of north, west, south, and east; the roman numerals identify the number of the lot oracle on each side.

70. Judicial affairs: see A.XIII; D.LI; economic decisions: see C.XXX; C.XXXIV; C.XXXVIII; C.XLIV; D.LIII; D.LV; travel: see A.III; A.XX; C.XLIII; marriage: see A.XXV.

71. A.I; see also A.XI.

oracles caution that one has to "obey the gods and be hopeful."[72] But the danger of showing *hybris* is also strongly underscored at several junctures:

> 13334.14. Of Poseidon. One Chian, three threes and one four, the god proclaims: You are kicking against the goads, you are struggling against the waves that oppose you. You are looking for a fish in the ocean, don't hurry into the matter. It is not profitable for you to force the gods inopportunely.[73]
>
> 44446.22. Of Poseidon. Throwing seeds and writing letters on the ocean, both are pointless toil and a fruitless task. Since you are a mortal do not force the god, who will do you some harm.[74]

Despite promises of the future arrival of salvation,[75] the total powerlessness of the enquirer to effect any change to the decision meted out by the gods is occasionally spotlighted:

> 43366.22. Of Ares Thourios. Do not go on the road which you intend to, stranger, for this road no one (travels). A great fiery lion wanders about—be on guard against it—a terrible one. The oracle is one against which nothing can be done. Wait in a calm manner.[76]

In sum, the grace of the gods cannot be presumed upon: tread warily, the ancients were advised, because the temperament of deities was unpredictable and especially vindictive towards the ritually disobedient.[77] The latter point finds confirmation in the many inscriptions dedicated in antiquity to deities who had previously imposed punishment upon their suppliants.[78]

---

72. C.XXXI.
73. B.XIV. Similarly, B.XV: "Don't devise awful thoughts or make prayers against the Daimones." Once again: "Don't strive in vain, like the bitch that gave birth to a blind whelp" (B. XXI; see also C. XXXII).
74. C.XLV.
75. C.XLII: "you will arrive at a day of salvation."
76. C.XLVI.
77. Note in this regard the warning in an inscription from Sounion (Attica): "Anyone who interferes with the god's possessions or is meddlesome, let him incur sin against Men Tyrannos which he certainly cannot expiate" (Greg. H. R. Horsley, "Expiation and the Cult of Men," *NewDocs* 3 [1983]: §6, 21).
78. For examples, see Greg J. Horsley, "Two Confession Texts from Graeco-Roman Phrygia," *NewDocs* 1 (1981): §7; Horsley, "Expiation and the Cult of Men,"

To say this is not denying that there were spontaneous and intensely felt celebrations of the mercy of the gods by grateful suppliants in antiquity.[79] But often the mercy was conditional, being somehow dependent on the worthiness of the worshiper.[80]

1.3. Alphabetic Oracles: A Case Study of Hierapolis

Alphabetic oracles were a widespread phenomenon in the Greek world.[81] A particularly interesting oracle is that of Apollo Kàreios from Hierapolis (second–third centuries CE).[82] It consists of twenty-four verses that represent Apollo's replies to the anticipated consultations of his faithful enquirers. A system of lot oracles (cleromancy) operated, whereby the devotees of the cult extracted a letter by lot. The priest then issued one of the oracular responses for the enquirer, indicated in each case by the same letter at the beginning of the verse as the enquirer had received on the lot.

---

§6, 27; R. MacMullen and E. N. Lane, eds., *Paganism and Christianity 100—425 CE: A Sourcebook* (Minneapolis: Fortress, 1992), §7.10, 104-105.

79. For example, see the text cited in MacMullen and Lane, *Paganism and Christianity 100–425 CE*, §7.3.

80. For example, see the dedication to the demigod Heracles by Lucius Mummius, destroyer of Corinth in 146 BCE. He concludes with this appeal to the god: "for this and other gifts grant thy blessings to a deserving man" (*CIL* 1.2). For a translation, see Frederick C. Grant, ed., *Ancient Roman Religion* (New York: Liberal Arts Press, 1957), 230. See, too, Mark Strom's discussion (*Reframing Paul: Conversations in Grace and Community* [Downers Grove, IL: InterVarsity Press, 2000], 118–19) of the Isis aretalogy in this regard.

81. For other examples, see *SEG* 18.592 (provenance: Soli in Cyprus; second century CE); *SEG* 38.1328 (provenance: Tymbriada in Pisidia, Asia Minor [second century CE]); *SEG* 38.1338 (provenance: Aspendos in Pamphylia, Asia Minor [second century CE]); *TAM* 2.3.947 (provenance: Olympos in Lykia, Asia Minor); *CIG* 4379 (provenance: Adada Pisidia, Asia Minor); Horsley and Mitchell, *Inscriptions of Central Pisidia*, §159 (Kokaaliher [second–third centuries CE). On Tymbriada and Soli, see Nollé, *Kleinasiatische Losorakel*, 265–76.

82. For the Greek text, English translation, and brief commentary, see Ritti, *Epigraphic Guide*, §39. In Italian, see Ritti, *Hierapolis I: Fonti Letterarie ed Epigrafiche*, Archeologica 30 (Rome: Giorgio Bretschneider, 1985), 127–37. Additionally, Ritti, "Oracoli alfabetici a Hierapolis di Frigia," *Miscellanea greca e romana* 14 (1989): 245–86, not sighted by me; Ritti, "Appendice II: Oracoli a Hierapolis," in *Hierapolis di Frigia IX: Storia e istituzioni di Hierapolis* (Istanbul: Ege Yayinlari, 2017), 248–67. See also Nollé, *Kleinasiatische Losorakel*, 253–63; additionally, see the fragmentary alphabet oracle of Hierapolis on 263–65.

The alphabetic oracle represents the type of popular wisdom known to us through the Delphic canon of the seven Greek sages and the Roman moralist Pubilius Syrus, among other expressions of proverbial teaching.[83] The veneration of the main god of Hierapolis, Apollo, had found its oracular expression through the local god Kàreios, who is represented for us visually though a damaged cult statue and its dedication (Κά[ρ]ειος Ἀπόλ|λων).[84] But, like the delegations of Laodicea, the residents of Hierapolis had consulted Apollo at the famous oracular sanctuaries of Klaros and also at Delphi.[85] Despite the fact that the oracular responses are dispensed in a random manner to their recipients in the lot process, we should not forget that the inscription unifies all the oracles on one monument, thereby asserting that the Apolline oracular mentality, in its local expression at Hierapolis, was also to be understood holistically by its readers.[86]

In the case of our alphabet oracle, Κάρειος "concedes fortune to him to whom the god is favourable," underscoring the unpredictability of divine grace, while affirming the soteriological power of the oracles of Κάρειος.[87] Apollo, with the glorious bow, is depicted more generically as giving strength and activity. Furthermore, the fickleness of fortune necessitates the help of "venerable Tyche" in making good decisions: the (cultic?) appeasement of Nemesis ensures that the enquirer can "have faith in (his) action." Given the caveat of appeasement, the enquirer should be confident that Nemesis (Retribution) "swings for mortals the balance of Dike (Justice)." The divine world, it seems, is extremely "touchy" about how it is contacted and thus preserves the right to dispense favor and justice to those who are faithful and responsive to the local oracles of Kàreios as much as to oracular

---

83. See Teresa Morgan, *Popular Morality in the Early Roman Empire* (Cambridge: Cambridge University Press, 2007); James R. Harrison, "The Seven Sages, The Delphic Canon and Ethical Education in Antiquity," in *Ancient Education and Early Christianity*, ed. Matthew Ryan Hauge and Andrew W. Pitts (London: Bloomsbury T&T Clark, 2016), 71–86.

84. Ritti, *Epigraphic Guide*, §39: "Arator, as the proverb says, you are taking a viper to your bosom"; Ritti, *Epigraphic Guide*, §40.

85. Klaros: Ritti, *Epigraphic Guide*, §16; Delphi: Ritti, *Epigraphic Guide*, §§12, 14, 23, 24, 43.

86. The original site of the monument is not known, since the inscription was found in a marble shrine, with the stone having being reused, in an octagonal building in honor of Saint Philip (Ritti, *Hierapolis I*, 130). On the Apolline oracular mentality, see Busine, *Paroles d'Apollon*.

87. For the quotation and what follows, see Ritti, *Epigraphic Guide*, §38.

Apollo in his other sanctuaries. Notwithstanding, some type of all-embracing soteriological transformation is imminent: "Know that purification of the soul and of the body is arriving." Consequently, the beneficent god, "that looks over you," will dispense "unexpected joy." But concerted action is also required: "Take, divide, and receive thus joy." Humans, it seems, have to balance the unpredictability of the gods with the gods' commitment to beneficence and the justice of the gods with their arbitrariness. How then should humans live according to the oracular mentality of Kàreios?

The moral advice is to wait, not to rush into action unnecessarily, to appreciate the right time for such decisions and to persevere patiently, thus avoiding being consumed with anxiety.[88] Notwithstanding the counsel of ethical caution, one oracle nevertheless says: "Resolutely take action and take it to its finish."[89] There is a paradox here for the reader of the inscription. How does one discern between the requirement of timely caution and the requirement of resolute action? How does one decide which has priority? Furthermore, one oracle counsels against navigating the waves of life alone but totally rejects local counselors in preference for "foreign counselors" in another oracle.[90] But why reject the local counselor? We are left guessing the answer, but ethical caution is the underlying motive for the unexpected choice. In sum, the oracular advice rejects extremes in moral decisions by imposing strong boundaries around the ever-present danger of unthinking impulsiveness, opting for instead, I would argue, an Aristotelian mean in ethics.[91] Finally, the social hierarchy of the aristocratic elites is endorsed in the operation of ancient friendship rituals: "Avoid worthless friends [φίλους], trust only the best ones [ἀρίστοις]."[92] The status quo is paramount and perhaps this throws light on the reason for the continuous refrain of timely caution for the elite audience at which this alphabet oracle is aimed.

1.4. The Confession Inscriptions and the Oracles of Zeus

Ever since the appearance of Georg Petzl's 1994 corpus, the number of extant confession inscriptions has swelled to well over 142 publications.[93]

---

88. Ritti, *Epigraphic Guide*, §39.
89. Ritti, *Epigraphic Guide*, §39.8.
90. Ritti, *Epigraphic Guide*, §39.14, 17.
91. See Harrison, "Seven Sages."
92. Ritti, *Epigraphic Guide*, §39.21.
93. Angelos Chaniotis, "Constructing the Fear of Gods: Epigraphic Evidence from

Each inscription has been found in the general region of Lydia and Phrygia in Asia Minor, an unusual feature that requires explanation, but so far there is no solution to the puzzle.[94] The time range of the confession inscriptions congregates around 115–210 CE, with the only first-century texts being a fragmentary inscription datable to 57/58 CE, itself questionably a confession text, as well as a complete text belonging to 81/82 CE.[95] The confession inscriptions were inscribed on stone stelae and were erected in sanctuaries. The offenders confessed to a series of "sins": religious misdemeanors, civic crimes, and personal offences. While the stela was erected voluntarily, as far as we can discern, the prior punishment of the gods invariably precipitated the supplicant to seek atonement with the gods.[96] Release from punishment was only accomplished when the stela was erected.

One confession inscription, relating to Theodoros's sexual misdemeanors, exhibits oracular elements:

> In the year 320, on the 12th of the month Panemos. In accordance with the fact that I was instructed by the gods, by Zeus and the great Men Artemidoros: "I have punished Theodoros on his eyes according to the

---

Sanctuaries of Greece and Asia Minor," in *Unveiling Emotions: Sources and Methods for the Study of Emotions in the Greek World*, ed. Angelos Chaniotis (Stuttgart: Steiner, 2012), 215–23. For new publications up to 2007, see Angelos Chaniotis, "Ritual Performances of Divine Justice: The Epigraphy of Confession, Atonement, and Exaltation in Roman Asia Minor," in *From Hellenism to Islam: Cultural and Linguistic Change in the Roman Near East*, ed. Hannah M. Cotton et al. (Cambridge: Cambridge University Press, 2009), 116 n. 7.

94. For the sites, see Chaniotis, "Constructing the Fear of Gods," 3–4.

95. Aslak Rostad ("Human Transgression—Divine Retribution: A Study of Religious Transgressions and Punishments in Greek Cultic Regulations and Lydian-Phrygian Reconciliation Inscriptions" [PhD Thesis, University of Bergen, 2006], 144) argues that the text is possibly an ex-voto inscription. For the dates of Petzl's epigraphic corpus in chronological order, see Rostad, *Human Transgression—Divine Retribution*, 142–44. See also Georg Petzl, "Die Beichtinschriften Westkleinasiens," *EA* 22 (1994): 1–143.

96. See Angelos Chaniotis, "Under the Watchful Eyes of the Gods: Aspects of Divine Justice in Hellenistic and Roman Asia Minor," in *The Greco-Roman East: Politics, Culture, Society*, ed. Stephen Colvin (Cambridge: Cambridge University Press, 2004), 1–43 for a useful summary of the transgressions confessed. Also see Clinton E. Arnold, "'I Am Astonished That You Are So Quickly Turning Away!' (Gal 1.6): Paul and Anatolian Folk Belief," *NTS* 51 (2005): 443.

transgressions (κατὰ τὰς ἁμαρτίας) he committed." I had intercourse with Trophime, the slave of Haplokomas, wife of Eutykhes, in the *praetorium* (?) [εἰς τὸ πλετώριν]. He removed the first transgression [τὴν πρώτην ἁμαρτίαν] with a sheep, a partridge and a mole. The second transgression [Δευτέρα ἁμαρτία]: Even though I was a slave of the gods [δοῦλος τῶν θεῶν] in Nonu, I had intercourse with Ariagne, who was unmarried. He removed the transgression with a piglet and a tuna. At the third transgression [Τῇ τρίτῃ ἁμαρτίᾳ] I had intercourse with Arethusa, who was unmarried. He removed the transgression with a hen (or cock), a sparrow and a pigeon; with a *kypros* of a blend of wheat and barley and one *prokhos* of wine. Being pure he gave a *kypros* of wheat to the priests and one *prokhos*. As intercessor [παράκλητον], I took Zeus. (He said): "Behold! I hurt his sight because of his deeds, but now he has reconciled the gods [εἰλαζομένου αὐτοῦ τοὺς θεούς] and written down (the events) on a stele and paid for his transgressions [τὰς ἁμαρτίας]." Asked by the council (the god proclaimed): "I will be merciful [εἴλεος εἴμι], because my stele is raised on the day I appointed. You can open the prison; I will release the convict when one year and ten months has passed."[97]

Chaniotis argues that the confessions of Theodoros "alternate with quotations of oracles given by Zeus, thus creating the impression of a dialogue between the sinner and the god."[98] The text sounds like the minutes taken in a case presided over by an unidentified "council" (perhaps, as we will see, of priests or village elders?).[99] The case is straightforward enough. Theodoros, who was a temple slave (δοῦλος τῶν θεῶν), should have been committed to sexual abstinence, but he had violated the slave wife of Eutykhes in the *praetorium* (?).[100] The charge of adultery would be much less serious than in modern society because it only involves the penetra-

---

97. Petzl, "Die Beichtinschriften Westkleinasiens," §5.
98. Chaniotis, "Under the Watchful Eyes of the Gods," 27.
99. Chaniotis, "Under the Watchful Eyes of the Gods," 27. Petzl ("Die Beichtinschriften Westkleinasiens," 10) proposes that it represents the actual trial proceedings, with a priest acting out the role of Zeus. Alan Cadwallader has drawn my attention to a "council of the gods" (σύνκλητος τῶν θεῶν) in another confession inscription (*SEG* 57.1186). This nuance is certainly a possibility in terms of our inscription, but the lack of specification of the "council" being "of the gods," as in *SEG* 57.1186, perhaps points to a human council in this instance, with the priest acting as Zeus.
100. Chaniotis, "Under the Watchful Eyes of the Gods," 27. For the identification of εἰς τὸ πλετώριν with the praetorium, see Petzl, "Die Beichtinschriften Westkleinasiens," 9.

tion of a slave's body.[101] Much more important is the fact that the sin was compounded by the fact that Theodoros had brought cultic impurity upon his role as a sacred slave in the temple.[102] Two further sexual sins are confessed. But, as Theodoros obfuscates, his sexual immorality did not matter because he only seduced unmarried women.[103] Nevertheless, Zeus upholds the importance of purity in sexual relationships in cultic matters,[104] not accepting Theodoros's casuistry that he was only deflowering unmarried women and roundly condemning both his adultery and, as is clearly implied, the abdication of his celibacy as a temple slave. Zeus, therefore, damages the eyesight of Theodoros as punishment.[105] How is this cultic crisis, which is the primary issue, resolved? Zeus only acts as intercessor for Theodoros after the offender has reconciled the gods by erecting his confession stela, with the god then forgiving him his sins (εἴλεος εἰμι). Significantly, the divine mercy is elicited by the appropriate ritual and the cultic flashpoint has been resolved. As Aslak Rostad remarks, Theodoros "can no longer be accused of breaking the rules surrounding his status as a *hierodoulos*."[106]

In sum, there can be, as was the case with the alphabetic oracle of Hierapolis, oversight of ethical issues on the part of the god, coupled with propitiatory sacrifices in this instance, in order to resolve the crisis created by the cultic impurity of Theodoros. But, unlike the alphabetic oracles, the

---

101. See Jennifer A. Glancy, *Slavery in Early Christianity* (Oxford: Oxford University Press, 2002).

102. On Greek cultic relations and the importance of ritual purification after sexual activities, see Rostad, *Human Transgression – Divine Retribution*, 109–112.

103. Rostad (*Human Transgression–Divine Retribution*, 198) writes that Theodoros stresses that the two women were unmarried because "he wants to avoid being accused of having had sex with other men's wives."

104. Cultic purity rather than the morality of sexual ethics is the issue at hand. Rostad (*Human Transgression—Divine Retribution*, 227) succinctly states: "With the exception of a few regulations from Asia Minor [e.g., *LSAM* 20], sexual activity ... is not regarded as wrong, provided the pollution is properly dealt with before one enters a shrine."

105. Regarding punishment in the eyes, note the confession inscription at Sardis: "To Artemis Anaitis Ammias, daughter of Matris, erected this because chastised in her eyes – – –" (ISardBR 7.1.95, with the iconographic incision of two eyes under the second line of the text). For discussion, see Louis Robert, *Nouvelles Inscriptions de Sardes* (Paris: Librairie d'amérique et d'orient, Adrien Maisonneuve, 1964), 27–33. See also the eye in a relief in Petzl, "Die Beichtinschriften Westkleinasiens," §90.

106. Rostad, *Human Transgression—Divine Retribution*, 198.

god has seemingly intervened first, unilaterally blinding Theodorus for his sins, eliciting propitiatory sacrifices from the suppliant, and then reconciling upon the erection of the confession stela. The oracular responses simply chart the unveiling of guilt and the process of reconciliation. The legal proceedings ratify the resolution of this process, because of the seriousness of the disruption to open communication with the gods caused by the misdemeanors of the *hierodoulos*.

1.5. Disease and Plague Oracles: Sardis, Troketta, and Pergamum

Inscriptions from the Asian cities reveal how the civic elites summoned the saving presence of the gods through oracular revelation when handling outbreaks of disease and plague during the Second Sophistic.[107] Since we have already briefly discussed how an outbreak of plague was addressed by an oracle at Hierapolis,[108] three further examples will suffice.

First, faced with an outbreak of a plague probably imported by the armies of Lucius Verus returning from Mesopotamia after 165 CE, the city of Sardis, in another oracle of Apollo, is summoned by the god to request Ephesus to send to the city an image of the virgin huntress goddess Artemis and then place her in a temple.[109] Both cities are also addressed

---

107. For discussion, see J. F. Gilliam, "The Plague under Marcus Aurelius," *AJP* 82.3 (1961): 234–36; Robinson, *Theological Oracles*, 68–73.

108. Ritti, *Epigraphic Guide*, §16a, b. Additionally, see the fragmentary IGBulg 224 (ll. 6–7: "[…] I (consulted?) Apollo at Klaros […] I dispelled the plague"; provenance, Odessos, in Bulgaria, southeastern Europe [second century CE]), translated in Robinson, *Theological Oracles*, C-18, 301–03.

109. James R. Harrison, "Artemis Triumphs over a Sorcerer's Evil Art," *NewDocs* 10 (2012): §8. See also the Apolline oracle from Klaros inscribed at the city of Kallipolis, southern part of East Thrace (Merkelbach and Stauber, "Die Orakel des Apollon von Klaros," §9.20–25). It is designed to counter the effects of the disease by erecting a statue of Apollo with a bow in front of the city gate and by offering a magical milk libation. The curse designed to effect the deliverance is as follows (ll. 17–19): "[…] if they (the demons of the plague) exhibit fear of *kateuche* ('curse') so that they move fast at once into the inmost part of the netherworld, where the foundation of Tartaros appears […]." For discussion and partial translation, see Zsuzsanna Várhelyi, "Magic, Religion, and Syncretism at the Oracle of Claros," in *Between Magic and Religion: Interdisciplinary Studies in Ancient Mediterranean Religion and Society*, ed. by Sulochana Ruth Asirvatham, Corrine Ondine Pache, and John Watrous (Lanham, MD: Rowman & Littlefield, 2001), 19–21; Andrzej Wypustek and Izabella Donkow, "Christians and the Plague in Second Century Asia Minor," *Palamedes* 1 (2006): 127–28.

with oracles in Revelation (2:1–7; 3:1–6). Explicit instructions are given to the city about honoring Artemis with thanksgiving sacrifices, feasts, and dances, coupled with a stern warning about "the penalty of fire" should they not obey the oracle of Apollo. In response, the divine "straight-hitting shooter of arrows," Artemis, would act decisively against the besieging powers of the plague and its occult instigators:

> she will provide escape from (your) sufferings and will dissolve the man-destroying poison (or "magic") of plague, having melted down with (her) fire-bearing torches by nightly flame the kneaded (figurines) of wax, the signs of (the) evil art of a sorcerer [μάγου].[110]

The reference to the "evil art of a sorcerer" in this oracle shows how the oracular phenomena of the Second Sophistic could be wielded against practitioners of magic as requited, reflecting in part the similar concern of Revelation regarding deleterious effects of sorcery (Rev 18:23; 21:18).

Second, in the preface to an oracle from Kaisareia Trakotta (in Lydia, west of Sardis),[111] the Klarian god requests the citizens to set up a statue of Apollo *Soter* (*IGRR* 4.1498.2–5). Undoubtedly, the pilgrims to Klaros attempted to appease the god Apollo with the purificatory rituals and the erection of the statue prescribed in the oracle proper (ll. 22–28). The reason for these propitiatory ceremonies was the outbreak of a calamitous plague in the city, the origins and nature of which are not specified. Is it an agricultural plague of some sort (locusts? mice? an unknown pollution [l. 12]?), affecting the crops and causing humans to perish from famine (ll. 10–11)?[112] Or is this simply to confuse the oracular imagery with what is actually occurring at the city? Alternatively, the evidence for some type of disease can only be inferred from the hyperbolic references to widespread deaths (ll. 11, 25). The precise circumstances, therefore, are not known, but the tenor of the oracle may have reminded early Christian readers of the elaborate apocalyptic imagery employed in the book of Revelation:

---

110. Harrison, "Artemis Triumphs over a Sorcerer's Evil Art," §8.6–9.
111. *IGRR* 4.1498 (second century CE). For translation (below), see Robinson, *Theological Oracles*, C-14, 283–87, cited in adapted form by Busine, "Oracles and Civic Identity," 192.
112. Robinson (*Theological Oracles*, 286), drawing on previous scholarship, suggests "a local famine caused by the loss of crops, which threatens sickness and death."

The oracle:
1 You who inhabit Troketta by snowy Tmolos,
2 Who are honored by Bromios and the mighty son of Kronos,
3 Why now, amazed, do you approach the threshold
4 Restrained from drawing near to the ground of truth?
5 To you who attend I shall shout forth an infallible oracle.
6 Alas, alas, a mighty calamity leaps to earth
7 An inexorable plague, wielding with one
8 Hand an avenging sword, with the other raising
9 Bitterly lamented phantoms of recently-struck mortals.
10 It distresses on every side the plowed ground.
11 It mows down the seedlings—the whole race perishes;
12 By oppressing men with pollution, it drives them out.
13 And such are the evils at hand that it contrives ...
— — — — — — — — — —
20 But as you yearn to see an escape, as is lawful, from these things, O mortals,
21 Who are now so very anxious to approach for my aid,
22 From seven springs seek to prepare for yourselves a pure drink,
23 Which you ought to sulphur from a distance and quickly draw out,
24 And sprinkle (your) houses at once with the nymphs (water), who are lovely,
25 That at least those mortals left untouched on earth
26 May without end accomplish excellent things from their revived increase.
27 Moreover, prepare to set up (an image of) Phoebus in the midst of the land,
28 In one hand wielding (the bow) ...

At the outset of the oracle, the mythological origins of Kaisareia Trakotta are proudly asserted (ll. 1–2). On the basis of such prestige and the healing power of Apollo ("wielding [the bow]": l. 28), the city and the pressed inhabitants of the earth can look forward to their revived increase in the future (ll. 25–26). More telling, however, are the veracity claims made on behalf of the oracular site of Klaros. Such claims, to be observed in two further oracles below, have relevance for the oracular mentality in the book of Revelation.[113] In coming to Klaros, the pilgrims approach "the ground of truth" and the oracle conferred there is "infallible" (ll. 5–6). The oracle must be heeded for revival to occur. But what is noteworthy

---

113. See Stephen R. Llewelyn, "Faithful Words," *NewDocs* 9 (2002): 14.

is the exotic imagery employed to describe the effects of the plague: a sword-wielding and phantom-raising menace that decimates the natural world and humanity at large. This is why the ποιητὴς παράδοξος, noted above, accompanied the Laodicean delegation to Klaros. The Klarian poet who rendered the oracle for Kaisareia Trakotta would have had similar literary skills.

Third, an inscription found in Pergamum, in which the city asserts its precedence over the other Asian cities,[114] sets out extensively the richness of its Greek mythological origins in lines 1–9. Clearly the city was asserting its Greek identity, as many others did in the Second Sophistic, negotiating a respected place for their Homeric ancestry ("people of Aiakides," l. 6) in the face of the ever-present realities of Roman provincial rule. Significantly, it is asserted that the traditional Greek gods still have the capacity to protect from "baneful diseases" (l. 6), even though the Pergamum delegation to Klarian Apollo is born out of the current experience of "painful disease" resulting from the plague (ll. 10–16, 26–28). The oracle, without its preamble, is set out below, but it is worth recalling that Pergamum too, like six other Asian cities, also had its own oracle directed to its church in Revelation (2:12–17):

1   To the children of Telephos, who, honored by King Zeus, son of Kronos,
    more than others, inhabit the land of Teuthras,
    and also (honored by) the family of the thundering Zeus,
4   Athena, who is warring and inexorable,
    and Dionysos, who banishes care and gives life,
    and also the Physician, saviour from baneful diseases;
    among whom Ouranos' sons, the Kabeiroi, first
8   kept watch on the heights of Pergamon over the new-born
    Zeus the lightener, when he opened the maternal womb;
    I would accurately tell a defence with truthful words [ἀψευδέσιν],
    lest for too long the people of Aiakides be born out
12 by painful disease; it shall be that which is pleasing to my
    son. Therefore I urge you, O leader of the delegation to the oracle,
    to divide into four parts under leaders all those

---

114. The oracle of Klarian Apollo, inscribed at Pergamum, asserts its preeminence thus (IPergamon 324): "which oracle the Council and People of the first metropolis of Asia and twice neokoros, the city of the Pergamenes, resolved to inscribe on steles and to erect both in the market place and in the temples."

> who beneath the sacred tower wear the *chlamys* (*ephebes*),
> 16 and to make them follow the four leaders in columns.
> The first of these (will sing) of Kronos' son with a
> hymn, the next of (Dionysos) Eiraphiotes,
> another of Trito-born (Athena), a maiden bold in war,
> the other of Asklepios, my dear son.
> 20 For seven days let them over thigh-bones on the altars,
> burning to Pallas those of a pure, unmated, two-year-old
> calf, those of a three-year-old ox to Zeus and Zeus Bacchus;
> likewise also sacrificing to Koronis' son (Asklepius) the thigh-bones
> 24 of a domesticated bull, prepare a sacrificial meal,
> you youths who wear the *chlamys*, as many of you as are
> not without your own fathers. But with each libation
> as you pour, request from the immortals a noble remedy
> for the plague, that into a distant land of hostile men it might go far
> away. (IPergamon 324)[115]

The delegation was directed to appease Zeus, Dionysos Eiraphiotes, Athena, and Asklepius with sacrifices and hymns (ll. 17–29). We have already seen that the traditional healing power of Dionysos is enunciated in the inscription. The reference to Zeus, whose birth at Pergamum is claimed in the oracle (ll. 1, 9–11, 17), "refuted a host of competing cities which claimed that they, not Pergamum, had received the newly born god."[116] But the mention of Asklepius (ll. 19, 23), the healing god, in the Apolline oracle was also apposite, because Asklepius was the son of Apollo. Moreover, the presence of the famous Asklepion at Pergamum, with its promises of healing through incubation at the sanctuary,[117] also makes the reference to Asklepius in the oracle particularly potent. But whether this clever therapeutic gambit came from the initiative of the Klarian officials themselves,[118]

---

115. Datable between Trajan and Caracalla. For translation, see Robinson, *Theological Oracles*, C-16, 291–96, cited in adapted form by Busine, "Oracles and Civic Identity," 193–94.

116. Robin Lane Fox, *Pagans and Christians in the Mediterranean World from the Second Century AD* (Harmondsworth: Viking, 1986), 232.

117. See Louise Wells, *The Greek Language of Healing from Homer to New Testament Times*, BZNW 83 (Berlin: de Gruyter, 1998), 83–95.

118. See Gil H. Renberg, *Where Dreams May Come: Incubation Sanctuaries in the Greco-Roman World*, vol. 1 (Leiden: Brill, 2016), 138–45. Busine ("Oracles and Civic Identity," 186) writes: "For Klarian officials, this could be a way of asserting the influence of their Apollo."

in order to secure the influence of Klarian Apollo at Pergamum, or from the strategizing of the socially powerful Pergamum delegation, in order to ensure a more locally favorable outcome in terms of the oracle, is difficult to say. The local competition in Asia between the various gods at their prestigious oracular and incubatory sites in antiquity is revealed implicitly in this inscription.

1.6. Political Oracles: Hadrianoi

What is particularly surprising in the Greco-Roman documentary literature is the almost total absence of oracles legitimizing the house of Julio-Claudian rulers and their political heirs from the early imperial period to the Second Sophistic. Conversely, it is equally surprising that there are no oracles critical of the imperial rulers, apart from the sole exception of the book of Revelation, reminiscent to some extent of the famous Egyptian Potter's Oracle from the Hellenistic age. Only one example, so far as I know, exists from the Julio-Claudian period:

> I, Gaurus, have obtained the prophet's
> faithful words [πιστοὺς λόγους] and inscribed
> the victory of Caesar [νίκην Καίσαρος] and the contests
> of the gods [ἄ(θ)λους θεῶν], through whom by prayers [κατευχαῖς]
> I grasped all things from start to
> finish, and repaying ungrudgingly
> the gifts [δῶρα ἀμισῶς ἀποδίδων], I exult.
> Gaurus, son of Asclepiades, from Torea
> (set up) the statue at his own expense.[119]

Stephen R. Llewelyn has argued that this prophecy, emanating from an oracular site at Hadrianoi, Mysia, in Asia Minor, has come from an unidentified prophet at the site.[120] The original editor argues that Gauros was a scribe from the office where oracles were recorded [χρησμογράφιον: IDidyma 31, 32][121] and had copied down our oracle. This is proposed on the original editor's restoration of ἄ[λ]λους θεῶν as opposed to ἄ[θ]λους

---

119. Llewelyn, "Faithful Words."
120. For the names of prophets mentioned in the Hadrianoi epigraphic corpus, see Llewelyn, "Faithful Words," 9.
121. Elmar Schwertheim, *Die Inschriften von Hadrianoi und Hadrianeia*, IGSK 33 (Habelt: Bonn, 1987), §24, 21–24.

θεῶν in lines 3–4 in our text. If the original editor is correct, the text would be translated as "inscribed the victory of Caesar and the others of the gods." However, a new restoration, proposed by Llewelyn,[122] understands the reference as ἄ[θ]λους θεῶν ("contests of the gods"). This is more likely. Given that the "victory of Caesar" must refer to *both* Caesar's victory at Pharsalus and Augustus's victory at Actium,[123] then the "contests of the gods" could well allude to the coalition of the gods, headed by Apollo, the tutelary deity of Augustus, who defeated the loathsome Egyptian gods and commanders of Antony and Cleopatra at Actium (Vergil, *Aen.* 8.698–713; see also Anth. Pal. 9.553; Dio Cassius, *Hist. rom.* 51.1.2–3; Horace, *Carm.* 3.4.60–64; Propertius, *Eleg.* 4.6.37–84; Ovid, *Trist.* 3.1.39–46).

Other aspects of the oracle have intrinsic interest. The prayers of Gauros to the gods are said to have aided his comprehension of the oracle and its sacral significance from beginning to end, allowing him to repay their unspecified beneficence by erecting the statue (of Augustus?) and its inscription. The importance of understanding and rendering the oracle accurately is seen in the nature of the prophetic communication itself: the prophet's words are "faithful"—a concept of revelation that has already been reflected to some degree in the references to "infallible oracle" and "truthful words" in the plague and disease oracles above.

Having investigated the place of the oracular in Asia Minor in the first three centuries, it remains to ask what pertinence this documentary oracular evidence has for the early Christian prophecy of Revelation, widely considered by scholars to be critiquing the Asian imperial cult under Flavian rule as opposed to being concerned about the local oracular sites.

2. The Prophecy of Revelation and the Asian Oracular Inscriptions

Scholars have expended considerable energy in discussing the challenges posed by the imperial cult for believers living in Asia Minor,[124] focusing

---

122. Stephen R. Llewelyn, "Contests of the Gods," *EA* 32 (2000): 147–49.
123. See Llewelyn, "Faithful Words," 9, for the arguments.
124. See David E. Aune, "The Influence of Roman Court Ceremonial on the Apocalypse of John," *BR* 2 (1983): 5–26; Adela Yarbro Collins, *Crisis and Catharsis: The Power of the Apocalypse* (Philadelphia: Westminster, 1984); Thompson, *The Book of Revelation*; Richard Bauckham, *The Climax of Prophecy: Studies on the Book of Revelation* (Edinburgh: T&T Clark, 1993); J. Nelson Kraybill, *Imperial Cult and Commerce in John's Apocalypse*, JSNTSup 132 (Sheffield: Sheffield Academic, 1996); Kraybill, *Apoca-*

on how the rhetoric of Revelation addresses the threats posed for the seven churches, both in terms of accommodation to its seductions (2:6, 14, 20; 3:17; 18:1–24) and the very real danger of martyrdom for Christ (Acts 2:13). Indeed, the oracle honoring Julius Caesar and Augustus for their victories at Pharsalus and Actium, discussed above, shows how the representatives of the indigenous oracular mentality of Asia Minor had ingratiated themselves with the new Julian rulers. Somewhat overlooked in the scholarly literature, however, are the threats that the local indigenous revelatory cults still posed to the early Asian Christians, though the challenge issued by revelatory magic in Revelation (9:20–21; 21:8; 22:15; see also 13:13–15; 19:20) has been comprehensively addressed by Aune and Rodney Lawrence Thomas.[125] But, as we have seen, the strong resurgence of the oracular sites in the Second Sophistic had already begun by the late first century BCE and continued to grow steadily during the first century CE. The provincial elites of Asia Minor were just as deeply immersed in the quest of honor, benefiting the oracular sites and acquiring their priestly and prophetic offices, as were the elites in advancing their family fame through prestigious posts of the imperial *cursus honorum*. How is the threat of the indigenous revelatory oracles

---

lypse and Allegiance: Worship, Politics, and Devotion in the Book of Revelation (Grand Rapids: Brazos, 2010); Wes Howard-Brook and Anthony Gwyther, *Unveiling Empire: Reading Revelation Then and Now* (New York: Orbis, 1999); Barbara R. Rossing, *The Choice between Two Cities: Whore, Bride and Empire in the Apocalypse* (Harrisburg, PA: Trinity Press International, 1999); Hans-Josef Klauck, "Do They Never Come Back? Nero Redivivus and the Apocalypse of John," *CBQ* 63 (2001): 683–98; Steven J. Friesen, *Imperial Cults and the Apocalypse of John: Reading Revelation in the Ruins* (Oxford: Oxford University Press, 2001); Friesen, "Satan's Throne, Imperial Cults and the Social Settings of Revelation," *JSNT* 27.3 (2005): 351–73; Christopher A. Frilingos, *Spectacles of Empire: Monsters, Martyrs, and the Book of Revelation* (Philadelphia: University of Pennsylvania Press, 2004); Craig R. Koester, "Roman Slave Trade and the Critique of Babylon in Revelation 18," *CBQ* 70 (2008): 766–86; Koester, "Revelation's Visionary Challenge to Ordinary Empire," *Int* 63 (2009): 5–18; Koester, "The Number of the Beast in Revelation 13 in Light of Papyri, Graffiti, and Inscriptions," *JECH* 6 (2016) 1–21; Michael Naylor, "The Roman Imperial Cult and Revelation," *CurBR* 8 (2010): 207–39.

125. See David E. Aune, "The Apocalypse of John and Graeco-Roman Revelatory Magic," *NTS* 33.4 (1987): 481–501; Rodney Lawrence Thomas, *Magical Motifs in the Book of Revelation*, LNTS 416 (London: T&T Clark, 2010). See also the excellent neglected study of Bruce J. Malina, *On the Genre and Message of Revelation: Star Visions and Sky Journeys* (Peabody, MA: Hendrickson, 1995).

handled in Revelation, even if it is somewhat oblique to the main purpose of the prophecy? Our approach will be suggestive rather than exhaustive.

First, in several of the oracles above the importance of the veracity and faithfulness of the words has been spotlighted. Significantly, similar motifs recur throughout Revelation. Christ is identified as the "faithful witness" (ὁ μάρτυς ὁ πιστός: Rev 1:5), the "faithful and true witness" (ὁ μάρτυς ὁ πιστὸς καὶ ἀληθινός: 3:14; see also 19:11), as is his martyr Antipas at Pergamum (ὁ μάρτυς ὁ πιστός μου: 2:13). Conversely, the opponents of the early Christians are labelled "liars" (ψεύδονται: 3:9: see also 2:9) and practitioners of "falsehood" (ποιῶν ψεῦδος: 22:15), whereas believers are blameless because no lie is found in their mouths (14:5; see also 2:18; 3:7). The judgements of God are also described as just and true (ἀληθιναὶ καὶ δίκαιαι: Rev 16:6–7). The key representative of the oracular culture in Revelation is the "false prophet" (ψευδοπροφήτης: 16:13; 20:10), depicted as a demonic figure (16:13a, 14a) and symbolic of "deceit and falsehood at any time and in any place."[126] The term ψευδοπροφήτης perfectly encapsulates the relentless fabrication emanating from the second beast from the earth (13:13–14; 19:20). He deludes the nations with counterfeit miracles, drawing his deceptive power from the "ancient serpent" (12:9), the cosmic "deceiver of the nations" (20:3, 8, 10).[127] This beast on the earth, probably symbolizing the high priest of proconsular Asia, stages cultic wonders in the local Asian theatres as part of the imperial cult before awestruck audiences (Rom 13:13–15), not only breathing life into the Roman ruler's image by cleverly staged conceits but also by erecting, in liaison with the provincial elites, honorific statues of the Roman ruler throughout the entire province.[128] While the primary referent of ψευδοπροφήτης is clearly imperial, later prophetic pretenders such as Alexander of Abonuteichos also staged fraudulent oracles (Lucian, *Alex.* 12–26). Aune is correct in saying that no evidence exists of imperial cult images being

---

126. Stephen S. Smalley, *The Revelation of John: A Commentary on the Greek Text of the Apocalypse* (London: SPCK, 2005), 345

127. Grant R. Osborne, *Revelation*, BECNT (Grand Rapids: Baker Academic, 2002), 514

128. George Raymond Beasley-Murray, *The Book of Revelation*, NCB (London: Oliphants, 1974), 216–17; Paul Barnett, *Apocalypse Now and Then: Reading Revelation Today* (Maryborough: The Book Printer, 1989), 110; Stephen J. Scherrer, "Signs and Wonders in the Imperial Cult: A New Look at a Roman Religious Institution in the Light of Rev 13:13–15," *JBL* 103.4 (1984): 599–610; Thompson, *Book of Revelation*, 162–63; Osborne, *Revelation*, 514–15.

"believed to actually give oracles."[129] But, if our sole Julian oracle from Hadrianoi had an accompanying imperial statue, as we have suggested, then the connection between the statue and oracle would be visually clear in its symbolism: the member of the Julian house, whoever he might be, presides over the oracle, endorsing perpetually the divinely waged Julian victories. Although only one such oracle has survived, there must have been others erected either by local prophets or provincial benefactors in Asia. Pivoted against all types of false prophecy, indigenous and imperial, is the spirit of prophecy (Rev 14:13b; 19:10; 22:17a), who inspires a special group of Christian prophets within the churches (11:18; 16:6; 18:20, 24; 22:9) and provides life-changing ministry within the Asian churches.[130]

Second, whereas in the case of Klaros and Didyma the delegations come to the oracular site, the messenger carrying the prophecy of John, who was exiled to Patmos at the time (Rev 1:9), would have passed through Miletus on his way to the first church, Ephesus (Rev 2:1–7). However, the idea of a circular postal road connecting the seven churches in the order of progression of Rev 2:1–3:22 has found no archaeological confirmation.[131] It may be the case that the messenger simply followed the route that John had regularly chosen as a peripatetic pastor and teacher before his exile. The crucial difference between the oracles of Klaros and Didyma and the prophecy of John is that the initiative comes from the delegation cities or individuals who approached the oracular centers, whereas in the case of Revelation the initiative originates with the God-given ἀποκάλυψις from Jesus Christ. The ἀποκάλυψις is entirely unsolicited by John, but it is conveyed to him by an angel and is addressed to God's servants in the Asian cities (Rev 1:1). The striking chain of revelatory command—God, Christ, the angel, and, last, John—accords "an unheard-of authority to the content of John's prophecy,"[132] differentiating its claim to legitimacy from the famous oracular sites of antiquity.

Third, in terms of actual allusions to the Asian oracular sites and their gods in Revelation, the first horseman in Rev 6:2—crowned, bow-holding, riding a white horse and conquering—has been proposed to be the god Apollo on the basis of the crown and bow imagery.[133] Thus the figure is

---

129. David E. Aune, *Revelation 6–16*, WBC 52b (Nashville: Nelson, 1998), 764.
130. Bauckham, *Climax of Prophecy*, 160–62.
131. David E. Aune, *Revelation 1–5*, WBC 52a (Nashville: Nelson, 1997), 131.
132. Smalley, *Revelation of John*, 51.
133. Kerkeslager, "Apollo, Graeco-Roman Prophecy."

said to be symbolic of the rise of false messiahs and false prophecy in Asia Minor, particularly Klarian Apollo.[134] Many commentators shy away from such an identification, seeing the imagery as more reflecting the bow-carrying Parthian hordes. The Parthians, for example, included some of their sacral white-colored horses in their armies and remained a continuous threat of conquest at the eastern edges of Asia Minor (e.g., 53 and 35 BCE; 62 CE). The military threat associated with the Parthians, it is argued, fits better the conquest envisaged in Rev 6:2 than the Apolline referent.[135] However, this overlooks the role of Apollo as the commander of the gods in bringing military victory to Augustus at Actium.[136] Apollo can adopt either a warlike or peaceful persona in the Julian ideology of rule, being both avenger and savior.[137] A multivalent image, therefore, embracing both Parthian and Apolline elements, is more likely in this instance.

This vignette has been brought into dialogue with Rev 9:11 where there is mention of the Angel of the Abyss, "whose name in Hebrew is Abaddon, and in Greek Apollyon [Ἀπολλύον]." Although both names mean "Destroyer," the majority of Revelation commentators see in the name Ἀπολλύον a punning reference to the god Apollo.[138] The locust (Rev 9:3–10) was one of several symbols of Apollo.[139] As we have seen, Apollo was the patron deity of Augustus, having been his divine protector at the battles

---

134. G. K. Beale, *The Book of Revelation*, NIGTC (Grand Rapids: Eerdmans, 378), 1999.

135. See Benjamin Witherington III, *Revelation*, NCBC (Cambridge: Cambridge University Press, 2003), 133, for a detailed exposition of the Parthian elements underlying Rev 6:2.

136. For discussion, see Karl Galinsky, *Augustan Culture: An Interpretive Introduction* (Princeton: Princeton University Press, 1996), 215–20; Carste Hjort Lange, "Res publica constituta: Actium, Apollo and the Accomplishment of the Triumviral Assignment" (PhD thesis, University of Nottingham, 2008), 142–86; John F. Miller, *Apollo, Augustus, and the Poets* (Cambridge: Cambridge University Press, 2009). Robert Alan Gurval (*Actium and Augustus: The Politics and Emotions of Civil War* [Ann Arbor: University of Michigan Press, 1995]) is unsuccessful in trying to diminish the centrality of Apollo in the Augustan conception of rule.

137. Galinsky, *Augustan Culture*.

138. J. Sweet, *Revelation*, TPINTC (London: SCM, 1979), 170; Wilfred J. Harrington, *Revelation*, SP 16 (Collegeville, MN: Glazier; Liturgical Press, 1993), 110.

139. However, R. H. Charles (*A Critical and Exegetical Commentary on the Revelation of St. John*, ICC [Edinburgh: T&T Clark, 1920], 246–47) is ambivalent about the suggestion and symbolism: "This is possible but not probable."

of Pharsalus (42 BCE), Naucholos (36 BCE), and Actium (31 BCE).[140] In 40–41 CE Caligula annexed a temple at the site of Didyma, situated within the territory of Miletus and being built for Apollo, for the purposes of his own cult (Dio Cassius, *Hist. rom.* 59.28.1).[141] Famously, Caligula liked to appear in public dressed as one of the gods, including Bacchus and Apollo (Philo, *Legat.* 95–96). Claudius, in his 52 CE letter to Delphi,[142] flatters the citizens of Delphi, writing regarding Delphic Apollo: "For long have I been well-disposed to the city of Delphi, and I have always observed the cult of Pythian Apollo." Coins show Nero with either a laureate head or radiate head (symbolizing divinity) on the obverse, with Apollo—or Nero impersonating Apollo—advancing to the right with a lyre on the obverse.[143] The likelihood of impersonation is stronger because Nero had identified himself with Apollo the citharode (Suetonius, *Nero*, 39; Tacitus, *Ann.* 15.10–16; Dio Cassius, *Hist. rom.* 63.6.2; 63.20.5; Calpurnius Siculus, *Ecl.* 4.159).[144] There is, however, no Roman literary evidence for Domitian identifying himself with the god Apollo, as is widely reported by Revelation commentators.[145] Rather Minerva was Domitian's patron deity, as her empaneled image placed above the famous frieze in his Forum Transitorium at Rome visually demonstrates.[146] Nevertheless, as J. Nelson

---

140. On Augustus and the cult of Apollo, see Galinsky, *Augustan Culture*, 213–24.

141. IDidyma 148.4–6, trans. in Robert H. Sherk, *The Roman Empire: Augustus to Hadrian* (Cambridge: Cambridge University Press, 1988), §43: "when Gnaeus Vergilius Capito was high-priest of the temple of Gaius Caesar in Miletus for the first time." See A. A. Barrett, *Caligula: The Abuse of Power*, 2nd ed. (London: Routledge, 2015), 193–94.

142. James H. Oliver, "The Epistle of Claudius which Mentions the Proconsul Junius Gallio," *Hesperia* 40.2 (1971): 239–40. Trans. Jerome Murphy-O'Connor, *St Paul's Corinth*, 3rd ed (Collegeville, MN: Glazier; Liturgical Press, 2002), 161–69.

143. RPC 1.1752 (laureate head issue); Kraybill, *Apocalypse and Allegiance*, 63 fig. 3.10 (radiate head issue).

144. Edward Champlin, "Nero, Apollo and the Poets," *Phoenix* 57.3-4 (2003): 276–83. For Apollo on the Neronian coinage, see 277. On Nero as New Apollo, see *IG* II/III² 3278, cited Champlin, "Nero, Apollo and the Poets," 277 n. 7.

145. Robert H. Mounce, *The Book of* Revelation, NICNT (Grand Rapids: Eerdmans, 1978); Beasley-Murray, *Book of Revelation*, 162–63; Aune, *Revelation 6–16*, 535; Smalley, *Revelation of John*, 234; Osborne, *Revelation*, 374; Beale, *Book of Revelation*, 504.

146. On the centrality of Minerva to Domitian's ideology, see Eve D'Ambra, *Private Lives, Imperial Virtues: The Frieze of the Forum Transitorium in Rome* (Princeton: Princeton University Press, 1993), 3–18. Martial's cryptic reference to "Palatine

Kraybell notes, coins of Domitia, the wife of Domitian, show their infant child depicted as the naked sun god Apollo, seated on a zoned globe, with his arms stretched out and surround by seven stars—the globe indicating world dominion and the stars denoting the divine nature of the young son.[147] The close connection between the imperial cult and Apollo in Asia Minor is well illustrated by Sagalassos in Pisidia, southwest Turkey. There the indigenous worship of Apollo was integrated with the worship of the Roman ruler from the time of Vespasian onwards,[148] with Sagalassos sending delegations to Klarian Apollo.[149] In conclusion, Apollo was incorporated into the Julio-Claudian conception of rule, with Caligula, in particular, opportunistically monopolizing the glory associated with the oracular site of Didyma.

Therefore, Rev 9:11 could possibly allude to the Apollo-impersonating Nero, highlighting how "the destructive host of hell had as its king the emperor of Rome!"[150] The implications of this, if George Raymond Beasley-Murray's proposal has validity, would have been sobering for any believers from Neronian Rome who might have relocated to Asia Minor after the 64 CE persecution of believers in the capital, if Revelation was written in 69 CE. The popular rumor abroad was that the dead Nero would reappear *redivivus* at the head of the Parthian armies and ascend to a throne in the East (Jerusalem or Parthia), with the appearance of various Nero pretenders soon to follow (69, 80, 88 CE).[151] The strong Julio-Claudian attachment to the god Apollo in the early empire, therefore, would have

---

Minerva" (*Epigr.* 5.5.1), signals the transition from the Augustan worship of Apollo on the Palatine at Rome to the worship of Minerva at the site under Domitian.

147. *RIC* 2.179; Ernst Janzen, "The Jesus of the Apocalypse Wears the Emperor's Clothes," in *Society of Biblical Literature 1994 Seminar Papers*, ed. Eugene H. Lovering Jr., SBLSP 33 (Atlanta: Scholars Press, 1994), 645–47. Janzen, however, identifies the child as the naked Jupiter.

148. See Peter Talloen and Marc Waelkens, "Apollo and the Emperors (I): The Material Evidence for the Imperial Cult at Sagalassos," *Ancient Society* 34 (2004): 171–216; Talloen and Waelkens, "Apollo and the Emperors (II): The Evolution of the Imperial Cult at Sagalassos," *Ancient Society* 35 (2005): 217–49.

149. Ferrary, *Les mémoriaux de délégations*, §§60, 80, 97, 358–359.

150. Beasley-Murray, *Book of Revelation*, 163.

151. Rev 13:3; 17:8–11; Sib. Or. 4.119–124; 5.137–141; 5.361–396; Dio Chrysostom, *Or.* 21; Tacitus, *Hist.* 1.2; 2.8–9; Dio Cassius, *Hist. rom.* 46.19.3; Suetonius, *Nero* 40; *Dom.* 57. The case for a 69 CE date for Revelation is argued by John A. T. Robinson, *Redating the New Testament* (London: SCM, 1976), 221–53.

lent additional prestige to the revival of the two major Apolline oracular sites in first-century Asia Minor. But John encourages his auditors, upon the sounding of the seventh angelic trumpet (Rev 11:15; see also 8:7, 8, 10, 12; 9:1, 13), that the growing threat posed by the Apolline oracular sites and, relatedly, the incorporation of Apollo into the imperial cult and the ideology of Julio-Claudian rule, would soon be supplanted by the advent of the eternal kingdom of God and his Christ (11:15b–18). Last, while there are clear intertextual echoes of the Exodus plagues in Rev 9:11,[152] we do not have regard this, as G. K. Beale does, as the "best background" for identifying the Angel of the Abyss." Rather, allowance has to be made for the polyvalent nature of John's imagery.

Fourth, throughout Revelation John continuously refers to the outbreak of plagues and famine (Rev 6:8b; 9:18, 20; 11:6; 15:1, 6, 8; 16:2, 9, 11, 21; 18:4, 8; 22:18). We have no evidence for plagues in first-century Asia Minor. However, in the second century there is the famous Antonine plague that occurred under the reign of Marcus Aurelius (161–180 CE),[153] destroying the entire population in some areas and elsewhere decimating the Roman army. Undoubtedly, this event lies behind many of our disease oracles discussed above. But to invoke a possible (unknown) first-century plague as conceptual background for the Revelation references, given the parallelism between the seven trumpets (Rev 8:3–11:19) and seven bowls of God's wrath (15:1–16:21) with the Exodus plagues,[154] would be perilous. Nevertheless, as noted, the graphic imagery of the disease oracles in Revelation may have resonated with Greco-Roman audiences later in the second century CE. But, in the case of the oracles of Klarian Apollo at Sardis and Kallipolis, the disease is interpreted as the result of the malevolent arts of magicians, whereas in Revelation the plagues represent the cosmic outpouring of God's wrath against sin and idolatry. The conceptual worlds—that is, the power of oracular Apollo over magic as opposed to John's proclamation of God's eschatological judgement—are vastly different.

---

152. Beale, *Book of Revelation*, 504.

153. For discussion and sources, see David Magie, *Roman Rule in Asia Minor to the End of the Third Century after Christ*, 2 vols. (Princeton: Princeton University Press, 1950), 1:663; 2:1533–34.

154. Beasley-Murray, *Book of Revelation*, 238–41; Beale, *Book of Revelation*, 121–32, 808–12; Smalley, *Revelation of John*, 393–94; Mitchell G. Reddish, *Revelation* (Macon, GA: Smyth & Helwys, 2001), 164, 306.

Fifth, the collision between the traditional understanding of honorific culture in Asia Minor and its redefinition by John in Revelation is revealing. As far as coronal rituals, the crowning of prophets in the sanctuary inscriptions of Didyma, noted above, demonstrated the centrality of the quest for honor and offices on the part of the Asian provincial elites at the oracular sites. However, in Revelation the indigenous and imperial coronal honorific system is inverted.[155] Thus, in Rev 4:10, while the four living creatures continuously hymn God (4:8), the twenty-four gold-crowned elders cast off their crowns before the heavenly throne. Uncrowned, they eulogize their beneficent God as worthy to receive all glory, honor, and power (Rev 4:10–11). Moreover, all creation hymns the Enthroned One and his reigning Lamb (Rev 5:6–14). Importantly, not only does this puncture the relentless boasting and quest for glory on the part of the provincial elites, but also it dismisses the coronal rituals associated with the Artemis cult at Ephesus, including the disputes emerging over the crowning of its priests during the reign of Claudius (IEph 1a.18a.11–17), as well, importantly for our context, the stipulation of an Apolline oracle from Sardis that the devotees of Artemis should wear myrtle crowns.[156] But, because similar coronal rituals are also found in the imperial cult and are reflected in its numismatic and gem iconography,[157] we must again acknowledge the polyvalence of John's honorific imagery, which pinpricks both the imperial and oracular quest for ancestral honor. Significantly for believers in the Asian churches, the honor of crowning is postponed until the eschaton, given in reward for their faithful discipleship under suffering in the face of strong opposition from the indigenous and imperial cults (Rev 2:10; 3:11).

Another example of the polyvalent nature of John's honorific imagery is also found in the hymns being sung to God and the continuous rejoicing punctuating the heavens in Revelation.[158] Significantly, the song sung by believers is a new song, embodying in their praise the eschatological newness of Christ's Kingdom they are experiencing (Rev 5:9; 14:3).

---

155. For discussion, see James R. Harrison, "'The Fading Crown': Divine Honour and the Early Christians," *JTS* 54 (2003): 509–18.

156. Harrison, "Artemis Triumphs over a Sorcerer's Evil Art," §8.15–16; see also IEph 5.1448.

157. Harrison, "'Fading Crown,'" 511–13.

158. Rev 1:5b–6; 4:8, 11; 5:9–10, 12, 13b, 14; 7:10, 12; 11:15, 17–18; 12:10–12; 14:3; 15:3–4; 16:5–6, 7b; 18:2–3, 4–7, 10, 16–17a, 19, 20, 21–24; 19:1b–3, 4, 5, 6b–8.

The polemical parallelism against the imperial cult here is clear enough.¹⁵⁹ Tacitus tells us that Nero was followed everywhere by 5000 equestrians who continually acclaimed him: "Then it was that Roman knights were enrolled under the title of *Augustiani*, men in their prime and remarkable for their strength.... Day and night they kept up a thunder of applause, and applied to the emperor's person the voice and epithet of deities" (*Ann.* 14.15). But, the Apolline cult at Klaros also experienced a continuous flow of delegations from eastern Mediterranean cities, which hymned the god at his sanctuary in preparation for their consultation and after his reply, bringing with them in the case of Laodicea the "marvelous poet for life [ποιητὴς παράδοξος ὁ διὰ βίου], teacher of hymns [διδάσκολος τῶν ὕμνων]." Thus the implicit polemic against the earthly counterparts to John's heavenly choirs is aimed equally at imperial and Apolline cultic worship in Asia Minor.

Sixth, how does John counter the ethics promulgated by the Apolline cults in Asia Minor? We have seen how the provincial elites were attached to the indigenous oracular cults, gaining prestigious offices through them, and flaunting in some cases the importance of their cities through their delegations. Some of the prophets of Didyma, we have argued, had significant contacts with Rome. Furthermore, I have proposed that the alphabetical oracle of Hierapolis advocates the Aristotelian mean, cautiously navigating between the excesses of the virtues and vices. Moreover, the prosperity theology that undergirded the lot oracles was also noted, allowing the enquirer confidence about a prosperous outcome if the god was rightly reverenced. While Revelation does not touch on these aspects of oracular culture directly, John does savagely criticize the prosperity accumulated by the provincial elites and their merchants under Roman rule (Rev 18:1–24; see also 3:17a; 12:16–17),¹⁶⁰ the reciprocity system that ties together its patrons and clients by gift-giving (11:10), and the folly of charting the middle course of least ethical resistance by ethical compromise (3:15; cf. 2:14, 20). The powerful figures of this world will be swept aside (Rev 19:18) and the just judgements of God effected (16:5–6), surpassing in scope the divine judgements of the confession inscriptions. Since the oracular cults of Apollo were inextricably entwined with the Julio-Claudian regime, it is

---

159. See Paul Barnett, "Polemical Parallelism: Some Further Reflections on the Apocalypse," *JSNT* 35 (1989): 111–20.

160. Bauckham, *Climax of Prophecy*, 338–83; Kraybill, *Imperial Cult and Commerce in John's Apocalypse*, passim.

hard to see how this critique did not also apply to the oracular mentality of Asia.

Seventh, how does John allay the deep anxiety aroused by the reemergence of powerful oracular sites in the first century CE? These centers of Apolline revelation were not only serviced by prophets but they were also increasingly visited by elite delegations from across the eastern Mediterranean basin, thereby reinforcing the social and religious honor that accrued to the local Apolline cults and their status-conscious personnel. The inability of the Asian churches to withstand the rapid urban expansion of such idolatrous cults demonstrated how precariously exposed they were as a religious group in the large cities of Asia Minor. Compromise with idolatry would have been tempting for some believers who were anxious to acquire or maintain social status (Rev 2:14, 20; 3:4, 17). Indeed, the fact that the early believers were publicly mocked in the oracular responses of the god at Didyma and Miletus[161] points to their personal vulnerability, high visibility, and social powerlessness in their Asian cities (Rev 3:8: μικρὰν ἔχεις δύναμιν). Moreover, in terms of the imperial cult, the economic isolation of believers was precipitated by their refusal to accept the ink-mark of the beast on their wrist or forehead (Rev 13:16–17; 20:4), accompanied by a sacrificial pinch of incense on the imperial altar, rituals which would allow them entry into the city market. The decision to refuse the mark and to refrain from its accompanying sacrifice resulted in their exclusion "from the trading community—an implied apartheid policy such as was eventually put into regular effect."[162]

Furthermore, it was popularly rumored that the Apollo-impersonating Nero, having committed suicide in 68 CE, would soon appear *redivivus* at the head of the Parthian armies, with a view to establishing anew his imperial throne somewhere in the East. Would the site be located in Jerusalem or Parthia? Public speculation was unable to specify. We do not know the extent to which the popular imagination spiraled out of control regarding Nero's projected return, but one could conceive that early believers were unsettled by such rising fears and wondered whether their Apolline persecutor might seek them out this time in the Greek East in contrast to the Latin West previously. But John the Seer does not shy away

---

161. Note 17, supra.

162. Edwin A. Judge, "The Mark of the Beast, Revelation 13:16," in *The First Christians in the Roman World: Augustan and New Testament Essays*, ed. James R. Harrison, WUNT 229 (Tübingen: Mohr Siebeck, 2008), 425.

from addressing the great cost of following Christ. He reminds his believing auditors of past martyrs (Rev 6:9–11; see also 20:4)—presumably the casualties of Nero's recent persecution at Rome (64 CE)—and of a more recent local martyr at Pergamum (2:13).[163] Persecution was still very much a present reality and would remain a continuing experience well into the future (Rev 2:10). The fear and unease experienced by Asian believers is all the more explicable if Revelation was written at the time when the social fabric of the Roman Empire was totally unraveling: the chaotic year of the four emperors (69 CE).

It is therefore highly significant that "fear" terminology regularly surfaces in the book of Revelation: that is, φοβέομαι (Rev 1:17; 2:10; 11:18; 14:7; 15:4; 19:5) and φόβος (11:11; 18:10, 15). What is fascinating is how John turns the believer's contemporary experience of fear topsy-turvy, but in ways that are commensurate with traditional Jewish scriptural teaching.[164] John's usage of the verb φοβέομαι consistently highlights how fear is appropriately reserved for the believer's relationship with God and his risen Son of Man. All other sources of fear—whether they are the Apolline cults, the threat of Nero *redivivus* and persecution, exclusion from the city's markets, or death itself—are ruled out. The fear envisaged is reverence for God (Deut 10:20; Ps 34:11 [MT 34:12]), expressing itself in unwavering faithfulness, no matter the status of the believer.[165] Crucial for the believer's personal comfort here is the placement of the Son of Man's hand gently on John (Rev 1:17a) who had fallen before the Son of Man's feet "as though dead" (Rev 1:17b). Significantly, the admonition Μὴ φοβοῦ ("Do not fear": Rev 1:17) of the risen Christ, accompanied by this intimate and very tangible gesture, is given right in the midst of John's suffering congregations. The imminence and presence of the Conqueror of death and hades among them (1:18–19) is strongly emphasized.[166] Finally, the noun φόβος in Rev 18:10, 15 is reserved for the fear that Rome's unbelieving and self-sufficient merchants feel as they witness the devastating

---

163. F. Gerald Downing, "Pliny's Prosecutions of Christians: Revelation and 1 Peter," *JSNT* (1988): 105.

164. On the rhetoric of fear in Revelation, see Robyn J. Whitaker, *Ekphrasis, Vision, and Persuasion in the Book of Revelation*, WUNT 2/410 (Tübingen: Mohr Siebeck, 2015), 71–103.

165. Whitaker, *Ekphrasis, Vision, and Persuasion*, 98.

166. Whitaker, *Ekphrasis, Vision, and Persuasion*, 99–100.

judgment that is divinely dealt out to Rome: believers, in sharp contrast, will be exempted from such eschatological terror.

3. Conclusion

This chapter has looked at how the oracular mentality of Asia intersected with the genre of epigraphic evidence and how the early Christians responded to the revival of oracular sites spanning the late first-century BCE to the third century CE. We have argued that although this corpus of inscriptions largely post-dates the New Testament documents, there is sufficient evidence to assume that the oracular explosion that occurred under the Second Sophistic had its first glimmerings from the late first century BCE to the mid first century CE onwards. Thus John, in his written προφητεία, is engaging the rise of the oracular in Asia, which had become integrated with the ideology and imperial cult of the Julio-Claudian rulers in its Apolline form, highlighting in sharp contrast the beneficial presence of believing prophets in the house churches and the continuously transformative impact of the "Spirit of prophecy" in the lives of believers.

We can posit a series of interpretative scenarios for John's prophecy depending upon when Revelation was written. If we date Revelation to the late first century CE, assuming with the majority of scholars that the work is a product of the Domitianic persecution, then the author shows considerable Spirit-given prescience about the problem that the oracular mentality would eventually pose for early believers, not to mention the current imperial challenge. But if the work is dated to the early second century CE, then it represents the vigorous response of an early Christian seer to the explosion of renewed interest in the oracular sites in the early Second Sophistic period. Last, if the work is dated to the year of the four emperors (68–69 CE), then the recent persecution of believers at Rome would be fresh in the memory of believers throughout the empire. There would have been the very real fear among Asian believers that Nero *redivivus* would reestablish his capital somewhere in the East, if popular rumors were true, continuing not only his commitment to the Apolline cult but also his vendetta against Christians. Perhaps this last scenario best explains John's full-blown rhetorical response to the dramatic events occurring around him.

One final set of questions remains: How do we explain the emergence of anti-Christian oracles at the Apolline sites? What provoked these? What is common in each oracular response is, to borrow a Pauline phrase, the derision of the foolishness of the cross. But why did delegations feel that it was worth bringing news of this new eastern cult to the attention of the Apolline oracular sites? Why not, alternatively, inform the Roman authorities about their growing destabilization of the status quo? The unsolicited and noncultic nature of early Christian inspired speech, available for nonbelieving outsiders to observe (1 Cor 14:24–25), was a phenomenon with little precedent.[167]

What made it intolerable was the ludicrous claim that their crucified and risen founder figure had poured out his prophetic πνεῦμα impartially upon the nonelites. The prestigious cult-sites and the quest for honor on the part of the provincial elites had been bypassed by this new competitor, threatening as a result the social concord with the gods. The coercive magic of occult practitioners, too, no longer posed sufficient threat to the early Christians because of their superior pneumatic power and thus was marginalized. The very success of the early Christians in democratizing access to Jesus's revelatory and indwelling πνεῦμα, which orchestrated an ever-expanding ministry across the eastern Mediterranean, would become a serious liability in the estimation of their opponents.

Bibliography

Arnold, Clinton E. "'I Am Astonished That You Are So Quickly Turning Away!' (Gal 1.6): Paul and Anatolian Folk Belief." *NTS* 51 (2005): 429–49.
Aune, David E. "The Apocalypse of John and Graeco-Roman Revelatory Magic." *NTS* 33.4 (1987): 481–501.
———. "The Influence of Roman Court Ceremonial on the Apocalypse of John." *BR* 2 (1983): 5–26.
———. *Prophecy in Early Christianity and the Ancient Mediterranean World*. Grand Rapids: Eerdmans, 1983.
———. *Revelation 1–5*. WBC 52a. Nashville: Nelson, 1997.
———. *Revelation 6–16*. WBC 52b. Nashville: Nelson, 1998.
Barnett, Paul. *Apocalypse Now and Then: Reading Revelation Today*. Maryborough: The Book Printer, 1989.

---

167. Forbes (*Prophecy and Inspired Speech*, 307) argues that there is only evidence for (at the very most) six examples of unsolicited and inspired prophecy in the first centuries BCE and CE.

———. "Polemical Parallelism: Some Further Reflections on the Apocalypse." *JSNT* 35 (1989): 111–20.
Barrett, Anthony A. *Caligula: The Abuse of Power*. 2nd ed. London: Routledge, 2015.
Bauckham, Richard. *The Climax of Prophecy: Studies on the Book of Revelation*. Edinburgh: T&T Clark, 1993.
Bean, E. "Notes and Inscriptions from Caunus (Part 2)." *JHS* 74 (1954): 85–87.
Beale, G. K. *The Book of Revelation*. NIGTC. Grand Rapids: Eerdmans, 1999.
Beasley-Murray, George Raymond. *The Book of Revelation*. NCB. London: Oliphants, 1974.
Beatrice, Pier Franco. "Monophysite Christology in an Oracle of Apollo." *International Journal of the Classical Tradition* 4.1 (1997): 3–22.
Busine, Aude. "Oracles and Civic Identity in Roman Asia Minor." Pages 175–96 in *Cults, Creeds, and Identities in the Greek City after the Classical Age*. Edited by Richard Alston, Onno van Nijf, and Christiana Grace Williamson. Leuven: Peeters, 2013.
———. *Paroles d'Apollon: Practiques et traditions oraculaiues dans l'Antiquité tardive (IIe—VIe siècles)*. RGRW 156. Leiden: Brill, 2005.
Champlin, Edward. "Nero, Apollo and the Poets." *Phoenix* 57.3-4 (2003): 276–83.
Chaniotis, Angelos. "Constructing the Fear of Gods: Epigraphic Evidence from Sanctuaries of Greece and Asia Minor." Pages 205–34 in *Unveiling Emotions: Sources and Methods for the Study of Emotions in the Greek World*. Edited by Angelos Chaniotis. Stuttgart: Steiner, 2012.
———. "Ritual Performances of Divine Justice: The Epigraphy of Confession, Atonement, and Exaltation in Roman Asia Minor." Pages 115–53 in *From Hellenism to Islam: Cultural and Linguistic Change in the Roman Near East*. Edited by Hannah M. Cotton, Robert G. Holyand, Jonathan J. Price, and David J. Wasserstein. Cambridge: Cambridge University Press, 2009.
———. "Under the Watchful Eyes of the Gods: Aspects of Divine Justice in Hellenistic and Roman Asia Minor." Pages 1–43 in *The Greco-Roman East: Politics, Culture, Society*. Edited by Stephen Colvin. Cambridge: Cambridge University Press, 2004.
Charles, R. H. *A Critical and Exegetical Commentary on the Revelation of St. John*. ICC. Edinburgh: T&T Clark, 1920,

Collins, Adela Yarbro. *Crisis and Catharsis: The Power of the Apocalypse.* Philadelphia: Westminster, 1984.
Coutras, Andrew J. *Chaos and Clairvoyance: Apollo in Asia Minor and in the Apocalypse.* PhD thesis, Asbury Theological Seminary, 2018.
Crone, Theodore M. *Early Christian Prophecy: A Study of Its Origin and Function.* Baltimore: Saint Mary's University Press, 1973.
D'Ambra, Eve. *Private Lives, Imperial Virtues: The Frieze of the Forum Transitorium in Rome.* Princeton: Princeton University Press, 1993.
Downing, F. Gerald. "Pliny's Prosecutions of Christians: Revelation and 1 Peter." *JSNT* (1988): 105–23.
Edwards, James R. "The Rider on the White Horse, the Thigh Inscription, and Apollo: Revelation 19:16." *JBL* 137 (2018): 519–36.
Eitrim, Samson. *Orakel und Mysterien am Ausgang der Antike.* Zürich: Rhein, 1947.
Ferrary, Jean-Louis. *Les mémoriaux de délégations du sanctuaire oraculaire de Claros, d'après la documentation conserve dans le Fonds Louis Robert.* Vol. 1–2. Des inscriptions et belles-lettres Tome 40. Paris: Mémoires de l'Académie, 2014.
Fontenrose, Joseph. *The Delphic Oracle: Its Responses and Operations.* Berkeley: University of California Press, 1981.
———. *Didyma: Apollo's Oracle, Cult, and Companions.* Berkeley: University of California Press, 1988.
Forbes, Christopher. *Prophecy and Inspired Speech in Early Christianity and Its Hellenistic Environment.* Peabody, MA: Hendrickson, 1997.
Fox, Robin Lane. *Pagans and Christians in the Mediterranean World from the Second Century AD.* Harmondsworth: Viking, 1986.
Friesen, Steven J. *Imperial Cults and the Apocalypse of John: Reading Revelation in the Ruins.* Oxford: Oxford University Press, 2001.
Frilingos, Christopher A. *Spectacles of Empire: Monsters, Martyrs, and the Book of Revelation.* Philadelphia: University of Pennsylvania Press, 2004.
Galinsky, Karl. *Augustan Culture: An Interpretive Introduction.* Princeton: Princeton University Press, 1996.
Gillespie, Thomas W. *The First Theologians: A Study in Early Christian Prophecy.* Grand Rapids: Eerdmans, 1994.
Gilliam, J. F. "The Plague under Marcus Aurelius." *AJP* 82.3 (1961): 225–51.
Glancy, Jennifer A. *Slavery in Early Christianity.* Oxford: Oxford University Press, 2002.

Grant, Frederick C., ed. *Ancient Roman Religion*. New York: Liberal Arts Press, 1957.
Grudem, Wayne A. *The Gift of Prophecy in 1 Corinthians*. Lanham, MD: University of America Press, 1982.
Guichard, Celeste L. "Travels and Traversals in the Hellenistic Oracular Temples at Klaros and Didyma." PhD diss., Columbia University, 2005.
Gurval, Robert Alan. *Actium and Augustus: The Politics and Emotions of Civil War*. Ann Arbor: University of Michigan Press, 1995.
Hall, A. S. "The Klarian Oracle at Oenoanda." *ZPE* 32 (1978): 263–68.
Harrington, Wilfred J. *Revelation*. SP 16. Collegeville, MN: Glazier; Liturgical Press, 1993.
Harrison, James R. "Artemis Triumphs over a Sorcerer's Evil Art." *NewDocs* 10 (2012): 37–47.
―――. "'The Fading Crown': Divine Honour and the Early Christians." *JTS* 54 (2003): 493–529.
―――. "Paul and the *Agōnothetai* at Corinth: Engaging the Civic Values of Antiquity." Pages 271–326 in *The First Urban Churches 2: Roman Corinth*. Edited by James R. Harrison and L. L. Welborn. Atlanta: SBL Press, 2016.
―――. "The Seven Sages, The Delphic Canon and Ethical Education in Antiquity." Pages 71–86 in *Ancient Education and Early Christianity*. Edited by Matthew Ryan Hauge and Andrew W. Pitts. London: Bloomsbury T&T Clark, 2016.
Herda, Alexander. *Der Apollon-Delphinios-Kult in Milet und die Neujahrsprozession nach Didyma: Ein neuer Kommentar der sog. Molpoi-Satzung*. Mainz: Philipp von Zabern, 2006.
―――. "How to Run a State Cult: The Organisation of the Cult of Apollo Delphinios in Miletos." Pages 57–93 in *Current Approaches to Religion in Ancient Greece: Papers Presented at a Symposium at the Swedish Institute at Athens, 17–19 April 2008*. Edited by Matthew Haysom and Jenny Wallensten. Stockholm: Swedish Institute at Athens, 2011.
Herrmann, P. "Inscriptions of Miletos." *Chiron* 1 (1971): 291–98.
Hill, David. *New Testament Prophecy*. London: Marshall, Morgan & Scott, 1979.
Horsley, Greg H. R. "Expiation and the Cult of Men." *NewDocs* 3 (1983): 20–31.
―――. "Two Confession Texts from Graeco-Roman Phrygia." *NewDocs* 1 (1981): 32–33.

Horsley, Greg H. R., and Stephen Mitchell, eds. *The Inscriptions of Central Pisidia: Including Texts from Kremna, Ariassos, Keraia, Hyia, Panemoteichos, the Sanctuary of Apollo of the Perminoundeis, Sia, Kocaaliler, and the Döşeme Boğazı*. Bonn: Habelt, 2000.

Howard-Brook, Wes, and Anthony Gwyther. *Unveiling Empire: Reading Revelation Then and Now*. New York: Orbis, 1999.

Janzen, Ernst. "The Jesus of the Apocalypse Wears the Emperor's Clothes." Pages 637–57 in *Society of Biblical Literature 1994 Seminar Papers*. Edited by Eugene H. Lovering Jr. SBLSP 33. Atlanta: Scholars Press, 1994.

Jones, Tamara. "Seating and Spectacle in the Greco-Roman World." PhD diss., McMaster University, 2008.

Judge, Edwin A. "The Mark of the Beast, Revelation 13:16." Pages 424–26 in *The First Christians in the Roman World: Augustan and New Testament Essays*. Edited by James R. Harrison. WUNT 229. Tübingen: Mohr Siebeck, 2008.

Kerkeslager, A. "Apollo, Graeco-Roman Prophecy, and the Rider on the White Horse in Rev. 6:2." *JBL* 112 (1992): 116–21.

Klauck, Hans-Josef. "Do They Never Come Back? *Nero Redivivus* and the Apocalypse of John." *CBQ* 63 (2001): 683–98.

Koester, Craig R. "The Number of the Beast in Revelation 13 in Light of Papyri, Graffiti, and Inscriptions." *JECH* 6 (2016) 1–21.

———. "Revelation's Visionary Challenge to Ordinary Empire." *Int* 63 (2009): 5–18.

———. "Roman Slave Trade and the Critique of Babylon in Revelation 18." *CBQ* 70 (2008): 766–86.

Kraybill, J. Nelson. *Apocalypse and Allegiance: Worship, Politics, and Devotion in the Book of Revelation*. Grand Rapids: Brazos, 2010.

———. *Imperial Cult and Commerce in John's Apocalypse*. JSNTSup 132. Sheffield: Sheffield Academic, 1996.

Lampinem, Antti. "Θεῷ μεμελημένε Φοίβῳ—Oracular Functionaries at Claros and Didyma in the Imperial Period." Pages 50–88 in *Studies in Ancient Oracles and Divination*. Edited by Mika Kajava. Direttore degli Acta Instituti Romani Finlandiae 40. Rome: Instituti Romani Finlandiae, 2013.

Lange, Carste Hjort. "Res publica constituta: Actium, Apollo and the Accomplishment of the Triumviral Assignment." PhD thesis, University of Nottingham, 2008.

L'Hôte, Eric. *Les lamelles oraculaires de Dodone*. Geneva: Droz, 2006.

Llewelyn, Stephen R. "Contests of the Gods." *EA* 32 (2000): 147–49.
———. "Faithful Words." *NewDocs* 9 (2002): 9–14.
MacMullen, Ramsay, and Eugene N. Lane. *Paganism and Christianity 100–425 CE: A Sourcebook*. Minneapolis: Fortress, 1992.
Magie, David. *Roman Rule in Asia Minor to the End of the Third Century after Christ*. 2 vols. Princeton: Princeton University Press, 1950.
Malina, Bruce J. *On the Genre and Message of Revelation: Star Visions and Sky Journeys*. Peabody, MA: Hendrickson, 1995.
Merkelbach, Reinhold, and Josef Stauber. "Die Orakel des Apollon von Klaros." *EA* 27 (1997): 1–54.
Miller, John F. *Apollo, Augustus, and the Poets*. Cambridge: Cambridge University Press, 2009.
Morgan, Teresa. *Popular Morality in the Early Roman Empire*. Cambridge: Cambridge University Press, 2007.
Moretti, Jean-Charles. "Le temple d'Apollon mis en chantier à Claros à la fin du ive s. av. J.-C." Pages 585–600 in ΑΡΧΙΤΕΚΤΩΝ: τιμητικός τόμος για τον καθηγητή Μανόλη Κορρέ. Edited by Kostas Zambas et al. Athènes: Melissa, 2016.
———. "Le temple de l'oracle d'Apollon à Claros." Pages 1–23 in *Archéologies et espaces parcourus*. Edited by Olivier Henry. Istanbul: Institut français d'études anatoliennes, 2012.
Moretti, Jean-Charles, with Liliane Rabatel, eds. *Le sanctuaire de Claros et son oracle*. Maison de l'Orient et de la Méditerranée 65. Lyon: Jean Poulloux, 2014.
Mounce, Robert H. *The Book of Revelation*. NICNT. Grand Rapids: Eerdmans, 1978.
Murphy-O'Connor, Jerome. *St Paul's Corinth*. 3rd ed. Collegeville, MN: Glazier; Liturgical Press, 2002.
Nasrallah, Laura. *An Ecstasy of Folly: Prophecy and Authority in Early Christianity*. Cambridge: Harvard University Press, 2004.
Naylor, Michael. "The Roman Imperial Cult and Revelation." *CurBR* 8 (2010): 207–39.
Nollé, Johannes. *Kleinasiatische Losorakel: Astragal- und Alpabetchresmologien der hochkaiserzeitlichen Orakelrenaissance*. Munch: Beck, 2007.
Nutton, V. "The Doctor and the Oracle." *RBPH* 47 (1969): 37–48.
Oliver, James H. "The Epistle of Claudius which Mentions the Proconsul Junius Gallio." *Hesperia* 40.2 (1971): 239–40.
Osborne, Grant R. *Revelation*. BECNT. Grand Rapids: Baker Academic, 2002.

Parke, H. W. *The Oracles of Apollo in Asia Minor*. London: Croom Helm, 1985.

———. *The Oracles of Zeus: Dodona, Olympia, Ammon*. Oxford: Blackwell, 1967.

———. "The Temple of Apollo at Didyma: The Building and Its Function." *JHS* 106 (1986): 121–31.

Petzl, Georg. "Die Beichtinschriften Westkleinasiens." *EA* 22 (1994): 1–143.

Picard, Charles. "Un Oracle d'Apollon Clarios à Pergame." *BCH* 46 (1922): 190–97.

Reddish, Mitchell G. *Revelation*. Macon, GA: Smyth & Helwys, 2001.

Renberg, Gil H. *Where Dreams May Come: Incubation Sanctuaries in the Greco-Roman World*. Vol. 1. Leiden: Brill, 2016.

Ritti, Tullia. "Appendice II: Oracoli a Hierapolis." Pages 248–67 in *Hierapolis di Frigia IX: Storia e istituzioni di Hierapolis*. Istanbul: Ege Yayinlari, 2017.

———. *Epigraphic Guide to Hierapolis (Pamukkale)*. Translated by P. Arthur. Istanbul: Italian Archaeological Mission at Hierapolis, 2006.

———. *Hierapolis I: Fonti Letterarie ed Epigrafiche*. Archeologica 30. Rome: Giorgio Bretschneider, 1985.

———. "Oracoli alfabetici a Hierapolis di Frigia." *Miscellanea greca e romana* 14 (1989): 245-86.

Robert, Louis. "Un oracle grave à Oinoanda." *Comptes rendus des séances de l'Académie des Inscriptions et Belles-Lettres*. 115.3 (1971): 597–619.

———, ed. "Les inscriptions." Pages 247–389 in *Laodiée du Lykos: Le nymphée*. Edited by J. des Gagiers et al. Quebec: L'Université Laval, 1969.

———. *Nouvelles Inscriptions de Sardes*. Paris: Librairie d'amérique et d'orient, Adrien Maisonneuve, 1964.

Robert, Jeanne, and Louis Robert. *Le plateau de Tabai et ses environs*. Vol. 2 of *La Carie: Histoire et géographie historique avec le recueil des inscriptions antiques*. Paris: Librairie d'Amérique et d'Orient, Adrien-Maisonneuve, 1954.

Robinson, John A. T. *Redating the New Testament*. London: SCM, 1976.

Robinson, Thomas Lonzo. "Theological Oracles and the Sanctuaries of Claros and Didyma: A Thesis." PhD diss., Harvard University, 1981.

Rossing, Barbara R. *The Choice between Two Cities: Whore, Bride and Empire in the Apocalypse*. Harrisburg, PA: Trinity Press International, 1999.

Rostad, Aslak. "Human Transgression—Divine Retribution: A Study of Religious Transgressions and Punishments in Greek Cultic Regulations and Lydian-Phrygian Reconciliation Inscriptions." PhD Thesis, University of Bergen, 2006.

Scherrer, Stephen J. "Signs and Wonders in the Imperial Cult: A New Look at a Roman Religious Institution in the Light of Rev 13:13–15." *JBL* 103 (1984): 599–610.

Schwertheim, Elmar. *Die Inschriften von Hadrianoi und Hadrianeia*. IGSK 33. Habelt: Bonn, 1987.

Sherk, Robert H. *The Roman Empire: Augustus to Hadrian*. Cambridge: Cambridge University Press, 1988.

Smalley, Stephen S. *The Revelation of John: A Commentary on the Greek Text of the Apocalypse*. London: SPCK, 2005.

Strom, Mark. *Reframing Paul: Conversations in Grace and Community*. Downers Grove, IL: InterVarsity Press, 2000.

Sweet, J. *Revelation*. TPINTC. London: SCM, 1979.

Talloen, Peter, and Marc Waelkens. "Apollo and the Emperors (I): The Material Evidence for the Imperial Cult at Sagalassos." *Ancient Society* 34 (2004): 171–216.

———. "Apollo and the Emperors (II): The Evolution of the Imperial Cult at Sagalassos." *Ancient Society* 35 (2005): 217–49.

Thomas, Rodney Lawrence. *Magical Motifs in the Book of Revelation*. LNTS 416. London: T&T Clark, 2010.

Turner, Max. *Power from on High: The Spirit in Israel's Restoration and Witness in Luke-Acts*. Sheffield: Sheffield Academic, 2000.

Várhelyi, Zsuzsanna. "Magic, Religion, and Syncretism at the Oracle of Claros." Pages 13–31 in *Between Magic and Religion: Interdisciplinary Studies in Ancient Mediterranean Religion and* Society. Edited by Sulochana Ruth Asirvatham, Corrine Ondine Pache, and John Watrous. Lanham, MD: Rowman & Littlefield, 2001.

Villiers, Pieter de. "Oracles and Prophecies in the Graeco-Roman World and the Book of Revelation in the New Testament." *APB* 8.1 (1997): 79–86.

Wells, Louise. *The Greek Language of Healing from Homer to New Testament Times*. BZNW 83. Berlin: de Gruyter, 1998.

Whitaker, Robyn J. *Ekphrasis, Vision, and Persuasion in the Book of Revelation*. WUNT 2/410. Tübingen: Mohr Siebeck, 2015.

Wilson, Mark. "The Ephesian Elders Come to Miletus: An Annaliste Reading of Acts 20:15–18a." *VeEc* 34.1 (2013): art. #744, pp. 1–9. http://dx.doi. org/10.4102/ve.v34i1.744.

———. "The Rise of Christian Oracles in the Shadow of the Apollo Cults." *Ekklesiastikos Pharos* 90 (2008): 162–75.

Wire, Antoinette Clark. *The Corinthian Women Prophets: A Reconstruction through Paul's Rhetoric*. Minneapolis: Fortress, 1994.

Witherington, Benjamin, III. *Revelation*. NCBC. Cambridge: Cambridge University Press, 2003.

Wypustek, Andrzej, and Izabella Donkow. "Christians and the Plague in Second Century Asia Minor." *Palamedes* 1 (2006): 123–32.

Contributors

Clinton E. Arnold studied New Testament exegesis at Aberdeen University and graduated from the doctoral program in 1986. He also did postdoctoral research at the Eberhard Karls University of Tübingen in 1991. Arnold is dean and professor of New Testament at Talbot School of Theology (Biola University) in La Mirada, California. His monographs include *Ephesians: Power and Magic* (Cambridge University Press, 1989) and *The Colossian Syncretism* (Mohr Siebeck, 1995). He is the general editor of the Zondervan Exegetical Commentary: New Testament and wrote *Ephesians* (2012) for that series.

Peter Arzt-Grabner studied theology and classics at the University of Salzburg and at the Pontifical Gregorian University in Rome, graduating from the doctoral program of Biblical Studies at the University of Salzburg in 1991. Since 2007 he has been associate professor of papyrology at the Department of Biblical Studies and Ecclesiastical History, University of Salzburg. He has edited several papyri (documentary and semiliterary) and is the chief editor of the series Papyrologische Kommentare zum Neuen Testament—Papyrological Commentaries on the New Testament (Vandenhoeck & Ruprecht), in which he authored volume 1 on *Philemon* (2003) and volume 4 on *2. Korinther* (2014).

Allen Brent read classics and theology at Cambridge University (Emmanuel College) and was awarded a higher doctorate (DD) of that university (in 2008) following peer examination of the corpus of his published works. Until recently he was professor in early Christian history and iconography at King's College, University of London, and professore invitato at the Augustinianum (Lateran University), Rome. He has been an affiliated lecturer in Cambridge University's Faculty of Divinity (2008–2010), and acting dean of Saint Edmund's College (2012–2013) where he continues with a fellowship. He has continued to publish extensively, and among his principal monographs are *Cyprian and Roman Carthage* (Cambridge University Press, 2010), *Ignatius of Antioch and the Second Sophistic* (Mohr Siebeck, 2006), and *A Political History of Early Christianity* (T&T Clark, 2009).

Alan H. Cadwallader, a doctoral graduate of Flinders University in 2003, is a researcher and Anglican priest, combining interests in archaeology, Scripture, and contemporary issues. His most recent monograph is *The Politics of the Revised Version* (T&T Clark, 2019). He has written extensively on the ancient site of Colossae, authoring *Fragments of Colossae* (ATF Press, 2015) and editing, with Michael Trainor, *Colossae in Space and Time: Linking with an Ancient City* (Vandenhoeck & Ruprecht, 2011), with a forthcoming monograph on the Letter to the Colossians and material culture (Eerdmans, 2021). He is also a foundation member of the Earth Bible Project, currently completing an ecological commentary on Mark's Gospel (T&T Clark, 2020). He is a research fellow at the Centre for Public and Contextual Theology at Charles Sturt University in Canberra, Australia.

Rosemary Canavan studied theology at Flinders University and graduated with a PhD in the area of biblical studies in 2011. Canavan is senior lecturer in New Testament and academic dean at Catholic Theological College, University of Divinity. Her doctoral thesis was published as *Clothing the Body of Christ at Colossae: A Visual Construction of Identity* (Mohr Siebeck, 2012). Recent book sections include "Armor, Gladiators and Peace: A Visual Exegesis of Ephesians 6:10–20" (*The Art of Visual Exegesis: Rhetoric, Texts, Images*, SBL Press, 2017) and "Weaving Threads: Clothing in Colossae" (*Fragments of Colossae*, ATF Press, 2015). Her current major work is a sociorhetorical exploration commentary (SREC) on 1 and 2 Thessalonians. She is a member of the editorial team for SREC series (SBL Press).

James R. Harrison studied ancient history at Macquarie University and graduated from the doctoral program in 1997. Harrison is Professor of New Testament and the research director at the Sydney College of Divinity. His recent monographs include *Paul and the Imperial Authorities at Thessalonica and Rome* (Mohr Siebeck, 2011), *Paul and the Ancient Celebrity Circuit* (Mohr Siebeck, 2019), and *Reading Romans with Roman Eyes* (Fortress, 2019). He is the chief editor of *New Documents Illustrating the History* *of Early Christianity*, volumes 11–15, and is editor of the Cascade collection (2019) of E. A. Judge, *The Conflict of Cultures: The Legacy of Paul's Thought Today*. Harrison is a Fellow of the Australian Academy of the Humanities.

Ulrich Huttner, DPhil.habil. (DPhil 1995 Munich, habilitation 2001 Leipzig), is professor of ancient history at the University of Siegen (Germany). He has published several monographs on ancient history and currently focuses on early Christianity in Asia Minor. His recent work on the topic is *Early Christianity in the Lycus Valley* (Brill, 2013).

Harry O. Maier studied patristics at Oxford University and graduated with a DPhil in 1987. Maier is professor of New Testament and early Christian studies at Vancouver School of Theology and Fellow at the Max Weber Center for Advanced Cultural and Social Studies at the University of Erfurt. His recent monographs include *Picturing Paul in Empire: Imperial Image, Text and Persuasion in Colossians, Ephesians and the Pastoral Epistles* (T&T Clark Bloomsbury, 2013) and *New Testament Christianity in the Roman World* (Oxford University Press, 2018), and he is editor of *Seeing the God: Image, Space, Performance, and Vision in the Religion of the Roman Empire* (Mohr Siebeck, 2018).

Angela Standhartinger studied Protestant theology at the Universities of Frankfurt/Main, Munich and Heidelberg. She graduated at Frankfurt in 1994 (dissertation) and 1998 (habilitation). Since 2000 she has been professor of New Testament at the Philipps-Universität Marburg, Germany. Her recent publications include the following: "Polis and Ekklēsia at Philippi: A Response to Kathy Ehrensperger, Paul Holloway, and Julien Ogereau," in *The First Urban Churches 4: Roman Philippi* (SBL Press, 2018); "Der Kolosserhymnus im Lichte epigraphischer Zeugnisse," in *Epigraphical Evidence Illustrating Paul's Letter the Colossians* (Mohr Siebeck, 2018); and "Colossians and the Pauline School," *NTS* 50 (2004): 572–93. Currently she is finishing a commentary on Paul's Letter to the Philippians.

Michael P. Theophilos studied New Testament at Oxford University and graduated from the doctoral program in 2008. Theophilos is senior lecturer in ancient languages and biblical studies at the Australian Catholic University. In addition to over twenty articles and book chapters, his monographs include *Jesus as New Moses in Matthew 8–9: Jewish Biographical Typology in First Century Greek Literature* (Gorgias, 2011); *The Abomination of Desola-*

tion in Matthew 24:15 (T&T Clark, 2012); *Numismatics, Lexicography, and the New Testament* (Bloomsbury, 2019); and the forthcoming *Matthean and Lukan Sondergut* in the Papyrologische Kommentare zum Neuen Testament series (Vandenhoeck & Ruprecht).

Michael Trainor is senior lecturer in biblical studies at Australian Catholic University. In 2007 Trainor received an Order of Australia (AM) for his services to theology, archaeology, and interfaith relations. His latest books include *Earth's Child: An Ecological Listening to the Gospel of Luke* (Sheffield Phoenix, 2012); *The Body of Jesus and Sexual Abuse: How the Gospel Passion Narratives inform a Pastoral Response* (Wipf & Stock, 2015); and, most recently, coauthored with Paul Babie of Adelaide University Law School, *Owning and Consuming: Neo-liberalism and the Biblical Voice* (Routledge, 2018). He is a contributor to the forthcoming volume, *Enabling Dialogue about the Land: A Resource Book for Jews and Christians* to be published by Paulist Press/Stimulus Foundation.

L. L. Welborn (PhD Vanderbilt University) studied New Testament and early Christianity at Yale University and Vanderbilt University and is currently professor of New Testament and early Christianity at Fordham University and honorary professor of ancient history at Macquarie University. His recent publications include *An End to Enmity: Paul and the "Wrongdoer" of Second Corinthians* (de Gruyter, 2011), *Paul's Summons to Messianic Life* (Columbia University Press, 2015), and *The Young against the Old: Generational Conflict in First Clement* (Fortress, 2018).

Primary Sources Index

Old Testament

Genesis
- 46:2 — 131

Deuteronomy
- 10:20 — 405
- 28:22 — 45
- 28:28–29 — 45

Psalms
- LXX 34:11 [MT 34:12] — 405
- 92 — 124
- 93:2–5 — 124, 131
- 117:22 — 358

Proverbs
- 25:6–7 — 30

Isaiah
- 28:16 — 358

Daniel
- 7:13 — 131

Deuterocanonical and Pseudepigraphical Books

1 Maccabees
- 10:36–37 — 134
- 13:40 — 134

2 Maccabees
- 8:20 — 134

Sibylline Oracles
- 4.106 — 22
- 4.119–124 — 400
- 5.137–141 — 400
- 5.361–396 — 400

Testament of Solomon — 182

Wisdom of Solomon
- 4:27 — 183

Ancient Jewish Writings

4Q405
- 23 I, 8–10 — 181

Josephus, *Antiquitates Judaicae*
- 4.115–116 — 135
- 12.137–153 — 135
- 12.148–153 — 132, 243
- 12.149 — 135
- 12.150 — 134
- 12.152 — 134–35
- 12.152–153 — 134
- 12.401 — 134
- 14.241–243 — 243

m. Avodah Zarah
- 1:1–3 — 58

Philo, *In Flaccum*
- 46 — 133

Philo, *Legatio ad Gaium*
- 45 — 133

Philo, Legatio ad Gaium (cont.)
95–96	399
281	133
311	133

Sepher Harazim 182

New Testament

Matthew
5:31–32	211
6:1–10	31
19:19	211
19:30	31
20:16	31
22:15–22	263
22:20	263
24:23	43

Mark
10:31	31
12:13–17	263

Luke
2:1	206
2:1–3	203
13:30	31
14:7–11	31
14:12–14	31
18:9–14	31
20:20–26	263
22:25–27	32

John
8:44	124

Acts
2:10	119, 133
2:13	395
8:27	340
14:11–12	42
16:6	119, 239
18:23	119–20, 239
19	182, 184
20:17	368
20:18–31	368
20:23	369
21:4	369
21:10–12	369

Romans
12:8	32
12:16	32
13:13–15	396
16	120
16:1	305–6
16:2	306

1 Corinthians
4:9	55
4:10	55
4:12	230
4.16	98
7:11	211
8:6	166
8:10	166
9:6	230
11:1	98
12:24	32
14:24–25	407
15:30–32	55–56
15:32	55
16:15	216

2 Corinthians
5:19	302
6:5	214
10:1	98
11:23	214

Galatians
5:23	98

Ephesians
1:21	41
3:16	358
5:14	358

Colossians
1:1	303 250

1:2	310	4:12–13	251
1:3–8	310	4:13	251, 277, 282, 302, 312
1:6	250	4:13–16	124
1:7	239	4:15	277, 282, 313, 315
1:7–8	251	4:15–16	364
1:10	250	4:16	250–51, 277, 282
1:12	97	4:17	216
1:13	97, 100		
1:15	76	1 Thessalonians	
1:16	167	1:6	98
1:18	100, 250	2:9	230
1:21	251	2:14	98
1:24	250–51		
1:29–2:1	74	2 Timothy	
2:1	120, 251, 277, 282	4:20	368
2:8	99, 167		
2:9	99	Philemon	73, 303
2:10	99	1–2	211
2:11	100, 251	2	16
2:13–23	319	5–6	216
2:15	277, 319	9	214
2:16	88	11	309
2:16–19	164	13	216, 226, 230
2:17	100	15–16	309
2:18	75, 88, 127, 130, 175, 180, 183, 247	17	225, 230
		22	307, 310
2:19	101, 250	23	251
3:1–3	319		
3:9–14	216, 225	Revelation	
3:10	82, 97, 101	1:1	397
3:11	14, 77, 82, 95, 132, 140, 247, 249, 313	1:1–8	316
		1:3	365
3:12	82, 97, 98, 101	1:5	396
3:14	82, 101	1:5–6	403
3.18–19	211	1:8	277
3:18–4:1	310	1:9	397
3:22	223, 322	1:9–3:22	316
3:22–25	216, 222	1:11	277, 282
3:23	223–24	1:17	405
4:1	216	1:17	405
4:3–4	251	1:18–19	405
4:8	250	2–3	36, 274
4:9	211–13	2:1	37
4:11	251	2:1–7	316, 389, 397
4:12	74, 239	2:1–3:22	397

Primary Sources Index

Revelation (cont.)

Reference	Pages
2:6	395
2:8	37
2:8–11	316
2:9	396
2:10	402, 405
2:12	37
2:12–17	316
2:13	396, 405
2:13–23	319
2:14	395, 403–4
2:18	37, 396
2:18–29	316
2:20	395, 403–4
3:1	37
3:1–6	316, 389
3:4	404
3:7	37, 396
3:7–11	316
3:8	404
3:9	396
3:11	402
3:14	37, 277, 282, 284, 396
3:14–21	250, 295
3:14–22	316–18, 364
3:15	403
3:15–22	166
3:16	35
3:17	283–84, 395, 403–4
3:17–18	22, 166, 317
3:18	284
3:19	283, 317
3:20	317
3:21	284
4:8	402
4:10	402
4:10–11	402
4:11	402
5:6–14	402
5:9	402
5:9–10	402
5:12	402
5:13	402
5:14	402
6:2	397–98
6:8	401
6:9–11	405
7:10	402
7:12	402
8:3–11:19	401
8:7	401
8:8	401
8:10	401
8:12	401
9:1	401
9:3–10	398
9:11	398, 400–401
9:13	401
9:18	401
9:20	401
9:20–21	395
11:6	401
11:10	401
11:11	405
11:15	401–2
11:15–18	401
11:17–18	402
11:18	397, 405
12	367
12:9	396
12:10–12	402
12:16–17	403
13:3	400
13:4	283
13:13–14	396
13:13–15	395
13:14–17	283
13:16–17	404
14:3	402
14:5	396
14:7	405
14:9	283
14:13	397
15:1	401
15:1–16:21	401
15:2	283
15:3–4	402
15:4	405
15:6	401
15:8	401

16:2	283, 401	22:15	395–96
16:5–6	402–3	22:17	397
16:6	397	22:18–19	365
16:6–7	396	22:21	277
16:7	402		
16:9	401	Early Christian Literature	
16:10	396		
16:11	401	2 Clement	
16:13	396	13.1	222
16:14	396		
16:21	401	Acts of John	120, 124
17:8–11	400		
18:1–24	395, 403	Acts of Pagan Martyrs	129
18:2–3	402		
18:4	401	Acts of Philip	120, 124, 129, 131
18:4–7	402	2.18	131
18:8	401		
18:10	402, 405	Acts of Thecla	121
18:15	405		
18:15–17	302, 318	Apollonius Citiensis, *Hippocratis de articulis commentaries*	
18:16–17	402		
18:19	402	1.7	126
18:20	397, 402		
18:21–24	402	Asterius of Amasea, *Homilies*	
18:23	389	3	122
18:24	397	4	122
19:1–3	402	9	123
19:4	402	10	122
19:5	402, 405		
19:6	367	Augustine, *De civitate Dei*	
19:6–8	402	19.23	369
19:7–10	36		
19:10	397	Clemens Romanus, *Epistula ad Corinthios*	
19:11	396	2.7.6	353
19:16	277		
19:18	403	Clement of Alexandria, *Protrepticus*	
19:20	283, 395–96	2.32–41	127
20:3	396		
20:4	283, 404–5	Constantine Porphyrogenitus, *Peri thematōn*	
20:8	396		
20:10	396	1.3	117
21:8	395		
21:18	389, 401	Eusebius, *Chronicon*	
22:7	365	2.154	243
22:10	365		

Primary Sources Index

Eusebius, *Historia ecclesiastica*
5.16.3 330

Gregory of Nazianzus, *Orationes*
4.77 129

Gregory of Nyssa, *De sancto Theodoro*
PG46:741B 122
PG46:741D 122
PG46:744A 122
PG46:744D–745A 122
PG46:745A 122

Historia Augusta
Comm. 7.7 329

Ignatius, *To Polycarp*
6.1 162

Ignatius, *To the Ephesians*
4.1–2 162
7.1 162

Ignatius, *To the Magnesians*
2.1 162
3.2 162
4.1 162
7.1 162
13.1–2 162

Ignatius, *To the Philadelphians*
inscrip. 162–63
4.1 162
7.1 162
7.2 162
8.2 162
10.1 162

Ignatius, *To the Smyrnaeans*
8.1 162
8.2 162
9.1 162
12.12 162

Ignatius, *To the Trallians*
2.2 162
3.1 162
7.1–2 162

John Chrysostom, *Homilies on Colossians*
3.1 250

John Malalas, *Chronicle*
13.19 128

Justin Martyr, *Dialogue with Trypho*
85 330

Lactantius, *Epitome divinarum institutionum*
4.13.11 369

Martyrdom of Philip 131
9 131
[15]26 131
21 131
26 131

Melito, *On Pascha*
67 353

Michael of Chronai = Bonnett, *Miraculo a Michaele Archangelo Chonis Patrato*
1–2 (Bonnet, 1.5–3.7) 123
3.1 (Bonnet, 3.8–10, 11–12, 14) 123, 127
3.2 (Bonnet, 3.15, 17–19) 123
3.2–4 (Bonnet, 3.14–5.3) 123
3.3 (Bonnet, 4.2, 9–10) 127, 131
3.5 (Bonnet, 4.5, 17; 5.2–3) 123–24, 128
3.6 (Bonnet, 5.3–5) 123
4.1 (Bonnet, 5.6, 6–9) 123–24
4.2 (Bonnet, 5.10) 123
4.4 (Bonnet, 4.16–17) 127
5.2–4 (Bonnet, 8.13–9.11) 123
5.4 (Bonnet, 9.9–10) 128
7.3–4 (Bonnet, 11.5–12.4) 123
7.4 (Bonnet, 11.10, 12) 123, 128

8.2 (Bonnet, 12.13)	124	PG 620D	127
8.2–3 (Bonnet, 12.8–13.2)	123		
10.1–3 (Bonnet, 13.16–14.7)	123	Theodoret, *Interpretatio in xiv epistulas sancti Pauli*	
11.1 (Bonnet, 14.11–15)	124, 131		
12.3 (Bonnet, 17.13–14)	131	PG 82.628.4	250
12.4 (Bonnet, 18.13–14)	127		

Theophanes, *Chronicle*

62	131

Nicetas Choniates, *Chronica*

88	132

Vita Sancti Abercii

Orosius, *Historiarum Adversum Paganos Libri VII*

		1–6	325
		2–8	330
7.12	243	9	353
		9–11	326
		13	330

Pseudo-Hippolytus, *Refutation of All Heresies*

		20–23	326
5.7.30–34	358	33	326
5.9.60	352	33–43	326
7.29.4–7	349	36	330
9.15.67	330	39–40	334, 349
		40	330

Severus of Antioch, *Epistles*

		45–49	326
5.6	128	47–50	326
		48	328

Shepherd of Hermas, *Similitudes*

		48–49	327
93(9.16).4	353	48–51	334
		50–51	326

Socrates, *Historia ecclesiastica*

		51	339
2.20.7–11	127	52–56	326
		55	355

Synod of Laodicea

		56	326
7–8	126	65	334, 350
11	126	65–66	326
29	130	66	331, 350
32–34	126	69	340
35	6, 130, 248	76	335
37	130	76–77	326
38	130	77	335, 337–38

Tertullian, *De baptismo*

Zonaras, *History*

1.3	355	13.12	128

Theodoret, *Interpretatio epistulae ad Colossenses*

PG 82.613	127

Primary Sources Index

Greco-Roman Literature

Aelius Aristides, *Orationes*
33.6	179
48.38–39	179
51.25	179

Aelius Aristides, *Sacred Tales*   363

Ammianus Marcellinus, *Res gestae divi Augusti*
22.5.4	125

Anthologia Palatina
9.553	394

Appian, *Bellum Mithridaticum*
62–63	21

Apuleius, *Apologia*
55	354

Apuleius, *Metamorphoses*
11.23	178

Arrian, *Anabasis*
4.4	134

Calpurnius Siculus, *Eclogue*
1.42–88	76
4.10	76
4.84–159	76
4.159	399

Cicero, *Epistulae ad Atticum*
5.15.2	279
5.16	22
6.3.9	29

Cicero, *Epistulae ad familiares*
2.17.2	22
3.5.4	22, 279
12.14–15	328

Cicero, *De amicitia*
27.1	98

Cicero, *Pro Flacco*
28	133, 243, 285
67–68	133

Demosthenes, *De Falsa Legatione*
251	85

Digesta
21	218
21.1.1.1	218
21.1.17.14	221

Dio Cassius, *Historiae romanae*
46.19.3	400
51.1.2–3	394
59.28.1	399
63.6.2	399
63.20.5	399
71.2.4	179
80.9–10	354

Dio Chrysostom, *Orationes*
21	400

Diodorus Siculus, *Bibliotheca historica*
14.80.8	109

Diogenes Laertius, *Lives and Opinions of Eminent Philosophers*
8.76	349

Epictetus, *Dissertationes*
4.5.16–19	263

Herodian, *History of the Empire*
5. 5.6–7	354

Herodotus, *Historiae*
7.30	109, 240

Homer, *Odyssey*
24.6–8	358

Primary Sources Index

Horace, *Carmina*
3.4.60–64 — 394

Iamblichus, *De mysteriis*
3.11 — 177

Julian, *Orationes*
3 — 122
5 — 122
5.180.A — 353

Julian, Contra Galileios
96C–E — 131

Julian, *Fragmentum epistolae*
295C–D — 131

Justin, *Epitome historiarum Trogi Pompeius*
15.4.3–9 — 111

Lucian, *Alexander the False Prophet*
12–16 — 363, 396

Martial, *Epigrams*
5.5.1 — 400

Ovid, *Tristia*
3.1.39–46 — 394

Pausanias, *Graeciae descriptio*
7.2.8–9 — 121

Philostratus, *On Heroes* — 45

Philostratus, *Vitae sophistarum*
2.24 — 49

Pliny the Elder, *Naturalis historiae*
2.232 — 177
5.29 — 241
5.105 — 20, 22
8.73.190 — 279
10.96.7 — 330
21.9.27 — 22
21.27.51 — 247
25.9.67 — 22

Plutarch, *Table Talk*
1.2.2 — 119

Plutarch, *On the Obsolescence of Oracles* — 363

Polyaenus, *Stratagems in War*
7.16 — 109

Polybius, *The Histories*
5.57.5 — 21
5.772 — 21

Propertius, *Elegies*
4.6.37–84 — 394

Seneca, *Apolocyntosis*
 — 75
4.21–32 — 76

Seneca, *De clementia*
2.2.1 — 97, 101

Stephanus, *Ethnica*
163 — 121

Strabo, *Geographica*
12.8.13 — 22, 241
12.8.16 — 246, 267–68, 279–80
12.8.20 — 278
13.4.2 — 21
13.4.14 — 35

Suetonius, *Vitae caesarum*
 Domitianus 13 — 283
 Domitianus 57 — 400
 Nero 7.2 — 75
 Nero 39 — 399
 Nero 40 — 400
 Tiberius 8 — 22, 268–69

Tacitus, *Annales*
2.54 — 177
4.55 — 241

Tacitus, Annales (cont.)
12.58	75
14.15	403
14.27	22, 243, 269, 280
15.10–16	399

Tacitus, *Historiae*
1.2	400
2.8–9	400

Vergil, *Aeneid*
8.698–713	394

Vitruvius, *De architectura*
8.3.14	22, 279

Xenephon, *Anabasis*
1.2.6	109
1.3.6	241

Inscriptions and Papyri

L'Année Épigraphique
(1913) 2	137
(1993) 1521	116
(2001) 1347	11

Alt. v. Hierapolis
169	139
170	139
195	139
216	139
339	52

Anderson, "A Summer in Phrygia II"
90, no. 25	245
90, no. 26	245

Ascough, Harland, and Kloppenborg, *Associations in the Greco-Roman World*
148–58	57
150–51	46
152	91
154	90

Aydaş, "New Inscriptions from Asia Minor"
EA 37 (2004): 124	183

Bean, "Notes and Inscriptions"
85–87, no. 2	371

Bulletin de correspondance hellénique
11 (1889): 353f., no. 16	246
107 (1983) 352, no. 9	11

Bulletin épigraphique
(1939) 392	10
(1970) 584	10
(1979) 15	10
(1984) 421	137
(2013) 407	11

Berlin Griechische Urkunden
1.27	190
1.28	194–96
1.110	194
1.111, col. 2	194–95, 199
1.124	205
1.232	205
1.252	207
1.183	207
1.316	219
2.243	215
2.372	202
2.632	215–16
3.859	221
3.887	188, 190–91, 219
3.887–9.22–23	219
3.987	221
3.913	188
4.423	190
4.632	190
4.1059	221
4.1103	111
4.1141	122, 223
9.56	226
11.2020	194–95
13.2228	205
15.2471	231
16.2615	215

16.2617	215	6:20	194
16.2618	215	6:66	198
		6:69	228

Berichtigungsliste der griechischen Papyrusurkunden aus Ägypten

1:9	194, 196	6:172	207
1:21	194	6:198	226
1:22	205	7:10	207
1:24–25	207	7:16	188, 190, 219
1:45	215	7:66	219
1:58	190, 215	7:93	198
1:74	221	7:113	190
1:77	188, 190	7:129	227
1:82	188, 190	7:216	227
2:141	217	7:216–17	227
2:154	207	8:6	188
1:245	205	8:9	198
1:290	190	8:19	205
1:319	207	8:20	207
1:320	227	8:27	190, 215
1:350	188, 190, 219	8:35	221
1:390	207	8:36	190
2:2	194, 203	8:42	222
2:94	207	8:55	205, 219
3:6	198	8:186	190
3:15	188, 190–91, 219, 221	8:198	190
3:17	222	8:324	190
3:34	219	8:427	198
3:37	190	8:461	202, 210
3:39	190	8:479	194
3:61	196	8:481	194
3:94	202	9:20	190, 215
3:101	198	9:141	190
3:170	228	9:162	190
3:236	203	9:170	207
3:242	226	9:179	227
4:2	198	9:243–44	203
4:6	188, 190	9:356	226
4:32	196	10:12	205
5:10	207	10:98	205
5:54	202	10:137–38	202
5:81	190	10:269	203
6:10	194, 196	11:25	222
6:19	194	11:72	194
6:19–20	195	11:112	202

Berichtigungsliste (cont.)

11:143	202
11:238	191
11:268	194
11:278	193
12:10	190
12:11	207
12:16	191
12:248	207
12:284	199
12:268	194
12:279	194
12:284	188

Cadwallader, "Honouring the Repairer of the Baths" 11, 246

Cadwallader, "A New Inscription"

109, no. 1	10
111, no. 2	9, 246
112–18, no. 3	14

Cadwallader, "One Man, Two Women"

168	11
171	11

Cadwallader, "Revisiting Calder"

56.108	10

Carter, *Gladiatorial Spectacles*, "Catalogue of Inscriptions"

341–48	54
344	55
351–55a	29

C.Epist.Lat.

1.16–71	190
1.87–88	190
3.88bis.1–4843	190

Chaniotis, "Epigraphic Bulletin for Greek Religion"

25	15

Ch.L.A.

11.477	190
12.547	189

Corpus Inscriptionum Graecarum

3538	176
3955	8–9
3956	8–9
4379	382
4380k3	8, 11, 213

Corpus inscriptionum judacarum

2.760	45
2.775	138

Corpus inscriptionum Latinarium

1.2	382
1.2.728	114
2.3349	271
3.6	189
3.7	189
3.14195	271
4.91–94	271
8.15447	272

Clerc, "Inscriptions de la vallée du Méandre"

353, no. 10	10, 245
353, no. 11	10
353, no. 12	10

Codex Coislinianus (H) 145	337

Codex Parisianus graecus

(A) 1480	337
(M) 1484	337
(C) 1495	337
(D) 1494	337
(E) 1501	337
(F) 1512	337
(G) 1503	337
(P) 1540	337

Cotton, Cockle, and Millar, "The Papyrology of the Roman Near East"
214–35   189

Corpus Papyrorum Raineri
15.24   194

C.Ptol.Sklav.   220

Dieterich, *Die Grabschrift des Aberkios*
12–16   350

Epigraphica Anatolica
17 (1991): 53–54, no. 3   217

Ferrary, *Les mémoriaux de délégations*
4   376
27   378
31   307
32   378
34   378
37   378
40   378
42   379
43   378
45   378
50   378
54   378
60   400
63   378
80   80
96   378
97   400
101   378
105   378
107   378
111   378
112 n. 20   374
134   378
136   374–75
139   378
168   375
200   378
209   378
223   378
224   378
247   378
251   375
281   378
283   378
287   378
289   378–79
290   378
341–352   378
358–359   400

Fontenrose, *Didyma*
A6   371
B2   372
B4   372
B5   373
2   370
9   370
10   370
11   370
12   370
14   370
17   371
18   370
19   370
20   370
21   371
22   371
23   372
25   371
28   370
29   371
30   371
31   370
177–244   370

French, *Roman Roads and Milestones*
101, no. 266   20
106, no. 279   20
111, nos. 294–295   20

Greek, Roman, and Byzantine Studies
48 (2009) 334   10

Harland, *North Coast of the Black Sea, Asia Minor*, vol. 1
 116 — 242

Herrmann, "Inscriptions of Miletos"
 292 — 371

Horsley and Mitchell, *The Inscriptions of Central Pisidia*
 5 — 380–82
 159 — 382

IBoubon
 102 — 11

ICUR
 2.1 proemium XV–XVII — 352

IDenizli
 126 — 306

IDidyma
 11 — 370
 25 — 371
 29 — 371
 132 — 370
 148 — 399
 229 — 372
 277 — 371
 280 — 372
 282 — 373
 496A — 371
 496B — 371–72
 499 — 370
 504 — 370–71
 505 — 371
 517 — 371

IEph
 1a.18a.11–17 — 402
 1a.26 — 52
 3.987 — 52
 5.1799 — 328
 7.2.3157 — 328

IGBulg
 224 — 388

Inscriptiones graecae ad res romanas pertinentes
 3.174 — 119
 3.175 — 119
 4.353 — 354
 4.468 — 115
 4.469 — 115
 4.834 — 138
 4.841 — 304–5
 4.868 — 307
 4.868–869 — 245
 4.869 — 10, 12, 124, 245
 4.870 — 6, 10, 246, 297
 4.871 — 10
 4.1033 — 22
 4.1436 — 354
 4.1498 — 389–90

Inscriptiones Judaicae Orientis 2 — 4, 138
 184 — 133
 187 — 56
 187–209 — 242–43
 188 — 56
 189 — 56, 138
 191A — 138
 191B — 140
 192 — 156
 192–93 — 138
 192–94 — 56
 193 — 56, 138, 306
 196 — 56–57
 196.n — 242–43
 198 — 56, 139
 199 — 56
 200 — 56
 201–3 — 56
 202 — 56
 203 — 56
 204 — 56
 205 — 56
 205–9 — 56
 206 — 56

Primary Sources Index

207	139	48	267
212	139, 243	49	284
212–13	45	50	92
213	139, 243	51	89
		53	22, 36

Inschriften griechischer Städte aus Kleinasien

		59	23
		62	42
23.440	10	62A	42
59.56	105	65	43
59.57	105	67	42, 377, 379
59.95	105	68–69	42
59.96	105	70	42
5169	105	73–78	28
59.170	105	73	29
		75	29

ILaodikeia

		78	29
1	20, 42	81	44
2	31–32	81A	28
3	42	82	43–44, 267
4	20	83	30
4b	32	84	43
5	20, 31, 42	125	42
6	20		
8	42	IMagnesia	
9	30, 50	115	137
10	41		
11	34, 42	IMilet	
12	33, 42	1.3.150	370
13	30, 34, 42	1.7.205	370
14	36, 42	1.7.205b	371
15	30, 42, 272		
16–17	32	IMylasa	
18	33, 42	306	137
19	20, 42		
21	42	IPergamon	
22	42	324	374, 391–92
23	42		
24	42	ISardBR	
24b	43, 309, 277	1.89	379
29	31	7.1	387
30	31		
31	20, 31	ISmyrna	
32–33	31	67	379
34	31	440	246
47	297		

IStratonikeia
- 186 — 137
- 256 — 137

Jewish Inscriptions of Western Europe
- 2.306 — 133, 139

Journal of Hellenic Studies
- 18 (1898): 25 — 10
- 18 (1898): 26 — 10
- 35 (1915): 22–65, no. 2 — 189

Jur.Pap.
- 36 — 189

Konakçi-Duman, *Denizli Sempozyumu*
- 1.61, no. 8 (pl. 12b) — 11

Le Bas and Waddington, *Inscriptions grecques et latines*
- 1220. — 11
- 1693B — 10

Lois sacrées d'l'Asie Mineure
- 20 — 387
- 50 — 369
- 72 — 370

MacMullen and Lane, *Paganism and Christianity 100—425 CE*
- 7.3 — 382
- 7.10 — 382

Macridi, "Altertümer von Notion"
- 165, no. 2.2 — 176
- 168, no. 4/5.4 — 247
- 170, no. 5.4 — 176

Macridi, "Altertümer von Notion II"
- 46, no. 1.1 — 176
- 46, no. 2 — 247

Magie, *Roman Rule*
- 986 n. 22 — 10

Monumenta Asiae Minoris antiqua
- 2.1.194 (IIa) — 136
- 4.276 — 306
- 4.276A (I) — 118
- 4.276A (III) — 118, 124, 136
- 4.276B — 118
- 4.277A (I) — 112
- 4.277A (II) — 118–19
- 4.279 — 119
- 4.281 — 119
- 4.283 — 119
- 4.289 — 119
- 4.297 — 20, 301
- 6 — 139
- 6.1–37 — 24
- 6.38–49 — 8
- 6.39 — 10, 245
- 6.40 — 10, 139, 246
- 6.41 — 9
- 6.42 — 10
- 6.44 — 9
- 6.45 — 9
- 6.46 — 9
- 6.47 — 10, 84–85, 246
- 6.48 — 10
- 6.49 — 10
- 6.50 — 8, 10, 246
- 6.51 — 8, 9
- 6.52 — 10
- 6.53 — 9
- 6.87 — 87
- 6.142 — 8
- 6.156 — 75
- 6.177 — 139
- 6.335 — 45
- 6.666 — 276
- 8 — 8
- 9.9 — 136

Meer, *Ostia*
- 29 — 298
- 54 — 298
- 70 — 298
- 71 — 298
- 90–91 — 298

92	298	O.Brux.	
94–97	298	14	199
103	298		
107–108	298	O.Cret.Chers	189

Merkelbach and Stauber, "Die Orakel des Apollon von Klaros"

		O.Did.	
9	388	412	187–88
		438	225

Merkelbach and Stauber, *Steinepigramme aus dem griechischen Osten* vol. 1

Orientis Graeci Inscriptiones Selectae

		229	137
262	349	238	135
		530	176
		669	137

Meyboom, *The Nile Mosaic of Palestrina*

		P.Abinn.	
37	7	64	219, 221

Milner, *An Epigraphical Survey in the Kibyra-Olbasa Region*

		P.Amh.	
3.4.11	7, 11	2.76	205
128	105		
152	105	P.Ant.	
		1.37	198

Miranda, "La comunità giudaica di Hierapolis di Frigia"

		P.Berl.Cohen	
16	138	12	194–95

Mitteilungen des Deutschen Archaeologischen Instituts, Atheniasche Abteilung

		P.Bingen	198
16:199	10	77	187
18:206, no. 3	10	105	192, 197

NewDocs 1 (1981)		P.Cair.Masp.	
7	381	1.67120	219

NewDocs 3 (1986)		P.Cair.Preis.	
6	381	1	220

NewDocs 10 (2012)		P.Cair.Zen.	
5	393	1.59036	190
8	49, 388–89	1.59037	190
17	11	1.59056	190
		1.59758	230

Nollé, *Griechische und lateinische Inschriften (5–16)*

		P.Choix	
497, no. 497	217	10	210

P.Col.		1974	10
1.inv. 480	220	2005	7, 246
8.231	196		
10.262	203	P.Euphrates	189
10.267	223		
		P.Fam.Tebt	
P.Corn.		30	198
18	196–97	33	198
		34	198
P.Diog.			
2	198, 371	P.Fay.	
2–4	198	28	194
3	198		
		P.FuadUniv.	
P.Dime		13	196
3	207		
3.39	207	P.Gen.	
3.40	210	12.16	202
		4.162	194, 199
P.Dura	189		
		Papyri Graecae Magicae	
Pennacchietti, "Nuove iscrizioni di Hierapolis Frigia"		1.296–300	182
7	139	P.Hamb.	
22	139–40	1.63	219
Petzl, "Die Beichtinschriften Westkleinasiens"		P.Hever	189
5	386	Picard, "Un Oracle d'Apollon Clarios"	
90	387	190–97	176
110	119		
		P.Jud.Des.Misc	
Pflaum, *Les Carrières*		2	189
1.262, no. 109	10	4–6	180
		5	189
Pfuhl and Möbius, *Die ostgriechischen Grabreliefs*		16–19	189
236	7, 246	P.Köln	
594	10, 246	2.87	196–97
1146	246		
1607	7, 246	P.Laur.	
1634	7	3.79.3	226
1665b	7, 246		
1920	7, 246	P.Lond.	
1973	7, 246	1.229	219

Primary Sources Index

2.208	212	12.1552	196
2.229	190	13.2858	200
2.324	205	14.1765	226
3.904	202	18.2191	190
3.1178	190	38.2858	196–97
		43.3136	196–97
P.Masada	189	43.3137	196
		43.3183	196
P.Mich.		49.3491	210
2	228	50.3593	90
3	192, 229	54.3754	197
3.170	228	65.4489	197
3.171	228	66.3295	196
3.172	228	74.4993	196
5.264	221	74.4994	196–97
5.265	221	74.4995	196–97
5.278	221	74.4999	196
5.279	221	78.5166	220
5.355	226	38.2855	196
8.487	190		
8.490	190	P.Oxy.Hels.	
8.491	190	29	226
8.501	190		
9.546	190	P.Petaus	
11.603	195	1–2	195–96, 200
P.Michael		P.Petra	189
30	230		
		P.Rain.Cent.	
P.Münch.		166	190
3.63	190		
		P.Ryl.	
P.Murabba'ât	189	2.154	207, 209
		4.654	230
P.Oxy.			
43	195	P. Scholl.	
237	16	5.3	223
447	16	9	225
2.254	202		
2.265	207	PGI (Vitelli, *Papiri greci e latini*)	
2.288	227	1.36a	207
2.275	227–28	3.164	196
3.497	210	6.690	217
6.905	210	8.393	196
10.1267	196–97	8.902	226

PGI (*cont.*)
  12.1257   196

P.Sijp.
  45   220

P.Stras.
  6.505   221
  7.634   197–98

P.Tebt.
  34   198
  2.292   194
  2.298   194
  2.299   193
  2.384   296

P.Turner
  22   189–91, 199, 212, 219, 221

P.Ups.Frid.
  6   192, 197

P.Vind.Bosw.
  2   198

P.Warr.
  2   194–95

P.Wisc.
  1.4   228

P.Yadin
  1   189
  2   189
  16   205

Ramsay, *Cities and Bishoprics*
  212   10

Reasoner, *Roman Imperial Texts*
  138–39   11

Ricl, "Les ΚΑΤΑΓΡΑΦΑΙ"
  30   113

Ritti, *An Epigraphic Guide to Hierapolis*
  12   49, 51, 383
  14   51, 383
  16   49, 376
  16a   377, 388
  16b   377, 388
  20   51
  21   49
  22   49, 51
  22–23   53
  23   383
  24   383
  29   51
  32   89
  34   51, 89
  36   51
  38   49, 377, 383
  39   382–84
  43   53, 383
  54   56

Ritti, *Fonti Letterarie ed Epigraphi*
  97–101   54
  100 plate 11b   55
  102 plate 13   55
  102–03, plate 12d   55

Ritti, *Hierapolis di Frigia IX*
  388–95   301

Ritti, *Museo Archeologico di Denizli-Hierapolis*
  19   50
  27–47   52
  27   53
  31A   52
  31B   52
  32–34   52
  37   52
  42   52
  48   50
  59   8, 245, 11
  60–61   54
  62–63, plates 62–63   54
  73   8, 10, 246

Primary Sources Index   441

80	8, 246	Sammelbuch griechischer Urkunden aus Aegypten	
113	8, 100		
		3.6016	221
Ritti, Grewe, and Kessner, "Water-Powered Stone Saw Mill"		3.6260	190
	54	3.6204	190
139	298	3.6304	219
145	299	3.6695	217
		3.6696, col.	217
Ritti, Şimşek, and Yıldız, "Dediche"		5.8007	219, 221
34, no. K44.		8.9557	190
		10.10220	227
Robert, *Les gladiateurs dans l'orient grec*		10.10236	227
116	29	12.11103	198
123	55	16.12742	198
124	54	16.12743	197
		16.12764	212
Robert, "Inscriptions"		16.12950	217
1	378	20.14284	202
3	378	20.14440	202
4	378	22.15538	191
5	378	22.15765	189
8	378	24.16253	229
11	378	24.16257	223–24
12	378		
13	378	Schubart and Olsson, *Papyrusbriefe aus der frühesten Römerzeit*	
14	378		
15	378	9	222
18	378		
19	378	*Supplementum Epigraphicum Graecum*	
21	378	2.447	116
22	378	8.1328	382
23	378	18.592	382
24	378	20.411	135
		24.1109	118
Robert, "Monuments des gladiateurs"		26,16803	184
140 (plate 16)	29	29.1391	10
		32.1252	134
Robert, *Opera Minores*		33.1128	306
3.1587, no. 53	11	37.961	354
		38.1328	382
Robert and Robert, *La Carie* vol. 2		38.1338	382
146	376	40.1109	370
		41.1336	217
		42.1791	137
		43.711	116

Supplementum Epigraphicum Graecum (*cont.*)

47.1745	137
54.1330	306
57.1382	15
57.1383	9
57.1384	10
57.1385	9
57.1186	386
57.1385	6, 9, 246
61.1160	15
62.1235	11

Sylloge inscriptonum graecarum

530	370

Şimşek, "Laodikeia Water Law" 34–35

Şimşek and Guizzi, "A Dedication of the Praeses Dyscolius" 32

Şimşek, Okunak, and Bilgen, *Laodikeia Nekropulü*

229	38
414	37
416	37
506	38
1149	37

Studien zur Palaeographie und Papyruskunde

18	194
20.11	203
20.15	210
22.37	194
22.100	194
38	194

Spratt and Forbes, *Travels in Lycia*

2.289	11

Straus, *L'achat et la vente des esclaves*

265	221
279	221

Strubbe, ΑΡΑΙ ΕΠΙΤΥΜΒΙΟΙ

285	52

Tituli Asiae Minoris

2.194	5
2.3	382
5.1	134

T.Dacia

6	221

T.Hercul.

	218
60	189, 219
62	189, 219, 221

Thonemann, "Abercius of Hierapolis"

Grabschrift 3, 6	336
Grabschrift 4, 6	351
Grabschrift 7–9	336
Grabschrift 12	335
Grabschrift 13–16	355
Grabschrift 14, 16	356
Grabschrift 20–22	333
Grabschrift 36–43	344

T.Jucundus 189

T.Sulpicii

40	189
42	219
43	189, 219, 221

T.Vind. 190

T. Vindol. 190

Warmington, *Remains of Old Latin IV*

1. Inscriptions Proper, 23	21

Coins

Armstrong, "Roman Phrygia"

179–219, nos. B65–66	39
199	39
268–70, nos. 95–110	23

271–76, nos. 120–58	23	Domitian 2.179	400
279, nos. 174–174	23	Nero 1.48	272
351, no. 12	244	Tiberius 1.55	272
357, no. 28	245	Trajan 2.750	116

BMC Phrygia

1.1–7, plate 2.1	109		
11	74		
54–66 plate XXX.6	112		
64	87		
2891	244		

Roman Provincial Coinage 1

1269–1270	269
1271	272
1286	39
1294	39
1294	39
1553	273
1752	399
1842–1863	284
1937–1938	284
2096	284
2143	273
2467	51
2469	51
2473	51
2486	51
2632	51
2893–2896	39
2893	276–77
2893–2895	269
2894	276–77
2895	278, 284
2896	277
2896–2897	269
2897	39, 279
2898	39, 284
2898–2900	269
2901	39, 276–77
2901–2005	269
2903	39, 278–79
2904	279
2905	39, 279
2906	277
2906–2907	269
2907	39, 87, 278, 284
2908	39, 276–77
2908–2910	269
2909	39, 279
2910	39, 279
2911	39, 269

Houghton and Lorber, *Seleucid Coins*

1.20	111
1.32–33	110
1.343–344	110
1.355–356	110
1.418	111
1.420	111
1.423	111
1.528–59	111
1.625–26	110
1.635–37	110
1.638	110
1.162.2	111
1.173.16	112
1.174.9	112
1.165.1	112
1.169	112
1.177.1	112
1.179	112
1.188	112
1.900–03	113
1.989–98	113
2.223	112

Newell, *The Coinage of the Western Seleucid Mints*

894	109
922 plate 17.5, 6	111
946–51	109

Roman Imperial Coinage

Augustus 1.72	272
Galba 1.35	272

Primary Sources Index

Roman Provincial Coinage 1 (*cont.*)

2912	272–73, 278, 283	920	272
2912–114	29	1079–1093	272
2912–16	269	1268	274, 278
2913	274, 278	1268–70	39
2914	272, 278	1269	274, 278, 280
2915	40	1269–1270	269
2916	274	1270	278
2917	274, 278	1271	39, 269, 283
2917–2918	269	1272–1280	30, 269
2918	40	1273	114, 274
2919	274, 278	1275	114
2920	278, 280	1276–78	39
2920–2925	269	1277	114
2921	278	1278	279
2922	278	1279	114, 279
2923	278	1279–80	40
2924	114, 279	1280	279
2924–2925	39	1281	274–75, 283
2925	114, 279, 284	1281–95	40
2926	39	1281–1296	269, 274
2926–2927	269	1282	39, 274, 278–79
2927	39, 278, 284	1283	274
2928	29, 40, 269, 272–73, 283	1284	274, 283
2969–2973	73, 77	1286	274, 283
2969	77	1287	274, 283
2970	78	1280	274
2971	77–78	1281	283
2972	78	1282–83	40
2973	74, 78	1284	275
2971	77	1286	275
2973	74	1287	275
2988	273	1288	39, 278
3898	277	1290	274–75, 283, 295
5445	273	1290–92	40
5446	273	1291	274–75, 283, 295
		1292	39, 278
		1293	274

Roman Provincial Coinage 2

		1294	274, 279
227	12	1295	40, 274, 279
447	12	1297	279
471–482	115	1297–1299	269
548	114	1299	284
550	12	1317	272
551	12	1332	272
559–653	115	1369	272

Roman Provincial Coinage 3
2309	12
2310A	13
2313A	212
2316	116

Roman Provincial Coinage 4
1083	115
2070	212
9991–3	212

Sylloge Nummorum Graecorum Copenhagen
513	87

Sylloge Nummorum Graecorum von Aulock
2.43–46	107
2.83–94	245
2.443–46	241
2.448–52	17, 112
2.455–57	115
2:458–60	108, 112
2.471–82	108
2.483	112
2.487–93	112
2.496–506	112
2.515–17	112
2.518–19	115
2.534–36	108
2.545	114
2.546	112
2.546–47	108
2.547	12
2.548	245
2.547	125
2.564	112
2.580	108
2.588	108
2.590	108

Modern Authors Index

Abel, Adolphe   339–41, 343, 348, 358
Adams, J. N.   249, 252
Aitken, Ellen Bradshaw   45, 63
Akıncı, E.   16, 60
Alberigo, Giuseppe   128, 145
Alföldi, Andreas   76, 78
Alkac, A.   26, 68
Allen, Pauline   146
Alston, Richard   374, 408
Amandry, Michael   244, 253
Ameling, Walter   46, 59, 131, 135, 139, 141–42, 242–43, 252
Anagnostou-Laoutides, E.   9, 60
Anderson, Janice C.   12, 59
Anderson, J. G. C.   245–46, 252, 260, 286
Andorlini, Isabella   208, 238
Annese, Andrea   193, 231
Aperghis, Gerassimos G.   136, 142
Armstrong, Andrea J.   18, 20–23, 38–41, 59, 242, 244–45, 252
Arnaoutoglou, Ilias   207, 231
Arnold, Clinton E.   5, 18, 59, 108, 142, 173, 176, 181, 183–84, 247, 252, 385, 407
Arundel, V. J.   6–9, 59
Arzt-Grabner, Peter   5, 193–94, 197, 203, 207, 210, 213–14, 218–19, 221–23, 225, 226, 229–32, 235, 308, 319
Ascough, Richard S.   45, 59, 90–91, 102
Ashton, Richard A.   112, 142
Asirvatham, Sulochana R.   179, 186, 388, 414
Aulock, Hans von   12, 17, 59, 107–8, 112, 114–16, 125, 142, 241, 244–45, 256

Aune, David E.   14, 69, 365, 367, 394–95, 397, 399, 407
Austin, Michel M.   20, 60
Avramea, Anna   327, 358
Aydaş Murat   183–84
Aytaçlar, P. O.   16, 60
Badian, Ernst   270, 286
Bagnall, Roger S.   107, 195, 201–3, 206, 232–33, 294, 320
Bain, Katherine   296, 300, 306, 314, 320
Balabanski, Vicky   212, 232, 295, 320
Bang, Peter F.   294 320, 322
Barber, E. J. W.   85, 102
Barclay, John M. G.   133, 142, 182, 185
Bar-Kochva, Bezalel   107, 137, 142
Barnett, Paul   396, 403, 407–8
Barrett, Anthony A.   77–78, 399, 408
Barth, Markus   108, 142, 181, 185
Barton, Tamsyn   39, 60
Bauckham, Richard   317, 320, 394, 397, 403, 408
Baysal, H. Hüseyin   50–51, 67, 149, 255, 276
Bazzana, Giovanni   230, 232
Bean, E.   371, 408
Bean, Georg   241, 252
Beale, G. K.   398–99, 401, 408
Beasley-Murray, George R.   396, 399–401, 408
Beatrice, Pier Franco   369, 408
Beck, Astrid B.   185
Beê, N. A.   121, 142
Bejor, Giogio   19, 28, 60
Bélis, Annie   191, 232
Bell, G.   10, 60

Belley, A. 7, 9, 60
Bellia, Andria 191, 232
Benda-Weber, Isabella 94, 102, 242, 252
Bennett,Robert 18, 60
Benson, Bailey 47–49, 60
Berenson McLean, J. K. 45, 63
Bergamasco, Marco 226, 232
Bevere, Allan R. 181, 185
Bianchini, Mariagrazia 218, 237
Bibauw, Jacqueline 225, 238
Bieżuńska-Małowist, Iza 212, 225
Bilgin, M. 26, 37–38, 69
Billows, Richard A. 107, 142
Binder, Gerhard 76, 78
Bird, Michael 181, 185
Birley, Anthony R. 12, 60, 116, 142
Biscottini, Maria Valentina 226–27, 233
Blanke, Helmut 108, 142, 181, 185
Blanton IV, Thomas R. 293, 320
Blois, Lukas de 288
Blümel, Wolfgang 176
Blumell, Lincoln H. 191, 233
Bobrinskoy, Boris 355, 360
Böcher, Otto 250, 255
Boer, W. den 275, 288
Boissonarde, Jean F. 338, 359
Boiy, T. 134, 142
Bolden, Ron 266
Bombardieriet, Luca 261, 291
Bonnet, Max 123, 142
Bonetto, Jacopo 28, 60
Boretius, Alfred 128 142
Bormann, Lukas 12, 15–16, 60, 75, 78, 108, 245, 249, 252
Bosch, Clemens 258, 286
Bourke van der Meer, I. 298, 320
Bovon, François 129, 149
Bowersock, Glen W. 328, 358
Brennan, Peter 262, 286
Brent, Allen 5, 325–61, 333–54, 356–57, 359
Breytenbach, Cilliers 55, 64
Brink, Laurie 333, 360
Brixhe, Claude 249, 252
Brock, Ann Graham 129, 149

Brooke, C. 263, 287
Broughton, T. R. S. 243, 252
Brubaker, Rogers 164, 168
Bruce, F. F. 23, 60
Brunt, P. A. 206, 233, 270, 286, 294, 321
Buckler, William H. 8, 24, 85, 140
Bujard, Walter 239, 253
Bülow-Jacobsen, A. 187
Bundy, David 341, 359
Burnett, Andrew 47, 67, 114, 244, 253
Busine, Aude 363, 373–76, 382, 389, 392, 408
Buttrey, T. V. 281, 286
Cadwallader, Alan 3, 5–11, 58, 60–61, 85–86, 88, 102–3, 118, 125, 128, 143–44, 225, 233–34, 240, 244–46, 249–50, 253–54, 256, 300, 306, 309, 314, 320, 322, 386
Calder, W. M. 8, 24, 85, 140, 337, 348, 352, 359
Callaghan, Allen Dwight 308, 311, 320
Callu, Jean Pierre 273, 286
Caltabiano, M. Caccamo 261, 286
Camilleri, V. G. 6, 69
Camodeca, Giuseppe 218, 233
Campagna, L. 261, 286
Campbell, J. B. 118, 144
Canavan, Rosemary 5, 15, 18–19, 62, 85, 86, 88, 96, 97, 101–2, 118, 144, 225, 233, 249, 253
Capozza, Maria 232–33
Carlebach, Elisheva 131, 144
Carletti, Carlo 343, 359
Carney, T. F. 303, 320
Carter, Michael J. D. 29, 55, 62
Carter, Warren 261, 286
Cary, M. 270, 286
Castelli, Emanuele 343, 359
Champlin, Edward 399, 408
Chaniotis, Angelos 15, 62, 249, 253, 384–86, 408
Charles, Robert Henry 398, 408
Christol, Michel 5, 62, 119, 125, 136, 144
Claytor, W. Graham 202, 233

Cleland, Liza	85, 102	Dölger, Franz Joseph	355–57, 359
Clerc, Michel Armand	10, 62, 245, 253	Dominik, William J.	76
Cockle, Walter E. H.	189, 233	Donkow, Izabella	388, 415
Cohen, Getzel M.	107, 137, 144	Downing, F. Gerald	405, 409
Cole, R. A.	226	Drew-Bear, Thomas	5, 62, 119, 125, 136, 144
Collins, Adela Yarbro	394, 409		
Colvin, Stephen	385, 408	Drexhage, H.-W.	187–88, 220, 234, 237, 242, 254
Concannon, C. W.	29, 62		
Cooper, Kate	300, 320	Drijvers, H. Jan Willem	110, 144
Corsten, Thomas	3, 19, 24, 29–30, 36, 60–62, 70, 89, 102, 110, 143, 213, 231, 253, 304, 314, 320–21	DuBois, Thomas A.	178, 185
		Duchesne, Louis	334, 340, 343–44, 359
		Duff, Paul B.	166, 168
Costa, V. M. da	258, 286	Duman, B.	11, 17, 26, 63, 68, 92, 103, 240, 254
Cotton, Hannah M.	46, 59, 131, 148, 189, 206, 233, 385		
		Duncan-Jones, Richard	265, 287, 294, 321
Coutras, Andrew J.	367, 409		
Coynbear, Frederick C.	340, 359	Dunn, Geoffrey D.	118, 143
Cramer, John A.	130, 144	Dunn, James D. G.	132, 144, 174, 185
Crawford, Michael H.	261, 263, 286–87	Dyer, K. D.	261, 287
Crone, Theodore M.	365, 409	Eck, Werner	73, 78, 130, 148, 328, 359
Cross, Lawrence	118, 143	Eden, P.T.	76, 78
Cuvigny, Hélène	187	Edwards, James R.	273, 287, 365, 367, 409
D'Agostino, Anacleto	291		
Dain, Alphonse	11, 15, 62	Eger, Otto	218, 234
D'Aiuto, F.	121, 144	Eitrim, Samson	363, 409
D'Ambra, E. Eve	399, 409	Elsner, Jaś	179, 186
D'Andria, Francesco	3–4, 19, 26, 47–48, 53, 62, 65, 67–68, 242, 244, 253, 304	Elton, Hugh	258, 290
		Emrys-Evans, D.	10, 63
Daniell, Edward T.	8, 69	Erdemir, Hatice	86, 103, 225 234
Daniell, Patrice	13, 69	Erdkamp, Paul	265, 288, 294, 321
Daubner, Frank	107, 134, 144	Erim, Kenan T.	89, 104
Davies, Glenys	85, 102	Esler, Philip	95, 103
Davila, James R.	182, 185	Esty, Warren W.	281, 287
Dehandschutter, Boudewijn	146	Fairchild, Mark R.	25, 63
Deissmann, Adolf	202, 216, 233	Fears, J. Rufus	262, 280, 287
Delattre, Daniel	191, 232	Ferrary, Jean-Louis	248, 254, 306, 321, 366, 373–79, 400, 409
Delmaire, Roland	327		
Dennis, George T.	140, 144	Ferrua, Antonio	335, 359
Destro, Adriana	193, 231	Ficker, Gerhard	340, 342, 344, 348, 352–53, 359
Devambez, Pierre.	245, 255, 291		
Dibelius, Martin	174–75, 185, 248, 254	Filges, Axel	240, 254
Dieterich, Albrecht	342, 348–50, 353–54	Fine, Steven	131, 144
		Fink, Robert O.	137
Dignas, Beate	327, 361	Finley, M. I.	294, 321
Dittmann-Schöne, Imogen	242, 254	Fitzmyer, Joseph A.	308, 321

Flavianus, K.-M. 245
Flexsenhar, M. 17, 60
Fontenrose, Joseph 363, 370–73, 409
Forbes, Christopher 365, 407, 409
Forbes, E. 8, 69, 366
Foss, C. 10, 63
Foster, Paul 12, 15, 63
Fox, Robin Lane 392, 409
Fragiadakis, Charilaos 212, 234
Francis, Fred O. 174, 176, 180, 185
Franco, Carlo 328, 359
Franke, Peter R. 188, 234, 258, 273, 287
French, David 20, 63
French, David H. 217, 234
Frerichs, Ernest S. 130, 146
Frier, Bruce W. 195, 201, 203, 232, 294, 320
Friesen, Steven J. 17, 60, 275, 287, 294, 296, 298, 321, 395, 409
Frilingos, Christopher A. 395, 409
Fugmann, Joachim 76, 78
Funke, Peter 271, 287
Gagniers, Jean des 19–20, 24, 32–33, 63, 65, 68, 245, 255, 275, 277–78, 287, 291, 413
Gagos, Traianos 218, 232
Galinsky, Karl 76, 78, 398–99, 409
Garnsey, Peter 270, 287
Garthwaite, John 76, 78
Gauger, Jörg-Dieter 133, 145
Gauthier, Philippe 133, 145
Gemünden, P. von 260, 292
Gianotto, Claudio 223, 232
Gielen, Marlis 212, 234
Gilles, Carole 86, 94, 104
Gillespie, Thomas W. 365, 409
Gilliam, Johnson Frank 137, 388, 409
Ginouvès, René. 245, 255, 291
Glancy, Jennifer A. 387, 409
Gleba, Margarita 94, 242, 252
Gnilka, Joachim 175, 185
Grabbe, Lester L. 133, 145
Graf, Fritz 176, 178–79, 185
Grainger, J. D. 133, 136, 145
Grant, Frederick C. 382, 410

Grant, Michael 259, 287
Grant, Robert 285
Green, David 168, 243, 254, 260, 333, 360
Greeven, Heinrich 175, 185
Grégoire, H. 337, 360
Grenfell, B. P. 228
Grewe, Klaus 54, 68, 298, 320, 323
Grierson, Philip 111
Grudem, Wayne A. 365, 410
Guarducci, Guido 291
Guarducci, Margherita 333, 339, 355, 360
Guichard, Celeste L. 178, 185, 364, 410
Guizzi, F. 32, 67, 69, 149, 255, 276
Gurval, Robert Allan 398, 410
Gwyther, Anthony 395, 411
Haacker, Klaus 250, 255
Habicht, Christian 275, 287–88
Habinek, Thomas N. 115, 145
Halfmann, H. 12, 63
Hall, A. S. 370, 410
Halla-Aho, Hilla 208, 235
Hamilton, W. J. 6, 24, 63
Hans, Linda-Marie 264, 288
Harland, Philip A. 46, 56–59, 63–64, 84, 90–91, 102–3, 138–39, 145, 242–43, 254
Harnack, Adolf von 154, 168, 334, 340, 342, 360
Hanson, Ann E. 224, 234
Harrill, J. Albert 234
Harrington, Wilfred J. 398, 410
Harris, William V. 270, 288
Harrison, James R. 3–5, 24, 36, 42, 44, 49, 52, 55, 63, 262, 289, 379, 383–84, 388–89, 402, 404, 410
Harrison, Stephen 179, 186
Hathaway, Stephanie L. 128, 143
Hauge, Matthew Ryan 383, 410
Haverfield, Francis H. 270, 288
Haysom, Matthew 369, 410
Head, Barclay 108
Hefner, Herbert 134
Heftner, Herbert 188, 235

Hekster, Olivier	265, 288, 294, 321	Ikeguchi, Mamoru	294, 322
Heller, Anna	106, 124, 145	Instone-Brewer, David	207, 235
Hellholm, David	353, 361	Isaac, Benjamin	270, 288
Hemer, Colin J.	285, 288	Ismaelli, Tommaso	299, 322
Hengstl, Joachim	226, 229, 234–35	Jackson, John	280, 291
Henry, Olivier	364, 412	Jakab, Éva	217–18, 235
Herda, Alexander	363, 369, 410	Janse, Mark	249, 252
Herrmann, Johannes	226, 235	Janzen, Ernst	400, 411
Herrmann, P.	372, 410	Johnson, Sherman E.	24, 64
Hernández, Juan P. S.	137, 147	Johnston, Ann	4, 64, 114, 145, 257–59, 281, 288–89
Herz, Peter	188, 235		
Herzer, Jens	216, 237	Jones, A. H. M.	293–94, 321
Heuchert, Volker	47, 67, 114	Jones, Christopher	75, 79
Hill, David	365, 410	Jones, Horace Leonard	268, 291
Hirschmann, Vera	340, 352, 360	Jones, Tamara	31, 65, 373, 411
Hock, Ronald F.	119, 145	Jones, Tom B.	258, 289
Højte, Jakob Munk	75, 79	Jongman, Willem	294, 321–22
Holmes, Michael	162–63, 168	Jördens, Andrea	198
Hölscher, T.	264, 288	Judeich, Walther	52, 65, 139, 145
Holtheide, Bernard	73, 79	Judge, Edwin A.	262, 289, 404, 411
Homann, Margit	216, 237	Jütte, Robert	135, 141
Hombert, Marcel	201, 235	Kagan, Y. O.	7, 65
Hopkins, Keith	294, 321	Kahil, Lilly	33, 66, 245, 255, 291
Horsley, Greg H. R.	44, 64, 380–82, 410–11	Kajava, Mika	364, 411
		Kampmann, Ursula	258, 289
Horsley, Richard A.	277, 288, 311, 320	Karanastasi, P.	145, 216
Horst, Peter W. van der	45, 64, 132, 139, 145	Katsari, Constantina	304, 320
		Kaufmann, Carl Maria	342, 360
Houghton, Arthur	109, 112–13, 145	Kearsley, Rosalinde A.	42, 65, 88, 103, 105, 115, 146, 306, 309, 322
Howard-Brook, Wes	395, 411		
Howgego, Christopher	47, 67, 109, 114, 145, 263, 265, 281, 288	Keenan, James G.	205, 236
		Keddie, G. Anthony	17, 61
Hoyland, Robert G.	59, 142	Kehoe, Dennis P.	294, 322
Hoz, María Paz de	137, 147	Kelp, Ute	249, 254
Huber, Lynn R.	34–36, 39, 64	Kerkeslager, A.	365 397, 411
Humann, Carl	4, 64, 139	Kerschbaum, Saskia	73, 79
Hunt, A. S.	228	Kessner, Paul	54, 68, 298, 320
Huttner, Ulrich	4–5, 10, 18–19, 64, 73–74, 79, 81, 83–84, 88–89, 91–92, 94–95, 98, 103, 112, 118–20, 123–30, 133, 139–40, 153–54, 158–60, 163, 168, 219, 235, 242–43, 247–48, 250–51, 254, 275–76, 278, 282, 288, 293, 300, 306, 308–9, 314–16, 318, 321	Kienast, Dietmar	74, 79, 273, 289
		Kiley, Mark Christopher	311, 322
		Kim, David W.	128, 143
		Kinns, Philip	281, 289
		Klauck, Hans-Josef	395, 411
		Klauser, Theodor	343, 360
		Kleijn, Gerda de	288, 294, 321
Hyatt, Adam	218, 232	Kleiner, Fred S.	266, 289

Kloppenborg, John S.	46, 59, 89–91, 102, 366	Lefebvre, Henri	167, 168
		Leitz, Christian	225, 237
Klöpper, Albert	311, 322	Leiwo, Martti	208, 235
Klose, Dietrich O. A.	115, 146, 273, 289	Leschhorn, Wolfgang	74, 79, 234, 258–59, 267, 281–82, 287, 289
Klutz, Todd E.	182, 185		
Kneissl, Peter	275, 289	Lesses, Rebecca M.	182, 185
Knox, John	308, 322	Levick, Barbara	108, 146, 271, 289
Knuf, Hermann	225, 237	Lewis, Peter	266, 289
Koch, Dietrich-Alex	210, 235	L'Hôte, Eric	364, 411
Koester, Craig R.	34–35, 65, 395, 411	Lieu, Judith	366
Koester, Helmut	109, 150, 258, 289	Lightfoot, J. B.	127, 146
Kolb, F.	113, 146	Limberis, Vasiliki M.	123, 146
Konakçi, E.	11, 17, 63, 65, 92, 103, 240, 254	Lindemann, Andreas	243
		Lindgren, Henry Clay	28, 66, 255
Konstan, David	43, 65	Lintott, Andrew	284, 290
Kooten, George H. van	248, 254	Llewellyn-Jones, Lloyd	85, 102
Kosmin, Paul J.	110, 146	Llewelyn, Stephen R.	390, 393–94, 412
Kovacs, Frank L.	28, 66	Lohse, Eduard	175, 186, 250, 255
Kraabel, A. Thomas	56–57, 65, 130 146	Long, Lea Emilia	30, 66
Kraft, Konrad	257, 289	Longenecker, Bruce W.	296, 322
Krampe, Christoph	218, 233	Lorber, Catharine C.	109, 112–13, 145
Krause, Victor	128, 142	Lotz, John Paul	41, 66
Kraybill, J. Nelson	394, 399, 403, 411	Lovén, Lena Larsson	86, 103
Kreinecker, Christina M.	229, 235	Lovering, Eugene	400, 411
Kreitzer, Larry J.	53, 65	Luckensmeyer, David	118, 143
Kretschmar, Georg	355, 360	Lüdtke, Willy	325, 360
Kritzer, Ruth E.	207	Luijendijk, AnneMarie	191, 235
Kruse, Thomas	192, 195–96, 199–200, 229, 235	Lyon, C. S. S.	281, 290
		Ma, John	133–34, 146
Kumsar, Halil	22, 65	MacDonald, David	247, 255
Kupisch, Berthold	218, 235	MacDonald, Margaret	132, 147
Kustermann, Abraham P.	135, 141	MacMullen, Ramsay	382, 412
Labahn, Michael	183, 186	Macridy, Theodore	176, 186, 248, 255
La Genière, Juliette de	248, 254	Magie, David	10, 18, 20, 66, 109, 147, 401, 412
Laiou, Angeliki E.	327, 358		
Lamberz, Erich	127, 146	Magness, Jodi	111, 147
Lampakis, G.	9, 65	Maier, Harry O.	5, 13, 19, 66, 74, 77, 79
Lampe, Peter	219, 235, 308, 322	Malay, H.	134–35, 137, 147
Lampinem, Antii	364, 411	Malbon, Elizabeth S.	356, 360
Lane, Eugene N.	278, 289, 382, 412	Malherbe, Abraham J.	56, 66
Lang, Markus	203, 231	Malina, Bruce J.	316, 322, 395, 412
Lange, Carste Hjort	398–99, 411	Malouta, Myrto	205, 236
Latyšev, Basilius	121, 146	Manders, Erika	260, 290
Leemans, Johan	122, 146	Manning, Joseph G.	205, 236
Leeming, David	280, 289	Manthe, Ulrich	218, 233

Mare, W. Harold 9, 66
Marshall, Anthony J. 133, 147
Martin, Beatrice 76, 78
Martin, Katharina 18, 66
Marucchi, Orazio 339–40, 343, 360
Maschek, Dominik 299, 322
Masino, Filippo 31, 69
Matthews, Christopher R. 129
Matthews, Elaine 139, 149
Mattingly, David J. 274, 290, 292
Mattingly, Harold 261, 274
Mauritsch, Peter 220, 237
Mayer, Wendy 6, 61, 118, 125, 143, 146
McDowell, Robert H. 109, 133, 147
McKechnie, Paul 19, 66
McLaren, James S. 14, 61, 132, 143, 250, 253
Meadows, Andrew 107
Meeks, Wayne A. 174, 185
Merkelbach, Reinhold 10, 66, 176, 186, 244, 246, 248, 255, 328–30, 340–41, 350, 352, 360, 363, 388, 412
Meshorer, Yaʿakov 263, 290
Metcalf, William E. 114, 147, 259, 267, 282, 290
Meyer, H. G. 270, 286
Meyboom, P. G. P. 7, 66
Michon, E. 11, 66
Mighetto, Paolo 31, 69
Milanese, Marco 304, 324
Mileta, Christia 106, 147
Millar, Fergus G. B. 189, 233
Miller, John F. 398, 412
Millett, Martin 270, 290
Milne, J. Grafton 111, 147
Milner, N. P. 11, 66, 105, 147
Minnen, Peter van 226, 236
Miranda, Elena 56, 66, 76, 138, 149, 255, 276
Mitchell, Margaret M. 308, 333–35, 341, 346–47, 353, 360
Mitchell, Stephen 20, 25, 28, 44, 66, 126, 147, 267, 271, 290, 304, 320, 322, 327, 361, 380, 382, 411
Mitteis, Ludwig 201, 238

Möbius, Hans 7, 67, 246, 255
Moffatt, James 154, 168
Mols, Stephan T. A. M. 288
Mommsen, Theodor 271, 290
Montevecchi, Orsolina 201, 207, 225, 236
Moretti, Jean-Charles 364
Morgan, Teresa 383, 412
Mørkholm, Otto 111, 148, 266, 290
Morris, Ian 294, 321, 323
Mounce, Robert H. 399, 412
Müller, Brigitte 234
Müller-Luckner, Elisabeth 130, 148
Murphy-O'Connor, Jerome 399, 412
Nasrallah, Laura 365, 412
Naylor, Michael 395, 412
Neil, Bronwyn 6, 9, 60–61, 125, 143
Nesbitt, John W. 140, 144
Neusner, Jacob 130, 146
Neverov, O. Y. 7, 65
Newell, Edward T. 109, 148, 111
Ng, Diana Yi-man 47–48, 50, 67
Nicholson-Smith, Donald 168
Nissen, Theodor 325, 337–38, 352, 360–61
Noe, Sydney P. 266
Nollé, Johannes 130, 148, 188, 217, 234, 236, 364, 380, 382, 412
Norden, Eduard 76, 79
Nordling, John G. 218, 236
Norwich, John J. 225, 148
North, John A. 56, 63
Nosch, Marie-Louise B. 86, 94, 104
Noy, David 139, 148
Nutton, V. 372, 412
Ogereau, Julien M. 230, 236
Oikonomides, Nicolas 140, 144
Okunak, M. 26, 37–38, 69
Öhler, Marcus 3, 15, 19, 60–61, 70, 110, 143, 203, 213, 231, 314, 321
Oldfather, W. A. 263, 290
Oliver, James H. 399
Olshausen, Eckart 273, 287
Olsson, Bror 222, 236
Önal, Mehmet 191, 236

Ormerod, H. A. 83–84, 103
Orsi, Valentina 291
Osborne, Grant R. 396, 399, 412
Osborne, Robert E. 55, 67
Ozan, Ali 19, 67
Pache, Corrine Ondine 388, 414
Palme, Bernhard 201, 236
Papadopoulos-Kerameus, A. 121, 148
Papathomas, Amphilochios 222, 236
Papazoglou, Fanoula 138, 148
Parke, H. W. 363, 413
Parker, Barry F. 134, 148
Parker, Robert 110, 148
Parkin, Tim G. 311, 322
Parrish, David 4, 62, 242, 253
Pastori, Franco 218, 237
Pásztókai-Szeöke, Judit 94, 242, 252
Peachin, Michael 311, 323
Pearl, O. M. 229
Peerbolte, B. J. Lietaert 182, 183, 186
Peers, Glenn 118, 148, 248, 255
Pennacchietti, Fabrizio A. 139, 148
Peregrine, Peter 106, 149
Pesce, Mauro 193, 231
Petzl, Georg 119, 148, 384–86, 413
Pflaum, H-G. 10, 67
Pfuhl, Ernst 7, 67, 246, 255
Picard, Charles 176, 186, 413
Pickett, Raymond 293
Pinzone, A. 261, 286
Pippidi, D. M. 282
Pitts, Andrew W. 383, 410
Pizzuto, Vincent A. 244, 255
Pleket, Henri W. 354, 361
Poblome, Jeroen 93–94, 103
Pohl, Daniela 188, 234
Pollard, J. 263, 287
Pomeroy, Arthur 311
Posner, Daniel N. 130, 148
Porter, S. E. 36, 64
Pratscher, Wilhelm 203, 231
Préaux, Claire 201, 235
Price, Simon R. F. 47, 56, 63, 67, 74, 79, 115, 142, 273, 283, 290
Psoma, S. 109

Rabatel, Liliane 364, 412
Rajak, Tessa 138, 148
Ramelli, Ilaria 355, 361
Ramsay, William M. 10, 23, 67, 83, 85, 103, 247–48, 255, 259–60, 276, 290, 340, 344–48, 352, 361
Rathbone, Dominic W. 206, 237
Ratté, Christopher 105, 148
Rea, John R. 195
Reasoner, Mark 11, 14, 67
Rebillard, Éric 58, 67, 164–65, 168
Recklinghausen, Daniel von 225, 237
Reddish, Mitchell G. 401, 413
Reger, Gary 258, 290
Reike, Bo 243, 255
Reinach, Salomen 347, 361
Reinmuth, Eckart 77
Reiter, Fabian 225, 237
Renberg, Gil H. 392, 413
Ricl, M. 112, 149
Ripollès, Pere Pau 244, 253
Ritti, Tullia 4–5, 8, 10–11, 20, 39, 47, 49–56, 62, 67–68, 89, 103, 118, 135, 149, 243, 245–46, 255, 276, 291, 298–99, 301, 305, 320, 322–23, 376–77, 382–84, 388, 413
Robert, Carl 345, 361
Robert, Jeanne 179, 186, 328, 361, 376, 413
Robert, Louis 10–11, 24, 29, 54–55, 68, 179, 186, 245, 255, 278, 291, 328, 370, 376–78, 387, 413
Robbins, Vernon 95, 100, 103, 254
Robinson, John A. T. 400, 413
Robinson, Thomas Lonzo 363, 366, 374–75, 388–89, 392, 413
Roche, Paul A. 76
Romeo, Ilaria 49, 62
Rosler, Andrés 271, 291
Rossing, Barbara R. 395, 413
Rostad, Aslak 385, 387, 414
Rouéché, Charlotte 105, 149
Ruffing, Kai 187–88, 220, 234
Ruggeri, Paolo 304, 324
Rüpke, Jörg 263, 292

Modern Authors Index

Rupprecht, Hans-Albert 218, 237
Russel, Ben 298, 320, 323
Rutherford, Ian 179, 186
Rutledge, Steven H. 73, 79
Ryan, Judith M. 308
Saller, Richard 270, 287, 294, 323
Sampley, J. Paul 29, 61
Sánchez-Moreno Ellart, C. 192, 196–97, 199–200, 237
Sanctis, George de 340, 359
Sbardella, Francesca 223, 232
Scardozzi, Giuseppe 299, 322
Schacter, Jacob J. 131, 144
Schalit, Abraham 134, 149
Scheidel, Walter 201, 237, 294, 298, 321, 323
Scherrer, Stephen J. 396, 414
Scholl, Reinhold 216, 220, 237
Schreiber, Stefan 77
Schubart, Wilhelm 222
Schuler, Christof 75, 79
Schultze, Victor 259, 291
Schumacher, Leonhard 311, 323
Schuman, V. B. 229
Schütte, Anke 188, 234
Schwertheim, Elmar 393, 414
Scullard, Howard H. 270, 291
Segre, M. 133, 149
Sekunda, Nicholas 136, 149
Ševčenko, Nancy Patterson 221, 149
Sezgin, M. A. 5, 31, 69
Sheppard, A. R. R. 217, 291
Sherk, Robert H. 399, 414
Sim, David C. 14, 61, 132, 143, 250, 253
Şimşek, Celal 3, 5, 19, 22–23, 25–28, 30–34, 37–38, 53, 62, 65, 67–69, 94, 103, 118, 131, 148–49, 274, 291, 304, 323
Sitlington Sterrett, J. R. 325, 336, 339, 346–48, 361
Slater, R. N. 129
Slootjes, Dani-Elle 294, 321
Smalley, Stephen S. 396–97, 399, 401, 414
Smith, Michael E. 106, 149
Smith, R. R. R. 85, 89, 104–5, 148, 327, 361
Sobra, Giorgio 31, 69
Soja, Edward 167–68
Solin, Heikki 237
Soriano, Isabel Velázquez 190
Sperti, Luigi 25, 69
Spinelli, Marianna 261, 291
Spratt, T. A. B. 8, 69
Staab, Karl 130, 149
Standhartinger, Angela 5, 18–19, 68, 249–50, 256, 310, 323
Stauber, Josef 10, 66, 244, 246, 248, 255, 341, 350, 360, 363, 388
Stegemann, Ekkehard W. 300, 323
Stegemann, Wolfgang 300, 323
Strelan, Rick 15–16, 69, 249
Stephens, Christopher W. B. 127, 150
Stevens, Gerald L. 284, 291
Steward, B. 263, 287
Stewart, Eric C. 156, 168, 256
Strachan, Lionel R. M. 202, 233
Straus, Jean A. 212–13, 220–21, 224–25, 237
Strom, Mark 382, 414
Strootman, Rolf 107, 150
Strubbe, Johann 52, 69
Swain, Simon 179, 186, 249, 252
Sweet, John 398, 414
Tabbernee, William 126, 150
Talloen, Peter 400, 414
Tanriver, C. 137, 140, 147, 150
Taubenschlag, Rafael 201, 224, 238
Teichmann, Jutta 188, 234
Temin, Peter 293–98, 310, 323
Tenney, Frank 243, 252
Temporini, Hildegard 114, 150
Theophilos, Michael P. 5
Thomas, Rodney L. 395, 414
Thompson, Leonard L. 14, 69, 166, 168, 316, 323, 394, 396
Thonemann, Peter 20, 40, 69, 107, 112, 118, 126, 142, 147–48, 150, 166, 218, 240, 249, 254, 256, 266–67, 272, 276, 291, 301–2, 323, 327–31, 346, 348–49, 361
Tomaschitz, Kurt 134, 188, 235

Tougher, Shaun 128, 150
Threatte, Leslie 115, 150
Thurston, Bonnie Beattie 308, 323
Tolmie, D. Francois 220, 231, 308, 320
Trainor, Michael 3, 5, 12, 17, 42, 61, 65, 69, 86, 88, 103, 118, 120, 143, 149, 225, 234, 240, 253, 256, 295, 309, 312, 322–23
Travaglini, A. 6, 69
Traversari, Gustavo 19, 25, 27–28 31–32, 60, 69
Trebilco, Paul 45, 69, 119–20, 130, 150
Triado, Jésus Bermejo 304, 323
Trinkl, Elisabeth 92, 104
Tuplin, Christopher 136, 150
Turner, Max 365, 414
Turner, Michael 262, 286
Unwin, James R. 29, 69
Uphus, Johannes B. 127, 146
Valentini, Stefano 291
Valero, Carlos Molina 137, 147
Vanacker, Wouter 284
Várhelyi, Zsuzsanna 179, 186, 388, 414
Velázquez, Soriano 190, 238
Verboven, Koenrad 294, 324
Verheyden, Joseph 3, 15, 19, 60–61, 70, 110, 143, 150, 213, 231, 314, 321
Veyne, Paul 122, 270, 292
Villiers, Pieter de 365, 414
Vismara, Cinzia 304, 324
Volk, T. 263, 287
Waelkens, Marc 400, 414
Waetzoldt, Hartmut 94, 104
Wallace, Sherman L. 201, 220, 238
Wallensten, Jenny 369, 410
Walsh, Kevin 117, 150
Walter, Christopher 122–23, 150
Walters, James 109
Warmington, E. H. 21, 70
Wasserstein, David J. 59, 142
Watrous, John 388, 414
Weber, Leo 4, 70
Weiss, Peter 114, 115
Weissenrieder, Annette 260, 292

Welborn, Laurence L. 23–24, 44, 56, 63–64, 70, 379, 410
Welles, Charles Bradford 137
Wells, Louise 392, 414
Wendt, Friedericke 259, 260, 292
Werner, M. 157, 169
Westermann, William L. 226, 238
Westermark, Ulla 111
Wet, Chris de 118, 143
Whitaker, Robyn J. 405, 414
White, L. Michael 119, 145
Whitmarsh, Tim 44, 66
Whittaker, C. R. 270, 273, 292
Wilcken, Ulrich 201–2, 238
Wild, John Peter 225, 238
Williams, Jonathan 263, 292
Williams, Margaret H. 139
Wilpert, Joseph 334, 361
Wilson, C. 10, 70
Wilson, H. L. 217, 292
Wilson, Mark 366, 368–69, 415
Winter, Bruce W. 271, 292
Winter, Engelbert 187, 234
Winter, John G. 229, 238
Winter, Sarah 308, 324
Wiotte-Franz, C. 15, 70
Wire, Antoinette Clark 365, 415
Wischmeyer, Wolfgang 337, 339, 346, 354, 361
Witherington III, Ben 181, 186, 398, 415
Wolff, Hans Julius 206–8, 239
Wolter, Michael 214, 238
Wörrle, Michael 20, 70, 135
Wright, Nicholas L. 107, 111, 113, 262, 286
Wypustek, Andrzej 388, 415
Yamauchi, Edwin 26, 30, 70, 265, 292
Yarbrough, O. Larry 119, 145
Yiftach, Uri 209, 238
Yiftach-Firanko, Uri 205, 207–9, 236, 238
Yıldız, H. 118, 149
Yilmaz, Salim 54, 68
Young, Robin Darling 14, 69
Zambas, Kostas 364, 412

Zambon, Angela	226, 238
Zanker, Paul	264, 292
Zgusta, Ladislav	16, 70
Ziche, Harmut G.	294, 322
Zimmerman, B.	157, 169
Zuiderhoek, Arjun	284

www.ingramcontent.com/pod-product-compliance
Lightning Source LLC
Chambersburg PA
CBHW021231300426
44111CB00007B/500